The Republic of St. Peter

THE MIDDLE AGES

a series edited by
EDWARD PETERS
Henry Charles Lea Professor
of Medieval History
University of Pennsylvania

The Republic of St. Peter

THE BIRTH
OF THE PAPAL STATE,
680–825

THOMAS F. X. NOBLE

UNIVERSITY OF PENNSYLVANIA PRESS
Philadelphia

88244

Design by Design for Publishing, Bob Nance

Copyright © 1984 by the University of Pennsylvania Press

Library of Congress Cataloging in Publication Data

Noble, Thomas F. X.
   The Republic of St. Peter.

   (Middle Ages)
   Bibliography: p.
   Includes index.
   1. Papal States—History—To 962.   I. Title.
II. Series.
DG797.1.N62   1984   945'.6   83-21870
ISBN 0-8122-7917-4

Printed in the United States of America

For My Wife
LINDA

Contents

Maps

Abbreviations

AHP	*Archivum Historiae Pontificiae.*
ASR	*Archivio Storico Romano.*
BEC	*Bibliothèque de l'école des chartes.*
BEHE	*Bibliothèque de l'école des hautes études.*
BM	Johann Friedrich Böhmer, Englebert Mühlbacher, et al., eds., *Die Regesten des Kaiserreichs unter den Karolingern*, vol. 1 of *Regesta Imperii* (reprint, Hildesheim, 1966).
BZ	*Byzantinische Zeitschrift.*
DA	*Deutsches Archiv für Erforschung des Mittelalters.*
FMSt	*Frühmittelalterliche Studien.*
FSI	*Fonti per la storia d'Italia.*
HJB	*Historisches Jahrbuch der Görresgesellschaft.*
HZ	*Historische Zeitschrift.*
IP	Paul Fridolin Kehr, et al., eds., *Italia Pontifica*, 10 vols.
Jaffé, *RP*	Philippus Jaffé, *Regesta Pontificum Romanorum*, vol. 1, 2d ed. (reprint, Graz, 1956).

LD   Hans Foerster, ed., *Liber Diurnus Romanorum Pontificum* (Bern, 1958).

LP   Louis Duchesne, ed., *Le Liber Pontificalis*, 3 vols. (Paris, 1955).

MAH   *Mélanges d'archéologie et d'histoire.*

Mansi, *Concilia*   J. D. Mansi, ed., *Sacrorum Conciliorum Nova et Amplissima Collectio*, 53 vols.

MGH   *Monumenta Germaniae Historica.*

Series in *MGH*

Cap	*Capitularia Regum Francorum.*
Conc	*Concilia Aevi Karolini.*
DK	*Diplomata Karolinorum.*
DO	*Diplomata Ottonum.*
EKA	*Epistolae Karolini Aevi.*
SS	*Scriptores.*
SSrG	*Scriptores rerum Germanicarum in usum scholarum.*
SSrL	*Scriptores rerum Langobardicorum et Italicarum.*

MIÖG   *Mitteilungen des Instituts für Österreichische Geschichtsforschung.*

PL   Jacques-Paul Migne, ed., *Patrologia Latina*, 221 vols.

QFIAB   *Quellen und Forschungen aus italienischen Archiven und Bibliotheken.*

RF   Ignazio Giorgi and Ugo Balzani, eds., *Il Regesto di Farfa*, vol. 2 (Rome, 1879).

SSCI   *Settimane di studio del Centro Italiano di studi sull'alto medioevo.*

ZKG   *Zeitschrift für Kirchengeschichte.*

ZRG	*Zeitschrift der Savigny-Stiftung für Rechtsgeschichte.*
——, *gA*	*germanistische Abteilung.*
——, *kA*	*kanonistische Abteilung.*

Acknowledgments

BOOKS HAVE their histories too. This one is the somewhat unexpected result of a project I started almost ten years ago. At that time I thought that I would expand on some material that had been included in my doctoral dissertation and write a longish article on the papal privileges of Louis the Pious. Various attempts to solve certain problems that kept confronting me caused me to pester a goodly number of learned and patient scholars who were unfailingly courteous and encouraging. Slowly it became clear to me that a book was called for; even more slowly I grasped the shape the book would have to assume and admitted, reluctantly at first, that Louis could not play a central role in it. The scholars who helped me to reach these conclusions are not to be held responsible for any shortcomings that remain in this book. Indeed, they are responsible for much of any merit that it may be found to possess. Anyway, my long article has become a long book and I have, in a deep and personal way, come to understand the words with which St. Augustine closed *De civitate Dei*.

Some at least of those who assisted me in one way or another must be singled out for special mention. Richard Sullivan, once and always my teacher, read my manuscript more than once in different forms, talked with me about complex issues, and encouraged me when I needed it most. John Contreni read and criticized the whole of this work several times and extended to me so many kindnesses that I cannot count them all. David Miller read an early draft of several chapters and offered much sage advice. He, and also David Sefton, passed many an hour with me discussing papal history. Karl Morrison graciously allowed me to draw upon his wisdom and erudition, and he gave me searching criticisms of several chapters. Bruce Hitchner talked with me about things Byzantine, suggested books and articles for me to read, and criticized my early chapters. Duane Osheim, on numerous occasions, talked with me about Italy and in talking taught me a very great deal. He also read my whole manuscript and made some helpful suggestions. Erik Midelfort attacked my manuscript with his rapier-like criticism and forced me to improve it in many ways. His were some of the most incisive, and therefore helpful, comments I received. Eddie Ayers gave me the priceless gift of friendship, which in my reckoning meant that I could (and did) bother him about almost anything at almost any time. He also read my whole work with the eyes of a non-medievalist and helped me to purge specialist's jargon and to write in something approaching idiomatic English. Philip Grierson talked with me about early papal coinage and made some very helpful suggestions. To Edward Peters I am grateful for his confidence and encouragement.

One person who both helped and encouraged me is now beyond the reach of these words. For several months in 1972-73 I went every other Wednesday morning to the home of François-Louis Ganshof. I hope that my work shows, at least in some small way, the benefits I received from my private tutoring in Carolingian history by one of the real masters of the subject. His enthusiastic encouragement was, however, his greatest gift to me. He liked the best some of my boldest ideas and I cannot help but wonder what he would have thought of this book in its final form.

Some sections of this book are polemical and may turn out to be controversial. In writing these sections I was very conscious that my attitude to the work of my predecessors both living and dead may seem a bit uncharitable. I hope, in fact, that my notes and bibliography will make it absolutely clear that I owe an incalculable debt to all of the scholars whose work has preceded my own. In this connection I should make special mention of the late Walter Ullmann with whose work I am frequently at variance but whose *oeuvre* has been a constant inspiration to me. I could say much the same thing about Schramm, whose work is, to me, brilliant; or about Caspar, whose learning was compendious. But I also disagree with them, and with many others too. I hope I have done so respectfully.

Far behind this book stands a dissertation the research for which was made possible, at least in part, by a Fulbright-Hays Fellowship. In subsequent years the American Philosophical Society, the National Endowment for the Humanities, Texas Tech University, and the University of Virginia provided crucial material assistance. The Small Grants Committee of the University of Virginia provided a subsidy toward the cost of having my maps drawn. The Corcoran Department of History at Virginia provided funds for me to employ a research assistant. To all of these institutions and organizations I am grateful.

My maps were drawn by Christina Sharretts with whose work I am very pleased. The references in my bibliography and then in my notes were verified by Robin Good. My daughter Kirby helped with some of the proofreading. The acquisitions and Inter-library Loan staffs of Alderman Library at the University of Virginia acceded promptly and efficiently to my every request. I shall be eternally thankful for the grace, good humor, and skill of the secretaries who helped me, especially Lottie McCauley, Kathleen Miller, and Ella Wood. They taught me word-processing, came to my rescue every time the machines got the best of me, incorporated copy editor's corrections and computer coding on the magnetic disks from which this book was produced, made at least a million last-minute changes, and helped with the index.

It is, finally, easy to record but impossible to measure what I owe to my wife, Linda. She helped me with many thankless and boring editorial tasks, kept the household together while I was away, sometimes for several weeks at a time, doing research, and rearranged her schedule time after time so that I could work steadily. She does not care at all about these old popes, but she does care about me. And so she made it possible for me to write this book and I repay her—it hardly seems fair—in the only way I can now. I give this book back to Linda through its dedication.

Charlottesville
Feast of the Dedication of St. John Lateran
9 November 1983

Introduction

MODERN TELECOMMUNICATIONS made it possible for a good portion of the world to observe the highest dramas and most solemn rituals of the Roman Catholic Church in the summer and again in the early autumn of 1978. Pope Paul VI died and the cardinal clergy gathered from all points of the compass to elect his successor. After a few days of deliberations, whose inner workings were immunized by ancient traditions from the glare of klieg lights and microphones, the cardinal deacon of the Church, Pericle Felice, appeared on a small balcony above St. Peter's square and intoned to the throng assembled below a venerable and many times repeated chant: "*Annuntio vobis gaudium magnum, habemus papam.*" Albino Luciani, formerly the patriarch of Venice, entered into the line of succession to St. Peter. After only a few weeks Luciani died and the cardinals returned to Rome. This time their deliberations resulted in the election of Karol Wojtyla, a Pole and the first of his nation ever to sit on Peter's throne.

Journalists were repeatedly frustrated in their attempts to penetrate behind the mysterious workings of the Vatican in order to report to a curious world the details of the two papal elections that had just taken place. Still, if perceptive observers could not fully understand the procedures that produced the elections, they must have noticed certain not very subtle events that immediately followed them.

Luciani and Wojtyla both took double names, John Paul I and John Paul II, respectively. This was novel but not, perhaps, particularly significant. More important was that each man elected not to be crowned with the tiara, the triple crown that signifies the pope's universal episcopate, supremacy of jurisdiction, and temporal rule. The crown in one form or another had been

worn for nearly twelve centuries and its renunciation was an event of considerable proportions.[1]

Why was the crown abandoned? Quite simply because it symbolized
realities that had ceased to exist. The abandonment may have owed something to the humble, unassuming, and unpretentious personality of Albino
Luciani, or to the essentially pastoral instincts of Karol Wojtyla, but, more
likely, the world was afforded a rare opportunity to watch the deeply traditional Catholic Church make, without press conferences or fanfare, a subtle
adjustment to the inexorable march of history. The pope, despite his vast
following, is no longer universal bishop. Peter's successors no longer exercise
universal jurisdiction within the Christian world, and frequently the pope
has difficulty gaining universal allegiance within his own church. Finally,
Vatican City is but a pale reminder of the vast temporal dominion once held
by the papacy. Virtually everything that the tiara once represented has passed
away; now too the tiara itself.

The modern visitor to Vatican City can only with great difficulty imagine
that for more than a millennium the pope ruled as direct sovereign an
expanse of territory in Italy that extended from Campania south of Rome
to the neighborhood of Ravenna far off to the northeast. The wars and
political settlements of the *Risorgimento* in the nineteenth century really put
an end to these "Papal States," but the Church did not definitively relinquish
its claims to them until the Vatican signed an accord with Mussolini's government in 1929. The pope thus remains a sovereign, but his tiny state,
however resplendent in its Renaissance grandeur and beauty, hardly merits a
crown.

In the early Middle Ages, however, the chiefs of this state, that is, the
popes, won the right to wear a crown and they maintained that right for a
remarkably long time. Few political entities in the western world have lasted
for more than a thousand years, and fewer still have exerted so profound an
influence on the shape and nature of the historic heritage of the West. A
comprehensive history of the Papal States would be a worthy undertaking,
but also a vast one. It is enough, as a start, to describe how this state came
into being, and why.

This book constitutes a descriptive and analytical treatment of the origins
and early history of the Papal State, but its primary purpose is to argue a
single thesis. To the extent that this thesis can be reduced to a few words, it

---

[1] On the history of the tiara see Bernhard Sirch, *Der Ursprung der bischöflichen Mitra und
päpstlichen Tiara* (St. Ottilien, 1975), pp. 48–187, esp. p. 49ff for Pope Constantine I (708–
15).

is this: Beginning in the last years of the seventh century a series of resolute and like-minded popes acting in concert with the local Roman nobility deliberately emancipated central Italy from the Byzantine Empire and transformed the region into a genuine state, the Republic of St. Peter. After the middle of the eighth century, the popes sought from the new Carolingian monarchy defense and protection for their fledgling state. These requests were granted by the Carolingians and the continued existence of the Republic was assured.

It would be idle to suggest that this story has not been told before. Indeed, a dauntingly voluminous literature has accumulated over the years, and many parts of the story seem very well known. There remain gaps in our knowledge, however, and the scope and perspectives of the present study differ significantly from the ones usually met in the scholarship on the subject. An attempt will be made in these pages to develop a perspective that has not been adopted before. The focus here is on central Italy, and on its history, during the century and a half from the 680s to the 820s.

Depending upon one's point of view, the thesis and perspective just enunciated may seem either distorted or unoriginal. In the past scholars have tended to absorb the history of the origins of the Papal State into either Byzantine or Frankish history. Habitués of either of these perspectives may find my Italian one distorted. As to the actual origins of the Papal State, it has been customary to place them in the 750s after the fall of the Byzantine government in central Italy and during the first military intervention south of the Alps by the Carolingians. Thus, it may be thought, this book cannot claim originality on the grounds of having discovered the birth of a Papal State in the eighth century. In fact, however, this study places the emergence of the Papal State well before the 750s, and it tries to demonstrate that this emergence was a process and not an event. It actually took, later chapters will argue, about a century and a half for this process to be completed. The scope of this work, reaching as it does far behind and beyond the 750s, is quite unprecedented.

There is today very little consensus about the origins of the Papal State, and there is ample room for a fresh investigation of the subject. A brief review of the major trends in the literature will therefore help to place the intended goals of this study into sharper focus. It may be useful to begin with the title. This book has not been entitled, nor has the state created by the papacy in the eighth century been called, *The Republic of St. Peter* out of a desire to be innovative. The name has been carefully chosen because it approximates very closely what the eighth-century popes actually called their new state. We shall see in later chapters how and why this name came to be used. For now it suffices to say that, as Erich Caspar pointed out forcefully years ago, conventional designations like Papal State(s), *Kirchenstaat, Etat de l'église,* and so forth are anachronistic when applied to the eighth or ninth century.[2] These terms only appeared in the later Middle Ages. On the subject of nomenclature, it will also be noted that the word *curia* is not used to refer to the papal administration during the period treated by this study. This word, as a vague reference to the papal government, and as a specific name for the papal court in the narrower sense, only became current in the late eleventh century.[3] I use the word *Lateran* whenever I wish to speak in a general way about the central institutions of the Church or of the Republic. This use of Lateran, once again, agrees with the language of the contemporary sources.

Turning to more substantive issues, this book departs from what might be called the "Byzantine view" of the subject.[4] According to many scholars, central Italy remained an integral part of the Byzantine Empire at least until the dissolution of the Exarchate of Ravenna in 751, and perhaps until the West received a new emperor in the person of Charlemagne in 800. It follows from this line of interpretation that the efforts and energies of the papacy between about 680 and 750 were primarily expended within the context of Byzantine history. Proponents of this view do acknowledge that central Italy eventually loosened itself from the grip of Constantinople, but to understand how this happened they assume that it is necessary to take a vantage point on the Bosporus and to observe the responses of the papacy and of the inhabitants of central Italy to various overtures by the imperial government.

The Byzantine view introduces some distortions into the historical record. It ignores, or insufficiently appreciates, a long and remarkably consistent set of deliberate, calculated steps taken in Italy to throw off the Byzantine yoke and to replace it with a different kind of rule at the hands of new masters. In other words, it is not particularly helpful to chronicle the gradual eclipse of Byzantine authority in central Italy because such chronicling runs the risk of missing the fact that there gradually emerged a new, more effective, and more permanent kind of authority in the lands that had formerly been Byzantine. In addition, the Byzantine view often fails to take into account the tensions and dynamics present in Italian society in the eighth century,

---

[2]Erich Caspar, *Pippin und die römische Kirche* (Berlin, 1914), p. 155.

[3]Lajos Pasztor, "L'histoire de la curie romaine, problème d'histoire de l'Eglise," *Revue d'histoire ecclésiastique* 64 (1969): 353.

[4]The literature pertinent to the Byzantine view is cited and discussed *in extenso* in chapters 2 and 3 below.

and the extent to which the birth of the Republic of St. Peter was a product of historical forces that had little to do with the constitutional regime of which Italy was theoretically a constituent part. In short, the Byzantine view treats Italian history as a mere annex of Byzantine history and, in so doing, stops short of comprehending fully the course of events in Italy itself.

It is impossible to deny that developments at Byzantium played a key role in precipitating or exacerbating crises in Italy. But those crises—and there were many of them—can often be fitted into specifically Italian contexts in order to show that the emergence of the Republic was an Italian response to Italian problems. Likewise, little can be gained by stipulating the validity of the extreme constitutionalist point of view that until 751, or perhaps until some later date, Italy was legally a part of the Byzantine Empire. As we shall see, after the 730s, perhaps after the 720s, the Byzantine writ ceased to run in Italy, and numerous actions undertaken there prove quite compellingly that most people no longer considered themselves to be subjects of the Basileus. To argue, therefore, that central Italy was legally Byzantine is to elevate constitutional and legal history to a level of abstraction suitable only to metaphysics. This book does not, therefore, treat epiphenomena in Byzantine history but central and crucial developments in the history of Italy. Likewise, it assumes that many people, and not just popes and emperors, played decisive roles in the unfolding story recorded in the following pages.

A second line of interpretation from which the present study parts company holds that the history of the Republic is actually a chapter in Frankish history. This view has won numerous adherents and is today almost the textbook orthodoxy. The "Frankish view" has two essential components.

The most concise statement of the first component of the Frankish view was made by Louis Halphen when he called the "Donation of Pepin" the "foundation charter" of the Papal State.[5] According to all who adhere to this view, the Papal State, or, as I call it, the Republic, was actually created by the Carolingians between 754 and 756. This interpretation is open to challenge on three counts. First, Pepin only "donated"—it is legitimate to argue that Pepin did not truly donate anything—a small portion of the lands that eventually constituted the Republic. Second, Pepin was not asked by Pope

---

[5]Louis Halphen, "Les origines du pouvoir temporel de la papauté," in his *A travers l'histoire du moyen âge* (Paris, 1950), p. 39. This article first appeared in 1922, and by 1947 when Halphen wrote his *Charlemagne and the Carolingian Empire*, trans. Giselle de Nie (Amsterdam, 1977), esp. pp. 27–31, he had moderated this view somewhat. It remains, however, an accurate statement of a broad school of thought. Further examples will be found in chapters 3, 5, 8, and 9.

Stephen II to create anything. He was asked to defend something, namely, the Republic, which was already in existence. Third, the Frankish view, in its first manifestation, tends to ignore what had been going on in Italy for a half-century before Pepin set foot across the Alps.

The second component of the Frankish view is more subtle, but no less widely held than the first. It maintains that after 754, or at any rate certainly after 774, the Republic became a constituent part of the vast Frankish realm. This interpretation denies the very existence of a republic. Some serious objections to this interpretation can also be raised. In later chapters it will become apparent that down to 800, when Charlemagne was crowned emperor, the Republic and the Frankish kingdoms were distinct entities and were totally independent of one another. After 800 matters became more complex, but it can be demonstrated that the Republic remained an autonomous region with only the slenderest of formal ties to the Carolingian emperors.

That the two sides of the Frankish view are contradictory seems not to have occurred to anyone before. Indeed, how could the Carolingians have created something that did not truly exist because it had been absorbed into another political entity? There is, perhaps, no need to try to resolve this contradiction because it is possible to approach the subject of Franco-papal relations somewhat differently than has been customary in the past. In 1896 Theodor Lindner said that Franco-papal relations form the single most important subject in medieval history.[6] Today most medievalists would rightly dispute that contention or at least suggest that it is badly exaggerated. Still, changing scholarly interests have not relegated the history of Carolingian relations with the papacy to second-class status. This is evident both from the almost yearly flow of new contributions to the subject, and also from the fact that many controversial issues unresolved in Lindner's time are no less so in our own. In a sense, though, Lindner's observation provides a sharp insight into certain problems connected with many histories of the early Republic.

If one takes even a hasty look at the literature on the origins of the Republic, it will be discovered that the bulk of it treats in detail only the years from 754 to 774. In the first of these years Pope Stephen II appeared in Francia and received certain promises and assurances from King Pepin. In the latter year Charlemagne visited Rome and confirmed his father's promises. These promises, and the historical circumstances that produced them,

---

[6]Theodor Lindner, *Die sogenannten Schenkungen Pippins, Karls des Großen und Ottos I. an die Päpste* (Stuttgart, 1896), p. 1.

are frequently interpreted as *the* crucial events in the emergence of the Republic. To these promises and all their attendant problems we shall return frequently, but for now it is important to note that this narrowness of focus has distorted the field of vision. It puts the Franks into the central place on that field when in fact they ought to be accorded only an auxiliary role. Moreover, there are few good reasons for beginning a study of Franco-papal relations in 754 and no reasons at all for concluding the story in 774. These are not the most critical distortions in much of the existing literature, however. The greatest mistake has been to assume that the origins of the Republic are to be sought in the context of Franco-papal relations on the one hand, and of Carolingian history on the other. In fact, Franco-papal relations form only one part of the story, and it is neither the introduction nor the central theme. Just as those who embrace the Byzantine view deny the Republic its own history, so too those who adhere to one or another version of the Frankish view make the history of the Republic an epiphenomenon in somebody else's history, in this instance that of the Franks.

If this study is original, then its originality derives from the novel context in which the origin of the Republic of St. Peter is placed and from its chronological scope. This book reclaims for the Republic its own history and locates that history squarely in Italy during several decades that were decisive for the historical development of that ancient land. Byzantines and Franks must be written into the drama, along with Anglo-Saxons, Bavarians, Lombards, and others, but always in supporting roles. On this stage the choice parts are played by Italians, and they are seen to be acting out their own history.

There is also a scholarly tradition quite different from the Byzantine and Frankish views that have just been discussed. Many historians simply do not believe that before the thirteenth century there really existed an entity that can legitimately be called a *state* inside the lands that eventually became, after Innocent III, the "real" Papal State. Wilhelm Sickel was the first to argue in detail that, in the eighth century, the Roman Church possessed only ecclesiastical institutions, and that these were inadequate to the task of government. Too much of the Roman secular ruling apparatus had been lost, he thought, for a state in any meaningful sense to have existed.[7] Recent work by Daniel Waley and Peter Partner has tended to agree with Sickel. According to the former, the Papal State first truly emerged in the thirteenth century, and was a dual product of the papacy's long struggle with the Hohenstaufen and the elaboration of an ideology, during the Investiture

---

[7]Wilhelm Sickel, "Alberich II. und der Kirchenstaat," *MIÖG* 23 (1902): 5off.

Controversy, that was appropriate to temporal rule. Waley's fine book, *The Papal State in the Thirteenth Century*,[8] is in many ways a model of what a historical monograph should be, but it does not appreciate the significance of those far-off developments that are actually the early chapters of the very subject to which he has devoted his estimable talents. Peter Partner, in *The Lands of St. Peter*,[9] at least acknowledges that the story begins in the eighth century, but he also seems to diminish the importance of the earlier period by looking at events before the thirteenth century as a history of the papal patrimonies rather than as the history of a papal state. Pierre Toubert's magisterial study of the medieval Lazio maintains that something more than mere patrimonial administration characterizes what he almost grudgingly calls the "First Papal State," but he concludes by hewing close to the standard view that a real Papal State did not emerge before the time of Pope Innocent III.[10] So pervasive are the interpretations represented by Sickel, Waley, and Partner that they are more or less implicitly accepted in a synthetic article by Eugenio Dupré-Theseider and in a major new study of Innocent III by Manfred Laufs.[11] Running through all of this scholarship, moreover, is a tacit judgment that after 754 the Republic was too dependent upon the Carolingian monarchy to merit being thought of as an independent political entity, a tendency that is very close to one of the components of the Frankish view.

Certainly a deliberate and articulated desire to be free and independent, a clear sense of territorial claims within recognized frontiers, and the conscious deployment and refinement of institutional structures designed not only to administer a church but also to govern in all legitimate and necessary respects may be taken as distinguishing characteristics of a true state. All of these conditions were met by the end of the eighth century and most of them had been met by the middle of the century. Chapters 1 through 5 of this book examine in detail the emancipation of central Italy from the Byzantine empire, the efforts of the popes to build and to control a state within the emancipated lands, and the political or diplomatic factors that produced the precise territorial configurations of the Republic. Chapters 6 and 7 describe

---

[8]Daniel Waley, *The Papal State in the Thirteenth Century* (London, 1961).

[9]Peter Partner, *The Lands of St. Peter* (Berkeley, 1972).

[10]Pierre Toubert, *Les structures du Latium médiéval*, 2 vols. (Rome, 1973), 2:935–36, 941 n.1, 1038–39.

[11]Eugenio Dupré-Theseider, "Sur les origines de l'état de l'église," *L'Europe aux IXᵉ–XIᵉ siècles: Aux origines des états nationaux*, ed. Tadeusz Manteuffel and Aleksander Gieysztor (Warsaw, 1968), pp. 93–103; Manfred Laufs, *Politik und Recht bei Innozenz III* (Cologne, 1980).

the secular and ecclesiastical structures that were employed to govern the Republic. Much of these two chapters is devoted to explaining institutional changes and refinements that reflect deliberate adjustments to the papacy's assumption of temporal rule. Chapters 8 and 9 study the Franco-papal alliance in an attempt to determine whether or not the Republic was at any time absorbed into the Frankish realm. The conclusion takes up the complex matter of the application of the term *state* to the Republic of St. Peter. Although the various chapters of this book examine different aspects of the early history of the Republic, three questions are always foremost: Was there in Italy a desire to be free and independent? Was there a clearly articulated sense of the exact lands that were to enjoy freedom? Was there an effective and unfettered government within those lands?

Because the present study seeks to make a contribution to our understanding of the history of central Italy, it should not be construed as being a book about papal history alone. The papacy looms large in the pages that follow, but papal history properly comprehended would involve many subjects concerning which this study has little or nothing to say. For example, liturgical texts and canonical collections are drawn upon for evidence, but little effort is made to offer explicit comments on the papacy's role in the historical development of liturgy or canon law. Likewise, the intrinsic theological issues involved in several doctrinal controversies are not treated, although the political implications of those quarrels will engage us frequently. The pastoral and hierarchical responsibilities of the popes in Italy figure prominently in some chapters, but not the pope's role as the head of a universal church. Finally, only occasionally will attention be drawn to the development and elaboration of papal ideology. Although somewhat sympathetic to Jeffrey Richards's comment that in recent times too much attention has been devoted to the ideological side of papal history, this book inclines more to the position of Peter Partner that " 'Papalism' is something which modern men think of primarily as a system of general ideas. But like much else in Christianity, it is more the product of local history than of abstract thought."[12] This is a book about local history, and during the period that it treats the papacy did not articulate a comprehensive ideology to justify or explain its actions in creating the Republic. This is not to imply that the period was without important ideological formulations. Even Richards, who eschews an ideological approach to papal history, begins his *The Popes and the Papacy in the Early Middle Ages* with a long and solid assessment of

---

[12]Jeffrey Richards, *The Popes and the Papacy in the Early Middle Ages* (London, 1979), pp. 1–5; and Partner, *The Lands of St. Peter*, p. 1.

papal ideology which relies heavily on the work of Walter Ullmann who is, without ever being named, the scholar whose approach Richards condemns. Ullmann, along with Ottorino Bertolini, Erich Caspar, Friedrich Kempf, David Miller, and Karl Morrison, to name but a few major contributors, have already exhaustively mined the scanty sources, and they have reported quite fully what they have to say about the conceptual foundations of papal thought and action in the early Middle Ages. My work relies at various points on the contributions of these scholars, but my aims are different from theirs. Occasionally it will be necessary to say something about the relationship between thought and action, but ideology in its own right is never my principal focus. Just as this study may be a useful complement to the works of those who write papal history in broader compass, so too, even with its admittedly and intentionally limited ideological and theoretical component, it may add something to what Ullmann and both his adherents and detractors have taught us.

This study commences in the last decades of the seventh century not because central Italians generally or the papacy in particular experienced then for the first time serious disagreements with the imperial administration but because, in about 685, the historical record contains the first clear evidence of a pervasive willingness in Italy to ignore Byzantine dicta. By the 720s the imperial government in Constantinople had come to be regarded by most people in central Italy as ruthless and oppressive. Rebellions against imperial authority broke out everywhere, and the popes began trying to refashion the imperial legacy in central Italy into a new and more durable and cohesive political entity. Papal efforts were constantly challenged by the possibility of Byzantine reprisals, particularism in Italy itself, and real or potential pressure from the Lombards. Eventually the Franks were called into Italy by the popes to supply a military and diplomatic counterbalance to the papacy's enemies. Papal diplomacy was effective insofar as it finally achieved a definitive removal of the Byzantine and Lombard threats to the Republic. Italian particularism, however, was never genuinely overcome, and its perseverance had important implications for the geographical and political contours which the Republic finally assumed. Moreover, from 754 to 824 the popes and the Franks tried repeatedly to define the terms of their own relationship in a way that guarded the legitimate interests of each party. The story stops in the 820s for two reasons. First, in 824 Pope Eugenius II and Louis the Pious set down in the *Constitutio Romana* what was to have been the definitive resolution of all of the terms of their personal and diplomatic relationships. Second, during the 820s certain developments began unfolding both in Francia and in Italy which had the net result of deflecting the course of the Republic's history onto unforeseen paths.

Despite an interruption of continuity in the ninth century, there is still a discernibly consistent history in central Italy that runs from the Republic of St. Peter through the Papal States to Vatican City. Seen in this perspective, the events of the thirteenth century, although they undoubtedly possess great historical significance, should be regarded as only one among many alterations in a much longer historical process. Before Innocent III one might note the decline of Carolingian rule in Italy, the attacks of the Muslims, the transformations of the Roman aristocracy, the imperialism of Saxon Germany, the conquests of the Normans, and the emergence of the so-called Papal Monarchy. After Innocent's time significant changes attended the papacy's absence from Italy during the Avignon period, the almost continuous local warfare of the Renaissance epoch, Napoleon's grand schemes, the wars for Italian unification, the regime of "Il Duce," and the renunciation of the tiara in 1978. We turn now, therefore, to what might be thought of as the first chapters of a very long book whose story was a millennium in the making.

FRANKISH
KINGDOM

L O M B A R D

Pavia

K I N G D O M

Aquileja

Venice

ISTRIA

Ferrara

Comacchio

EXARCHATE

Bologna

Ravenna

Imola

Classe

Faenza

Forli

Forum Populie

Rimini

Cesena

La Cattolica

Pesaro

PENTA

Fano

Montefeltro

POLIS

Senigallia

Urbino

Ancona

Fossombrone

Umana

TUSCANY

Cagli

Jesi

Osimo

Citta di Castello

Gubbio

Perugia

DUCHY

OF

Spoleto

SPOLETO

Bomarzo

Amelia

Terni

Bieda

Orte

Rieti

Narni

Sutri

Farfa

DUCHY

Rome

Sora

OF

Arpino

Arce

ROME

Aquino

Terracina

DUCHY

Gaeta

Benevento

OF

Capua

Naples

BENEVENTO

Salerno

CORSICA

SARDINIA

C A L A B R I A

S I C I L Y

ITALY
IN THE EARLY
EIGHTH CENTURY

Map 1

Map 2

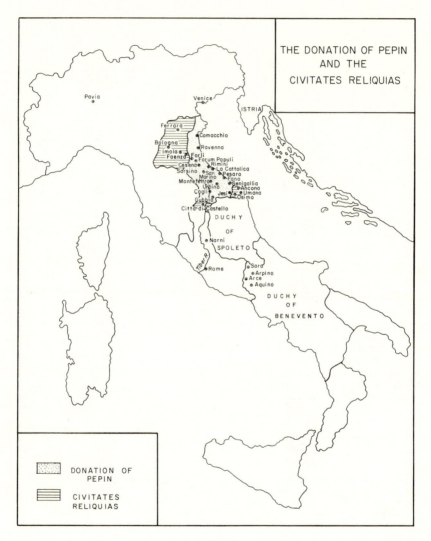

THE DONATION OF PEPIN
AND THE
CIVITATES RELIQUIAS

Pavia

Venice

ISTRIA

Ferrara
Comacchio
Bologna
Ravenna
Imola
Forlì
Faenza
Forum Populi
Cesena
Rimini
Sarsino
San
La Cattolica
Marino
Pesaro
Montefeltro
Fano
Urbino
Senigallia
Ancona
Coglia
Jesi
Umana
Gubbio
Osimo
Città di Castello

DUCHY
OF
Narni
SPOLETO

Tiber R.

Rome
Sora
Arpino
Arce
Aquino

DUCHY
OF
BENEVENTO

DONATION OF
PEPIN

CIVITATES
RELIQUIAS

Map 3

Citta di Castello

Orvieto
Bagnorea
Amelia
Bomarzo
Orte
Viterbo
Galese
Biejia
Sutri
Nepi
Toscanella
Civitavecchia

Sovana

Rosellae

Populonia

Forta

Tivoli

Rome
Porto
Ostia

Tiber R.

Albano
Velletri
Segni
Anagni
Veletri
Patrica
Ferentino
Frosinone
Alatri
Sqra
Arpino
Arce
Aquino
Terracina
Gaeta

THE DUCHY OF ROME AND
THE FRANCO-PAPAL SETTLEMENTS
781–787

Pre–781 Border — — — —
Post–787 Border —————

Map 4

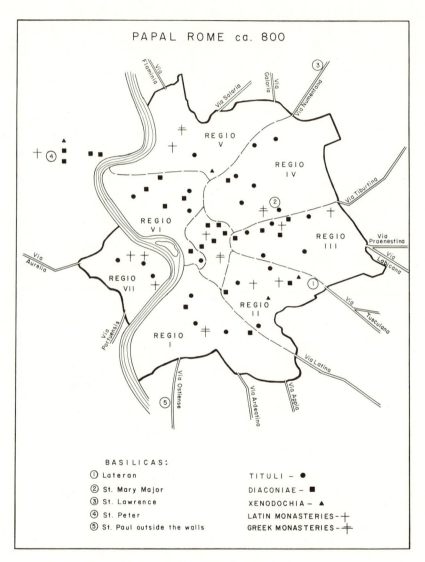

PAPAL ROME ca. 800

Via Flaminia
Via Solaria
Via Galaria
Via Numentana
Via Tiburtina
Via Praenestina
Via Labicana
Via Tusculana
Via Latina
Via Appia
Via Ardeatina
Via Ostiense
Via Portuensis
Via Aurelia

REGIO V

REGIO IV

REGIO VI

REGIO III

REGIO VII

REGIO II

REGIO I

BASILICAS:
① Lateran
② St. Mary Major
③ St. Lawrence
④ St. Peter
⑤ St. Paul outside the walls

TITULI – ●
DIACONIAE – ■
XENODOCHIA – ▲
LATIN MONASTERIES – ✝
GREEK MONASTERIES – ✚

Map 5

One

Pax Italiae

IN ABOUT 680 or 681 the Byzantines and the Lombards finally concluded peace in Italy on the basis of the status quo in terms of territorial possessions.[1] Lombard hostilities against Byzantine Italy ceased, and the imperial regime finally recognized the ineradicable reality of a Lombard kingdom in northern Italy. By about 680 the final remnants of Lombard Arianism had disappeared, and this also contributed to a relaxation of tensions between the heretical and Catholic segments of the population of Italy.[2] Likewise the years 680–81 marked, with the decisions of the Sixth Ecumenical Council at Constantinople, a healing of the old and bitter theological rift between Rome and the imperial capital.[3] After the brutal Gothic wars (535–55), the Lombard conquests and settlements (post 568–69), the long war of attrition waged by the heretical and ferocious Lombards against what remained of imperial Italy, and the constant, acrimonious religious squabbling between East and West, the peace of 680–81 appeared to create brighter prospects for Italy than this ancient land had known for two or three centuries. If we are to understand the complex set of developments that would in the long

---

[1]Ludo Moritz Hartmann, *Geschichte Italiens im Mittelalter*, 3 vols. in 5 (Gotha, 1897–1911), 2.1:272–73, 279–80 n.3, states that the peace could have been concluded any time between 677 and 681. Erich Caspar, *Das Papsttum unter byzantinischer Herrschaft* (Tübingen, 1933), p. 724, gives 681 as the date. Ottorino Bertolini, *Roma e i longobardi* (Rome, 1972), p. 27, says 678–81. See also Paolo Delogu, "Il regno longobardo," in *Longobardi e bizantini*, vol. 1 of *Storia d'Italia*, ed. Giuseppe Galasso (Turin, 1980), pp. 99–100.

[2]Steven C. Fanning, "Lombard Arianism Reconsidered," *Speculum* 56 (1981): 241–58, makes an impressive case, against all the literature, for the relative weakness and insignificance of Lombard Arianism. Even if he is correct, and I have my doubts, his argument does not change the fact that Arianism was defunct by about 680. For a more traditional and, to me, still persuasive assessment of Lombard Arianism see: Donald Bullough, "Germanic Italy," in *The Dawn of European Civilization*, ed. David Talbot Rice (New York, 1965), p. 173.

[3]This council will be discussed more fully later. For a brief treatment see: Louis Bréhier and René Aigrain, *Grégoire le Grand, les états barbares et la conquête arabe (590–757)* (Paris, 1947), pp. 192–93.

run radically transform what Louis Duchesne once called the "political archaeology" of Italy, it is necessary to have in mind a clear sense of the Italian
scene in the last half of the seventh century and in the first decades of the
eighth.

The Transformation of Byzantine Italy

Continental Italy, primarily consisting of the valley of the Po, constituted the
firm basis of the *Regnum Langobardorum*. This area was conquered very
early by the Lombards, who likewise took its two great cities, Milan and
Pavia, the latter of which served as capital of the kingdom.[4] Neither to the
east nor to the west did the Lombard kingdom reach the modern borders of
Italy. The Franks had, since the sixth century, held the passes through the
French and Swiss Alps along with the lands immediately on the Italian side
of the mountains.[5] In the east, the coastal regions of Venetia and Istria
remained in Byzantine hands and the headwaters of the Adriatic were possessed by the Avars. The *regnum* extended into peninsular Italy only in
Tuscany, but there it reached to within thirty or forty miles of Rome.

The Lombard conquests had not stopped short in the north. Much of
central and southern Italy had been overrun also, and within a generation
of the initial Lombard invasion two large duchies had been created south of
the *regnum*. The Duchy of Spoleto occupied the center of the peninsula from
the Sabine hills east of Rome to the Adriatic. Below Spoleto was the larger
Duchy of Benevento which stretched from sea to sea and occupied the
territory south of Spoleto and north of the Byzantine duchies of Calabria
and Naples.[6] In theory the Lombard dukes were subject to the kings at Pavia,
but in practice they were virtually autonomous. The ruling apparatus in each
duchy was relatively sophisticated, modeled on the royal administration at
Pavia, and a potent agent for the preservation of ducal independence.[7]

---

[4]The clearest account of the Lombard conquest remains Thomas Hodgkin, *Italy and Her
Invaders*, vol. 5, *The Lombard Invasion* (Oxford, 1895). For recent assessments see: Delogu,
"Il regno longobardo," pp. 12–28, and Bullough, "Germanic Italy," pp. 171–73.

[5]Georgine Tangl, "Die Passvorschrift des Königs Ratchis und ihre Beziehung zu den Verhältnis zwischen Franken und Langobarden vom 6.–8. Jahrhundert," *QFIAB* 38 (1958): 6–
10; Robert Holtzmann, *Die Italienpolitik der Merowinger und des Königs Pippin* (Darmstadt,
1962), pp. 9ff, 15ff.

[6]Hodgkin, *Italy and Her Invaders*, vol. 6, *The Lombard Kingdom* (Oxford, 1895), pp.
62–96.

[7]H. Pabst, "Geschichte des langobardischen Herzogthums," *Forschungen zur deutschen
Geschichte* 2 (1862): 414–15, 467–69, 471–73. See also: Bullough, "The Writing Office of
the Dukes of Spoleto in the Eighth Century," in *The Study of Medieval Records: Essays in*

From the Lombards' first appearance in Italy in 568–69 until the peace of 680–81, they represented for the Byzantines, who were in theory masters of all of Italy, unwelcome intruders against whom, with neither cease nor success, war was "suspended and begun again a hundred times in every part of Italy."[8] This constant state of warfare, or war-preparedness, produced a profound transformation in the regime created by Justinian's Pragmatic Sanction of 554 at the conclusion of the Gothic wars. Whereas Justinian had envisioned a typical Roman administration with sharply distinct civil and military jurisdictions, there gradually arose a tightly knit institutional, political, and social structure that was fundamentally military in both design and function.[9]

The Byzantine province of Italy consisted of the Exarchate of Ravenna[10] and several duchies: Istria, Venetia, Ferrara, the Pentapolis, Rome, Perugia, Naples, and Calabria.[11] Naples and Calabria, which figure only marginally in this study, were extensively Hellenized by 700[12] and had been transferred

---

Honor of Kathleen Major (Oxford, 1971), pp. 1–21; Stefano Gasparri, *I duchi longobardi* (Rome, 1978), pp. 7–44.

[8]Giovanni Tabacco, "La storia politica e sociale," in *Storia d'Italia*, ed. Giulio Einaudi (Turin, 1974), p. 42.

[9]Tabacco, *Storia d'Italia*, pp. 42–44; Charles Diehl, *Etudes sur l'administration byzantine dans l'Exarchat de Ravenne* (Paris, 1888), pp. 4–5, 81–92; Piero Rasi, *Exercitus Italicus e milizie cittadine nell'alto medioevo* (Padua, 1937), pp. 168–69; Chris Wickham, *Early Medieval Italy: Central Power and Local Society, 400–1000* (London, 1981), pp. 27, 75–76. T. S. Brown, "Social Structure and the Hierarchy of Officialdom in Byzantine Italy, 554–800 A.D." (Ph.D. diss., Nottingham, 1975), p. 11, points out that too much should not be made of the envisioned separation of civil and military jurisdictions, because in practice it would have been very difficult to divide them in sixth-century Italy.

[10]Ironically no document uses the term Exarchatus Ravennatis until after the dissolution of the Exarchate in 751. The term has become standardized in historical discourse but sometimes introduces certain confusions, because often without warning, it is used to denote either the whole Exarchate or just the region of Ravenna proper. See Brown, "Social Structure," pp. 59, 91 n.54.

[11]Diehl, *L'administration byzantine*, p. 5; Paul Goubert, *Byzance avant l'Islam* (Paris, 1965), 2: 39–48.

[12]Lynn T. White, "The Byzantinization of Sicily," *American Historical Review* 42 (1936): 1–21; Peter Charanis, "On the Question of the Hellenization of Sicily and Southern Italy During the Middle Ages," ibid. 52 (1946): 74–86. Extensive Hellenization is not in question; its source is. White argues for fugitives from the Muslims. Charanis emphasizes immigrants from the Balkans fleeing Slavs, Bulgars, and Avars. Both make impressive cases, which suggests that exclusive interpretations ought to be avoided. For additional perspectives on the Hellenization of southern Italy see: Bernhard Bischoff, "Das griechische Element in der abendländischen Bildung des Mittelalters," *BZ* 44 (1951): 28; Jean Irigoin, "La culture grecque dans l'occident latin du VIIe au XIe siècle," *SSCI* 22 (1975): 428–31.

to the authority of the patrician of Sicily.[13] The other duchies were administered by the exarch of Ravenna, the highest Byzantine magistrate.

It is not known exactly when the first exarch was sent to Italy. In all probability this occurred in the last decades of the sixth century, after which time exarchs continued to be appointed to the province until 751. It seems that the exarchs were originally officers with an essentially military mandate, but rather soon they began to combine both civil and military functions. They were always sent to Italy from Constantinople and rarely had served in any capacity in Italy before being named exarch. Usually, in fact, they were selected from among the high officers of the palace administration. The exarch was the emperor's direct representative in Italy, and in theory he had a very narrow scope for personal initiative. Only on rare occasions did his term of office exceed six or seven years. His duty was to lead the *exercitus Italicus*, administer the province during the pleasure of his imperial master, publish laws and canons of church councils, and appoint most subordinate officials.[14]

The territory ruled by the exarchs was very diverse and plagued everywhere by separatist tendencies. Regional separatism was a constant problem for the Byzantine Empire in the seventh century, and Italy was no exception.[15] Within Italy itself the Exarchate was a fragile creation that owed more to military exigencies than to a coherent historical development. It threatened to split apart at any moment. The area was more Latinate than the profoundly Hellenized south, but Greeks and easterners of various kinds formed more than 40 percent of the population in the region of Ravenna itself, and there is no reason to believe that this high percentage would have been noticeably lower in other major regions such as Rome.[16] Religious and civil institutions forged some bonds of unity but diversity and divisiveness

---

[13]André Guillou, "L'Italia bizantina dall'invasione longobarda alla caduta di Ravenna," in *Longobardi e Bizantini*, vol. 1 of *Storia d'Italia*, ed. Giuseppe Galasso (Turin, 1980), p. 237.

[14]Ludo Moritz Hartmann, *Untersuchungen zur Geschichte der byzantinischen Verwaltung in Italien, 540–750* (Leipzig, 1889), pp. 4–34; Diehl, *L'administration byzantine*, pp. 168–84; Goubert, *Byzance avant l'Islam* 2:33–38, 49–55; Guillou, "L'Italia bizantina," pp. 238–40.

[15]Guillou, *Régionalisme et indépendence dans l'empire byzantin au VIIᵉ siècle: L'example de l'Exarchat et de la Pentapole d'Italie* (Rome, 1969), pp. 11–13; Karl Bosl, *Gesellschaftsgeschichte Italiens im Mittelalter* (Stuttgart, 1982), pp. 13–14, 16–18.

[16]Guillou, *Régionalisme*, pp. 77–88, 95; idem, "Demography and Culture in the Exarchate of Ravenna," *Studi Medievali*, 3d series, 10 (1969): 201–19; Diehl, *L'administration byzantine*, pp. 241–88. Brown, "Social Structure," pp. 206–8, notes that Guillou's figures are based on too little evidence to be taken very precisely. They seem to me to be more valid in general terms, however, than Brown will admit.

were more often the rule.[17] Ravenna, with its proud late-imperial associations, its lordly archbishops, and its position as the seat of the Exarchate, rarely desired to work in unison with the rest of Byzantine Italy.[18] The Pentapolis, a region of coastal cities of some commercial vitality, was located to the south of Ravenna and time and time again sought to loosen its ties with that city.[19] To the north of Ravenna, Venice, as always in its history, looked out for itself first.[20] Perugia was something of a historical accident whose only reason for being was to secure communications between Rome and Ravenna, two cities which, incidentally, gave frequent notice of not desiring to be in very close communication with one another.[21] The old via Flaminina was in Lombard hands after the conquest of Spoleto and, as a result, a new road, the via Amerina, had been traced across Perugia to provide transit and communications between Rome and Ravenna. This narrow artery was almost always threatened with closure and supplied only the most tenuous linkage between the two poles of central Italy. Finally, there was Rome and its duchy, theoretically extending to the one-hundredth milestone along each of the great roads leading out of the city, but in fact much reduced in size on all sides by the incursions of the Lombards. Rome had, as always, its proud historical traditions, but these could not mask the decline and disrepair of the Eternal City.[22]

The fundamentally military organization of Byzantine Italy appears to have emerged not only as a response to constant pressure from the Lombards but also as a corrective to the territorial complexity of the region.[23] Beneath

---

[17]Guillou, *Régionalisme*, pp. 43–76.

[18]Guillou, *Régionalisme*, p. 224; Paul Luther, *Rom und Ravenna bis zum 9. Jahrhundert* (Berlin, 1889), pp. 9–12; Hermann Josef Schmidt, "Die Kirche von Ravenna im Frühmittelalter," *HJB* 34 (1913): 729–80; T. S. Brown, "The Church of Ravenna and the Imperial Administration in the Seventh Century," *English Historical Review* 94 (1979): 13–18.

[19]Guillou, *Régionalisme*, p. 43ff; Diehl, *L'administration byzantine*, pp. 59–63.

[20]Roberto Cessi, *Storia della Repubblica di Venezia* (Milan, 1968), 1:13–15.

[21]Tabacco, *Storia d'Italia*, p. 41, and Jules Gay, *L'Italie méridionale et l'empire byzantine* (Paris, 1904), pp. 26–27, point out that while Perugia kept Rome and Ravenna in contact with one another, the duchy also served to keep the Lombard *regnum* out of touch with the Duchies of Spoleto and Benevento.

[22]Diehl, *L'administration byzantine*, pp. 63–68; Louis Heinrich Armbrust, *Die territoriale Politik der Päpste von 500 bis 800 mit besonderer Berücksichtigung der römischen Beamtenverhältnisse* (Göttingen, 1885), p. 58. We are informed of the jurisdiction of the Urban Prefect out to the hundredth milestone by Procopius and Cassiodorus, but by the late seventh century the Lombards of the *regnum*, Spoleto, and Benevento had significantly attenuated these earlier limits.

[23]Tabacco, *Storia d'Italia*, p. 43.

the exarch in this structure there were dukes, who possessed military and civil authority in the duchies enumerated above, and tribunes or counts, who led individual detachments of troops called *numeri* and who also had important civil functions in particular localities. In the sixth century, local detachments constituted garrisons at *castra* throughout the countryside and along all strategic borders. By the seventh century the *castra* still existed, but probably were less significant as permanent garrisons than as rallying points for local defense. Although we still hear of *iudices* and *consules* in seventh- and eighth-century documents, these titles no longer signified distinct civil offices but instead were among the titles used to describe the civil functions accumulated by the dukes and tribunes.[24] Taken together this structure represented the officer corps and chief troops of the *exercitus Italicus*. In theory there was only one Italian army under the exarch, but in practice the armies of the most important duchies functioned almost autonomously.[25] Each major city also possessed an urban militia which was made up of the adult, male citizenry who could be called up, or dragooned, into service to defend the city as the situation might warrant.[26]

Not surprisingly, the gradual shift to an almost exclusively military organization produced a radical and, at any rate from the Byzantine point of view, unforeseen social transformation of the province. Originally the Byzantine authorities intended to garrison Italy from the east with seasoned troops and generous contingents of barbarians from the Balkans, but in time the lack of available troops, the existence of more pressing military problems in the Near East, Asia Minor, and the Balkans, and a rising feeling at Constantinople that Italy ought to have to defend itself led to the local recruitment of troops.[27] The Gothic wars and the Lombard conquest had destroyed the landed nobility of the late empire,[28] but slowly, through a variety of pro-

---

[24]Diehl, *L'administration byzantine*, pp. 141–56, 300–303; Hartmann, *Byzantinischen Verwaltung*, pp. 52–73; Rasi, *Exercitus Italicus*, p. 49; Goubert, *Byzance avant l'Islam*, pp. 65–72; Tabacco, *Storia d'Italia*, pp. 42–43. The fullest discussion of Byzantine military practices in general is Agostino Pertusi, "Ordinamenti militari, guerre in occidente e teorie di guerra dei Bizantini (secc. VI–X)," *SSCI* 15 (1968): 631–700. The most detailed study of the military structures of Italy proper is Brown, "Social Structure," pp. 51–104.

[25]Diehl (*L'administration byzantine*, pp. 311, 317) holds for one army as does Guillou (*Régionalisme*, pp. 149 n.7, 158, 159–60; and "L'Italia bizantina," p. 265) who criticizes Rasi (*Exercitus Italicus*, pp. 54–57) for arguing on behalf of separate armies. From the constitutional point of view Diehl and Guillou are doubtless correct, but Rasi's interpretation is closer to historical reality.

[26]Rasi, *Exercitus Italicus*, pp. 120, 124–125, 147–148, 152.

[27]Rasi, *Exercitus Italicus*, p. 50; Bertolini, *Roma e i longobardi*, pp. 30–31; Tabacco, *Storia d'Italia*, p. 45; Guillou, "L'Italia bizantina," p. 264.

[28]Tabacco, *Storia d'Italia*, pp. 43–44; Bosl, *Gesellschaftsgeschichte*, pp. 5–6.

cesses, a new class of great landholders arose from the officer corps of the *exercitus Italicus*. These people acquired their lands by purchase, gift, force, fraud, and quite frequently by obtaining emphyteusis contracts from the church, more especially from the churches of Rome and Ravenna.[29] These landed magnates began very early to seek preferments from the Byzantine authorities and achieved them easily from a government that was eager to win them over.[30] With the eventual emergence of an entirely locally recruited army in Italy there came an almost perfect convergence between the governmental and the socioeconomic hierarchies in the province.[31] With the exception of the exarchal office, the officer corps of the *exercitus Italicus* was made up of large landholders. Lower officers were drawn from the less richly endowed and the ordinary troops came from the small landholders. A person's place in political (i.e., military) society was dictated by his place in the landed economy.

By the end of the seventh century one begins to find everywhere in the sources terms like *proceres* or *optimates militiae* signifying an increasingly closed and hereditary land and officeholding aristocracy. These people formed the key social class in late Byzantine Italy. Alongside the *proceres* one begins to find two other designations, *exercitus* and *universus populus*. *Exercitus* referred to the soldiers generally, but more precisely to the medium landholders. *Universus populus* was a catchall designation, apparently, for merchants, artisans, laborers, and all other people who were not necessarily landholders and who generally had no place in the military hierarchy.[32] Perhaps the clearest indication of the enhanced role of the military aristocracy can be seen in its role in papal elections. In the time of Pope Gregory I (590–604) papal elections were accomplished by "clergy, senate and people." By the late seventh century the *proceres* and the *exercitus* played the manifestly decisive roles.[33]

---

[29]Diehl, *L'administration byzantine*, pp. 293–99; Guillou, *Régionalisme*, pp. 189–91.

[30]Diehl, *L'administration byzantine*, pp. 300–303.

[31]Tabacco, *Storia d'Italia*, pp. 45–46.

[32]Paolo Brezzi, *Roma e l'empero medioevale (774–1252)* (Bologna, 1947), pp. 4–7; Bertolini, *Roma e i longobardi*, p. 31; Rasi, *Exercitus Italicus*, p. 51. For a remarkable assessment of the social structure of late Byzantine Rome, and of the system of values and attitudes that sustained it see: Evelyne Patlagean, "Les armes et la cité à Rome du VIIᵉ au IXᵉ siècle, et le modèle européen des trois functions sociales," *MAH* 86 (1974): 25–62.

[33]The transformation is evident in papal election formulae. See: *LD*, nos. 60–63, pp. 114–21. That these formulae date from a little after 682 was proved by Louis Duchesne, "Le *Liber Diurnus* et les élections pontificales au VIIᵉ siècle," *BEC* 52 (1891): 5–30. For assessments of these circumstances see: Caspar, *Das Papsttum*, pp. 620–21; Richards, *Popes and the Papacy*, p. 205. I return to this subject in Chapter 6.

The steadily growing prominence of the military officers of Byzantine Italy was only one feature of the region's social transformation. After the profound demographic decline of the sixth century, many indicators suggest that the population was recovering, even expanding, in the seventh.[34] Several important developments accompanied this demographic recovery.

In the first place, many abandoned sites were reinhabited, and some entirely new centers of population emerged.[35] In the second place, people began to return to the countryside. Despite what one scholar has called "an embarrassing wealth of variation" in settlement patterns,[36] it seems clear that more people were working the soil in the seventh century than in the sixth and also that more land was under cultivation. The old Roman pattern of widely dispersed rural settlements was not generally replicated, however, except in the sector of the Duchy of Rome north of the city and west of the Tiber.[37] Across most of central Italy nucleated settlements were growing up around the Byzantine *castra*.[38] As more land was coming into cultivation, the population increase was sustained and even propelled forward.[39] This process tended to increase the population of many rural centers and also to make them more prosperous.

The gradual increase in the number of centers of population and cultivation is an important fact in its own right, but it is closely connected with other crucial developments. Traditionally, political and military historians have examined the numerous *castra* of central Italy, and they have pronounced the verdict that these fortified centers were essentially defensive, and therefore socially and economically static.[40] In reality, they were dynamic nuclei around which there steadily emerged complex local societies.[41] These societies were dominated by military officers but they included small landholders as well as dependent peasants whose social and legal status varied

---

[34]Guillou, "Demography and Culture," pp. 203–5; Philip J. Jones, "L'Italia agraria nell'alto medioevo: Problemi di cronologia e di continuità," *SSCI* 13 (1966): 65–73.

[35]Giulio Schmiedt, "Le fortificazioni altomedievali in Italia viste dall'aereo," *SSCI* 15 (1968): 860–85, 885–92.

[36]Wickham, "Historical Aspects of Medieval South Etruria," in *Papers in Italian Archaeology* (Oxford, 1978), 1: 381.

[37]Wickham, "Medieval South Etruria," pp. 375–77.

[38]T. S. Brown, "Settlement and Military Policy in Byzantine Italy," in *Papers in Italian Archaeology* (Oxford, 1978), 1: 325ff, 327ff; A. W. Lawrence, "Early Medieval Fortifications near Rome," *Papers of the British School at Rome* 32 (1964): 89–122.

[39]Jones, "L'Italia agraria," p. 77.

[40]For example, Pertusi, "Ordinamenti militari," pp. 684–87.

[41]Brown, "Settlement and Military Policy," pp. 323–38 passim. This is a crucial article for anyone who seeks to understand Byzantine Italy. See also Bosl, *Gesellschaftsgeschichte*, pp. 6, 11–12.

considerably from place to place.[42] Even local clergy, including bishops, were drawn into the social life of these centers. Just as the local recruitment of troops had produced what might be called an "Italianization" of Byzantine Italy, so too the progressive development of towns and villages was producing a "localization" of society.

The importance of this social transformation of Byzantine Italy cannot be stressed too strongly. By the end of the seventh century Italy was led, politically, socially, and economically, by men whose careers, families, and fortunes were increasingly tied to particular local communities. A new military aristocracy had grown up, and alongside it a complex social structure that did not necessarily identify with its imperial masters in Constantinople, or with the emperor's representatives in Ravenna. This situation was ripe with possibilities for particularism within Italy, and for tension between West and East.

In time, the secular aristocracy of Italy joined with its clerical counterpart to redefine Italy's relationship to the Byzantine Empire. That redefinition forms one of the central themes of this study. Moreover, even this brief introduction to the Italian social scene in about 700 provides one clue to the fact that the eventual creation of a republic was by no means solely the work of the papacy and of the Lateran bureaucracy. It was a product of Italy's seventh-century social transformation in which many people had played integral parts. On this historical basis I will argue that in the eighth century the papacy led, but did not drive, Italy out of the Byzantine Empire. We shall also be able to see why some areas in Italy rallied to the cause of the republic while others sought independence from Byzantium on their own terms or elected to retain bonds of some sort with the imperial regime.

The Place of the Roman Church

Within Byzantine Italy there existed an institution that was older, richer, and potentially more significant than the whole secular ruling apparatus. This was the Roman Church. From the time of Pope Gregory I the Church had become de facto the key power in Italy.[43] There were two principal reasons why this had happened.

From the fifth century on, in the absence of a continuously effective imperial administration, the Church had begun to care for widows, orphans,

---

[42]Jones ("L'Italia agraria," pp. 81–89) rightly emphasizes the diversity and complexity of local social structures.

[43]Peter Llewellyn, *Rome in the Dark Ages* (London, 1971), p. 107.

minors, and prisoners. The Lateran took over responsibility for public spectacles and urban conveniences ranging from the water supply to public health and sanitation. A system of ecclesiastical courts assumed ever greater responsibility not only for adjudicating disputes among clients of the Church but also for ruling in civil cases between laymen and clerics. Given that one must construe the term *cleric* extremely liberally in this period, and that so much litigation would have touched the church's interests at one point or another, it is probably safe to suggest that most judicial business was now passing before the church's courts. Gregory I accelerated and expanded the scope of previously secular business handled by the Church as no other pope in history. He did this not as a grasping politician but instead as a pastor with a profound sense of his responsibilities. Although statistical evidence is entirely lacking, one will not go wrong in suggesting that a huge proportion of the population of Byzantine Italy was affected every day by some aspect of the church's government.[44] Indeed, although the papal government was already large in Gregory's day, it had doubled in size by the beginning of the eighth century and was by then appreciably larger, and more efficient and responsive, than its secular counterpart.[45]

Not only did the Roman Church possess the most sophisticated government in Italy, but it was also Italy's greatest landholder; perhaps the greatest in the whole Byzantine Empire.[46] A ninth-century biographer of Gregory I, John the Deacon, provides us with a tolerably complete accounting of the papal patrimonies in the days when his subject lived.[47] Apart from a few minor errors and omissions, his list enables us to grasp the vast landed wealth of the early medieval papacy. The pope held lands in every part of Italy, on the adjacent islands of Sicily, Sardinia, and Corsica, and even in southern Gaul and North Africa.[48] It is impossible to formulate a precise estimate of the worth of these estates, but it is known that, in the time of

---

[44]These facts are generally well known, and I wish only to lay special emphasis on the tremendous bonds of clientage that existed between the papal government and the population of Byzantine Italy. For up-to-date discussions see: Bertolini, "Le origini del potere temporale e del dominio temporale dei papi," *SSCI* 20 (1973): 231–55; Richards, *Consul of God: The Life and Times of Gregory the Great* (London, 1980), pp. 70–125.

[45]Caspar, *Das Papsttum*, pp. 630.

[46]This is the plausible suggestion of August Schäfer, *Die Bedeutung der Päpste Gregor II und Gregor III für die Gründung des Kirchenstaates* (Montjoie, 1913), pp. 10–13.

[47]*Vita S. Gregorii*, 2.53, *PL* 75:110.

[48]For lists of the patrimonies and their locations see: Hartmann Grisar, "Ein Rundgang durch die Patrimonien des heiligen Stuhles um das Jahr 600," *Zeitschrift für katholische Theologie* 1 (1877): 321–60; Edward Spearing, *The Patrimony of the Roman Church in the Time of Gregory the Great* (Cambridge, 1918), pp. 5–18; Vincenzo Recchia, *Gregorio Magno e la società agricola* (Rome, 1978), pp. 11–14.

Emperor Leo III (i.e., 732), the revenues from Sicily and Calabria alone amounted to three and one-half talents (350 lbs.) of gold.[49] Gregory I, and his successors, considered the patrimonies to be an endowment for the poor.[50] In practice, this meant that the revenues from the patrimonies were applied to the cost of the numerous previously secular responsibilities assumed by the Church. Nothing, however, can conceal the fact that the patrimonies of the Roman Church created additional, potent bonds between the religious authorities and a good part of the Italian population. In part, this resulted from the role played by the patrimonies in financing the social services provided by the Church, but no less important was the enormous number of people who lived and worked on the church's estates.

The services provided by the church's government and the patrimonies were, then, two factors that contributed to the papacy's preeminence in Italy. At the same time, the church's administration and landholdings produced various kinds of complications and tensions in central Italy. Most of the revenues generated by the patrimonies flowed into Rome and were spent there for the immediate advantage of the Roman populace. While papal charity and largesse were undoubtedly appreciated in Rome, they may have been somewhat less highly esteemed in the dozens of rural communities whose local exertions paid for them. Such tensions are difficult to document but a few examples will come to light later in this study. In legal terms, furthermore, ecclesiastical patrimonies and publicly or privately held lands were quite distinct, but in practice certain developments had effected a blurring of the distinctions between them.[51] Numerous public charges were sustained by the patrimonies. Their inhabitants paid taxes to the imperial authorities and also rendered dues in money and in kind to the agents of the papal administration. The former payments maintained, in part at least, the *exercitus Italicus* along with the officials of the Byzantine government, while the latter financed the ecclesiastical projects of the Church plus the many secular responsibilities that had been assumed by the papacy. For many people in the Italian countryside it must have been difficult to distinguish between the imperial and papal agents who came around regularly to collect the fruits of their labors. Although it might have been that Italy's rural population would have disliked equally its papal and imperial masters, we shall later see that the popes intervened on behalf of the peasants when the emperor tried to raise their taxes. Moreover, during several periods of strai-

---

[49]Grisar, "Rundgang durch die Patrimonien," p. 330. His source is the Byzantine chronicler Theophanes whom all scholars seem to follow on this point.

[50]Richards, *Consul of God*, pp. 95–96.

[51]Patlagean, "Les armes et la cité," pp. 56–57.

tened circumstances in the seventh century, the popes pleaded for and obtained a reduction of the tax burdens on the patrimonies. These interventions must have helped the rural population to decide where to lodge their ultimate loyalties.[52]

An additional blurring of the distinction between private and ecclesiastical property resulted from the possession, usually by means of long-term emphyteusis contracts, of substantial tracts of patrimonial land by the military aristocracy.[53] Why exactly the Church had leased out so much of its land is not clear. André Guillou argues, plausibly enough, that economic and demographic shortfalls had produced a situation wherein the Church possessed more land than it could effectively exploit.[54] The consequences of the passage of considerable amounts of patrimonial land into aristocratic hands are, however, readily to be apprehended. Inadvertently or otherwise, the Roman Church became deeply enmeshed with the economic, and thus with the political and social, strivings of the Italian landed aristocracy. Although friction between the clerical and secular authorities was not uncommon, cooperation, based upon a convergence of interests, was more frequent.[55] Ecclesiastical and secular potentates in Italy, both of whose livelihoods were increasingly tied to the same pieces of land, had to pursue a common Italian policy that would eventually put them both at odds with the essential interests of the imperial government.

The Sixth Ecumenical Council

Prospects for peace within Italy, and between Italy and the East, were also enhanced in 680–81 by the Sixth Ecumenical Council convoked by Emperor Constantine IV at Constantinople. This council had formally restored the

---

[52]Brown, "Social Structure," pp. 193–94, argues that Byzantine taxes, which were both heavy and burdensome, played a key role in producing disaffection between Italy and the imperial regime.

[53]See above n. 29. On emphyteusis contracts see, for a lucid and brief introduction: Gabriele Pepe, *Le moyen âge barbare in Italie*, trans. Jean Gonnet (Paris, 1956), pp. 198–200. I return to this subject much more fully in chapter 7.

[54]Guillou, *Régionalisme*, pp. 189–91.

[55]Bertolini, "Le origini del potere temporale," pp. 252–53; Richards, *Consul of God*, p. 90; Schäfer, *Bedeutung*, pp. 10–13; Wickham, *Early Medieval Italy*, pp. 78–79. Brown, "Social Structure," pp. 181–83.

Byzantine Empire to Chalcedonian orthodoxy on essentially Roman terms.[56] The seemingly interminable monophysite, and then monothelite, policies of the imperial government had long estranged Rome from Constantinople, and much of Italy from the Byzantine government generally and from the exarchs specifically. These long theological quarrels were by no means idle intellectual games indulged in by a few clerical zealots. Everything suggests that people took these controversies very seriously, quite apart from the degree of comprehension which they brought to them. This is true whether one thinks of amusing anecdotes about the likelihood of a person's getting his throat slit in a barber shop for holding views contrary to the barber's, or whether one reflects on the public riots and armed mutinies that usually accompanied either subtle or significant shifts in religious policy. Moreover, the controversies quite regularly evoked intense and heated discussions of the proper relationship of secular to religious authorities. Generally, the religious powers denied the emperor's right to interfere in matters of dogma, and the ultimate heritage of these denials was twofold. On the one hand, imperial authority was somewhat diminished by having, as it were, its theological prerogative circumscribed. On the other hand, respect for the imperial will and majesty in general was endangered by the staunch and steady opposition by the Church to matters considered gravely significant at the palace. Sometimes theological quarrels resulted in little more than recondite disputations. Occasionally, however, outright brutality was visited upon the opponents of the will of the Basileus. For example, Pope Martin I (649–653) was seized, dragged to Constantinople, publicly humiliated, tortured and sent away to die in exile. Such heavy-handed conduct by the Byzantines could not fail to have serious repercussions in Italy, where the place of the pope was already becoming paramount.[57] Indeed, at the time of Martin's arrest there is evidence that the imperial government realized that it would have to proceed cautiously because its religious policies had thrown into question the loyalty of the military aristocracy around Rome.[58]

Such, in brief outline, was the shape of Italy at the time of the various

---

[56]On the council see: George Ostrogorsky, *A History of the Byzantine State*, trans. Joan Hussey, rev. ed. (New Brunswick, N.J., 1969), pp. 127–28; Richards, *Popes and the Papacy*, pp. 198–201.

[57]For two penetrating analyses of East-West tensions in the seventh century see: Bertolini, "Riflessi politici delle controversie religiose con Bisanzio nelle vicende del sec. VII in Italia"; and Paul Lemerle, "Les répercussions de la crise de l'empire d'orient au VIIe siècle sur les pays d'Occident," *SSCI* 5 (1958): 733–89, 713–31. On the social and political importance of the popes see also Bosl, *Gesellschaftsgeschichte*, p. 12.

[58]Guillou, "L'Italia bizantina," p. 260, cites *in extenso* the pertinent source.

peaces concluded in about 680. In reality, every component of this general peace was more illusory than real. The imperial government had carefully fashioned a military structure in Italy to defend the province from the Lombards. The Lombards were for the moment quiescent, but no one could well have predicted whether or not hostilities would recur. During the seventh century the imperial government had not been notably successful in protecting its Italian subjects, so the cessation of hostilities must have been welcome. The key question in many people's minds must have been: Will the peace hold, and if it does not, can the emperor do anything about it? The canons of the Sixth Ecumenical Council were certainly greeted with enthusiasm in Italy, but again, people had to have been pondering the likelihood of permanent religious peace. Ever since the fourth century religious and secular authorities had been debating not only specific points of dogma but also the trickier question of whose duty and responsibility it was to effect authoritative theological formulations. What would happen in Italy if, as experience made eminently likely, the Basileus decided to embark upon a new round of theological contention? Finally, within Byzantine Italy itself all sorts of tensions threatened to pass from latent to overt. Would the "Italianized" and "localized" aristocracy remain loyal to the empire? Would the ancient rivalry between Rome and Ravenna flare up again? Would the new communities dotting the Italian countryside grow resentful of their larger and always domineering neighbors such as Rome and Ravenna? Would the Roman Church continue to forge bonds of unity with much of central Italy's population, and thereby enhance its leadership role, or would it face opposition from the numerous people who were at once its beneficiaries and dependents? Would the popes and the exarch find themselves competing for the loyalty of the inhabitants of central Italy? If a future exarch were called upon to execute against a pope an imperial command considered unpopular in Italy, would the military aristocracy, regardless of its opinions about the command in question, side with the pope, whose lands they held in lease tenure, or with the exarch, who was their lawful superior?

Later in this study there will be ample opportunity, in fact a clear necessity, to answer all of these questions. For now it suffices to anticipate just a bit and say that each question would receive an answer that was simultaneously rooted in Italian realities and deleterious to imperial interests. Thus it would be fairer to say that Byzantine Italy was fragile, rather than peaceful, in 680.

Two

St. Peter's Peculiar People

WHEN ITALY was subjected to new pressures by the imperial government, by the Lombards, and by its own social dynamics both creative and destructive forces were unleashed. Slowly at first, but with an ever quickening momentum, people of every station from all over central Italy, with the popes in the lead, destroyed Italy's bonds with Byzantium. In the process a new state was created, the Republic of St. Peter. For a long time this Republic was a strange agglomeration of territories that were ill-defined, insecure, and of decidedly uncertain prospect. The obvious fragility of the *Pax Italiae* allows us in retrospect to invest the outcome of Italy's long crisis, or many crises, with a certain inevitability that simply cannot have been perceived by people at the time. We know what actually happened; they did not know what was going to happen. An understanding of the Italian crisis from about 680 to 750, then, requires a suspension of judgment, a patient accumulation of details, and eventually an ability to see pattern and meaning amidst the seemingly bewildering welter of events.

Peace Betrayed: Byzantines

The *Pax Italiae* was broken within a half-dozen years of its institution and there can be no doubt about who broke it. The culprit was the new Byzantine emperor, Justinian II. This mercurial figure enjoyed some military success in the East but was twice deprived of his throne and once disfigured by having his nose cut off. His western policy was, in a word, disastrous.[1]

---

[1]Constance Head, *Justinian II of Byzantium* (Madison, Wis., 1972), is a naive attempt to rehabilitate Justinian. Ostrogorsky, *Byzantine State*, p. 129, comes down squarely on both sides of the issue: Justinian was "a gifted ruler with a clear perception of the needs of the state" but

For no apparent reason Justinian wrote to Pope Conon—actually he wrote to Pope John V who had died and Conon received the "*divalem iussionem*"—on 27 February 687 telling him that he had found a copy of the canons of the Sixth Ecumenical Council and, further, that he had established their authenticity.[2] The authenticity of these canons was not then in doubt, and the council itself had played a key role in improving Byzantine-papal relations. Evidently, Justinian was seeking to lay claim to the traditional, and to the papacy galling, imperial authority in dogmatic issues.[3] Nothing much came of this affair but another, and profoundly more serious, squabble was about to erupt.

For some reason Justinian decided to convene a great church council in 691–92. Perhaps he was revealing a sense of duty and religious devotion,[4] or possibly he just wanted to go down in history with the other great Byzantine emperors who had had "their" councils.[5] Whatever the reason, he assembled in the Trullan Hall of the imperial palace a council that has come to be called the "Quinisextian" because it issued a set of 102 disciplinary canons designed to complement the purely theological canons of the Fifth and Sixth Ecumenical Councils.[6] The *vita* of Pope Sergius I says that his representatives in Constantinople signed the canons because they had been deceived, but goes on to say that they were compelled to sign.[7] Confusing or contradictory sources notwithstanding, it seems clear that Sergius and his agents had not willingly endorsed the Quinisextian council. Justinian then had six "Tomes" prepared, that is, six copies of the 102 canons: one for himself, one for the pope, and one for each of the four eastern patriarchs. These Tomes were sent to Sergius for his signature but he bluntly refused to sign and sent the canons back to Constantinople.[8] Most of the canons were actually unobjectionable enough in themselves, but some would have had the effect of making binding in the West certain rites and rules of the eastern church that already differed radically from western practices. The pope may

---

"he possessed neither the astute circumspection nor the balanced judgment of a true statesman, for he was by nature passionate and impulsive. . . . He also had the autocratic spirit . . . and this took the form of a ruthless despotism."

[2]*LP* 1:368 (Conon); Mansi, *Concilia* 11:737. Bréhier and Aigrain, *Grégoire le Grand*, pp. 192–93.

[3]Franz Görres, "Justinian II und das römische Papsttum," *BZ* 17 (1908): 437–40.

[4]Ostrogorsky, *Byzantine State*, p. 138.

[5]Head, *Justinian II*, pp. 66–67.

[6]For the canons: Mansi, *Concilia* 11:921–1006.

[7]*LP* 1:372.

[8]*LP* 1:373.

also have disliked in principle a council's having been called without his explicit permission or approval.[9]

Justinian was evidently surprised by papal opposition to his council and sent the *Protospatharius* Zachary to Rome to haul Sergius unceremoniously to Constantinople to answer for his conduct. Zachary arrived in Rome but soon thereafter he was to be found in mortal fear hiding under the pope's bed while a howling mob surrounded the Lateran and demanded his head. The armies of Ravenna and the Pentapolis had meanwhile marched to Rome to prevent any evil from befalling the pope.[10] The army of Rome is not mentioned, but as it had played a key role in electing Sergius, did not oppose the Ravennese and Pentapolitans, and provided no succor to Zachary, one may safely assume that the leading Romans acquiesced in the obviously generalized opposition to the *protospatharius*.[11] The loyalty of the Roman army to the pope may also be inferred from the fact that when Sergius was elected in 687 he had had a rival who tried to bribe the exarch, John Platyn, into securing the papal office for him. John marched on Rome, and the Roman army refused to admit him and did not permit him to interfere in Sergius's election.[12] It is, thus, possible that Zachary had been sent to Rome because the exarch's authority had been severely compromised. Sergius managed to calm the crowd, and thanks to the pope's efforts, Zachary escaped with his life.[13] The Quinisextian canons remained unsigned, and Sergius unchastized. This whole incident indicates the extent to which, under certain circumstances, Italian loyalties could be shifted from the imperial to the papal banner.

Byzantine authority in Rome had been challenged twice within the space of a few years by deliberate, overt actions. Almost simultaneously a third, and this time exquisitely subtle, challenge was thrown before the Basileus. One of the Quinisextian canons had forbidden the representation of Christ as a lamb, and shortly after the abortive promulgation of those canons Sergius commanded that the hymn "*Agnus Dei*" (Lamb of God) be chanted in the eucharistic liturgy at the fraction rite.[14] The significance of this action by the pope cannot have been lost on anyone in Italy or in the Empire.

---

[9]Görres, "Justinian II," pp. 440–50; Ostrogorsky, *Byzantine State*, pp. 138–39.

[10]*LP* 1:373–74 (Sergius); Paul the Deacon, *Historia Langobardorum*, 6.11, MGH, SSrL, p. 168.

[11]That the Roman army played a central role in effecting Sergius's election is clear: *LP* 1:372. See also: Guillou, *Régionalisme*, pp. 209–11.

[12]*LP* 1:371–72.

[13]*LP* 1:374.

[14]Mansi, *Concilia* 11:978–79, c. 82; *LP* 1:376; Ordo I, c. 105, *Les* Ordines Romani *du*

It is true that it had been the religious authority of the emperor that was challenged in each of these instances, but it is particularly significant that, in the heat of two of the struggles, an exarch and a special imperial envoy had been prevented from carrying out their duties by important laymen in Italy. Moreover, the religious and secular authority of the Basileus were as two sides of the same coin. A defacement of the obverse implied a devaluation of the reverse. In short, it would be a serious mistake to regard the pope and the emperor as the only combatants, or to assume that the issues were exclusively spiritual ones.

At Byzantium, meanwhile, Justinian was not first in the hearts of his countrymen and was, accordingly, deprived of his throne and his nose and sent into exile among the barbarians. Tiberius II was no more pleased with Sergius than his predecessor had been, and in 701 he sent the Exarch Theophylact from Sicily to Rome to discipline the pope. Theophylact found Sergius dead and John VI in the Lateran, but the "*militia totius Italiae*" rose up to defend the new pope. Theophylact went away, like Zachary before him, empty-handed.[15] Although the sources are cryptic, it appears that many prominent Italians had arisen again in defense of the pope. It is also clear that, with new men in the palace and in the Lateran, the struggles of the last few years cannot be attributed to personal animosity between Sergius and Justinian II.

In 705, as a result of circumstances that are of no concern to us, Justinian II recovered his throne. Almost immediately he wrote to the pope, now John VII, and asked him to reconsider the papacy's position on the Quinisextian canons. He offered the pope a compromise whereby the latter might assent to only those canons which he did not find offensive, but John would have none of it.[16] If no open hostilities ensued between John and Justinian, this did not prevent the pope from waging a subtle ideological battle in Rome. He created a new bishop's palace on the Palatine Hill, perhaps contemplating a transfer of the papal government from the Lateran precincts in the southeast corner of the city to the old urban center.[17] The Palatine was

---

haut moyen âge, ed. Michel Andrieu, 5 vols. (reprint, Louvain, 1961), 2:101, and Andrieu's comments, 2:48–51.

[15]*LP* 1:383 (John VI). Duchesne, ibid, p. 384 n.1, says nothing can be known about Theophylact's mission. I disagree and follow the interpretation of Bertolini, "I papi e le relazioni politiche di Roma con i ducati longobardi di Spoleto e di Benevento. III. Il secolo VIII: da Giovanni VI a Gregorio II," *Rivista di storia della chiesa in Italia* 9 (1955): 2–3.

[16]*LP* 1:385–86 (John VII). Görres, "Justinian II," pp. 451–52, depicts John VII as totally unreasonable; likewise, Head, *Justinian II*, pp. 132–33.

[17]Llewellyn, *Rome in the Dark Ages*, p. 170; Richard Krautheimer, *Rome: Profile of a City, 312–1308* (Princeton, 1980), p. 100.

the site of the imperial palace in Rome and John's schemes were rich with ideological significance. Recent popes had denied the emperor's authority in dogma, and Italian troops had protected the pope against imperial reprisals. Now the pope would have a residence, and the seat of his government, where heretofore only the emperor lived. John's plans were cut short by his death, but their symbolic meaning is not difficult to grasp.

John also sponsored the production of a remarkable set of frescoes in the church of Santa Maria Antiqua in Rome near the old forum, a region which, like no other in the city, symbolized all that Rome had been. While all of these frescoes are of profound interest to students of early medieval Byzantine and Roman art,[18] some are particularly relevant to the present discussion. In one panel John had four popes depicted in an aura of sanctity: Leo I, Martin I, an unidentifiable pope, and John himself.[19] The three popes who can be identified were all champions of Roman orthodoxy. Martin had been brutalized for his opposition to monothelitism and John himself, like his two immediate predecessors, had been imposed upon in matters of dogma by Justinian II and Tiberius II. It is difficult to escape the conclusion that John was sending a message to Constantinople about the sanctity and uprightness of popes who had stood up to Byzantine tyranny and religious perversity.[20] That he broadcast this message from the Roman forum can only have added power to it. Another fresco depicts the Virgin enthroned and, nearby, a donor who may be John himself.[21] Peter Llewellyn presumably had this panel in mind when he spoke of the papacy receiving the symbols of its office from a Virgin crowned and robed as an empress. He went on to conclude that "the papacy, secure in divine patronage, needed little from earthly authority."[22] The panel is unfortunately in such woeful condition that Llewellyn may have read more into it than is there. Nordhagen, the great student of Santa Maria Antiqua, drew no such conclusions. Even so, the general ideological tendencies of John VII's work are unmistakable. The pope would govern his church without imperial interference and would set his own conditions for the admission of imperial officials into what was becomimg more and more papal Rome.

In 709 a curious set of events began to unfold. First, Justinian sent a fleet under Theodore Monstraticus to seize Archbishop Felix of Ravenna and to

---

[18]Per Jonas Nordhagen, *The Frescoes of John VII in S. Maria Antiqua in Rome* (Rome, 1968).

[19]Nordhagen, *Frescoes of John VII*, pp. 41–43, with plates XLVI–LI.

[20]Nordhagen, *Frescoes of John VII*, p. 95ff, with a discussion of the difficulties of applying ideological interpretations to John's program.

[21]Nordhagen, *Frescoes of John VII*, pp. 84–85, with plate CIII.

[22]Llewellyn, *Rome in the Dark Ages*, p. 170.

punish the Ravennese.[23] It has usually been assumed that Justinian was intent on exacting revenge from certain citizens of Ravenna who had played a role in his deposition.[24] While an indecipherable passage in Agnellus may support such a conclusion,[25] I suspect that Justinian actually had in mind the humiliation of the *Protospatharius* Zachary caused by the Ravennese in 693. In any event, Archbishop Felix was blinded and made a prisoner at Constantinople while other prominent citizens were either mutilated or killed.

Then, with exemplary courtesy, Justinian invited Pope Constantine to the imperial city. Late in 709 the pope departed from Rome and, all along the way, he was accorded virtually imperial honors. At the capital he was honorably received, handsomely treated, and sent home in a spirit of deep fraternity and amity.[26] This last visit by a pope to Constantinople until Paul VI appears at first sight to stand in contradiction to both papal and imperial policy since 692 but, in reality, an enormously complicated game was afoot.

Felix of Ravenna had, after his election, sought consecration from the pope, an action which archbishops of Ravenna had been studiously avoiding for decades. Shortly afterward, however, he made only partial satisfaction on a set of demands laid before him by Constantine. These demands would have had the result of making him and his church fully dependent upon Rome. Neither Felix nor the Ravennese would tolerate so effective an intrusion of the pope's influence into Ravenna.[27] An earlier archbishop of Ravenna, Maurus, had some years before extorted a privilege from Emperor Constans II to the effect that elections in the Church of Ravenna were to be free of control by Rome.[28] While Constantine was in Constantinople Justi-

---

[23]*LP* 1:389 (Constantine). The *terminus post quem* is summer 709 when Felix became archbishop: Ernst Stein, "Beiträge zur Geschichte von Ravenna in spätrömischer und byzantinischer Zeit," *Klio* 16 (1919): 59. Head (*Justinian II*, pp. 137–39) argues that Justinian punished Felix because of the emperor's "flourishing good relations" with the pope. This has things out of chronological sequence. First Felix was punished and then Justinian and the pope were to some extent reconciled. Paul Gordon Wickberg, "The Eighth-Century Archbishops of Ravenna: An Ineffectual Alternative to Papalism," *Studies in Medieval Culture* 12 (1978): 29, follows Head.

[24]Luther, *Rom und Ravenna*, pp. 46–47; Llewellyn, *Rome in the Dark Ages*, pp. 161–62; Ostrogorsky, *Byzantine State*, p. 143.

[25]*Lib. Pont. Rav.*, c. 137, MGH, SSrL, p. 367.

[26]*LP* 1:390–91; Paul, *Hist. Lang.*, 6.31, MGH, SSrL, p. 175. For chronology: Jaffé, *RP*, p. 248.

[27]*LP* 1:389 (Constantine). This account grimly states that Felix got what he had coming from Justinian for disobeying the pope. The reasons for the quarrel are explained by Guillou, *Régionalisme*, pp. 211–14.

[28]Richards, *Popes and the Papacy*, p. 196. The course of this dispute can be followed in *LP*

nian "renewed all his privileges" and among these was one that restored papal control over archepiscopal elections at Ravenna.[29] Justinian was also persuaded to release Felix, who returned to his see in 712.[30] Scholars suppose, in addition, that some mild compromise on the Quinisextian canons was worked out.[31] This is not impossible, though no source expressly says so. It is reasonable to assume that Constantine gave up something in return for getting renewed control over Ravenna. Perhaps something like Justinian's earlier offer to John VII was now accepted.

It would, however, be wrong to conclude from Constantine's visit to the capital that papal-imperial tensions had been eased. The pope did not have to respond to Justinian's invitation, after all, and it is hard to believe, in view of recent events, that the emperor could have compelled him to come. On the subject of the Quinisextian canons it is significant to note that no surviving manuscript bears a papal signature. Thus, Constantine surely did not cave in and abandon the policy of his predecessors. If he did compromise— and this has always been a mere conjecture—he could have done so without great sacrifice because most of the Quinisextian canons were inoffensive. Actually, Constantine got a restoration of papal influence in Ravenna and, as far as can be determined, he gave up very little. Since an emperor had stripped away the pope's rights there, only an emperor could effectively reestablish them. Constantine got what he wanted, apparently, but what Justinian wanted or obtained cannot be determined.

The events of 709 are also revealing of certain trends in Italy. First, the quarrel between Felix and the pope is indicative of the longstanding hostility between Rome and Ravenna. An earlier archbishop had used the emperor to circumvent the pope, and this time a pope used the emperor to bring down the archbishop. Second, Constantine's interest in Ravenna reflected a perennial papal desire to control that city; a desire which will come repeatedly to our attention in the pages that follow. Finally, Justinian's ability to seize and to punish Felix should not be taken as an indication of the emperor's ability to coerce his Italian subjects. Felix's willingness to be consecrated by the pope and his apparent willingness to meet at least some of Constan-

1:348 (Donus), 360 (Leo II), 368 (Conon). For the "*Typus autocephaliae*" acquired by Maurus see *MGH, SSrL*, p. 350.

[29]*LP* 1:390–91; Paul, *Hist. Lang.*, 6.31, MGH, SSrL, p. 175. Luther, *Rom und Ravenna*, pp. 46–47.

[30]Luther, *Rom und Ravenna*, p. 47.

[31]Görres, "Justinian II," pp. 452–53; Head, *Justinian II*, p. 135; Richards, *Popes and the Papacy*, p. 214.

tine's demands had estranged him from many people in Ravenna who were not so much loyal to the imperial regime as jealous of their independence from Rome.[32] They allowed Felix to be taken, and then Constantine used the emperor to secure his rights in Ravenna. Only under these circumstances could Theodore act decisively in Ravenna. The contrast with Zachary's failure in 693 is striking.

While Constantine was in the east Justinian showed his true colors, and from an imperial point of view, conditions in Italy deteriorated even further. No sooner had Constantine left Rome than the new exarch, John Rizocopus, arrived there from Sicily and murdered some papal officials who were held to be guilty of unspecified offenses.[33] His bloody work in Rome done, John went on to Ravenna, where the populace showed its affection for the new imperial representative by murdering him.[34] In a typically incomprehensible passage Agnellus says that the Ravennese elected, to what office we do not know, a certain George who urged his fellow citizens "not to show their backs to the haughty Greeks" and who organized the military defenses of the city, apparently in anticipation of an attack.[35] Erich Caspar, following Ludo Moritz Hartmann, sees this as the beginning of the "Italian Revolution" against Byzantium.[36] It seems more likely that, despite Pope Constantine's presence in Constantinople at that very moment, the "revolution" was already two decades old.

With his brutalities finally coming home to roost, Justinian was deposed for a second time and murdered in 711. His successor was an Armenian, Philippicus-Bardanes, of no particular talent but of monothelite, and possibly even monophysite, religious tendencies.[37] The new emperor tried to impose his religious will and, in the West, Pope Constantine responded with the strictest sanctions allowed by contemporary diplomacy. Neither the pope nor the Romans paid him the customary honors due to the emperor: His image was not displayed publicly, his coins were not accepted, and his name was not included in liturgical intercessions. In addition, the Romans refused to admit the new *Dux Romae*, Peter, whom Philippicus had deputed to the

---

[32]Guillou, "L'Italia bizantina," pp. 287–88, 295–96. I cannot accept his chronological reconstruction.

[33]*LP* 1:390. Richards, *Popes and the Papacy*, p. 213, supposes a scheme to plunder the papal treasury. Guillou, "L'Italia bizantina," pp. 286–87, thinks John's mission was to break local resistance to the Trullan canons in the pope's absence.

[34]*LP* 1:390. Guillou, *Régionalisme*, pp. 215–16.

[35]*Lib. Pont. Rav.*, c. 140, *MGH, SSrL*, pp. 369–70.

[36]*Das Papsttum*, p. 643; Hartmann, *Geschichte Italiens* 2.2:78–81.

[37]Ostrogorsky, *Byzantine State*, pp. 144–45, 152–53.

city. In fact, there was bloody fighting in Rome and the pope had to compose the situation.[38] Once again the West had decided for itself under what circumstances it would accept, not this time a particular imperial policy, but the very person of the emperor himself.

From 711 to 717 the Byzantine Empire passed through a period of short reigns, usurpations, instability, and severe threats from the Arabs. The Greeks were neither willing nor able to pay much attention to Italy. In the years since 685, when Justinian II had ascended the throne, the fragile East-West peace of 680–81 had been ruptured in ways that, even if unforeseen at the time, were to prove irreparable. The Ravennese and the Romans, however resentful of one another they may have been, had worked together to defend Italian interests against the imperial government.[39] The Italians had served frequent and forceful notice that they did not wish to be coerced, which means, in effect, that they did not wish to obey their lawful superiors. That the quarrels were usually religious makes no difference in view of the genuine and generalized Italian responses. That it was usually the pope who bore the brunt of the imperial wrath makes no difference, because Italians from both Rome and Ravenna rose up to defend him. Possibly a new regime in Constantinople might have salvaged the situation had not the Lombards renewed their depredations in Italy in the midst of these difficulties. The Italians of the Byzantine province were learning, to their dismay, that even at the price of tolerating religious perversity and murderous meddling, they could get no protection from their barbarian neighbors. But the Italians did not want to tolerate actions like those recently perpetrated, and therefore when no military assistance was forthcoming, an already grim situation was made incalculably worse.

Peace Betrayed: Lombards

The first hint that the Lombards were about to break the peace came in 702 when Duke Gisulf of Benevento attacked Campania, that is, the southern flank of the Duchy of Rome. He seized the cities of Sora, Arce, and Arpino and ravaged Campania with fire and sword, seizing hostages along the way,

---

[38] *LP* 1:391–93; *Gesta epis. neapol.*, c. 35, MGH, SSrL., p. 421.

[39] Luther, *Rom und Ravenna*, pp. 47–49, notes that only a common anti-Byzantine policy kept Rome and Ravenna together down to 751. As we shall see, an anti-Lombard policy was important too.

as far as Horrea, a *fundus*, or estate, five miles out from Rome on the Via Latina.[40] Gisulf's actions represented, until then and for some time to come, an isolated instance of renewed Lombard aggression. At roughly the same time King Aripert II took the heretofore unprecedented step of restoring to the papacy its massive patrimony in the Cottian Alps.[41] This action makes it clear that there was no general Lombard offensive. Possibly Gisulf was encouraged to venture his bold stroke by the recent and manifest inability of the imperial government to impose its will on Rome.[42] Whatever the case, the fact remains that just as East-West tensions were being heightened the papacy, and perhaps Byzantine Italy generally, had again to take the Lombards, or adventurism by individual Lombards, into account.[43]

In the Lombard *regnum* the years from 700 to 712 were a time of deep instability. Ansprand and his son Liutprand spent these twelve years at the Bavarian ducal court and then, with Bavarian aid, returned to Italy in 712 to contest for the Lombard crown. Ansprand defeated Aripert II, but survived his victory by only three months. He was succeeded by Liutprand, a figure with whom we shall be much occupied in the following account.[44]

Liutprand spent the early years of his long reign (712–44) successfully consolidating the royal position in northern Italy.[45] He was to all appearances a devout man, and he moved quickly to establish good relations with Pope Gregory II (715–31) by confirming the pope's possession of the Cottian Alps patrimony.[46] By 717, however, Liutprand had revived the traditional

---

[40]*LP* 1:383 (John VI); Paul, *Hist. Lang*, 6.27, MGH, SSrL, p. 174. Duchesne, *LP* 1:384 n.2, identifies Horrea.

[41]*LP* 1:385 (John VII); Paul, *Hist. Lang.*, 6.28, MGH, SSrL, p. 174; *Codice Diplomatico Langobardo* (hereafter *CDL*), 3.1, ed. Carlrichard Brühl (*FSI* vol. 64 [Rome, 1973]), no. 3 pp. 298–99 (A.D. 705–7). On this patrimony see: Paul Fabre, "Le patrimoine de l'église romaine dans les Alpes cottiennes," *MAH* 4 (1884): 283–420.

[42]Bertolini, "Relazioni politiche," pp. 6–10.

[43]Bertolini, *Roma e i longobardi*, pp. 31–32. Hartmann, *Geschichte Italiens*, 2.2:75, argues that despite Gisulf's plunderings the Lombards were not a menace. I disagree.

[44]Hodgkin, *The Lombard Kingdom*, pp. 320–26, 389–90; Reinhard Schneider, *Königswahl und Königserhebung im Frühmittelalter* (Stuttgart, 1972), pp. 51–52; Hermann Fröhlich, *Studien zur langobardischen Thronfolge von den Anfängen bis zur Eroberung des italienischen Reiches durch Karl den Grossen*, 2 vols. (Tübingen, 1980), 1:182.

[45]Hodgkin, *The Lombard Kingdom*, p. 390ff; Fröhlich, *Thronfolge* 1:187ff.

[46]Paul, *Hist. Lang.*, 6.44, MGH, SSrL, p. 179; *CDL*, 3.1, ed. Brühl, no. 4, p. 299. Hartmann, *Geschichte Italiens*, 2.2:87. Brühl will offer only 715–31 as dates for the confirmation, but because Liutprand had strained relations with Gregory on several occasions after 717, and because it appears that he moved quickly to enter into good relations with the pope, I would date the confirmation 715–17.

Lombard dreams of a territorial unification of Italy. Doubtless he was encouraged to do so by the severe difficulties then being suffered by the Byzantine Empire, plus the palpably weak Byzantine position in Italy.

In 717, or possibly in 718, Liutprand attacked the Exarchate of Ravenna and seized Ravenna's port of Classe.[47] Almost simultaneously Duke Faraold of Spoleto seized the *castrum* of Narni from the Duchy of Rome,[48] and Duke Romuald of Benevento took the *castrum* of Cumae on the southern side of the Roman duchy.[49] The simultaneity of these events is striking, but it would be wrong to suppose that Liutprand had engineered a single, broad offensive.[50] Rather, opportunism reigned on all sides. Everyone could see that Byzantine Italy was vulnerable at many points, and with the Arabs before the walls of Constantinople, no reprisals had to be feared at that moment from the East. Liutprand had next to no power in the southern duchies and could neither have caused nor prevented the actions of the dukes.[51]

The crisis passed fairly quickly, and more easily than might have been expected. When Emperor Leo III defeated the Arabs, and then sent the patrician Paul to Italy as exarch, Liutprand restored Classe to him.[52] Liutprand's actual intentions and motivations at this time are a bit hard to fathom because Duke Faraold of Spoleto had taken Classe in the first place only to lose it to Liutprand, who restored it to Paul.[53] Perhaps Liutprand was not quite ready to go on the warpath, or he may have wished to pause

---

[47]*LP* 1:403 (Gregory II); Paul, *Hist. Lang.*, 6.49, *MGH, SSrL*, p. 181.

[48]*LP* 1:403; Paul, *Hist. Lang.*, 6.48, *MGH, SSrL*, p. 181.

[49]*LP* 1:400; Paul, *Hist. Lang.*, 6.40, *MGH, SSrL*, p. 179.

[50]Bertolini, "Relazioni politiche," pp. 13–15, assumes this as does Delogu, "Il regno longobardo," p. 148.

[51]Pabst, "Herzogthums," pp. 474–75; Hartmann, *Geschichte Italiens* 2.2:87. Although no comparable evidence survives from Benevento, it is clear that royal power was virtually nonexistent in Spoleto. Spoletan charters in this period are not dated by royal years: *RF*, vol. 2, nos. 2–9, pp. 22–27. There are historical and diplomatic problems with these early Spoletan charters (as with all of them before 724: Carlrichard Brühl, "Chronologie und Urkunden der Herzöge von Spoleto," *QFIAB* 51 [1971]: 10–11), but for present purposes one can rely on the honesty and competence of Gregory of Catino, who compiled the Farfa register. See: Herbert Zielinski, *Studien zu den spoletinischen 'Privaturkunden' des 8. Jahrhunderts und ihrer Überlieferung im Regestum Farfense* (Tübingen, 1972), pp. 25–34.

[52]Bertolini, "Relazioni politiche," pp. 17–18.

[53]Paul, *Hist. Lang.*, 6.44, *MGH, SSrL*, p. 180, says Faraold took Classe but was compelled to give it back on Liutprand's order. Otherwise the sources (*LP* 1:403) say Liutprand took Classe. Perhaps Faraold actually did take it, along with Narni, and then Liutprand took it away from him fearing that this would represent an unacceptable augmentation of the already considerable power of the Duke of Spoleto. This is Bertolini's opinion: "Relazioni politiche," pp. 10–12, 17–18.

and gauge the intentions and capacities of Leo III, whose reputation can only have been enhanced by his defeat of the Arabs. Liutprand may also have wished to check the ambitions of his unruly dukes. In later years he worked with imperial representatives to limit and control the dukes; so it is not impossible that he did so in 717–18. The Spoletans kept Narni. It would remain in Lombard hands for many years. The Romans recovered Cumae but the way in which this was accomplished was rich with implications for the future.

When Cumae fell Gregory II had no luck with negotiations for its restoration and turned to Duke John of Naples and to Theodimus, who was rector of the papal patrimonies in Campania. They drove out the Beneventan Lombards and then Gregory paid Duke Romuald 70 pounds of gold for the *castrum*.[54] Henceforth the papacy treated Cumae in the same way as it treated its own patrimonies.[55] This represents the first instance wherein the pope undertook to arrange for the defense of the Duchy of Rome while at the same time securing for himself a title to a piece of public land. In time the popes would come to treat the whole Duchy of Rome along with, later, a sizeable portion of central Italy, in this same fashion. A step along the road to the formal creation of a papal republic had been taken.

In the midst of all of this confusion two more future players in the Italian drama appeared on the scene. Duke Theodo of Bavaria visited Rome in 716. He came of his own volition and sought papal help to erect a regular ecclesiastical hierarchy in Bavaria. Gregory II was only too happy to comply, but his plans for the Bavarian church remained unrealized for many years. The pope did, however, open Bavaria to Roman influences and initiated a long and close connection between the papacy and the Bavarian ducal house.[56] In 719 the great Anglo-Saxon missionary Boniface visited Rome for the first

---

[54]For the sources see n.49. Bertolini ("Relazioni politiche," p. 27) thinks that Cumae was church property inside the Neapolitan patrimony. He has no evidence and his argument is unlikely for two reasons. First, Cumae was a *castrum*, thus public land. Second, the *castrum* belonged to the Duchy of Rome and its defense was procured by the rector of the Campanian patrimony, not by a Neapolitan patrimonial officer. That John of Naples was called in signifies nothing in particular. He was the only local authority who could provide aid. The issue is important for it matters very much whether Gregory recovered one of his own patrimonies or a piece of public land. All scholars except Hodgkin (*The Lombard Kingdom*, pp. 442–43) agree that the gold was paid to Romuald, not to John of Naples. See further: Kehr, *IP* 8, no. 9, p. 420; Jaffé, *RP*, no. 2154.

[55]Schäfer, *Bedeutung*, pp. 15–16; Caspar, *Das Papsttum*, pp. 726–28.

[56]*LP* 1:398. Kurt Reindel, "Grundlegung: Das Zeitalter der Agilolfinger (bis 788)," in Max Spindler, ed., *Handbuch der bayerischen Geschichte* (Munich, 1971), 1:122; Theodor Schieffer,

time, pledged his loyalty to the papacy, and set out to win the heathens of central Germany for Rome and the pope.[57]

Through his work in the north Boniface exerted a profound influence in Italy itself; his role will be taken up in due course. For the moment Theodo's démarche is more interesting. Liutprand was married to Guntrut, daughter of either Theodo or his son Theudebert.[58] Because Liutprand and Gregory were on good terms in 716, the fact that the pope welcomed Theodo so cordially suggests that he may have been trying to cement together a larger network of papal friendships in northern Italy and beyond. Gregory may even have been thinking of the Bavarians as a potential restraining force on Liutprand should one ever be needed. Gregory was, throughout his life, a supremely competent diplomat, and it is not at all farfetched to suppose that in 716 he was already thinking of more than the Bavarian Church.

In the early 720s Liutprand extended or consolidated the Lombard possessions in northeastern Italy in the region of Aquileia.[59] More than a century and a half earlier, when the Lombards had first penetrated into this region, Venice had lost much of its hinterland and the patriarchal see of Aquileia had been transferred to Grado.[60] The patriarchs at Grado were, until 607, separated from Rome over the "Three Chapters" controversy.[61] When Rome and Grado composed their differences in 607, Grado's suffragan bishops located in Lombard territory elected a new patriarch of Aquileia and this see remained schismatic until the end of the Three Chapters controversy, more than a century later. By Liutprand's time the "new" patriarchs of Aquileia had a long tradition behind them. I say "new" because these patriarchs refused to acknowledge the authority of the "old" or, actually, former patriarchs of Aquileia now and for a long time already resident at Grado. Accordingly, with the Three Chapters controversy settled at last and the

---

Winfrid-Bonifatius und die christliche Grundlegung Europas, reprint with corrections (Darmstadt, 1980), p. 95. S. J. P. VanDijk, "The Urban and Papal Rites in Seventh- and Eighth-Century Rome," *Sacris Erudiri* 12 (1961): 438, says that Gregory was the first pope to promote the use of Roman liturgical books north of the Alps.

[57]Boniface, ep. no. 12, ed. Tangl, *MGH*, pp. 17–18.

[58]Reindel, "Zeitalter der Agilolfinger," p. 120.

[59]Benedict of St. Andrea, *Chronicon*, ed. Giuseppe Zucchetti (*FSI* 55 [Rome, 1920]): 64.

[60]Cessi, *Storia della Repubblica di Venezia*, pp. 9–12; Kretschmayr, *Geschichte von Venedig*, pp. 22–28; F. X. Murphy, "Aquileia," *New Catholic Encyclopedia* (New York, 1967), 1:710–11; O. P. Sherbowitz-Wetzor, "Grado," ibid, 6:85.

[61]For a brief, clear discussion of the Three Chapters, see: Bréhier and Aigrain, *Histoire de l'église*, pp. 43–44, 398, 408.

Lombards now Catholic, Liutprand asked Gregory II to send a pallium to Serenus of Aquileia. Gregory willingly complied but warned Serenus not to interfere with Grado.[62] Gregory also wrote to Donatus of Grado telling him that Serenus had been granted the pallium on condition that he leave Grado alone.[63] All of this took place in 723 and tends to prove that, after the difficulties of 717–19, Liutprand and the pope were again on good terms, a situation that was fortunate for Italy because the Byzantines were about to disturb the scene again.[64] Before turning to this renewal of contention between East and West, however, it is necessary to emphasize strongly this recent papal solicitude for Venice and Aquileia. Within a few years the popes would be claiming these lands for their new republic.

Twin Challenges: Iconoclasm and Lombards

After having met the Arab threat to Constantinople, Emperor Leo III, with his throne finally secure, decided to shore up imperial rule in Italy while at the same time making Italy assume a greater measure of the cost of its own defense.[65] He raised, perhaps doubled, taxes on all estates in Italy.[66] This new tax burden fell also on the Church's patrimonies, and Gregory II resolutely refused to pay. Gregory's act may have had economic implications and motivations, but it was inherently political. The pope had raised the standard of rebellion in Italy.[67]

For the next several years events in Italy moved with astonishing rapidity. It is unfortunate that the best source, sometimes the only source, is the *vita* of Gregory II in the *Liber Pontificalis*. This is not to imply that this source is palpably tendentious. The account given by Gregory's anonymous biographer is a valid perception of the course of events as they were seen through

---

[62]*Epp. Lang.*, no. 8, MGH, EKA 3:699.

[63]*Epp. Lang.*, no. 9, MGH, EKA 3:700.

[64]Delogu, "Il regno longobardo," pp. 146–47.

[65]Caspar, *Das Papsttum*, pp. 643–44.

[66]*LP* 1:403.

[67]Caspar, *Das Papsttum*, p. 646; Guillou, *Régionalisme*, pp. 218–19; Armbrust, *Territoriale Politik*, pp. 38–39; David Harry Miller, "The Roman Revolution of the Eighth Century: A Study of the Ideological Background of the Papal Separation from Byzantium and Alliance with the Franks," *Mediaeval Studies* 36 (1974): 100–101, 109. Richards, *Popes and the Papacy*, p. 218, thinks Gregory's actions were taken for essentially economic reasons, to prevent the bankruptcy of the Church. I believe that this was only one factor among many.

Italian eyes. The problem with the *vita* is that, first, its chronological se-
quences are difficult to establish, and second, it makes the motivations and
intentions of individual participants difficult to decipher.

Leo III's tax decree must have been issued in 722 or 723, and his
dispatch of Exarch Paul to punish the pope's rebellion can with fair certainty
be placed in 725.[68] Perhaps not long after Gregory refused to pay the taxes,
three individuals, a duke named Basil, a *chartularius* named Jordanes, and a
subdeacon named John Lurion, formed a plan to kill the pope, and they
won the assent of the *protospatharius* Marinus, who was then duke of
Rome. The time was not ripe, however, and the conspiracy came to nothing.
The Romans, though, learned of the conspiracy and put Jordanes and John
to death while also making a monk out of Basil. We are not told what
happened to Marinus, but evidently, a new duke of Rome was appointed.[69]
Probably this plot represented an effort by some zealous local officials and a
disgruntled cleric to curry favor with the Byzantines. What is, however, most
significant and interesting is the powerlessness of the duke of Rome and the
continued willingness of the Romans to protect the pope.

In 725, then, Exarch Paul collected troops in the Ravennate and the
Pentapolis and set out for Rome to discipline the pope, or to kill him if the
vita can be believed. The sources—the *vita* is here supplemented by Paul the
Deacon—imply that Paul did not enjoy full success in raising the necessary
forces.[70] When Paul got to Rome the Romans, the Lombards of Spoleto, and
possibly the Beneventans rose up to defend the pope.[71] Paul had to return
abjectly to Ravenna. For all practical purposes imperial authority in the city
and region of Rome had ceased to exist. Neither Paul nor the new duke of
Rome was able to impose the imperial will in the city. The taxes, as far as
is known, were never collected, and the pope was spared the humiliation
meted out to his predecessors Vigilius and Martin.

For about two years no further troubles are reported in Italy. At Constantinople, however, Leo III commenced a policy that would have world-histor-
ical significance. In 726 or 727 he initiated Byzantine iconoclasm. Apparently the emperor did, at this time, issue a first, formal decree against icons,
and he put his henchmen to tearing down certain particularly revered ones
in the capital while making known to one and all his personal distaste for

---

[68] I follow here, with minor variations, the chronology of Bertolini ("Relazioni politiche,"
pp. 31–33) and Guillou (*Régionalisme*, pp. 218–19).

[69] *LP* 1:403.

[70] *LP* 1:403–4; *Hist. Lang.*, 6.49, *MGH, SSrL*, p. 181.

[71] *LP* 1:404.

pictorial representations in sacred art.[72] The emperor somehow communicated his new policy to the pope for the *vita* says that Gregory was expected to comply if he wished to have the emperor's grace.[73] Gregory had been getting along fine without such grace for several years already, and he did nothing to win the favor of the Basileus at this moment. The pope's biographer says that "despising the vulgar command of the prince, he armed himself against the emperor as against an enemy, denounced his heresy, and wrote to Christians everywhere to be on their guard wherever such impiety might arise." The *vita* implies that Paul had been mandated to execute the emperor's command, so perhaps some subordinate of the exarch had brought the decree to Rome. In any event, the pope obviously feared no one, and with good reason.

In 727 the armies, that is, the military aristocracies, of Ravenna, Venice, and the Pentapolis rose up against the iconoclastic policy of Leo III. They boldly announced that they would defend the pope against any hostile action by Exarch Paul or any of his agents.[74] This sedition was serious enough, but it was only the beginning. First, Italians everywhere elected their own dukes. It cannot be determined how we are to understand election in this context, but there can be no doubt that all over central and northern Italy people were openly declaring an end to Byzantine rule. Defense of the pope and of the orthodox faith played roles in this rebellion, certainly, but at least in Ravenna and Venice traditional desires for autonomy were also critical motivating factors.[75] Second, some sort of struggle broke out between papal and imperial factions in Ravenna and the exarch lost his life in the fray.[76] It seems clear that by this time imperial rule was dying in all those parts of central Italy where it had not already expired a few years earlier. Third, the Lombards re-entered the Italian scene.

---

[72]For the traditional view that no formal decree was issued in 726–27 see: Ostrogorsky, *Byzantine State*, p. 160ff. But for a persuasive argument that such a decree was indeed issued see: Milton V. Anastos, "Leo III's Edict Against the Images in the Year 726–27 and Italo-Byzantine Relations Between 726 and 730," *Byzantinische Forschungen* 3 (1968): 5–41, esp. 5–25.

[73]*LP* 1:404.

[74]*LP* 1:404. John, *Chronicon Venetum, MGH, SS* 7:11; Paul, *Hist. Lang.*, 6.49, *MGH, SSrL,* p. 181. Cf. Regino of Prüm, *Chronicon, MGH, SS* 1:553.

[75]Delogu, "Il regno longobardo," pp. 149–50; Cessi, *Storia della Repubblica di Venezia,* pp. 13–15; Guillou, *Régionalisme,* pp. 11–13; Pier Silverio Leicht, "Il termine 'communitas' in una lettera di Gregorio II," *Archivum Latinitas Medii Aevi* 1 (1924): 171–75.

[76]*LP* 1:405: "Igitur discussione missa in partibus Ravennae, alii consentientes pravitati imperatoris, alii cum pontifice et fidelibus tenentes, inter eos contentione mota, Paulum patricium occidunt." This is all we know.

In recent years Liutprand had maintained good relations with Rome, and there is no evidence that he had been disturbing Ravenna. In 725, probably in concert with his ally Charles Martel, the mayor of the palace in Francia, Liutprand attacked his erstwhile Bavarian friends from the south while Charles attacked from the north. Charles carried off a Bavarian bride, Swanahild, and Liutprand rounded off the northern frontier of his kingdom.[77] Throughout his reign Liutprand sought to keep peace with the Franks and the Avars,[78] and this policy may lie behind his attack on Bavaria, a land that was situated exactly in the middle of the Lombards, Franks, and Avars. From Liutprand's point of view friendship with the Franks had become more important than his old good relations with those very Bavarians who had assisted his rise to kingship.

His kingdom thus augmented, Liutprand watched with great interest as the Italian rebellion exploded anew just beyond his borders. Perhaps because, as a devout man, he was scandalized by iconoclasm, or possibly seeing an opportunity to fish in troubled waters, Liutprand proclaimed himself the pope's ally and hit the exarchate with a vengeance.[79] Some cities he conquered, while others apparently regarded him as a liberator and threw open their gates.[80] He even took Sutri, a *castrum* on the border between the Duchy of Rome and Lombard Tuscany.[81] Some have supposed that Liutprand and the pope were allies until the fall of Sutri,[82] but a more likely assessment of the situation is that Gregory was cool to Liutprand's apparent zeal in defense of the faith because that very zeal seemed to be bringing with it a dismemberment of Italy.[83] Since at least the time of Gregory I, the popes had had a visceral fear of the prospect of becoming glorified Lombard bishops. Nothing that Gregory II ever did suggests that he was immune to that fear, and this pope was too prudent not to have realized that an alliance with Liutprand would have been the end of him.

---

[77]*Annales mettenses priores*, ed. Bernhard Simson, *MGH, SSrG*, p. 26; *Fredegarii Continuatio*, c. 12, ed. John Michael Wallace-Hadrill (London, 1960), p. 90. Hartmann, *Geschichte Italiens*, 2.2:125; Reindel, "Zeitalter der Agilolfinger," pp. 123–24; Theodor Breysig, *Jahrbücher des fränkischen Reiches*, 714–741 (Leipzig, 1869), pp. 51–54.

[78]Paul, *Hist. Lang.*, 6.58, *MGH, SSrL*, p. 187.

[79]*LP* 1:405; Paul, *Hist. Lang.*, 6.49, *MGH, SSrL*, pp. 181–82. Bertolini, *Roma e i longobardi*, pp. 33–42, makes an impressive case for the importance of Liutprand's religious convictions. See also his "Relazioni politiche," pp. 37–38.

[80]Caspar, *Das Papsttum*, p. 727.

[81]*LP* 1:407.

[82]Fröhlich, *Thronfolge* 1:189; Hartmann, *Geschichte Italiens*, 2.2:86–87.

[83]Hodgkin, *The Italian Kingdom*, p. 450; Bertolini, "Relazioni politiche," pp. 39–40.

In the middle of all of this chaos Gregory took two steps. He refused to countenance, indeed actively opposed, all efforts by the insurgents in Venice and Ravenna to create a new emperor.[84] Gregory was astute enough to realize that the anarchy that would inevitably attend the creation of a pretender was not an attractive alternative to the present disruption of the Italian scene. Moreover, the Basileus was far away and totally ineffectual. An emperor of any kind resident in Ravenna might present real problems for the pope, particularly if he could win the allegiance of the army in those regions.[85] Ravenna, it must be remembered, had always been hostile to Roman influence, and recent popes had displayed a marked desire to exert authority there. Gregory also pleaded with Liutprand for 140 days to return Sutri to him. The king finally handed it over, minus its surrounding territory and a good deal of booty, "to the blessed apostles Peter and Paul."[86] The pope had thus acquired a title of sorts in his own right to a second piece of public property; Cumae had been the first.

Gregory was in a supremely difficult position. He knew that if the rebellion proceeded much further only the Lombards would profit from it. The Lombards were now Catholic and their king was a self-proclaimed defender of the faith, but the papacy was a universal institution and an accommodation between the papacy and the Lombards over, for example, the control of bishops exercised by Frankish kings would have been unthinkable.[87] If Gregory tolerated the complete collapse of the Byzantine position in Italy then there would have been nothing to prevent the Lombards from conquering the whole peninsula. But caving in on Byzantine policies such as iconoclasm in order to win imperial support against the Lombards was also out of the question. An alliance with Liutprand against the Greeks might very well have handed Italy to the king with no assurances that he could be controlled. Thus, in the end, Gregory warned his countrymen to be loyal to the emperor and stated that he himself hoped to convert the prince.[88] He wrote two

---

[84]*LP* 1:404–5.

[85]Hodgkin, *The Italian Kingdom*, p. 450; Armbrust, *Territoriale Politik*, p. 39; Schäfer, *Bedeutung*, pp. 25–26; Hartmann, *Geschichte Italiens*, 2.2:94–95; Bertolini, "Relazioni politiche," pp. 39–40; Guillou, *Régionalisme*, pp. 219–21.

[86]*LP* 1:407: "donationem beatissimis apostolis Petrum [*sic*] et Paulo ante fatus emittens Langobardus rex."

[87]Duchesne, *The Beginnings of the Temporal Sovereignty of the Popes*, trans. Arnold Harris Mathew (London, 1908), p. 94. The best, albeit controversial, treatment of papal ideology in the early Middle Ages is Walter Ullmann, *The Growth of Papal Government in the Middle Ages*, 3d ed. (London, 1970), pp. 1–48 passim.

[88]*LP* 1:404–5.

letters to Leo to try to correct his errors. These letters are in no way conciliatory. The pope condemned iconoclasm in blunt terms and also rejected the emperor's right to make authoritative pronouncements on questions of doctrine. The emperor had evidently written to Gregory and said at some point that he was "priest and king." The pope wrote back to say that the emperor was no such thing; that priests and kings were distinct and that each should keep to his proper sphere.[89] Gregory's dilemma was that he was calling for support of a regime that he and many others regarded as heretical, fiscally treacherous, and murderously oppressive.

Some scholars have depicted Gregory as a revolutionary, while others have seen in him a loyal and hard-pressed subject of the emperor.[90] Both of these views are wrong. Gregory was a man, a Roman it ought to be noted,[91] who was trying to secure Italian interests against both Byzantines and Lombards. He was no more, but also no less, revolutionary than his predecessors going back to 685. He faced graver issues and issued stiffer responses, but the differences between Gregory and his immediate predecessors existed in the realm of degree, not of kind.

A de facto secession of much of Italy from Byzantine control had taken place. Gregory had not caused the secession by himself, although he had played a decisive role in it. The problem now was could he control this volatile situation, and in whose interests would that control be exercised. In Ravenna and Venice, for example, iconoclasm was despised, but the insurgents had risen up primarily to secure local liberties, not to join some new state under papal sovereignty. And even in Rome Gregory's position was

---

[89]Ostrogorsky, *Byzantine State*, p. 151 and n.5. Scholarship on Gregory's letters follows today, with a few insignificant exceptions, Caspar, "Papst Gregor II und der Bilderstreit," *ZKG* 52 (1933): 29–70. Caspar's interpretations have been confirmed by Hans Grotz, who also demonstrates that the letters to Leo were written in Greek in the first place. It has always been thought that we had only late and interpolated Greek translations of Latin originals: "Beobachtungen zu den zwei Briefen Papst Gregors II an Kaiser Leo III," *AHP* 18 (1980): 9–40. The letters themselves are now available in a truly critical edition which far surpasses Caspar's (*art. cit.*, pp. 72–89): Jean Gouillard, "Aux origines de l'iconoclasme: Le témoinage de Grégoire II," *Travaux et memoires: Centre de recherche d'histoire et civilisation byzantines* 3 (1968): 243–307, esp. 276–97 for ep. no. 1, and 298–307 for ep. no. 2. Gouillard provides a good French translation. For the passages mentioned above see: ep. no. 1, pp. 291, 291–93, ep. no. 2, pp. 299, 302.

[90]Armbrust, *Territoriale Politik*, pp. 38–39; Schäfer, *Bedeutung*, pp. 19–22; Hartmann, *Geschichte Italiens*, 2.2:86–87; and Caspar, *Das Papsttum*, pp. 655–62, see Gregory as a revolutionary. Ostrogorsky, *Byz. State*, pp. 162–65; and Duchesne, *Temporal Sovereignty*, p. 5, describe him as a loyal subject.

[91]*LP* 1:396.

perilous. During the insurrections in the north a duke, Exhilaratus, and his son, Hadrian—apparently Campanians—rallied some people to a plot to kill the pope in order to please the emperor.[92] Actually, Hadrian held a grudge against Gregory because, a few years earlier, he had eloped with a deaconness named Epiphania and had been condemned for this indiscretion by a Roman synod in 721.[93] When the Romans learned of the plot they put the ringleaders to death and even blinded the duke of Rome, Peter, who had been writing to the emperor against the pope.[94] Peter's fate demonstrates, once again, that imperial control in Rome itself was effectively at an end, but the plot against Gregory shows, at the same time, that the pope's leadership was not unanimously acknowledged.

None of the weird schemes and plots hatched by the emperors in recent years was well calculated to impress upon Italians generally, or on the Romans and the pope, the virtues and rewards of Byzantine rule. But, as the 720s were drawing to a close, the Italian situation was so complex and dangerous that no clear alternatives to the old order readily suggested themselves. Since the time of Justinian II that order had shown itself to be morally and religiously bankrupt, and now it could not provide defense against the Lombards, and its political agents were powerless. Crises were now following one another so rapidly that the Italians and, chief among them, the pope would begin contemplating radical new departures.

At this juncture the emperor sent a new exarch, Eutychius, to Italy. He landed in Naples because the north was obviously unsafe for an imperial representative, and he let it be known that the pope might be killed with impunity.[95] Gregory's position was not seriously endangered, but leaving nothing to chance, he forged an alliance with the dukes of Spoleto and Benevento.[96] Since the Spoletans had already defended the pope against Paul, this alliance was not really an innovation, and for the next decade solidarity with the duchies would be a cornerstone of papal policy. In Rome, the ducal alliance must have been seen as equally effective against Eutychius or Liutprand.[97] The alliance was probably concluded in 728 or 729, and from it we get a glimpse of a new papal policy that would tend in the direction of full

---

[92]*LP* 1:405.

[93]Mansi, *Concilia* 12:263–64.

[94]*LP* 1:405.

[95]*LP* 1:405–6. Gregory also mentions this threat to his life in his ep. no. 1, ed. Gouillard, p. 295.

[96]*LP* 1:406. In his ep. no. 1, ed. Gouillard, pp. 295, 297, Gregory told Leo that the emperor could not coerce him, that he was safe in his own domain, and that the West would rise up to protect him.

[97]Eugen Ewig, "The Papacy's Alienation from Byzantium and Rapprochement with the

autonomy for central Italy.[98] The pope would henceforth decide whether and under what circumstances the imperial writ would run in Italy, and the Lombard dukes, along with the Roman militia,[99] would supply the muscle necessary to protect the pope from both the emperor and the king.

Liutprand, for his part, simply did not understand the papacy's violent reaction to his "assistance" against the Greeks, and he utterly failed to comprehend the social dynamics in the Exarchate. Although some cities in the Pentapolis may have seen him as a liberator, these people generally desired liberation from Ravenna itself as much as from the Greeks. Liutprand himself was unloved in the whole region.[100] Moreover, the king cannot have liked the spectacle of a Roman-Spoletan-Beneventan alliance that might be turned against him just as easily as against the Greeks.[101] Until 728–29 the king had shown little interest in the southern duchies.[102] In 719–20 the Spoletans had ejected his ally Faraold and replaced him with Transamund, the deposed duke's son,[103] but Liutprand had done nothing. When the pope rebuffed Liutprand's aid, demanded back Sutri, and then allied with the dukes, Liutprand took immediate action. He entered Spoleto for the first time, and astonishingly, he concluded an alliance with Eutychius.[104]

It has always been assumed that Liutprand wanted to incorporate all of Byzantine Italy into his kingdom and that this desire made him the inevitable enemy of the pope. Recently, however, Hallenbeck has reviewed the evidence and he argues persuasively that Liutprand was for a long time willing to leave the Duchy of Rome unmolested until the pope allied with the dukes of Spoleto and Benevento.[105] The king had genuinely sought good relations with the pope, but he considered the pope's alliance with the Lombard dukes a

Franks," in Hubert Jedin and John Dolan, eds., *Handbook of Church History*, vol 3, trans. Anselm Biggs (New York, 1968), p. 20.

[98]Schäfer, *Bedeutung*, pp. 19–22; Hartmann, *Geschichte Italiens*, 2.2:94–95; Bertolini, "Relazioni politiche," p. 33. For a different chronology and some conclusions which I am unable to follow, see: Jan T. Hallenbeck, "The Roman-Byzantine Reconciliation of 728: Genesis and Significance," *BZ* 74 (1981): 29–41.

[99]On their role see: *LP* 1:406. Rasi, *Exercitus Italicus*, p. 152.

[100]Bertolini, *Roma e i longobardi*, pp. 38–42.

[101]Hodgkin, *The Italian Kingdom*, pp. 457–58; Bertolini, "Relazioni politiche," pp. 45–50; Fröhlich, *Thronfolge* 1:189–90.

[102]Pabst, "Herzogthums," pp. 474–75. No charters in this period were issued in the king's name or with his regnal years.

[103]Fröhlich, *Thronfolge* 1:189; Brühl, "Chronologie," p. 19; cf. Paul, *Hist. Lang.*, 6.44, *MGH, SSrL*, p. 180.

[104]*LP* 1:407.

[105]Hallenbeck, *Pavia and Rome: The Lombard Monarchy and the Papacy in the Eighth Century* (Philadelphia, 1982), pp. 21–29.

deliberate and unprovoked act of aggression. It is the papal-ducal alliance, therefore, that explains the king's otherwise inexplicable *volte face* in forging an entente with Eutychius.

In return for Eutychius's aid in subjecting the two duchies, Liutprand agreed to help restore the exarch's authority in Rome.[106] Such were the terms of this unholy alliance, but it is important to realize how one-sided it was, for Liutprand was holding all the cards. Eutychius was virtually powerless and had to grasp at any opportunity. Liutprand, meanwhile, could by allying with the exarch cover his actions with a cloak of imperial legitimacy and make himself the arbiter of Italy.[107] The events of 728–29 make Gregory's perspicacity in refusing to anchor his policies in an alliance with Liutprand in 727 quite clear. What would happen next was anybody's guess.

Liutprand, having entered Spoleto, received the submission of the dukes along with hostages as a pledge for their loyalty.[108] The king then marched his army to the Campus Neronis, a small plain situated between the Vatican, the Monte Mario, and the Tiber,[109] and entered into negotiations with Gregory. It seems possible that Eutychius was with Liutprand, but this is not expressly stated.[110] Nor are we told by the *vita* what subjects formed the basis for the negotiations, although with a bit of reasoned speculation it is possible to discern their broad outlines. Gregory did not suffer any indignity. Eutychius was not allowed to carry out any reprisals against the pope or the "*optimates Romae.*" The iconoclastic decrees of Leo III were not imposed. Probably the pope had to give up his alliance with Spoleto and Benevento and, perhaps in return for this concession, Liutprand laid down his royal insignia at the confession of St. Peter and received them back at the hand of the pope. Doubtless the king also gave up his alliance with Eutychius.[111] Liutprand, for whom religious scruples were always an animating force, may have momentarily persuaded the pope of his sincerity and reliability as an ally so long as the pope did not take countermeasures like allying with the dukes. Liutprand, whether by fair means or foul, had become the arbiter of Italy, and Gregory, for his part, could do no more than make a virtue of

---

[106]*LP* 1:407.

[107]Bertolini, "Relazioni politiche," pp. 50–57; Hartmann, *Geschichte Italiens* 2.2:98; Hallenbeck, "Roman-Byzantine Reconciliation," pp. 37–38.

[108]*LP* 1:407. Hartmann, *Geschichte Italiens*, 2.2:131–32.

[109]Duchesne, *LP* 1:413 n.39.

[110]This seems likely from the circumstances, and from the fact that, after reporting these events, *LP* 1:408 says: "Igitur exarcho Roma morante."

[111]*LP* 1:408.

necessity by going along with the king. After all, he had not lost anything significant in this démarche. It is also worth noting that Gregory seems never to have considered any sort of rapprochement with Eutychius.

After the interview on the Campus Neronis, Liutprand disappears from the Roman sources for a couple of years. Immediately after that interview, however, the abject weakness of Eutychius was made manifest to all. A new imperial pretender, otherwise unknown, named Tiberius Petasius, appeared in Tuscany and won some of the inhabitants of that region over to his cause. In this context, it should be noted, Tuscany means "Roman" Tuscany, that is, the region just north of the city, and not historic Tuscany, which was in those days always called "Lombard" Tuscany. The exarch was "profoundly disturbed" on hearing this report but the pope "comforted him" and placed Roman troops at his disposal with whose aid Tiberius was rapidly defeated.[112] The rebel's head was sent to Leo III but "not even this gesture won for the Romans the full grace of the emperor."[113]

Several inferences can be drawn from the affair of Tiberius. First, the exarch had authority in Rome only during the pope's pleasure. Second, the pope would not support the creation of rival emperors, for just as had been true a few years earlier, only anarchy could result. Gregory was not so much loyal to Leo III as aware of the potential unreliability of Liutprand and, as against Leo III, convinced of the strength of his own position in Rome. Gregory was acting more like an ally of the emperor than a subject.[114] Third, in the vicinity of Rome itself the pope's position of leadership was not totally secure. Two rebellions against the pope had arisen in Campania and now a third in Roman Tuscany. The city itself seems to have been solidly papal by 729, but its region was somewhat less secure. In this region many members of the *exercitus Romanus* had estates,[115] and the Church possessed extensive landholdings. It may be that the papal administration and elements within the military aristocracy had conflicting economic interests in the countryside around Rome, and that some *milites* were seeking to draw personal advantage from the pope's discomfiture at the hands of the Lombards and the Greeks. With the Byzantines and the Lombards both a continuing menace, the pope could hardly tolerate anarchy or serious rivals in his own neighborhood, and it appears that he had adequate support and resources to meet any local challenge. Fourth, the *vita* says that Gregory placed at Eutychius's

---

[112]*LP* 1:408.
[113]*LP* 1:409.
[114]Schäfer, *Bedeutung*, pp. 29–30.
[115]Kehr, *IP* 2:3–13 passim, showing grants of *fundi* to *milites* 5 to 15 miles from Rome.

disposal *"proceres ecclesiae atque exercitus."* Here one has a splendid testimony to the pope's control of the civil and ecclesiastical life of the city and of its duchy, even if that control was not yet absolute. From 729 on, and in certain respects for several years already, it is meaningless to speak any longer of imperal Rome. Some new but still inchoate papal Rome now existed.

Leo III had an uncanny knack for taking a bad situation and making it worse. Having tolerated the iconodule patriarch, Germanus, for a number of years, the emperor now deposed him and installed a lackey, Anastasius, in his place.[116] On 17 January 730 Leo convoked an imperial *Silentium*, or council meeting, and issued another formal decree against icons.[117] Gregory vigorously protested against the deposition of Germanus and once again condemned iconoclasm, but to no avail.[118] Gregory's tumultuous pontificate came to an end in February 731 and the learned and zealous Gregory III was elected in his place. The new pope had no more esteem for iconoclasm than his predecessor and almost immediately dispatched a priest named George to Constantinople to recall the emperor from his errors. George set out but was struck with terror and returned to Rome. Gregory thought about degrading him but instead, by his own persuasion and that of the *"optimates,"* convinced George to try again. Here was another instance of the pope and the Roman nobility acting in concert to oppose the will of the emperor. George departed again but was this time detained by imperial agents in Sicily.[119] Leo's iconoclastic policies had precipitated a massive revolt in 726, and now those policies were being confirmed and perhaps given added legal force. Imperial agents had already proved incapable of breaking Gregory II's opposition, and by 731–32 it must have become clear in Constantinople that Gregory III, with prominent Romans arrayed behind him, would be no less inflexible than his predecessor.

Diplomatic representations having accomplished nothing, Gregory now decided to respond to iconoclasm by a more direct and formal method. He summoned a Roman synod to meet 1 November 731 for the purpose of condemning this hateful heresy.[120] Unfortunately the conciliar *acta* are lost, but from Gregory's *vita* one can conclude that the acta contained an impas-

---

[116]*LP* 1:409.

[117]Ostrogorsky, *Byzantine State*, p. 164; Aikatherine Christophilopulu, "SILENTION," *BZ* 44 (1951): 79–85.

[118]For this correspondence see n.89.

[119]*LP* 1:415–16 (Gregory III).

[120]*LP* 1:416; *Chron. pat. grad.*, c. 12, *MGH, SSrL*, p. 396; *Epp. Lang.*, no. 13, *MGH, EKA* 3:703; Jaffé, *RP*, no. 2232. Gregory's letter to Antonius of Grado gives us the chronology.

sioned defense of icons. Even without the *acta*, enough is known about the synod to form some impression of East-West relations at this critical juncture. Gregory summoned the patriarchs of Grado (Venice) and Ravenna "along with the rest of the bishops of these western regions." The meeting took place in Rome in the presence of the Roman clergy and nobility and "the rest of the Christian people."[121] Gregory was turning the Roman synod into a focal point of Italian national life.[122] What Leo had done in the East Gregory would undo in the West. That prominent laymen participated alongside the clergy is highly reflective of attitudes in Italy. Gregory sent a *defensor*, Constantine, to the capital with another letter in defense of images, but he too was detained in Sicily. Letters were also sent "to the totality of this province of Italy" and more letters were sent to Constantinople.[123] Imperial religious policy, which was a cornerstone of Leo III's regime and a key imperial prerogative under any circumstances, had been rejected in Italy by all classes of people both lay and clerical. Moreover, the references to "eastern" and "western" regions in papal correspondence suggest that people were beginning to think of Italy and the empire as separate entities.

Leo's response to all of this Italian fulmination was a punitive naval raid against Ravenna. The ships were wrecked in the Adriatic before reaching their destination. After the failure of this venture, which must have struck the emperor as one more example of his inability to manage affairs in Italy, in 732 or 733, Leo transferred the ecclesiastical provinces, and with them the papal patrimonies, of southern Italy, Sicily, and Illyricum to the jurisdiction of the patriarch of Constantinople.[124] Eugen Ewig concludes that this action was designed to "condemn Rome to insignificance" or to "abandon old Rome, fallen from its former height, to its own fate."[125] These interpre-

---

[121]*LP* 1:416.

[122]Llewellyn, *Rome in the Dark Ages*, p. 129.

[123]*LP* 1:416–17.

[124]Ewig, "Papacy's Alienation from Byzantium," p. 7, gives the traditional view. Dominic Mandic, "Dalmatia in the Exarchate of Ravenna from the Middle of the VI until the Middle of the VIII Century," *Byzantion* 34 (1964): 347–74, discusses what the pope lost in Illyricum. The attempt of Venance Grumel ("L'annexion de l'Illyricum oriental, de la Sicile et de la Calabre au patriarchat de Constantinople," *Recherches de science religieuse* 40 [1952]: 191–200) to date the transfer of these provinces to the 750s has found little acceptance except by Ostrogorsky (*Byzantine State*, p. 170 and n.1). The definitive study is Anastos, "The Transfer of Illyricum, Calabria and Sicily to the Jurisdiction of the Patriarchate of Constantinople in 732–33," *Studi bizantini e neoellenici* 9 (1957): 14–31.

[125]Ewig, "Papacy's Alienation from Byzantium," p. 7. Similar views are held by: Schäfer, *Bedeutung*, pp. 36–37; Llewellyn, *Rome in the Dark Ages*, pp. 168–69; Peter Classen, "Karl

tations are not mutually exclusive, and both contain a large measure of the truth. Southern, Hellenized Italy was richer, more strategically significant in the face of the Arabs and had been conspicuously loyal in recent years. Illyricum was beyond effective papal control in any case, and an important vantage point for defense of the Balkans. The papacy did not for two generations raise objections to the transfer, and it was accomplished with apparent ease.[126] The Duchy of Rome was now de facto an autonomous region under the pope. The emperor had cut his losses by securing tightly those regions he could control and casting adrift those which he could not. The exarch, Eutychius, was not recalled by his government, and so it would be an exaggeration to say that the Byzantines absolutely renounced their authority in central Italy. But the complete powerlessness of the Byzantine administration there makes the de jure position of the exarch meaningless.

The forces that would eventually compel a separation of central Italy from its Byzantine masters had been set in motion in the 680s. By 729 a turning point had been reached and by 733 a new history had commenced. The creation of a papal Republic may be dated to the years between 729 and 733. The pope, with the Italian nobility arrayed behind him, had thrown off almost every vestige of imperial authority, and the Basileus had recognized the new ordering of affairs by reorganizing the territories where his power was still effective. Some difficult questions remained, however. What sort of relationship would exist between this new state in Italy and the empire of which it had formerly been a part? Would the whole of the old Exarchate be included in the Republic, or only the region of Rome? Would the Lombard menace reappear, and if it did, would the new Republic be able to muster the forces necessary to defend itself?

New Lombard Threats and Shifting Papal Diplomacy

When we left Liutprand he had, after mediating the false peace of 729, and with his kingdom appreciably augmented by the subjection to it of Spoleto and Benevento, disappeared from the scene for a while. Transamund of Spoleto remained loyal to the king for a time, and when Romuald II of

---

der Große, das Papsttum und Byzanz," in Wolfgang Braunfels, ed., *Karl der Große*, 4 vols. (Düsseldorf, 1965), 1:538–39.

[126]Gay, *Italie méridionale*, p. 8.

Benevento died, Liutprand intervened there to secure royal interests. The date of Romuald's death cannot be fixed precisely, but it must have fallen between 730 and 732.[127] Romuald left only a minor son, Gisulf, and a faction of Beneventans rose up in support of a *referendarius* of the dead duke. Liutprand intervened, sent Gisulf off into honorable residence at Pavia, and installed his own nephew Gregory as duke.[128] Control of Benevento was important to the king for many reasons, not the least of which was that the massive duchy served to insulate central Italy from the still Byzantine south. After Leo III had transferred the pope's former church provinces, the Exarchate was completely open and exposed to Liutprand, but for several years he did not seek to draw profit from the situation. In 735 he was ill for a time, causing the Lombards to elect his nephew Hildeprand co-regent.[129] Perhaps his illness or, what is more likely, some aspect of his agreement with Gregory II prevented him from taking any action. There was general peace in Italy for several years.

During Liutprand's illness or maybe shortly thereafter Duke Agatho of Perugia attacked and tried to reconquer Bologna, which the king had taken during his push into Emilia some ten years earlier.[130] Agatho's raid was beaten back with little difficulty, but it signaled an end to the calm that had prevailed for several years. Concluding, perhaps justifiably, that the "Romans" had broken the truce, Hildeprand and Paradeo, the duke of Vicenza, attacked and actually captured Ravenna. Ravenna's fall probably took place in 738.[131] The exarch was forced to flee to Venice. Gregory III wrote to Duke Ursus of Venice and to Antonius of Grado asking them to come to the aid

---

[127]Hodgkin, *The Italian Kingdom*, p. 470, says the year 730; Hartmann, *Geschichte Italiens*, 2.2:132 says 731–32; Fröhlich, *Thronfolge* 1:190, says 732.

[128]Paul, *Hist. Lang.*, 6.55, *MGH, SSrL*, p. 184.

[129]Fröhlich, *Thronfolge* 1:197ff.

[130]Paul, *Hist. Lang*, 6.54, *MGH, SSrL*, p. 184. Only Hallenbeck (*Pavia and Rome*, pp. 31–32) and Delogu ("Il regno longobardo," p. 156) place Agatho's attack *before* the Lombard raid on Ravenna. I enthusiastically accept their reconstruction of the order of events but not their absolute chronology.

[131]Paul, *Hist. Lang.*, 6.54, *MGH, SSrL*, pp. 183–84; John, *Chron. Ven.*, *MGH, SS* 7:12. The chronology is very difficult to establish. Jaffé, *RP*, no. 2178, and Kehr, *IP*, vol. 7, pt. 1, no. 20, p. 38, say 729 but this is either far too early or a confusion with earlier events. Many historians have held for 732: Hartmann, *Geschichte Italiens*, 2.2:133; Caspar, *Das Papsttum*, p. 728; Bertolini, *Roma di fronte a Bisanzio e ai Longobardi* (Rome, 1941), pp. 457–58; Fröhlich, *Thronfolge* 1:191. Kretschmayr, *Geschichte von Venedig* 1:47–48, says 739 and Cessi, *Storia della Repubblica di Venezia*, p. 18, says 740. Hodgkin, *The Italian Kingdom*, says 737 or shortly thereafter. The chronology is very important, so a review of the evidence is in order.

of Eutychius and of Ravenna.[132] Aid was provided and Ravenna was retaken. Paredeo was killed and Hildeprand held captive for a while.[133]

The language used by Gregory in his letters to Ursus and Antonius is fascinating. He asked them to restore Ravenna to the "holy republic" and to "the imperial service of our sons Leo and Constantine." Ravenna thus belonged to a "holy republic" and the pope saw it as his own responsibility to assure its safety. But, why would Gregory appeal to the Venetians to restore Ravenna to Leo III and his son? There are several reasons. De jure Ravenna was still a part of the empire. No one in Rome had yet denied that. Ravenna and Venice had never taken kindly to the idea of falling under papal sway, and so an appeal on behalf of the emperor was more likely to effect the immediate objective of getting the Lombards out than an appeal on behalf of the pope himself. Finally, there remained the possibility, however slim, that the Greeks might yet offer aid against the Lombards. The reality of the situation has been aptly summarized by Jeffrey Richards, who says that "by defending Catholic interests against the emperor and imperial interests against the Lombards the papacy was in effect defending its own interests against all comers."[134] Liutprand probably regarded Gregory's intervention on behalf of the Ravennese as both surprising and decidedly unfriendly. For ten years he had avoided attacking the Duchy of Rome or in any other way provoking the pope. In the king's calculus Rome and Ravenna represented separate entities and the former had no business taking up the cause of the latter.[135] For his part Gregory was, like his predecessor, acting like an ally of

---

Paul the Deacon places the attack on Ravenna close in time to Liutprand's helping Charles Martel in Provence against the Muslims. This campaign took place in 739: *BM*, no. 41b; Breysig, *Jahrbücher*, p. 94. In 740 Gregory wrote to Charles (*Codex Carolinus* [hereafter CC], no. 2, p. 477) saying "preterito anno" Ravenna had been taken. This would mean 739 if Gregory's letter must be placed in 740 and if his words are to be taken absolutely literally. Neither thing is certain, however. After Ravenna had been captured, Gregory wrote to Duke Ursus of Venice (see n.132) who died in 737. He was murdered, so it is possible that Gregory did not have immediate knowledge of this fact. John the Deacon says that Eutychius fled to Venice during the rule of Hypatius, who was one of the people who ruled Venice, after the fall of Ursus, from 737 to 741: Kretschmayr, *Geschichte von Venedig* 1:48; Cessi, *Storia della Repubblica di Venezia*, p. 48. My best estimate is 738.

[132]*Epp. Lang.*, nos. 11, 12, *MGH*, *EKA* 3:702; Jaffé, *RP*, no. 2177. Hartmann (*Geschichte Italiens*, 2.2:153 n.8) and Caspar (*Das Papsttum* p. 729 n.1) consider the letter to Ursus to be a forgery. Bertolini (*Roma*, p. 457) shows that there are insufficient grounds for this opinion.

[133]Paul, *Hist. Lang.*, 6.54, *MGH*, *SSrL*, p. 184; John, *Chron Ven.*, *MGH*, *SS* 7:12.

[134]Richards, *Popes and the Papacy*, p. 46.

[135]This is, with some modifications, Hallenbeck's reconstruction: *Pavia and Rome*, p. 31ff. In broad outlines, but not in all details, I find it superior to all previous ones.

the emperor in coming to Ravenna's aid. The pope had been willing for a number of years to live in peace with both the exarch and the king. He would not, however, tolerate a substantial alteration of the territorial situation which might have worked to the advantage of either of his potential foes.

The Lombard attack on Ravenna may have been a signal for a general opening of hostilities. Transamund of Spoleto seized the *castrum* of Gallese, a strategic point that protected Roman communications with Ravenna. Gregory then paid Transamund to restore Gallese to the "holy republic" and the "Christ-loved Roman army."[136] It is important to note that the pope handled this case (*"potuit causam finire"*) without appeal to the emperor or exarch or other Italian cities. Gregory was acting as the sole competent authority for Rome and its army, which may be taken to mean the city's leading citizens.[137]

The pope was also mixing his metaphors. He had received Gallese into his own possession much as his predecessors had obtained Cumae and Sutri. Gallese was purchased by the pope for a "holy republic," which can only mean, in this context, the Duchy of Rome. At almost the same time, however, he had helped to recover Ravenna for a "holy republic," which in that context can only refer to the Byzantine Empire. By the 750s this ambiguity in terminology will have disappeared, but in the late 730s the pope was beginning to call his new state a republic and to equate it with the Byzantine one.[138]

Transamund of Spoleto had shown real independence in seizing Gallese and then selling it to the pope. Liutprand may not have liked this in view of the Roman attack on Bologna and his recent difficulties in Ravenna, but he must have been even less pleased when Duke Gregory of Benevento died and a separatist faction elected Godescalc duke.[139] Gregory, who had already repaired the walls of Rome and Civitavecchia, perhaps in anticipation of trouble in his sector of Italy, quickly moved to strike an alliance with Transamund and Godescalc.[140] Clearly the pope was trying to shore up central Italy against the king, doubtless fearing that after the Lombards had attacked

[136]*LP* 1:420–21.
[137]Bertolini, *Roma e i longobardi*, pp. 45–46.
[138]Delogu, "Il regno longobardo," p. 158.
[139]Paul, *Hist. Lang.*, 6.56, *MGH, SSrL*, p. 185.
[140]*LP* 1:420, 421. Bertolini, *Roma e i longobardi*, pp. 47–48; Schäfer, *Bedeutung*, pp. 41–44.

Ravenna military operations against Rome were altogether possible in retaliation for the aid given the Ravennese by the pope.

These displays of independence on the part of the dukes in the south goaded Liutprand into action. By 16 June Spoleto was in his hands and he had installed Hilderich as duke.[141] Transamund managed to flee to Rome. Godescalc was allowed to hold Benevento for a time. Liutprand had entered Spoleto from the Pentapolis and on his march part of his army had been attacked by Spoletans and "Romans" who were probably Pentapolitans.[142] The king may have reasoned that Spoleto was insufficiently secure to permit campaigning farther south in Benevento. Besides, Liutprand had a score to settle with the pope for harboring Transamund and allying with the dukes. As a result he laid siege to the Duchy of Rome. It does not appear that Liutprand actually intended to conquer the duchy. His objectives were probably limited to forcing Gregory to hand over Transamund and to abandon his alliance with the dukes. A papal-ducal alliance, in 738–39 as in 728, posed a dire threat to the integrity of the Lombard kingdom.[143] Gregory's reasons for concluding the alliance may have been rooted in hostility to the the king, or in a feeling that after the Lombard attack on Ravenna it was necessary to fortify Roman Italy against any eventuality. In any case, Liutprand's decisive actions had left the pope in straitened circumstances.

His position having become untenable, the pope sent two clerics, Anastasius and Sergius, by sea to Charles Martel in Francia to implore his aid.[144] The letter to Charles is revealing.[145] The pope told the mayor of the palace that as a true son of St. Peter he must rush to the defense of Peter's church and the pope's "*peculiarem populum.*" The Church of St. Peter was being oppressed by the Lombards and, after God, only Charles could help. The pope concluded by telling Charles that if he hoped to have eternal life he had to come to the defense of the Church. Liutprand had attacked the Roman duchy but this had become, in Gregory's mind, St. Peter's land. Liutprand was capturing Romans and tonsuring them "*more Langobardorum,*" but these Romans are now St. Peter's, that is, the pope's, "peculiar

---

[141]Pabst, "Herzogthums," p. 479; Brühl, "Chronologie," p. 20; Fröhlich, *Thronfolge* 1:192. For the date: *CDL*, 3.1, ed. Brühl, no. 14, pp. 63–67.

[142]Paul, *Hist. Lang.*, 6.56, MGH, SSrL, p. 185. Delogu, "Il regno longobardo," pp. 160–61, thinks that Transamund had made some sort of bargain with Eutychius and that this explains the attack on Liutprand by Pentapolitan forces. I am not completely persuaded by this argument because there are serious chronological problems that Delogu has not solved.

[143]Hallenbeck, *Pavia and Rome*, pp. 34–35.

[144]*LP* 1:420.

[145]*CC*, no. 1, p. 497.

people." The pope wrote like a head of state seeking a defensive alliance. Not once in his letter did Gregory mention the emperor or the exarch.

The pope's appeal was not well calculated to bring immediate results. Liutprand had always pursued a policy of friendship with Charles. In 725 they had, acting in concert, attacked Bavaria. In about 737 Charles had sent his second son, Pepin, to Liutprand for a ceremonial haircut that established a bond of fictive kinship between the two ruling houses.[146] In August 739 Liutprand gave up his siege of Rome to rush to the aid of Charles, who was then campaigning against the Muslims in Provence.[147] The Frankish mayor and the Lombard king were, in short, fast friends when Gregory appealed to the former against the latter.

In Liutprand's absence Gregory commissioned the Roman army to restore Transamund to Spoleto. When the king had marched north he had retained in his control the four cities of Amelia, Orte, Bomarzo, and Bieda. Transamund, as the price of the help of the Roman army in restoring him, agreed to help the Romans recover the four cities.[148] By December 739 Transamund was back in Spoleto but, perhaps because he feared Liutprand, he refused to carry out his part of the bargain with the Romans.[149] The four cities remained in Lombard hands.

It is crucial to realize how difficult the pope's position was in 739–40.[150] No military help had come from Charles, and none was likely. The Spoletan alliance had backfired. The exarch was useless. Liutprand had attacked Rome, seized four of its cities, and then left temporarily, but his return had to have been expected at any moment. Despite all of the talk in the sources about the Roman army, its forces were obviously inadequate to the task of meeting a major Lombard offensive.

Perhaps grasping at straws, Gregory wrote to Charles Martel a second time. It is unfortunate that more details do not survive concerning this exchange between Rome and Francia. Charles must have responded in some way to Gregory's first letter, because the pope's second one was carried to Francia by Anthat, a *fidelis* of Charles.[151] Many years later Charlemagne said that his grandfather, Charles Martel, had undertaken defense of the Roman

---

[146]Paul, *Hist. Lang.*, 6.53, MGH, SSrL, p. 183.

[147]Fröhlich, *Thronfolge* 1:193; Bertolini, *Roma*, p. 467.

[148]*LP* 1:426 (Zachary).

[149]Brühl, "Chronologie," p. 21; Pabst, "Herzogthums," p. 479.

[150]Hartmann, *Geschichte Italiens*, 2.2:139–40.

[151]CC, no. 2, pp. 477–79. This letter can be dated December 739 or very early 740. This bears on the subjects treated in n.131.

Church,[152] and between late 739 and 742 we have no reports of further Lombard attacks on Rome. Thus it is possible that Charles interceded in some way for the pope.

One wonders what could have persuaded Gregory to appeal to Charles Martel in 739 when he had to have known that Charles and Liutprand were then, and had been for many years already, allies. It may have been Boniface who suggested to Gregory the idea of an appeal to Charles. In 737 the great missionary visited Rome for a second time and stayed there nearly a year.[153]

Gregory's second letter urged Charles not to believe Lombard lies. Liutprand seems to have persuaded Charles that the pope had wronged him by supporting rebels. He must have meant the Spoletans and Beneventans who, the pope himself said, had committed only this crime: "They refused to attack Rome and to destroy the property of the holy apostles and to plunder their peculiar people." Again Charles was urged to come to the defense of St. Peter's Church which now, in the pope's thinking, was coterminous with the old Duchy of Rome. It seems safe to suggest that when Liutprand went to join Charles in Provence the latter had already received Gregory's first letter and that the king provided Charles with his own version of affairs in Italy. Probably Charles sent Anthat to Rome to make inquires and, perhaps, to argue Liutprand's case. By means of Anthat, then, Gregory responded to the inquiries put to him, jointly in a sense, by Charles and Liutprand. This is all that can be learned from the pope's letter, and the *Liber Pontificalis* supplies no details at all. The Frankish sources, however, cast a completely different light on the situation.[154]

Gregory, the better to impress Charles Martel, sent him the keys to the tomb of St. Peter, a link from the saint's chains, and other gifts. This deeply impressed the Frankish chroniclers who observed that no pope had ever before sent such things to Francia. Charles also sent back gifts of his own with Grimo, the abbot of Corbie, and Sigebert, a monk of St. Denis. Perhaps these men played some role in mediating the quarrel between Gregory and Liutprand,[155] although that role may also have been played by Anthat. Up to this point, apart from minor differences in detail, the Frankish and papal sources really only complement each other. There remains, however, a re-

---

[152]*MGH, Cap.*, vol. 1, no. 45, c. 15, p. 129.

[153]Schieffer, *Winfrid-Bonifatius*, p. 172. In 745 Boniface definitely suggested, although in connection with a different matter, that Pope Zachary ought to appeal to the Franks: Boniface, ep. no. 60, ed. Tangl, *MGH*, p. 122.

[154]*Fredegarii Continuatio*, c. 22, ed. Wallace-Hadrill, p. 96; *Annales mettenses priores*, ed. Simson, pp. 30–31; *Chronicon moissacense, MGH, SS* 1:291–92.

[155]Ewig, "Papacy's Alienation from Byzantium," p. 20, thinks so. The Anthat mentioned in *LP* is not mentioned in Frankish sources.

markable notice in the Frankish sources which appears nowhere in the papal records. Fredegar's continuator, who was a relative of Charles Martel,[156] and the anonymous Metz and Moissac annalists say that the pope and the Roman people proposed that they would depart from the empire and place themselves under Charles's protection.

Not surprisingly, these revelations have been the source of some controversy. That Gregory and the Romans formally proposed to secede from the Byzantine Empire and transfer themselves under the protection of the Franks is a common but slightly strong interpretation of the passage in the Frankish sources.[157] In reality, central Italy had seceded some years earlier from Byzantium, but it is certainly true that a defense alliance with the Franks was being sought in 739. The most controversial issues about Gregory's proposal, however, turn on the form taken by the pope's approach to Charles. Ever since Bruno Krusch edited Fredegar for the *MGH*, scholars have been trying to emend *"romano consulto"* into *"romano consulato"* in order to interpret the passage in such a way that Gregory was conferring the consulate on Charles.[158] Eduard Hlawitschka has argued persuasively that this interpretation has two fatal flaws.[159] No surviving document assigns Charles a consular title and no manuscript of Fredegar has *consulato*. In fact, the *Annales iuvavenses breves*, which quote Fredegar's continuator, have *consulto*.[160] Another line of interpretation holds that *"romano consulto"* is the correct reading and that it means that a decree of the Roman Senate, a *senatus consultum*, had been issued as a formal basis for securing an alliance.[161] The problem with this point of view is that there is absolutely no reliable evidence that the Roman Senate had survived into the eighth century.[162] *Romano consulto* means quite simply that the Romans, certainly the leading individ-

---

[156]Wattenbach-Levison-Löwe, *Deutschlands Geschichtsquellen im Mittelalter* (Stuttgart, 1953), p. 161ff.

[157]Gina Fasoli, *Carlomagno e l'Italia* (Bologna, 1968), 1:30–31; Eduard Hlawitschka, "Karl Martell, das römische Konsulat und der Römische Senat: Zur Interpretation von Fredegarii Continuatio cap. 22," in Werner Besch, ed., *Die Stadt in der europäische Geschichte: Festschrift Edith Ennen* (Bonn, 1972), pp. 81, 90, with the older literature.

[158]Englebert Mühlbacher, *Deutsche Geschichte unter den Karolingern* (Stuttgart, 1896), p. 42; Hartmann, *Geschichte Italiens*, 2.2:170, 199; Caspar, *Pippin und die römische Kirche*, p. 1.

[159]Hlawitschka, "Das römische Konsulat," pp. 80, 87, 90.

[160]*MGH, SS* 3:123.

[161]The most passionate defender of this thesis is Arrigo Solmi, *Il senato romano nell'alto medioevo* (Rome, 1944), pp. 11–14, 25ff. Solmi is certainly correct to emphasize the degree to which the Romans drew on their own rich history to support their own interests. Fasoli (*Carlomagno*, p. 32 n.2) agrees with Solmi as does Bertolini (*Roma*, pp. 464–65).

[162]Hlawitschka, "Das römische Konsulat," pp. 83–84, 87, 90, with further literature.

uals in the city, had been *consulted* before Gregory appealed to Charles, and that they approved of the appeal.[163]

From the limited evidence relevant to Gregory's approach to Charles it is possible to form some impression of the solution to the Italian crisis that was beginning to take shape in Roman circles. An independent state, belonging to St. Peter, inhabited by Peter's "peculiar people," governed by the pope, and protected by the Franks was to replace the old Byzantine Duchy of Rome. This state would include, at a minimum, the Duchies of Rome and Perugia, and possibly the region of Ravenna. There is no reason whatsoever to believe that by 739–40 prominent Romans, the pope among and probably leading them, had not decided to abandon definitively their former associations with Byzantium.[164] Freedom from Byzantium had always carried with it the spectre of total isolation for central Italy,[165] and it was to alleviate that isolation that the letters to Charles were drafted and dispatched. When Charles failed to respond, the papacy was in no worse shape than it had been before the approach to the Franks, and the future possibility of securing a Frankish alliance could be added to the repertoire of papal defensive tactics that already included such devices as alliances with the Lombard duchies.

From early 740 until late 741 it is difficult to form a clear sense of what was taking place in Italy. One suspects that very little was happening as all parties watched and waited. Possibly through Charles's good offices Liutprand and Gregory were temporarily at peace. If so, it was a peace based on the status quo as of late 739, which means that Liutprand still held Amelia, Orte, Bieda, and Bomarzo, while Transamund possessed Spoleto and Godescalc Benevento. Neither king nor pope can have been happy with this state of affairs. In 740, after his appeal to Charles Martel had failed, Gregory had written to the bishops of Lombard Tuscany asking them to be mindful of their oaths of office and reminding them to work for the interests of the Church against the attacks of Liutprand.[166] This action by the pope may have struck the king as a subtle but effective reminder that Rome was not without means of stirring up trouble in the *regnum.* Finally, in 741, three of

---

[163]Irene Haselbach, *Aufstieg und Herrschaft der Karolinger in der Darstellung der sogenannten Annales Mettenses Priores* (Lübeck, 1970), pp. 94–95.

[164]Hlawitschka, "Das römische Konsulat," p. 90; Fasoli, *Carlomagno,* pp. 30–31.

[165]Karl Schmid, "Zur Ablösung der Langobardenherrschaft durch den Franken," *QFIAB* 52 (1972): 1–2.

[166]*Epp. Lang.,* no. 16, *MGH, EKA* 3:708. For the date: Jaffé, *RP,* no. 2253, 15 October 740. To compare this letter to episcopal oaths of office see: *LD,* ed. Foerster, nos. 75, 76, pp. 136–38. For interpretation see: Caspar, *Das Papsttum,* p. 727.

the great actors in this drama died: Gregory, Charles Martel, and Leo. No one can have predicted the likely policies of the successors of each ruler and prudence may have imposed caution on everyone in 741, and into 742.

Gregory III died 29 November 741 and his successor Zachary was elected on 3 December.[167] The conventional wisdom, misinterpreting a key passage in Zachary's *vita*, holds that he was the last pope to send a formal notice of his election to the emperor for confirmation.[168] In fact, Zachary, as a true son of St. Peter's Republic, did no such thing. The *vita* actually says that Zachary sent to Constantinople "*synodicam simulque et aliam suggestionem.*"[169] Ottorino Bertolini has correctly penetrated the nuances of this passage.[170] A synodical letter was sent, but this was a purely formal document attesting to the pope's orthodoxy. It is quite reasonable to assume that the letter contained a fresh denunciation of iconoclasm. As a significant diplomatic sidelight, the name of the patriarch to whom the letter was sent—synodica were exchanged among clergy, they had nothing to do with the emperor—is not given. The heretical interloper Anastasius was then presiding over the Byzantine Church. The "*aliam suggestionem*" was, on the other hand, surely some sort of letter to the emperor requesting him to desist from iconoclasm.[171] No election decree can have been involved for several reasons. Since the late seventh century these went to the exarch and not to the emperor and, in any event, five days, the length of time between Gregory's death and Zachary's consecration, would not have been long enough for the necessary documents to have traveled back and forth between Rome and Ravenna. The place in Zachary's *vita* where the "*suggestio*" is mentioned makes it clear that it was at least 742 or 743 before this document went east, and Zachary was elected in 741. Finally, Zachary had played a bit of a game in the East by recognizing during parts of 741 and 743 and all of 742 an iconodule rebel against Constantine V named Artavasdus.[172] Zachary

---

[167]Jaffé, *RP*, p. 262.

[168]E.g., Caspar, *Das Papsttum*, p. 738.

[169]*LP* 1:432.

[170]Bertolini, "I rapporti di Zaccaria con Costantino V e con Artavasdo nel racconto del biografo del papa e nella probabile realta' storica," *Archivio della società romana di storia patria* 78 (1955): 1–21.

[171]This is what Hadrian I thought years later: Mansi, *Concilia* 12:1061.

[172]On Artavasdus see: Ostrogorsky, *Byzantine State*, pp. 165–66, whose chronology differs from Bertolini's (as in n.170). On the chronology of Artavasdus's revolt, I follow Paul Speck, *Artabasdos, der rechtgläubige Vorkämpfer der göttlichen Lehren: Untersuchungen zur Revolte des Artabasdos und ihrer Darstellung in der byzantinischen Historiographie* (Bonn, 1981), pp. 1–133. I am dubious about his argument that Artavasdus did not attempt to restore icons.

eventually recognized Constantine, and in gratitude the new emperor gave the pope two valuable estates at Nimfa and Norma near Rome.[173] Thus it was not the pope who sought confirmation from the emperor but, in a sense, the emperor who was confirmed by the pope.

Nearer to home Zachary stood aside while Liutprand reestablished royal authority in Spoleto and Benevento. Zachary made representation to the king concerning the four cities taken in 739, and Liutprand promised to return them. Generally, Liutprand had shown direct hostility to Rome only when the popes allied themselves with the duchies, and the dukes had not always proved reliable.[174] Thus Zachary elected to give up his predecessors' policy of allying with the dukes, and he even dispatched troops to help the king in his reconquest of Spoleto.[175] In 742 Liutprand invaded Spoleto and removed Transamund, who was powerless without Roman assistance, to a monastery. He then installed his nephew Agiprand as duke and headed for Benevento. Just the news of the king's approach terrified Godescalc, who tried to flee but was caught and killed. As duke of Benevento, Liutprand introduced his kinsman and long-time guest at Pavia, Gisulf.[176]

Zachary had assuredly come to the realization that his predecessors' policy of allying with the dukes was flawed because of the weakness and unreliability of the dukes in the face of a king who was determined to control the southern duchies.[177] The pope had decided that a direct confrontation with Liutprand was his only hope for the future, but the papal-ducal alliance had served some useful purposes. It had kept the Byzantines out of Rome on more than one occasion and had also distracted Liutprand and had prevented him from overwhelming the Duchy of Rome in 739.[178] On balance it had been a wise and worthwhile policy because the territorial independence of central Italy had been achieved through the alteration of the balance

---

[173]*LP* 1:433; Duchesne, *Temporal Sovereignty*, p. 19.

[174]Hartmann, *Geschichte Italiens*, 2.2:126.

[175]*LP* 1:427.

[176]Paul, *Hist. Lang.*, 5.56–57, *MGH, SSrL*, p. 185. Brühl, "Chronologie," p. 21. Gisulf was related to Liutprand through his mother, Gumperga, who was a daughter of the king's sister Aurona: Paul, *Hist. Lang.*, 6.50, *MGH, SSrL*, p. 182.

[177]Bertolini, "Carlomagno e Benevento," in *Karl der Große* 1:609–10; Hartmann, *Geschichte Italiens*, 2.2:139–40; Richards, *Popes and the Papacy*, p. 225, is especially critical of the alliance because of its potential for confrontation.

[178]Rasi, *Exercitus Italicus*, pp. 85–87. Hallenbeck, *Pavia and Rome*, p. 37ff, does not think Liutprand ever intended to conquer Rome. I am not sure that by 739 conquest had not begun to appear necessary to the king, not so much as an end in itself but as a means to cut off the only ally available to his rebellious southern dukes.

of power in Italy produced by the papacy's ties with the duchies. For a brief time, the pope had tipped that balance in his own favor.[179] Gregory II and III had eased the Republic out of the Byzantine Empire thanks in part to this alliance, and their skillful diplomacy merits high marks. Zachary, however, found himself in a situation calling for a reorientation of papal diplomacy if all of central Italy were to be kept out of the Lombard *regnum*.

After restoring order on his own terms in the duchies, Liutprand hesitated to restore the four cities which, in the words of an Italian source, he had taken "from the right of the Roman pontiff, Gregory."[180] This singular turn of phrase indicates quite clearly the new order that had dawned in Italy and explains why Zachary, with no appeal to any other authority, set out to recover "his" cities. Zachary's biographer says that the pope, "as a good pastor to the people committed to him by God" went to Terni to meet King Liutprand.[181] For the next quarter of a century similar pastoral terminology would be used repeatedly by papal biographers to describe the pope's efforts on behalf of the Republic. In fact, there is an interesting "pastoral" dimension to the phrase "*peculiaris populus*" that the popes had been using for several years to refer to the people of the Republic. "Peculiar," in English, connotes "odd," "strange" but it can bear the meaning "special." Surely it is this sense of uniqueness or distinctiveness that the popes wished to convey in using the word. What is interesting, then, is the fact that "*peculiaris*" derives from the same Latin root as "*pecu*" which means a flock or a herd. Another related word, "*peculium*," means one's private property. The pope's "peculiar people" were his "special people" in just the same way that a shepherd's flocks are special to him.

Zachary and Liutprand held a series of remarkably cordial meetings at Terni and, at their conclusion, the king restored the four cities taken from the Duchy of Rome in 739, along with Narni and at least some of the Church's patrimonies in the Sabina, which had been seized by the Spoletans thirty or more years earlier. In addition, the Pentapolitan cities of Osimo, Ancona, and Umana were restored as well as the land around Sutri; the actual *castrum* of Sutri had been seized and restored in 727–28. All of these restorations were made "*per donationis titulo*," that is by a formal royal act, and in each instance the recipient was "*beato Petro apostolorum principi*."[182] All captives or hostages then held by the Lombards were repatriated and

---

[179]Carl Rodenberg, *Pippin, Karlmann und Papst Stephan II* (Berlin, 1923), pp. 3–4.
[180]*Pauli continuatio tertia*, c. 14, MGH, SSrL, p. 207.
[181]*LP* 1:427.
[182]*CDL*, 3.1, ed. Brühl, no. 5, pp. 299–300.

Liutprand concluded a twenty-year peace with the Duchy of Rome. The pope and the king then dined together amicably, and Liutprand is said to have remarked that he had never enjoyed himself more. The following day royal and papal officers made a circuit of the four frontier cities of Amelia, Orte, Bieda, and Bomarzo and each of them was formally handed over to the pope's agents. The *vita* says, significantly, that the party traveled "*per circuitum finium reipublicae.*"[183] Zachary returned home to a joyous reception.

Many things are positively striking about this encounter at Terni. The Duchy of Rome was now for the first time unambiguously called a republic, and its eponymous head is St. Peter whose agent is the pope. In 738–39 Gregory III had made veiled and ambiguous references to a "holy republic," but he may have been referring to the empire on the occasion when it was the region of Ravenna that was in dispute, and to the the Roman duchy when it was a question of Gallese. The meeting at Terni also marks the first time that a pope had ever left Roman soil to negotiate with a Lombard king. The pope now negotiated matters of public law and concluded treaties in his own name, or, perhaps, on behalf of St. Peter, which amounts to the same thing. Zachary worked not only as an agent of St. Peter but also as the representative of the *populus Romanus*. No imperial or exarchal officials were even minutely involved in the proceedings.[184] Theodor Schieffer notes that although Zachary still issued his public documents under the regnal years of the emperor at Constantinople, this must strike us as "hopelessly anachronistic and contrary to reality."[185] Indeed, Zachary functioned as the head of an independent state under the patronage of St. Peter. As to the dates: The regnal years of the Basileus were the most widely recognized ones in the Christian world and it is not at all surprising that the pope continued to use them. Eventually popes would date by their own pontifical years and, after that, they would use Carolingian imperial years.

Liutprand had gained a good deal from the peace of Terni, or so he thought. He achieved a renunciation of papal-ducal alliances and evidently he believed that by recognizing the independence of the Duchy of Rome he had been left a free hand to intervene in Ravenna.[186] Accordingly, in 743, he

---

[183]*LP* 1:428–29.

[184]Caspar, *Das Papsttum*, p. 735; Pepe, *Moyen âge barbare in Italie*, pp. 168–69; Fasoli, *Carlomagno*, p. 35; Bertolini, *Roma e i longobardi*, pp. 56–57.

[185]*Winfrid-Bonifatius*, p. 188.

[186]Hartmann, *Geschichte Italiens*, 2.2:142–43; Caspar, *Das Papsttum*, p. 735; Fasoli, *Carlomagno*, p. 35. For a very different reconstruction of the following events see: Hallenbeck, *Pavia and Rome*, p. 45ff.

attacked Ravenna and siezed Cesena, a *castrum* near the frontier between
Ravenna and the *regnum*, and located at a strategic point on the via Aemilia
which road Liutprand may have hoped to secure as a means of access to
Spoleto.[187] The exarch, still Eutychius, and the archbishop of Ravenna, John,
sent a plaintive appeal to Zachary asking him to intercede on their behalf.
Zachary dispatched a legation to Liutprand consisting of a bishop who was
also the papal *vicedominus*, Benedict, and the *primicerius* of the notaries,
Ambrose. Such were conditions in Italy that only the pope and officers of
his government were competent and capable of dealing with the Lombards.

When Liutprand refused to budge, Zachary "committed the city of Rome
to the duke and patrician Stephen for safe-keeping" and set out "as a true
pastor to recover the rest of his flocks and the things which they had lost."[188]
Here is another piece of evidence that confirms papal rule in the Republic.
The duke of Rome, now a subordinate official, rules only in the pope's
absence.[189] The exarch and a great concourse of the Ravennese came out
fifty miles to meet the pope and on his approach acclaimed him with the
words "Happy are we to see the approach of our pastor who, having left his
flocks, has come to liberate us who are lost."[190] Four interesting points must
be noted in this account. First, it was the exarch who came out to meet the
pope whereas imperial protocol had always required the opposite. And, at
that, the pope was required to go one mile out from Rome to receive an
exarch but here the exarch traveled *fifty miles*. Second, the Romans and the
Ravennese had always had their differences but now the pope was claiming
the latter as his "flocks" while they simultaneously served notice that only
the pope could free them from their present predicament. Third, the exarch
appears completely powerless. Fourth, the pastoral terminology applied by
Gregory III to Rome and its environs was now being used by Zachary to
refer to Ravenna.

Zachary sent a deputation to Pavia to Liutprand announcing his intention to visit the king. When the legates crossed over into Lombard territory
they learned that they were to be prevented from seeing the king and they
so informed Zachary. The pope himself then headed for Pavia. At Pavia the
king was "struck with grief and did not wish to see the pope." Nevertheless,
on 28 July Zachary reached the Lombard capital and was received honorably. Zachary told Liutprand that he should cease attacking the "province of

---

[187]*LP* 1:429.

[188]*LP* 1:429.

[189]Armbrust, *Territoriale Politik*, pp. 88–89.

[190]*LP* 1:430.

Ravenna" and that he should return the cities he had taken from the Ravennese. After contemplating the matter, Liutprand decided to restore two-thirds of Cesena "*ad partem reipublicae*" while retaining the other third until the first of June next (i.e., 744) or until his envoy should return from Constantinople.[191]

After the Peace of Terni Liutprand seems to have continued to believe that the Duchy of Rome and the remnants of the Exarchate not already in his hands were two separate entities. By concluding peace with the former he had supposedly won a free hand in dealing with the latter.[192] This would explain why, after taking Cesena, he made representation to the emperor about keeping the *castrum*. It must be noted that when Zachary got to Pavia Liutprand's envoy had already gone to the imperial city. To the pope, however, both regions were now being claimed for his Republic and their inhabitants were all his flocks, his "peculiar people." Zachary's acquisition of Cesena, moreover, is interesting because it was the first piece of soil in the old Exarchate to which any pope had secured a title. One is reminded of the papacy's acquisition of Cumae and Sutri a generation earlier. Whether the Ravennese still considered themselves subjects of the empire is not known, but does not really matter. They did understand Italian realities, and when Liutprand captured Cesena they did not turn to the emperor for aid but to the pope. The king probably was saddened when he learned that the pope intended to plead for Ravenna's safety. He never dreamed that the pope would be solicitous of exarchal Ravenna, from which quarter his predecessors had suffered so many indignities. Bertolini supposes that at Terni the pope had acted as a sovereign working on behalf of his own state, but that at Pavia Zachary had functioned as a representative of the exarch.[193] In fact, Zachary acted like a sovereign on both occasions. No source says he drew a distinction between the Romans and the Ravennese. Quite the contrary is true. The papal biographer calls both peoples the pope's "flocks." Once Liutprand had dreamed of taking all of Italy, but the popes allied with his unruly dukes and brought that scheme to naught. Then Liutprand made peace with the pope, brought his dukes to heel, and assumed Ravenna was his for the taking. This plan came undone when Zachary took up the cause of the Ravennese just as vigorously as ever the popes had supported Rome.

Liutprand had to bend before ineradicable realities. If he could not divide

---

[191]*LP* 1:430–31.

[192]Hartmann, *Geschichte Italiens*, 2.2:144; Caspar, *Das Papsttum*, p. 735; Fasoli, *Carlomagno*, pp. 36–37; Bertolini, *Roma e i longobardi*, pp. 59–60.

[193]*Roma e i longobardi*, pp. 57–58.

Italy, he could not conquer it. Even if he did not wish to conquer all of Italy, he needed a secure route from the *regnum* to Spoleto. The attack on Cesena suggests that the king only intended to carve out a highway through the Exarchate and the Pentapolis, but the pope would have peace only on the basis of the status quo of Terni. Zachary had renounced an alliance with the dukes, but as long as the duchies were separated from the *regnum* by a band of territory outside Liutprand's control the king could not effectively dominate his always unruly southern duchies. The king was also a man of sincere religious sentiments and he did not relish having to make war on the pope. He had only rarely, and only after being—in his view at least—provoked, attacked Rome and its duchy and now he must have been gravely disappointed to learn that even an attack on Ravenna was to be construed as an act of war against St. Peter. Finally, the king was now an old man. He had been seriously ill in 735–36 and, perhaps, he had never recovered his former vigor. By early 744 he was dead. The papal biographer says that the king's decease was a divine judgment for his evil ways. One suspects that in Pavia things were viewed somewhat differently.

For the next few years events in Italy took a sharp turn in favor of papal interests. After Liutprand's death, which probably occurred in March 744, his nephew and co-regent Hildeprand assumed the royal mantle until he was deposed in, it seems, September of that year.[194] That Hildeprand was deposed is clear, but it is difficult to determine precisely why this happened.[195] It has usually been assumed that Hildeprand represented the aggressive, anti-Roman party among the Lombards and that philoromans rose up, threw him out, and replaced him with Ratchis.[196] There is nothing implausible in this theory, but in support of it one can only cite indirect and circumstantial evidence. Ratchis was a deeply religious man and, upon succeeding to the

---

[194]The date of Liutprand's death cannot be fixed, but on 22 March 744 Hildeprand issued a document at Pavia: *CDL*, vol. 3, pt. 1, ed. Brühl, no. 18, pp. 80–85. Fröhlich, *Thronfolge* 1:204, inexplicably dates this document 31 March. *Pauli continuatio cassinense*, c. 2, *MGH, SSrL*, p. 198, says Hildeprand ruled for seven months. See: Fröhlich, *Thronfolge* 1:204; Schneider, *Königswahl und Königserhebung*, p. 56.

[195]*Pauli continuatio tertia*, c. 19, *MGH, SSrL*, p. 207: "Hildeprandum . . . a Langobardis reprobatur." Schneider, *Königswahl und Königserhebung*, p. 56, misconstrues this passage. He believes it refers to March 744 and means that the king was "again approved." This is not what the Latin says. Similarly: *Pauli continuatio romana*, c. 1, *MGH, SSrL*, p. 200, says that Hildeprand was deposed. For a correct assessment see: Konrad Bund, *Thronsturz und Herrscherabsetzung im Frühmittelalter* (Bonn, 1979), pp. 213–14.

[196]Fasoli, *Carlomagno*, p. 38; Bertolini, *Roma*, p. 490; Maria Pia Andreolli, "Una pagina di storia langobarda: 'Re Ratchis,' " *Nuova rivista storica* 50 (1966): 311–12.

throne, confirmed Liutprand's twenty-year peace with the pope. Zachary's biographer says that "all Italy was quiet."[197] Ratchis was married to a Roman, Tassia, and was an energetic patron of the Church.[198] From all of this it is concluded that Ratchis was philoroman and, given that his predecessor was deposed, it follows that Ratchis was elected by philoromans. Another factor in his favor may have been that he either tolerated or promoted a reaction by those forces in the Lombard kingdom that opposed the centralizing policies of Liutprand.[199] He had been duke of Friuli before his election as king and, shortly after his election, the royal name disappears from Spoletan documents.[200] In his legislation, Ratchis treated Spoleto and Benevento as territories that did not belong to the kingdom.[201] Perhaps his election owed something to persons who believed that as a former duke Ratchis would not attempt to impose too strict a regime on the other dukes. As viewed from Rome, these developments must have been most welcome. A peaceful, philoroman, and religious man was on the Lombard throne, and the kingdom itself was dissolving into its constituent parts, which made it a much less formidable foe.

In 749 Ratchis effected a volte-face in foreign policy and attacked Perugia and several cities in the Pentapolis.[202] Why he did this is not clear. Hartmann thought that Zachary had somehow broken the Peace of Terni, but he advances this notion without the benefit of evidence.[203] More likely is the position adopted by those who believe Ratchis was goaded into action by the Lombard nationalist party. Presumably this party had been quiescent for a few years and now reasserted itself.[204]

Zachary again left Rome to negotiate. He met Ratchis at Perugia and once more worked his magic on a Lombard king. Ratchis was prevailed upon to abandon Perugia and, a few days later, he laid down his crown and became a monk at Zachary's hand.[205] Some suppose that by giving up the

---

[197]*LP* 1:431.

[198]Andreolli, "Re Ratchis," pp. 281–327 passim, is an excellent study of this king which analyzes all of the details cited above. See also, for briefer accounts: Hallenbeck, *Pavia and Rome*, pp. 51–52; Delogu, "Il regno longobardo," pp. 163–68.

[199]This is Bertolini's view: *Roma*, p. 490.

[200]*RF*, vol. 2, nos. 14–22, pp. 29–33.

[201]Tangl, "Passvorschrift," pp. 25–28.

[202]*LP* 1:433.

[203]*Geschichte Italiens*, 2.2:149.

[204]Bertolini, *Roma*, p. 497; Andreolli, "Re Ratchis," pp. 310–14; Bund, *Thronsturz*, pp. 214–15.

[205]*LP* 1:434.

siege of Perugia Ratchis enraged the nationalists who therefore deposed him.[206] Others feel that the king may have had a genuine crisis of conscience that led him to abandon the world.[207] Whatever it was that motivated Ratchis, his departure from the scene was not a good omen for Rome. The Lombards elected in his place the redoubtable Aistulf, and Italy was abruptly awakened from its years of relative repose.

On 3 or 4 July 749 Aistulf became king[208] and in short order restored royal authority in the southern duchies. By 751 Duke Lupus of Spoleto was dead and Aistulf was thereafter content to rule the duchy in his own name by means of powerful local families who were loyal to him.[209] In the summer or fall of 751 Gisulf of Benevento died and was succeeded by his minor son Liutprand. Until at least 755 his mother, Scauniperga, served as regent. Benevento again recognized royal authority under Scauniperga's regency.[210] These were impressive achievements by Aistulf, but by far his greatest accomplishment was the conquest of Ravenna in 751. No contemporary source describes this feat, but from a royal diploma dated 4 July 751 we learn that Aistulf was then in residence in the city.[211] The later *Chronicon salernitanum* says Eutychius handed the city over to Aistulf, and this same chronicle suggests that Aistulf also conquered Comacchio, Ferrara, and Istria.[212] Aistulf may actually have attacked Istria but we shall later have occasion to see that it was almost twenty years before Lombard authority there became real. In 752 Aistulf attacked the Duchy of Rome, but by then Zachary had died, and a new chapter in the history of the Republic was about to open.

The Birth of a Papal Republic

From the time when Justinian II assumed the purple at Constantinople, Italy began loosening its ties to Byzantium. Imperial religious policies, fiscal oppression, punitive raids, murderous attacks on Italian officials, and deten-

---

[206]Bund, *Thronsturz*, pp. 214–15; Hartmann, *Geschichte Italiens*, 2.2:149; Fröhlich, *Thronfolge* 1:209.

[207]Fasoli, *Carlomagno*, p. 40; Karl Heinrich Krüger, "Königskonversionen im 8. Jahrhundert," *FMSt* 7 (1973): 169–202.

[208]Schneider, *Königswahl und Königserhebung*, p. 58.

[209]Brühl, "Chronologie," pp. 35, 46; *RF*, vol. 2, nos. 23, 37–42, pp. 33, 43–46.

[210]Fröhlich, *Thronfolge* 1:218.

[211]*CDL*, vol. 3,pt. 1, ed. Brühl, no. 23, pp. 111–15.

[212]C. 2, ed. Ulla Westergh (Lund, 1956), p. 4.

tion of ambassadors produced a crisis of immense and irreparable proportions. The "Italianization" of Italy in the seventh century had made the
region ripe for a separatist movement, but it was the Greeks who forced the
issue. Separation from Byzantium, however, was not so easy as it might
seem, because lurking in the background were the Lombards, ever ready to
pounce on a defenseless Italy. The Italians knew perfectly well that to pull
away from the East was to leave themselves open to conquest unless they
could unite, or alleviate the Lombard threat, or both.

Unity requires a leader and a cause. The cause was clear, an end to
Byzantine oppression and defense against the Lombards. The leader was the
pope who rejected, or who took the lead in rejecting, every kind of imperial
policy after about 685, and who also organized the defense of Italy from the
kings at Pavia. Much of Italy, however, had profound reasons to mistrust or
to dislike Rome. This was especially true of Ravenna and Venice. Naturally,
these cities could and did unite with Rome against Lombards, or in defense
of the faith, but nothing could mask the ancient and deep-seated animosities
that divided one region of Italy from another. Thus the leader could only
lead on certain occasions, and the unity was more apparent than real.

Still, it was the papacy that defined the terms of the solution to the
Italian crisis. The inhabitants of Rome, of the Ravennate, and of the Pentapolis, were the pope's "flocks." Together they lived in a republic and St. Peter
was its patron and eponymous hero. The appearance of the term *respublica*
and its association with St. Peter establishes beyond a reasonable doubt that
a new political entity was coming into being. Scholars have noticed that the
ideological foundations of the Republic took shape beginning with Gregory
II, but they have often underestimated the extent to which this ideology
actually reached maturity under Gregory II and III.[213] "These western lands"
or "this province of Italy" or "the republic" were inhabited by a "peculiar
people" who were the pope's "flocks" or else his "lost flocks" when the
Lombards seized them. The Lombards took lands "from the right of the
Church" and restored them "to the prince of the apostles, St. Peter." What
could be clearer than this? It is certainly true that in succeeding decades

---

[213]Wilhelm Sickel, "Die Verträge der Päpste mit den Karolingern," *Deutsche Zeitschrift für
Geschichtswissenschaft* 11 (1894): 316–18; Henri Hubert, "Etude sur la formation des états
de l'église," *Revue historique* 69 (1899): 30; Wilhelm Gundlach, *Die Entstehung des Kirchenstaates und die curiale Begriff Res Publica Romanorum* (Breslau, 1899), p. 31; Armbrust,
Territoriale Politik, pp. 61–64; Duchesne, *Temporal Sovereignty*, pp. 16, 18, 28; Brezzi, *Roma
e l'empero*, p. 3; Miller, "Roman Revolution," pp. 109–10. Miller's study is the best of the lot,
and the only one that comes close to seeing the maturity of papal thought in these years. The
other studies tend to see this period as a prologue to the Carolingian era.

some rigor in conceptualization and some precision in terminology entered papal documents. But the differences were not great and the early eighth-century popes would have understood perfectly the conduct of their successors. A series of remarkable popes had steered the Republic of St. Peter out of the Byzantine Empire.

By the time of Zachary's death in 752 two questions remained in suspense. The first was whether the Republic would consist of all of the former exarchate or only the Duchies of Rome and Perugia. Within this latter area the pope's authority was unchallenged. Gregory II and Gregory III rebuilt Rome's walls and the latter restored the fortifications of Civitavecchia in Tuscany. Gregory III and Zachary may have issued coins in their own names,[214] and in all their correspondence these popes called the Romans their own people. Gregory III and Zachary negotiated legally for Rome and the latter allowed the duke of Rome and, surely, the secular authorities generally to govern only in his absence. Cesena, Cumae, Sutri, and the massive restorations of Liutprand were given not to the empire, or to the Romans, but to St. Peter and the pope. After Gregory III the pope no longer notified the emperor of his election and, from about 730 on, there is no longer evidence of a resident papal *apocrisiarius* in Constantinople.[215] Finally, in the *Ordines Romani* it is possible to see the elaboration of a papal court ceremonial bearing all the trappings of a sophisticated, sovereign state.[216]

If papal rule in the Duchies of Rome and Perugia was an established fact by 752, it is much less clear how things stood elsewhere. Gregory III had called upon the Venetians to save the Ravennese when Hildeprand took the city, and his letters to Charles Martel evince his solicitude for the region. Zachary marched out to save the Ravennese from Liutprand and called them his flocks. The popes certainly thought in terms of Ravenna's belonging to their Republic but, except under emergency circumstances, those feelings probably were not reciprocated and may have become irrelevant in view of Aistulf's conquests.

When Aistulf took Ravenna the Venetians may have aided him because

---

[214]Serafini (*Le monete e le bulle plumbee pontificie*, vol. 1 [reprint, Bologna, 1964], p. 3, and Tavola 1, nos. 1, 2) considers the copper "objects" minted by Gregory III and Zachary in their own names to be coins. These may have been tokens of some sort, perhaps for pilgrim's offerings. Philip Grierson suggested to me that they might have been weights; he is quite certain that they were not coins.

[215]Llewellyn, *Rome in the Dark Ages*, pp. 117, 119.

[216]Ordo I, ed. Andrieu, 2:67–108. See also: Llewellyn, *Rome in the Dark Ages*, p. 126. VanDijk, "Urban and Papal Rites," pp. 467–69, believes that the elaboration of papal chant was influenced by Byzantine court etiquette and served to enhance the position of the pope.

he divided the region of Ravenna in such a way as to leave a portion of Venice's territory outside the *regnum*. Aistulf never ruled in Venice and it is difficult to believe that the city could have withstood his attack.[217] The Venetians, always vigilant in defense of their liberty, wanted no part of the Republic. In Ravenna, it appears that Archbishop Sergius effected an accommodation with Aistulf whereby he was to be independent of Rome.[218] Agnellus says Sergius behaved "like an exarch,"[219] and we shall see in differing contexts in the next several chapters that Ravenna's relations with the Republic were usually strained and always complicated.

The second question was whether the Republic would be able to withstand Aistulf's onslaught. The answer to this question would emerge after another appeal to the Franks.

---

[217]Bertolini, *Roma e i longobardi*, p. 64, drawing upon a capitulary of Lothair I: *MGH, Cap.*, vol. 2, no. 233, c. 26, p. 135; Cessi, *Storia della Repubblica di Venezia*, p. 21.

[218]Luther, *Rom und Ravenna*, pp. 49–52; Schmidt, "Ravenna," pp. 749–50.

[219]Agnellus, *Lib. pont. rav.*, c. 159, *MGH, SSrL*, p. 380.

Three

St. Peter's Strong Right Arm

GIVEN, as we are, the luxury of hindsight, we know that the papal appeal of 753 to the Franks was accorded a full measure of success. But precisely because we do know what actually happened, we can be seduced into assuming its inevitability. The question of whether or not a papal appeal to the Franks in the early 750s for aid against the Lombards was likely to be successful appears difficult to answer if one takes, for posing the question, a vantage point in almost any year between the unsuccessful attempt by Gregory III and the successful one of Stephen II. Moreover, one's interpretation of why the papacy sought aid in Francia, and of why the Franks finally agreed to supply assistance, will depend heavily upon how one interprets papal history, Frankish history, and Franco-papal relations in the 740s and very early 750s.

Boniface, the Popes, and the Franks

It is a commonplace of the historical literature that Boniface struggled mightily, from the 720s until his martyrdom in 754, to spread Roman and papal influences in Francia, and that his work facilitated, perhaps even rendered inevitable, the Franco-papal alliance of 753–54. In fact, Boniface's labors in Francia, and the whole history of Franco-papal relations before the early 750s, raise some very complex questions. It can be argued, for instance, with Theodor Zwölfer and Johannes Haller, that because of a profound and pre-existing veneration for St. Peter on the part of the Franks, Boniface had great and prompt success in disseminating papal influences.[1] Or it can be argued,

---

[1] Theodor Zwölfer, *Sankt Peter, Apostelfürst und Himmelspförtner: Seine Verehrung bei den Angelsachsen und Franken* (Stuttgart, 1929); Johannes Haller, *Das Papsttum*, 5 vols. (Basel, 1951), 1:391ff.

with Albert Hauck and Erich Caspar, that Boniface's labors were of limited success because of persons in Francia who desired to maintain a Frankish provincial church in preference to a "Rome-bound" church.[2]

The facts are more subtle than this straightforward polarity of views suggests. The idea implied in the second argument that the Frankish Church was free of Roman influences before Boniface's time is manifestly false. In canonical, liturgical, and other traditions there were distinct similarities between Frankish and Roman practices, and there is little direct evidence of Frankish hostility to the penetration, by whatever means, of Roman norms.[3] Actually, there had been very little contact between the two churches, which is not at all the same as saying that there existed friction between them. Similarly questionable is the idea that, in Francia, people feared domination by a monarchical papacy. What Boniface sought to spread were Roman norms in dogma, canon law, liturgy, and to a lesser extent, principles of ecclesiastical organization. These kinds of things, more than any sort of direct and daily papal rule, were at the heart of his labors.[4] Likewise, one ought not to make the mistake of supposing that papal rule in the mid-eighth century meant anything like what that rule would come to mean in the high Middle Ages. The eighth-century popes lacked the panoply of governmental and jurisdictional tools necessary for an aggressive and constant exercise of papal authority.[5] In short, it is pointless to argue that some atavistic Frankish tradition rose up in righteous indignation before the agent of a grasping papal Romanization.

It is equally pointless to argue that Boniface enjoyed unqualified success in spreading even limited kinds of papal influence. In fact, the great missionary encountered pointed opposition in his efforts to improve the morals and structure of the Frankish Church. In letters to Rome Boniface frequently detailed his disappointments, frustrations, and failures.[6] There were basically two root causes for the tensions Boniface engendered. He angered powerful members of the Frankish nobility whose loyalty was essential to the rising Carolingian family, and he interfered, probably quite inadvertently, in Frankish political schemes.

---

[2]Albert Hauck, *Kirchengeschichte Deutschlands*, 5 vols., 5th ed. (Leipzig, 1935), 1:418ff; Caspar, *Das Papsttum*, p. 695ff.

[3]Schieffer, *Winfrid-Bonifatius*, pp. 48–49.

[4]Schieffer, *Winfrid-Bonifatius*, pp. 139–57.

[5]Friedrich Kempf, "Chiese territoriali e chiesa romana nel secolo VIII," *SSCI* 20 (1973): 294–96.

[6]Boniface, *epp.* nos. 50, 58, 60, 61, 63, ed. Tangl, *MGH*, pp. 80–86, 107, 122–24, 125–27, 129–32.

During the years when Charles Martel was mayor of the palace, the Frankish Church was generally in a deplorable state, and some of the lands in central Germany where Boniface worked longest and hardest possessed only limited traces of Christianity and virtually no ecclesiastical organization.[7] The clergy as a whole was usually drawn from prominent members of powerful local families, and as Charles Martel sought to consolidate his power, he had both to appease and to win over these families. When Boniface attempted to institute more regular ecclesiastical procedures he ran into hostility from these families, and Charles was forced to side with them against the missionary, whose work he really did not oppose in principle.[8] Charles died in 741, and because his sons and successors, Carlomann and Pepin, were somewhat more kindly disposed to the goals of the Bonifatian reforms, Boniface had a season of success in a series of great reform councils. By about 744, however, opposition from the nobility again forced the mayors to take a prudent course that put them on the side of the nobility.[9] In 747 Pope Zachary responded favorably to a request by Pepin for a set of canons.[10] Pepin was unable to promulgate them, however, because of opposition from the nobility.[11] Moreover, it appears that Pepin had circumvented Boniface in requesting the canons directly from the pope; no source mentions Boniface's having played a role in their procurement. The old missionary's influence seems not to have been very strong by the late 740s.

The early Carolingians were neither cynical nor duplicitous in their dealings with Boniface. Pepin and Carlomann, at least, were genuinely religious men who surely saw the wisdom and value of what Boniface was trying to accomplish. They were also practical men who appreciated the difficulties for themselves of the rigorous application of Boniface's Roman norms. Boniface's failures can be attributed to the displeasure of the Frankish nobility

---

[7]For concise and competent assessments of the Frankish church in the early eighth century see: Bréhier and Aigrain, *Histoire de l'église*, pp. 329–90, esp. 357ff; Ewig, chap. 2 and 3 in *Handbook of Church History*.

[8]Schieffer, *Winfrid-Bonifatius*, pp. 130–33, 139–57; Heinrich Büttner, "Bonifatius und die Karolinger," *Hessisches Jahrbuch für Landesgeschichte* 4 (1954): 27–28; Heinz Löwe, "Bonifatius und die bayerisch-fränkische Spannung: Ein Beitrag zur Geschichte der Beziehungen zwischen dem Papsttum und den Karolingern," in *Zur Geschichte der Bayern*, ed. Karl Bosl (Darmstadt, 1965), pp. 269–70.

[9]Schieffer, *Winfrid-Bonifatius*, pp. 226–32; Emile Lesne, *La hiérarchie épiscopale, 742–882* (Lille, 1905), pp. 45–47; Friedrich Prinz, *Klerus und Krieg im früheren Mittelalter* (Stuttgart, 1971), pp. 8–10.

[10]CC, no. 3, pp. 479–87. Zachary praises Pepin for his zeal in Church reform.

[11]Schieffer, *Winfrid-Bonifatius*, pp. 240–43.

at certain features of his work. Powerful families had long held bishoprics and monasteries as something akin to private property, and Boniface's work would have put an end to the most flagrant abuses of canonical prescriptions. These families simply would not give up control of the church in their territories, and the Carolingians had to take these families seriously into account. Frankish politics and raison d'état impeded Boniface's work much more than anxieties about papal influence.

Boniface may have interfered in Frankish politics while carrying out his missionary work in Bavaria. We noted earlier that in 725 Charles Martel and Liutprand had jointly attacked Bavaria. From that time forward the Franks claimed overlordship in the duchy, but the Bavarians were never especially willing to submit themselves. In 736 Odilo succeeded to the ducal office, and within a few years he had made his duchy virtually independent of the Franks. When Charles divided his mayoral responsibilities between Pepin and Carlomann in 741, he did not even mention Bavaria.[12]

In 739 Boniface entered Bavaria, doubtless on Odilo's request, to continue the work of ecclesiastical organization begun there by Gregory II after Duke Theodo's visit to Rome in 716.[13] Bavaria had enjoyed fairly good relations with Rome ever since 716, and Odilo himself was fast becoming the key figure in a massive Bavarian, Saxon, and Alemannian alliance against the Franks.[14] Odilo apparently saw the strict ecclesiastical organization of his duchy by Boniface as a further means of avoiding Frankish influence.[15] Boniface had thus quite unwittingly played a role in a rebellion against Frankish authority by his work in Bavaria.

In 743 Pepin and Carlomann were ready to deal with the rebellious Odilo. Bavaria was a problem in its own right for the Carolingians, but the area posed a threat for other reasons as well. Odilo was married to Chiltrudis, a daughter of Charles Martel and sister of the mayors.[16] In addition, Grifo, Charles Martel's son by his second marriage, to the Bavarian princess Swanahild, was a continual source of trouble for his half-brothers and a frequent meddler in both Frankish and Bavarian affairs.[17] Bavaria was there-

---

[12]Reindel, "Zeitalter der Agilolfinger," pp. 124–25.

[13]Gregory III to Boniface, *apud* Boniface, ep. 45, ed. Tangl, *MGH*, pp. 71–74.

[14]*Fredegarii continuatio*, cc. 25, 26, ed. Wallace-Hadrill, pp. 98–99; *Annales mettenses priores*, ed. Simson, p. 33.

[15]Büttner, "Bonifatius," pp. 28–29; Löwe, "Bonifatius und die bayerisch-fränkische Spannung," pp. 281–86.

[16]*Annales mettenses priores*, ed. Simson, p. 33; *Fredegarii continuatio*, c. 25, ed. Wallace-Hadrill, p. 98.

[17]*Annales mettenses priores*, ed. Simson, p. 32, says Grifo was born of a concubine. Grifo's

fore not only a rebellious province but also a land that harbored blood relatives and potential rivals of the Carolingians.

In 743 Bavaria was successfully invaded, and during the time the duchy was being subdued, a papal envoy named Sergius was captured. He claimed he had been sent by Zachary to prevent war between the Franks and the Bavarians.[18] Zachary may very well have turned to Odilo after his predecessor had gotten no decisive assistance from Charles Martel.[19] Charles was the ally of the pope's enemy, Liutprand, Bavaria had a score to settle with both Charles's heirs and Liutprand for the attack of 725, and since 716 the papacy had been cultivating good relations with the Bavarian ducal house. In 743 the Lombards were still very much a threat in Italy, and Zachary, no less than his predecessors, was looking for allies. Perhaps he did not realize the extent to which a papal alliance with Bavaria would offend the Franks, or it may be that he was an honest broker and did not wish to see open hostilities between the only two peoples who could possibly provide aid against the Lombards. There can be no question, however, that when Zachary sought an alignment with Bavaria he produced tensions between Rome and Francia. Boniface, meanwhile, was caught in the middle of all of this. Odilo apparently decided that the missionary was no longer of any use to him, and he himself had turned directly to Rome.[20] In the end, neither Zachary's nor Boniface's role in Bavaria contributed to the promotion of good relations between the papacy and the Carolingians.

Politics in Francia: A New Dynasty

Developments in Francia after the death of Charles Martel were likewise so intricate and fraught with difficulties that appeals from the outside were not likely to be well received.[21] Although the Arab threat had subsided, others had emerged to replace it. Aquitanians, Bretons, Frisians, Saxons, Alemannians, and Bavarians were a constant source of trouble for Pepin and Carlo-

---

legitimate birth has been proved by Hanns Leo Mikoletzky, "Karl Martell und Grifo," in *Festschrift E. E. Stengel* (Munster, 1952), pp. 130–56.

[18]*Annales mettenses priores*, ed. Simson, pp. 34–35.

[19]Reindel, "Zeitalter der Agilolfinger," p. 125; Löwe, "Bonifatius und die bayerisch-fränkische Spannung," pp. 288–89; Walter Mohr, *Studien zur Charakteristik des karolingischen Königtums im 8. Jahrhundert* (Saarlouis, 1955), pp. 23–24.

[20]Schieffer, *Winfrid-Bonifatius*, pp. 207–8.

[21]Mohr, *Karolingischen Königtums*, pp. 19–20.

mann.[22] The Frankish monarchy had long claimed overlordship over these peoples but had only infrequently exercised any genuine authority over them. Since 737 the Merovingian throne had been vacant. The mayors had been content to rule in their own names. By the early 740s regions that had long sought autonomy may have used the vacant throne as a pretext to refuse to obey the mayors Pepin and Carolmann.[23] In 743 the Merovingian Childeric III was placed on the throne and the Carolingians, now acting in his name, set out to put down the rebellions that were flaring up everywhere.[24] The survival of the Frankish kingdom itself was very much an open issue throughout the 740s.

Within the Carolingian family itself there were also deep difficulties. Grifo, the offspring of Charles's second marriage, was a constant source of trouble for his half-brothers until he was murdered in 753.[25] Grifo fomented or participated in insurrections in Saxony, Aquitaine, and Bavaria, and at the end of his life, he was attempting to stir up trouble in Lombardy. What made him so dangerous, apart from his reckless ambition, was his Carolingian and Agilolfing blood. He was the social equal of anyone in the kingdom, and because he apparently enjoyed some support in various regions it was impossible for Pepin and Carlomann summarily to remove him from the scene.[26] Whether Grifo's support was an embodiment of opposition to his half-brothers, or whether loyalty was accorded to him personally is difficult to say, but amounts to the same thing. So long as Grifo was abroad in the land, Pepin and Carlomann could never be totally secure.

After 747 conditions in Francia were simultaneously complicated and clarified by the abdication of Carlomann. Despite prodigious efforts to do so, no one has succeeded in proving that Pepin forced Carlomann to abdicate so that he could assume for himself the mayoral office in all of Francia.[27]

---

[22]The fullest treatment of these years remains, remarkably, Heinrich Hahn, *Jahrbücher des fränkischen Reiches, 741–752* (Berlin, 1863).

[23]Werner Affeldt, "Untersuchungen zur Königserhebung Pippins," *FMSt* 14 (1980): 112, 125–26; Löwe, "Bonifatius und die bayerisch-fränkische Spannung," pp. 294–95.

[24]*BM*, no. 45a; for the campaigns: nos. 45b, c, 48a, b, 49a, b.

[25]Affeldt, "Königserhebung Pippins," p. 113, emphasizes the problems caused by Grifo. Mohr, *Karolingische Königtums*, pp. 13–47 passim, correctly notes the importance of Grifo during these years but offers interpretations, including one suggesting that Charles actually intended for Grifo to be his sole heir (pp. 21–23), that are eccentric. Grifo's checkered career can be followed in Hahn, *Jahrbücher*, pp. 16ff, 92ff, 115ff, 156ff, 212ff.

[26]Haselbach, *Aufstieg und Herrschaft der Karolinger*, p. 102; Reindel, "Zeitalter der Agilolfinger," pp. 125–26.

[27]The most recent attempt is Dieter Riesenberger, "Zur Geschichte des Hausmeiers Karlmann," *Westfälische Zeitschrift* 120 (1970): 271–86. He reviews the older literature quite well.

Quite simply, Carlomann seems to have had a genuine desire, by no means unprecedented in his age, to give up the life and toil of the world and enter a monastery.[28] In 747 he abandoned Francia for Rome where, at the hands of Zachary, he became a monk.[29] He had taken with him to Rome some of his supporters, and he was soon paid visits by many others. Eventually this traffic disturbed his repose sufficiently that he removed to the greater solitude of Monte Cassino.[30]

Carlomann's abdication temporarily simplified things in Francia by unifying the mayoral office in the hands of one man, Pepin. At the same time, however, Carlomann's departure rendered Grifo's threat more real and dangerous, while also making the absolutely powerless position of the Merovingian king, Childeric III, vividly clear to everyone. In addition, Carlomann left sons behind in Francia for whom, although they were very young, he may have foreseen some future role.

Pepin tried, with no lasting success, to compose his difficulties with Grifo without sharing power with him. Those difficulties only ended with Grifo's death in 753. Pepin's eventual solution to his relationship with Childric was to have himself made king, but we cannot know exactly when Pepin decided upon this course of action. Probably he made his decision shortly after Carlomann abdicated. What must be appreciated is that it cannot, under the circumstances, have been an altogether easy decision to make.

Late in 749, or early in 750, Pepin sent Bishop Burchard of Wurtzburg and Fulrad, later the abbot of St. Denis, to Rome with the now famous question for Pope Zachary: Was it right or not that the king of Franks at that time had absolutely no power but nevertheless possessed the royal office? Zachary responded that this was a disruption of the proper "order" and that he who had the power ought also to be king.[31] Accordingly, in 751, Pepin was elected king "by the custom of the Franks," and anointed by Boniface or else by Frankish bishops. All of this happened "on the command of" or "with the approval of" or "on the authority of" Pope Zachary.[32] Quite

---

[28]Affeldt, "Königserhebung Pippins," pp. 115–17, notes that there may have been some pressure on Carlomann but that his religious motivations must not be doubted. See also: Krüger, "Königskonversionen," pp. 175–202; Schieffer, *Winfrid-Bonifatius*, p. 250. Krüger tries to ascertain what influences might have affected Carlomann (pp. 175–83, 187–97, 200–202) but concludes that personal, religious factors were probably decisive (p. 185).

[29]*LP* 1:433; *BM*, no. 52a.

[30]*BM*, nos. 52b, c.

[31]Virtually every surviving source mentions these events: *Annales regni Francorum, anno* 749, ed. Kurze, p. 8; *Annales qui dicuntur Einhardi, anno,* 749 ed. Kurze, p. 9; *Fredegarii continuatio,* c. 33, ed. Wallace-Hadrill, p. 102.

[32]Einhard, *Vita Karoli,* c. 3, ed. Louis Halphen (Paris, 1938), pp. 13–15; *Fredegarii contin-*

naturally, Pepin's elevation to kingship, and Zachary's participation in that act, have attracted an enormous amount of attention. Here we must confine ourselves to two central questions: First, why did Pepin turn to Zachary? Second, did Pepin, in turning to the pope, oblige himself to any particular course of action on behalf of the Republic?

As a prelude to answering the first of these questions it will be well to set out clearly the difficulty of Pepin's position in 750–51. While he certainly had nothing to fear directly from Childeric III,[33] there were many people who could allege loyalty to the Merovingians as an alibi for failing to support him.[34] Merovingian law, moreover, knew no precise procedure for deposition in a formal sense, so in addition to real or feigned loyalty for Childeric, there was a problem involved in getting the throne declared vacant so that Pepin could assume it.[35] Additionally, all was not well within Pepin's own family. Grifo's support has already been mentioned in other contexts, and it is reasonable to assume that if people supported Grifo while Pepin was mayor, then some at least of these same people would have supported Grifo against any effort by his half-brother to become king. Carlomann had also left his own children, especially his son Drogo, in Pepin's care.[36] Should Pepin seek the royal office then there would have been adherents of Carlomann to come forward and advance the cause of the latter's son.[37] The Frankish nobility, and the non-Frankish dukes in Saxony, Bavaria, and Aquitaine, cannot have been pleased at the prospect of seeing an energetic man on the throne. Charles Martel and Pepin and Carlomann had been nuisance enough to these people as mayors of the palace. As kings the Carolingians would have been seen as dire threats to provincial autonomy and aristocratic independence. Frankish noblemen may also have disliked the meteoric rise of a family they regarded as no better than themselves, and without the support of this nobility Pepin could not hope to become, or to remain, king.[38] Finally,

---

uatio, c. 33, ed. Wallace-Hadrill, p. 102; *Annales regni Francorum*, annis 749, 750, ed. Kurze, pp. 8–10; *Annales qui dicuntur Einhardi*, annis 749, 750, ed. Kurze, pp. 9–11; *Annales mettenses priores*, anno 750, ed. Simson, p. 42; *Annales fuldenses*, anno 752, ed. Kurze, MGH SSrG, p. 6; *Chron. moiss.*, MGH, SS 1:292; *Ann. laurr. min.*, MGH, SS 1:116.

[33]Bund, *Thronsturz*, pp. 367–68. The classic description of the hapless Childeric is Einhard, *Vita Karoli*, c. 1, ed. Halphen, pp. 8–10.

[34]Affeldt, "Königserhebung Pippins," pp. 112, 122ff.

[35]Bund, *Thronsturz*, pp. 344ff, 381–82.

[36]Rodenberg, *Pippin, Karlmann und Papst Stephan II*, pp. 27–30; Jörg Jarnut, "Quierzy und Rom: Bemerkungen zu den 'Promissiones Donationis' Pippins und Karls," *HZ* 220 (1975): 270–71.

[37]Affeldt, "Königserhebung Pippins," p. 176.

[38]Bund, *Thronsturz*, pp. 367–68; On the crucial political significance of the nobility see:

there may have been questions surrounding Pepin's ability to legitimize a coup d'état before the Romanic elements in the population of Francia.[39]

Any one of these potentially debilitating political liabilities, let alone all of them operating together, might have been enough to induce Pepin to look for an ally or benefactor outside the sphere of internal Frankish affairs. The authorities of the church were likely candidates, but as we have seen, Pepin's relations with the church in Francia, as well as with the head of the church in Rome, had not been uniformly smooth and cordial. One must, therefore, avoid the temptation of assuming that the pope was the obvious or only court of last appeal for Pepin.

Still, the pope did represent that court, so it is necessary to seek more evidence for what pushed Pepin to seek help in Rome. Historians believe that there was a certain sanctity, a certain charisma, that coursed through the veins of Germanic kings.[40] Over time the church, never enthusiastic about kings with mysterious long hair or ancestors who were sea gods, began to redefine kingship in Christian terms.[41] The royal office came to be defined as a divinely instituted ministry, and in influential circles in Francia the idea may have slowly emerged that the church could declare null and void the charisma of the Merovingians while at the same time asserting that that charisma had been transferred, by God through his churchmen, to Pepin.[42] A cynical line of reasoning must be carefully avoided here because Pepin

---

Affeldt, "Das Problem der Mitwirkung des Adels an politischen Entscheidungsprozessen im Frankreich vornehmlich des 8. Jahrhunderts," in *Aus Theorie und Praxis der Geschichtswissenschaft: Festschrift für Hans Herzfeld*, ed. Dietrich Kurze (Berlin, 1972), pp. 404–23; Karl Ferdinand Werner, "Important Noble Families in the Kingdom of Charlemagne: A Prosopographical Study of the Relationship Between King and Nobility in the Early Middle Ages," in *The Medieval Nobility: Studies in the Ruling Classes from the Sixth to the Twelfth Century*, ed. and trans. Timothy Reuter (Amsterdam, 1978), pp. 137–202; Karl Brunner, *Oppositionelle Gruppen im Karolingerreich* (Vienna, 1979); Jürgen Hannig, *Consensus Fidelium. Frühfeudale Interpretationen des Verhältnisses von Königtum und Adel am Beispiel des Frankenreiches* (Stuttgart, 1982) pp. 130–51, 170–78.

[39] This issue was raised by Hans Walter Klewitz, "Germanisches Erbe im fränkischen und deutschen Königtum," *Die Welt als Geschichte* 7 (1941): 206. Affeldt, "Königserhebung Pippins," p. 173, is not sure this is a real problem.

[40] Although this subject has been raised and refined many times, it is still worthwhile to go back to the study of Otto Höfler, "Der Sakralcharakter des germanischen Königtums," in *Das Königtum*, ed. Theodor Mayer (Constance, 1956), pp. 75–104. Affeldt, "Königserhebung Pippins," p. 122ff, provides an up-to-date discussion of sacral kingship, with the literature.

[41] Ewig, "Zum christlichen Königsgedanken im Frühmittelalter," in *Das Königtum*, pp. 7–73, esp. 41ff.

[42] Fritz Kern, *Kingship and Law in the Middle Ages*, trans. S. B. Chrimes (New York, 1970), pp. 9–12; Büttner, "Aus den Anfängen des abendländischen Staatsgedankens," in *Das Königtum*, pp. 155–67.

was, by the standards of his day, a religious man, and he surely desired a divine sanction for his kingship.[43] God was not merely a clever device by means of which to detach Childeric from his throne. After Pepin had been elected by the Franks—and this was assuredly the constitutive act—he was anointed by the clergy.[44] He was the first Frankish king whose royal office received this visible and public divine confirmation.

The pope stood outside Frankish politics and, as the head of the ecclesiastical hierarchy, he was placed closest to the heavenly source of royal ministry. He was, in the end, the best person to whom Pepin could appeal. The first question can therefore be answered by saying that no higher authority could be found than the pope, and this made Pepin turn to him. That Pepin turned to Rome, however, is not proof, nor was it a result, of good relations between the papacy and the Carolingians prior to 751. Likewise, there is no solid evidence here for a Frankish predilection for St. Peter and his vicar.

That brings us to the second question: Did Pepin oblige himself to Zachary? It has usually been assumed that he did.[45] According to this interpretation, Pepin paid a price for his successful appeal to Zachary, and that price was a vague promise of some sort to become the pope's ally and protector. We have already seen that the papacy was totally isolated in Italy and in severe need of protection. Thus, the idea that Zachary set a quid pro quo for his affirmative answer to Pepin's famous query is eminently plausible on logical grounds. Historical evidence, however, does not always play by the rules of logic. No Frankish source says that Pepin incurred any debts to the pope. Perhaps, one might say, these sources are tendentious and deliberately avoided setting forth the terms of the bargain that was struck. Again, this is plausible. But how do we then interpret the fact that neither the *Liber Pontificalis* nor the *Codex Carolinus* ever mentions the mission to Rome or Zachary's response? These critical papal sources seem not to have attached any particular significance to these events. In later years, after the Carolingians had indeed obliged themselves to St. Peter and to his vicar, the popes never tired of demanding fulfillment of those obligations. Here, however,

---

[43]Hans von Schubert, *Geschichte der christlichen Kirche im Frühmittelalter* (Tubingen, 1921), p. 314; Franz Kampers, "Rex et Sacerdos," *HJB* 45 (1925): 502ff; Ernst Perels, "Pippins Erhebung zum König," *ZKG* 53 (1934): 408–9.

[44]Heinrich Brunner, *Deutsche Rechtsgeschichte*, vol. 2, 2d ed. by Claudius Freiherr von Schwerin (Leipzig, 1928), p. 35; Perels, "Pippins Erhebung," pp. 406–7. The whole series of acts whereby Pepin was made king is more complicated than has sometimes been assumed. For a penetrating analysis see: Karl Hauck, "Von einer spätantiken Randkultur zum karolingischen Europa," *FMSt* 1 (1967): 68–74.

[45]Hauck, *Kirchengeschichte Deutschlands* 2:14ff; Hartmann, *Geschichte Italiens* 2.2:174; Perels, "Pippins Erhebung," pp. 405, 415; Mohr, *Karolingischen Königtums*, p. 32ff.

there is only silence. Was Zachary in a position to strike a bargain? Probably not, for it can hardly be assumed that Pepin had left his fate entirely in the pope's hands.[46] Perhaps Pepin knew ahead of time that he would get a favorable answer to his famous question. There were people in Francia who knew Zachary well and who knew his mind. Boniface and his pupil Burchard were two such people, and they may have known that the pope would view the current state of affairs in Francia as a disruption of the Augustinian *"ordo."*[47] Or Pepin and his associates may have laid their predicament before Zachary in hopes that the pope would see the justice in their case and an opportunity of getting improved relations with Pepin at little or no cost to himself.[48] The critical fact is this: We must not imagine Pepin waiting anxiously for an answer that might have been no. Pepin simply did not, indeed could not have, left his career entirely in Zachary's hands. Zachary, therefore, had no leverage to extort an alliance or a promise of protection. None of this precludes the possibility that Zachary made representation to Pepin concerning his plight in Italy, but there are no grounds for talking about bargains.

Pepin's elevation to the royal office cannot have been viewed with indifference in Rome even if papal sources took no note of it. Pepin was a religious man, and as we shall see, he did have a deep reverence for St. Peter and the pope. His approach to Zachary cannot but have improved the complex and often tense relationship between Rome and Francia. But all of the problems that Pepin faced in the year he became king did not go away after 751. Thus, even if Franco-papal relations were better when Stephen II became pope in 752 and found himself in hideous difficulties, Pepin's situation was not such as to make it likely that he could or would intervene in Italy. This, then, is how matters stood in 752 and 753 as the Republic of St. Peter faced Aistulf's juggernaut.

The Italian Crisis and the Franco-Papal Alliance

Stephen II was consecrated on 26 March 752. By this date Aistulf had conquered Ravenna and its region, including the Pentapolis, he had attacked

---

[46] Affeldt, "Königserhebung Pippins," pp. 183–84.

[47] Affeldt, "Königserhebung Pippins," pp. 148–67, esp. 165–67. The reference to Augustine would be *De civitate Dei* 19:13. The critical problem is that it is impossible to be absolutely certain that Zachary had this in mind.

[48] The point here is that there probably were negotiations of some sort in Rome, even though the sources have lost all trace of them: Perels, "Pippins Erhebung," pp. 167–71.

Istria and had made a separate peace with Venice, and he was making menacing gestures toward Rome.[49] The Republic was totally isolated in Italy and Stephen had no choice except to negotiate. He sent his brother Paul and the *primicerius* Ambrose—it is worth noting that these were Lateran officials—to Aistulf, who promptly concluded a forty-year treaty in June 752.[50] Within four months Aistulf had broken the treaty, and he began attacking the Duchy of Rome. What is more, he demanded a tax of one solidus from every inhabitant of the duchy as a sign of submission to him.[51] With the *regnum* secure and the southern duchies submitted to his will, and with Ravenna in his hands, Aistulf had only to absorb the Duchy of Rome to fulfill the old Lombard dream of a unified Italy; unified, that is, except for the extreme south which was still effectively Byzantine and which had never been the object of Lombard desires.

Certain aspects of the course of events in 752 are puzzling. Several times during the early months of that year, and evidently on into the summer, Stephen appealed to the Byzantines for aid.[52] It had not yet occurred to Stephen to request assistance from the Franks. The lack of an approach to Pepin tends to confirm the fact that no defense pact had been concluded between the Frankish king and Zachary in 751. The Byzantines represented, therefore, the only possible source of assistance. The pope was not, however, acting as a loyal subject of the Basileus. He was acting like a sorely pressed ally.[53] The papal appeal to the Greeks is not as difficult to understand as is the treaty between Stephen and Aistulf that was signed and violated within so short a time. Bertolini thinks that Aistulf simply perjured himself; he bought time with the treaty but never intended to fulfill it.[54] Hallenbeck, on the other hand, believes that by continuing to appeal to the Byzantines after the signing of the accord with Aistulf, Stephen broke the treaty.[55] In fact, Delogu has grasped the reality of the situation.[56] Aistulf's schemes were

[49]*LP* 1:441; *Pauli continuatio cassinense*, c. 4, MGH, SSrL, p. 199.

[50]For date: Jaffé, *RP*, p. 271.

[51]*LP* 1:441; *Pauli continuatio tertia*, c. 23, MGH, SSrL, p. 208.

[52]*LP* 1:442.

[53]Guillou, "L'Italia bizantina," p. 231, reflects the view of most Byzantinists that Stephen was acting throughout as an imperial subject.

[54]Bertolini, "Il primo 'periurium' di Astolfo verso la chiesa di Roma, 752–753," *Miscellanea Giovanni Mercati*, vol. 5 (Vatican City, 1946), pp. 161–205.

[55]Hallenbeck, *Pavia and Rome*, pp. 52–61. Hallenbeck actually doubts that Aistulf represented a real threat to Rome in 752. Although this interpretation is both original and plausible, I am unpersuaded by it.

[56]Delogu, "Il regno longobardo," pp. 170–72.

wrecked on the same miscalculation that had brought down the plans of Liutprand and Ratchis. The pope regarded all of the inhabitants of formerly Byzantine Italy as his "peculiar people." Aistulf assumed that he could take Ravenna and still have peace with Rome. The pope was quite willing to have peace in his own neighborhood, but he would not stand by idly while the Lombards turned the Ravennese into "lost sheep." Moreover, Aistulf's peace with Rome was neither full nor generous because in demanding tribute from the Romans the Lombard king was announcing his intention of rendering the Duchy of Rome tributary to his kingdom. It may seem pertinent to ask why Aistulf did not, without further ado, add Rome to his other impressive conquests in 752 when all of the evidence suggests that nothing could have prevented him from doing so. The answer to this question exposes a dilemma that had been faced numerous times already by Liutprand and Ratchis. As devoutly Catholic kings, the Lombard rulers did not relish the spectacle of making outright war on the pope. At the same time, Aistulf knew, a pope left absolutely independent was always a menace to the king's essential interests. Aistulf had, at the moment, the southern duchies under his control, but how many times in the past had the popes found support in them? Ravenna was in his hands and Venice was bought off in some way, but the pope might be able to stir up trouble in that quarter; Gregory III had used the Venetians to dislodge the Lombards from Ravenna once before. Stephen was appealing repeatedly to the Greeks. Could they do anything? Finally, without at least some possessions in the Exarchate and the Pentapolis, particularly key cities lying astride the major roads, Aistulf was cut off from his southern duchies. At a bare minimum he needed a corridor to the south. Stephen was hardly pleased by Aistulf's whirlwind conquests, but it is difficult to believe that the pope really wanted to see a Byzantine army marching about the Italian countryside. Italy in 752 was a land of multiple and conflicting dilemmas.

In the face of this crisis Stephen continued to ply the tools of diplomacy. In about October 752 he sent the abbots of the two great Beneventan monasteries of Monte Cassino and San Vincenzo of Volturno to Aistulf to demand a treaty of peace. Aistulf spurned them.[57] At this point an imperial *silentarius*, John, arrived in Rome with a letter from Constantine V demanding that Stephen try again to negotiate with Aistulf "to get him to restore to their rightful lord the places diabolically usurped from the Republic." The Greeks had not, obviously, relinquished their own claims to Ravenna and

---

[57]*LP* 1:441–42; *Pauli continuatio cassinense*, c. 4, *MGH, SSrL*, p. 199.

they hoped to use the pope, as an ally, to get the city back. Stephen sent John and his brother Paul to Aistulf who quickly dismissed them "with a vain answer."[58] The pope then sent John and his own envoy to Constantinople to ask the emperor "to free this city of Rome and the whole province of Italy" from Aistulf. Stephen also demanded that the emperor restore images.[59] The papal biographer goes on to say that Stephen continued to intercede for his "lost sheep, indeed for the whole Exarchate of Ravenna and this whole province of Italy." Stephen's biographer was clearly articulating the papacy's claims to those very lands that the Basileus wanted restored to himself. At this critical juncture, precise details break off.

At the close of 752, then, the Republic was in severe danger. Stephen had used diplomacy throughout the year in an abortive effort to ameliorate the situation. He had sent three, and perhaps more, embassies to Aistulf. He had not, it should be repeated, appealed to the Franks. As far as the imperial representative is concerned, his role is easy to explain. First, Stephen acted like an ally, not like a subject, of the emperor. Second, the emperor still wanted Ravenna back, but he had to turn to the pope in his effort to recover it. This illustrates vividly the realities of the Italian situation and the powerlessness of the emperor to intervene there. Third, although the emperor was claiming Ravenna, Stephen was too. A deep interest in Ravenna had been a marked aspect of papal policy for a generation, but except for the acquisition of Cesena in 743, papal claims there had been expressed in somewhat ambiguous terms before 751. Fourth, by asking Constantine to come to Italy the pope put himself in a position to determine once and for all if the emperor could intervene there. Papal leadership in Rome was unassailable by the 750s, and as far as Ravenna was concerned, papal claims there had always been grander than actual papal authority. Thus, if the emperor came to Italy, defeated Aistulf, and reestablished imperial control in Ravenna, the pope had little to lose and probably much to gain from the destruction of Aistulf. If, on the other hand, the emperor did nothing, Stephen's position was no worse, and his claims in Ravenna became potentially more effective. The crucial problem was Aistulf, not Constantine.

Some time elapsed and Stephen saw that the emperor was not going to play a significant role in Italy. Therefore, in 753, the pope sent a message to Pepin secretly through a pilgrim. He asked the Frankish king to send envoys to bring him to Francia. By this time the Lombards were pressing Rome

---

[58]*LP* 1:442.
[59]*LP* 1:442; Jaffé, *RP*, no. 2308.

harder and had seized Ceccano on the southern flank of the Duchy of Rome.[60] Pepin sent the abbot Droctegang to Rome to see Stephen, and the pope sent back two letters with Droctegang and a Roman cleric named John. One letter was addressed to Pepin and one to "*Omnibus ducibus gentis francorum*."[61] An understanding of certain features of the contents of these letters is of extreme importance for the subsequent course of events.

The first, to Pepin, says that the pope, in the presence of Pepin's protector St. Peter, gives thanks to God for so pious and resolute a king. The letter goes on to say that the pope has responded fully to certain queries put to him by Droctegang and that the abbot will himself report back fully. The pope concludes by saying that he expects a response. All of this is nothing if not enigmatic. Would that the letter itself told us of Stephen's and Droctegang's conversations! The second letter, to the Frankish magnates, is also curious, not least because it was unprecedented for a pope to write such a letter. Stephen says he expects the Franks to struggle with all their might for their protector St. Peter and for the needs of the Church. Acquitting themselves well in this struggle will, he assures them, merit eternal salvation, and the pope did not neglect to remind the magnates who holds the keys of the kingdom of heaven. Stephen also tells them that they must rally to Pepin, who is about to struggle "to secure the interests ["*utilitate*"] of your patron St. Peter the Prince of the Apostles."

In reading these letters one almost gets the impression that a secret language is being spoken. Is it possible to penetrate the veiled references and queer circumlocutions of these missives? Can a clear relationship between the two letters be established? By employing the method of working from the known to the unknown, it may just be possible to answer the questions posed above. When the pope appealed to Pepin for aid, the Frankish kingdom was in a state of turmoil. Yet Pepin did exchange ambassadors with the pope, so he must have been willing to entertain the pope's pleas. Now, to help the pope obviously meant to intervene in Italy, and there were powerful voices in Francia that strongly opposed abandoning the traditional Frankish friendship with the Lombards.[62] Pepin was not a reckless man; so it must be that he was willing to consider intervening in Italy because the advantages of that course of action were likely to outweigh the disadvantages. The traditional view is that Pepin had nothing to gain politically from going to

---

[60] *LP* 1:444. The "pilgrim" had to travel incognito because the Lombards had closed the Alpine passes: Tangl, "Passvorschrift," pp. 60–61.

[61] *CC*, nos. 4, 5, pp. 487–88.

[62] Holtzmann, *Die Italienpolitik der Merowinger*, pp. 5–7, 39–42.

Italy,[63] but it has also been suggested that becoming the pope's protector and establishing hegemony over the Lombards may have been seen in some quarters as potent enhancements of Pepin's young and none too secure kingship.[64] Moreover, the Frankish monarchy had recently been secured by an appeal to a pope, and if the papacy should be overwhelmed by the Lombards this might have had serious implications for Pepin.[65] Finally, Boniface's reforms, however much tension they may have caused in Francia, were beginning to take root, and certain influential and "reformed" clerics were among the most ardent supporters of the new regime. People like Burchard, Fulrad, and Chrodegang were among Pepin's closest associates. Perhaps these people persuaded Pepin to intervene in Italy,[66] or it may be that the king simply could not run the risk of offending these people by leaving the pope in his current difficulties.[67] However one looks at it, there were definitely advantages to be gained by intervening in Italy. But there was also opposition to overcome. There are two issues here. The first is straightforward: how to overcome the opposition. The second is more complex. Pepin may have seen in Italy an opportunity to overcome an opposition that must have been a real hindrance to him for years already.

For the moment the key question is, How could Pepin overcome the domestic opposition to his plans, assuming that his plans involved rendering assistance to the beleaguered pope? The answer was to have the pope himself write to the Franks. We noted above that Stephen's letter to Pepin says almost nothing substantive while referring in vague terms to a message given orally to Droctegang. It seems reasonable to suppose that Pepin wanted to help the pope and sent the abbot to Rome with information about potential opposition in Francia and how this might be overcome. In response, then, Stephen wrote to the Frankish magnates but did so in a very peculiar way. In a letter of only twenty-five lines Stephen invoked St. Peter six times. It is Peter, or on one occasion Peter's church, who needs help. The pope personally recedes into the background in this letter. He does not mention the

---

[63]Miller, "The Motivation of Pepin's Italian Policy, 754–768," *Studies in Medieval Culture* 4, no. 1 (1973): 45–46, 50.

[64]Martin Lintzel, "Der Codex Carolinus und die Motive von Pippins Italienpolitik," *HZ* 161 (1939): 35–36.

[65]Jarnut, "Quierzy und Rom," pp. 271–72.

[66]Léon Levillain, "L'avènement de la dynastie carolingienne et les origines de l'état pontifical (749–757)," *BEC* 94 (1933): 227–28, supposes that Fulrad was the "*animateur*" of Pepin's policy. This is possible, but others could be suggested as well, such as Burchard or Chrodegang.

[67]Lintzel, "Motive von Pippins Italienpolitik," p. 35; Miller, "Motivation of Pepin's Italian Policy," pp. 50–54.

Lombards, and he uses no political or geographical language of any kind. From this letter it is not possible to form any notion of why St. Peter needs help, or against whom. Pepin may very well have suggested to Stephen that a direct appeal to the magnates would be helpful, but then the pope himself decided to mobilize his most powerful weapon: St. Peter.[68] Earlier I suggested that it is overly simple to derive Frankish intervention in Italy from the especially exalted place occupied by St. Peter in Frankish spirituality. This caution is a necessary one, but it need not be taken to imply that veneration for St. Peter should not be carefully considered in close connection with other important factors. It is also important to observe that the pope cast the whole letter in religious terms. There can not have been any doubt that Stephen was calling for a war to be waged by the Franks against the Lombards. Ordinarily the Church, and its leaders especially, ought to have been opposed to war, but Stephen was spelling out a doctrine that war against the enemies of the Church was not only justified but a positive obligation for Christians. In this connection it is crucial to see that it is always the Church or St. Peter who is in trouble, never papal or Byzantine Italy. Stephen's request for Frankish warriors to fight on behalf of St. Peter marked an important step in the transformation of Christian attitudes toward war.[69]

Pepin, then, did want to intervene in Italy, and he had good cause for wishing to do so. There is no reason to suppose that Pepin's religious sensibilities were not genuinely offended by Aistulf's attacks upon the pope, but there were practical considerations involved as well. The two papal letters to Francia, when placed meticulously into context, are neither obscure nor disjointed. The Petrine references represent neither rhetorical flourishes nor a secret language, but the best technique the pope could employ under the circumstances to overcome opposition in Francia to an intervention by Pepin in Italy. The two letters are related in that the first is a courteous response to Pepin and the second a letter either actually requested by Pepin himself, or else apprehended as a useful device by Droctegang and Stephen during their deliberations in Rome. Stephen wanted help and Pepin wanted to help

---

[68]Haller, "Die Karolinger und das Papsttum," *HZ* 108 (1912): 53–59; Caspar, *Pippin und die römische Kirche*, pp. 5–7; Zwölfer, *Sankt Peter*, pp. 115–29; William M. Daly, "St. Peter: An Architect of the Carolingian Empire," *Studies in Medieval Culture* 4, no. 1 (1973): 55–69; Ewig, "Der Petrus- und Apostelkult im spätrömischen und fränkischen Gallien," in his *Spätantikes und fränkisches Gallien*, 2 vols. (Munich, 1979), 2:318–354. This crucial study proves that the Petrine cult was older than the Bonifatian missions but less influential than some have thought.

[69]Hauck, "Randkultur," p. 78ff; Carl Erdmann, *The Origin of the Idea of Crusade*, trans. Marshall W. Baldwin and Walter Goffart (Princeton, 1977), pp. 3–13, 22–23, 23 n.1.

him. The two papal letters of 753 provide the first hints that ways were being found to overcome the obstacles that stood in the path of the mutual accommodation of the wishes of pope and king.

Diplomatic traffic between Rome and Francia was time consuming, and events in Italy were not standing still. A few weeks after Droctegang left Rome the *silentarius* John reappeared bearing news that no troops were forthcoming but "commanding" the pope to go to Pavia and negotiate with Aistulf for the return of the Exarchate.[70] This must rank as one of history's emptier commands. Stephen sent news to Aistulf that he was coming and began making preparations for his journey. Just as the pope was departing from Rome, Bishop Chrodegang of Metz and Duke Autchar appeared carrying an invitation for Stephen to come and visit Pepin.[71] On 14 October 753 Pope Stephen II left Rome and commenced a fateful journey.

As he traveled to Pavia, Stephen must have seen that his position was not altogether bad. His previous diplomatic approaches to Aistulf had enjoyed no success, but his predecessor Zachary had obtained astonishing results in face-to-face meetings with Lombard kings. Perhaps by means of a direct encounter—we would call it a summit meeting today—he would have similar success. The Byzantine command that he go to see Aistulf was meaningless, but useful. Stephen now knew for sure that the Greeks were not going to be a complicating factor in Italy. Aistulf may not have known this, however. Thus, if by some unlikely chance Aistulf gave in to the imperial command that he evacuate the Exarchate, Stephen's position would have been immeasurably improved with no foreign intervention whether Greek or Frankish. If Aistulf proved recalcitrant, which was more likely, Stephen's position would not thereby have deteriorated. Finally, if Aistulf proved absolutely impervious to Stephen's suasions, the pope could play his Frankish card. Taking everything into consideration, Stephen's position was a relatively strong one when he reached the gates of Pavia.

It is deeply frustrating that more cannot be known about what transpired at Pavia. Stephen's position as governor of the Roman duchy, which at this time was all the territory remaining to the Republic, was clear. He had taken with him to Pavia "certain priests and others of the clerical order along with nobles of the militia." When this entourage reached the outskirts of Pavia, Aistulf sent news that the pope was not to mention "Ravenna and the

---

[70] *LP* 1:444–45: "ob recipiendam Ravennantium urbem et civitates ei pertinentes." Note that the Duchy of Rome is not mentioned. The empire had long given up any meaningful claim to it.

[71] *LP* 1:445.

Exarchate or the rest of the places of the republic" that he and his predecessors had captured. Stephen refused to be intimidated, entered Pavia, exchanged gifts with Aistulf—diplomatic protocol seems never to be suspended—and vigorously reclaimed his cities and his lost sheep. The *silentarius* presented Aistulf with the emperor's letters, but to no avail.[72] The Lombard king was totally unavailing, and at length the Frankish envoys asked him to give the pope leave to go to Francia. Aistulf asked the pope if this was his will and he said it was. The next day, after trying but failing to persuade the pope not to go, the king asked him again if he was absolutely determined to do so. The pope gave the same answer as the day before and then departed "very quickly" for the Alpine passes. He actually left the Lombard capital on 15 November.[73]

All of this seems clear enough until the dates involved are noticed carefully. Stephen left Rome on 14 October. He had a large entourage but he was traveling through hostile territory on an urgent mission. There is no reason to assume that he did not make the best time he could. Allowing a generous reckoning, let us assume that it took about three weeks for him to reach Pavia.[74] Let us suppose further that a couple of days were devoted to preliminary negotiations while Stephen was in the outskirts of the city and to diplomatic festivities immediately after the pope's formal arrival. The pope finally left the Lombard capital on 15 November, so he had to have spent one to two weeks, let us say ten days, there. Why would he have stayed so long if Aistulf had refused to budge from the moment when the pope first appeared? Ten days is not enough time for an exchange of correspondence between Pavia and Rome or Constantinople or Francia; so further diplomacy can be ruled out. There would have been no need anyway to consult Rome, since Stephen had with him representatives of the clerical and secular nobilities of the city. I suspect that when Aistulf saw the relatively strong position of the pope he took some time to calculate the merits of obstinacy on his own part. Aistulf certainly knew that the Republic, left alone, could not withstand his attacks forever. He also learned that the emperor could do nothing, or he would have sent an army and not a bureaucrat. The Franks alone must have been the source of Aistulf's consternation. What would they

---

[72]*LP* 1:446.

[73]*LP* 1:446–47.

[74]Pierre Riché, *Daily Life in the World of Charlemagne*, trans. Jo Ann McNamara (Philadelphia, 1978), pp. 22–23, says travelers could cover 30–40 kilometers per day. He also notes that in 875 Charles the Bald, with a large following and in no particular hurry, took three weeks to go from Rome to Pavia.

do? Aistulf eventually decided that obstinacy vis-à-vis Rome and the pope was a gamble worth taking, but he did not leave too much to chance, because he labored strenuously to prevent the pope from going on to Francia. The Lombard king cannot have been ignorant of recent events and currents of opinion in Francia, and he must have been betting that the pope would not be able to get the Franks to restrain him in any significant way. In the end, he had to let the pope go because, with Frankish envoys in the pope's entourage, he did not dare provoke an incident so outrageous as to overcome the very opposition in Francia upon which he was evidently banking. So many things would be clearer to us if we had more details concerning the pope's visit to Pavia!

Many aspects of Stephen's sojourn in Francia are controversial and difficult to understand. The pope crossed the Great St. Bernard and arrived at St. Maurice at Agaune where he was met by Fulrad and Rothard who had orders to bring him to the king.[75] Pepin, meanwhile, was at Diedenhofen, and one source hints that he did not know whether to expect the arrival of the pope or not. When he finally heard that Stephen was coming he was "filled with joy."[76] He sent his son Charles to meet the pope and to accompany him to Ponthion.[77] Obviously Pepin had everything in readiness for a papal visit, should one actually take place, but one detects in the sources a genuine sense of uncertainty. The Franks cannot have known for sure whether or not the pope would strike a bargain with Aistulf. They could not really have known whether the pope would leave Rome to visit a northern kingdom. No pope had ever done so. Finally, it seems clear that Pepin wanted very much for the pope to come. The king knew he was going to be asked to protect Rome, and it stands to reason that he had something to gain from the pope as well.

Pepin and Stephen met at Ponthion on 6 January 754.[78] This is virtually the last fact for a year and a half that can be stated with certainty and without controversy. For example, Stephen's biographer says that Pepin prostrated himself before the pope and then did groom service for him, while the usually well informed Moissac chronicler has the pope prostrating himself before Pepin.[79] It would be possible to go on endlessly citing discrepancies of this sort, but to do so would avail us little. It suffices to say that Frankish

---

[75] *LP* 1:447.

[76] *Annales mettenses priores*, ed. Simson, p. 44.

[77] *Fredegarii continuatio*, c. 36, ed. Wallace-Hadrill, p. 104.

[78] Jaffé, *RP*, p. 272.

[79] *LP* 1:447; *Chron. moiss.*, *MGH, SS* 1:293.

and papal writers took somewhat different views of what transpired while the pope was in Francia.

Stephen came seeking protection. The sources all agree on this, but we must pause and notice the language they employ. The pope's biographer says that he asked "that through a treaty of peace he [i.e., Pepin] might dispose of the affairs of St. Peter and the Republic of the Romans."[80] Another Italian source, which depends heavily on the *Liber Pontificalis*, says almost the same thing.[81] The Frankish sources are not radically different. Two say that Stephen begged for help for himself and for the "Roman people."[82] Another source has the pope asking for help only for himself.[83] A very important annal reports that the pope requested aid for the Roman Church.[84] Finally, three Frankish annals say that the pope sought defense from the Lombards and the recovery of the "*iustitiis Sancti Petri*," the "rights of St. Peter."[85]

The pope is responsible for a republic. The Republic and the Roman Church are fundamentally the same. The patron of both is St. Peter, and it is St. Peter's rights that have been infringed. This is the same language that Zachary had used a decade and more earlier, and it is approximately the language used by Gregory III. In the Lateran some precision had been introduced, but not as much as would appear in a year or two. It is surely no cause for concern that some of the critical words and terms appear in Frankish sources and some in papal ones. These records were all written later, and as Bertolini has shown, their terminology is all papal. Probably the Franks learned it in their discussions with the pope.[86]

At Ponthion Pepin acceded to the pope's wishes. They entered into a pact of personal friendship, and the king swore on oath to restore to the Republic its "*iura seu loca*," including the Exarchate.[87] Precise details concerning how this was to be accomplished were left to be worked out later.[88] The nature,

---

[80]*LP* 1:448.

[81]*Pauli continuatio tertia*, c. 34, MGH, SSrL, pp. 209–10.

[82]*Chron. moiss.*, MGH, SS 1:293; *Ann. mettenses priores*, ed. Simson, p. 45.

[83]*Fredegarii continuatio*, c. 36, ed. Wallace-Hadrill, p. 104.

[84]*Annales qui dicuntur Einhardi*, *anno* 753, ed. Kurze, p. 11.

[85]*Ann. laurr.*, *anno* 753, MGH, SS 1:138; *Ann. laurr. min.*, MGH, SS 1:116; *Annales regni Francorum*, *anno* 753, ed. Kurze, p. 10.

[86]Bertolini, "Il problema delle origini del potere temporale dei papi nei suoi presupposti teoretici iniziali: Il concetto di 'restitutio' nelle prime cessione territoriali alla Chiesa di Roma (756–757)," in his *Scritti scelti di storia medioevale*, ed. Ottavio Banti, 2 vols. (Livorno, 1968), 2:514–25.

[87]*LP* 1:448.

[88]Ewig, "Papacy's Alienation from Byzantium," p. 22.

significance, and implications of the oaths and engagements undertaken by Stephen and Pepin at Ponthion are of the utmost importance for the subsequent history of Franco-papal relations dealing with the Republic. Consequently, they will form the initial subject matter of chapter 8 of the present study, which is devoted to the legal and moral dimensions of the Franco-papal bond. For now it is enough to say that Pepin obliged himself by oath to come to the aid of the pope, the Church, and the Republic. In practical terms, this meant he had agreed to force the Lombards to restore their conquests.

Because it was winter, and because the pope was fatigued from his travels, Pepin sent him to St. Denis to await the advent of spring.[89] Pepin also sent envoys to Aistulf urging him "out of reverence for the holy apostles Peter and Paul" to make amends with the Romans. Aistulf summarily refused.[90] Pepin also must have been working feverishly to overcome the opposition of those who disliked his plan to aid the pope against the Lombards. Exactly who opposed Pepin, and why, is something that can never be known for sure. Einhard, who tells us of the opposition and who was very close to the royal family, provides no details.[91] Presumably, support for Carlomann's heirs and a disinclination to intervene in Italy were significant factors. Aistulf, in March or April of 754, played upon these tensions by getting Carlomann to leave Monte Cassino and travel to Francia. Apparently Aistulf compelled the abbot of Monte Cassino to let Carlomann depart, and then commissioned him to oppose the pope's plans and keep Pepin from invading Italy.[92] Historians assume that Carlomann, who had now been a monk for six or seven years, agreed to go both to intercede for his sons and to prevent his brother from embarking upon an anti-Lombard policy.[93] Both possibilities are plausible. Furthermore, it is reasonable to suppose that Carlomann would have possessed a sufficient understanding of affairs in Francia to give him hope of succeeding in his enterprise. But Carlomann failed, was placed under house arrest in a Frankish monastery, and soon died. Pepin's had been

[89]*LP* 1:448.

[90]*Annales mettenses priores, anno* 753, ed. Simson, p. 45.

[91]*Vita Karoli*, c. 6, ed. Halphen, pp. 19–21.

[92]Leo, *Chron. cass.*, c. 7, *MGH, SS* 7:585; *Pauli continuatio tertia*, c. 35, *MGH, SSrL*, p. 210; *Pauli continuatio cassinense*, c. 4, *MGH, SSrL*, p. 199; Benedict, *Chronicon*, pp. 77–78; *Annales regni Francorum, anno* 753, ed. Kurze, p. 10; *Annales mettenses priores, anno* 754, ed. Simson, p. 46.

[93]Rodenberg, *Pippin*, pp. 27–29; Tangl, "Die Sendung des ehemaligen Hausmeiers Karlmann in das Frankenreich im Jahre 754 und der Konflikt der Brüder," *QFIAB* 40 (1960): 2–6, 16–17; Jarnut, "Quierzy und Rom," pp. 267–69; Bund, *Thronsturz*, p. 363.

a busy but successful winter. His brother had been unable to make trouble and the magnates, at least some of them, had been won over to the pope's cause. How exactly this happened we do not know, but when the Franks gathered in public assembly at Quierzy in April they agreed to come to the pope's assistance.

In the words of Walter Ullmann, "Pippin's promise at Ponthion was solemnized at Easter (14 April), ratified at Kierzy."[94] This clear and simple formulation is perfectly accurate but conceals the fact that the events that took place at Quierzy are among the most controversial in medieval history. This controversy applies to both the events themselves and their implications, for no single source reports fully on the assembly at Quierzy and this forces the historian to reconstruct events from a whole catena of documents. The precise order of any attempted reconstruction, the relative value assigned to this or to that document, will naturally affect the interpretations attached to Quierzy.

At Ponthion Pepin had personally promised to come to the pope's assistance, but as we saw, he and Stephen left the details to be worked out at a later date. This meant that Pepin had to win the assent of his nobility, and the precise question of what might be done in Italy had to be resolved. On 1 March Pepin called an assembly at Berny, and there "having taken counsel with his magnates" he agreed to go to Italy if necessary.[95] At Quierzy, probably in the presence of the pope, solemn, public force was given to Pepin's promise of Ponthion as a result of the agreement won at Berny. The promise of Quierzy was no more binding upon Pepin that his earlier one at Ponthion. This time, however, it had the support of the Franks. Where the promise of Quierzy differed from its predecessor was in spelling out what the Franks would do in Italy in the event that they had to go there.

We already observed that Stephen came to Francia seeking the "rights of St. Peter" and defense for himself, the Roman Church, and the Republic. At Ponthion matters were allowed, for the moment, to remain at this very vague and general level. At Quierzy a written document was produced specifying the pope's claims in Italy. It is this document, known today only from a brief

---

[94]Ullmann, *Papal Government*, p. 56.

[95]*BM*, no. 73g; *Annales mettenses priores*, anno 754, ed. Simson, p. 46; *Fredegarii continuatio*, c. 37, ed. Wallace-Hadrill, p. 105. Levillain, "L'avènement de la dynastie carolingienne," p. 294, dates this assembly of Berny 755 and changes most of the familiar chronology of early 754. I accept the traditional dates here. See: Halphen, *Charlemagne and the Carolingian Empire*, pp. 27–28; Ludwig Oelsner, *Jahrbücher des fränkischen Reiches unter König Pippin* (Leipzig, 1871), p. 129ff.

excerpt contained in the later life of Pope Hadrian I, that has been the focal point of much of the controversy surrounding Stephen's visit to Francia.

In 774 Charlemagne, in Rome, confirmed his father's promise of Quierzy. After saying this, Hadrian's *vita* goes on to spell out the contents of that promise.[96] It says that Pepin had promised to hand over lands "within defined boundaries" from Luni with the island of Corsica to Soriano, to Monte Bardo (i.e., Berceto), to Parma, to Reggio, to Mantua, and on to Monselice, plus the Exarchate "as it formerly was" (including the Pentapolis, Istria, and Venetia) and the duchies of Spoleto and Benevento. All of this is remarkable because neither Pepin nor Charlemagne ever handed over to the pope all of these territories. Plainly, the Quierzy document is a problem.

One venerable school of thought denies the authenticity of the passage in the *Vita Hadriani* that refers to Quierzy. These scholars believe that no such document as Hadrian's biographer cites ever existed and that, furthermore, at Quierzy Pepin made public and formal only the vague and private promises of Ponthion.[97] Another view is that some written document was issued at Quierzy but that the version contained in Hadrian's *vita* is either forged or interpolated in some respects, especially those having to do with the line from Luni to Monselice.[98] There are insuperable problems with this interpretation, not the least of which is that it asks us to believe that in 774 Charlemagne confirmed a forged copy of a document originally signed in his very presence twenty years earlier. This is not likely.

A way out of the difficulties began emerging in the last two decades of the nineteenth century when a number of scholars, chief among them the editor of the *Liber Pontificalis*, Louis Duchesne, proved beyond a doubt that the critical passage in the *Vita Hadriani* is both authentic and accurate.[99]

---

[96]*LP* 1:498.

[97]Wilhelm Martens, *Die römische Frage unter Pippin und Karl dem Großen* (Stuttgart, 1881), pp. 18–22, 31–39; Louis Saltet, "La lecture d'un texte et la critique contemporaine. La prétendue promesse de Quierzy dans le 'Liber Pontificalis,' " *Bulletin de litterature ecclésiastique* 41 (1940): 176–207; 42 (1941): 61–85; Elie Griffe, "Aux origines de l'état pontifical: Apropos de la Donation de Constantin et de la Donation de Quierzy," ibid. 53 (1952): 216–31; idem, "Aux origines de l'état pontifical: Charlemagne et Hadrian Ier," ibid. 55 (1954): 65–89.

[98]Martens, *Die römische Frage*, pp. 283–99, 302–6; Armbrust, *Territoriale Politik*, pp. 72–73; Paul Scheffer-Boichorst, "Pipins und Karls des Grossen Schenkungsversprechen: Ein Beitrag zur Kritik der Vita Hadriani," *MIÖG* 5 (1884): 194–97; Adolf Schaube, "Zur Verständigung über das Schenkungsversprechen von Kiersy und Rom," *HZ* 72 (1894): 199–203; Hodgkin, *The Frankish Invasion*, pp. 379–97; Albert Hauck, *Kirchengeschichte Deutschlands* 2:24 and n.2; Rodenberg, *Pippin*, pp. 32–34, 82–83.

[99]Duchesne, *LP*, 1:ccxxxiv–ccxxxvii; idem, *Temporal Sovereignty*, pp. 95–96; Paul Kehr, "Die sogennante karolingische Schenkung von 754," *HZ* 70 (1893): 391–98; Ernst Sackur,

This determination only solved one problem, however. It established that a document, of which at least some of the contents can be precisely known, was actually issued at Quierzy. A problem remained because the terms of the document as we know them from Hadrian's *vita* were never fulfilled and the papacy never complained about this apparent breach of promise. Thus, what exactly was the Quierzy document?

All the Quierzy document did, according to two scholars, was define the papal and Lombard spheres of influence in Italy.[100] But no evidence can be adduced in support of this theory. Another historian suggested that only patrimonies were involved. Pepin agreed to restore all of the pope's patrimonies south of the Luni-Monselice line.[101] This interpretation conflicts with the clear language of the document. It was Paul Kehr who finally solved the dilemma by proposing that the Quierzy document was a "contingent treaty."[102] According to Kehr, Pepin and Stephen surely held serious discussions about what would happen if Pepin invaded Italy. The Quierzy document did not mention the Duchy of Rome. It goes without saying that if Pepin did come to the defense of St. Peter he would have had to restore places like Ceccano recently taken from the duchy, and perhaps a very limited intervention in Italy would have involved no more than relatively minor restorations of this sort. In the most extreme case, however, Pepin might wreak utter devastation upon the Lombards, and here is where the Quierzy document would have come in. By its terms the Lombard kingdom would have been divided along the Luni-Monselice line. Presumably the division would have been between Stephen and Pepin with the former adding Tuscany and the southern Lombard duchies to the Republic and the latter attaching the heart of the *regnum* to his own kingdom. It is not impossible, however, that Stephen and Aistulf would have been the contracting parties with Aistulf having to endure a radical diminution of his kingdom to a point where it would no longer be a threat to the Republic.

"Die Promissio Pippins vom Jahre 754 und ihre Erneuerung durch Karls des Grossen," *MIÖG* 16 (1895): 387; Pepe, *Moyen âge barbare en Italie*, p. 182; Classen, "*Karl der Große, das Papsttum und Byzanz*," p. 551; Ewig, "Papacy's Alienation from Byzantium," p. 22; Jarnut, "Quierzy und Rom," pp. 278–81.

[100]Hubert, "Etude sur la formation des états de l'église," p. 265; Caspar, *Pippin und die römische Kirche*, pp. 148–50.

[101]Lindner, *Schenkungen*, pp. 47–86.

[102]Kehr, "Sogennante Schenkung," p. 436ff; Duchesne, *Temporal Sovereignty*, p. 96 n.1, agrees completely with Kehr; Caspar, *Pippin und die römische Kirche*, p. 104, follows Kehr only up to a point. See also: Gustav Schnürer, *Die Entstehung des Kirchenstaates* (Cologne, 1894), pp. 44–47, 82–83.

This theory is altogether the best possible explanation of the enigmatic Quierzy document. On Rome's side, there is nothing striking about the papal claims, with one exception. The Luni-Monselice line, probably taken over from a papal-Lombard treaty of about 600,[103] would have carved off Lombard Tuscany from the *regnum*.[104] The claim raised against Spoleto and Benevento may seem a bit extreme, but the papacy had long followed a policy of allying with the duchies. Claiming the duchies outright went a good deal beyond earlier papal schemes, but was not totally out of step with them. Ravenna, Istria, and Venetia were areas in which the papacy had long shown interest. The popes had always had trouble making effective their control in these areas, but for Stephen to have claimed them from Pepin was perfectly consistent with papal policy for a generation. On Pepin's side, the document left him some freedom of action. It represented a maximum scheme beneath which any number of lesser enactments might have been necessary, expedient, or acceptable. Historically, the great significance of the Quierzy document is that it displays unambiguously what can be called the papacy's "maximum plan" for the territorial dimensions of the Republic. In the best possible circumstances, the Republic would have consisted of all of formerly Byzantine central Italy, plus Lombard Tuscany and the two greatest Lombard duchies. Lombard Tuscany was doubtless seen as a buffer zone between Rome with its immediate environs and the *regnum*, whether the *regnum* passed into Frankish hands or remained under Lombard control. Since the 720s the Lombards had been laying waste the *castra* and towns in Roman Tuscany, and thus for the Republic to acquire Lombard Tuscany would have been an excellent security measure. Acquisition of Spoleto and Benevento would have added to the Republic's security in two respects. On the one hand, the *regnum* would have been further weakened by their loss and, on the other hand, the duchies would have provided a broad buffer zone between Rome and the still Byzantine south of Italy.

---

[103]Peter Rassow, "Pippin und Stephan II," *ZKG* 36 (1916): 499, puts the problem well by saying that if the Luni-Monselice line means little to us, it must have been clear and significant to people in the mid-eighth century. Caspar, *Pippin und die römische Kirche*, pp. 133–42, established that the line came from a treaty no earlier than 598 and no later than 640. He supposes it was originally a system of roads used as a line of demarcation and his view has won support: Classen, "Karl der Große, das Papsttum und Byzanz," p. 551; Fasoli, *Carlomagno*, p. 131; Ewig, "The Age of Charles the Great," in *Handbook of Church History*, p. 58. Ewig points out that the mention of Corsica is perhaps the most difficult territorial issue to solve but Adelheid Hahn, "Das Hludowicianum," *Archiv für Diplomatik* 21 (1975): 78–82, traces Corsica through all documents of the age and concludes that it does go back to 754.

[104]Duchesne, *LP* 1:cxxxvii, notes that only the claim on Lombard Tuscany represents any novelty and even here Città di Castello had earlier been claimed.

In July, at St. Denis,[105] Stephen rewarded Pepin for his efforts and commitments on behalf of the Republic. He consecrated and anointed Pepin, his wife, and his sons.[106] He also invested Pepin and his sons with the title *Patricius Romanorum*, which was designed to create a legal entitlement for Pepin's having assumed the obligation of defending the Republic.[107] The constitutional significance of this title, which Pepin never used but with which the papacy always addressed him, will be analyzed in detail in chapter 9.

A new Roman title was perhaps something which Pepin could do without, but a confirmation of his royal office by the pope himself, rather than on the pope's orders as in 751, must have been a welcome enhancement of Pepin's still young kingship. The new anointing alone, however, is not enough to establish why Pepin wanted the pope to come to Francia in the first place. The crucial piece of evidence is a curious little treatise entitled *Clausula de unctione Pippini regis* written at St. Denis in about 767.[108] This document had no public, legal force and probably reflected only the views of its author.[109] Still, it was written at St. Denis, a monastery closely associated with the Carolingian family and presided over by Fulrad, one of Pepin's most intimate advisers. Thus, the *Clausula* can be taken as an accurate account of what happened at St. Denis at the time of Pepin's anointing, and as a clear reflection of what Pepin considered most important about that act. Quite simply, the *Clausula* says that the pope solemnly forbade the Franks ever to choose a king from another family.[110] With one stroke, the highest moral authority the world then knew had set aside the claims of the Merovingians, of Carlomann and his sons, and of any jealous or ambitious Frankish mag-

---

[105]Oelsner, *Jahrbücher*, p. 155ff; *BM*, no. 76a. Halphen, *Charlemagne*, p. 34, represents a tradition that places these events in the spring of 754.

[106]*LP* 1:448; *Annales regni Francorum*, *anno* 754, ed. Kurze, p. 12; *Annales qui dicuntur Einhardi*, *anno* 754, ed. Kurze, p. 13; *Annales mettenses priores*, *anno* 754, ed. Simson, pp. 45–46.

[107]*Annales mettenses priores*, pp. 45–46; *Clausula de unctione Pippini regis*, ed. Bruno Krusch, *MGH, SS rer. Merov.* 3:465.

[108]Its authenticity used to be thought questionable: Maximilian Buchner, *Die Clausula de unctione Pippini, eine Fälschung aus dem Jahre 880* (Paderborn, 1926). Léon Levillain, "De l'authenticité de la *Clausula* . . . ," *BEC* 88 (1927): 20–42, proved its authenticity. See now: Affeldt, "Königserhebung Pippins," pp. 103–9. For the importance of the ideas contained in the little treatise a good discussion is: Josef Fleckenstein, *Early Medieval Germany*, trans. Bernard S. Smith (Amsterdam, 1978), pp. 58–59.

[109]This is Halphen's opinion: *Charlemagne*, pp. 33–34. Affeldt, "Königserhebung Pippins," pp. 103–9, takes much the same view.

[110]*Clausula*, ed. Krusch, *MGH, SSrer. Merov.* 3:465.

nates. This strengthening of his royal office is what Pepin wanted from the pope, and he wanted it done in Francia by St. Peter's vicar before the very persons who might contest his rule.[111] Stephen, however, waited until after he had received confirmation from *both* Pepin and the Frankish nobility that they would come to his aid before he acted to secure Pepin's throne. Neither man, it seems, was in a position of great strength, and each one played out his diplomatic trump cards slowly, cautiously, and at just the right moment.

After his unction on 28 July, the king sent two more sets of envoys to Pavia to try to get peace and restitutions in Italy.[112] These efforts failed, and in the early spring of 755 Pepin collected his army and set out for the south.[113] It seems that Pepin did not take a very large force to Italy.[114] Perhaps there was still opposition to his plans and he could not risk a general mobilization. Or, with the frontiers of his realm so insecure he may not have wished to march his whole army out of the kingdom. On the way to Italy Pepin and Stephen made one last appeal to Aistulf, but as always, he refused to budge.[115] Pepin even offered to pay 12,000 solidi to Aistulf if he would only do justice to St. Peter.[116]

Aistulf sought to block the Alpine passes but failed. The Franks entered Italy, battle was joined, and the Lombards were defeated. Aistulf fell back on Pavia but Pepin besieged the city and after a short time the Lombard king had to capitulate.[117] It is interesting to note that Aistulf sent representatives

---

[111]Rodenberg, *Pippin*, pp. 13–14.

[112]*LP* 1:449.

[113]Here I follow the chronology of Levillain, "L'avènement de la dynastie carolingienne," pp. 271–74. Hodgkin, *Italy and Her Invaders*, vol. 7, *The Frankish Invasion* (Oxford, 1899), pp. 229–34, was the first to place this campaign in 755 and not in 754. Halphen, *Charlemagne*, p. 40, and F. L. Ganshof, "The Frankish Monarchy and Its External Relations from Pippin III to Louis the Pious," in his *The Carolingians and the Frankish Monarchy*, trans Janet Sondheimer (Ithaca, 1971), p. 182 n.3, accept Levillain's chronology. The traditional view places the campaign in 754: Oelsner, *Jahrbücher*, p. 193ff; *BM*, no. 76b. Ewig, "Papacy's Alienation from Byzantium," p. 23, is indicative of German scholarship which still adheres to 754. French, English, American, and Italian scholars are today about equally divided on the question. The evidence is extremely difficult to interpret, but I find Levillain's arguments persuasive. Delogu, "Il regno longobardo," p. 175 and n.3, holds for 754 on the basis of two Lombard charters the testimony of which is more ambiguous than he thinks. See: *CDL*, vol. 1, ed. Schiaparelli, nos. 114, 117, pp. 333, 353.

[114]Jarnut, "Quierzy und Rom," pp. 85–86.

[115]*LP* 1:450.

[116]*Annales mettenses priores*, anno 754, ed. Simson, p. 47.

[117]For basic details on the campaign see: Oelsner, *Jahrbücher*, pp. 193–202. Hallenbeck, *Pavia and Rome*, pp. 78–80, offers some alternative interpretations.

to the Frankish nobility to seek peace.[118] Here is another of those tantalizing bits of evidence that relate to Pepin's problems with his nobility, and one more indicator that Aistulf knew of those problems and hoped to draw profit from them. Aistulf was compelled to pay an indemnity of 30,000 solidi, to deliver forty hostages, and to promise never to withdraw from Frankish overlordship.[119] A peace treaty was also concluded "among the Romans, Franks and Lombards."[120] According to its terms, Aistulf swore on oath to return Ravenna and, in the words of the *Liber Pontificalis, "diversis civitatibus."* The Metz annals enable us to fill out this report. Narni, Ceccano, and the Pentapolis were the other cities besides Ravenna.[121] This oath and treaty were written down and together make the "First Peace of Pavia."[122]

The Quierzy document, produced just a year before, necessarily went unfulfilled, because the Lombard kingdom had not been dissolved. Pepin charged Fulrad to escort Stephen back to Rome, and Pepin himself returned to Francia.[123] On the whole both Stephen and Pepin had reason to be satisfied with the First Peace of Pavia. Pepin had fulfilled his obligation to intercede for St. Peter. He had campaigned in Italy, but in a fairly limited way so as not to antagonize any more than he had to those who favored traditional Franco-Lombard friendship. The pope got back Narni and Ceccano, which had been taken from the Duchy of Rome, and Aistulf was compelled to hand over Ravenna and the Pentapolis, where the papacy had been showing interest for years. Venetia and Istria,[124] Tuscany, and the Duchies of Benevento and Spoleto were not mentioned at Pavia, as they had been at

---

[118]*Fredegarii continuatio*, c. 37, ed. Wallace-Hadrill, p. 105.

[119]*Annales regni Francorum, anno* 755, ed, Kurze, p. 12; *Annales mettenses priores, anno* 754, ed. Simson, pp. 46–47; *Ann. laurr., MGH, SS* 1:138.

[120]*LP* 1:451.

[121]*Anno* 754, ed. Simson, p. 47.

[122]*LP* 1:451: "per scriptam paginam"; *Pauli continuatio tertia,* c. 39, *MGH, SSrL,* p. 210: "per scriptam paginam"; Benedict, *Chronicon,* p. 80: "per precepto." Caspar, *Pippin und die römische Kirche,* pp. 71–90, goes through an elaborate effort to prove that no precise written documents accompanied the First Peace of Pavia. Ullmann, *Papal Government,* p. 57 n. 5, accepts Caspar's judgment, but it is against the evidence. It may have been, as *LP* implies, that the territorial prescriptions were vague and general. Still, the preponderance of the evidence makes it clear that there was a written instrument.

[123]*Annales regni Francorum, anno* 755, ed. Kurze, p. 12.

[124]For reasons not at all clear to me Caspar (*Pippin und die römische Kirche,* pp. 71–90) and Jarnut ("Quierzy und Rom," pp. 285–86) say Venetia and Istria were given back to Byzantium. There is no evidence for this notion, although these scholars are right to call attention to the pope's failure to acquire these regions.

Quierzy, but with Aistulf under Pepin's overlordship, and Pepin's loyalty beyond question, Stephen must have thought that he had little more to fear from the Lombards.

The First Peace of Pavia had a serious flaw. It depended on the willingness of Aistulf to honor its terms. Pepin had no sooner regained his kingdom than Aistulf refused to make any restitutions to the Republic, and began attacking the Duchy of Rome from all sides. Aistulf was certainly a bit reckless, but unless he is to be taken for a complete fool it must be supposed that he had elected for a second time to run a calculated risk. Pepin had shown integrity in honoring his commitment to help the pope, but he had not shown marked enthusiasm for an Italian campaign. At least three times he had sent ambassadors to Italy while Stephen was in Francia, and later, when his army was en route to Italy, Pepin sent envoys once more, persuaded the pope to do the same, and finally tried to bribe Aistulf. After defeating Aistulf, Pepin let him off somewhat easily. A Frankish chronicler says that Pepin "merciful as always was moved as an act of grace to grant him his life and his crown."[125] Apparently Aistulf thought that Pepin had gone as far as he dared in 755 and would not intervene again. He must have read Pepin's caution as a sign of inability or unwillingness to proceed to total victory in Italy. It would be interesting to know whether or not Aistulf had knowledge of the Quierzy document. If he did, which I think is likely, then when he saw how far short of its terms the Pavia treaty had fallen he must have been appreciably emboldened.[126]

Whereas Frankish sources note simply that Aistulf went back on the offensive,[127] it is Italian sources, specifically letters 6 to 10 in the *Codex Carolinus*, and the *Liber Pontificalis*, that supply details. The basic course of events is not difficult to establish. "A little while" after Pepin and Stephen had parted company, Aistulf "refused to fulfill the things he had promised" and commenced "a general mobilization of the whole people of his kingdom

---

[125]*Fredegarii continuatio*, c. 37, ed. Wallace-Hadrill, p. 106.

[126]Certainly Aistulf's goal in 755 and 756 was the total conquest of the Duchy of Rome. He never seems to have realized that the popes would be implacable enemies of his dreams of Italian unification: Bertolini, *Roma e i longobardi*, p. 62. Hallenbeck ("Rome Under Attack: An Estimation of King Aistulf's Motives for the Lombard Siege of 756," *Mediaeval Studies* 40 [1978]: 195–98, 201–3, and *Pavia and Rome*, pp. 81–85) argues that Aistulf saw the Franks as an impediment to his annexing Rome, disliked the dismemberment of his kingdom in the Peace of Pavia and sought, therefore, to drive Rome into a position of neutrality. Only in 752 did Aistulf actually attempt to conquer Rome. This argument is questionable.

[127]*Annales mettenses priores*, anno 755, ed. Simson, p. 48. Many sources say that Aistulf broke faith with Pepin and went on the offensive.

of the Lombards against this Roman city." This account, taken from the biography of Stephen, compresses things severely.[128] Pepin had left Italy before mid-year in 755, and Aistulf's siege of Rome began 1 January 756.[129] For developments in the last months of 755 it is necessary to turn to two letters from the pope to Pepin.

In the first, Stephen reminds Pepin of his obligation to be assiduous in seeking the rights of St. Peter and he cites the *"donacionis paginam"* whereby Pepin had made restitutions to the saint.[130] This oblique reference must be to the Pavian peace treaty and not to the Quierzy document. He goes on to say, somewhat intemperately, that the perverse, mendacious, diabolical, and perjurious Aistulf had refused to hand over "a palm's breadth" of land "to St. Peter and to the Holy Church of God, the Republic of the Romans." All Christians know, Stephen says, that St. Peter can only have justice by the strong right arm of Pepin. Peter, the pope insists, anointed Pepin king, is his protector, and personally received Pepin's promise of protection and restitution. Pepin should never forget that St. Peter holds the keys of the kingdom of heaven. The second letter of 755 is a bit longer but says much the same thing.[131] This time Stephen tells how St. Peter instructed him to make a long and arduous journey into a far-off province to seek salvation from the iniquity of the Lombards. Again, Pepin is asked to make good his promises.

These letters make only vague and veiled references to new conquests by Aistulf. Primarily they demand fulfillment of the terms of the Peace of Pavia. It is not possible to date either letter precisely. When the first one was written Fulrad was still in Rome. The second letter talks of envoys and hints, I believe, at Fulrad's imminent departure for Francia. Apparently, Aistulf had refused rather quickly to fulfill the requirements of the treaty and then watched attentively as envoys passed back and forth between Rome and Francia. No support came to Stephen in the second half of 755, and this probably encouraged the king to attack Rome, which he did on the first of the new year. His gamble in refusing to hand over "a palm's breadth of land" was paying off, and now he could, evidently with impunity, attack Rome itself.

We have no record of further correspondence from Stephen until late February 756 when he dispatched three letters simultaneously to Francia. The first says that Rome had now been under siege for several weeks by

---

[128]*LP* 1:451.
[129]Levillain, "L'avènement de la dynastie carolingienne," pp. 282–83.
[130]CC, no. 6, pp. 488–90.
[131]CC, no. 7, pp. 490–93.

Aistulf and the Beneventans.[132] Narni had been seized—had Aistulf perhaps restored and then retaken it?—and the Lombards had penetrated to St. Peter's. Aistulf had told the Romans that if they would hand over the pope he would have mercy on them. People in the countryside around Rome were being killed. With all the rhetorical power of a biblical prophet Stephen paints a picture of gloom and destruction and pleads for salvation. The pope sent this letter to Pepin with two *missi* of his own who were to accompany Pepin's own *missus* Warnehar back to Francia. The second says virtually the same thing as the first, but the address is interesting.[133] It was sent to Pepin and his sons, to the bishops, abbots, priests, and monks of Francia, to the dukes, counts, and all the soldiers of the provinces of the kingdom. Here is the same strategy that had been employed in 753: A letter to Pepin and a second letter directly to the Franks who were still, it seems, reluctant about campaigning in Italy. The third is one of the most fascinating in the whole *Codex Carolinus.*[134] It is, like the second, addressed to the kings, clergy, and magnates of the Franks, but its author purports to be St. Peter himself. The letter begins "*Ego Petrus apostolus . . . ,*" but then goes on to say pretty much the same things as the first two. Obviously the pope was going to all possible lengths to save the Republic from the Lombards. He made every kind of appeal he could possibly make.

The pope's appeals finally achieved the desired result. Pepin collected his forces and headed for Italy again. The campaign was just as successful as the one of the previous year, but this time Pepin took firmer action upon its conclusion.[135] Pepin "acceded to his nobles' wishes" and once more granted Aistulf his crown and a head on which to wear it. The Lombard king was, however, compelled anew to hand over hostages, yield one-third of his treasury, pay an annual tribute, and swear oaths to make restitutions.[136] Once more a treaty document, "The Second Peace of Pavia," was drawn up and, Stephen's biographer says, deposited in the archives of the Roman Church. This instrument spelled out exactly what cities Aistulf was to hand over, and to insure that the transfer actually took place, Pepin sent Fulrad to each named city to receive its keys and hostages. Fulrad then deposited the keys and the treaty documents at St. Peter's.[137]

---

[132]CC, no. 8, pp. 494–98.

[133]CC, no. 9, pp. 498–500.

[134]CC, no. 10, pp. 501–3.

[135]For details on the campaign: Oelsner, *Jahrbücher*, pp. 254–69; Halphen, *Charlemagne*, pp. 44–46; Hallenbeck, *Pavia and Rome*, pp. 83–85.

[136]*Fredegarii continuatio*, c. 38, ed. Wallace-Hadrill, p. 108; *Annales mettenses priores*, *anno* 755, ed. Simson, p. 49.

[137]*LP* 1:453–54. The cities were: Ravenna, Rimini, Pesaro, Conca (= La Cattolica), Fano,

Generations of history students have been told of a "Donation of Pepin." The treaty documents of 756 constitute that "Donation," but it was really a donation only in an odd and limited sense. Pepin donated nothing of his own to the pope. Rather, he defeated Aistulf and forced him to give back to the papacy certain cities that he or his predecessors had taken from the Exarchate of Ravenna over many years' time, or from the Republic quite recently. Although Aistulf had taken Narni and Ceccano from Rome, the majority of his conquests had, in strict legal terms, been at the expense of the Byzantine Empire in the Ravennate and Pentapolis. It could perhaps be argued that in defeating Aistulf, Pepin took title to Aistulf's lands and then "donated" a portion of them to Stephen, but so to argue would be to rush far ahead of the evidence. The "Donation of Pepin" was really a parcel of land—actually several widely scattered parcels—that Pepin forced Aistulf to donate to the papacy. If Pepin had deposed Aistulf and taken his kingdom by right of conquest, then the "Donation of Pepin" would have to have followed the terms of the Quierzy document, but in 756, as in 755, Pepin stopped far short of wreaking maximum devastation on the Lombards.

As Pepin was crossing the Alps in 756 two Byzantine officials appeared in Rome, having been sent to Pepin by the emperor. The pope told them Pepin was on his way to Italy, but the imperial envoys doubted this, and so joined by a papal *missus*, they set out for Marseilles. Upon arriving there they learned that they had missed Pepin. The papal *missus* tried to detain the imperial ones, but they headed for Italy and met Pepin at Pavia where they hotly demanded that the king hand over Ravenna to them. Pepin, we may suppose, left these sophisticated Byzantine officials nonplussed when he said that all his actions had been undertaken not for earthly reward but for the love of St. Peter and for the remission of his sins.[138] In reality, then, Pepin had donated that which was not his to donate, but there are three mitigating factors. First, affairs in Italy were being regulated by power, not by constitutional niceties.[139] Second, in the midst of the Franco-papal entente the Byzantines held, in 754, an iconoclastic council which far surpassed in rigor and theological sophistication anything that had preceded it.[140] Stephen II, as a result of this council, sought from Pepin protection not only from the

---

Cesena, Sinigaglia, Jesi, Forlimpopoli, Forli (with Sussubio), Montefeltro (= San Leo), Arcevia, Mons Lucatium (a site near Cesena), Serra dei Conti, San Marino, Sarsina, Urbino, Cagli, Cantiano, Gubbio, Comacchio, Narni. For identification of them: Duchesne, *LP* 1:460; Hodgkin, *The Frankish Invasion*, pp. 222–23.

[138]*LP* 1:452–53.

[139]Mühlbacher, *Deutsche Geschichte*, p. 69.

[140]Ostrogorsky, *Byzantine State*, pp. 171–75.

Lombards but also from the heresy of the Greeks. From this time forward, papal letters to the Franks regularly requested that the rights of St. Peter be secured and that the "*catholica fides*" be kept inviolate.[141] Third, the papacy had been making claims on Ravenna for a generation already, so there was nothing radical about Pepin's having honored those claims in 755 and 756.

Sanctae Dei Ecclesiae Reipublicae Romanorum

The historic significance of Stephen II is that he found a way to break through all the dangers and difficulties separating Rome from Francia. In so doing he acquired the protector the Republic so desperately needed. "The Frankish monarchy," writes Walter Ullmann, "appeared to the papacy as the instrument by which the plan of emancipation could be brought to a successful conclusion."[142] This is the customary interpretation of the Franco-papal alliance, but it is somewhat distorted. The papacy had emancipated itself from Byzantium years before Pepin set foot in Italy. The Franks played no role at all in freeing the popes from the Byzantines. Rather, they saved the papal republic from liquidation by the Lombards. After the dismal failures of Eutychius in 728–29, the Byzantines were a feeble and inconsequential presence in Italy. In the 730s and 740s the papacy picked up the remnants of Byzantine central Italy and forged them into a Republic. With the advent of Aistulf the continued existence of that Republic was called into question. Emancipation and survival are two very different things. The former was a fait accompli by the 730s. The latter was no certainty until after 754.

Many historians have seen that the papacy began creating a state in the 730s and the 740s, and that a splendid ideological apparatus was created to define that state and to defend its existence.[143] Unfortunately, virtually everyone who has written on papal history in this period has been so accustomed to attach fundamental significance to the Franco-papal alliance that perspectives have been warped. By Zachary's time the pope governed the Duchies of Rome and Perugia and claimed to rule in some fashion in Venice and

---

[141]Bertolini, "Problema della origini," pp. 539–41.

[142]*Papal Government*, pp. 53–54.

[143]The best accounts, both of which cite the older literature, are: Ullmann, *Growth of Papal Government*, pp. 44–57; Miller, "Roman Revolution," pp. 83–114.

Ravenna. The inhabitants of this region, called a Republic,[144] were the pope's "peculiar people." St. Peter was the patron of the Republic. In the 750s there emerged an intensification of these ideas, but no really new developments, with one possible exception. Bertolini thinks that whereas earlier popes expressed a sense of pastoral solicitude for their lost sheep, Stephen II sought to exercise genuine authority over them.[145] Bertolini performs a notable service in showing how the papacy used pastoral terminology to advance its territorial claims, but then, at the last moment, he fails to draw out the full significance of his own ideas. Bertolini, like so many others, like Ullmann in the lines quoted just above, cannot grant the existence of papal rule in Italy before there are Franks involved. David Miller says that Stephen II was faced with the necessity of providing an ideological explanation for the fact that, since Gregory II, the popes had stood at the head of an independent state. Stephen's answer was the curious phrase "*sanctae Dei ecclesiae, reipublicae Romanorum.*"[146] Why, one may ask, is Stephen so significant? Did not his three immediate predecessors have just as urgent a need to explain what they had done? Miller is virtually the only scholar who flatly admits that Gregory II began building a state, but like so many others, Miller is entrapped by the need to have Franks on the scene before the process can be regarded as complete. It is particularly odd that Miller and Ullmann push final explanations down to the time of Stephen II, because they, more than any of the countless others who have written on papal ideology in the eighth century, have seen the clarity and precision of that ideology well before the time of Stephen. Stephen did nothing radically new. He did something successful. He got a commitment from the Franks to protect the Republic of St. Peter.

If Stephen did nothing radically new, he did nevertheless take a small step forward with the fascinating and enigmatic title he gave to his state. The preponderance of the evidence for the pontificate of Stephen uses the kind of varied and ambiguous language that could have come from the chanceries of his three immediate predecessors; so one must be careful not to read too much into the new title. For example, the word *republic* is met, along with *St. Peter's people*, and *rights*. Then, however, in a letter from 755 there appears "*sanctae Dei ecclesiae, reipublicae Romanorum.*" Does

---

[144]This point has been known since the end of the last century: Martens, *Die römische Frage*, p. 20; Lindner, *Schenkungen*, pp. 23, 30.

[145]Bertolini, "Problema della origini," pp. 499, 510.

[146]"Roman Revolution," p. 121; Lindner, *Schenkungen*, pp. 41–42, had already said much the same thing.

the coining of this phrase in Stephen's Lateran represent a new departure? Only a careful analysis of the evidence can answer this important question.

From the reign of Stephen II this "Roman Republic" appears in documents twice: One is from the *Liber Pontificalis* and one from the *Codex Carolinus*.[147] It will be helpful for the following discussion to set out the examples in full.

> sanctae Dei ecclesiae reipublice Romanorum (*LP*)
> sanctae dei ecclesiae reipublice Romanorum (*CC*)

These same documents also supply several variations. Again I cite them in exactly the grammatical forms in which they originally appear in their respective contexts.

> sancte Dei ecclesie reipublice (*LP*)
> sanctaeque Dei ecclesiae rei publice (*CC*, 6)
> cunctus noster populus rei publice Romanorum (*CC*, 7)
> sanctam Dei ecclesiam et nostrum Romanorum rei publice (*CC*, 8)

This list constitutes a series of similar juxtapositions: Either "The Holy Church of God" with the "Republic of the Romans" or "all our people" with the "Republic" or with the "Republic of the Romans." In the past, the juxtapositions have been understood to imply either a subordination of the Church to the Republic, or just the opposite. In fact, the terms are appositive, equivalent, complementary.[148] Miller says that "the ecclesiastical state was, as its title implied, the Roman Empire."[149] In fact, had the Lateran wished to say this, it would have used *respublica romana*.[150] The point of the papacy's formulation was to identify the Holy Church, which was not iconoclastic and heretical, with the Republic of the Romans, that is, with the *real* Romans, the Catholic ones, and not with the heretical and vain Greeks who lived not on the Tiber but on the Bosporus and who called themselves

---

[147]Stephen's *vita* in the *LP* was probably written shortly after his death. The term appears in the *vita* at a point where Stephen was still in Francia, but actually, the first time it was used was in the *Codex Carolinus*. LP 1:449; CC, no. 6, p. 489.

[148]Franz Kampers, "Roma aeterna und Sancta Dei Ecclesia rei publicae romanorum," *HJB* 44 (1924): 240–43 (subordination); Caspar, *Pippin und die römische Kirche*, pp. 156–57 (opposition); Gundlach, *Entstehung des Kirchenstaats*, p. 27; Miller, "Roman Revolution," p. 122 (apposition).

[149]Miller, "Roman Revolution," pp. 123–24.

[150]Ullmann, *Papal Government*, p. 61.

"Romans" in Greek: *romaioi*.[151] This term could be applied in unequivocal terms to all of formerly Byzantine central Italy only after the First Peace of Pavia, because only after 755 did the papacy have a secure deed to most of the emperor's erstwhile holdings.[152] It is worth remarking that the new title, in any of its forms, appears only after the middle of 755.

There was, then, a new formulation of the Republic's title, but it would be a mistake to make too much of it. In the same documents where this new title appears, there exist many older, more traditional expressions: "*In istis partibus Romanis*," "*eius* [i.e., *Petri*] *civitatibus et locis*," "*totius nostrae* [i.e., *papae*] *provintiae*," "*hac Romana provintia*," "*res beati Petri*," "*iustitiam beati Petri*."[153] In view of the simultaneous appearance of these expressions, it may not be wise to attach much significance to *sanctae Dei ecclesiae, reipublice Romanorum*. There is no evidence at this early date that the Lateran developed and deployed only a single name for the Republic and it would be a mistake to read too much into any particular turn of phrase. In the aggregate, papal language makes it clear that Pepin was called upon to defend a Republic that belonged to St. Peter.

Pepin's role in Italy was, there is no denying it, critical. Without him the Republic's history would in all probability have ceased in the middle 750s after a brief existence of some two decades' duration. Thanks to Pepin that history went on for more than a millennium. Pepin was not, however, a founding father of the Republic, and neither, for that matter, was Pope Stephen II.

Perhaps it will be objected that Pepin's role was more distinctive than the foregoing account admits. Did he not make massive restitutions to the pope and thereby secure for him lands that he had not possessed before? Surely, but taken by itself this action was not original. Cumae had been given to the pope by the Duke of Naples, and Liutprand had handed over the Cottian Alps patrimonies, Sutri, Amelia, Orte, Bomarzo, Bieda, and Cesena. Gallese had been bought from the Duke of Spoleto. The papacy had been acquiring titles to pieces of Italy in various ways, from various people, for a long time. Pepin's restitutions thus fit into a longer tradition. Is it important that Pepin was named *Patricius Romanorum*? Probably not, because on the one hand, popes had been naming officials of all kinds in Italy for more than a century, and on the other hand, Pepin never used the title. It seems not to have meant anything to him. Finally, was not the appeal to the Franks

---

[151]Ullmann, *Papal Government*, p. 61ff.

[152]Lindner, *Schenkungen*, pp. 12–j21; Hartmann, *Geschichte Italiens*, 2.2:184.

[153]CC, nos. 2, 6–9, pp. 477–98.

important? It was, in fact, important only because it was successful. In a certain sense the appeal of 753 was no more important than the earlier one of 739. Each appeal was based on a similar set of circumstances in Italy, and each sought essentially the same thing. Moreover, in past difficulties, popes had turned to Naples, Benevento, Spoleto and, in sheer desperation, even to Constantinople for assistance.

Unanswered Questions

The events of the early 750s had added a major new actor to the Italian drama, but they did not bring the curtain down. The Byzantines had raised a claim on Ravenna in 756. What role would they, could they, play in the years ahead? Shortly after Pepin returned to Francia in 756 Aistulf, "while he was contemplating how he might avoid fulfilling his promises," was killed in a hunting accident.[154] Who would the new Lombard king be? What attitude would he take toward the Republic? If it became necessary, could Pepin be prevailed upon again to raise an army and come once more to the defense of St. Peter? Given the wide differences between the papacy's maximum territorial plan, as seen in the Quierzy document, and the much attenuated restorations of 755 and 756, what would the ultimate shape of the Republic be? Now that the pope had a legal title to the old Exarchate, in the narrow sense, could he hold it and govern it if the Ravennese decided to oppose him? What about Venice and Istria: Would they be restored to Byzantium, become independent, or enter into the Republic?

The birth of the Republic of St. Peter was a process and not an event, and in 756 much of that process still lay in the future.

---

[154] *Annales qui dicuntur Einhardi, anno* 756, ed. Kurze, p. 15.

Four

Our Beloved Son Desiderius . . .
That Foul and Pestiferous Lombard

ST. PETER fared both well and ill during the seventeen years that separated Pepin's second Italian campaign from Charlemagne's first. The new Lombard king, Desiderius, at first conciliatory, later proved to be just as aggressive as, but far more cunning than, his predecessors. Inside the Republic, the first direct challenges to papal rule began to disturb the unity of the region. The lands newly added to the Republic in 755 and 756, chiefly Ravenna, sought by fair means and foul to remain independent of Rome. In Francia domestic political and military difficulties, coupled with changes of rulers in 768 and again in 771, precluded the possibility of direct intervention in Italy. If the events of the 750s do not loom quite so large in the history of the Republic when viewed from the perspective of the 730s and 740s, then those events seem extremely tentative and provisional when viewed from the 760s.

New Rulers, New Opportunities, Old Antagonisms

The last month of 756 and the early ones of 757 were propitious for the papacy and its Republic. In some ways this period is reminiscent of late 744 when Zachary had had the pleasure of witnessing the death of his redoubtable foe Liutprand and the succession of the pious and, so it was thought, pliable Ratchis. After Aistulf died in December 756 Ratchis abandoned his monastic retreat at Monte Cassino and returned to Pavia.[1] Whether he became king for a second time, or merely served as some sort of a regent, is difficult to determine. A Pisan diploma uses the odd words "*guvernante domino Ratchis famulo Christi Jesu principem gentis Langobardorum anno*

---

[1] For details see Andreolli, "Re Ratchis," pp. 322–25.

primo."² This weird formulation had never before been used by a Lombard ruler, though in later times the *princeps* title among the Lombards was virtually the equivalent of a royal title.³ Perhaps because Aistulf had died without issue Ratchis did return to Pavia as a regent,⁴ but the *communis opinio* is that he did indeed become king once again.⁵ Quite possibly Ratchis was recalled by the Lombard magnates who desired to retain the family of Aistulf on the throne, but who also wished to dissociate themselves from the ruinous policies of the late king.⁶ Whatever Ratchis's motives and constitutional position may have been, it is a fair assumption that the pope would have had mixed feelings about Ratchis. Would he be the pious philoroman of 744 or the aggressive expansionist of 749?

At this juncture another candidate for the throne emerged. This was Desiderius, a wealthy Brescian, former constable to Aistulf, and at the time of the king's death, a duke in Tuscany.⁷ He began, probably shortly after Ratchis had returned to Pavia, to collect his troops in order to seize the throne.⁸ Immediately after his intentions became known, certain prominent Lombards, apparently the very ones who were supporting Ratchis, opposed him vigorously.⁹ Possibly the opposition was rooted in the idea that Desiderius was so completely a creature of Aistulf that he would continue the latter's policies and thereby cause the Franks to revisit Italy.¹⁰ Desiderius, however, short-circuited the opposition by the remarkably clever device of turning for support to Stephen II.

Stephen had held aloof from the Lombard succession controversy until Desiderius appealed to him.¹¹ Stephen then sent his brother Paul, the *primi-*

---

²*CDL*, vol. 2, ed. Luigi Schiaperelli, no. 124, p. 367.

³Hans H. Kaminsky, "Zum Sinngehalt des Princeps-Titels Arichis' II. von Benevent," *FMSt* 8 (1974): 81–92.

⁴Andreolli, "Re Ratchis," pp. 323–24; Fasoli, *Carlomagno*, p. 55.

⁵Fröhlich, *Thronfolge* 1:224–31 provides a full discussion and an evaluation of the literature. See also: Hallenbeck, *Pavia and Rome*, pp. 85–86.

⁶Hartmann, *Geschichte Italiens*, 2.2:206–7; Bertolini, *Roma*, p. 574.

⁷*Pauli continuatio romana*, cc. 4, 5, MGH, SSrL, p. 201; *Annales qui dicuntur Einhardi*, *anno.* 756, ed. Kurze, p. 15; *LP* 1:454. Hartmann, *Geschichte Italiens*, 2.2:244 n.2; Fröhlich, *Thronfolge* 1:231–32.

⁸Schneider, *Königswahl und Königserhebung*, p. 60, assumes that Desiderius was king from the moment he claimed the throne. Fröhlich, *Thronfolge* 1:232, argues that Ratchis was king and that Desiderius had to try to unseat him and win recognition.

⁹*LP* 1:454–55; *Pauli continuatio romana*, c. 4, MGH, SSrL, p. 201; *Chronicon salernitanum*, ed. Westerbergh, pp. 9–10.

¹⁰Andreolli, "Re Ratchis," pp. 324–25.

¹¹*LP* 1:455. Fröhlich, *Thronfolge* 1:233.

cerius Christophorus, and Fulrad to Tuscany to meet with Desiderius.[12] The pope was in a particularly advantageous position. Desiderius had to have help and was therefore ripe for extortion. The papal envoys accordingly extracted from him a promise to live in peace with the Republic and to restore to it "the cities which remained" in Lombard hands. Specifically, Desiderius offered to hand over Ancona, Ferrara, Faventia, Umana, Imola, and Osimo, plus Bologna, which he and two other dukes jointly agreed to restore.[13] These cities represented essentially the old conquests of Liutprand,[14] and their recovery would have placed the pope in possession of virtually the whole of formerly Byzantine central and northern Italy except for Venice and Istria. Stephen drove a hard bargain, but Desiderius was really in no position to negotiate.

After his envoys had returned to Rome, Stephen wrote to Pepin to win him over to the settlement, and he offered Desiderius armed assistance, should it be needed, to secure the crown. The pope's willingness, and more especially his ability, to provide Desiderius with troops is clear testimony to papal control in and around Rome, and to the degree to which people there accepted the pope's leadership. He also sought, successfully as it turned out, to persuade Ratchis to return without incident to his monastery.[15] On 3 or 4 March 757 Desiderius became king of the Lombards.[16] Perhaps Desiderius's entente with Stephen allayed the suspicions of those who had been opposing him. No further opposition is reported.

A group of Frankish sources relate these events quite differently. North of the Alps various writers asserted that it was Pepin who had made Desiderius king.[17] There is actually no evidence that Pepin took an active role in

---

[12]*LP* 1:455. Duchesne, *Temporal Sovereignty*, p. 72, says it is "more than probable" that Christophorus was the key instigator of the papacy's maximum territorial aspirations. This has become, rightly, the prevailing interpretation.

[13]*LP* 1:455; *CC*, no. 11, p. 506. For some reason Seppelt (*Geschichte der Päpste* 2:133) says Desiderius promised to give these cities to Pepin who would then hand them over to the pope.

[14]Hodgkin, *The Frankish Invasion*, p. 241.

[15]*LP* 1:455.

[16]Oelsner, *Jahrbücher*, p. 439.

[17]*Fredegarii continuatio*, c. 39, ed. Wallace-Hadrill, p. 109; *Annales mettenses priores*, ed. Simson, p. 49; *Chron. moiss.*, *MGH, SS* 1:295. The *Chronicle of Benedict of St. Andrea* (ed. Zuchetti, p. 81) says Lombards chose Desiderius to keep Pepin from invading again. Perhaps this attitude conceals an assumption that Pepin played some role. The "Einhard Annals" (ed. Kurze, p. 15) say simply that Desiderius "successit in regnum" and the *Annales regni Francorum* (*anno* 756, ed. Kurze, p. 14) offer the cryptic statement, "Et quomodo et qualiter

Italian affairs at this time,[18] but it may be that because of Fulrad's continuing presence in Italy and participation in the negotiations surrounding Desiderius's succession, later Frankish writers simply assumed a decisive role for Pepin. Moreover, in view of the overlordship established by Pepin in 755 and 756, writers in the north might well have taken it for granted that Pepin had made Desiderius king.[19] In reality, Pepin wanted neither more nor less than peace in Italy, and this had apparently been achieved. Parties in both Rome and Francia had good reason to be content with the surprising turn of events that had seated Desiderius on the Lombard throne.

Stephen left nothing to chance, however. His letter to Pepin, dispatched in March or April 757, is an interesting and revealing document.[20] After a lengthier than usual bit of diplomatic flattery, the pope reminds Pepin of his duty to struggle for the liberation and the security of the people of the Republic. He also tells Pepin to work for the restitution of the "*civitates reliquias*," which Desiderius had just promised him. As far as is known, the Treaties of Pavia had not mentioned these "remaining cities" of formerly Byzantine Italy. Because, presumably, of the Promise of Ponthion, Pepin had incurred, in the pope's mind, the responsibility of defending all territories that the pope might acquire at any time by any means. As one continues reading Stephen's letter, this becomes clear. Stephen recounts in detail the promises made by Desiderius and then enjoins Pepin to make certain that they are carried out. One brief passage in the letter is a bit puzzling, however. The pope tells Pepin to be mindful of fulfilling what is contained "in the pacts confirmed by your goodness." This cannot, in the context, refer to the Pavian treaties, and so it must mean that when Paul, Christophorus, and Fulrad met Desiderius in Tuscany a document (*pactum*) was drawn up. Stephen evidently, and perhaps correctly, saw Fulrad as Pepin's plenipotentiary and therefore went on to assume that Pepin was a full partner to the agreement concluded with Desiderius. It is interesting and important to observe how Stephen sought to win Pepin over to, and then make him guarantor of, the revised territorial situation in Italy.

Stephen's letter to Pepin also contains a startling bit of news. Shortly

---

missus est Desiderius rex in regno, postea dicamus." Unfortunately, the author never returned to the subject. It would, of course, be interesting to know what meaning the author wished "missus est" to bear.

[18]Hartmann, *Geschichte Italiens*, 2.2:207–8.

[19]Holtzmann, *Italienpolitik*, pp. 39–40.

[20]CC, no. 11, pp. 504–7. Gundlach and Jaffé (*RP*, no. 2335) give as the date March or April.

after Aistulf's death the Duchies of Benevento and Spoleto had commended themselves, through Stephen, to Pepin.[21] There is no evidence that Pepin regarded the dukes as his vassals in the strict, feudal sense, or that he had invited them to declare their independence from Pavia.[22] Probably traditional dynamics of Italian politics were at work. Liutprand of Benevento had been loyal to Aistulf, although more out of fear than because of any genuine feeling of allegiance, but now took the separatist path of his predecessors.[23] In Spoleto, which Aistulf had ruled directly from 751 to 756, the death of the king induced the locals to elect a new duke, Alboin.[24] Both of these dukes were, by turning to Rome and to Francia, following very traditional policies but embracing new methods. Stephen, who did nothing to oppose and may have encouraged the ducal strivings for independence, was returning in a way to a policy that reached back to Gregory II. Surely, the pope's willingness to see the duchies detach themselves from the *regnum* was thought of as a security measure directed against Pavia. This measure Stephen strengthened by having the dukes commend themselves to Pepin thereby making the king of the Franks the guarantor of this dismemberment of the Lombard kingdom.[25] This policy in various forms had worked tolerably well in the past and could have been expected to work even better now that Pepin was the pope's protector.

Late in April 757 Stephen died.[26] His pontificate had been an important one for the Republic, but it remained to be seen whether his successors would be able to hold, or perhaps to expand upon, his solid achievements. His brother Paul was elected a few days after his death, but was not consecrated until 29 May.[27] Paul sent a notification of his election to Pepin, using in his letter formulae, drawn from the *Liber Diurnus*, which had formerly been used to inform the exarch of a new election,[28] but the delay between election and consecration cannot be attributed to this correspondence with

---

[21]CC, no. 11, p. 506.

[22]Hartmann, *Geschichte Italiens*, 2.2:244 n.1.

[23]Oelsner, *Jahrbücher*, p. 444; Gasparri, *I duchi longobardi*, pp. 96–98.

[24]Fröhlich, *Thronfolge* 1:238; Brühl, "Chronologie," pp. 46–47; Gasparri, *I duchi longobardi*, pp. 81–82.

[25]Hartmann, *Geschichte Italiens*, 2.2:207; Bertolini, *Roma e i longobardi*, pp. 85–86; Fröhlich, *Thronfolge* 1:237–38.

[26]He was buried 26 April. The time between death and burial was rarely more than a day or two. See: Jaffé, *RP*, p. 277.

[27]Jaffé, *RP*, p. 277.

[28]CC, no. 12, p. 508; cf. *LD*, no. 59, ed. Foerster, pp. 113–14. Hartmann, *Geschichte Italiens*, 2.2:209–10; Seppelt, *Geschichte der Päpste* 2:139.

Francia. The king of the Franks did not possess, and had never claimed, any right to approve papal elections. What is more, Paul did not seek approval from Pepin. He merely informed him of his election and sought to confirm and renew the alliance already concluded between Stephen and Pepin.[29] Paul also sent to Pepin a letter written by "*Omnis Senatus atque Universa Populi Generalitas*" of Rome thanking Pepin for his help in the past and requesting his continued intercession for the Republic.[30] The reason for the delay of several weeks between Paul's election and consecration was that the election itself had been contested. Some people had favored the archdeacon Theophylact whereas "the greater part of the officials and the people" held for Paul.[31] Open and bitter struggles did not last more than a few weeks, and after Paul's consecration whatever opposition there had been to him seems to have collapsed.

Thus far 757 had been a good year for the papacy. Aistulf had died and a seemingly friendlier regime had assumed rule in Pavia. The Republic had been appreciably augmented and a new alliance with Benevento and Spoleto had been established. A change in the see of Peter had not damaged the Franco-papal alliance. The papacy's good fortune continued into the early months of Paul's pontificate when some old problems with Ravenna were composed, and for the first time, the pope was able to exert some genuine influence in the Ravennate. Actually, Stephen and Paul played complementary roles in introducing papal rule into Ravenna, and the process moved through several distinct stages. At various critical junctures our only source is the usually incomprehensible Agnellus who, even when he appears to make sense, was deeply hostile to Rome. Still, the broad outlines of what happened can be discerned.

The story of the introduction of papal rule into Ravenna begins when a married nobleman named Sergius was elected archbishop at Ravenna in, probably, 752. He faced serious domestic opposition and therefore traveled to Rome to seek consecration. He may also have sought some sort of an understanding with Aistulf. This obeisance to Rome, however nominal, caused Sergius further difficulties at home.[32] The archbishops of Ravenna had al-

---

[29]*CC*, no. 13, p. 508.

[30]*CC*, no. 13, pp. 509–10. The letter does not say that Paul had it sent but I consider this a safe assumption. Solmi, *Il senato*, pp. 27–28, believes that this letter is another proof of the continued existence of the Roman Senate but we have already seen that *Senatus* was merely an anachronistic designation for the leading social class at Rome.

[31]*LP* 1:463. Neither *CC* 12 nor *CC* 13 mentions these problems.

[32]Agnellus, *Lib. pont. rav.*, c. 154, *MGH*, *SSrL*, p. 377. Ravennese chronology is difficult

ways been the second personages in their city, and with the demise of the exarch in 751 the position of the archbishop had become paramount.[33] Sergius himself was, as Agnellus suggests, hoping to become the heir of the exarch in Ravenna, and thus he bowed to the pope only to secure the episcopal office.[34] For Stephen to have consecrated Sergius, even under difficult circumstances for the archbishop, was still a considerable gain for the pope precisely because it was a significant concession for the Ravenna prelate to have made.

When it became clear, as a result of the Franco-papal alliance, that Ravenna was not going to remain independent of Rome but would, in fact, be handed over to the pope, Sergius and the Lombard king concluded some sort of alliance.[35] Sergius had never intended to hand himself or his city over to Rome. He needed papal consecration as a means of securing a personal power base at home where he may have suffered further unpopularity for the relationship with Aistulf mentioned by Agnellus. In 755 Stephen visited Ravenna, where plots against his life were hatched. The sources do not say so, but Sergius was almost certainly implicated in these plots. Affairs in Italy were not turning out at all well for Sergius with the decline of Aistulf's power and the enhancement of the pope's. Perhaps Sergius opposed the pope as any patriotic Ravennese would have, or it may be that he was now trying to win the favor of his neighbors. Stephen managed to bring Sergius and a number of other malefactors to Rome and kept them there for two or three years.[36] For the time being Sergius's grand schemes had come to no good end, and the Ravennese had to bow to the pope.

Stephen did not rest content with a chastisement of the archbishop. He also sent to Ravenna a priest, Philippus, and a duke, Eustachius, to take over rule in the old Exarchate on behalf of the Republic.[37] These two officials

---

to establish for the early years of Sergius's career. He could have become archbishop any time between 742 and 752 (See: Holder-Egger's note *Lib. pont. rav.*, p. 377 n.7) but I follow Hodgkin (*The Frankish Invasion*, p. 333) in placing Sergius's accession in 752. Bertolini has written the best and fullest account of Sergius's career, but I cannot accept all of his interpretations: "Sergio, arcivescovo di Ravenna," in his *Scritti scelti* 2:549–91.

[33]Guillou, *Régionalisme*, pp. 166–67; Schmidt, "Ravenna," pp. 749–50.

[34]*Lib. pont. rav.*, c. 159, *MGH, SSrL*, p. 380.

[35]*Lib. pont. rav.*, c. 157, *MGH, SSrL*, p. 379. Hodgkin, *The Frankish Invasion*, pp. 333–38; Fasoli, *Carlomagno*, p. 41.

[36]*Lib. pont. rav.*, c. 157, 158, *MGH, SSrL*, pp. 379–80. Agnellus connects these events with Paul, but it is easy to see that he has made an error on this point. Schmidt, "Ravenna," pp. 749–51, makes pretty good sense of these problems. See also: Bertolini, *Roma e i longobardi*, pp. 87–88.

[37]The term *Exarchate of Ravenna* appears for the first time in papal sources of the mid-

were to oversee the rest of Ravennese officialdom and send all local officials to Rome for their *praecepta actionum*.[38] Agnellus passes on some murky stories about fears in Ravenna that the pope was going to rifle the city's treasury, but one suspects that his account is a garbled narrative of this first introduction of direct papal rule in Ravenna.[39] After Stephen died Paul allowed Sergius to return to Ravenna,[40] and he restored the monastery of St. Hilarion to the Church of Ravenna after Stephen had taken it away.[41] Sergius and Paul got along tolerably well thereafter, and it may be that Paul relaxed somewhat the strict terms of Stephen's provisions for ruling the Exarchate.[42] Nevertheless, in 757 the papacy had for the first time some semblance of genuine authority in a city and region whose inhabitants had long been claimed as the Republic's "lost sheep."

If one were to adopt a vantage point in almost any year between about 680 and 757, it would be difficult to predict the profound peace and security of papal Italy that Stephen and Paul had achieved. But, just as earlier peaces had always proved illusory, this one would too. Popes Stephen and Paul may have been, as Duchesne put it, "the sovereign disposers of Italy,"[43] but Desi-

---

750s as a designation for the city of Ravenna and its immediate surroundings. Technically, of course, the Exarchate of Ravenna included all of Byzantine central and northeastern Italy but the papal usage of the term is the one that has become commonest among historians. See: Hartmann, *Untersuchungen*, pp. 26, 135.

[38]This we learn from a letter of Pope Hadrian I to Charlemagne: *CC*, no. 49, p. 569. The best studies are both by Bertolini: "Gli inizi del governo temporale dei papi sull'esarcato di Ravenna," *Archivio della società romana di storia patria* 89 (1966): 25–35, esp. 29ff, and "Le prime manifestazioni concrete del potere temporale dei papi nell'esarcato di Ravenna," in his *Scritti scelti*, 2:593–612, esp. 601ff. The latter study shows that the pope required of Ravennese officials oaths analogous to those sworn by rectors of the patrimony (p. 606) and refers to *LD*, no. 75, ed. Foerster, pp. 136–37. The comparison is plausible but formula no. 75 is an episcopal *Indiculus*.

The only major point at which I part company with these excellent studies by Bertolini is over his belief that Ravenna still belonged to Byzantium after 755. This is simply not possible, and Bertolini seems to prove the case against himself by his excessively intricate arguments over whether public law or private law was at issue in Stephen's Ravenna program. He correctly concluded that public jurisdiction was taken over by the pope and then tries to explain away this fact which is awkward for his a priori assumptions about Ravenna being Byzantine.

[39]*Lib. pont. rav.*, c. 158, *MGH, SSrL*, p. 380.

[40]*Lib. pont. rav.*, c. 157, *MGH, SSrL*, p. 379. Agnellus implies that Sergius bribed Paul but there is no other evidence for this.

[41]Kehr, *IP*, vol. 5, no. 75, p. 34.

[42]Luther, *Rom und Ravenna*, pp. 52–53; Schmidt, "Ravenna," p. 753; Bertolini, "Gli inizi del governo temporale," p. 35.

[43]Duchesne, *Temporal Sovereignty*, p. 47.

derius was a force to be reckoned with. In the early months of 758 the Italian peace was shattered by the Lombard king. To explain why Desiderius abandoned the irenic policies he had pursued in 757 there are two possibilities. Either he was an unrelenting cynic who wanted the crown so badly that he had been willing to say or do anything to get it, or else he came gradually to the realization that he simply could not tolerate the dismemberment of his kingdom.

In early 758 Paul wrote to Pepin to say that the Lombards, displaying their customary perfidy, had not yet handed over the cities promised in 757. Pepin was asked to intercede to get Desiderius to fulfill his pledges.[44] The tone of the letter is not particularly anxious; it does not seem that conditions in Italy had yet deteriorated badly. A bit later in the year, however, Paul's tone was radically different, and with good reason.

In May 758 Desiderius marched into Spoleto and deposed Duke Alboin, of whom nothing more is ever heard.[45] For about a year Desiderius either ruled Spoleto himself, or had it governed by loyal agents. In April 759 Gisulf was appointed duke and he served in that capacity until mid-761. For another year or so Desiderius ruled the duchy himself and then he introduced Theodicius, who served until 773.[46] Having secured Spoleto in 758, Desiderius swept into Benevento and Duke Liutprand fled to Otranto. Desiderius installed Arichis, who would rule the duchy for thirty years.[47]

The king's subjection of the two rebellious duchies, and his refusal to date to make good on his earlier promises to Stephen, might well have angered Paul, but Desiderius's next step truly flabbergasted the pope. After he had reestablished his authority in Benevento, Desiderius traveled to Naples and met with a Byzantine emissary, George, who had recently visited Francia. Desiderius proposed to him a Lombard-Byzantine alliance whereby he would help the Greeks to recover Ravenna and they would in turn hand over to him Liutprand, the deposed Beneventan duke.[48] Desiderius then marched to Rome and met with Paul to tell him that he genuinely desired peace and

---

[44]CC, no. 14, p. 512.

[45]Oelsner, *Jahrbücher*, p. 442; Brühl, "Chronologie," p. 47; Fröhlich, *Thronfolge* 1:238.

[46]Oelsner, *Jahrbücher*, pp. 442–43; Brühl, "Chronologie," pp. 47–48. For Gisulf's charters see: *RF*, vol. 2, nos. 49–56, pp. 49–55. Nos. 57 and 58 (pp. 55–56) from 762 bear only Desiderius's name. With no. 59 (p. 56) for 763 begins the series of Theodicius's charters. Incidentally, *CC*, no. 17, p. 515, says only that Alboin was taken prisoner. See also: Gasparri, *I duchi longobardi*, pp. 82–84.

[47]*Chronicon salernitanum*, c. 9, ed. Westerbergh, p. 10; *Annales beneventani*, *MGH, SS* 3:173; *Chron. vulturnense*, pp. 154–55. Oelsner, *Jahrbücher*, pp. 444–45.

[48]CC, no. 15, p. 512.

would hand over Imola if Paul would write to Pepin and request repatriation of the Lombard hostages then held in Francia.[49]

Paul in fact wrote three letters to Pepin.[50] One was very brief, only mentioning the Byzantine-Lombard alliance. The second was moderate in tone and inquired about the Lombard hostages. The third was written to cancel the second which, the pope said, he had been compelled to write. Paul's letters show that he judged his position to be perilous in the extreme, but the reality was quite different. Desiderius was moving very cautiously, doubtless to avoid provoking the Franks. He had taken nothing new from the Republic and appeared willing to renegotiate his promises of 757.[51] As to the Byzantines, Desiderius's approach to them actually points out sharply how isolated *he* was. He had to seek allies wherever he could find them. Moreover, the Greeks were in no position to interfere in Italy, but papal paranoia about them was such that Deiderius could conjure mightily with the prospect of an alliance. Paul, it seems, either misunderstood Desiderius's true intentions, or else he was deeply angry at the potential demise of his and his brother's carefully wrought schemes to augment the Republic. The king wanted only a slightly improved settlement than he had contracted in 757, and some assurances that his newly won kingdom would not atomize before his very eyes.

It is necessary to speak in rather general terms about what happened between 759–60 and 764–65. The sequence of events cannot be pinned down precisely, and the motives and policies of the contending parties cannot be established with the degree of certainty that one would like to have. All problems stem from the fact that virtually the only source is the *Codex Carolinus*, or more exactly, about twenty letters from this collection. These letters accurately reflect papal views, but they provide only diffused and filtered glimpses of what Pepin and Desiderius were thinking and doing. Even if details cannot always be established, however, a tolerably accurate picture of the basic issues can be fashioned.

During these five or six years Paul wrote repeatedly to Pepin to ask him to get the Lombards to fulfill their promises. On three occasions Paul wrote to Pepin's sons, Charles and Carlomann, to remind them of their responsibilities to defend the Church.[52] Once the pope wrote to the Franks to praise

---

[49] CC, no. 16, pp. 513–14.

[50] CC, nos. 15, 16, 17, pp. 512–17.

[51] Hartmann, *Geschichte Italiens*, 2.2:212; Seppelt, *Geschichte der Päpste* 2:142. The most thoughtful assessment of Desiderius's motives and objectives between 757 and 765 is Hallenbeck's (*Pavia and Rome*, pp. 85–106) although I cannot accept all of his interpretations.

[52] CC, nos. 26, 33, 35, pp. 530–31, 539–40, 542–43.

them for their zeal on behalf of St. Peter.[53] The tone of Paul's letters is always insistent, but the attentive reader can also detect in them an air of resignation. Rome seems gradually to have realized that Pepin had serious distractions in Francia,[54] and that he was not going to come to Italy to intervene militarily.[55] On several occasions Paul felt compelled to write to Pepin to dispel rumors. In one letter he accused Desiderius of engaging in what we would call today a disinformation campaign.[56] In another letter Paul asked about reports that Pepin would not aid the Church in its hour of need.[57] Finally, Paul had to assure Pepin that he had not lent his personal support to Tassilo, the rebellious Duke of Bavaria and son-in-law of Desiderius.[58] Paul constantly reported on his discussions with Frankish *missi*, and on the work of Lombard and papal *missi*. One gets the clear impression that negotiations of all kinds were going on without rupture. Paul protested continuously and vigorously that he truly wanted peace with Desiderius.[59] Apparently, Pepin, Paul, and Desiderius differed in their views of what was necessary to get peace, but their quest seems to have been genuine and mutual. It should also be noted that Pepin and Paul treated a variety of matters—monastic foundations, felicitations concerning Pepin's youngest child, exchanges of books, commissioning of chant masters, etc.—which had nothing to do with the affairs of the Republic.[60] Some of Paul's letters, then, repeat the ancient litany of Lombard treachery while others show us papal business as usual. Cordial relations between Pepin and Paul persisted throughout, an indication that there were no great tensions between the allies. Pepin also was obviously never very alarmed about Desiderius, and so the latter may not have repre-

---

[53]*CC*, no. 39, pp. 551–52.

[54]From 758 until the end of his reign Pepin campaigned almost without interruption in Saxony and Aquitaine. See: *Annales regni Francorum, annis* 758–68, ed. Kurze, pp. 16–26; *Annales qui dicuntur Einhardi, annis* 758–68, ed. Kurze, pp. 17–27. In *CC*, no. 27, pp. 531–32, Paul expresses concern over Pepin's campaigns in Aquitaine and in *CC*, no. 28, p. 532, Paul notes that Pepin has been busy and hopes that all is going well for him.

[55]Miller, "Papal-Lombard Relations During the Pontificate of Paul I: The Attainment of an Equilibrium of Power in Italy," *Catholic Historical Review* 55 (1969): 370–71.

[56]*CC*, no. 21, pp. 523–24.

[57]*CC*, no. 29, p. 534.

[58]*CC*, no. 36, pp. 545–46. Already in no. 29, p. 534, Paul had told Pepin he would never support his enemies. On Tassilo's rebellion see: *Annales regni Francorum, anno* 763, ed. Kurze, pp. 20–22; *Annales fuldenses, anno* 763, ed. Kurze, p. 7. Reindel, "Zeitalter der Agilolfinger," pp. 127–28; Fröhlich, *Thronfolge* 1:240–41.

[59]*CC*, no. 38, p. 551. Gundlach and Jaffé (*RP*, no. 2369) date this letter 758–67 but I follow Classen (who follows Kehr) in dating it 759–60: "Karl der Große, das Papsttum und Byzanz," p. 541 n.4.

[60]*CC*, nos. 18, 23, 24, 41, 42, pp. 518–19, 526–29, 553–56.

sented a huge threat. In the end it seems that three men were groping about sincerely but a bit blindly for solutions to problems whose contours were not at all clear.

Among all these contradictory and confusing hints and signals, the following issues can be discerned. Desiderius, no more than any of his predecessors, could not allow the separation from his kingdom of Benevento and Spoleto.[61] The king retook the duchies and, after some initial complaints, Paul let the matter drop. Pepin, as far as we know, said nothing about them, which tends to prove that he had had nothing to do with their having commended themselves to him in 757. The question of the cities promised to Stephen II in 757 is more complicated, and at the time proved more intractable. Liutprand had on several occasions seized properties and then restored them promptly. Aistulf achieved truly impressive conquests but they were lost to him, and restored or given to the Republic, within four or five years. The cities promised by Desiderius in 757 represented conquests made as far back as the time of Gregory II. Handing these cities over to the Republic proved difficult because precise boundaries were hard to determine, and because integral restorations would have forced the submission of significant numbers of Lombards to the social and political jurisdiction of the Republic without any safeguards for them.[62] The Roman notion of territoriality of the law was here in sharp conflict with the Germanic idea of personality of the law. Desiderius was not unwilling to work out boundary problems, and to effect some compromise on the legal status of persons, but he wanted to do these things before handing over the cities. Paul evidently wanted the cities first, with a resolution of outstanding problems to follow conveyance.[63] Pepin did send *missi* to try to arrive at an acceptable solution, but neither Desiderius nor Paul would give ground.[64] At one point, Desiderius increased pressure on Rome by seizing Sinigaglia and a *castrum* in Campania, but even these menacing gestures did not move Paul.[65] As Duchesne has put it, Pepin eventually decided that Paul and Desiderius should settle on the basis of *uti possidetis*.[66] Finally, both Paul and Desiderius realized that

---

[61]Bertolini, *Roma e i longobardi*, pp. 85–86; Miller, "Papal-Lombard Relations," pp. 367–68.

[62]See, e.g., CC, no. 19, pp. 519–20.

[63]Hartmann, *Geschichte Italiens*, 2.2:214–15, appears to be the only scholar who has figured this issue out.

[64]CC, no. 19, pp. 519–20.

[65]CC, no. 21, pp. 523–24.

[66]Duchesne, *Temporal Sovereignty*, pp. 55–56.

Pepin was not going to intervene directly in Italy. Paul satisfied himself that the Franks had not abandoned him, and Desiderius became aware that the pope had moderated his claims and that peace could be had on the basis of the Pavian treaties. The promises of 757 became a dead issue, but the Lombard king did grant the pope some territorial concessions in Tuscany, Spoleto, and Benevento.[67] Under the circumstances, this must be understood to mean that some long alienated patrimonies were restored. The crucial point is that peace was maintained.

Paul's *vita* mentions none of this. The official papal view must have been that Paul was a failure because he could neither get nor hold what had been promised to Stephen II. Seppelt argues, quite correctly, that Paul failed only in his maximum schemes, which were too bold in design, but otherwise gained considerably in terms of clarification and consolidation for the territorial structure of the Republic.[68] The major gains of 755–756 were not thrown open to challenge. Miller notes, additionally, that Paul, Pepin, and Desiderius achieved an authentic modus vivendi in Italy and that this was a remarkable accomplishment.[69] All parties did want peace, and they finally had it, but only on the basis of the status quo as in 756.

Another theme that runs through Paul's correspondence is the pope's fear of, one might almost say his obsession with, the Greeks. As we have seen, Desiderius entered into an alliance with the Byzantines in 758, and in 757 Pepin himself had opened a friendly intercourse with them.[70] Paul's anxieties about the Byzantines thus had two bases. On the one hand, he genuinely feared a Greek-sponsored invasion directed against his Republic and led by Desiderius,[71] and on the other hand, he shared his predecessors' aversion to iconoclasm.[72] For a time Paul feared that Pepin might abandon him and that Desiderius might actually help the Greeks to recover some of their losses in Italy. Gradually, however, there emerges in Paul's letters a tone of contentment as he came to the double realization that neither Pepin nor Desiderius would assist in handing him over to the Byzantines[73] and that

---

[67]CC, no. 37, p. 549.

[68]Seppelt, *Geschichte der Päpste* 2:144.

[69]Miller, "Papal-Lombard Relations," p. 375 and passim.

[70]*Annales regni Francorum, anno* 757, ed. Kurze, pp. 14–16; *Fredegarii continuatio,* c. 40, ed. Wallace-Hadrill, p. 109.

[71]CC, nos. 20, 30, 31, pp. 521, 536, 537.

[72]LP 1:464.

[73]This is implicit, not explicit, in the sources. I follow the interpretations of Hartmann (*Geschichte Italiens,* 2.2:215) and Delogu ("Il regno longobardo," pp. 180–84). Hallenbeck's account (see n.51) is helpful as well.

Pepin remained steadfast in his defense of the true faith.[74] Paul knew too that left to their own devices the Byzantines represented no direct threat to him, but if that Constantinopolitan diplomatic acumen which is the true stuff of legend had managed to enlist Desiderius as an ally, or to detach Pepin from Rome, things might have turned out very differently.

Paul died 28 June 767.[75] His pontificate had been in many ways less significant for the Republic than those of his four immediate predecessors. But, then, he never had to face the dire threats which they had encountered. In that sense he was never really tested. In the minor crises—and they were minor even if Paul did not always think so—that filled his pontificate, he acquitted himself well. By his time the existence of the Republic of St. Peter was a fait accompli that no one wished, or was able, to challenge. Paul played the role of a continuator and consolidator, not of a builder. Nonetheless, he played his role well. On his death the Republic was at peace, and if it was no larger than he had found it, it was no smaller either.

A Crisis Inside the Republic

The peace that Paul had managed to achieve proved to be ephemeral. A contested papal election ushered in nearly seven years of turmoil within the Republic itself. On the death of Sergius of Ravenna the old Exarchate loosened its already tenuous ties with the Republic. Desiderius began, perhaps for the first time, to threaten the Republic, and he took Istria, which the papacy had long claimed. Finally, serious doubts began to arise about the ability or willingness of the Franks to come to the Republic's aid in times of peril. It is really astonishing to observe how rapidly Italy degenerated from peace and security to crisis on all fronts. Perhaps, therefore, it is better to argue that the peace of the 760s, although ardently sought by all parties, was laid on unstable foundations and had not resolved the underlying issues that had been disturbing Italy for generations.

As Paul I lay dying at San Paolo fuori le mura, a military potentate from Roman Tuscany, Duke Toto of Nepi, gathered a formidable band of troops and approached Rome. His goal, evidently, was to influence the papal election that was, given Paul's illness, in prospect. The *primicerius* Christopho-

---

[74]This is clear in several letters. No. 36, pp. 544–45, is an especially good example.
[75]Jaffé, *RP*, p. 283.

rus, long one of the most influential Lateran bureaucrats, met Toto and exacted from him a promise not to interfere in the election of a new pope, and not to introduce "rustics" into the city for the purpose of making a disturbance. When Paul finally died, on 28 June, Toto broke his oath, forced his way into Rome by the gate of San Pancrazio, and convoked a meeting of his associates at his house in the city. Working in concourse with his brothers Constantine, Passibo, and Paschal, and supported by troops and "rustics" from Tuscany, Toto had his brother Constantine elected pope, while he himself became Duke of Rome. Bishop George of Praeneste was forced to ordain Constantine, who was then a layman, and a few days later George, along with Bishops Eustratius of Alba and Citonatus of Porto consecrated Constantine pope.[76]

Since the seventh century, the people in the the cities of Italy, but especially Rome and Ravenna, had forged societies composed of clerical and military aristocracies whose interests converged in many ways.[77] During the first seven decades of the eighth century, in Rome, the clerical and military orders had usually worked together harmoniously, not only because their domestic interests converged, but also because they faced common external threats. There had been some minor opposition to the pope by laymen from both Roman Tuscany and Campania in the latter years of the pontificate of Gregory II, but thereafter the clergy and the local nobility had generally cooperated. Once the Byzantine menace to the Republic effectively disappeared, and after Paul and Desiderius concluded peace, tensions long latent burst into the open. Toto's actions in 767 mark the first instance wherein the military aristocracy acted specifically as a result of the certain knowledge that the papal office was the highest one in the Republic, and that control within the Republic was impossible without seizing the papacy.[78] The clerical bureaucracy, with the pope at its head, was larger, wealthier, and more sophisticated than anything that the military aristocracy could, or in fact did, erect to confront it. But, the military potentates possessed power and influence that had to be taken into account and, over the years, there had

---

[76]For basic details we have only the introductory section of the *vita* of Stephen III, Constantine's successor: *LP* 1:468–69. No *vita* of Constantine exists. Some details can be learned from a deposition made before the Roman synod of 769 by Christophorus. These survive in a ninth-century Verona MS published in Mansi, *Concilia* 12:717, and, after Cenni, by Duchesne, *LP* 1:480–81 n.3. For modern reconstructions of events see: Hartmann, *Geschichte Italiens*, 2.2:231–32; Seppelt, *Geschichte der Päpste* 2:147–49.

[77]Rasi, *Exercitus Italicus*, pp. 193, 196; Patlagean, "Les armes et la cité," passim.

[78]A. Hauck, *Kirchengeschichte Deutschlands* 2:72–73; Classen, "Karl der Große, das Papsttum und Byzanz," p. 544; Marcel Pacaut, *La papauté* (Paris, 1978), p. 72.

been a good deal of blending of the lay and clerical orders.[79] Stephen II and Paul I, for example, came from a wealthy, aristocratic family.[80] Toto's role in getting Constantine elected demonstrates the emergence of a new, and potentially at least, highly disruptive factor in the internal life of the Republic: a conflict between the lay and clerical orders for control.

No sooner had Constantine been elected than he wrote to Pepin. He sought to confirm the formal alliances and the personal friendship concluded by his predecessors with the Frankish king. The language of Constantine's letters is marked by the formulaic humility so typical in ecclesiastical, or it might be said in diplomatic, documents generally. Constantine, unwilling and unworthy, had been borne to the lonely and burdensome pinnacle of papal power by the unanimous suffrages of his countrymen.[81] This was, to be sure, an egregious distortion of the truth, but it seems to have evoked no response in Francia. Pepin was still too bogged down in his various military campaigns to concern himself with internal Roman affairs and he had, after all, pursued a laissez-faire policy in Italy throughout the 760s. Moreover, Pepin's apparent failure to register any opinion concerning the events of 767 probably derives as well from the fact that he never saw himself as an emperor or an exarch, and thus he did not regard papal elections as processes in which he had any rights or obligations. Constantine, or at least the Tuscan military, was firmly in control in Rome and it must have seemed to outside observers that nothing was to be done. Conceivably the Franks had little sure information about Roman affairs, but even if they had had a full dossier from Constantine's opponents, we probably ought to suppose that the pope's letters, letters from the vicar of St. Peter, heaven's gatekeeper, would have done much to allay suspicions.

As far as can be determined, Constantine and Toto did not carry out any purges in Rome. Their military control, the weakness of the loyalist duke, Gregory, in Campania,[82] and the fact that the Franks were unwilling to play a role must have either chastened or disheartened Christophorus and his son Sergius, who were the leaders of the Lateran bureaucracy and the chief representatives of the former order. Christophorus and Sergius begged leave to go to Rieti and enter the monastery of St. Savior, and they were permitted to do so. No sooner had they entered Spoletan territory, however,

---

[79]Solmi, *Il senato*, p. 32; Haller, *Das Papsttum* 1:441–42; Partner, *Lands of St. Peter*, pp. 25–26.

[80]Duchesne, *Temporal Sovereignty*, p. 49.

[81]CC, nos. 98, 99, pp. 649–52.

[82]His role is well discussed by Hartmann, *Geschichte Italiens*, 2.2:233.

than they sought to win the good offices of Duke Theodicius with Desiderius. They wanted Desiderius to help them effect the redemption of the *sancta Dei ecclesia.*[83] It is easy in retrospect to argue that the pope and Toto were naive to let Christophorus and Sergius leave Rome. But, in a fairer assessment, there was no reason then to believe that Pepin could be induced to intervene, and no way to have predicted that the most bitterly anti-Lombard man in Rome, and his son, would have turned for help to the ancient enemies of the Republic.

Desiderius must have been both amazed and delighted to have Christophorus appear before him as a suppliant. With no initiative on his part, the Lombard king was afforded an unprecedented opportunity of winning influence in Rome; or so he thought. He instructed Theodicius to supply soldiers to Christophorus and Sergius, and he sent along, as his personal envoy, a Lombard priest named Waldipert. The forces thus assembled headed for Rome, crossed the Tiber, and entered the city through the gate of San Pancrazio, which was opened by the *secundicerius* Demetrius and a *chartularius* Gratiosus, who were, respectively, a Lateran officer and a minor military official. Both were partisans of Christophorus. The account in the *Liber Pontificalis* is not entirely clear, but it seems that after some desultory fighting Toto was killed and Sergius and Waldipert entered the heart of the city and took Constantine captive.[84] By the beginning of August 768 the revolution of 767 was at an end. What would happen next, however, was very much an open question.

Immediately after he had entered the city, Waldipert fetched an obscure priest named Philip from the monastery of St. Vitus and got a few Romans to elect him pope.[85] Certainly this had been accomplished with Desiderius's knowledge, and perhaps on his orders.[86] The possibilities of a Lombard-dominated papacy must have absolutely dazzled the king at Pavia. Christophorus was not, to all appearances, similarly dazzled. In a stunning display of haughtiness he appeared before the city—exactly where he had been during the fighting is not clear—and declared that he would not enter Rome until Philip was removed from the Lateran. Gratiosus and some Romans

---

[83]*LP* 1:469.

[84]*LP* 1:469–70. It is interesting to note that the defeat of Toto and the capture of Constantine are attributed to "huius Romanae urbis militiae iudices." The Lombards are not mentioned in the account of the victory and their role in entering Rome is minimized by calling them timorous and hesitant in the face of Toto's men.

[85]*LP* 1:470–71.

[86]Haller, *Das Papsttum* 1:443; Seppelt, *Geschichte der Päpste* 2:149–50.

thus moved promptly to return Philip to his monastery.[87] Christophorus then entered Rome and assembled a great concourse of lay and clerical dignitaries in the old Roman forum and effected the election as pope of the titular priest of St. Cecilia, Stephen.[88] Apparently the Lateran had triumphed over the laity, and Desiderius's interests had been neatly set aside.

For a short time Rome was the scene of random and gratuitous violence. At Alatri in Campania a tribune, that is, a minor military official, Gracilis, held out for Constantine. The *"universus exercitus Romanae urbis seu Tuscie et Campaniae"* was sent to Alatri, and Gracilis was brought to Rome a prisoner. Quickly some "evil persons" from Campania entered Rome and mutilated Gracilis. In 767 Campania had been loyal but ineffectual under Gregory. In 768, it seems, the area was divided in its allegiance. Shortly after the Gracilis affair a column of troops under Gratiosus went to Cellanova and blinded Constantine. Finally, in the midst of all these difficulties, a rumor spread that Waldipert had entered into a plot with Theodicius and "some Romans" to kill Christophorus. Waldipert was seized and mutilated. He died a few days later.[89] The Lateran had clearly regained the upper hand, but its hand was bloody and its support was far from unanimous.

Stephen III was consecrated 7 August 768,[90] and he immediately sent Sergius to Francia bearing a letter to confirm Franco-papal relations and to invite Pepin to send Frankish bishops to a Roman synod which was to treat the affair of Constantine.[91] On his arrival in Francia, Sergius found that Pepin had died and that Charles and Carlomann were now *reges Francorum*.[92] They agreed to send bishops to Rome for the synod and confirmed the pact of friendship between themselves and the pope.

In just a year Rome had become a very different place. Violence had been used to elect three popes, and unspeakable brutalities had been visited upon the partisans of each successive loser. Such conduct must have gone far toward poisoning the atmosphere in the city, and although Christophorus and his party were back in power their reputations had probably suffered. The countryside, in Campania and especially in Tuscany, was now riven by

---

[87]*LP* 1:471.

[88]*LP* 1:471: "omnes sacerdotes ac primatus cleri et optimates militiae atque universum exercitum et cives honestos, omnes populi Romani coetum, a magno ad parvum." Doubtless this account is wishful thinking and reflects a degree of consensus hoped for but not attained by the Lateran.

[89]*LP* 1:471–73.

[90]Jaffé, *RP*, p. 285.

[91]Jaffé, *RP*, no. 2376; *LP* 1:473. The letter does not survive.

[92]He died 24 September 768: *BM*, no. 115a.

clerical and military factions and even in Rome there were citizens arrayed behind each party. Such turmoil would have been disastrous had there been a serious Lombard threat at the moment, but fortunately Desiderius had thus far contented himself with stealth and subterfuge. Never again, however, would the Republic present a united front to its old enemy, and he knew it.

The years from 769 to 773 were profoundly difficult ones for the Republic. Internal discord continued, threats from the Lombards reappeared, and the nature of the Franco-papal alliance sustained several modifications. These years have been intensively and minutely scrutinized by historians, but little genuine consensus has emerged, and some startlingly exotic interpretations have been advanced. Most of the difficulties that lurk behind all efforts to interpret the events of these years stem from the fact that almost all of the sources are papal and deeply partisan. Partisan here must be understood in two distinct senses. On the one hand, nothing good is said about the Lombards and some plainly erroneous things are said about the Franks. On the other hand, because strife in Rome continued, and because the winners got to write the history, some key facts have been mutilated and others obliterated.

The year 769 opened auspiciously for the Republic. On 12 April[93] a synod of forty-nine bishops, including twelve from Francia, was convoked to deal with the usurpation of Constantine.[94] Predictably the council looked into Constantine's "election" and condemned both it and him.[95] Then the council passed a remarkable decree on papal elections. Henceforth the election was closed to Roman laymen; only the clergy could participate as electors, and only specified clerics were eligible for election. Soldiers from Tuscany and Campania were specifically forbidden to intrude on the electoral process.[96] Christophorus, Sergius, and the Lateran bureaucrats were securely in power. Their candidate, Stephen, was pope and Christophorus's relative, Gratiosus, had succeeded Toto as duke of Rome.[97] As Hartmann astutely observed years ago, the Lateran leaders had decided to develop institutional continuity as a replacement for a less durable continuity based

---

[93]Jaffé, *RP*, p. 285.

[94]For the canons see: *MGH, Conc.* 2.1:74–92. For general discussions: Hartmann, *Geschichte Italiens* 2.2:238–41; Seppelt, *Geschichte der Päpste* 2:151–52; Ullmann, *Papal Government*, pp. 87–88; Harald Zimmermann, *Papstabsetzungen des Mittlelaters* (Graz, 1968), pp. 13–14, 19.

[95]*MGH, Conc.* 2.1:81–86.

[96]*MGH, Conc.* 2.1:86–87.

[97]Ewig, *Handbook*, p. 25; Llewellyn, *Rome in the Dark Ages*, pp. 225–26; Bertolini, *Roma e i longobardi*, pp. 91–92.

solely on the person of the pope.[98] This was, unquestionably, the goal of the Republic's leaders in 769, but the whole policy was flimsy because it did not rest upon a genuine social and political consensus within the Republic.[99] Nothing in the evidence suggests that the *proceres ecclesiae* and *iudices militiae* had been reconciled after the fall of Toto, and in the future violent disturbances would again upset the Republic. For the moment, nevertheless, the clergy had the upper hand.

As if to drive home with particular force the point that Byzantine rule in Rome was at an end, the synod had met "*regnante Domino nostro Jesu Christo.*"[100] One would, in earlier times, have found imperial regnal years instead of this singular expression. Moreover, the council fathers took pains to declare themselves for the veneration of images,[101] and they implored Constantine V to restore them.[102]

The Roman synod, or, more specifically, the list of bishops in attendance, can also tell us something about the extent of papal rule in Italy, and about the current state of the Republic's relations with Desiderius. Several Lombard bishops attended: the bishop of Tortona representing Milan, legates of the bishop of Pavia, and the bishops of Acquapendente, Toscanella, Bagnorea, Populonia, and Luni.[103] Certainly it would have been well within Desiderius's power to prevent the attendance of bishops from his kingdom, so from their presence it may be inferred that the king, despite his rude setback in 768, had not yet openly broken with Rome. Likewise, the papacy seems to have been winning some measure of influence in the *regnum* after a couple of centuries during which the Lombard bishops had had only weak ties with Rome. Legates of the archbishop of Ravenna also appeared, indeed they are given pride of place in the list of participants, along with the bishops of Cesena and Faenza, two cities dependent upon Ravenna.[104] From this it can be deduced that Sergius of Ravenna was still loyal, or at least not openly disloyal, to Rome.[105] The fact that the vast majority of the bishops present came from the immediate environs of Rome demonstrates quite clearly where

---

[98]Hartmann, *Geschichte Italiens*, 2.2:240.

[99]Ullmann, *Papal Government*, pp. 87–88.

[100]*MGH, Conc.* 2.1:79. Classen, "Karl der Große, das Papsttum und Byzanz," p. 545.

[101]*MGH, Conc.* 2.1:87.

[102]Jaffé, *RP*, no. 2337.

[103]For the list: *MGH, Conc.* 2.1:75–76, 80–81, and *LP* 1:474–75. For analysis: Duchesne, *LP* 1:482 n.33.

[104]Sources and analysis in n.103.

[105]Luther, *Rom und Ravenna*, p. 53.

the real strength of the Republic was to be found: in Rome and its suburbs, Roman Tuscany, and Campania.[106]

Roman affairs were no sooner settled than there appeared a fresh problem in Ravenna. Sergius died 8 August 769[107] and a contested election ensued. The Ravennese archdeacon, Leo, was apparently properly elected but could not assume his see because Duke Maurice of Rimini, with the aid of Desiderius, got the layman Michael, a *scrinarius* of Ravenna, elected and seated. Michael, Maurice, and the *iudices Ravennantium*, that is, the leading laymen of the city, wrote to Pope Stephen and offered him gifts to consecrate Michael. Stephen refused and Michael redirected his largesse to Desiderius, thereby reducing Ravenna to poverty according to the papal account.[108]

Several things are interesting and significant about these events in Ravenna. First, it is obvious that Sergius's truce with Rome went to the grave with him. This is not so much evident from the contested election itself as from the role played in it by the aristocracy of Ravenna. Second, as Hartmann saw, the role of Duke Maurice in Ravenna almost exactly parallels that of Toto in Rome.[109] Rome and Ravenna had had roughly similar historical developments during the last century. In both cities there were military and clerical elites whose interests converged in the face of Lombard or Byzantine hostilities but who now found themselves, with real or potential external threats much diminished, in confrontation with one another.[110] In each city the immediate aftermath of the demise of Byzantine rule had been an ascendancy of the clerical order and now, in both, the lay order was asserting itself. Third, it is particularly interesting to observe Desiderius's role in Ravenna. He had just been rebuffed in Rome in 768, and so he now turned to another important Italian city in an effort to insinuate his influence. Although we have no report of a Ravennese counterpart to Waldipert, the cases are otherwise remarkably similar. Each time, parties within the cities appealed to Desiderius for help, and each time he answered the call. In neither case, it should be noted, did Desiderius manage to draw any long-term advantages. In Rome it had been the clerical party, whereas in Ravenna it was the laymen, who emitted the cry for help. Still, the parallels are striking

---

[106]Armbrust, *Territoriale Politik*, pp. 56–57.

[107]Luther, *Rom und Ravenna*, p. 53.

[108]*LP* 1:477; CC, no. 85, p. 621. See: Luther, *Rom und Ravenna*, pp. 53–54; Schmidt, "Ravenna," p. 753; Hodgkin, *The Frankish Invasion*, pp. 339–40.

[109]Hartmann, *Geschichte Italiens*, 2.2:242–43.

[110]The best concise analysis of Ravennese development is Brown, "The Church of Ravenna and the Imperial Administration," pp. 1–28, which deals with much more than its title suggests.

and it is impossible to escape the conclusion that Desiderius was trying to make himself arbiter of those parts of central Italy not already in his grasp.

Intrigue was not the only device used by Desiderius in 769, however. At about the same time that he was abetting Michael of Ravenna, Desiderius marched into Istria. Everything that can be known about this affair comes from a letter of John of Grado to Stephen and two letters of the pope, one of them to John and the other to the bishops of Istria.[111] Lands of the Church of Grado had been occupied and Istrian bishops were being impeded from carrying out their duties. Although Desiderius did send troops into Istria, it does not seem that he attempted an outright conquest. Thus it may be that, here again, he was only trying to become arbiter of the region's fortunes. Stephen promised to bring solace to John and his suffragans, but this promise turned out to be a hollow one for reasons that no one could have foreseen at the moment.

By the end of 769 the pope's position was unclear, and dangerous to the very extent that it was unclear. The Roman end of the Republic was peaceful, and for the time being at least, safely under the control of the Lateran. How long this would last, however, was anyone's guess. At the Ravennese end of the Republic losses had been suffered. The key city of Ravenna, and, in its region, the important city of Rimini which could dominate the Pentapolis, were in hostile hands. This was serious in itself, but matters were complicated by Desiderius's involvement. Moreover, Desiderius had in some fashion involved himself in Istrian affairs, and this was a region long claimed but never yet ruled by the Republic. In 768 the Lombard king had tried to take control of Rome through the ploy of getting a Lombard-controlled pope. He had failed in this effort but then used the next year or so to make important gains at the expense of the Republic in northeastern Italy. What now was to prevent him from turning back to Rome? Presumably the kings of the Franks, St. Peter's protectors, but there were also problems on that front, perhaps, actually, the most serious ones Stephen was then facing.

Late in 769, or early in 770, Stephen wrote to Charlemagne and Carlomann to say that he had learned that the brothers were having difficulties, and to express his hope that they would settle their differences amicably. There is a genuinely pastoral tone in the letter, but a practical one as well. Stephen desired peace in Francia so that the brother kings could effectively demand the *iustitiae* of St. Peter from the Lombards.[112] This can only refer

---

[111]*Epp. Lang.*, nos. 19–21, MGH, EKA 3:711–15; cf. Kehr, *IP*, vol. 7, pt. 2, nos. 24ff, pp. 39ff.

[112]*CC*, no. 44, pp. 558–60. For a very different interpretation and chronological reconstruction of the following events see: Hallenbeck, *Pavia and Rome*, p. 113ff.

to Desiderius's recent incursions into Ravenna and perhaps Istria, for the Republic had not otherwise raised any territorial claims against the Lombard king since the Paulician peace of the mid-760s, and Stephen had told John of Grado he would appeal to the Franks concerning Istria. It may also be that, although the evidence from the Roman synod of 769 shows that the zone of the Republic's effective control was limited to the environs of Rome, the papacy had not abandoned the maximum territorial schemes of the 750s. One may doubt that Stephen's use of *iustitiae* refers in any way to the Quierzy document, but it is possible that he was reverting to Desiderius's promises of 757. Or, it may be that the pope was claiming Istria as a "right" of St. Peter. Bertolini takes this letter to be evidence that Christophorus and Sergius, the former of whom had been a "maximum-schemer" back in the 750s, were still very much in control in Rome.[113] I agree, but I still cannot say for certain what lands were being referred to in this letter. The hand of Christophorus can also be seen behind the next letter sent into Francia, a letter which reveals a dawning awareness of the full and potentially horrible implications for the Republic of the current squabbles beyond the Alps.

In what must count as one of the most exquisitely intemperate letters ever written, Stephen expressed his utter shock and dismay at a rumor that the Franks were about to conclude a marriage alliance with the Lombards.[114] The pope omits no term of opprobrium, no invective, in his description of the "vile and pestiferous" Lombards. The king is characterized as a total wretch undeserving of Frankish friendship, and the Franks are reminded of many evil consequences that would inevitably attend their proposed pact with the Lombards. The letter makes it clear that Stephen did not know who was to marry whom, so it must have been written in an atmosphere of rumor and deep anxiety. The pope's language—it may be Christophorus's— surely appears excessive, but his concern was eminently sensible. If the Franks gave up their protectorate over the Republic and traded it for a Lombard alliance, then, given Desiderius's recent behavior and the conduct of his predecessors, the Republic was finished.

What, exactly, was going on in Francia? To answer this question fully would take us deep into some intricacies of Carolingian history that possess only marginal relevance for the history of the Republic. But, precisely because the pope was deeply concerned about developments in the *regna Francorum*, and also because those developments, however dimly perceived or

---

[113]Bertolini, "Carlomagno e Benevento," pp. 610–11.

[114]Einhard, *Vita Karoli*, c. 3, ed. Halphen, p. 14; *Fredegarii continuatio*, cc. 53, 54, ed. Wallace-Hadrill, pp. 120–21.

understood in Rome, would severely impinge on the Republic's freedom of action, we must turn to the north.

When Pepin died in 768 he divided his kingdom between his two sons. The sources provide conflicting pictures of who received what, but patient efforts by scholars have disentangled most of the problems posed by the evidence.[115] Each son received a capital in Neustria, but Carlomann obtained a relatively compact block of lands in the center of the *regnum*, while Charlemagne inherited a strip of territory that formed a wide arc around his brother's possessions. Carlomann's holdings bordered on Bavaria and Italy, two areas that had recently been troublesome for the Franks. Charlemagne, however, received the lands in Francia, especially Saxony and Aquitaine, that had been most bothersome to Pepin. From October of 768 until at least April of 769, when they jointly sent delegates to the Roman synod, the brothers were on good terms. Sometime during the summer of 769 Carlomann met Charlemagne at Duasdives in Poitou and there refused to lend aid for a campaign in Aquitaine.[116] From this time forward the two brothers were openly hostile to one another and, as we have seen, news of this hostility reached Rome.[117] In early 770, perhaps in March, the queen mother, Bertrada, visited Carlomann at Selz to try to mediate peace between her sons.[118] She then passed through Bavaria, to Pavia, and on to Rome. In the course of her travels she effected a fundamental realignment of the diplomatic structure of continental Europe. She managed to get peace between Tassilo of Bavaria and Charlemagne, and to institute a marriage alliance between the latter and Desiderius by the terms of which Charlemagne would marry a daughter of the Lombard king. Since Tassilo was already married to another daughter of Desiderius, Bertrada's scheme put together a neat coalition of the three rulers.[119] Against whom was this coalition aimed?

---

[115]A. Kroeber, "Partage du royaume des Francs entre Charlemagne et Carlomann Ier," *BEC* 20 (1856): 341–50; Sigurd Abel and Bernhard Simson, *Jahrbücher des fränkischen Reiches unter Karl dem Grossen*, 2 vols., 2d ed. (Leipzig, 1883–88), 1:23–30; Halphen, *Charlemagne*, pp. 41–42.

[116]*Annales regni Francorum, anno* 796, ed. Kurze, p. 28; *Annales qui dicuntur Einhardi, anno* 769, ed. Kurze, p. 29. The most insightful interpretation of the meeting at Duasdives remains: Martin Lintzel, "Karl der Große und Karlmann," *HZ* 140 (1929): 2–6.

[117]The sources are late and lay the hostility at the feet of Carlomann's supporters. This is not impossible, but it should be remembered that we owe these accounts to partisans of Charlemagne: Einhard, *Vita Karoli*, c. 3, ed. Halphen, p. 14; *Annales qui dicuntur Einhardi, anno* 769, ed. Kurze, p. 29.

[118]*Annales qui dicuntur Einhardi, anno* 770, ed. Kurze, p. 31: "locuta pacis causa."

[119]Reindel, "Zeitalter der Agilolfinger," pp. 130–31; Abel and Simson, *Jahrbücher* 1:65ff; Hartmann, *Geschichte Italiens* 2.2:251; Lintzel, "Karl und Karlmann," pp. 9–10.

Carlomann seems the obvious candidate, and ever since the mid-ninth century this has been accepted as true.[120] Probably the whole plan was a consequence of Bertrada's inability to restore good relations between her sons when she saw Carlomann at Selz. Until Bertrada got to Rome, however, and explained herself to Stephen, it is easy to see how this coalition, or the first faint news of its formation, would have moved Stephen to draft the vicious letter number 45 of the *Codex Carolinus*. In Rome no conclusion seemed possible except that in Francia political tensions had been resolved in such a way as to rupture the Franco-papal alliance and replace it with a Franco-Lombard bond at the very time when Desiderius was up to his old tricks in Ravenna and Istria. The very survival of the Republic must have seemed doubtful before Bertrada got to Rome. Indeed, Stephen's fear was so great that he dispatched a letter to Carlomann alone in which he expressed his desire to stand as *compater* for Carlomann's newborn son, Pepin.[121] Since the 750s all papal letters to Francia, except for those to the Frankish magnates, had been addressed to Pepin and his sons, and since 768 to Charlemagne and Carlomann jointly. Stephen was desperate, but he must also have been in possession of a little more news about the new diplomatic coalition because, realizing that it was directed against Carlomann, he wrote to him.

When Bertrada arrived in Rome she was able to persuade Stephen that Charlemagne's Lombard alliance was not a threat to the Republic.[122] She also brought news that, as the price of friendship with the Franks, Desiderius had promised to make restitutions to St. Peter.[123] She also offered the pope Charlemagne's services to settle the recent problems in Ravenna, and to recover some long-lost papal patrimonies in the Duchy of Benevento. Charlemagne actually delivered on both of these counts. A count named Hugbald seized Michael of Ravenna and took him to Rome, thus making possible the

---

[120]Andrea of Bergamo (*Historia*, c. 3, MGH, SSrL, p. 223) was the first, in the ninth century, to report that the alliance was directed against Carlomann. See also: Lintzel, "Karl und Karlmann," pp. 9–11; Holtzmann, *Italienpolitik*, pp. 41–42; Etienne Delaruelle, "Charlemagne, Carloman, Didier et la politique du mariage franco-lombard (770–771)," *Revue historique* 170 (1932): 213–17, believes that Bertrada worked consistently to reconcile her sons. This point of view cannot be squared with the evidence.

[121]To arrive at this interpretation, I follow Lintzel, "Karl und Karlmann," p. 14 n.1, in dating CC, no. 47, pp. 565–66, after no. 45 and before nos. 46 and 48. Both Jaffé and Gundlach date no. 47 770–71. In fact, it must be 770, but before Bertrada got to Rome, and after the first rumors began circulating about Charlemagne's Lombard marriage plans.

[122]Seppelt, *Geschichte der Päpste* 2:153–54; Delaruelle, "Mariage franco-lombard," p. 17.

[123]*Ann. laurr.*, MGH, SS 1:30; *Chron. moiss.*, MGH, SS 1:295.

consecration of the papally approved candidate Leo.[124] Another Frankish *missus*, Itherius, secured the restitution of the Beneventan patrimonies.[125] Stephen's worst fears were not realized, and during the last half of 770 a new and potentially more solid peace had descended upon Italy. Charlemagne and Carlomann remained unreconciled, but Charlemagne was by far the stronger of the two and for the time being at least he was the Republic's proven ally. He was also of course Desiderius's ally, but the Lombard king was then behaving himself and Stephen had every reason to believe that Charlemagne was, at least in part, responsible for Desiderius's good conduct. In the course of a year Stephen's perception of the political constellation around his Republic had undergone a radical transformation. In spite of his earlier fears, the pope must have seen the new state of affairs as a decided improvement over the former one.

Perhaps Stephen had only made a virtue of necessity. Certainly he had no realistic alternative except to fall in line with Bertrada's new diplomatic alignments. Still, those realignments had serious repercussions within the Republic. They alienated Christophorus and his party, who, apart from a brief eclipse in 768, had for at least fifteen years directed Lateran policy.[126] That policy had been based on close alliance with the Franks for the principal purpose of bringing maximum pressure to bear upon the Lombards. An acceptance of Frankish peace with the Lombards was the very antithesis of everything that Christophorus stood for. Stephen cannot have been ignorant of the implications of Bertrada's plans for influential circles in the Lateran. Thus it seems reasonable to suggest that in 770 Stephen, for the first time, asserted himself as the Republic's true leader. The traditional view of Stephen is that he was a weak and easily dominated man. Recently Hallenbeck has reviewed the evidence and pronounced the old verdict unjust.[127] Indeed, Charlemagne and Bertrada provided Stephen with an opportunity, which he rapidly seized, to become his own man.

Under the circumstances, freedom of action for Stephen meant freedom from Christophorus and Sergius. Early in 771 Stephen wrote to Charlemagne that these men, along with a *missus* of Carlomann named Dodo, were plotting against him.[128] It appears that Christophorus and Sergius were

---

[124]*LP* 1:477–78; *CC*, no. 85, p. 621. Luther, *Rom und Ravenna*, pp. 53–54; Schmidt, "Ravenna," p. 753. Duchesne, *LP* 1:484 n.55, dates this late 770.

[125]*CC*, no. 46, p. 564. Bertolini, "Carlomagno e Benevento," pp. 610–11; Classen, "Karl der Große, das Papsttum und Byzanz," p. 546.

[126]Bertolini, *Roma e i longobardi*, p. 89; Haller, *Das Papsttum* 1:443.

[127]Hallenbeck, "Pope Stephen III: Why Was He Elected?" *AHP* 12 (1974): 287–99.

[128]*CC*, no. 48, p. 566.

as isolated in Rome as Carlomann was in Francia. This made them natural allies. In Lent of 771[129] Desiderius approached Rome, ostensibly to pray but actually to meet with Stephen to discuss their common enemies, Christophorus and Sergius.[130] While the pope and king were meeting at St. Peter's, Christophorus and his son closed the gates of the city. Presumably they were defending Rome against the Lombards, but it looks as though in reality they were trying to pressure Stephen into an anti-Lombard position. Stephen did make representation to Desiderius about the lands he had promised Bertrada to restore, but nothing came of this. Stephen then asked his opponents to come to him, and to enter into monasteries. The pope did not want a bloody purge, but he did desire an end to the influence of Christophorus and Sergius. The two held out for a time, but slowly Rome, at least some prominent Romans, turned against them. Their cause hopeless, they finally went to St. Peter's to turn themselves over to the pope. Instead, Desiderius seized them and turned them over to his henchman in Rome, a new figure on the scene, Paul Afiarta. While these events were taking place, Stephen felt himself to be in Desiderius's debt and wrote accordingly to Charlemagne.[131] At length, however, Stephen's attitude changed. He had continued pressing Desiderius for restorations, and finally the Lombard king told him that it was enough that he had helped him to get rid of Christophorus and Sergius "who were dominating him" and that questions about restorations should be set aside.[132]

Two developments here call for comment. First, it is almost amusing to watch the rise and fall of Desiderius's stock in Rome. Stephen II called him a "beloved son." Paul I and Stephen III had employed less flattering adjectives, some of them suggesting both literally and figuratively that Desiderius did not smell very good. Then Stephen III decided that Desiderius was beloved again only to change his mind in a short time. Second, the frustratingly thin dossier of evidence on Roman affairs between 767 and 771 makes it impossible to understand how Christophorus could have been firmly in the saddle in 767, unhorsed later in that year, remounted in 768, and then retired for good in 771.

Paul Afiarta took Christophorus and Sergius from St. Peter's into Rome

---

[129]Jaffé, *RP*, p. 287.

[130]Delaruelle, "Politique du mariage," pp. 218–19. The following account is drawn primarily from *LP* 1:478–80. Halphen studied all the sources for these events and concluded that, although not without problems, the *LP* version is the best: "La papauté et le complot lombard de 771," in his *A travers l'histoire du moyen âge*, pp. 51–57.

[131]*CC*, no. 48, p. 566.

[132]*LP* 1:487.

and there they were blinded. Christophorus died three days later but Sergius lived on for almost another year.[133] Thus had ingloriously ended two distinguished Lateran careers.[134] Desiderius had gotten rid of his two most implacable foes in Rome, and had done so, to all seeming, as the pope's ally. What Desiderius had failed to achieve in 768 now seemed to have been won by him. He had a foothold in the city. Stephen, as succeeding events will show, had merely traded masters. He was now under the tutelage of Paul Afiarta, an unscrupulous and ambitious minor officeholder, who may have wished to become pope, or who may, with Desiderius's aid, have been content to be the power behind the papal throne.[135] Usually it is argued that Stephen was victimized by a "Lombard party" in Rome.[136] Actually, there is no certain evidence that such a party existed, and it is difficult to see how one could have existed.[137] The Republic had long had, of course, a violently anti-Lombard party led by Christophorus and Sergius. There was also a party that accepted the peaceful diplomatic realignment arranged by Bertrada. Finally, there were unsavory characters like Paul Afiarta whose only allegiance was devoted to the advancement of their own careers. The events of 770–71 indicate, therefore, the extent to which the poisoned atmosphere and factional strife of 767–68 had persisted, and had grown more complex. The Republic was lurching from crisis to crisis. Desiderius had not fulfilled his promises of 770, and now he had an agent in Rome. Moreover, there was a rumor circulating that Carlomann was contemplating a campaign in Italy.[138] He lacked the wherewithal to do any such thing, but the rumor about his intentions is reflective of the perilous position in which the Republic imagined itself to be.

Late in 771 Paul Afiarta imprisoned or sent into exile a number of people who, we may confidently assume, had been partisans of Christophorus and Sergius.[139] Evidently Paul was attempting to remove all opponents to his

---

[133]*LP* 1:480.

[134]The fullest study of these tangled problems is Bertolini, "La caduta del primicerio Cristoforo (771) nelle versioni dei contemporanei e le correnti antilangobarde e filolangobarde in Roma alla fine del pontificato di Stefano III (771–72)," in his *Scritti scelti* 1:19–61. I do not agree with all of Bertolini's conclusions.

[135]The best study is Hallenbeck, "Paul Afiarta and the Papacy: An Analysis of Politics in Eighth-Century Rome," *AHP* 12 (1974): 22–54.

[136]A. Hauck, *Kirchengeschichte Deutschlands* 2:80–83; Seppelt, *Geschichte der Päpste* 2:159. Examples could be multiplied.

[137]Hallenbeck, "The Lombard Party in Eighth-Century Rome: A Case of Mistaken Identity," *Studi medievali*, 3d series, 15 (1974): 951–66.

[138]*LP* 1:487.

[139]*LP* 1:486–87.

complete assumption of behind-the-scenes rule. Stephen disappears entirely from the sources until his death in early 772. Whatever the pope's ultimate intentions may have been, Paul Afiarta was effectively governing the Republic during the latter months of 771 and the first weeks of 772.

North of the Alps politics began changing again in 771 in ways that would bear significantly on the Republic. The key fact is that, in late summer or early fall of 771, Charlemagne repudiated his Lombard bride.[140] Obviously this action signaled an end of the Franco-Lombard alliance, but less obvious are the reasons why Charlemagne sent Desiderius's daughter back to her father. Perhaps he disliked the passive Italian policy to which Bertrada's diplomacy had committed him. Maybe he took umbrage at Desiderius's and Paul Afiarta's high-handed conduct in Rome. Possibly he had at last so weakened and isolated Carlomann that he no longer needed allies against him. Finally, we do have a report that Carlomann fell ill in the summer of 771, and Charlemagne may have had reason to anticipate his brother's imminent decease.[141] Lacking firm testimony we can only speculate about Charlemagne's reasons for breaking his Lombard connection. It is enough to realize that by mid-771 Charlemagne and Desiderius were no longer allies.

Carlomann did die on 4 December, and the magnates of his kingdom immediately went over to Charlemagne.[142] Gerberga, Carlomann's widow, and her children fled to Desiderius, and so as 771 closed, the political situation outside the Republic cleared up considerably. Charlemagne, now unopposed in Francia and demonstrably friendly to Rome, and Desiderius, now insinuating his influences into the Republic, were openly hostile. A traditional policy of Franco-papal alliance against the Lombard king appeared to be in order, but with Desiderius's protegé Paul Afiarta seemingly in control, it was not clear that such a policy could be implemented.

Stephen III died 24 January 772[143] and Hadrian I was elected and consecrated, apparently without violence or opposition, on, respectively, 1 and

---

[140]There is consensus that Charlemagne and Desiderius's daughter were married in late summer or early fall of 770: Abel and Simson, *Jahrbücher* 1:65ff, 94ff; Hartmann, *Geschichte Italiens* 2.2:251; A. Hauck, *Kirchengeschichte Deutschlands* 2:75. Einhard (*Vita Karoli*, c. 18, ed. Halphen, p. 54) says Charlemagne repudiated her after one year. For a substantial but not especially original study of this whole problem see: Mikel V. Ary, "The Politics of the Frankish-Lombard Marriage Alliance," *AHP* 19 (1981): 7–26. Generally speaking I agree with Ary's conclusions but I disagree with the premises upon which they rest. In particular, my reading of Bertrada's role differs from his.

[141]The various possibilities are discussed by Lintzel, "Karl und Karlmann," p. 17ff; Delaruelle, "Politique du mariage," p. 214ff.

[142]*Annales regni Francorum*, anno 771, ed. Kurze, p. 32.

[143]Jaffé, *RP*, p. 288.

9 February.[144] Hadrian came from an old and prominent family of the military aristocracy. His family's lands were located in Roman Tuscany, near those, it ought to be noted, of the late Toto of Nepi. In the city, Hadrian's family had holdings in the Via Lata region where other important military aristocrats had possessions. The new pope's parents had died while he was young and he had been reared by an uncle, Theodotus, who had been duke of Rome before 755 and who became *primicerius* of the notaries under his nephew.[145] Hadrian's election, therefore, sheds light on the events of late 771. First, it is clear that Paul Afiarta's position was not impregnable. Probably he had no real body of supporters behind him and relied primarily on Desiderius's influence. Second, Paul's purges had not fully eliminated those who had once supported the policies, if not necessarily the persons, of Christophorus and Sergius. The military aristocracy had always been anti-Lombard and Hadrian's election, because he came from this class, proves that its influence had not been rooted out. Because of the election decree of 769, moreover, it is possible to argue for a considerable absorption into the Lateran bureaucracy of men from the military order. These very people had to have been Hadrian's electors. The new election created for the first time since 767 a potential social and political consensus in Rome. Hadrian was a Lateran careerist *and* a military aristocrat. His elevation to the leadership of the Republic was a crucial step towards domestic peace after several years of chaos.[146]

Hadrian's first official act as pope was to recall from exile the people *"tam de clero quam de militia"* who had been dismissed by Paul Afiarta. The new pope also opened the jails.[147] These actions can only have been

---

[144]Jaffé, *RP*, p. 289.

[145]*LP* 1:486. Ewig, *Handbook*, p. 56; Bertolini, *Roma e i longobardi*, pp. 105–6; Duchesne, *LP* 1:514 nn.1,2.

[146]Much nonsense has been written about Hadrian's election and its implications for Roman politics. The sanest account is David S. Sefton, "Pope Hadrian I and the Fall of the Kingdom of the Lombards," *Catholic Historical Review* 65 (1979): 207, 209–10, 214–15, 219–20. But see also: Bertolini, *Roma e i longobardi*, p. 105; Classen, "Karl der Große, das Papsttum und Byzanz," pp. 548–49. A. Hauck, *Kirchengeschichte Deutschlands* 2:83, sees Hadrian's election as a victory of the Frankish party over the Lombard party. Neither of these "parties" existed. Mohr, *Charakteristik des Königtums*, pp. 72–86, believes that Hadrian was originally a member of the Lombard party and then switched sides. To "prove" this contention he challenges the authenticity of the early chapters of Hadrian's *vita*. Löwe ("Zur Vita Hadriani," *DA* 12 [1956]: 493–98) compellingly vindicates Hadrian's *vita* from Mohr's attack. Hallenbeck once argued that the Lombard party was so strong in early 772 that Hadrian's election must have been a coup d'état: "The Election of Pope Hadrian I," *Church History* 37 (1968): 261–70. In light of his own later work I suspect Hallenbeck no longer holds this view.

[147]*LP* 1:486–87.

designed to embarrass Paul and to remove the last vestiges of his influence. Sometime after the middle of February envoys from Desiderius appeared in Rome seeking peace and friendship. Hadrian stated that he wished to live in harmony with all Christians, and that Desiderius could have peace at any moment on the basis of the Treaties of Pavia. The pope went on to say that the king had defrauded Stephen, and he blamed him for the murders of Christophorus and Sergius. At a bare minimum, Hadrian said, Desiderius would have to fulfill his promises to Stephen III if he truly desired peace. To negotiate on this matter Hadrian sent to Pavia the *sacellarius* Stephen and Paul Afiarta.[148] Hadrian must have had a sublime sense of the ironic to have sent Paul Afiarta to his patron to demand territorial concessions!

Hadrian's envoys had traveled only as far as Perugia when the pope learned that Desiderius had seized Faenza, Ferrara, and Comacchio. Within two more months Ravenna itself was threatened and Archbishop Leo wrote to Hadrian imploring his help. Desiderius, meanwhile, insolently stated that he would return nothing until Hadrian came to see him. The Lombard king was harboring Gerberga and her sons. He wanted Hadrian to anoint the boys kings of the Franks "desiring to foment division in the kingdom of the Franks and to separate the most blessed pontiff from the love and affection of the most excellent King Charles, and to subject the city of Rome and all of Italy to his Lombard kingdom."[149] Desiderius was no fool, and his plan was well conceived. It failed in the end because he could neither coerce nor cajole Hadrian into submitting to it. Paul, meanwhile, continued to display his true colors by telling Desiderius that he could force Hadrian to appear before him.[150]

In all probability Hadrian had assigned Paul his mission only to get him out of Rome. While Paul was absent evidence began accumulating on his role in the deaths of Christophorus and Sergius. Hadrian decided to open a full inquest into Sergius's death, but he feared Paul would learn of this and flee. The pope therefore sent Julian, a tribune, to Leo of Ravenna with instructions that Paul should be captured and held at Ravenna or Rimini.[151]

At Rome Hadrian's inquest turned up the fact that two clerics and a tribune, all of them from Anagni, had by night taken the already blinded Sergius out into the Campanian countryside eight days before Stephen's death. Thus had he met his end. They were asked who gave them their

---

[148]*LP* 1:487. For chronology: Jaffé, *RP*, p. 289.

[149]*LP* 1:487–88; *Pauli continuatio tertia*, c. 48, *MGH, SSrL*, p. 212; *Pauli continuatio romana*, c. 6, *MGH, SSrL*, p. 201.

[150]*LP* 1:489.

[151]*LP* 1:489.

orders and they answered Paul Afiarta, a regional *defensor* named Gregory, and Duke John. Hadrian turned the murderers over to the urban prefect for trial, and eventually they were sent to Constantinople.[152]

The pope now had the bodies of Christophorus and Sergius ceremoniously reinterred at St. Peter's. Their rehabilitation was posthumous but complete. Full particulars were sent to Leo of Ravenna along with further instructions that Paul should be sent into exile in Greece "via Venice, or via someplace else, however it could be arranged." Leo said he could not send Paul to Venice because Desiderius was then holding Duke Maurice's son prisoner and Maurice would merely exchange Paul for him. Leo believed that Paul should be killed. This was not a deeply pastoral position for the archbishop to have taken, but it should be remembered that in 769–70 Leo had been deprived of his see, at least in part, because of Lombard chicanery in Ravenna. Leo had very little affection for the likes of Paul Afiarta. Hadrian then sent envoys, again a cleric and a layman, to Ravenna to bring Paul back to Rome. On their arrival in Ravenna, they discovered that Paul was dead.[153] Hadrian did not wish to make a martyr of Paul and to give thereby to Desiderius a pretext for further troublemaking. Leo was bound neither by scruples nor by higher policy considerations.

Desiderius, meanwhile, still refused to restore the lands he had captured, and he would not fulfill his earlier promises to Stephen. Sometime during the early months of 772 Hadrian wrote to Charlemagne, but as far as can be determined, nothing came of his appeal for help against Desiderius.[154] Although the tempo of events in late 772 cannot be established, it is certain that Hadrian kept seeking an end to the impasse in Italy. Desiderius's response to continual papal pressure was the seizure of Sinigaglia, Jesi, Montefeltro, Urbino, Gubbio, and "other cities of the Romans."[155] In early 773 he sent the army of Tuscany to Blera and caused the deaths of a number of nobles in that frontier city. Subsequently Desiderius's troops carried their devastations all the way to the outskirts of Rome. Hadrian wrote repeatedly to Desiderius, to no avail, and he sent at least two impressive delegations to the Lombard king. Abbot Probatus of Farfa was sent, and he was followed a short time later by Pardus, *higoumen* of St. Saba, and Anastasius, the *primus defensorum*. Desiderius continued to demand that Hadrian come out

---

[152]*LP* 1:489–90.

[153]*LP* 1:490–91.

[154]Jaffé, *RP*, no. 2396, says "perhaps in February." This is possible, but the letter may have been sent a few weeks, or even months, later.

[155]*LP* 1:491; *Pauli continuatio tertia*, c. 49, *MGH, SSrL*, p. 212.

to meet him, while the pope adamantly insisted that Desiderius would first have to retreat from Rome and make full restitutions.[156]

Perhaps in April 773 Hadrian again appealed to Charlemagne.[157] His envoys had to travel by sea because Desiderius had by then declared a general mobilization of his forces and, with Gerberga and her children in tow, headed for Rome. Without waiting to see whether his most recent appeal to Charlemagne would have any effect, Hadrian called out the troops of the Duchy of Rome, of Perugia, and of the Pentapolis. He intended to defend the Republic as best he could. He also sent a delegation of three bishops to Viterbo with a bull of anathema for Desiderius.[158] Surprisingly, that gambit caused the king to back off, but he did not restore an inch of land and he retained Gerberga and her children. Hadrian had achieved a momentary truce, but the situation demanded a definitive resolution.[159]

In Francia, Charlemagne received the pope's emissaries, and he called for an assembly of the Franks. He won a favorable decision for a campaign in Italy, assembled a large army, and set out for the south. At the Alpine passes the army was divided so that two substantial columns would penetrate Lombardy. This major offensive stands in sharp contrast to the relatively modest forces that Pepin had twice led into Italy but, still, in the midst of the campaign Charlemagne offered Desiderius 14,000 solidi to make peace with Hadrian. Desiderius refused and settled in at Pavia. His son, Adelchis, along with Gerberga, went to Verona. Charlemagne laid seige to Pavia and continued the attack until June 774 when the city finally surrendered. Verona was also taken by storm and Carlomann's family fell into Charlemagne's hands. Adelchis fled, eventually arriving at Constantinople.[160] We shall hear of him again.

Charlemagne's answer to the Lombard problem was different from his

---

[156]*LP* 1:492–93.

[157]Jaffé, *RP*, no. 2403; *Annales qui dicuntur Einhardi, anno* 773, ed. Kurze, p. 35.

[158]*LP* 1:493.

[159]Fasoli, *Carlomagno*, 78–79, emphasizes the impact of the threatened excommunication. Haller, *Das Papsttum* 1:449, thinks Desiderius felt inadequate to the task of taking Rome. I incline toward Fasoli's interpretation. Delogu ("Il regno longobardo," p. 189) believes that the threat of excommunication was a factor but adds that, with prominent noblemen fleeing to the Franks, Desiderius was faced with a disintegrating kingdom.

[160]*Annales regni Francorum, anno* 773, ed. Kurze, pp. 34–36; *Annales mettenses*, pp. 59–60; *Chron. moiss., MGH, SS* 1:295; *Ann. laurr. min., MGH, SS* 1:150; *Pauli continuatio Romana, MGH, SSrL*, p. 201. For details on this campaign see: Abel and Simson, *Jahrbücher*, 1:135–54, 186–90; *BM*, nos. 158b, d; Halphen, *Charlemagne*, pp. 71–75. The most acute analysis of the fall of the Lombard kingdom is Schmid, "Langobardenreich."

father's. Instead of settling for an unenforceable overlordship, Charlemagne sent Desiderius into a monastery and assumed the Lombard crown for himself. Charlemagne's reasons for going to Italy, and for acting so decisively there, are not difficult to understand. He did not face the complicated domestic situation that had confronted his father from 751 to 756. He was, surely, offended by Desiderius's attacks on the Republic and a sense of duty was manifestly a prime motivation for his conduct. But Desiderius, because he kept trying to foment discord in Francia by getting Carlomann's sons anointed, represented a real threat to Charlemagne's own monarchy.[161] Desiderius had become an unbearable pest. He had to go, and Charlemagne unceremoniously got rid of him. Charlemagne spent only a few more weeks in Italy and then returned to Francia to meet a new threat from the Saxons. Charlemagne was always a practical and clear-sighted statesman. He could not afford to deal repeatedly with the treacherous and unreliable Lombards. Saxony was in open rebellion. Aquitaine was but recently subdued. Bavaria was quiescent at the moment, but the lessons of recent history would have taught Charlemagne to expect trouble from that quarter at any moment. In the midst of these problems, and of others as well, there was no room for a perpetual Lombard nuisance.

Hadrian and His Republic in 774

Let us, in conclusion, examine Hadrian's position and the position of the Republic after Desiderius's defeat and the removal of the last of Rome's major external enemies. A persistent tradition maintains that Hadrian still acknowledged Byzantine rule in central Italy.[162] We have seen that Byzantine authority effectively ceased two decades before the fall of the Exarchate, and that it had been repeatedly denied for a long time before that. Those who

---

[161] Karl Hauck, "Die Ausbreitung des Glaubens in Sachsen und die Verteidigung der römischen Kirche als konkurriende Herrscheraufgaben Karls des Großen," *FMSt* 4 (1970): 144. Desiderius was placed in the custody of Adalfrid, abbot of St. Amand and later bishop of Liège: *Annales Lobienses, MGH, SS* 13:228–29. Rosamond McKitterick, believes he spent his captivity at St. Amand: "Charles the Bald and his Library," *English Historical Review* 95 (1980): 43–44.

[162] Most recently: Bertolini, *Roma e i longobardi*, pp. 117–18 (he has made this point in numerous writings); Classen, "Karl der Große, das Papsttum und Byzanz," pp. 548–49; Guillou, "L'Italia bizantina," p. 232ff.

hold for continued Greek rule point to three things: Hadrian's turning over of the murderers of Sergius to the civil authorities in Rome; the sending into exile in the Greek east of the murderers, and the pope's desire to send Paul Afiarta there; a document from 772 dated with the imperial regnal years. Each of these pieces of "evidence" can actually be explained, or explained away, very easily.

The pope, as the civil and religious head of the Republic, was in complete control of all officials in the city of Rome. In fact, there is abundant evidence that he appointed them all, including the judicial officers.[163] Criminal jurisdiction was never taken over by the papal courts, so it was only natural that Sergius's murderers would be handed over to the Urban Prefect. This prefect was a papal appointee, and therefore nothing in this litigation proves, or even says anything at all about, Byzantine authority in Italy.

Hadrian had no choice but to send the exiles to Constantinople. Keeping them in Rome would have been dangerous for many reasons. Hadrian did not wish to murder them and either make martyrs of them or enable Desiderius to charge into Rome as their advocate. It was out of the question to send them to Desiderius, or into his kingdom, and in early 772 Francia did not offer good prospects as a refuge for exiles since Charlemagne had not yet explicitly declared his intentions vis-à-vis Rome. Hadrian in reality had no choice but to send his opponents to the East. Moreover, the Byzantines were totally powerless in central Italy, and so, leaving all other considerations aside, they were unlikely to be able to use Hadrian's enemies against him.

Finally, there is a letter written by Hadrian to Probatus of Farfa in 772 and dated by the regnal years of Constantine V and Leo IV.[164] Too much should not be made of this letter for several reasons. First, chancery practices could in medieval times be notoriously conservative. Second, very few papal documents from the eighth century survive with full date devices and one must be careful not to generalize about authoritative chancery policy at any particular moment. Third, given the universal traditions of the papacy, it would have been unthinkable for anyone in Rome to have adopted a dating system according to the regnal years of one or another of the "barbarian" kingdoms. Fourth, the Roman synod of 769 had met "*regnante domino nostro Jesu Christo*" and by 781 Hadrian's chancery had adopted "*regnante Domino et Salvatore nostro Jesu Christo.*"[165] There is some slight evidence

---

[163]See chap. 6 and 7 for details.

[164]*Reg. farf.*, vol. 2, no. 99, pp. 83–85.

[165]Percy Ernst Schramm, "Die Anerkennung Karls des Großen als Kaiser," in his *Kaiser, Könige und Päpste*, 4 vols. in 5 (Stuttgart, 1968–72), 2:223–24.

that this new style may have emerged by 774,[166] and it is certain that in Tuscany, between 774 and 796, documents were dated by papal years under the influence of Roman chancery practice.[167] The Farfa document, therefore, appeared at a time when the practices of the Roman chancery were changing, and when a definitive new dating system had not yet been selected. The document in no way proves an admission of Byzantine imperial rule.

Certain positive considerations can also be brought forward. The very Farfa document so often cited to prove Greek authority twice uses the phrase "*nostrae romanorum reipublicae.*"[168] When Desiderius in 772 and 773 seized cities in the vicinity of Ravenna, this was said to have been done at the expense of the "Romans."[169] This simply cannot refer to the Greek "*Romaioi*" in the East. Hadrian's letters to Leo of Ravenna concerning Paul Afiarta asked the archbishop to send Paul into exile "through Venice or some other place."[170] The clear implication is that Ravenna was not an imperial city, and neither was Rome. Evidently Venice and other places were, and Hadrian's letter admits this even though the papacy had long been claiming Venice. Finally, while the Lombard kingdom was disintegrating under the blows of the Franks, the Spoletans and the residents of several cities in Lombard Tuscany placed themselves under Hadrian's rule, and the pope named the heretofore unheard of Hildebrand as duke of Spoleto.[171] None of these areas seems to have thought it necessary to turn to Constantinople. The evidence is random and diverse, but it all urges one and the same conclusion: Hadrian was a head of state, and he acted like one, and he was so treated.

Furthermore, one of the most famous of all historical documents proves that, from an ideological point of view, the popes not only acted like heads of state but thought of themselves that way as well. I refer to the *Constitutum Constantini*, the forged "Donation of Constantine." This is not the place for a monographic or even a synthetic analysis of the *Constitutum*.[172] A few general and relevant points can be made, however.

---

[166]Josef Deér, "Die Vorrechte des Kaisers in Rom, 772–800," *Schweizer Beiträge zur allgemeinen Geschichte* 15 (1957): 10.

[167]Déer, "Vorrechte," p. 10; Classen, "Karl der Große, das Papsttum und Byzanz," p. 224 and nn. 20, 21.

[168]*RF*, vol. 2, no. 99, pp. 83–85.

[169]*LP* 1:491.

[170]*LP* 1:490.

[171]*LP* 1:496; *RF*, vol. 2, no. 100, p. 85, is even dated "temporibus Adriani pontificis." See: Brühl, "Chronologie," pp. 63–64; Gasparri, *I duchi longobardi*, pp. 84–85.

[172]A splendid edition is now available: *Constitutum Constantini*, ed. Horst Fuhrmann, *MGH, Fontes iuris germanici antiqui* (Hannover, 1968).

There is gradually emerging a consensus that the famous forgery was fabricated between the pontificates of Stephen II and Hadrian.[173] It seems clear that the text was written in the Lateran by a Roman cleric.[174] But, the penetrating researches of Horst Fuhrmann, building on those of Gerhard Laehr, have established conclusively that "all things considered, it is hard to prove that the papacy based its political conduct on the *Constitutum Constantini* in the eighth century."[175] The forgery was never trotted out publicly

---

[173]Levillain, "L'avènement du dynastie carolingienne," pp. 231–34, emphasizes a connection with Stephen II's journey to Francia. Caspar, *Pippin und die römische Kirche*, pp. 185–89, points to the pontificate of Paul I as did Scheffer-Boichorst, "Neuere Forschungen über die konstantinische Schenkung," *MIÖG* 10 (1889): 302–25. Von Schubert, *Kirche im Frühmittelalter*, p. 320, thinks Christophorus was the author, and Ullmann, *Papal Government*, p. 74 n.2, 87 n.1, admits this possibility. Thus, a date between the early 750s and 771. Nicolas Huyghebaert, "La donation de Constantin ramenée à ses véritables proportions," *Revue d'histoire ecclésiastique* 71 (1976): 62–67, says Stephen II to Paul I. Classen, "Karl der Große, das Papsttum und Byzanz," pp. 543–44, holds for Stephen II to early Hadrian I. In a series of articles Wolfgang Gericke tries to prove that the text of the *Constitutum* developed in four distinct stages in the years 754, 766–71, 790, and 796: "Wann entstand die Konstantinische Schenkung?" *ZRG, kA* 43 (1957): 1–88; "Das Constitutum Constantini und die Sylvester-Legende," *ZRG, kA* 44 (1958): 343–50; "Konstantinische Schenkung und Sylvesterlegende in neuer Sicht," *ZRG, kA* 47 (1961): 293–304; "Das Glaubensbekenntnis der konstantinische Schenkung," *ZRG, kA* 47 (1961): 1–76. Fuhrmann proves that Gericke's thesis is untenable, although he generally had the right period: "Konstantinische Schenkung und Sylvesterlegende in neuer Sicht," *DA* 15 (1959): 523–40. Elsewhere Fuhrmann says that the second half of the eighth century is surely the right time: "Das frühmittelalterliche Papsttum und die Konstantinische Schenkung: Meditationen über ein unausgeführtes Thema," *SSCI* 20 (1973): 263–64.

It seems safe now to dismiss as both incorrect and fruitless the efforts of many scholars to date the forgery after 800. See, for some examples: Griffe, "Aux origines de l'état pontifical: Le couronnement impérial de l'an 800 et la Donatio Constantini," *Bulletin de litterature ecclésiastique* 59 (1958): 202–9; Werner Ohnsorge, "Das konstantinische Schenkung, Leo III und die Anfänge der kurialen römischen Kaiseridee," in his *Abendland und Byzanz* (Darmstadt, 1958), pp. 79–110; idem, "Das Constitutum Constantini und seine Entstehung," in his *Konstantinopel und der Okzident* (Darmstadt, 1966), pp. 92–162; Maximilian Buchner, "Rom oder Reims die Heimat des Constitutum Constantini?" *HJB* 53 (1933): 137–68; Etienne Delaruelle and Jean-Remy Palanque, "La Gaule chrétienne à l'époque franque," *Revue de l'histoire de l'église de France* 38 (1952): 64–65, 65 n.7. It goes without saying that I cite only a few of the more important, or more representative, studies.

[174]"That the place of the famous forgery was the Roman chancery is indisputable": Ullmann, *Papal Government*, p. 74 n.2. Also: Fuhrmann, "Frühmittelalterliche Papsttum," p. 264.

[175]Fuhrmann, "Frühmittelaltrliche Papsttum," pp. 268–92, see also his "Konstantinische Schenkung und abendländisches Kaisertum," *DA* 22 (1966): 63–178; Laehr, *Die konstantinische Schenkung in der abendländischen Literatur des Mittelalters bis zur Mitte des 14. Jahrhunderts* (Berlin, 1926); see also: Huyghebaert, "Donation," p. 52; Raymond Loenertz, "*Constitutum Constantini*: Destination, destinataires, auteur, date," *Aevum* 48 (1974): 210, 217.

to make or to prove a point. Various papal letters that some historians believe
to echo the *Constitutum* were probably only influenced by one or another of
the Constantinian and Sylvestrian legends which enjoyed wide currency in
the eighth century.[176] None of these letters gives certain proof that any pope
acted with a text of the *Constitutum* before his eyes.

Ordinarily it is argued that the famous forgery was produced to legitimize papal usurpation in Italy.[177] This argument is not compelling. The
Franks required no such legitimization. Pepin, as he told the Greek envoys in
756, made donations to the pope for the love of St. Peter and for the
remission of his sins. Constantine's alleged largesse played no discernible
part in his calculations. The sophisticated and cynical Byzantines would have
laughed the *Constitutum* out of any court. There is no good reason to argue
that the papal government or the Romans would have required an establishment of the legitimacy of a policy that, by the 750s and 760s, they had been
pursuing for more than half a century, and the Romans would hardly have
tried to persuade themselves by means of a forgery of their own confection.
Thus it is tempting to agree with Nicholas Huyghebaert that it may have
been a private compilation.[178] Alluring too, however, is T. S. Brown's suggestion that the forgery may have been produced to secure the papacy's claim
to Ravenna,[179] although there is no evidence that the document was ever
used for that purpose. This most famous forgery was, then, without practical, political, juridical significance at the time of its composition. Still, the
document was written in the Lateran during the early years of the Republic's
existence and it may be read as an indicator of certain attitudes in that
crucial place, at that crucial time.

The essential ideological preoccupations of the *Constitutum* have always
been recognized and understood.[180] The document purports to represent a
massive donation made by Emperor Constantine to Pope Sylvester in the

---

[176]The letters adduced are, as far as I know: Jaffé, *RP*, nos. 2322, 2347, 2372, 2423, 2448.
Fuhrmann, "Konstantinische Schenkung" pp. 121–22, shows the danger in seeing these letters
as evidence of the Donation's influence. Wilhelm Levison, "Konstantinische Schenkung und
Sylvester-Legende," in *Miscellanea Francesco Ehrle* (Rome, 1924), 2:159–247, demonstrates
the connection between the forgery and the cycle of Sylvester legends. It is also worth noting
that many papal letters were composed upon models such as *LD* formulae, canon law collections, earlier papal letters, and other texts: Fuhrmann, "Zu kirchenrechtlichen Vorlagen einiger
Papstbriefe aus der Zeit Karls des Grossen," *DA* 35 (1979): 357–67.

[177]Examples: Hartmann, *Geschichte Italiens*, 2.2: 223–30; Caspar, *Pippin und die römische Kirche*, pp. 185–89; Seppelt, *Geschichte der Päpste* 2:137–38; Haller, *Das Papsttum*
1:435–37.

[178]Huyghebaert, "La donation," pp. 47–68.

[179]Brown, "Church of Ravenna," p. 27.

[180]A good discussion, with rich bibliography, is: Ullmann, *Papal Government*, pp. 74–86.

early fourth century. The actual donation appears toward the end of the text, however. First, the reader encounters rather long sections emphasizing Constantine's purity of faith[181] and the pope's universal dominion (*"principatus"*) within the Church.[182] Two points were clearly being made here. Constantine's supposed orthodoxy was being sharply contrasted with the heresy, that is with the iconoclasm, of recent emperors. Also the pope's unfettered right to define and control the dogmas of the *catholica fides* was asserted in very strong language.[183] One cannot help but see in this an affirmation of the pope's right, indeed duty, to condemn the iconoclasm of the Byzantine Church. Then, as the reader nears the actual passages detailing Constantine's "donation," a remarkable emphasis on Sts. Peter and Paul begins to emerge. At the point where the donation narrative commences there appear the words *"concedimus ipsis sanctis apostolis . . . beatissimis Petro et Paulo."*[184] This echoes in a clear way the ideology of the Republic of St. Peter since the 730s. Finally, the donation itself says that Constantine made over to Sylvester the Lateran palace, the symbols of the imperial office including the crown, and the western provinces of the empire including the city of Rome.[185] Taken as a whole, the *Constitutum* is not so much a justification as a description of the papacy's "emancipation from the constitutional framework of the Eastern empire," to use Ullmann's words.[186] The text grounds the pope's right to rule his Republic in descent from St. Peter, in spiritual primacy, and in a concrete act of the sovereign will of the first, and perhaps greatest, of the Christian emperors. Much more than this has been read into the *Constitutum*, perhaps legitimately. For present purposes it is enough to note that the famous forgery confirms the fact that an independent, papally governed Republic existed as a matter of stark reality. Because the document was almost totally devoid of practical significance or application in the time of its fabrication, I would not care to go further in interpreting it than to say that it shows us how clearly the Lateran saw, and believed to be justified, its own independence and rule in Italy. Ullmann says the forgery was a justification for the papacy's conduct. This interpretation is, perhaps, permissible as long as it is realized that the "justification" came ex post facto and was quite unnecessary.

---

[181]*Constitutum*, cc. 3–7, ed. Fuhrmann, pp. 59–71.

[182]*Constitutum*, cc. 8, 10, 12, etc., ed. Fuhrmann, pp. 71–74, 77–80, 82–84.

[183]*Constitutum*, c. 12, ed. Fuhrmann, pp. 82–83.

[184]*Constitutum*, c. 14, ed. Fuhrmann, pp. 86–87. St. Peter is named seventeen times in the text.

[185]*Constitutum*, cc. 14–19, ed. Fuhrmann, pp. 86–96.

[186]*Papal Government*, p. 87.

Five

Multis Documentis:
Hadrian, Charlemagne, and
the Republic of St. Peter

EINHARD in his biography of Charlemagne relates a Byzantine proverb according to which "if you have a Frank for a friend, he is surely not your neighbor."[1] With the fall of Pavia in 774 Charlemagne and Hadrian became neighbors, and during the next fifteen years their friendship was tested on several occasions. Hadrian sought to draw for the Republic maximum benefit from the fall of the Lombard kingdom; indeed he hoped to dismember it. Charlemagne, once he had become *rex Langobardorum*, acquired a new set of responsibilities in, and perspectives upon, the whole Italian situation. In the end Charlemagne honored, and even in some areas exceeded, his father's concessions to the Republic, but in several significant respects he induced Hadrian to moderate his more extreme demands. The Byzantine dictum quoted above notwithstanding, Hadrian and Charlemagne became and remained firm friends, and by the time of Hadrian's death in 795 the Republic had assumed its basic territorial configuration.

A Time of Uncertainty

Charlemagne, in the midst of his siege of Pavia, shortly before Easter 774, and quite before it had become clear what the exact outcome of this protracted siege would be, collected an impressive entourage and headed suddenly for Rome. Perhaps there is no reason to suppose that Charlemagne did not go to Rome, at least in part, to pray and to pass the Eastertide near the tombs of the holy apostles and martyrs, but practical considerations surely played a part in his actions as well.[2] Upon arriving at St. Peter's

---

[1] *Vita Karoli*, c. 16, ed. Halphen, p. 50.
[2] *Annales qui dicuntur Einhardi, anno* 774, ed. Kurze, p. 39.

Charlemagne did display extraordinary awe and reverence; altogether befitting a man whose piety Heinrich Fichtenau once expressively characterized as "massive."³ More than pious exertions were involved, however. First, while the siege of Pavia was in progress several key cities and the Duchy of Spoleto had handed themselves over to Hadrian, as we have seen already. Charlemagne may have felt a need to meet with Hadrian to determine the fate of Italy.⁴ Second, why did Charlemagne elect to cross Tuscany, a region where Desiderius had once been a duke, and why did he take substantial forces with him? Similarly, why did Hadrian, after he had recovered from the shock of learning that Charlemagne was coming to Rome, send the Roman militia out to the thirtieth milestone⁵—farther, that is, than would have been appropriate for the reception of an emperor or exarch? Perhaps Charlemagne feared he would have to use force to traverse Tuscany, and possibly Hadrian had not a clue about what the king's real intentions were and sent his own troops out thirty miles in a modest, yet impressive, display of strength.⁶ Franco-papal relations had not been uniformly good since 767, and the events leading up to the meeting between Charlemagne and Hadrian in 774 convey an impression of two uncertain men trying to gauge one another's intentions.

No blows were struck in any quarter, and Charlemagne and Hadrian began what would prove to be a long and fruitful working partnership. Felicitations, touring, meetings, and solemn liturgical celebrations occupied most of Charlemagne's time in Rome, but on the Wednesday after Easter (6 April) Hadrian asked Charlemagne to fulfill in all respects the promises of his father for the Republic.⁷ Various Italian sources say that Charlemagne restored to the pope the cities and territories seized by Desiderius.⁸ This, as it turned out, is not exactly true. Frankish sources virtually ignore Charlemagne's visit to Rome, except for Einhard who says only that the king restored what Desiderius had "stolen."⁹ The *Liber Pontificalis* says that Char-

---

³*LP* 1:497.

⁴Fasoli, *Carlomagno*, p. 131.

⁵*LP* 1:496.

⁶Bertolini, *Roma e i longobardi*, pp. 113–14.

⁷*LP* 1:497–98. For basic details see: *BM*, nos. 160b–63; Abel and Simson, *Jahrbücher* 1:154–86 passim.

⁸*Pauli continuatio tertia*, c. 58, *MGH, SSrL*, p. 214; Leo, *Chronicon cassinense*, 1.12, *MGH, SS* 7:589; *Chronicon vulturnense*, ed. Vincenzo Federici (*FSI*, vols. 58–59 [Rome, 1925]), p. 173.

⁹*Vita Karoli*, c. 6, ed. Halphen, p. 20.

lemagne confirmed the promise of Quierzy that had been sworn in 754.[10] We have already seen that repeated efforts to impugn the authenticity of the passage in Hadrian's *vita* concerning Charlemagne's promise of 774 and the Quierzy document upon which it was based have all failed.[11] Most of those who attack this key passage point to the fact that neither after 754 nor after 774 was this *promissio donationis* ever fulfilled. Thus, they reason, the critical passage in Hadrian's *vita* must be forged at worst or interpolated at best. As Etienne Delaruelle has put it, if Charlemagne had actually made the promise reported by Hadrian's biographer, then there ought to have ensued a state of Franco-papal cold war after 774.[12] But, we have also seen that Paul Kehr was able to explain the Quierzy document as a "contingent treaty,"[13] and it follows that its repetition in 774 represented another contingent treaty.[14] In each instance the emergence of certain contingencies, chief among them the demise of the Lombard kingdom, would have created a division of Italy between the Franks and the papacy along the Luni-Monselice line. The pope would have received everything south of this line, that is, Lombard Tuscany and a saddle of lands extending across the Apennines, plus Ravenna and the old Exarchate, Venetia, Istria, and the Duchies of Spoleto and Benevento.

In 754–56 the relevant contingencies never snapped into place. Pepin did not depose Aistulf and annex half of his kingdom. In 774, however, the fundamental contingency underlying the Quierzy-Rome pact does appear to have been met: Desiderius was deposed and the Lombard monarchy dissolved. To be sure, Pavia did not fall until two months after Charlemagne had visited Rome, but its conquest may already have been in prospect. Thus Charlemagne renewed the contingent treaty of Quierzy, and in so doing honored Hadrian's request that Pepin's promises be fulfilled. Hadrian was driving a tough but fully precedented bargain. He could have laid before Charlemagne for confirmation either of the Pavian treaty documents, or Desiderius's promises of 757, or Desiderius's promises to Stephen III. Yet Hadrian reverted to Quierzy, that is, to the papal maximum scheme for the Republic.[15]

---

[10]*LP* 1:498.

[11]See above chap. 3, pp. 84–85 and nn. 97–99.

[12]Delaruelle, "Charlemagne et l'église," *Revue d'histoire de l'église de France* 39 (1953): 175.

[13]See above chap. 3, pp. 85–86, n. 102.

[14]In addition to Kehr see Robert Folz, "Charlemagne and His Empire," in *Essays on the Reconstruction of Medieval History*, ed. Vaclav Mudroch and G. S. Couse (Montreal, 1974), p. 110 n.40. But Folz had not taken this position in *The Imperial Coronation of Charlemagne*, trans. J. E. Anderson (London, 1974), pp. 30, 34–35.

[15]Caspar, *Das Papsttum unter fränkischer Herrschaft*, p. 48.

When Pavia did finally fall, Charlemagne made a few temporary arrangements in Italy, assumed the Lombard crown for himself, and hastily returned home to meet a new Saxon revolt.[16] The Quierzy-Rome promise was left unfulfilled at that time, and as we shall see, its precise terms would never be met. Hadrian's *vita*, interestingly and importantly, narrates the fall of Pavia in bland terms, mentions Charlemagne's return to Francia, and then abruptly breaks off its narration of the historical details of the pontificate.[17] The *vita* does continue for sixteen quarto pages, making it one of the longer ones in the *Liber Pontificalis*. But, the concluding sections all deal with Hadrian's building projects and pious benefactions in and around Rome. Perhaps it is striking that the papal biographer did not pause to relish the grim details of the ultimate discomfiture of Desiderius, but it is deeply puzzling that no further words were written on the territorial settlement of the Republic. As already noted in the discussion of the Quierzy pact, Hadrian's *vita* was written in two parts.[18] The section dealing with the years 772 to 774 was authored shortly after the events it narrates. Thus, the absence of any mention of a definitive territorial settlement can mean one of two things. Either papal Rome regarded that Quierzy-Rome promise as definitive, or else shortly after the fall of Pavia it became apparent in the Lateran that the pact was not actually going to be fulfilled and, in an air of disappointment, Hadrian's biographer laid down his quill.

These possibilities are actually not mutually exclusive, and there exists a plausible connection between them. At least, a connection can be established if we do not have to assume that part one of Hadrian's *vita* was written in, say, 774 or 775. If the date of composition is pushed forward to about 778, then several dimensions of Franco-papal relations in the 770s that have always been troublesome for scholars fall neatly into place. More specifically, it becomes possible to see why there is no need to assume forgery in the *vita*, why the Quierzy-Rome pact was never literally fulfilled, why Hadrian and Charlemagne remained on cordial terms, and why there is no need to argue that Charlemagne was cynical and deceitful in his conduct after 774. Moreover, and for this study this is the crucial issue, it becomes possible to see why the Republic wound up with frontiers that conformed neither to the Quierzy-Rome promise nor to the Pavian treaties.

For the years after 774 a great deal can be learned from Hadrian's letters to Charlemagne in the *Codex Carolinus*. These documents provide some

---

[16]*Annales regni Francorum, annis* 773–74, ed. Kurze, pp. 38–39; *Annales mettenses priores*, ed. Simson, p. 62; *Poeta Saxo*, 1.26, *MGH, SS* 1:230.

[17]*LP* 1:499.

[18]See above chap. 3, pp. 84–85, n. 99.

valuable insights into Hadrian's thoughts and feelings, and sometimes, veiled references and even omissions give us some sense of Charlemagne's conduct and its basic motivation.

First, the pope several times requested that Charlemagne honor the promise and donation he had made *"coram sancti Petri."*[19] As an adolescent Charlemagne had been bound to honor the promises and donations of 754 and 756, but because Hadrian spoke in his letters of acts done in the presence of St. Peter he was referring not to past engagements but to the pact of 774. Thus, until at least 778 Hadrian still believed that the Quierzy-Rome promise was valid, and he was insistent on its literal and total fulfillment.

Second, Hadrian raised issues which indicate that he had concerns in Tuscany and in the Lombard duchies. He asked Charlemagne to compel the bishops of Lucca, Pisa, and Reggio to return to their sees,[20] and he demanded that a certain Raginald not be granted any rights in Tuscany.[21] Several times Hadrian raised complaints or suspicions about Dukes Hildebrand of Spoleto and Arichis of Benevento.[22] Neither Tuscany nor the duchies had ever been included in previous Carolingian donations, so the concerns Hadrian expressed about them show that he was acting on the assumption that both Lombard Tuscany and the duchies were his according to the terms of the Quierzy-Rome pact.

Third, Hadrian once asked what good it had been that the Lombards were defeated because no restorations had been made.[23] In this letter, as in several others,[24] Hadrian complained about Archbishop Leo of Ravenna who was refusing to acknowledge papal rule and who had seized several cities in the Pentapolis. Leo was also accused of intercepting a dispatch from Patriarch John of Grado to Rome, which suggests that Hadrian still considered Venetia to be part of the Republic.[25] Likewise, Hadrian complained about the expulsion by the Greeks of Bishop Maurice of Istria, which seems to indicate that the pope was still claiming this region as well.[26] Ravenna, Venetia, and Istria had long been claimed by the Republic, but as we have seen, these regions regularly refused to recognize that they belonged to it. Hadrian's demands concerning these territories need not, of course, be

---

[19]CC, nos. 51, 52, 53, 55, 56, 60, pp. 571, 574, 575, 579, 581, 587.
[20]CC, no. 50, p. 570.
[21]CC, no. 58, pp. 583–84.
[22]CC, nos. 56, 57, 59, 64, pp. 581, 582, 585, 591.
[23]CC, no. 49, p. 568.
[24]CC, nos. 53, 54, 55, pp. 575, 576–77, 579–80.
[25]CC, no. 54, pp. 576–77.
[26]CC, no. 63, p. 590.

understood as necessarily having been based on the Quierzy-Rome pact, because the Pavian treaties had assigned Ravenna to Rome and ever since the time of Gregory II the popes had evinced designs on Venice and Istria. Still, when they are taken in connection with the Tuscan and ducal claims, the impression is created that Hadrian was grounding his demands throughout on the promise of 774.

Fourth, the pope raised a whole series of specific and general complaints about his predicaments. He told Charlemagne not to believe vicious rumors,[27] and he demanded the return of two Roman malefactors who had apparently fled to Francia after committing crimes "the likes of which had not been seen since the beginning of the world."[28] Hadrian complained that his Campanian possessions were being ravaged,[29] and he expressed a fear that the Lombards and the Greeks were plotting to restore Lombard rule in Italy.[30] Finally, Hadrian often spoke of his eager anticipation of a new visit by Charlemagne only to sink into depression when the king did not appear, or when his *missi* transacted business in Italy without sojourning in the papal precincts.[31] All of these criticisms, complaints, and laments are very much like the ones that popes had been placing before the kings of the Franks since the days of Gregory III. Therefore, a close reading of Hadrian's correspondence between the years 774 and 778 might lead one to conclude that the Franks were either bad or indifferent neighbors.

Amidst the general and specific concerns mentioned in Hadrian's letters, two basic issues can be discerned. First, the pope seems to have been genuinely puzzled and perplexed about his position in Italy. Second, Charlemagne was not wholly aloof from the Italian scene. His *missi* were active there and his presence was expected at any time, but especially in late 775 and again in 778 after the birth of his son Louis. If we are to penetrate behind Hadrian's bewilderment, and to comprehend Charlemagne's conduct, we must turn initially to Italian and Frankish, but not papal, sources because Hadrian's letters provide only hints that cannot by themselves be explained.

When Charlemagne went to Rome in 774 he cannot have known very much about the overall situation in Italy. Some persons like Fulrad would have been available to tutor the king, but his direct, personal knowledge had to have been limited. Surely, while the siege of Pavia was underway, Charle-

---

[27]CC, no. 51, p. 572.
[28]CC, no. 51, p. 573.
[29]CC, no. 61, p. 589.
[30]CC, no. 57, p. 582.
[31]CC, nos. 51, 52, 55, 56, 60, pp. 571, 574, 578, 581, 586.

magne would have been aware that several important cities and the Duchy of Spoleto had handed themselves over to the pope. He would also have been acutely aware that Desiderius had not yet capitulated, and that his son Adelchis was hiding in Verona with Gerberga. Certainly a Frankish victory over Desiderius was in prospect, but its aftermath cannot have been easily foreseen. Under the circumstances, it is not surprising that Charlemagne sought to avoid disaffecting the pope at whose behest he had come to Italy in the first place. Thus the king went to Rome and renewed the contingent treaty of Quierzy.[32] In those tense and uncertain months of the late spring of 774 an ultimate settlement of the whole Italian situation had not yet formed in Charlemagne's mind; nor, perhaps, in Hadrian's. Charlemagne's actions in Rome do prove, however, that he intended to guarantee the territorial integrity of the Republic and to become in his own right its protector. This was a responsibility that Charlemagne took very seriously throughout his reign,[33] even though it was one that, under different circumstances, he had already incurred twenty years before when Stephen II had visited his homeland.

Even if Charlemagne had some interim settlement in mind in 774 that would have departed from the Rome pact, it had to be deferred because the king was compelled to rush home to deal with a new Saxon revolt.[34] For the next several years a number of military problems in Francia, including the famous misadventure at Roncevalles, precluded any concerted attention to Italian affairs. Charlemagne did return to Italy in 776, but only briefly and for the sole reason that he had to put down a rebellion by Duke Hrodgaud of Friuli.[35] The embers of revolt were extinguished easily and afterward a number of Italian cities and individual magnates made formal submission to Charlemagne.[36] Among these was, evidently, Duke Hildebrand of Spoleto.[37]

---

[32]Jarnut, "Quierzy und Rom," pp. 292–93.

[33]K. Hauck, "Die Ausbreitung des Glaubens," pp. 138–72, esp. 140–41.

[34]*Annales qui dicuntur Einhardi, anno* 774, ed. Kurze, p. 41.

[35]*Annales regni Francorum, annis* 775–76, ed. Kurze, pp. 42–44; *Annales qui dicuntur Einhardi, anno* 776, ed. Kurze, pp. 43–45; *Annales mettenses priores,* ed. Simson, p. 64; *Poeta Saxo,* 1.1–17, *MGH, SS* 1:232. Brunner, *Opositionelle Gruppen,* p. 45. *BM,* nos. 199b–203.

[36]Frankish sources report these events in 774 (*Annales regni Francorum, anno* 774, ed. Kurze, p. 38; *Annales mettenses priores,* ed. Simson, p. 62) but according to Francesco Manacorda they belong in 776: *Ricerche sugli inizii della dominazione dei Carolingi in Italia* (Rome, 1968), pp. 36–42.

[37]In 774 Hildebrand dated by Hadrian's years (*RF,* vol. 2, no, 100, p. 85) but in late 775 he was dating by Charlemagne's years (*RF,* vol. 2, no. 105, pp. 85–86). Brühl, "Chronologie," p. 65, says Hildebrand had recognized Charlemagne by January 776 and perhaps in December 775.

Probably Hildebrand's "defection" to Charlemagne explains Hadrian's low opinion of him.

Only after 776 is it possible to speak of the gradual introduction of genuine and effective Frankish rule into formerly Lombard Italy. Some Lombards remained in important and influential positions, but northerners began to take up duchies, counties, episcopacies, and abbacies. Charlemagne moved slowly over many years in introducing Frankish personnel and institutions into his Italian kingdom, and it is important to see that he began his transalpine reforms in 776, not in 774.[38] With so many urgent problems facing him on both sides of the Alps, Charlemagne had thus far had neither the time nor the inclination to deal with Rome.

Charlemagne did not visit Rome in 776, because he had to rush home to confront yet another Saxon menace.[39] Judging from one of Hadrian's letters the king did plan a visit to Rome in 778, but his Spanish campaign forced another postponement.[40] When Charlemagne did finally revisit Italy in 781, he began to work out with Hadrian, amicably it should be noted, a comprehensive territorial settlement for the Republic. That settlement differed in marked respects from both the Pavian and the Quierzy-Rome pacts. At this point we must ask why that should have been.

There are two reasons. After Pavia fell, Charlemagne assumed a new title: *Carolus gratia Dei rex Francorum et Langobardorum.*[41] Contained in this title is a fact that had subtle but crucial implications for the eventual Italian settlement. The contingent element in the Quierzy promise had been a dissolution of the Lombard monarchy. Consequent upon that dissolution there would have been a division of the *regnum* between the pope and the Frankish king. Charlemagne dispatched the Lombard line of kings in 774,

---

[38]Manacorda, *Dominazione dei Carolingi*, is the most recent general assessment of Charlemagne's impact on Italy but other important studies can be cited: Fasoli, *Carlomagno*, pp. 90–119; Joachim Fischer, *Königtum, Adel und Kirche im Königreich Italien, 774–875* (Bonn, 1965); Bertolini, "I vescovi del 'regnum Langobardorum' al tempo dei Carolingi," in *Italia Sacra, 5: Vescovi e diocesi in Italia nel medioevo* (Padua, 1964), pp. 1–26; Eduard Hlawitschka, *Franken, Alemannen, Bayern und Burgunder in Oberitalien, 774–962* (Freiburg, 1960), pp. 17–53; Gerd Tellenbach, "Der großfränkische Adel und die Regierung Italiens in der Blütezeit des Karolingerreichs," in *Studien und Vorarbeiten zur Geschichte des großfränkisches und frühdeutschen Adels* (Freiburg, 1957), pp. 40–70; Bullough, "Baiuli in the Carolingian 'regnum Langobardorum' and the Career of Abbot Waldo," *English Historical Review* 77 (1962): 625–37; idem, "The Counties of the *Regnum Italiae* in the Carolingian Period (774–888): A Topographical Study I," *Papers of the British School at Rome* 23 (1955): 148–68.

[39]*Annales regni Francorum, anno* 776, ed. Kurze, p. 44.

[40]CC, no. 60, p. 586.

[41]*MGH, DK*, vol. 1, no. 80, p. 114: Given at Pavia for Bobbio 5 June 774.

but preserved the *regnum Langobardorum* under his own sceptre. He did this because he could never have hoped to rule the former Lombard kingdom, with its old and distinctive traditions, as a mere annex to the *regnum Francorum*.[42] By preserving the Lombard crown, however, he called into question the essential contingency upon which the Quierzy-Rome promise rested. In strict terms, Charlemagne had avoided having to divide the Lombard kingdom with Hadrian by preserving an independent Lombard crown.[43] We ought not to regard this as a cynically clever move on Charlemagne's part designed to sidestep in June 774 an agreement that he had concluded in April. Rather, Charlemagne acted out of a sense of what was best for his far-flung realm as a whole. Peter Classen correctly notes that Hadrian did not like what Charlemagne had done, and that the silence of the *vita* speaks volumes about his displeasure.[44] As early as the second half of 774 papal Rome may have come to the realization that the foundations upon which its maximum territorial schemes had always been based had been shattered. Or, it may be that the Lateran came slowly to this realization between 774 and 778 as Hadrian based demands upon the Rome promise and saw his demands go unfulfilled. In April 774 Charlemagne apparently had not yet decided what he was going to do after the capture of Pavia. This enabled him to confirm the pact of Quierzy in good conscience. Then, when Charlemagne made his decision in June to assume the Lombard crown, it took several years for the full implications of that decision to become clear to all concerned parties.

In the second place, between 774 and 781, when a comprehensive settlement began taking shape, Charlemagne had both time and opportunity to learn a good deal about Italy. He spent several months there in 773–74 and again in 776. He sent envoys into the peninsula and had many exchanges of correspondence with Hadrian about it. He apparently received some fugitives from papal justice, and he was visited by Leo of Ravenna.[45] In 776 Charlemagne felt able to issue the first of his Italian capitularies, a sure sign that he was growing more comfortable with his new possessions.[46] When, after 781,

---

[42]Gustav Eiten, *Das Unterkönigtum im Reiche der Merowinger und Karolinger* (Heidelberg, 1907), pp. 18–34.

[43]I believe that this point was first made by Schnürer, *Kirchenstaat*, pp. 84, 94, but his book is rarely cited.

[44]Classen, "Karl der Große, das Papsttum und Byzanz," p. 549.

[45]CC, no. 54, p. 577. Fasoli, *Carlomagno*, p. 83, shows that Leo and Charlemagne were in contact.

[46]*MGH, Cap.*, vol. 1, no. 88, pp. 187–88. For the date: Manacorda, *Dominazione dei Carolingi*, pp. 37–38.

the frontiers of the Republic began to be defined, Charlemagne proved both generous and perspicacious, and Hadrian accepted, even concurred in, the final determinations. Thus, between 774 and 781 Charlemagne learned what he could and ought to do in Italy, and Hadrian learned by 778 that the Rome promise had been provisional.

The year 778 has been repeatedly emphasized as a crucial one in the relations between Hadrian and Charlemagne, and in the bearing of those relations upon the Republic. The reasons for this emphasis are based on Hadrian's letters written between 778 and 781. After 778 Hadrian gave up his general references to the promise of 774. He either turned to very specific references to named territories, Terracina, for example,[47] or the Sabine patrimonies,[48] or else he moved the discussion to a wholly different plane, as in letter number sixty where he adduced a reference to Constantine's having granted to Sylvester dominion *"in his Hesperiae partibus."*[49] I agree with those scholars who are reluctant to see in this letter a deliberate reference to the *Constitutum Constantini.*[50] The famous forgery is a valuable indicator of certain attitudes prevalent in the Lateran, but it is not safe to regard it as a bargaining chip in eighth-century papal diplomacy. Hadrian's reference to the Sylvester legends, and a curious passage in the same letter where the pope mentioned all sorts of titles and documents contained in the Lateran archives, suggest that the authorities of the Republic were earnestly trying to find some legitimate basis for their claims after coming to the realization that the Rome promise had apparently become a dead issue.[51] In this same vein, it is striking to read papal letters concerning Benevento and Spoleto wherein the pope spoke to Charlemagne of these regions being under *"vestra et nostra"* jurisdiction.[52] This odd formulation is not typical of the pre-778 correspondence. It seems to indicate that the pope knew he was not going to have the duchies all to himself, and so he was trying to retain some sort of a claim to them. Finally, in May 778 Hadrian wrote to Charlemegne that

---

[47]CC, no. 64, p. 591.

[48]CC, no. 68, p. 598.

[49]CC, no. 60, p. 587.

[50]See above chap. 4, n.176.

[51]CC, no. 60, p. 587: "Plures donationes in sacro nostro scrinio Lateranensae reconditas habemus. Tamen et pro satisfactione christianissimi regni vestri per iam fatos ad demonstrandam eas vobis direximus."

[52]CC, no. 64, p. 591: "sub vestra et nostra sunt dicione." Something like this is contained in no. 55 (27 October 775), p. 577, where Hadrian speaks of Arichis of Benevento "quamque reliquis nostris vestrisque inimicis" but in the 781 letter *lands* are referred to and the distinction can legitimately be drawn.

he was going to send the army of the Duchy of Rome out into Campania to drive out the Beneventans.[53] True, the same letter contains a plea to Charlemagne to restrain the Beneventans, but this only indicates that Hadrian was beginning to feel as though he would have to manage on his own in Italy.

It was suggested above that at the time of Hadrian and Charlemagne's first meeting in 774 both acted with caution and uncertainty. At this point it can be proposed that uncertainty reigned on both sides until 781. It took Hadrian until 778 to realize that the promise of 774 was not definitive, and between 778 and 781 the pope acted almost bewildered. Charlemagne, quite simply, was unable between 774 and 781 to effect a full, fair, and mutual resolution of open questions in Italy. Military problems in Francia coupled with an initially inadequate but slowly growing body of information about Italian conditions caused Charlemagne to postpone a reckoning of accounts with the pope. If, therefore, the years from 774 to 781 are interpreted as ones of uncertainty, it is possible to explain why the Quierzy-Rome promise was not fulfilled without having recourse to theories of forgery or interpolation, or to excessively intricate theories like Bertolini's which try to work out a pattern of relationships among *promissiones, donationes,* and *traditiones.*[54] Likewise, it is unnecessary to view Charlemagne's conduct as cynical and deceitful, or Hadrian's as shrill and paranoid.[55]

Problems with the Sources

The definitive determination of the Republic's boundaries came in two major stages, in 781 and 787–88, and in several minor stages. If we had only Italian or papal sources, we would never be able to figure out what happened, let alone why. In fact, most Frankish sources are not of much help either. There is one crucial document, the so-called *Pactum Ludovicianum* of 816–17, whose contents can, when properly evaluated, enable us to see what took place in the 780s. Before we can turn to the *Ludovicianum* and its contents, however, several preliminary considerations must be entertained. The *Ludovicianum* itself is a controversial document, and the applicability of its contents to the 780s has been a matter of some debate.

---

[53]CC, no. 61, p. 589.

[54]Bertolini, "Carlomagno e Benevento," p. 614ff.

[55]This still widely held view can be traced back to Ferdinand Hirsch, "Papst Hadrian I. und das Fürstentum Benevent," *Forschungen zur deutschen Geschichte* 13 (1873): 33–68, esp. 35–36, 44, 67–68.

In the last years of the nineteenth century, when the growth of papal territorial rule and Franco-papal relations both became serious subjects of historical inquiry, the *Ludovicianum* was not ordinarily drawn into discussions about Charlemagne and Hadrian. Julius Ficker had made the point that a passage in the *Ludovicianum* seemed to illuminate the settlement in the Sabina accomplished in 781, but he did not develop a detailed argument.[56] When Theodor Sickel studied the *Ludovicianum* he was looking forward in time to the *Ottonianum* of 962, rather than backward to the earlier Carolingian pacts.[57] Karl Lamprecht was the first to attempt a detailed demonstration of the possibilities of reconstructing the late eighth-century pacts from the early ninth-century *Ludovicianum*, but his particular conclusions were, in many instances, so manifestly wrong that his method was discredited.[58] Then, in a review of Theodor Lindner's fundamentally misguided *Die sogennanten Schenkungen*,[59] Paul Kehr showed that Lamprecht's method was sound, even if his conclusions were not.[60] Kehr was, however, like Sickel, more interested in the series of pacts between 817 and 962 than he was in the settlements of the eighth century. Edmund Stengel finally proved beyond a doubt that it is possible to reconstruct earlier pacts by working backward, but he too was primarily concerned with figuring out the details of the pacts between 817 and 962.[61] Only recently has Adelheid Hahn finally given the *Ludovicianum* the full diplomatic analysis it has always deserved.[62] She is the first scholar since Lamprecht to attempt a comprehensive reading of the *Ludovicianum* against the background of the pacts between 754 and 817; and where Lamprecht failed, she succeeds. That is, she succeeds in showing that the *Ludovicianum* can be drawn upon to explain the settlements of the 780s. Hahn does not, however, solve all of the specific territorial problems to which we shall turn soon.

A vindication of Lamprecht's method is not at all the same thing as a

---

[56]Ficker, *Forschungen zur Reichs- und Rechtsgeschichte Italiens*, 4 vols. (Innsbruck, 1868–74), 2:346–50.

[57]T. Sickel, *Das Privilegium Otto I. für die römische Kirche vom Jahre 962*. (Innsbruck, 1883). Harald Zimmermann has also made an important contribution to our understanding of the *Ludovicianum*, but, once again, his goal was to understand the *Ottonianum*: "Das Privilegium Ottonianum von 962 und seine Problemsgeschichte," *MIÖG, Erganzungsband* 20 (1962): 147–90.

[58]Lamprecht, *Die römische Frage* (Leipzig, 1889).

[59]Lindner argued for patrimonies, not territories, in the donations.

[60]Kehr, *Göttingische gelehrte Anzeigen* 158 (1896): 128–39.

[61]Stengel, "Die Entwicklung des Kaiserprivilegs für die römische Kirche, 817–962," in his *Abhandlungen und Untersuchungen zur mittelalterlichen Geschichte* (Cologne, 1960), pp. 218–48 (first pub. 1921).

[62]Hahn, "Das Hludowicianum," pp. 15–135.

vindication of the text to which he applied it. The *Ludovicianum* was long dismissed as a forgery, then later it was thought to be partly genuine though interpolated, but now it has finally come to be regarded as essentially authentic. It has, once again, taken just about a century for us to arrive at a proper understanding of this critical document. Some aspects of the old debate must be rehearsed here in order to establish exactly what the *Ludovicianum* was, under what circumstances it was composed, and what precautions must be taken in drawing testimony from it.

The *Ludovicianum*, as read in the Boretius-Krause edition of the Carolingian capitularies,[63] represents the imperial pact concluded between Louis the Pious, Charlemagne's son and successor, and Pope Paschal I in the first half of 817.[64] We now know that Louis had already concluded a pact with Stephen IV in October 816,[65] and it is today widely and correctly assumed that the pacts of 816 and 817 were essentially alike, perhaps identical.[66] The text is not long. It occupies slightly more than two quarto pages. It contains a remarkably precise and detailed listing of the lands of the Republic of St. Peter, and a variety of political, legal, and institutional prescriptions pertaining to those lands.

The potential significance of the document ought to be obvious. Because none of the full or official texts of any of the earlier Franco-papal pacts survives, the *Ludovicianum* stands as the first extant inventory of the lands granted or guaranteed by the Carolingians to the papacy. Louis made no new grants of his own, and there is no evidence to suggest that he at any

---

[63] *MGH, Cap.*, vol. 1, no. 172, pp. 352–55.

[64] Jaffé, *RP*, no. 2548. Hahn, "Hludowicianum," pp. 28–29, established that the *nomenclator* Theodore, who was present at the signing of the *Ludovicianum*, was still in Rome 1 February 817 (citing *RF*, vol. 2, no. 225, p. 187). When he left for Francia cannot be determined, nor can we fix the date of his arrival. The Aachen assembly of July is the *terminus ante quem*.

[65] *LP* 2:49; *Annales regni Francorum, annis* 816, 817, ed. Kurze, pp. 144–46; Astronomer, *Vita Hludowici*, c. 27, *MGH, SS* 2:621; Ermoldus Nigellus, *In honorem Hludowici christianissimi caesaris*, ed. Edmond Faral (Paris, 1932), vs. 936–40, 1034–39, 1040–47. The actual document may still have been in existence in 1105, and may have been seen by Gregory of Catino: *Chronicon farfense*, ed. Ugo Balzani (*FSI*, vol. 33 [Rome, 1903]), 2:255. For details and literature see: Hahn, "Hludowicianum," pp. 23–30.

[66] Von Schubert, *Geschichte der christlichen Kirche*, p. 397; Hildegard Thomas, "Die rechtliche Festsetzungen des Pactum Ludovicianum," *ZRG, kA* 11 (1921): 131; Ullmann, "The Origins of the Ottonianum," *Cambridge Historical Journal* 11 (1953): 117; Wolfgang H. Fritze, *Papst und Frankenkönig: Studien zu den päpstlich-fränkischen Rechtsbeziehungen von 754 bis 824* (Sigmaringen, 1973), p. 19; Folz, et al., *De l'antiquité au monde médiéval* (Paris, 1972), p. 378; Hahn, "Hludowicianum," p. 30.

time altered conditions as they had existed at the time of his father's death in January 814. Charlemagne made no territorial alterations in Italy that we know of after 787–88, so the contents of the *Ludovicianum* may be able to show us the status quo as of 788. Because there are important differences between the *Ludovicianum* and both the Pavian treaties and the Quierzy-Rome pact, the former document permits us to discern the scope of the territorial settlements of the 780s. Charlemagne, as we have just seen, made no major territorial adjustments affecting the Republic in the 770s, except for assuming overlordship in Spoleto, which clearly contravened the Rome promise. Actually, some adjustments in Istria, Venetia, and Ravenna may date back to the 770s, but this is a deeply complex matter to which we shall return. At any rate, it appears that by a subtle and complex process of extrapolation the *Ludovicianum* can be made to tell us the details of Charlemagne's arrangements with Hadrian in the 780s. That is, the document can provide such details to the extent that it can be considered authentic and uninterpolated.

It was in the eighteenth century, against long-held opinions, that Cenni asserted the authenticity of the *Ludovicianum*,[67] but his views gained no currency until Ficker suggested that the document was authentic.[68] Ficker's judgment caused Sickel to submit the document to a massive historical, diplomatic, and paleographical analysis, the result of which was that its basic authenticity was placed beyond doubt.[69]

Still, Sickel had raised grave doubts about some passages in the *Ludovicianum* and his doubts, plus those of other scholars, continued for a long time to find their way into discussions of the document.[70] Virtually all

---

[67]Cenni, *PL* 98:579ff.

[68]Ficker, *Forschungen* 2:284ff, 299ff, 332ff.

[69]T. Sickel, *Das Privilegium Otto I*. Obviously, as his title implies, he worked backwards from the *Ottonianum*. For Sickel to have reopened the question is a tribute to his integrity because a few years earlier he had dismissed it as a forgery: *Acta karolinorum digesta et ennarata* (Vienna, 1867), p. 381ff.

[70]There is no need here to do more than give some sense of the *guerre des savants*: Cenni discussed the views of his predecessors and contemporaries: *PL* 98:551ff; Thomas, "Pactum Ludovicianum," pp. 125–26, gives a resume of work before Sickel. The following take the text to be basically authentic: Amann, *L'époque carolingienne* (Paris, 1947), pp. 205–6; Halphen, *Charlemagne*, pp. 163–64; Brezzi, *Roma e l'empero*, p. 44; Seppelt, *Geschichte der Päpste*, 2:203–5. Among those with doubts are: Bernhard Simson, *Jahrbücher des fränkischen Reiches unter Ludwig dem Frommen*, 2 vols. (Leipzig, 1874–76), 1:180 n.7; Von Schubert, *Geschichte der christlichen Kirche*, pp. 396–97; Ferdinand Gregorovius, *Geschichte der Stadt Rom im Mittelalter*, 8 vols., 7th ed. (Stuttgart, 1922), 3:36–38; Thomas, ibid., pp. 155–65; Karl Heldmann, *Das Kaisertum Karls des Großen* (Weimar, 1928), p. 399ff; Heinrich Brunner,

problems caused by the *Ludovicianum* stem from the fact that we do not have an original copy of it. The text may have survived as late as 1245, but our only means of access to it today is through the works of canonists beginning with Deusdedit of Milan, Anselm of Lucca and, perhaps, Bonizo of Sutri.[71] It seems possible that these canonists had the original before their eyes,[72] but in compiling their works they were less concerned with transmitting verbatim extracts than with documenting a variety of ecclesiastical rights and claims. Thus, while there is no reason to accuse or to suspect them of deliberate forgery or interpolation, it is legitimate to have doubts about how faithfully or fully they reproduced their sources.[73] Moreover, because the manuscript traditions of the canonists' works are diverse and complex, it is difficult to have complete confidence about the literal accuracy of any particular passage taken from these manuscripts in the task of effecting an edition of the *Ludovicianum*.[74] To produce an edition, which Cenni did and Sickel did better—his text is behind Boretius's in the *MGH*—it is necessary to assemble a fair number of scattered passages from the canonists because none of them reproduces a full and continuous text of the *Ludovicianum*.

If there is ample room for doubt about the *Ludovicianum*, how much room is there for confidence? Fortunately a great deal in all that concerns the document's inventory of the Republic's properties. Sickel noticed the palpable similarity between the *Ludovicianum* and the *Ottonianum*, and then analyzed the canonical texts and manuscripts of the former in light of the latter, whose text is integrally transmitted. His findings were built and improved upon by Kehr and Stengel, and have been largely confirmed by Hahn.

Deutsche Rechtsgeschichte 2:118, 127 n.57. Examples could be multiplied almost endlessly on both sides of the argument.

[71]Anselm, *Collectio canonum una cum collectio minore*, 4.34, ed. Friedrich Thaner (1906; reprint, Aalen, 1965), pp. 210–14; Deusdedit, *Die Kanonessammlung des Kardinals Deusdedit*, 3.280, ed. Victor Wolf von Glanvell (1905; reprint, Aalen, 1967), pp. 385–89. On Bonizo see: Hahn, "Hludowicianum," p. 30 n.101, 34 n.119. Laufs, *Innozenz*, pp. 8–10, argues that the original text was no longer extant in Innocent's time.

[72]Hahn, "Hludowicianum," pp. 37–40. The eleventh century writer Leo of Monte Cassino seems to me to have seen a text given his extremely precise description of it: *Chron. cass.*, 1.16, *MGH, SS* 7:592.

[73]On these canonists see: Sickel, *Privilegium*, pp. 55–69; Paul Fournier and Gabriel LeBras, *Histoire des collections canoniques en occident*, 2 vols. (Paris, 1932), 2:26–27, 39–40; *Lexikon für Theologie und Kirche*, 1:596, 3:260; *New Catholic Encyclopedia*, 1:584–85, 4:823.

[74]The fullest and most up-to-date discussion of all textual problems is Hahn, "Hludowicianum," pp. 30–40.

The chief results of all this scholarship can be briefly formulated. Virtually the whole of the section in the *Ludovicianum* treating papal possessions is authentic and can therefore be used to reconstruct events of the 780s. The only passage that must be explained is the one that concerns the islands of Sicily, Sardinia, and Corsica. We shall study this passage in due course. Naturally, the information in the *Ludovicianum* must be controlled by, and interpreted in light of, surviving documents from the 780s but, and this is the crucial point, Louis's pact can stand at the center of the discussion. In later chapters there will be occasion to return to the legal, political, and institutional clauses of the *Ludovicianum*. These are the ones about which the most persistent doubts exist. For the present, however, these clauses need not detain us.

The Territorial Settlements of 781

During his meeting at Reims in October 816 with Pope Stephen IV, Louis directed his chancellor, Helisachar, to draw up a document for presentation to the pope.[75] Helisachar's text ultimately stands behind the *Ludovicianum* of 817 which we can read in the *MGH* edition of the Carolingian capitularies. In this latter document, after an enumeration of the territories that Louis guaranteed to the pope, the emperor is reported to have said "in like fashion, through this our decree of confirmation, we confirm the donations which our grandfather, the lord king Pepin of pious memory, and afterward our lord, king and father Emperor Charles handed over by their own will."[76] If this were all we had to go on it would be very difficult, perhaps impossible, to reconstruct the agreements concluded by Charlemagne and Hadrian because the *Ludovicianum* is not, and does not claim to be, a direct confirmation of any single earlier donation. In fact, it differs in marked respects from all earlier donations of which we have any knowledge. Clearly, however, Louis saw his pact as a confirmation of earlier ones. When Helisachar prepared his text, he did so in a highly rationalized fashion. That is, the clauses in the *Ludovicianum* detailing the Republic's territories are set forth in a precise, geographical order. This system of arrangement and narration made perfectly good sense in the ninth century, but a twentieth-century historian would have preferred a chronological organization of the material.

---

[75]*LP* 2:49; *Annales regni Francorum, anno* 817 (*sic*), ed. Kurze, pp. 144–46.

[76]*MGH, Cap.*, vol. 1, no. 172, p. 354.

Lacking a chronological organization, therefore, the historian cannot get much help from the external form of the document except for the certainty that it was a confirmation, and that its contents were the result of a recombination in geographical order of at least some elements from earlier pacts of Pepin and Charlemagne. To figure out how the text came to be constituted, it is necessary to apply a penetrating exegesis to its internal features. This means that one cannot start with the first clause and proceed in order straight through the document. Rather, it is necessary to dig out clues wherever they can be found, and to explain as much text as each clue permits before moving on to the next one.

The first great clue comes at the end of a clause that starts with a discussion of the old Exarchate and ends with the Sabine territory. This passage is revealing in a variety of ways and deserves to be quoted:

Eodem modo territorium Sabinense, sicut a genitore nostro Karolo imperatore beato Petro apostolo per donationis scriptum concessum est sub integritate, quemadmodum ab Itherio et Magenario, missis illius, inter idem territorium Sabinense atque Reatinum definitum est.[77]

The first critical element here is the mention of Itherius and Magenarius. Itherius was abbot of St. Martin of Tours and a trusted associate of Charlemagne and the very man who, in 774, had drawn up the copy of the Quierzy promise that the king had deposited at St. Peter's.[78] Scholars have noticed that, ever since the time of Fulrad, the Carolingians had what today's diplomats would call "Italian experts": one was Fulrad, of course; another was Itherius in the 770s; later there were Adalhard, Angilbert, Wala, Leo, and others.[79] To grasp the roles of Itherius and Magenarius it is necessary to turn to a series of letters in the *Codex Carolinus*.

Alas, one cannot simply take up Gundlach's edition of the letters and go to work. As is universally recognized, his edition is deeply flawed, and his dating is frequently erratic.[80] For present purposes, his chronology is what

---

[77]*Ludov.* (as in n.76), p. 353.

[78]*LP* 1:498.

[79]These "Italian experts" have been noticed by: Bullough, "Leo, *qui apud Hlotharium magni loci habebatur*, et le gouvernement du *Regnum Italiae* à l'époque carolingienne," *Le moyen âge* 67 (1961): 221–45; Hagen Keller, "Zur Struktur der Königsherrschaft im karolingischen und nachkarolingischen Italien," *QFIAB* 47 (1967): 129. The problem merits further study.

[80]Hahn, "Hludowicianum," p. 17 n.10, cites some of Gundlach's weaknesses and the literature on the problem.

must be rectified and, unfortunately, in one case relevant here it is not possible to turn to Jaffé's older edition for greater precision because he also seems to have made a critical mistake, although in many cases Jaffé does supply essential corrections to Gundlach's errors.

In a letter that must date from late 780 or early 781, Hadrian wrote to Charlemagne to say that Itherius and Magenarius had conducted an inquest at Foronovo concerning the papacy's ancient *patrimonium Savinense*.[81] He expected the king to do right and to return these lands to him. In a letter written a little later Hadrian again referred to the work of the *missi* and asked Charlemagne to make good on the grant of the *territorium Savinense* for "your most noble offspring."[82] Later, either late in 781 or early in 782, Hadrian reported that he had not yet received the *territorium Savinense*.[83] In yet another letter, the pope told Charlemagne that evil persons were preventing Itherius and Magenarius from handing over the Sabine territory to him.[84] In this letter Hadrian noted that Desiderius had once agreed to the restoration of certain estates in the Sabina "wherever they could be found" but that he had never contemplated handing over the whole territory as Charlemagne had done. Indeed, the pope expressed his gratitude for having "recently" ("*noviter*") been granted the Sabine territory. Finally, in a letter from 782 or 783, Hadrian talked of Charlemagne's promises, noted that problems still existed in their fulfillment, and mentioned "*multis documentis*" in his possession concerning the lands involved in the promises.[85]

---

[81]CC, no. 69, p. 599. Gundlach and Jaffé (his ed. of CC, no. 70, pp. 218–20) both date this letter May to September 781, but I believe that it must be placed before Charlemagne's visit to Rome in April of that year. First, Hadrian does not use "spiritalis compater" in the address of this letter. At Rome Hadrian baptized Charlemagne's son Pepin (*Annales regni Francorum, anno* 781, ed. Kurze, p. 56) and created thereby a bond of compaternity that helped to cement the Franco-papal bond as Arnold Angenendt has shown: "Taufe und Politik im frühen Mittelalter," *FMSt* 7 (1973): 143–68. True Hadrian calls himself "spiritalis compater" *in the letter* but this is the last time this is not found *in the address*. Hadrian knew already that Charlemagne was on his way to Rome, and he knew that he was going to baptize Pepin, so he could have been anticipating a bit. That is, he may have been trying to draw some advantage already from a powerful fictive kinship that was about to be created. Second, Hadrian's description of the Foronovo inquest suggests that its outcome was not yet clear. Third, Hadrian speaks of the *patrimonium Savinense* in this letter but all later ones refer to the *territorium Savinense*. This distinction is crucial and its significance will become clear below. Fourth, in a later letter Hadrian talks of Charlemagne's donation of the whole *territorium Savinense* "pro vestros nobilissimos proles," which must refer to the baptism of Pepin and the unction of Louis and Pepin.

[82]CC, no. 70, p. 600. Gundlach and Jaffé agree: May–Sept. 781.

[83]CC, no. 71, pp. 601–2. Gundlach and Jaffé agree: 781 or early 782.

[84]CC, no. 72, pp. 602–3. Gundlach says 782; Jaffé says 781*ex.*–783 April.

[85]CC, no. 68, pp. 597–98. Here is Gundlach's most serious error. He says 781*in.* which

Dating the *Ludovicianum*'s clause on the Sabina to 781 should now cause no problems. Itherius and Magenarius are mentioned in both the *Codex Carolinus* and the *Ludovicianum* in connection with the Sabina. Papal letters talk of documents, and Louis's pact speaks of a concession that was "*scriptum.*" The work of Itherius and Magenarius fell both before and after Charlemagne's visit to Rome in April 781, and one of Hadrian's letters says that, in part at least, it was because of events in Rome, that is, the baptism and consecration of the king's son Louis, that Charlemagne had made his donation. Lurking in these papal letters, then, are both an explanation of the passage from the *Ludovicianum* quoted above, and a first, precious insight into how Charlemagne and Hadrian worked together.

Let us begin with an explanation of the exact significance of the clause in the *Ludovicianum* pertaining to the Sabina. The old Byzantine Duchy of Rome had once had a precisely defined eastern border that crossed the province of Valeria in such a way that a part of the Sabine region was inside the duchy. Rieti was then the westernmost city of Spoleto.[86] Over the years Lombards entered the Roman Sabina in considerable numbers, and the easternmost part of this region was effectively lost to the duchy.[87] Since the time of Gregory II the Duchy of Rome had formed the core of the Republic, but actual control of the Roman Sabina was no more possible for the pope than it had been for the Byzantine authorities. Pope Zachary had received from Liutprand a promise to restore the patrimonies in the Sabina, and Desiderius had confirmed it.[88] Apparently, on the testimony of one of Hadrian's just discussed letters, little had been recovered by 781. Since the time of Zachary the papacy had begun to speak of a *territorium Savinense*,[89] which was the whole of the former Roman Sabina reconstituted at some point out of the old suburbicarian dioceses of Cures, Forum Novum, and Nomentum.[90] Natu-

---

simply cannot be. Jaffé (his ed., no. 74, p. 227) says 781*ex.*–783 April. For this whole series of letters Jaffé has the correct order and, with the exception of his date for no. 69 (Gundlach; Jaffé's no. 70) his dates are acceptable as long as they are viewed sequentially. Thus, Gundlach's sequence should be 69, 70, 71, 72, 68.

[86]Diehl, *Etudes*, p. 65; Toubert, *Latium* 2:938–39.

[87]Toubert, *Latium* 2:941–42; Otto Vehse, "Die päpstliche Herrschaft in der Sabina bis zur Mitte des 12. Jahrhunderts," *QFIAB* 21 (1929–30): 120.

[88]Duchesne, *LP* 1:ccxxxix.

[89]*LP* 1:426.

[90]Toubert, *Latium* 2:943 n.2. If Toubert is correct, and I believe that he is, that diocesan boundaries served as a basis for the Sabine settlement, then it is a real shame that we do not have more documents relevant to the whole series of territories enumerated in the *Ludovicianum*. The point is that, with such documents, one could take up an old but still crucial study

rally, as long as the Lombards reigned, the papacy had no control over a Sabine "territory" and had great difficulty holding or recovering patrimonies in that region. Thus, while the Lombard kingdom was disintegrating in 773–74, Hadrian sought to improve his situation to the east by getting control of Spoleto and, through this action, securing his possession of the Sabine region.[91] By late 775 Hildebrand of Spoleto had sworn allegiance to Charlemagne and Hadrian was back to his original position. From 778 to 781 Hadrian's concern was solely with his Sabine patrimonies,[92] and then in April 781 he was given the "*territorium Savinense sub integro*." Charlemagne's *missi*, after their inquest at Foronovo in the Sabina, fixed the eastern frontier of the region so as to incorporate into the Duchy of Rome the whole of the former Roman Sabina. The westernmost extent of the diocese of Rieti now formed the western border of the Duchy of Spoleto.[93] The long struggle over the Roman Sabina had, in Toubert's words, "a happy outcome for the papacy."

As Toubert correctly emphasizes, the clause in the *Ludovicianum* quoted above says "*inter idem territorium Sabinense atque Reatinum definitum est.*" Hadrian got the whole Roman Sabina, and not just papal patrimonies in the Sabine region as has been persistently argued.[94] The reasons why scholars doubt that the whole region was handed over turn around the monastery of Farfa. This house had been prominent under the Lombard dukes and held extensive properties throughout the Sabina.[95] In 775 Charlemagne granted Farfa, on the request of Abbot Probatus, freedom from episcopal control, free abbatial elections, and immunity.[96] How, it has been asked, could Charlemagne grant an immunity *inside* a territory he had conceded to Rome? Does this not imply that only patrimonies were handed over? This is a

---

by Duchesne ("Le sedi episcopali nell'antico ducato di Roma," *ASR* 15 [1892]: 478–503) and see if diocesan boundaries served in other instances as the basis for settlements. It looks as though this was true in the Liri valley (see below) and I cannot help wondering if it was elsewhere as well.

[91] Vehse, "Sabina," p. 121; Toubert, *Latium* 2:942.

[92] Toubert, *Latium* 2:942. He calls Hadrian's retreat "une ligne de conduite plus réaliste."

[93] Toubert, *Latium* 2:942–43 and his map no. 2.

[94] Vehse, "Sabina," p. 122ff, cites and discusses the older literature and says we cannot be sure. Hahn, "Hludowicianum," pp. 71–74, says only patrimonies and further states that no document was issued in 781. This conflicts with the testimony of the *Ludovicianum* and with Hadrian's letters.

[95] Vehse, "Sabina," pp. 123–26. One has only to leaf through the pages of the *Registrum farfense* to get a sense of its massive landholdings.

[96] *MGH, DK*, vol. 1, nos. 98, 99, pp. 141–42, 142–43.

complex question, and the documents demonstrate that contemporaries saw it as such.

Some friction had arisen between Hadrian and Farfa in 772 because of injuries done to the monastery "by men of the Roman Republic." Hadrian decreed then that henceforth all of Farfa's quarrels with Rome should be referred to the papal *vestararius*.[97] Then, in May 775, *before* Duke Hildebrand turned to Charlemagne, Abbot Probatus requested freedom from episcopal control and free abbatial elections. Charlemagne consented, but it is difficult to see whether he was trying to protect Farfa from Rome or Rieti. A few days later Charlemagne granted Farfa an immunity valid for all of its holdings wheresoever situated. In both of Charlemagne's diplomas there are some curious phrases. Each one speaks of Farfa "*in ducatu Spoletano vel fundatum in territorio Sabinensi.*" Thus we can see that, on the one hand, the Sabine lands were not then considered by the Franks to be part of the Duchy of Rome while, on the other hand, the Sabina was understood to be a discrete region of some sort. A bit further on the diplomas say that a privilege is being granted to Farfa "*sicut et caetera monasteria, quae infra regna nostra constructa esse videtur.*" The implication here is that Farfa is not in Charlemagne's kingdom. By extension, then, neither Spoleto nor the Sabine territory was in his kingdom in the spring of 775.[98] Evidently in early 775 Hadrian's claim to Spoleto was being recognized. When Hildebrand went over to Charlemagne in late 775, the Duchy of Spoleto went with him but Farfa's status did not change. Probatus apparently wanted to clarify his position and petitioned Charlemagne for a confirmation of all of Farfa's possessions granted by earlier kings and dukes. His request was honored in June 776.[99]

In the settlement of 781 Charlemagne, having learned before that the *territorium Savinense* was a distinct region and having also learned that the territory had once belonged to the Duchy of Rome and had recently been claimed by the pope, set his *missi* the task of defining its boundaries. Once they had done this he gave the whole territory to the Republic. This grant must have struck Hadrian as generous and unexpected for since Hildebrand's "defection" the pope had resigned himself to reclaiming only his old patrimonies. Within the territory, however, there remained the problem of Farfa. Charlemagne never withdrew his immunity, so in reality, Hadrian was

---

[97] Jaffé, *RP*, no. 2395.

[98] The phrase in question must be disjunctive and not conjunctive because otherwise it is superfluous. Moreover, it does not appear *in any other* immunity diploma of Charlemagne.

[99] *MGH, DK*, vol. 1, no. 111, pp. 156–57.

conceded effective possession of the whole *territorium Savinense* minus any lands within it held by Farfa.

Charlemagne's conduct, and Hadrian's acquiescence in it, can be explained on three grounds. First, in 774 Hadrian's claim to Spoleto had been recognized and then in late 775 Charlemagne realized that, like his Lombard predecessors, he could not tolerate a dismemberment of his newly acquired kingdom. Thus he assumed overlordship of Spoleto and compensated the pope by granting him the whole *territorium Savinense*, which had once been a part of the Duchy of Rome and whose cession reduced somewhat the western flank of the Spoletan duchy. At the same time it is not unlikely that Duke Hildebrand's desires were taken into account by the king. Second, Farfa kept its immunity because of its unusually significant position as a center of Lombard religious life. Since the middle of the eighth century the Franks had begun a subtle intrusion of influence into Lombard Italy through monasteries. Besides Farfa, Nonantula and San Vincenzo at Volturno and Monte Cassino are good examples of houses that radiated Frankish influence. Karl Schmid has said, astutely, that it is possible to talk of a "monastic conquest" of Italy by the Franks before their military takeover.[100] Farfa was historically too significant for Charlemagne to let it out of his grasp,[101] but even in keeping it, he still gave Hadrian more in the Sabina than the pope might have expected. Third, it may have been that Charlemagne simply did not think about the implications of introducing a Frankish legal and institutional practice, immunity, into a zone that lived by Roman territorial law. In any event, Farfa and the papacy got along peacefully for a generation.

A precise analysis of three and one-half lines from the *Ludovicianum* has enabled us to see the exact dimensions of Charlemagne's first definitive grant to Hadrian. Moreover, it is clear that, for a time, the Quierzy-Rome promise was in force and that, after it ceased being operative, Charlemagne acted in a generous way to effect compensations with one hand for territories he had taken away with the other. Above, the years from 774 to 781 were characterized as ones of uncertainty. The ultimate handling of the Sabina in 781 bears out that characterization. In addition, let us recall that in 782 or 783 Hadrian wrote to Charlemagne about "*multis documentis*." It has long been assumed—quite rightly as we shall see—that more than the Sabina was settled in 781. Again, our starting point must be the *Ludovicianum*.

---

[100]Schmid, "Langobardenreich," pp. 30–35.

[101]After Probatus, three late eighth-century abbots of Farfa were from Francia: Raginbald "in Gallia civitate ortus"; Altbert "Parisios civitate exortus Galliarum"; Maurold "natione Francus": *Chron. farf.*, ed. Balzani, 1:163–66.

It has been necessary to begin with the Sabina because the pertinent passage in the *Ludovicianum* mentions Itherius and Magenarius and thus allows us to fix the date of 781. Even though it is usually assumed that other territories were negotiated and settled at the same time, virtually all of the rest of the evidence is circumstantial and its interpretation raises a number of difficulties.

At this point we can return to the very beginning of the *Ludovicianum*. Louis began by confirming Paschal I, and probably Stephen IV already, in possession of "the city of Rome together with its duchy and suburbs."[102] Following this clause there is an enumeration of the cities and territories of Roman, or suburbicarian, Tuscany. Many of them, for example Bieda, Sutri, Nepi, Castrum Gallese, Orte, and Bomarzo, have attracted our attention already. They had always belonged to the Duchy of Rome, had always been claimed by the papacy, and had frequently been bones of contention between the popes and the Lombards. Among these cities only Narni[103] had been mentioned in one of Pepin's donations, and then only because Aistulf had seized it. Thus, the clause in the *Ludovicianum* concerning Roman Tuscany and the Duchy of Rome cannot date from the 750s or the 760s. It must, moreover, date from after 774 because it is clearly a rectification of the Quierzy-Rome promise, which did not itself contain a reference to Roman Tuscany. No pacts were concluded between 774 and 781, so the latter year is the first one in which the Tuscan clause can be placed.

The following clause in the *Ludovicianum* treats the Roman Campania. This is not surprising because the Roman duchy had always included the city as well as Roman Tuscany and Campania, and these lands had long formed the core of the Republic. Since 770, at the latest, the Roman duchy seems to have absorbed the former Duchy of Perugia.[104] It is mentioned at the end of the enumeration of Tuscan cities and just before the Campanian list. At the end of the Campanina list we read "*necnon et Tiburim cum omnibus finibus*. . . ." Thus, the *Ludovicianum* described the Duchy of Rome from north to south adding Perugia to Roman Tuscany and the large diocese of Tivoli to Roman Campania.[105] Just as the cities of Roman Tuscany had never been mentioned in an earlier donation, so too those documents had contained no references to Campania, not to mention Perugia or Tivoli. As on the Tuscan, so on the Campanian side of Rome, the *Ludovicianum*'s

---

[102]*MGH, Cap.*, vol. 1, no. 172, p. 353.
[103]*LP* 1:452.
[104]*LP* 1:493. Hahn "Hludowicianum," p. 65.
[105]Toubert, *Latium* 2:945–46.

information cannot come from a pact concluded before 781. This does not prove, however, that these two areas were actually negotiated in 781.

A great deal of circumstantial evidence points in that direction. First, we have seen how the old frontiers of the Duchy of Rome figured prominently in the Sabine settlement which definitely took place in 781. Might not that have been the ideal time to determine in a precise way all of the duchy's borders? Second, we have remarked that in 782 or 783 Hadrian wrote about "many documents" granted by Charlemagne "recently." We have also seen that the Sabina clause in the *Ludovicianum* was based on a written document. Thus it is reasonable to assume that other written documents were issued in 781. Third, we have collateral documents—letters—which prove that Campania was a regular subject of discussions between Hadrian and Charlemagne in the late 770s.

The southern sector of the Duchy of Rome, essentially Campania, was a complex region throughout the eighth century. Papal rule in the area was often tenuous, as we noted in the years after 767 when several plots and conspiracies were hatched there. In addition to internal problems, there were also two sets of frontier issues that disturbed the region. Along the coast, to the south of Gaeta and perhaps even from Terracina, the Byzantines still had a foothold. This area was, nominally at least, under the jurisdiction of the duke of Naples, who was himself subordinate to the patrician of Sicily. Ever since the western rejection of the iconoclastic decrees and the demise of the Exarchate, the Greeks had been a potential menace to the southern, coastal flank of the Republic. All along the coast, as far south as Naples, the papacy had lost valuable patrimonies to the Greeks in the 730s. Further inland the Republic had a long and rather mobile frontier with the Lombard duchy of Benevento. The Roman duchy had once reached into the Liri valley, but in 702 Duke Gisulf of Benevento seized several cities in that area and they had not been recovered by the 770s. Throughout the eighth century the Beneventan Lombards continually pressured the southern flank of Campania, and they also attacked the Greeks of Naples quite regularly. Benevento had only a very short coastline in the west, and its dukes desired access to the ports, and thus to the commerce, of Gaeta, Amalfi, Sorrento, and perhaps even Naples. Throughout this era the papacy, the Beneventans, and the Neapolitan Byzantines might have found all sorts of grounds for alliances of any two of them against the third had there not existed various long-standing hostilities among all three.[106]

---

[106]The Greek and Lombard south of Italy in the eighth century is badly in need of a careful study. There exists nothing comparable to Nicola Cilento's *Italia meridionale langobarda* 2d ed.

In view of these developments, it is no cause for wonder that Popes Stephen II and Hadrian sought, in the Quierzy-Rome promise, to add Benevento to the Republic. Such an acquisition would have secured, or insulated, Roman Campania while also isolating the Byzantines of Naples. For a couple of years after 774 Hadrian wrote to Charlemagne in terms that make it clear that he expected a literal fulfillment of the Quierzy-Rome promise in the south; a cession, that is, of Benevento.[107] Hadrian miscalculated on two grounds, however. He failed to take into account Charlemagne's desire to know more about his new kingdom, and he failed utterly to comprehend one of the remarkable men of the age, Duke Arichis of Benevento.

Arichis had been instituted as duke by Desiderius in 758, and in 774 he began styling himself *Princeps*. His intention, evidently, was to set himself up as heir to the fallen Lombard monarchy. He erected an elaborate court life at Benevento, fostered impressive cultural development, strengthened ducal resources, and carried on a lively diplomacy with all of his potential friends and foes.[108] He obviously had no intention of submitting himself to the papacy, but his attitude toward Charlemagne was more complicated.

During 775 and 776 two *missi* of Charlemagne, Possessor and Rabigaud, were active in central and southern Italy. Hadrian's letters from these years convey the impression that the pope was not being kept very fully informed about the activities of these *missi*.[109] By 776 the pope seems to have resigned himself to the fact that he was not going to get Spoleto and Benevento.[110] Hildebrand of Spoleto submitted himself to Charlemagne in

---

(Naples, 1971), which begins with the ninth century. The basic historical outline can be reconstructed from: Gay, *L'Italie méridionale*, pp. 3–39; idem, "L'état pontifical, les Byzantins et les Lombards sur le littoral campanien," *MAH* 21 (1901): 487–508; Giorgio Falco, "L'amministrazione papale nella campagna e nella marittima dalla caduta delle dominazione bisantina al sorgere dei communi," *ASR* 38 (1915): 677–707; René Poupardin, "Etudes sur l'histoire des principautés lombardes de l'Italie méridionale," *Le moyen âge* 11 (1907): 1–25; Hirsch, "Hadrian I und Benevent," pp. 33–50; Bertolini, "Carlomagno e Benevento," pp. 609–33; Vehse, "Benevent als Territorium des Kirchenstaats bis zum Beginn der avignonischen Epoche," *QFIAB* 22 (1930–31): 89–90.

[107] E.g., *CC*, nos. 51, 53, pp. 571, 575.

[108] The key study of Arichis's Benevento remains Hans Belting, "Studien zum Beneventanischen Hof im 8. Jahrhundert," *Dumbarton Oaks Papers* 16 (1962): 141–93. See also: Kaminsky, "Zum Sinngehalt des Princeps-Titels," pp. 81–92; Elisabeth Garms-Cornides, "Die langobardischen Fürstentitel" (774–1077)," in *Intitulatio*, ed. Herwig Wolfram, 2 vols. (Vienna, 1967–73), 2:354–75; Gasparri, *I duchi longobardi*, pp. 99–100. Kaminsky is preparing for *FSI* a new edition of the Beneventan charters which will be an essential aid to further research.

[109] *CC*, nos. 52, 55, 56, 57, pp. 573–74, 578–83. Bertolini, "Carlomagno e Benevento," p. 615 n.28, believes that no. 52 is actually the last in the sequence and dates it early 776.

[110] Bertolini, "Carlomagno e Benevento," p. 619.

late 775, and it seems that Arichis of Benevento made some perfunctory gesture of recognition also, probably in return for a guaranty that his duchy would not be assigned to the papacy.[111] In 776 Hadrian set a new tack. He wrote to Charlemagne to say that a massive revolt was brewing.[112] What Hadrian seems to have had in mind was an attempt to identify his own interests with Charlemagne's by lumping together the enemies of both pope and king.[113] In the end only Hrodgaud of Friuli did actually revolt, and Hadrian got no satisfaction in the south. From the pope's point of view an impasse had been reached. Spoleto and Benevento were not to be his, but he was still vulnerable in Campania and had no certainty about what help, if any, he might expect from Charlemagne in that region.

By 778 Hadrian was writing to Charlemagne that "the most wicked Beneventans" had joined forces with the citizens of Gaeta and Terracina and the patrician of Sicily to seize certain cities in Campania.[114] Hadrian said that repeated warnings from him had availed nothing, and now he wanted the king to restrain his enemies. This letter is interesting because it does not refer to promises. Rather, the pope, depicting his own position as a very precarious one, implored aid and said, at the end of the letter, that he might have to send his own army into Campania. What we have here is yet more evidence of the prevailing uncertainty in the late 770s.

In fact, Hadrian did send his troops out in 778 or 779 to recover Terracina, but then the Neapolitans and Beneventans took it back.[115] Hadrian then proposed a military alliance with the Franks to recover Terracina, and to attack Gaeta and Naples "for the purpose of recovering our patrimonies which are situated in Neapolitan territory." All of this is reminiscent of Hadrian's contemporary concerns about his Sabine patrimonies. In each instance he started by demanding a whole region and ended up asking only for his patrimonies.

In the south, however, conditions were more complicated than they were in Spoleto. Apparently the Neapolitans, after they had helped to retake Terracina, tried to strike a bargain with Hadrian in exchange for his patrimonies. In doing this they abandoned their alliance with Arichis, who then

---

[111]Hirsch, "Hadrian und Benevent," p. 44; Garms-Cornides, "Fürstentitel," pp. 370–71, supposes only a "non-aggression pact."

[112]CC, no. 57, pp. 582–83.

[113]Hirsch, "Hadrian und Benevent," pp. 37–38.

[114]CC, no. 61, pp. 588–89.

[115]CC, no. 64, pp. 591–92. Bertolini ("Carlomagno e Benevento," p. 622 n.75) dates this letter May 780, which is plausible, though an earlier date is possible. Gundlach says 779–80 as does Jaffé.

sought to establish stronger ties with the patrician of Sicily.[116] Arichis also seems to have entered into some sort of negotiations with the Byzantine court.[117] The duke of Benevento had found the Neapolitans unreliable and, with both Rome and Francia unsympathetic to his goal of independence, the Greeks of Sicily and Constantinople were the only potential sources of support for him. It was in the midst of this tangled set of circumstances that Hadrian was appealing to Charlemagne for assistance.

In a letter of 780 Hadrian reported of a meeting in Rome with a *missus* of Charlemagne, a deacon named Atto.[118] Bertolini's reading of this letter merits careful consideration.[119] He observes that there is no mention in it of the need for armed intervention in Campania. Perhaps, therefore, Atto related to Hadrian that Charlemagne was coming to Italy soon, and that southern affairs would be treated shortly. In fact, this is exactly what happened. After Charlemagne's visit to Rome in 781 peace reigned for several years in Campania and beyond. All of the tensions evident in the papal correspondence between 774 and 780 disappear,[120] and evidence concerning San Vincenzo at Volturno indicates that Charlemagne's rule in Benevento had finally been recognized.[121] We must ask how Arichis was brought under control, because virtually all of the intrigues of the preceeding few years are directly or indirectly traceable to him.

Amidst all of these confusing developments it may be helpful to review briefly the points that have been established thus far. From 774 to 776 Hadrian laid claim to Spoleto and Benevento, and then later gave up those claims and turned to a request for the restoration of his patrimonies inside the duchies. In Campania, unlike Sabina, the pope faced genuine threats from the Beneventans and perhaps from the Greeks of Naples to what he already held, and until the summer of 780 he repeatedly pleaded for assistance in this region. From 775 through 781 Charlemagne had *missi* operating almost constantly in central Italy. Surely he was trying to come to grips with the political contours of his new kingdom. Hadrian, for his part, knew about these *missi*, but could not obtain full disclosures about their activities.

---

[116]CC, no. 64, p. 591. Gay, "Littoral campanien," pp. 492–95; Poupardin, "Principautés," pp. 250–53; Bertolini, "Carlomagno e Benevento," pp. 622–24.

[117]Poupardin, "Principautés," p. 250, points to *Translatio S. Heliani*, c. 1, *MGH, SSrL*, p. 581, as evidence but this passage is difficult to date and interpret.

[118]CC, no. 65, pp. 592–93.

[119]Bertolini, "Carlomagno e Benevento," p. 624.

[120]Gay, "Littoral campanien," pp. 494–95.

[121]CC, nos. 66, 67, pp. 593–97. Hirsch, "Hadrian und Benevent," pp. 48–50; Bertolini, "Carlomagno e Benevento," pp. 625–30.

In 780, when Atto visited Rome, Hadrian was apparently assured that settlements to his liking were about to be concluded. We know that affairs in the Sabina were regulated in 781, and a good many indicators point to the likelihood of a Campanian settlement at the same time.

The reason for peace in the south, and to the south of the Duchy of Rome, lies in diplomacy. While Charlemagne was in Rome in 781 ambassadors from the Byzantine empress, Irene, came to him to conclude a marriage alliance. Charlemagne's daughter Rotrud was affianced to Irene's son, Constantine VI.[122] That the Greek envoys knew exactly where and when to find Charlemagne indicates that their meeting was prearranged.[123] Perhaps negotiations had been going on for some time; perhaps Atto reported to Hadrian on them in the summer of 780. The result of the Franco-Byzantine marriage alliance was that Arichis of Benevento was completely isolated.[124] He had to give up his plots and schemes and make peace with Charlemagne and Hadrian because even this remarkable character was no match for the Franks without allies.

The Sabine settlement, which definitely took place in 781, would have been possible any time after about 778. The Campanian settlement only became possible in 781 with the isolation of Arichis. Certainly Charlemagne had had important and pressing military concerns in Francia which delayed for a time his return to Rome, but only in 781 would a journey to Italy for the purpose of reckoning accounts with Hadrian have been feasible on the basis of purely Italian conditions. Thus it seems altogether correct to locate the *Ludovicianum*'s Campanian clause in 781 and to regard it as one of those "many documents" Hadrian later referred to.

The Campanian settlement, which was altered slightly in 787, differs in some interesting and important ways from the Sabine one. The latter was a generous adjustment of the Republic's eastern frontier worked out by Charlemagne and Hadrian as a compensation for the papacy's renunciation of its claims to, and expectations in, Spoleto. In Campania the settlement was less generous in terms of territory, for the named sites, Segni, Anagni, Ferentino, Alatri, Patrica, Frosinone, and Tivoli, "*cum omnibus finibus Campaniae*," represented for the Republic no territorial gains, unless the cession of the whole diocese of Tivoli marked a gain to the east. Still, the Campanian settlement was valuable because it set down precisely the Republic's borders

---

[122]Einhard, *Vita Karoli*, c. 19, ed. Halphen, pp. 58–60; *Ann. laurr., MGH, SS* 1:32; Theophanes, ed. de Boor, 1:455. Abel and Simson, *Jahrbücher* 1:384–86.

[123]Bertolini, "Carlomagno e Benevento," pp. 624–25.

[124]Bertolini, "Carlomagno e Benevento," p. 631; Garms-Cornides, "Fürstentitel," p. 372.

with Benevento and the Greek south. Charlemagne was sworn to defend the *"iustitiae sancti Petri*," and after 781 the territorial dimensions of those "rights" were clear to all parties. Given the unusually complicated political situation to the south of Rome, Hadrian had every reason to feel satisfied with the Campanian settlement. He obtained clear title to Campania, and not just to his patrimonies. He did not get back his church's former Neapolitan patrimonies, but with Arichis in check and the Greeks at peace he no longer had to fear attacks from the south.

The year 781 was a crucial one not only for the Republic but also for Carolingian Italy. Charlemagne made his son Pepin king of Italy in that year and issued a capitulary at Mantua that extended many features of Carolingian rule into the Italian *regnum*.[125] In view of these developments, and of the Sabine and Campanian settlements, is it possible that further arrangements between Hadrian and Charlemagne can be traced to 781?

After the long paragraph in the *Ludovicianum* that begins with Ravenna and ends with Sabina, we read a clause that says, "Likewise in Lombard Tuscany Città di Castello, Orvieto, Bagnorea, Farentum [Marino?], Viterbo[?], Orchia, Marta, Toscanella, Sovana, Populonia, Rosellae [Grosseto]." Lindner and Gundlach thought that this passage must date from 781,[126] but most scholars have placed it in 787.[127] There are substantial reasons for holding to 781. The sources for Charlemagne's visit to Italy in 787 make it absolutely clear that his journey was undertaken "for the purpose of settling affairs in the Beneventan area,"[128] and Hadrian's letters from the middle and late 780s never refer to Tuscany.[129] Let us see, then, how a case can be made for a Tuscan settlement in 781.

The Quierzy-Rome promise would have given the Republic most of Lombard Tuscany and a good deal of the Romagna south of the Luni-Monselice line. During the 770s Charlemagne gradually served notice that the Quierzy-Rome promise was not going to be fulfilled literally, but he

---

[125]*MGH, Cap.*, vol. 1, no. 90, pp. 190–91. See also no. 97, pp. 203–4, from 779–80. On these capitularies see: Manacorda, *Dominazione dei carolingi*, pp. 43–50, and for chronology, his "Tabella 1," p. 137.

[126]Lindner, *Sogenannten Schenkungen*, p. 58; Gundlach, *Kirchenstaat*, p. 67.

[127]Duchesne, *LP* 1:ccxi; Partner, *Lands of St. Peter*, p. 35; Hahn, "Hludowicianum," p. 75.

[128]*Annales regni Francorum, anno* 787, ed. Kurze, p. 74.

[129]*CC*, nos. 82–85, pp. 615–21. Hahn, "Hludowicianum," p. 75 and nn.489, 490, inexplicably cites these annals and letters as *proof* of a Tuscan settlement in 787. In fact, not a single document cited by her, or by anyone else, in this connection mentions Tuscany in any way.

displayed some uncertainty about his obligations under that promise, and at least in the Sabina, he later sought to make amends for his failure to fulfill it integrally. Generally, Charlemagne spent the late 770s learning about his new kingdom, and one of the things he learned was that he could not suffer its dismemberment by, for example, complete cessions of Spoleto and Benevento. Lombard Tuscany was no less significant to the *regnum* than the southern duchies, and at some point Charlemagne must have come to the stark realization that he could not afford to part with this region, even though he had once promised to do so.[130] From 774 to 781 Charlemagne displayed a noticeable reluctance to deal with Tuscany and the Romagna,[131] and on at least one occasion, Hadrian wrote to Charlemagne about three Tuscan bishoprics in terms which suggest that the pope considered the region to be his.[132] Then, shortly after his visit to Rome in April 781, Charlemagne began issuing diplomas, in quantity and of various sorts, for both Tuscany and the Romagna. The first of these dates from 8 June 781, and thereafter we have a long series of them.[133] The evidence from Charlemagne's diplomas only makes sense if it is assumed that some settlement pertaining to Tuscany was achieved before 8 June 781. This settlement, presumably, freed Charlemagne to handle affairs in a region where he had for seven years been displaying a discernible reluctance to exercise any authority at all. The only likely time and place is Rome in April of that year.

The settlement is, once again, an interesting one. The Duchy of Rome had never extended into Lombard Tuscany, and in 781 the precise northern frontier of the duchy itself was fixed and defined at its ancient limits in suburbicarian, or Roman, Tuscany. Then, Charlemagne added to the Republic a section of southern and coastal Lombard Tuscany which he detached from the *regnum*. It seems, again, that Hadrian was being compensated for the fact that the Quierzy-Rome promise was not literally fulfilled. The Republic received lands it had never held in return for abandoning claims that Charlemagne could not honor. There are, thus, striking similarities between

---

[130]The great study of this region remains Fedor Schneider, *Die Reichsverwaltung in der Toscana von der Gründung des Langobardenreichs bis zum Ausgang der Staufer*, vol. 1 (vol. 2 never appeared) (Rome, 1914).

[131]Two diplomas survive, from 776 and 780, both for Nonantula: *MGH, DK*, vol. 1, nos. 113, 131, pp. 159–60, 181–82. I would class these with the diplomas for Farfa discussed above. Nonantula was a key monastic center of Frankish influence in Italy.

[132]*CC*, no. 50, p. 570.

[133]*MGH, DK*, vol. 1, nos. 133 (Reggio), 147 (Modena), 150 (Arezzo), 155 (S. Miniato in Florence), 183 (Nonantula for lands in Bologna), 196 (Arezzo), etc., pp. 183–84, 199–200, 204, 210, 247, 263.

the Tuscan and Sabine settlements, but also a marked difference. The Republic did have a historic claim on the *territorium Savinense* which had many years earlier been absorbed into the Duchy of Spoleto. Charlemagne, in the Sabina, *gave back* lands he might well have considered to be his own after he had accepted Spoleto's submission. In Tuscany, on the other hand, Charlemagne made an outright concession to the Republic of lands to which the papacy had no historic right, and which he had every reason to regard as a part of his Italian kingdom.

If a Tuscan settlement was achieved in 781, then it follows that another clause in the *Ludovicianum* goes back to that year. The relevant clause says that Hadrian and Charlemagne entered into an agreement whereby certain revenues customarily paid to the palace at Pavia by Tuscany and Spoleto would henceforth go to the pope. Moreover, the text explicitly states that Hadrian got these revenues in exchange for abandoning his claims to Spoleto and Tuscany.[134] Once more we can see Charlemagne compensating Hadrian because the Quierzy-Rome promise was not precisely honored. This time, indeed, there is concrete proof that compensations were being effected. In addition, this enormously significant clause proves that Charlemagne did acknowledge that the pope had a legitimate claim on Spoleto and Tuscany. This claim can only have come from the Quierzy-Rome promise, so we can see here a confirmation that Charlemagne did feel himself bound to some extent by that pact. Finally, the "revenue clause" of the *Ludovicianum* brings to light another of those "many documents" from 781 to which Hadrian adverted in 782 or 783.

The preceding discussion has not quite exhausted all of the provisions of the general settlement of 781, for it seems that the *Ludovicianum*'s long clause on Ravenna, the Exarchate, and the Pentapolis also dates from that year. The clause in question appears to be a composite construction based on the Pavian treaties, the Quierzy-Rome promise, and a new version of

---

[134]*MGH, Cap.*, vol. 1, no. 172, 354: "Simili modo per hoc nostrae confirmationis decretum firmamus donationes, quas pie recordationis domnus Pippinus rex avus noster, et postea domnus et genitor noster Karolus imperator beato apostolo Petro spontanea voluntate contulerunt, necnon et censum et pensionem sui ceteras dationes, quae annuatim in palatium regis Langobardorum inferri solebant, sive de Tuscia Langobardorum, sive de ducatu Spoletino, sicut in suprascriptas donationibus continetur, et inter sanctae memoriae Adrianum papam et domnum ac genitorem nostrum Karolum imperatorem convenit, quando idem pontifex eidem de suprascriptas ducatibus, id est Tuscano et Spoletino, suae auctoritatis praeceptum confirmavit, eo scilicet modo, ut annos singulis predictus census ecclesiae beati Petri apostoli persolvatur, salva super eosdem ducatus nostra in omnibus dominatione et illorum ad nostram partem subiectione."

these older texts formulated in 781.[135] As with the Sabina, Campania, and Tuscany, so too concerning the Exarchate did Hadrian and Charlemagne correspond in the 770s.[136] The outcome in Ravenna and its region was, for the Republic, both better and worse than in the other areas under negotiation. The area of Ravenna, the Exarchate, and the Pentapolis, was not radically altered from what it had been when Aistulf took it in 751, or when Pepin demanded it be given back to Stephen II in 755 and 756. The cities of Bologna and Imola, along with the southern Pentapolitan towns of Ancona, Osimo, and Umana, were now added, but this was not really a novelty because together they formed the "remaining cities" that had been so hotly contested by Desiderius with Paul I, Stephen III, and Hadrian himself. In this regard Hadrian got exactly what he desired. In another regard, however, the old Exarchate, "*sicut antiquitus erat*," presents profound difficulties because Hadrian had, within the region, to endure a settlement that left his full rights limited and impaired.

Before 751 the papacy had consistently evinced a keen interest in Ravenna, and after that year the popes expressed outright and unambiguous claim to it. Pepin, Charlemagne, and Louis the Pious all guaranteed the Republic's possession of Ravenna and the old Exarchate, and in 756–57 Stephen II introduced papal officials into the area. All of this seems simple and straightforward, but the reality was infinitely more complex. The Ravennese had always been willing to cooperate with the papacy when their fundamental interests coincided, but quite frequently, at least from the point of view of the Ravennese, their interests diverged sharply.

Late in 774 Hadrian wrote to Charlemagne to complain that Leo of Ravenna had been sending envoys to the Frankish court, and to criticize Leo for retaining control of a number of cities in Emilia and the Pentapolis. Hadrian went on to say that Leo was personally ordering affairs in Ravenna, and that the demise of Desiderius had profited Rome nothing in the northeast of Italy.[137] On three occasions in 775 Hadrian wrote in similar terms, particularly specifying that papal officials were being prevented by Leo from carrying out their duties.[138] From these letters one can conclude that papal rule had become negligible in Ravenna.

For a variety of reasons both Hadrian's complaints and Leo's efforts

---

[135]Hahn, "Hludowicianum," pp. 68–71, handles this clause accurately and cites the relevant literature in her notes.

[136]CC, nos. 49, 53, 54, 55, pp. 568–69, 575, 576–77, 579–80.

[137]CC, no. 49, pp. 568–69.

[138]CC, nos. 53, 54, 55, pp. 575–76, 576–77, 579.

to escape papal domination are perfectly understandable. In Ravenna, as elsewhere, Hadrian was uncertain about his situation after 774 and he was seeking clarification. The Ravennese, for their part, had rarely been kindly disposed toward Rome, and the archbishops considered themselves to be the legitimate successors to the exarchs in the former lands of the Exarchate.[139] In fact, there are obvious parallels between the position the popes had assumed in Rome and the position that the archbishops were trying to assume in Ravenna. Local legends maintain that Leo had invited Charlemagne to Italy to fight Desiderius in 773, and that the two remained in league after the fall of Pavia.[140] If any credence can be lent to these legends then, after 774, Charlemagne may have felt some sense of obligation to Leo.[141] After all, Charlemagne's *missi* had played a key role in putting Leo on the archepiscopal throne after Desiderius's machinations in 767. It is also possible that Leo's envoys to the Frankish court, the ones attested to by Hadrian's letters, and Leo himself, who visited Francia, made out a case for Ravenna's legitimate historical interests. In the 750s it must have been easy for the Franks to have conceded Ravenna to Rome because, quite simply, Aistulf had captured it and the pope claimed it. Later, with fuller information available, the papacy's slender title to Ravenna became clear to Charlemagne at just about the same time that he realized that he had in some fashion to honor a long-standing promise to hand the region over to Rome. In the end, Hadrian's concerns about Ravenna after 774 seem analogous to his concerns about other regions. Charlemagne seems to have been unwilling to spell out his own views of Ravenna's relationship with the Republic before he entered upon the series of engagements undertaken in 781.

Leo, who had become Hadrian's implacable adversary, died 14 February 777,[142] and in 781 Charlemagne put Hadrian back in possession of the Exarchate. Within a couple of years, however, the pope again met serious opposition in Ravenna, where local officials refused to admit his agents and appealed against him to the Franks.[143] When Gratiosus of Ravenna died (ca. 788) Charlemagne's envoys participated in the election of his successor,[144] and in the years thereafter Ravennese officials continued to refuse to bend

---

[139]Guillou, *Régionalisme*, pp. 15–16; Wickberg, "Archbishops of Ravenna," pp. 25–33.

[140]Agnellus, *Lib. pont. rav.*, c. 160, *MGH, SSrL*, p. 381; *CC*, nos. 49, 54, pp. 568, 576–77.

[141]Luther, *Rom und Ravenna*, pp. 56–58; Fasoli, *Carlomagno*, p. 83.

[142]Schmidt, "Ravenna," p. 756.

[143]*CC*, no. 75, pp. 606–7.

[144]*CC*, no. 85, pp. 621–22.

to Hadrian's will.[145] At just about the same time that Franks, over the pope's protests, participated in the archepiscopal election, Hadrian was asked by Charlemagne to prevent Venetian merchants from trading in Ravenna and the Pentapolis. Simultaneously Hadrian and Charlemagne tried to restrain a duke, Garamannus, who had robbed the Church of Ravenna of some of its possessions.[146] The documents that reveal these facts certainly suggest that pope and king were cooperating in ruling Ravenna. Under Pope Leo III (795–816) we know of both Frankish and papal *missi* operating in the Exarchate,[147] and this again points to cooperation. When Martin was elected archbishop in 810, he sent envoys to Francia, perhaps to secure his own rights vis-à-vis Rome.[148] His ploy seems to have availed him little, however, for in 814 Louis the Pious responded to a complaint by Leo III touching Martin's behavior and dispatched Bishop John of Arles to Ravenna to take Martin to Rome to answer for his conduct before the pope.[149] By 816 papal relations with Ravenna were at least outwardly cordial because, while he was returning from his visit to Francia, Pope Stephen IV stopped at Ravenna and confirmed its privileges.[150] This evidence, scanty as it is, tells us only that the popes and archbishops were frequently at odds with one another, and that the Frankish crown played a mediating role between the antagonists.

Duchesne supposed that Charlemagne considered Ravenna ungovernable by the Republic and more or less traded a cession of papal claims in the old Exarchate for favorable settlements elsewhere.[151] There is probably some truth in this hypothesis, but it does not accommodate all of the evidence very well. Frankish donations always mention Ravenna, and no papal document renounces control of the region. Closer to the full truth is the suggestion of Tabacco that pope and king possessed concurrent rule in Ravenna.[152] This view seems very close to the few permissible deductions that can be drawn from the limited surviving evidence. I venture to suggest that Raven-

---

[145]CC, no. 94, p. 635.

[146]CC, no. 86, pp. 622–23; Kehr, *IP*, vol. 5, no. 89, p. 37.

[147]*Leonis Papae III Epistolae X*, no. 9, MGH, EKA 3:100–102. Schmidt, "Ravenna," p. 759.

[148]Schmidt, "Ravenna," p. 759.

[149]Agnellus, *Lib. pont. rav.*, c. 169, MGH, SSrL, p. 387.

[150]Kehr, *IP*, vol. 5, no. 94, p. 38.

[151]Duchesne, *LP* 1:ccxl–ccxli.

[152]Tabacco, *Storia d'Italia*, p. 78. This is close to the position taken long ago by Luther, *Rom und Ravenna*, pp. 56–58, and more recently by Bertolini, "Prime manifestazione," p. 606.

na's government can be characterized as a "double dyarchy." On the one hand pope and king shared rule, and on the other hand pope and archbishop divided authority. To be sure, no text says this in so many words, but the actual terms of the arrangements that covered Ravenna cannot be spelled out precisely on the basis of the extant documents. Nevertheless, all Carolingian privileges assign Ravenna to the Republic, and in this one zone only the pope's authority was less than complete. Strictly speaking, then, it is possible to say that in 781 Charlemagne guaranteed to the Republic possession of the old Exarchate within its historic territorial limits. Inside those limits, however, in 781 or at some later and undeterminable date, Charlemagne and Hadrian arrived at a compromise on the extent of papal jurisdiction.

Enveloped within the *Ludovicianum*'s clause on Lombard Tuscany there is another passage that was probably the result of a settlement dating from 781. After its enumeration of the cities in Lombard Tuscany granted to Hadrian in 781, the text continues by saying "and the islands of Corsica, Sardinia and Sicily, wholly, with all their adjacent maritime territories, coasts and ports." Scholarly opinion holds that the *Ludovicianum*'s text on these islands was tampered with sometime between 817 and the execution of the canonical collections from which the document today derives.[153] Can anything be retained from this passage? Can it be dated to 781? Can it be explained?

The first two of these questions can be handled together. Sardinia and Corsica had belonged to the Exarchate of Carthage before its conquest by the Arabs.[154] Thereafter they probably passed under the jurisdiction of the patrician of Sicily, who was in other respects the heir of the African exarchs. The islands were also Roman suburbicarian dioceses and had valuable patrimonies on them.[155] In the eighth century the Lombards conquered Corsica,[156] but there is no conclusive evidence that they ever took Sardinia. The Quierzy-Rome promise assigned Corsica to Rome,[157] and in 778 Hadrian mentioned it as yet another territory whose restitution he was expecting.[158]

---

[153]Sickel, *Privilegium*, p. 132, discusses the literature but also expresses some doubts about the "dogma of interpolation"; Hahn, "Hludowicianum," p. 78.

[154]Goubert, *Byzance avant l'Islam*, pp. 195–97; Tabacco, *Storia d'Italia*, p. 39, says Justinian submitted Corsica and Sardinia to Ravenna but, to my knowledge, there is no evidence for this contention.

[155]Schwarzlose, *Patrimonien*, p. 28ff; Hartmann, *Untersuchungen*, p. 100. As recently as 715 Pope Sisinnius appointed a bishop in Corsica: *LP* 1:388.

[156]This is not universally admitted, but I follow the reasoning of Schneider, *Toscana*, p. 79.

[157]*LP* 1:498.

[158]*CC*, no. 60, p. 587.

In 808 Pope Leo III committed Corsica to Charlemagne for safekeeping because of Muslim attacks on the island.[159] Sardinia may have passed under Arab control before 754, and of its fate after that date we can know little for certain. Corsica, however, appears to be an authentic component of the *Ludovicianum*'s contents, and a guaranty of it to Rome in 781 seems likely given that so many other territories mentioned in the Quierzy-Rome promise and in other documents dating from the years 774 to 781 were disposed of in that year. Sicily had been alienated from all Roman jurisdiction by Emperor Leo III after the rejection of the iconoclastic edicts and remained Byzantine for centuries.[160] It has no proper place in a document from 817, let alone in one from 781. In short, Corsica is a genuine grant of 781, Sardinia is a mystery, and Sicily is a later interpolation.

Interpolation can, of course, mean many things. It need not be concluded that Sicily, and perhaps Sardinia, were *inserted* into some later version of the *Ludovicianum*. A 781 text, taken up in 816–17, may have said something about these two islands. Ficker thought that lands outside Carolingian control may have been mentioned only to secure the legitimacy of papal claims to them.[161] In this regard the passage in the *Ottonianum* on Sicily is intriguing. Here Otto I granted "the patrimony of Sicily if God shall grant that it fall into our hands."[162] Perhaps the *Ludovicianum*, as well as its model, contained an additional clause like this which an interpolator working between 962 and the late eleventh century changed to Sicily "*sub integro.*" We do know, because Sickel proved it, that the *Ottonianum* took up almost verbatim the territorial provisions of the *Ludovicianum*, so Sicily, or more likely Sicilian patrimonies, may actually have been mentioned in 781 and again in 816–17. Sardinia, however, remains a mystery. It was not, as far as is known, mentioned between 754 and 781. The island appears in the *Ludovicianum* and disappears from the *Ottonianum*. This leads me to believe that, sometime after 962, whoever altered the Sicilian clause went a step further and inserted into the document a claim upon Sardinia. Then Anselm, Deusdedit, and Bonizo discovered a text with claims to all three islands and, knowing that the Church had venerable claims and interests on all of them, reproduced the words they found. I am assuming that none of them was the interpolator.

---

[159]Leo III, *Epp. X*, no. 1, *MGH, EKA* 3:88.

[160]Pope Leo III admitted that Sicily was Byzantine: Leo III, *Epp. X*, no. 6, *MGH, EKA* 3:96. Classen, "Karl der Große, das Papsttum und Byzanz," p. 541.

[161]Ficker, *Forschungen* 2:344; cf. Martens, *Römische Frage*, pp. 226–27.

[162]*MGH, DO*, vol. 1, no. 235, p. 325.

Corsica, then, may be regarded as an authentic donation of 781. Sicily "*sub integro*" can be dismissed as a donation, though there may have been some talk about Sicilian patrimonies. Sardinia must be left on the margin until new documents or sharper interpretations come to light. As for Corsica, its donation is analogous to the grant of the Exarchate in 755, 756, 774, and 781. It was a land seized by the Lombards from the Byzantines and then taken from the Lombards by the Franks and given to the Republic. Charlemagne could have kept the island as a part of his new Lombard kingdom, but he elected to honor in yet another respect the Quierzy-Rome promise, and so he gave it to Hadrian.

Several things ought now to be apparent. First, Charlemagne did feel himself bound to a considerable degree by the Quierzy-Rome promise and, at least until 778, Hadrian had assumed that the promise was in force. Still, because the Quierzy-Rome promise had been based upon certain contingencies that were never precisely met, there was always room for negotiation of the basic provisions of the agreement. Charlemagne assumed the Lombard crown, which simultaneously made it unnecessary for him to divide his new kingdom and unwise for him to dismember it. Hadrian desired, essentially, that same freedom and independence of action, coupled with territorial security, that all his predecessors since Gregory II had sought. In 781, after several years during which both king and pope tried to come to grips with their respective and mutual positions in Italy, a massive settlement was established. Hadrian got more for the Republic than it had ever possessed, but he obtained less than the papacy's maximum scheme had contemplated. Charlemagne gave, quite generously, in Tuscany, Spoleto, Corsica, and perhaps Tivoli. He also assigned revenues to Rome that had traditionally flowed to Pavia, and which he had every right to reckon among his own royal incomes in Italy. Envoys went back and forth carrying correspondence, and gradually the shape of the eventual settlement emerged. When it was at last signed in 781 it was fair and acceptable to all parties. Hadrian's tone in all his correspondence with Charlemagne, both before and after 781, is warm, cordial, and solicitous. Charlemagne, Einhard says, "wept as though he had lost a brother or a son" when he learned of Hadrian's death in 795.[163] If my interpretation of the years from 774 to 781 as ones of uncertainly is correct then, for the first time, it becomes possible to see how Charlemagne and Hadrian cooperated, and why they were so genuinely fond of one another. They were both remarkable men who accepted with grace and good humor reasonable solutions to their individual problems and acceptable accommo-

---

[163] *Vita Karoli*, c. 19, ed. Halphen, p. 60.

dations of their mutual ones. The late François-Louis Ganshof, in numerous publications, made an impressive case for the need to study Charlemagne's reign year by year so as to be able to take all factors into account simultaneously and thereby to avoid the inevitable distortions introduced by the standard topical approaches. The chief danger of the topical approach is that it yields a static picture by seeming to suggest that policies were formulated and applied once and for all. Ganshof's approach, which is basically the one adopted here, permits an appreciation of change, adjustment, development.[164]

By applying Ganshof's method to the seven years after 774, it becomes possible to see 781 as a year of enormous import in Carolingian history, in the history of Carolingian Italy, and in the history of the Republic of St. Peter. In this year Charlemagne concluded a marriage alliance with the Byzantines that temporarily isolated his greatest potential rival in Italy, Arichis of Benevento, and heightened his own prestige immeasurably. He introduced his son Pepin into Italy as king, and he issued the Mantuan capitulary which extended to Carolingian Italy the basic program of the earlier capitulary of Herstal. Finally, Charlemagne undertook a massive reckoning of accounts with Hadrian that addressed in novel ways problems latent in Franco-papal relations since 754, and in the history of the Republic since the 720s. At the same time, Hadrian must, after the papacy had bounded from crisis to crisis for nearly a century, have taken great pleasure at seeing all of Italy at peace and his Republic secure and in several areas augmented. Likewise, Hadrian's joy must have been complete at knowing with absolute conviction that his lands were guaranteed by "many documents."

The Territorial Settlements of 787–88

One more thing that the *Ludovicianum* does say, and two things that it does not say, need to be discussed before this account of the territorial development of the Republic of St. Peter can be brought to a close. The former has to do with Benevento again and can be precisely dated to 787. The latter concern Venetia and Istria and can be dated only approximately.

In a clause immediately after the one dealing with Lombard Tuscany the *Ludovicianum* says, "Likewise in the territory of Campania Sora, Arce,

---

[164]Some of the best of Ganshof's studies are collected in *The Carolingians and the Frankish Monarchy*.

Aquino, Arpino, Teano and Capua." In addition, this clause also gives title to patrimonies in Benevento, Salerno, upper and lower Calabria, and Naples. In all other areas the settlement of 781 was definitive; why therefore was a later adjustment necessary in the south? And why did this adjustment take the form that it did?

Late in 786, "having peace all around," Charlemagne decided to go to Italy to submit definitively "that region which was not yet subject to him, Benevento."[165] Arichis had never completely submitted himself to Charlemagne, but he had been neutralized in 781 by the Franco-Byzantine marriage alliance. For the next several years we hear of him only that he attacked Amalfi and was driven off by the Neapolitans.[166] Surely this was not enough to bring Charlemagne to Italy. Arichis's penchant for independence alone cannot have been the reason either, for if that had been the sole, critical objection of Charlemagne to the Beneventan duke then some opportunity could have been found to deal with him in 776 or in 781 when the Franks were already in Italy.

Peace in Francia in 786 afforded an opportunity, a pause, to deal with Arichis, but this particular time was chosen to deal with Benevento for two specific reasons. First, Charlemagne had decided to break off his marriage alliance with Byzantium. He did this formally when he was met at Capua by Greek envoys in 787.[167] Obviously any rupture in Franco-Byzantine relations would have restored the status quo as of 781. That is to say, Arichis would be free to seek an alliance with Constantinople. Just as importantly, though, Arichis personally posed a problem that, in the absence of diplomatic restraints, had to be met. He was a crowned, anointed prince with valuable ties to prominent Lombard families who had both opposed and supported Desiderius. He was a legitimate threat to the whole Carolingian regime in Italy. At the same time, Arichis was related by marriage to Duke Tassilo of Bavaria[168] who was in the late 780s in open opposition to the Carolingians. Charlemagne's family was still not absolutely secure on the throne, and he could not suffer gladly the independence of two powerful men, actually two powerful and related families, that were *Königsgleich*.[169]

---

[165] *Annales regni Francorum*, anno 786, ed. Kurze, p. 73; *Poeta Saxo*, 2.21–28, *MGH, SS* 1:241.

[166] *CC*, no. 78, p. 610.

[167] *Annales qui dicuntur Einhardi*, anno 786 (sic), ed. Kurze, p. 75. See: Abel and Simson, *Jahrbücher* 1:567–69; Bertolini, "Carlomagno e Benevento," p. 634.

[168] They were both sons-in-law of Desiderius.

[169] Brunner, *Oppositionelle Gruppen*, pp. 43–44, 47, 53; Hartmut Hoffmann, "Französische Fürstenweihen des Hochmittelalters," *DA* 18 (1962): 93–95; Garms-Cornides, "Fürstentitel," pp. 371–72.

Charlemagne spent Christmas 786 at Florence and headed for Rome early in the year. There he was met by Romuald, Arichis's son, who offered his father's submission if Charlemagne would stay out of Benevento. Charlemagne took counsel with both his magnates and Hadrian and decided to press forward. The king entered Benevento and went as far as Capua where he learned that Arichis had fled from the city of Benevento to Salerno. Arichis nonetheless sent hostages to Charlemagne, including his sons, and agreed to submit himself.[170] Southern Italy was notoriously malarial, and Charlemagne may not have had adequate forces for a protracted campaign.[171] Thus, for the time being, the king returned to Rome.

About this second visit to Rome in 787 several Frankish sources make what seems like an odd statement. They say that Charlemagne seized Benevento and gave it to St. Peter.[172] In fact, Charlemagne handed to Hadrian at this time title to a string of cities in the Liri valley along with the papacy's old patrimonies in several areas of southern Italy. One last time Charlemagne was generous. In 781 Charlemagne received from Hadrian a renunciation of the pope's claim to Benevento, but he only guaranteed to the pope the Campanian frontier as it had existed after Duke Gisulf II of Benevento had penetrated the Liri valley in 702. No more could effectively be done at that time because Benevento was outside direct Frankish control. When Arichis was brought to heel in 787 Charlemagne apparently did two things. First, and this is reminiscent of his handling of the *territorium Savinense*, he moved the Campanian frontier out to its ancient limits. Second, he compensated Hadrian's "loss" of Benevento with patrimonies in several areas of the south.

There is room for some legitimate suspicion about the passage in the *Ludovicianum* wherein Charlemagne and his successor supposedly guaranteed to the pope the Church's old patrimonies in southern Italy. Charlemagne did not control the areas of Naples and Calabria in 787 or at any other time; neither did Louis the Pious. These territories were in Byzantine hands. Charlemagne and Hadrian had corresponded about the Neapolitan patrimonies in the late 770s, and Hadrian had entered into some sort of negotiations concerning them with the duke of Naples when the duke had evidently sounded out the pope about an alliance against Arichis of Benevento. It is clear, therefore, that parties in Rome were interested in recovering the lands taken from the Church by Emperor Leo III. All things considered,

[170]*Annales regni Francorum, anno* 787, ed. Kurze, p. 74; *Annales mettenses priores*, ed, Simson, p. 74; *Ann. laurr. min., anno* 787, *MGH, SS* 1:118; *Chron. vult.*, pp. 179–80.

[171]Bertolini, "Carlomagno e Benevento," pp. 633–34; Poupardin, "Principautés," p. 258.

[172]*Annales iuvavenses minores, anno* 787, *MGH, SS* 1:88; *Annales maximiniani, MGH, SS* 13:21.

one cannot help wondering if a later interpolator did not work a bit of wizardry on the text of Louis's privilege. Perhaps, in other words, the original Neapolitan grant—if there was one—may have contained a disclaimer similar to the one that must have originally attached to the clause pertaining to the Sicilian patrimonies. Then an interpolator altered a conditional concession of southern patrimonies "if they should fall into our hands" into an outright concession. This reservation notwithstanding, the broad outlines of Charlemagne's second Campanian settlement are readily to be seen.

Throughout the second half of 787 Hadrian complained to Charlemagne that Arichis refused to hand anything over to the Republic.[173] We also have a report on Charlemagne's *missi* who had been sent to Benevento to identify and delineate the territories Hadrian was supposed to receive. They were bullied and threatened with murder.[174] Arichis, mainfestly, had reneged on the agreement he had made at Capua.

The reason for Arichis's boldness lies in the rupture of the Franco-Byzantine alliance. The Greek envoys whom Charlemagne had snubbed at Capua had gone on to Arichis and offered him the title of patrician. This would have made him the equal of the patrician of Sicily and the superior of the duke of Naples, with whom he had never enjoyed easy or cordial relations.[175]

Nothing came of Arichis's schemes, because he died 26 August 787. His son Romuald—Charlemagne had taken only Grimoald hostage—had already died in July, but for a few months Arichis's widow, Adelperga—a true daughter of Desiderius—carried on her husband's autonomist policies.[176] The Greeks, meanwhile, now played a trump they had been holding for years: Desiderius's son Adelchis. He was sent to Italy with an army, and another army was dispatched against Ravenna.[177]

Under the circumstances, and against Hadrian's advice, Charlemagne took an oath of submission from Grimoald and sent him to Benevento. In the short run this proved to have been a wise decision because Grimoald, along with Hildebrand and Winigis of Spoleto, met and repulsed the Greek threat.[178] In the long run, however, Charlemagne's judgment may have been

---

[173]CC, nos. 79, 80, pp. 611, 613.

[174]Published by Gundlach as appendices 1 and 2 to the CC, pp. 654–57; cf. CC, no. 82, pp. 615–16.

[175]CC, no. 83, p. 617. Poupardin, "Principautés," pp. 261–62; Gay, *Italie méridionale*, pp. 36–37; Bertolini, "Carlomagno e Benevento," p. 636; Garms-Cornides, "Fürstentitel," pp. 373–74.

[176]Bertolini, "Carlomagno e Benevento," p. 646.

[177]Bertolini, "Carlomagno e Benevento," p. 646ff.

[178]Poupardin, "Principautés," pp. 269–70.

faulty, for by 789–90 Grimoald had virtually detached himself from Frankish overlordship.[179] In 807 Grimoald was succeeded by his treasurer, also named Grimoald, and in 812 this character refused to pay tribute to the Franks, although he later submitted himself to Louis the Pious. In 817 this second Grimoald fell victim to a local conspiracy, and for all practical purposes, Frankish rule in Benevento ceased in both theory and practice.[180]

In 788 Hadrian was still complaining that he had not received his due in Benevento.[181] In fact, he never did; nor would any of his successors. The southern patrimonies certainly were not restored, and in the ninth century Sora, Teano, and Capua were integral components of the Duchy of Benevento.[182] Even in Hadrian's time, Sora, Arce, Arpino, and Aquino could not be absorbed into the Republic fully. The problem was not, as used to be thought, that Charlemagne handed them over conditionally.[183] Rather, the local aristocracies were, and had been for a century, Lombard and wanted no part of a transfer of allegiance.[184] The promise of 787, which was repeated in 816–17, was not made frivolously or in bad faith either time. Its successful fulfillment, however, was based on a policy, called by Bertolini a *"rischio calcolato,"* that Grimoald would turn out to be a loyal subject. He did not. Nor, for that matter, did any of his successors, and there was nothing, really, that the Franks could do about it. The Campanian-Beneventan settlement of 787 ought to be understood in ideal terms because we know, ideally, how Charlemagne and Hadrian proposed to handle the region. We also know that reality fell far short of that ideal.

Benevento in the end was simply too far from the Frankish heartlands, and represented too insignificant a threat to the Republic, to merit constant and massive military intervention. Moreover, the failure of the Byzantine attacks in 787 must have convinced the Romans and the Franks that little had to be feared from the East. At the same time, Hadrian and the Empress Irene effected a rapprochement of sorts in 787 when the Greeks held a second council at Nicaea and condemned iconoclasm. The major bone of contention between the Byzantines and the papacy for a half-century had been removed, and this surely contributed to a relaxation of tensions in

---

[179]According to Erchempert, *Historia*, c. 5, MGH, SSrL, p. 236, he married a niece of Constantine VI. On his independence see: Poupardin, "Principautés," pp. 268–69; Bertolini, "Carlomagno e Benevento," p. 649; Garms-Cornides, "Fürstentitel," p. 375 ff.

[180]Poupardin, "Principautés," pp. 270–74.

[181]CC, no. 84, pp. 619–20.

[182]Gay, *Italie méridionale*, p. 38; idem, "Littoral campanien," pp. 503–4.

[183]See, e.g., Vehse, "Benevent," p. 90.

[184]Toubert, *Latium* 2:946–47.

southern Italy. If Hadrian did not get all that he wanted, or all that he had been promised, he nevertheless knew that Charlemagne would never abandon him and that the Greeks could not, and now probably would not, attack him. Grimoald lacked the means to be a real nuisance all by himself, and the failure of Adelchis, coupled with the end of iconoclasm, had indeed left him quite alone. Thus Hadrian got peace, which was assuredly worth more than the Liri valley.

Venetia and Istria are unique among all the territories with which the Republic and the Franks were involved. They are the only lands mentioned in the Quierzy-Rome promise that were passed over in silence by the *Ludovicianum*. At some point, therefore, Charlemagne elected not to hand over these territories, and it is interesting to note that nowhere in Hadrian's correspondence is there a hint that they were ever the subject of claims or negotiations. Perhaps some discussion about them took place in 781, but this cannot be proved. That neither Charlemagne nor Hadrian ever wrote a line about them is puzzling, especially in view of the papacy's interest in them dating back to the 720s, but it may have been that both parties realized very early the practical impossibility of introducing direct papal rule in extreme northeastern Italy. Moreover, Charlemagne had good reasons of his own for not even attempting to hand over Venetia and Istria to the pope. In short, a few inferences can be drawn about these two regions, but that is all.

Einhard says, with no particular emphasis, that Charlemagne added Istria to his kingdom.[185] He does not say when this happened, but it had to have occurred before 791 when the region had a Frankish-installed duke,[186] and it may go back to the period just after Hrodgaud's rebellion. Brunner says of Istria that "here were intertwined too many threads of European power politics."[187] Istria was a frontier zone situated among Lombardy, Venice, Bavaria, the Avar lands, and Byzantine Dalmatia. It also straddled the headwaters of the Adriatic, in which sea Byzantine naval power was a force to be reckoned with. At one time or another Charlemagne had profound difficulties with all of these peoples, and sometimes with several of them simultaneously. He could never have afforded to grant Istria to anyone. Also, it is quite probably true that Hadrian could not have controlled Istria even if Charlemagne had been of a mind to give it to him.

The story of Venice is more complicated. The papacy had, since the days of Gregory II, been speaking of the Venetians as "lost sheep." We have

---

[185] *Vita Karoli*, c. 15, ed. Halphen, p. 44.

[186] Erich of Friuli, who was killed in 791: Einhard, *Vita Karoli*, c. 13, ed. Halphen, p. 40. See: Diehl, *Etudes*, p. 47; Bullough, "Counties in Italy," p. 165.

[187] Brunner, *Oppositionelle Gruppen*, p. 45.

learned that this was no vague expression of pastoral solicitude but, rather, a peculiar circumlocution designed to express a certain kind of claim to overlordship. The Venetians never, as far as can be determined, submitted to papal dominion, and they never had any intention of doing so. From the 730s, at least, what the Venetians wanted was independence. Sometimes they allied with the pope, sometimes with the Franks, and sometimes with the Byzantines.[188] The Byzantines always continued to claim Venice as their own, and the Venetians often acknowledged Byzantine claims, but only as a means of avoiding western entanglements. In the end, Venice always stood foursquare for Venice.[189] Charlemagne used Venice for years as a bargaining chip in his dealings with the Byzantines, and finally admitted the legitimacy of Greek rule there in about 812.[190] This is not the place to recount the long and tangled history of Carolingian relations with Venice. It suffices to say that neither the Lombards nor the Franks ever genuinely possessed Venice and that, therefore, neither Pepin nor Charlemagne was ever in a position to give it to Rome. Perhaps Venice, like Istria, possessed sufficient strategic significance that Charlemagne would not, in any situation, have given it to the Republic. There is no point in speculating. The histories of Venice and of the Republic of St. Peter touched lightly for a few decades in the middle of the eighth century and then went their separate ways.

The Frontiers of the Republic

On the whole, papal aspirations from the 720s to the early ninth century were markedly consistent, and they served as the basis for the reconstitution of the Republic by Pope Innocent III in the thirteenth century.[191] Throughout the eighth century, the popes laid claim to the Exarchate of Ravenna, but one must not be seduced by the temptation to regard the Exarchate and the Republic of St. Peter as coterminous. Eighth-century texts use the word

---

[188]For arguments based on the idea that various factions in Venice were pro-Byzantine, pro-Frankish, or pro-papal see: Kretschmayr, *Geschichte von Venedig* 1:53ff; W. Carew Hazlitt, *The Venetain Republic*, vol. 1 (London, 1915), p. 34ff; Abel and Simson, *Jahrbücher* 1:293–94; John J. Norwich, *Venice: The Rise to Empire* (London, 1977), pp. 41–43.

[189]Cessi, *Repubblica di Venezia*, pp. 23–25.

[190]Presumably as a part of the peace negotiated with the Byzantines. *Annales regni Francorum, anno* 812, ed. Kurze, p. 136.

[191]Waley, *Papal State in the Thirteenth Century*, p. 29. But Laufs, *Innozenz III*, p. 1ff and passim, attempts to prove that Innocent considered the old imperial privileges to be an inadequate basis for the papacy's claims.

exarchate in two distinct ways. Sometimes it meant the whole of formerly Byzantine central and northeastern Italy, but on other occasions it designated more precisely Ravenna and its immediate environs. In reality, the Duchy of Rome, in the attenuated shape left to it by the Lombard invasions of the seventh and very early eighth centuries, was always the firm base of the Republic. In the 760s, or possibly as early as the 740s, the old Duchy of Perugia was incorporated into the Republic, and in Charlemagne's massive settlements with Hadrian, the duchy reacquired lands to the south and east once lost to the Lombards, and also obtained for the first time, to the north, a bit of Lombard Tuscany. The popes sometimes claimed Spoleto and Benevento, and for a long time tried to establish title to the old Exarchate in the narrow sense along with Venetia and Istria. In these regions, however, the Republic's dominion was always either problematical or ephemeral.

The essential interests of the Lombard monarchy, under either Lombard or Frankish kings, made lasting papal rule in the great southern Lombard duchies quite impossible. Venice desired independence above all else. The Venetians were not above cooperating with the papacy when it was in their interest to do so, but they never submitted to direct papal rule. Istria was too far from Rome to be ruled effectively therefrom, and too strategically significant to be handed over. The papacy regarded the Venetians and Istrians as "lost sheep," but these flocks escaped the papal crook.

Ravenna presents complications unlike those found in any other area of the Republic. It had strong and independent traditions of its own, and archbishops who were, in Italy, second only to the popes in power, prestige, and influence. The Carolingians promised to hand over Ravenna to the Republic, and actually did so on more than one occasion but, in the end, the donation was conditional. The Republic finally consisted of the augmented Duchy of Rome, Perugia, and the old Exarchate in the restricted sense.

Slowly but surely, with growing confidence and determination, the popes had headed a movement which marched unflinchingly to the emancipation of the Republic of St. Peter from the Byzantine Empire. The pope became the definitive heir of the Byzantines by the 730s and 740s, and after those momentous decades only two questions remained unresolved. First, would the incipient papal Republic be swallowed by the Lombard monarchy, and second, what parts of the Byzantine territorial legacy in Italy would actually pass into the Republic's possession? The Carolingians played crucial roles in answering both of these questions. They defended the Republic from the Lombards, and they helped to define the boundaries of the Republic.

The Frankish role in Italy after 754 may be evaluated in different ways. Pepin and Charlemagne proved to be steadfast allies, but not disinterested or indifferent lackeys. It is no exaggeration to say that the Carolingians saved the Republic from the very real danger of extinction in the 750s and again in the 770s. Frankish campaigns in Italy were magnanimous gestures, but not entirely altruistic ones. Both Pepin and Charlemagne had very real, personal interests to serve in crossing the Alps. Likewise, the Carolingians did not acknowledge the papacy's maximum scheme for the shape of the Republic. Venice and Istria, and the Lombard duchies were not handed over, and Ravenna had to be shared. In these areas it might well be argued that the Franks caused the papacy to lose ground in spite of their love for St. Peter and the remission of their sins. But, then, direct and generous Frankish grants in 781 and 787 expanded the old Duchy of Rome quite beyond specific and articulated papal claims. On balance, it is difficult to escape the conclusion that the popes had every reason to be satisfied with their real estate dealings with the brokerage firm of Charlemagne. And, there can be no question that the Franks produced a peace and security in Italy unknown since the outbreak of the Gothic wars. Still, the Carolingians entered Italy at a late stage of the eighth-century crisis. This point cannot be overemphasized. They did not create the Republic of St. Peter, and they were not responsible for its creation.

If Hadrian knew of the Byzantine proverb with which this chapter begins, I would wager that it occasioned more than one wry smile from this able and determined pope. At the same time, I think Hadrian would have denied the truth of the proverb. Charlemagne was his neighbor for twenty-one years. The great Frank was also his friend.

Six

The Governors of the Republic

BYZANTINE ITALY was sundered by a relentless series of crises in the eighth century. The political map of the whole Italian region, from the Alps to Sicily, was redrawn. The popes had been principally responsible for the cartographic alterations that had taken place. Their rejection of Byzantine authority had resulted in the creation of a new state which was itself the most significant new element on the map of Italy. Then papal diplomacy, adroitly applied to a complex situation in central Italy, permitted that new state to survive and to assume secure and guaranteed frontiers. Now it is time to look inside the Republic and to learn as much as we can about the people who were its leaders and the means that were available to them to exercise their leadership.

It is necessary to begin with the popes themselves. They were the leaders of the Republic and, for that reason alone, deserve a prominent place in any discussion of the domestic life of the Republic. More importantly, however, they are the only people for whom, across the whole course of the Republic's history, there exists relatively abundant information. The fact that more evidence survives about the popes than about any other groups or individuals raises problems, but also offers opportunities. On the one hand, even though the popes could never have acted alone to accomplish all that they did, there is nevertheless much that simply cannot be known about the upper social classes at Rome who cooperated with the popes, and who sometimes opposed them. On the other hand, the popes were products of Roman society, and facts drawn from a succession of papal careers may permit some valid generalizations about the whole Roman scene.

In the immediately following account an attempt will be made to describe who the popes were, how they attained their office, and how they were prepared for it. The succeeding chapter will examine the secular and ecclesiastical structures over which the popes presided and by means of which they governed. The story of the creation and territorial definition of the Republic of St. Peter required a focus on the years from 685 to 788. To describe the governors and governance of the Republic it is necessary to add some four decades to the story and to push ahead into the 820s, specifically to the election of Gregory IV in 827. Just as the delineation of the frontiers of the Republic was a fluid and shifting process until the great settlements of the 780s, so too the development of the social, political, and institutional structures of the region was the result of a long and intricate evolution.

Papal Profiles

The ethnic and social backgrounds of the popes provide a first important indicator of developments inside the Republic. It used to be argued that the last years of the seventh century and the first half of the eighth marked a "Byzantine Captivity" of the papacy.[1] The key piece of evidence adduced to support this contention is that among the popes from John V to Zachary (685–752) only Gregory II was a Roman; the rest were either Syrian or Greek.[2] Recently, however, Jeffrey Richards has noted that throughout this period there is no evidence of successful imperial or exarchal interference in papal elections. Therefore, he concludes, there must have been a dramatic change in the ethnic composition of the Roman Church during these decades. The Roman clergy was "swamped" by easterners.[3] This interpretation tells only a part of the story. The fact is that the popes of this period, regardless of place of origin, had generally served long and well in the Roman Church before their elections. Also, the families of some of these popes may have been Greek or Syrian in origin but often they had been in Italy for a long time.[4] Conon (686–87), for example, came from an eastern family, but he was educated in Sicily and entered the Roman clergy young.[5] Sergius (687–

---

[1] Diehl, *Etudes*, pp. 241–47; cf. the title of Caspar's second volume: *Das Papsttum unter byzantinischer Herrschaft*.

[2] *LP* 1:367, 369, 376, 383, 386, 393, 410, 421, 435. In what follows I leave out of consideration Sisinnius who was pope for 20 days in 708 and Stephen who was elected but died before having been consecrated in 752.

[3] Richards, *Popes and the Papacy*, pp. 270–71.

[4] Much has been written on this subject. For some helpful, general comments see: G. Schreiber, "Levantinische Wanderungen zum Westen," *BZ* 44 (1951): 517–23; Anton Michel, "Die griechische Klostersiedlungen zu Rom bis zur Mitte des 11. Jahrhunderts," *Ostkirchliche Studien* 1 (1952): 32ff.

[5] *LP* 1:368–69.

701) came from a Syrian family, but he was born in Sicily and entered the Roman clergy during the pontificate of Adeodatus (672–76).[6] Constantine (708–15) was likewise a Syrian, but he had been a deacon and had traveled to Constantinople for a council in 680, twenty-eight years before he became pope.[7] Zachary (741–52), the last Greek pope, was born in Italy in 679, in Calabria, and he was a deacon in the Roman Church by at least 732.[8]

Richards's perception of an increase in the numbers of easterners in the Roman clergy corresponds with Guillou's determination that persons of eastern extraction formed a slightly larger percentage of Byzantine Italy's population in the late seventh century than they had earlier.[9] There may, however, be an explanation for the rising prominence of easterners in the Roman clergy that is independent of demographic realities. The seventh century had been a period of frequent and complex theological disputation. In spite of the temporary pause afforded by the Sixth Ecumenical Council, theological contention between East and West continued into the eighth century. Almost every doctrinal quarrel of the period arose in the East, either at Constantinople or in one of the other eastern patriarchates. The debates attending these quarrels were carried on in Greek, and at least down to the council of 680–81, there is abundant evidence that, in Rome, not many people still understood Greek.[10] Thus, even though the Roman ecclesiastical authorities showed a marked disinclination to debate matters of theology that, in the western view, had been definitively resolved at Chalcedon in 451, there can be no question that linguistic deficiencies in the West impeded a close following of the ever-shifting course of the debates. Under these circumstances the growing prominence of easterners in the Roman clergy may be a reflection of a tendency to promote men whose cultural heritage gave them ready access to the theological lucubrations arising in the eastern Mediterranean region.[11]

That these popes, or their families, had originally come from the East seems not to have predisposed them to think well of the imperial government. Once these men entered the Roman clergy, and served there for years, they worked for and supported the interests of Italy and of the Church,

---

[6]*LP* 1:371.

[7]*LP* 1:356, 385. Richards, *Popes and the Papacy*, p. 267.

[8]*LP* 1:336 n.1, 426. Giorgio S. Marcou, "Zaccaria (679–752): L'ultimo papa greco nella storia di Roma altomedioevale," *Apollinaris* 50 (1977): 274.

[9]Guillou, "Demography and Culture," pp. 202–8.

[10]Harold Steinacker, "Die römische Kirche und die griechischen Sprachkenntniße des Frühmittelalters," *MIÖG* 62 (1954): 28–66, esp. 40ff.

[11]Gay, "Quelques remarques sur les papes grecs et syriens avant la querelle des iconoclastes," *Mélanges offerts à M. Gustave Schlumberger* (Paris, 1924), 1:40–54.

which were fundamentally alike, against the imperial government. There is also no real evidence of tension between Italians and "easterners" in the Roman clergy. Nor did they adopt different postures vis-à-vis Constantinople. Sergius and Constantine rejected imperial authority in dogma just as forcefully as the Roman Gregory II. Gregory II refused to pay taxes and his "eastern" successors Gregory III and Zachary likewise refused to submit to imperial authority. What is noticeable, then, is a remarkable consistency in basic attitudes regardless of the ethnic or geographical backgrounds of the popes. Common formulations of religious and political policy were consistently made in the Roman Church by a series of steadfastly like-minded men. One cannot legitimately speak of a "Byzantine Captivity" of the papacy. Instead it seems that the highest ranks of the Roman clergy display that same "Italianization" and "localization," at least in terms of identifying with local Roman interests, that are apparent throughout Byzantine Italy.

Richards notices something else interesting about the popes from John V to Zachary. None of them was a Roman aristocrat.[12] The apparent lack of noble Romans at the upper level of the ecclesiastical hierarchy is at first sight a bit puzzling, but it may owe something to a preference on the part of important laymen to seek their fortunes in the military hierarchy or in the still functioning structures of Byzantine officialdom. Even if the local aristocracy did not enjoy prominence in the clergy, the efforts of the popes to reject Byzantine religious and political demands were supported by the lay magnates. On several occasions they protected popes from exarchs or special imperial envoys. The nobility and the clergy traveled along parallel paths in rejecting the authority of the Byzantine government.

Then, during the pontificate of Zachary, Richards sees a rising "Romanization" of the clergy.[13] This process can only be explained on the assumption that as a papal republic was coming into being members of the local Roman society began entering the clergy in greater numbers in order to gain high office and to reconfirm, through the Church, their traditional social and political importance in the vicinity of Rome. Actually, once the process of creating the Republic had begun to move across a broad political front, the local aristocracy began taking a more active and visible role. From Stephen II (752–57) to Gregory IV (827–44) all the popes were Romans except two. Stephen III (768–72), who had himself entered the clergy years before under Gregory III (731–41), was a Sicilian, and Leo III, an Apulian, was of either Greek or Arabic descent.[14] Moreover, Stephen II, Paul I, Hadrian I,

---

[12]Richards, *Popes and the Papacy*, pp. 245–46.
[13]Richards, *Popes and the Papacy*, p. 275.
[14]*LP* 1:440, 463, 486; 2:1, 49, 52, 69, 71, 73, for the Romans. For Stephen III, ibid.

Stephen IV, Paschal I, Valentinus, and Gregory IV were noble,[15] and only Stephen III and Leo III were demonstrably not from the nobility.[16]

Some clear conclusions can be drawn from the social and ethnic backgrounds of these popes. If the early and "eastern" ones began the emancipation of central Italy from the Byzantines, then the later and Roman ones supported their efforts and carried them forward. Likewise, the non-noble popes before 752 do not seem to have behaved differently than the noble ones did later. Actually, it appears that, in the 740s if not earlier, the Roman aristocracy made common cause with the clergy in creating the Republic of St. Peter. Indeed, the Roman aristocracy, which must always have been represented to some degree in the clergy of the Roman Church, gradually began to dominate that clergy and, through it, the Republic. It may be worth noting that the predominance of eastern and non-noble popes ceased at a moment when two forces converged. First, as an independent political entity was emerging the Romans, and chief among them the nobility, took over its leadership. Second, as the West definitively turned its back on Byzantine theology (iconoclasm) and church discipline (the Trullan canons) there was no longer, inside the Church itself, felt to be a need for leaders who could understand and respond to the subtleties of eastern divines. Gregory II, who knew Greek, wrote thoughtfully crafted letters to Leo III to recall him from his errors. Later popes, most of them Roman and noble, simply and bluntly instructed the emperors to desist from iconoclasm. The Republic thus began at an early stage in its history to represent the attitudes and aspirations of both the clerical and social elites of central Italy. Although it can no longer be maintained that there had been a "Byzantine captivity" of the papacy, it may be useful to replace that old notion with a more valid one: The Republic of St. Peter saw the emergence of a "noble-Roman captivity" of the papacy.

Papal Elections and Republican Politics

The question of how the Church, or in our period the Republic, elected its rulers is not an easy one to answer, but an attempt must be made to address this issue. Discussions based upon "eastern swamping," "intellectual fit-

---

1:468. On Leo see: Hans-Georg Beck, "Die Herkunft des Papstes Leo III," *FMSt* 3 (1969): 131–37. Eugenius II is problematical.

[15]Stephen II, Paul I, Hadrian, and Valentinus were from the Via Lata region of Rome. This was an aristocratic "address": René Vielliard, *Recherches sur les origines de la Rome chrétienne* (Rome, 1959), p. 134. For the others see: *LP* 2:49, 52, 73.

[16]*LP* 2:1, does not say he was noble and the nobility opposed him.

ness," or "rising Romanization" demand an understanding of the processes by which popes were put into office. A study of papal elections, and of certain political incidents during various pontificates, will help to confirm the "Romanization" of the Republic's leadership that has already become apparent in the preceding comments about the popes' ethnic backgrounds. This analysis will help to demonstrate how, why, and with what consequences the Roman aristocracy came to dominate the Church and, through it, the political and institutional life of the Republic.

By the early fifth century, and perhaps earlier, the popes were elected by the clergy and people of Rome. The bishops of Rome were, apparently, elected in much the same way as other bishops throughout the Roman world.[17] In 499, during the troubled pontificate of Symmachus, a Roman synod, pressured by the Ostrogothic king Theodoric, passed a decree requiring a majority of the clergy to decide only if the reigning pope had failed to designate a successor.[18] There were two novelties here: designation and restriction of the electoral process to the clergy. Neither was to have much success in later years, although Boniface II (530–32) tried again to establish the principle that the reigning pope could designate his successor.[19] As our period opens the pope was elected by the clergy and people of Rome, and was subject to confirmation by the emperor's representative, the exarch.

During the pontificate of Sergius I various sources began to refer to the papal government in a general way, as well as to the seat of that government, as the *patriarchium Lateranense*.[20] Understandably, therefore, most of the elections for which we have details took place in the Lateran precincts. It is not clear, however, that a particular building within the Lateran complex was regularly the scene of the elections.[21] John V was elected in the Constantinian basilica, the predecessor of today's St. John Lateran.[22] So was Conon, but an opposing faction met near the Lateran at the basilica of St. Stephen.[23]

---

[17]Paul Hinschius, *System des katholischen Kirchenrechts*, vol. 1 (reprint Graz, 1959), p. 218; Arnold Hugh Martin Jones, *The Later Roman Empire*, 2 vols. (Norman, Okla., 1964), 2:915–20.

[18]Mansi, *Concilia* 8:229. Hinschius, *Kirchenrecht* 1:218–19.

[19]*LP* 1:281.

[20]Willibald M. Plöchl, *Geschichte des Kirchenrechts*, vol. 1, 2d ed. (Munich, 1960), p. 317. Michel Andrieu shows that *episcopium Lateranense* had been in use since Gregory I and then discusses the change to *patriarchium* under Sergius: *Les Ordines Romani du haut moyen âge* 2:45–46. For evidence: *LP* 1:371, 373; Andrieu, *Ordo I*, nos. 7, 18, *Ordines* 2:69–70, 72.

[21]The medieval Lateran has been the subject of several studies: George Rohault de Fleury, *Le Latran au moyen âge* (Paris, 1877); Philip Lauer, *Le palais de Latran* (Paris, 1911); Krautheimer, *Corpus basilicarum christianarum Romae*, vol. 5 (Vatican City, 1977).

[22]*LP* 1:366. See: Vielliard, *Recherches*, pp. 63–65; Krautheimer, *Rome*, 21ff.

[23]*LP* 1:368.

On the election of Sergius there were again factions. The victorious party held the Lateran while the vanquished had operated out of the nearby Julian basilica and the oratory of St. Sylvester.[24] Stephen II was elected at St. Maria in Praesepe and then led to the Constantinian basilica.[25] Paul I had an opponent, a deacon Theophylact, who was elected in his own house, but the scheme came to nothing. Paul himself was elected in the Lateran.[26] Stephen III was elected in a corner of the Roman forum, but the city was then deeply troubled.[27] Later popes seem regularly to have been elected in the Lateran. There is no surviving document bearing a requirement that papal elections had to take place in the Lateran, but tradition and convenience seem to have made this the usual and natural place. It is quite possible that most elections took place in the Constantinian basilica. It cannot be mere coincidence that only the presence of factious contenders or political turmoil caused elections to take place elsewhere.

Given that elections regularly took place at the seat of the papal government, that is, in the Lateran, it would be easy to suppose that the clergy played a dominant role. The laity had a role, however, because the *Liber Pontificalis* often records instances of factions lining up behind one or more candidates, and on other occasions is virtually formulaic in saying that popes were elected "*cuncto populo.*" Such formulations are not very helpful and are probably wide of the mark for at least two reasons. First, it is inconceivable that everyone in Rome participated. Second, contested elections were rather common and therefore *cunctus* cannot be understood to mean unanimous, which was probably the biographers' intent. Even if we cannot form a precise impression of the people involved in the electoral assemblies—and it goes without saying that we know nothing about their procedure—then perhaps the contested elections themselves can shed some light on the people involved as candidates and electors. Although capable at times of disturbing degrees of deception, the papal biographers in our period seem to have been reliable in reporting the details of quite a few contested papal elections.

When Conon was elected in 686 the clergy assembled at the Constantinian basilica and the "army" at the basilica of St. Stephen. The clerics were desirous of electing the archpriest Peter whereas the army, which can only mean the civil-military aristocracy, preferred a priest named Theodore. Paschal, who was archdeacon under Conon, secretly wrote to the exarch and

---

[24]*LP* 1:371–72, 377 nn. 7, 8, 9. Also: Vielliard, *Recherches*, p. 69.
[25]*LP* 1:440.
[26]*LP* 1:463.
[27]*LP* 1:471.

offered a bribe for the exarch's help in making him pope. Paschal's plot failed, and the clergy finally settled on Conon, a Roman priest.[28]

When Conon died "the people of the city of Rome, as usual, were divided into two parties." One party held for the archpriest Theodore, while the other advanced the candidacy of the archdeacon Paschal. Duchesne assumes that the Theodore in question is identical with the priest who had been a candidate in 686.[29] This is very likely, and it may be that Conon had sought to compose his difficulties with his former rivals by offering them the prestigious offices of archpriest and archdeacon. Theodore's supporters held the interior of the Lateran, and Paschal's adherents worked from the outer buildings, the oratory of St. Sylvester and the Julian basilica. Something curious then happened. The "greater part of the principal officers, the militia of Rome and the clergy, especially the priests and a multitude of citizens" went to the imperial palace on the Palatine and elected Sergius, a priest of the *titulus* of St. Susanna. Sergius was elected because the party that supported him "was stronger." Theodore submitted immediately but Paschal appealed to Ravenna again. The exarch, John Platyn, came to Rome, but the "Romans" would do nothing until he recognized Sergius. John tried to obtain the 100 pounds of gold Paschal had promised him, but Sergius refused to pay. John then engaged in some retaliatory plundering at St. Peter's, Sergius was consecrated, and Paschal lost the archdeaconship.[30]

A few inferences can be drawn from this electoral strife. The emergence of the "army" is quite apparent and signifies that even if the popes of this period were neither noble nor Roman then the Roman secular nobility was by no means indifferent to the outcome of papal elections. The civil-military aristocracy supported some candidates and opposed others. In each instance a "stronger" party carried the day and, we are told, the Romans usually divided into two parties. Around what issues might these "parties" have coalesced? Leadership in the Church, prominence in Rome, and the ability to promote one's supporters may explain why certain individuals would have sought followers and then built out of them electoral factions. But this scenario, however likely, cannot explain the parties. Guillou detects in Ravenna a split between a majority of Latins and a minority of easterners who tended to support Byzantine against local interests.[31] It is just possible that a similar cleavage stands behind the electoral strife at Rome. If this hypothesis

[28]*LP* 1:368–69.
[29]*LP* 1:377 n.5.
[30]*LP* 1:371–72.
[31]"L'Italia bizantina," p. 284ff.

is correct, then some other developments become explicable. For example, the "stronger" party won each time, and the popes thus elected were all opposed to Byzantine religious policy. Assuming that this is not a coincidence, it looks as though a majority (meaning stronger?) in Rome supported the popes' religious policies. This hypothesis gains in force when it is remembered that several times the Roman "army" refused to permit the Byzantines to discipline the pope. It may also be significant in the same connection that on several occasions in the 720s the Roman "army" protected Gregory II from plots hatched by disgruntled clerics and military officers who were trying to win the favor of the duke of Rome or of the exarch. Perhaps these individuals represented the "weaker" party. Finally, it is just possible that the many eastern popes of this period achieved the papal office because they made common cause with the local Roman nobility in opposing Byzantine policies. These clerics, many of them fugitives from earlier Byzantine religious policies, would presumably have joined with a "stronger" party of Romans who had local and particular reasons of their own for opposing the Greeks. Thus, the polarity which Guillou discovered at Ravenna may have been reversed to some extent at Rome. In the latter city it was the eastern clergy who opposed the Greeks, whereas in the former it was apparently the easterners who supported the Byzantines.

In short, papal elections in the 680s, taken in conjunction with related developments down to the 720s, point to the emergence in Rome of a "party" that dominated the city and that was willing to use its domination to thwart the Greeks. It will be recalled that elections took place in the Lateran and that the winners in each case, except for Sergius, held the Lateran while their opponents worked from outside the main papal buildings. This leads one to suggest that an anti-Byzantine "Lateran party" united with an anti-Byzantine "army party" to secure control of the papal office. In a way, therefore, the higher levels of the clergy were Romanized in a political sense well before they were Romanized in an ethnic sense. The clergy and the Romans, at any rate a majority of the Roman military nobles, were marching in lockstep along a road that would, after the decisive events of the late 720s and early 730s, lead inevitably to a secession of a fair portion of Italy from the Byzantine Empire. Once the implications of their common enterprise became crystal clear, the Romans ceased playing an auxiliary role and took over.

Precise details on subsequent elections down to 757 are meager. No open disputes are recorded, however. In the face of Lombard and Byzantine menaces throughout the first half of the eighth century, but especially during the years after about 730, it is likely that the Romans, both lay and clerical, thought better of engaging in internecine struggles that might have provided their enemies with opportunities for meddling in the city. Moreover, one suspects that the "weaker party" was gradually overcome and then finally crushed amidst the abortive uprisings against Gregory II.

The election of Stephen II in 752 opened a period of decisive change in the history of papal elections and of the social position of the pope in the Republic. He was a Roman and an aristocrat, and his successors almost always shared these qualities. It should also be pointed out that Stephen and his brother Paul entered the Lateran under Gregory II, and received their first significant promotions under Zachary.[32] While their rise to prominence is a good piece of evidence for the Romanization of the Lateran detected by Richards, and may show that he placed the beginnings of that Romanization a bit too late, their nobility should be emphasized as well.[33] Stephen was elected at perhaps the most pivotal moment in the Republic's history. Emancipation from Byzantium was a fait accompli by 752, but utter defeat by Aistulf was in prospect, and no help from Francia could yet have been predicted. Under the circumstances the Romans sought to place the fate of the Republic in the hands of an ecclesiastical careerist who was also a local nobleman. Stephen was a personal embodiment of both the lay and clerical elites who had in the past generation created a state.

When Stephen died in 757 the Republic was reasonably secure because of his able diplomacy. The Lombards had been defeated, the Byzantines rebuffed, and the Republic had gained a powerful protector. The election of Stephen's brother Paul in 757 thus seems perfectly natural. But, Paul met opposition from the archdeacon Theophylact. We are told that the "greater part" of the clergy and the nobility supported Paul, and he eventually won out.[34] But the see of Peter was vacant for thirty-five days, so Theophylact was apparently a more formidable opponent than any of the sources suggest.[35]

The election of 757 was similar to those of 686 and 687 in that parties within both the nobility and the clergy were sharply divided. Baumont thought that Theophylact was the candidate of the military aristocracy.[36] This interpretation is too rigid. Theophylact was the archdeacon of the Roman Church

---

[32] *LP* 1:456, 465.

[33] Their nobility must be deduced from residence in the Via Lata. Duchesne confirmed the importance of this street. Also: Krautheimer, *Rome*, p. 255.

[34] *LP* 1:463.

[35] *LP* 1:465; Jaffé, *RP*, p. 277.

[36] Maurice Baumont, "Le pontificat de Paul Ier (757–767)," *MAH* 47 (1930): 8–9.

and therefore the head of the ecclesiastical personnel of Rome. His support must have come principally from a party within the clergy. Paul was the Roman nobleman, but later events would show that he did not have the unanimous backing of the local nobility. In addition, Paul had been in the clergy for more than twenty years and had to have had support in the Lateran. Indeed, his election was effected there while Theophylact's supporters had to gather elsewhere in a private house. Baumont also guessed, although there is no evidence, that Theophylact represented people who opposed Stephen's and Paul's policies, and that he had support among those who desired reconciliation with Byzantium.[37] Neither of these guesses is likely because both the clergy and the aristocracy had long since cut their ties to the Greeks, and both parties had to have realized full well that only the Frankish alliance could save the Republic from the Lombards. Moreover, we have already seen that in the past scholars have made too much of the pro-Frankish sentiments of Stephen and Paul. These popes were pro-Roman in the first place, and pro-Frankish only in the second place as a means to the end of defending the Republic against its redoubtable Lombard foes.

The election of 757 produced a division along factional lines, and it is profoundly unfortunate that no hard evidence exists to permit a precise determination of the issues dividing the factions. Paul and Theophylact were both high Lateran officers and both had to have had support among the clergy. Paul was a nobleman and, although there is no evidence that his opponent was noble, both men must have had some support among the nobility or a vacancy of five weeks would not have occurred. Because the "stronger" party, evidently a majority of the aristocracy and perhaps of the clergy as well, carried Paul's election, it is possible to discern, albeit dimly, two developments in the election of 757. First, a group in the clergy represented by Theophylact appears to have resented the growing prominence within the clergy of the Roman nobility. Second, factions inside the Lateran somehow corresponded with factions in Roman society, and the issues dividing the factions cannot this time have been attitudes toward Constantinople.

Paul was a *politique* who eventually sought a reconciliation among the Franks, the Lombards, the aristocracy, and the clergy.[38] This inference is

---

[37]Baumont, "Le pontificat de Paul Ier," p. 8. This position was also held by Diehl (*Etudes*, p. 232) and Gregorovius (*Geschichte der Stadt Rom im Mittelalter* 2:297) and also more recently by Guillou ("L'Italia bizantina," p. 232). C. Bayet, "Les élections pontificales sous les carolingiens au VIIIe et au IXe siècle (757–885)," *Revue historique* 24 (1884): 69ff, could not seem to make any sense out of the election of 757.

[38]I attach great significance to Miller's demonstration of the true character and significance

based upon the fact that throughout the 760s radical clerics like Christophorus were held in check, and after Paul died, the aristocracy reacted violently. Once the continued existence of the Republic had been assured, and because the institutions of the Church were the only effective government within the new state, it was only to be expected that the social elite, that is, the military aristocracy, would demand a greater role. Stephen and Paul were aristocrats, but they were also career Lateran bureaucrats. They managed to effect a delicate but temporary balancing of the orders that came crashing down in 767.

The effort, only momentarily successful, of Toto of Nepi to put a layman who was a military aristocrat on the papal throne represented an abortive revolution.[39] Had it been successful the late eighth-century papacy might have become as deplorable as the tenth-century institution under the domination of Marozia and Theophylact. The revolution proved abortive precisely because the two dominant clerics in the city, Christophorus and Sergius, turned to the Lombards to dislodge the military aristocracy from its control of Rome. Toto had not only named his own pope, Constantine II, but he had also proclaimed himself duke of Rome, and he installed other supporters, such as Gracilis in Campania, into key positions. The aristocracy had made a blatant effort to seize total control of Rome at the expense of the clergy, and it is crucial to see that the insurgents felt it necessary to control the papal office.

Desiderius, after being solicited by Christophorus and Sergius, had hoped to control the papacy himself through his agent Waldipert. Christophorus would have none of this, and when he returned to Rome he did two things. First he assembled his followers in a corner of the forum—Waldipert's people had the Lateran—and brought about the election of a non-noble Lateran careerist, Stephen III, as pope. Then, after he had secured control of the Lateran, he called for the Roman synod of 769.[40]

The Roman synod predictably investigated and condemned Constantine and all his works, but its truly momentous achievement was the promulgation of a decree governing papal elections. This decree forbade laymen to participate in papal elections, and reserved to them only the relatively insignificant right of acclaiming the newly elected.[41] But, it also went a step

---

of Paul's pontificate: "Papal-Lombard Relations" and "Byzantine-Papal Relations" cited frequently in chap. 4 above.

[39] *LP* 1:468–69.

[40] For details and a standard interpretation see: Ullmann, *Papal Government*, p. 87ff.

[41] *MGH, Concilia*, 2.1:86, c. 14.

further and limited the pool of *papabili* to the titular priests of Rome and the regional deacons of the Roman Church.[42] Even the suburbicarian bishops were excluded from candidacy, probably because three of them had bent to the will of Toto in 767 and had consecrated Constantine.

The decree of 769 spoke a clear message. Henceforth the clergy of the Roman Church would choose its leader among a small and elite circle of its own members. Aristocrats could, and did, hold distinguished offices in the Church, but they could aspire to leadership only by passing through the ecclesiastical hierarchy. Christophorus and his supporters in the clergy must have assumed that even if aristocrats like Stephen and Paul were to be elected under the new decree, they would be loyal to the Church first and to the secular interests inherent in their noble station second.

Who exactly were these clerics who were trying to retain their dominance in the Republic? The available evidence permits only a few guesses. In the first place, the "easterners" so common in the early eighth century cannot have simply disappeared. Moreover, the iconoclastic era produced new waves of voluntary immigrants and persecuted refugees.[43] In the second place, one prime line of access to the Church, as we shall have occasion to see in detail later, was the *schola cantorum* sometimes called the *orphanotrophium*. This route into the Lateran was principally followed by the poor and by people who were not nobles even if they were not poor. This is not much to go on but it suggests that the "clergy" tended to represent the lower and non-Roman rungs of the Roman social ladder. Over time, of course, the Roman nobility had begun making deep inroads into the erstwhile dominion of this "clergy," and this may very well explain the clergy's efforts to cement its leadership with the election decree of 769.

Christophorus's scheme failed because, like Toto's, it was too bold. In the first place, Christophorus could not maintain his own predominant position in Rome. By 771 Stephen III, who was a *politique* as Paul had been, did not wish to be dominated any longer by Christophorus and Sergius, and he used Desiderius to bring down his rivals.[44] In the second place, Stephen continued the by then traditional policy of promoting aristocrats to high

---

[42]*LP* 1:471. Only Carl Gerold Fürst, *Cardinalis: Prolegomena zu einer Rechtsgeschichte des römischen Kardinalskollegiums* (Munich, 1967), pp. 65–68, has drawn attention to the limitation of the number of *papabili*.

[43]See n.4 above.

[44]Hallenbeck's "Pope Stephen III: Why Was He Elected?" is very important for emphasizing Stephen's career and showing that he was not the nullity his many detractors have made him out to be.

positions in the Church. In the long run this policy would break down the barrier between the nobility and the clergy that is first detectable in 757.

The elections of the next two popes, Hadrian and Leo III, illustrate vividly the strengths and weaknesses of the system created by the decree of 769. Hadrian's election was carried out without difficulty, and his pontificate was without disturbing incidents in Rome. Hadrian's support among the clergy had to have been very great in order for him to have been elected under the terms of the decree of 769. He had been promoted to deacon by Stephen III, and so it may be assumed that he enjoyed that pope's confidence. Shortly after his own election he effected a posthumous rehabilitation of Christophorus and Sergius. That act had clear political implications because Hadrian was, at least in part, trying to embarrass his own nemesis Paul Afiarta. Still, one senses that Hadrian had support among all segments of the clergy—the radicals like Christophorus who wished to exclude the nobility from power as much as possible and the *politiques* like Stephen III who could see what lay beyond the horizon. The new pope's personal history is also very revealing. His family was from the Via Lata region of the city[45] and, like many aristocratic families, held lands in the countryside around Rome.[46] Specifically, Hadrian held an estate at *Capracorum* in Roman Tuscany which made him a neighbor of Toto of Nepi.[47] His uncle Theodotus had been a consul and duke and, later, *primicerius* of the Church.[48] Two of his relatives, Paschalis and Campulus, served as *primicerius* and *sacellarius* of the Church, and one of his nephews was for a time duke of Rome.[49] We thus see the quintessential Roman aristocrat serving harmoniously for twenty-three years while promoting other aristocrats, some of them relatives. Hadrian also ordained twenty-four priests and seven deacons, which means that he was able to put a very personal stamp on the Roman clergy.[50]

---

[45]*LP* 1:486.

[46]For a discussion of urban aristocrats with rural landholdings see: Andrea Castagnetti, *L'organizzazione del territorio rurale nel medioevo: Circonscrizione ecclesiastiche e civile nella 'Langobardia' e nella 'Romania'* (Turin, 1979), pp. 208–9, 211–12. Guido Mengozzi, *La città italiana nell'alto medioevo* (reprint, Florence, 1973), pp. 297–98, points out that in most Italian cities there were clear legal and political distinctions between a town and its suburbs, but that Rome formed an exception in that its city and suburbs were essentially one entity legally, politically, and socially.

[47]*LP* 1:510, 518 n.52.

[48]*LP* 1:486, 514 n.2. Halphen, *Etudes sur l'administration de Rome au moyen âge* (Paris, 1907), pp. 91–92.

[49]Halphen, *L'administration de Rome*, pp. 93, 136.

[50]*LP* 1:514.

There was a genuine clerical-noble symbiosis during Hadrian's pontificate and to it is attributable a long period of domestic harmony in the Republic. His is the first "republican" *vita* to make a statement such as "*Vir valde praeclarus et nobilissimi generis prosapia ortus et potentissimis romanis parentibus editus.*" Never before had a papal biographer laid such stress on the high birth of his subject. Hadrian's biographer goes on to say that, even as a youth, this pope was pious, studious, and chaste. Hadrian's social and religious qualifications were both spelled out quite explicitly. Indeed, he had acquired such a reputation for sanctity that he came to the attention of Paul I, who made him a cleric. Incidentally, the biographer's remark here inadvertently shows us Paul at work recruiting and promoting a real Roman blueblood. Hadrian's ecclesiastical *cursus honorum* is revealing. After taking minor orders, Hadrian was made a regional notary, one of the key offices in the Church, by Paul.[51] Privilege of social rank was certainly operating here. Then Hadrian became a subdeacon under Paul and deacon under Stephen III. When he was elected pope in 772 he must have been, from the Lateran's point of view, an ideal candidate: a powerful nobleman and a Lateran careerist all wrapped up in one. Hadrian was no rowdy, rustic thug like Toto. The Church could trust him. Likewise, the social class from which Toto came could look at Hadrian as one of its own.

Leo III lacked one of Hadrian's essential qualities. He was not a nobleman. He had, however, had an impressive career in the Church. In addition to making some ritual statements about his piety and decency, Leo's *vita* says that he had been a subdeacon, priest of the *titulus* of St. Susanna, and *vestararius* of the Church. We also learn that he was liberal in his largesse to the Roman clergy, and an enormously active builder and renovator of Roman churches.[52] Leo's election shows that the clerical party, to the extent that it can still be distinguished from the aristocratic, was strong in Rome at least until 795. It also casts a retrospective light on Hadrian's pontificate. Ironically Leo, a commoner, was promoted to a cardinal priesthood and a high Lateran office by the most aristocratic pope of the eighth century, a pope who on other occasions elevated nobles to high office. Again, we can see how those who had been responsible for the election decree of 769 had hoped to create in the Lateran, but also to control, a blending of the social and religious elites of the city.

---

[51] *LP* 1:486.

[52] *LP* 2:1, 3, 3–34 passim, 34 n.3. A glance at the index Krautheimer's *Rome* s.v. Leo III (p. 387) will convey some sense of his importance for the history of Rome's monuments.

Leo's was an unusually troubled pontificate, and this is not the place to get bogged down in an analysis of the myriad indignities inflicted on this pope.[53] A few key issues must be studied, however. Leo's election and consecration were rapid and uneventful, but the account in his *vita* raises doubts. It says Leo was elected "by divine inspiration, with one and the same will and concord, by all the priests and officials of the whole clergy, indeed by the nobility and the whole Roman people." We might dismiss all of this as harmless rhetorical excess were it not for two facts. First, according to the electoral decree of 769 the Roman nobility and people could only acclaim, not elect, a pope. Second, Leo was opposed very quickly by powerful interests in Rome, and it is doubtful that his election was really effected amidst such harmony. It is not enough to say that the language of the *vita* is formulaic and need not be taken at face value.[54] It reads like propaganda, and papal biographers always chose their words very carefully and to precise effect.

But to what effect? Evidently the biographer's intention was to portray as negatively as possible the lay and clerical magnates who in 799 perpetrated a vicious attack on Leo. It has been plausibly argued that Leo owed his election to those in the Lateran who opposed the rising tide of noble influence within the Church.[55] If this is true, and it must be at least in part, then Leo's biographer was trying to say that what everyone had agreed to in 795 a mean-spirited and mendacious faction tried to abrogate in 799. Why else would he have emphasized that high officials of the Church and great nobles of the city had concurred in the election?

While he was celebrating the major litanies, 25 April 799, Leo was attacked by a mob in a Roman street near the church of St. Lawrence in Lucina. The ringleaders were Paschalis, Campulus, and Maurus of Nepi. The first two were nobles, relatives of Hadrian and high officers of the Church. The third was a military aristocrat and a neighbor of both Toto of

---

[53]The fullest account is Horace Kinder Mann, *The Lives of the Popes in the Middle Ages* (London, 1925), 2:1–110. This study is badly dated and often more chatty than illuminating. Briefer, though better, are: Amann, "Léon III, " *Dictionnaire de théologie catholique* 9, no. 1 (Paris, 1926): 304–12; Ullmann, "Leo III," *Lexikon für Theologie und Kirche* 7 (Freiburg, 1963): 947–48; Richard E. Sullivan, "Pope St. Leo III," *New Catholic Encyclopedia* 8 (New York, 1967): 640.

[54]Bayet, "L'élection de Léon III, la révolte des romains en 799 et ses consequences," *Annuaire de la faculté des lettres de Lyon*, 1 (1883): 174.

[55]Bayet, "L'élection de Léon III," p. 174; Caspar, *Das Papsttum unter fränkischer Herrschaft*, p. 117; A. Hauck, *Kirchengeschichte Deutschlands* 2:98; Haller, *Das Papsttum* 2:16, argues that Leo was elected by Hadrian's followers but this seems doubtful.

Nepi and Hadrian's family. Leo, "*semivivus*," was thrown to the ground
and an attempt was made to mutilate him. Subsequently he was incarcerated
in the monasteries of Sts. Stephen and Sylvester and of St. Erasmus. During
the night a loyal papal *cubicularius* spirited Leo away from St. Erasmus to
Wirundus of Stavelot, a *missus* of Charlemagne, and Duke Winigis of Spoleto. Safe from the hands of his enemies, Leo set out on a long journey that
would take him to a conference with Charlemagne at Paderborn in Saxony
and on a return trip to Rome with an impressive entourage from Francia.
Some charges against Leo of simony and immorality were bruited about,
but with Franks in Rome no one would come forward to substantiate the
accusations. Sometime between late 799 and the autumn of 800 Charlemagne himself decided that he would have to travel to Rome to put an end
to Leo's difficulties. Finally, Leo exculpated himself by oath of any wrongdoing, and on Christmas day in 800 he crowned Charlemagne emperor at
St. Peter's. Shortly thereafter the persons who had been guilty of the attack
on Leo were sent into exile.[56]

A statement by Leo himself[57] and another by Alcuin[58] indicate that Leo's
enemies had sought to depose him. This is probably true, but the sources for
the early years of Leo's pontificate are all so partisan and tendentious that it
would be hazardous to venture any bold interpretations of the central
issues.[59] The only thing that is clear is that key noblemen, both lay and
clerical, opposed Leo and sought to get rid of him. Their gambit might have
succeeded had not Leo had some support in Rome and the protection of the
king of the Franks. The nobility obviously disliked losing the highest seat of
power in 795, but was not quite powerful enough to carry off a coup d'état.
Only by a coup, however, could the clerical party that had elected Leo under
the terms of the election decree of 769 be detached from its control of the
papal office. Hadrian had evidently not gone as far as some have suggested,
and as some of his contemporaries might have liked, in promoting noblemen
to positions within the Church generally and among the *papabili* specifically.
In view of the support that Hadrian had to have had among all factions of
the clergy to have been elected in 772, it is not surprising that he did not
simply hand the Church over to the nobility. Hadrian, rather like Paul one

---

[56]These facts are well known. See: *LP* 2:4–5; Jaffé, *RP*, pp. 308–9.

[57]Leo III, *Epistolae X*, no. 6, *MGH, EKA* 3:63.

[58]Alcuin, *Epp.* no. 179, *MGH, EKA* 2:297.

[59]The best studies are: Walter Mohr, "Karl der Große, Leo III und der römische Aufstand
von 799," *Archivum Latinitas Medii Aevi* 20 (1960): 39–98; Zimmermann, *Papstabsetzungen
des Mittelalters*, pp. 25–36.

suspects, was a gradualist in his perception of the need and desirability to "nobilize" the Church. Thus, after the nobility found that it could not elect one of its own in 795 powerful men resorted to the desperate tactic of planning and attempting to carry out a coup d'état in 799. All of this is reminiscent of Toto of Nepi's bold venture in 767.

Leo's opponents were down, but not out. In 815, shortly after Charlemagne had died, Leo discovered that certain noblemen were conspiring against him.[60] The pope rounded up the leaders and had them executed in a field near the Lateran.[61] Louis the Pious received news of this and dispatched his nephew, King Bernard of Italy, to investigate and to report back through a count named Gerold.[62] Louis's emissaries did go to Rome, and they did send a report to the emperor, but we have no details about its contents nor do we know anything about the mandate of the three papal envoys who traveled to Francia except that they filed a report of their own "concerning all that had befallen their lord."[63] Later in 815 a gang of hoodlums ravaged some papal estates outside Rome but, on orders of Bernard, Winigis of Spoleto was sent to put a stop to the plundering.[64] A short time later Leo died.

This series of events suggests that, on the one hand, the nobility was never reconciled to Leo and, on the other hand, only the threat of a new Frankish intervention between 800 and 814 prevented the nobles from at-

---

[60]Astronomer, *Vita Hludowici*, c. 25, MGH, SS 2:609, says "hoc anno cursum vertente, perlatum est imperatori . . ." which suggests late 814 or early 815 but *Annales regni Francorum*, anno 815, ed. Kurze, p. 142, says Louis learned of the attack while holding an assembly at Paderborn. BM, no. 587b, dates this assembly 1 July 815, so the conspiracy probably took place in the late winter or early spring of 815. All sources emphasize that noblemen were involved: *Annales regni Francorum*, p. 142: "Quisdam de primoribus"; *Annales fuldenses, anno* 815, ed. Kurze, p. 20: "Quidam primores"; *Annales sithienses*, MGH, SS 3:37: "Quidam primores"; Astronomer, c. 25, p. 619: "Aliqui potentes." References could be multiplied many times. The *LP* is silent on all of this.

[61]*Annales regni Francorum*, anno 815, ed. Kurze, p. 142; Benedictus, *Chronicon*, c. 24, MGH, SS 3:711, adds the detail "in campo Lateranensis" and says 300 were killed, a figure correctly judged grossly excessive by BM, no. 587a, and Simson, *Jahrbücher* 1:61 n.5.

[62]*Annales regni Francorum*, anno 815, ed. Kurze, p. 142; Astronomer, *Vita Hludowici*, c. 25, MGH, SS 2:619.

[63]*Annales regni francorum*, anno 815, ed. Kurze, pp. 142–43. The papal envoys included a duke, Sergius, a suburbicarian bishop, and a Lateran official, which shows that Leo did have supporters among all parties at Rome.

[64]*Annales regni Francorum*, anno 815, ed. Kurze, p. 143; Astronomer, *Vita Hludowici*, c. 25, MGH, SS 2:619. For no apparent reason Haller, *Das Papsttum* 2:25, calls this a peasants' revolt.

tacking Leo again while Charlemagne was still alive. When Leo was attacked the second time, in 815, Louis the Pious quickly sent representatives to Rome and this action must have demonstrated to the magnates a continuing Frankish resolve to protect the pope, and the inherent futility of further action on their part. Moreover, the fact that Leo was able to put down the rebellion of 815 before Frankish assistance arrived tends to indicate that the pope was not without at least some support in influential circles in Rome.

Events surrounding the election of Leo's successor, Stephen IV, are rich with clues about the domestic situation in Rome. Stephen was a nobleman who had entered the Lateran under Hadrian but whose promotions to deacon and subdeacon had come under Leo.[65] These aspects of Stephen's career illustrate, first, the penetration of noblemen into the clergy that had been a marked feature of the pontificate of Hadrian and, second, the fact that Leo was not unwilling to promote at least some noblemen, apparently those with whom he had served for a long time. The *Liber Pontificalis* does not mention any untoward incidents in connection with Stephen's election, but some events that followed that election cast a murky retrospective hue over it. Stephen's election, of course, ought to have been governed by the decree of 769. If it was, then Stephen might be regarded as a reconciliation candidate. He was a nobleman and a Lateran careerist who had enjoyed the confidence of Leo III. Perhaps the electors hoped, through Stephen, to replicate the harmonious conditions of Hadrian's pontificate. There are, however, reasons to suspect that in 816 the election decree of 769 had been subverted.

Immediately after his election Stephen departed from Rome to meet with Louis the Pious in Francia "to make satisfaction to the emperor concerning his election." He also hoped to gain release of the exiles then languishing in Francia on account of their plots and schemes against Leo.[66] About what, exactly, did Stephen wish to "satisfy" Louis? He cannot have been seeking formal, legal approval or confirmation of his election. The Carolingians had never been assigned, and never claimed, the old imperial prerogatives in papal elections. Among the various accomplishments of Stephen's journey, a very significant one was an adjustment of the electoral decree of 769. One of the legal prescriptions of the *Pactum Ludovicianum* reopened papal elections to "all the Romans."[67] Under the circumstances "*omnes Romani*" can

[65]*LP* 2:49.

[66]*Annales regni Francorum*, *anno* 815, ed. Kurze, p. 144; Astronomer, *Vita Hludowici*, c. 26, *MGH, SS* 2:620; Thegan, *Vita Hludowici*, c. 16, *MGH, SS* 2:594; *LP* 2:49.

[67]*MGH, Cap.*, vol. 1, no. 172, c. 10, pp. 354–55. Louis also specifically renounced any imperial rights over papal elections, which led von Schubert, *Geschichte der christlichen Kirche*,

only have meant, in practice, the nobility. Perhaps therefore the nobility had grown so tired of Leo and of the clerics who wished to exclude them from papal elections that they intruded upon the "conclave" of 816. Stephen, partly because of this irregularity and partly because Frankish bishops with royal approval had assented to the decree of 769, felt a need to "satisfy" Louis. The emperor was evidently persuaded to permit an extension of the franchise and apparently assured that peace could be maintained in Rome. As far as Louis's interests can be ascertained, they extended only to securing harmony in the pope's city.

How had Stephen been able to convince Louis of the likelihood of peace and harmony? Although he had been promoted by Leo, he was a nobleman and he went to Francia to plead the cases of other noblemen who had been Leo's implacable foes. Stephen's true allegiance lay not with those clerics who resented the nobility and who sought to obstruct their rising prominence in the Lateran, but instead with the nobles themselves who wished to take over control of the papal office and administration and, through them, the Republic. In the early ninth century the nobility had not yet achieved a dominant position among the clergy and, having grown impatient, they forced the issue in 816. Even noble clerics like Stephen, however, had to give some thought to both the political and the religious sides of the papal office. Therefore, the new election decree of 816 did not alter the narrow circle of *papabili*. The nobles got back the vote in 816, and they could henceforth vote for one of their own if they wished, but the candidates had to come from a relatively restricted group of high Church officers. The new decree was designed to assure that there would be no more popes like Leo III, but it had the concomitant effect of assuring that there would also be none like Constantine II.

Most popes after Stephen IV were noblemen, but the peaceful interlude that had been Hadrian's pontificate was seldom replicated. For example, in 823 reports reached Francia that two high Lateran officers and some other men had been blinded and then beheaded in Rome. The reports contained intimations that Pope Paschal I had been implicated and perhaps responsible.[68] Paschal soon sent a delegation to Louis consisting of both major

---

p. 397, to doubt the authenticity of this passage because he assumed that the Carolingians inherited the Byzantine right of confirmation. They did no such thing, as Bayet, "Les élections pontificales," pp. 69–72, long ago proved. On c. 10 of the *Ludovicianum* see, in general, Hahn, "Hludowicianum," p. 101ff.

[68] *Annales regni Francorum, anno* 823, ed. Kurze, p. 161; Astronomer, *Vita Hludowici*, c. 37, MGH, SS 2:627–28.

Lateran officers and lay dignitaries. Factional strife of some sort lurks behind
these events, but it is very difficult to detect the basic issues. When Paschal
died in 824 a disputed election ensued and, for a time, Paschal's former
opponents refused to permit him a decent burial at St. Peter's.[69] These events,
however little can be known about them, make it difficult to escape the
conclusion that once the nobility had secured its control of the papal office
and of the clergy, it imported into the Lateran that propensity for factious
strife that had been a familiar landmark on the Roman scene since the
Hannibalic war.

    Later in the ninth century both Nicholas I and John VIII tried to return
to the decree of 769, but they failed.[70] In the tenth century social tensions of
all sorts erupted in Rome, and the nobility almost totally diverted the papacy
from its religious missions and turned it for a while into little more than a
political office. This situation was eventually rectified by the election decree
of Nicholas II which basically returned the situation to what it had been
between 769 and 816. After 816, however, contested elections, factional
strife, and often violence became the almost inevitable companions of papal
elections.

    A study of the ethnic backgrounds of the popes illustrated the Romaniza-
tion of the clergy as the Republic was coming into existence. In chapter 2
of this book a case was made that Gregory III and Zachary were the first
popes to have presided over an independent, albeit roundly threatened, Republic. It is therefore worth emphasizing that the process of Romanization
is first discernible during these pontificates; indeed it may have begun under
Gregory II. From a study of papal elections it has been possible to detect, by
the 750s and 760s, another phenomenon. The nobility began to contest with
the clergy for leadership within the Republic. This was a perfectly natural,
probably inevitable, development, but for a time the clergy tried to retain
control on its own terms. By 816 the nobility had grown tired of waiting for
control to come to it gradually and had learned on two occasions that overt
violence would not work either. Thus the nobility intruded on the election
of 816 and then persuaded Louis to agree to an extension of the franchise
in papal elections that put the aristocracy into an unassailable position in
the Republic. Thereafter the leadership in the Roman Church mirrored the
secular, social leadership of the Republic.

    This process of identification between the clergy and the local society
might have been a positive development for the Republic if the delicate

---

[69]*BM*, no. 785b; Jaffé, *RP*, p. 320.
[70]Ernst Perels, *Papst Nikolaus I und Anastasius Bibliothecarius* (Berlin, 1920), pp. 53–54,
53 n.1 citing *PL* 119:795. For John VIII see: Mansi, *Concilia* 18:221.

balancing of forces achieved under Hadrian had persisted. Surely the conditions of the 680s, with factions in the "army" lining up behind factions in the clergy, would have been relentlessly disruptive. Unfortunately, once the clergy and the nobility had become socially indistinguishable, the aspirations and ambitions of the latter were shared by the former. Factional strife outside the Lateran, but inside the Roman nobility, was imported within the Lateran and this process, as the sorry record of the tenth century shows only too well, was also disruptive. Lateran offices, chief among them the papacy, became prizes in the games of Roman politics. Alas, almost all the rules of those games are in our period forever shrouded by the impenetrable silence of the sources.

Reflections on the Papal Office

As the popes became tightly enmeshed in the social and political struggles of Rome it might be thought that the papal office became unstable in direct proportion to the degree of its participation in those struggles. In addition, it might seem that the popes could not reconcile the conflicting demands of their simultaneous positions as heads of church and state. Wilhelm Sickel thought that, as an elective office subject to continuous political pressures, the papacy had to have lacked the stability and continuity that typify dynastic states. Sickel also believed that as an ecclesiastical office the papacy was fundamentally unsuited to the tasks and requirements of secular rule.[71] Sickel's views have contributed in an important way to the pervasive notion that the Republic of St. Peter was not a true state.

On closer inspection it will be seen that Sickel's interpretation has three components. The first speaks to the papal office as a guarantor of, or as an obstacle to, continuity and stability. The second addresses the papal office to be sure, but in a larger sense it demands reflection upon the Republic's government as a whole and on the place in that government of the pope. The third component is essentially ideological and goes to the heart of the matter of what actually constitutes a state, in the early Middle Ages or at any other time. At present only the question of the stability or instability of the papal office will be addressed. The next chapter of this book will treat the government of the Republic and the place of the pope in that government, and in the conclusion the definition of "state" will be confronted.

---

[71] W. Sickel, "Alberic und der Kirchenstaat," pp. 50–64.

The papal office as a guarantor of stability and continuity may be examined from several different perspectives. It may be well to start by specifying that kings or popes are individuals, but monarchy and papacy are institutions. The institutions are, in a sense, immortal and do not necessarily depend on the mortal and momentary holders of office. To some degree all regimes try to depersonalize institutions,[72] that is, for example, to separate king and crown. The question is, therefore, did dynastic states—or other kinds for that matter—as a rule separate office and officeholder any more or any better than the papacy did? Was an elective papacy a poor guarantor of order and stability? All of the evidence urges us to respond negatively.

The Lateran had potent traditions, many of which reached back authentically to the third century. No pope could fully escape them, and the available records indicate that few tried. From the Roman Empire to the present the papacy has been an awesome and awe-inspiring institution. No pope, however peculiar, single-minded, or charismatic, has been able entirely to escape the larger-than-life office to which he has ascended. The papacy has almost always constricted the popes and confined them within certain limits of action. Those limits have often been stretched, but they have seldom been broken. There has always been a sense that the papacy is bigger than any individual pope, and this sense had been responsible for much of the evident continuity in papal history.

In important respects the aura of the papacy was not conferred at the solemn moment of consecration. Rather, in the early Middle Ages, it was instilled gradually in the Lateran and in the Roman ecclesiastical community. Lateran bureaucrats tended, in our period, to enter the papal government young and to stay there all their lives. They cannot have avoided, and would not for any discernible reason have wanted to avoid, the slow but steady inculcation of Lateran traditions. In this connection it is important to remember that all of the popes in our period, with the exception of the intruder Constantine, were Lateran careerists. It is thus easy to understand why such a remarkably consistent policy was pursued from the 680s into the ninth century. Toward the middle of the eighth century Lateran and Roman traditions began to merge and the result, except during the troubled pontificate of Leo III, was a conjunction of lay and clerical traditions culminating in the papal office. The men who became pope were imbued with the traditions of their church and of their city, and the men who elected them were susceptible

---

[72]See, for example: Helmut Beumann, "Zur Entwicklung transpersonaler Staatsvorstellungen," in *Das Königtum: Seine geistigen und rechtlichen Grundlagen* ed. Theodor Mayer (Sigmaringen, 1956), pp. 185–224.

to the same influences. It is difficult to imagine an office more likely to proceed from, to represent, and to guarantee stability than the papacy.

The pope's term of office was another guarantor of continuity and provides some instructive comparisons with dynastic states which Sickel presumed to be more stable. Leaving out anti-popes, or momentary ones like Sisinnius in 708 and Philip in 768, the figures for average pontificates in our period are intriguing. In the 159 years from 685 to 844, that is, from John V to Gregory IV, there were twenty popes and they reigned for an average of 7.95 years. In the Byzantine period proper, from the Pragmatic Sanction of 554 to 685, there were twenty-three popes in 131 years for an average pontificate of 5.7 years. Our period also saw a number of unusually long pontificates: Gregory II, 16 years; Hadrian, 23 years; Leo III, 21 years; Gregory IV, 17 years. Eight years, the average pontificate under the Republic, does not compare unfavorably with modern standards of official tenure or with early medieval ones. For example, the twenty-eight Byzantine emperors from Justinian (527–65) to Theophilus (829–42) averaged 10.3 years on the throne, and the thirty-two patriarchs of Constantinople from Eutychius (552–65) to Methodius I (843–47) averaged 9.45 years. Casting a bit more widely for comparisons, we discover the following figures. Seventeen Carolingian kings averaged reigns of 17.0 years, while twenty-two Lombard kings averaged 9.4 years. Finally, the twenty-seven Visigoths who ruled in Spain averaged 9.1 years. These figures prove that, on the grounds of the frequency of the changes in office, the elective papacy was about as stable as any of its contemporary dynastic states.

The papal throne was vacant twenty times in the period under consideration, and these vacancies might be thought of as hindrances to stability and continuity. Two mitigating factors must be taken into consideration, however. First, and this was not necessarily true of a dynastic state, when the pope died the business of the Lateran did not cease. The archpriest, archdeacon, and *primicerius* of the notaries constituted a regency council which automatically ruled *sede vacante.*[73] Continuity was assured by these very high Lateran officers who would always have been close associates of the dead pope and who would later form part of the inner circle around the new one. Second, the intervals between the death of one pope and the consecration of another tended to be rather long in the Byzantine period, when imperial or exarchal confirmation was required, but became very short thereafter. For example, from John V, with whom this study begins, to Gregory III, proba-

---

[73]*LD*, no. 59, ed. Foerster, p. 113: "ill. archipresbyter ill. archdiaconus ill. primicerius notariorum seruantes locum sanctae sedis apostolicae."

bly the last pope who sought Byzantine confirmation, the average vacancy
was 62.4 days. From Zachary to Eugenius II—we have no figures for his
two immediate successors—9.9 days was the average vacancy, and if we
leave out the extraordinary interval of 35 days between Stephen II
and Paul I occasioned by the abortive candidacy of Theophylact, then the
more realistic figure is 6.8 days.[74] The nine-week intervals of the late Byzantine period may have been a minor nuisance, but with a regular regency
council in place it cannot have been an insuperable one. One-week intervals,
on the other hand, were no problem at all, and must have insured a very
prompt and orderly transition from one pontificate to the next.

Finally, although there was no set *cursus honorum* for popes, it is a
matter of no small consequence that, under the Republic, every pope except
the lay usurper Constantine II had had a long and varied career in the
Lateran before his elevation. In various contexts this fact has come to our
attention already but it may be helpful now to recapitulate with particular
emphasis some of the papal careers we have already encountered.

As to length of service, it has been noted that Constantine I was the
holder of a responsible office twenty-eight years before his election in 708.
Stephen II and Paul I entered the clergy under Gregory II (715–31) and were
elected in, respectively, 752 and 757. They had served in the Church for an
absolute minimum of twenty-one and twenty-six years. Stephen III entered
the clergy under Zachary (741–52) and was elected pope in 768. He had to
have spent at least sixteen years in the Lateran administration. Stephen IV
entered the Lateran under Hadrian I (772–95) and reached the papal office
in 816, at least twenty-one years later. For many popes there are no documents upon which to base a determination of length of service, but there
does not seem to be any reason to suppose that the lengthy ecclesiastical
careers of popes for whom evidence does exist were in any way extraordinary.

While they were in the clergy, future popes usually held a succession of
offices. No case has come to light of a republican pope serving in only one
office before entering into succession to St. Peter. Because there was no
predetermined *cursus honorum* papal careers differed markedly from one
another in terms of the previous offices that the popes had held. Papal
careers were alike, however, in being long, as just noted, and diverse. Some
popes had wide experience in the administrative side of the Lateran while
others had spent most of their time in the pastoral and liturgical staffs.

---

[74]The figures are computed from statements at the end of each *vita* in *LP*.

Most, however, seem to have had experience in both branches of the Lateran administration. Leo III, for example, was at one time *vestararius*, a major Lateran administrative dignity, but also served as a titular priest. Service as a regional notary and as a deacon preceded Hadrian's election. John VII (705–7) had been rector of the Campanian patrimony and later a deacon, from which office he was raised to the papacy.[75] Gregory II was a subdeacon and later a deacon, a diplomat, librarian, and a treasury officer before his election as pope.[76]

Representative evidence drawn from these papal careers permits several conclusions. First, it would be quite correct to speak of the popes as professionals. Their lengthy careers and wide experience appears to justify such a characterization. Second, long and varied service in the clergy had important implications for the papal office. The traditions of the clergy were ancient and distinctive. It may be presumed that years of service in the Church would have inculcated those traditions while at the same time mitigating the ethnic, social, or political traditions which the future popes brought with them into the clergy. There is no reason to suppose that Roman popes were not sensitive to local Roman interests, or that aristocratic popes did not sympathize with the aspirations of the aristocracy. Nevertheless, the Lateran would have had a sanitizing effect in that it cleansed men, beginning while they were still adolescents, of the uglier and more selfish traits of social class and political station. In short, the Lateran was a great machine that produced generations of clerics marked by a sense of the shared interests of their common enterprise. As political, administrative, social, and religious leaders it is difficult to imagine men more likely to assure continuity and stability that the "Lateranized" popes of the Republic.

The Papacy Within the Republic

Some of the most important internal developments in the Republic of St. Peter are mirrored in the personal histories of the popes from John V to Gregory IV. Late in the seventh century and during the first three decades of the eighth the popes were neither Roman nor noble, but they joined forces with a strong party of local Roman magnates to reject Byzantine religious policy and to prevent regularly appointed Byzantine officials from carrying

---

[75]*LP* 1:386 n. 1; Richards, *Popes and the Papacy*, p. 267.
[76]*LP* 1:410.

out their duties. During this forty– or fifty–year period there was a party at Rome, represented in both the clergy and nobility, that opposed the anti-Byzantine direction of the majority party, but this opposition was eventually overcome. Thus it would be wrong to attribute full credit for the emancipation of central Italy from the Byzantine Empire to the papacy. If the attitudes and policies of the popes had been out of step with those of the most prominent and numerous inhabitants of Rome, then either the early eighth-century popes would not have been elected or else some of them would have ended as humiliated exiles like Martin I. The "greater" or the "stronger" part of the Romans supported the popes, and so it was the exarchs who were repeatedly humiliated and, in a sense, exiled from Rome and its environs.

By the late 720s the dominant party at Rome began to see that secession from the Byzantine state was the only workable response to a long and bitter period of Byzantine oppression. The interests of the Romans had become, quite simply, local and Roman. The empire offered them nothing that they needed and much that was repulsive to them. As this realization dawned Romans began entering the clergy in greater numbers. Eastern popes ceased being elected and noble Romans began rising to the summit. Until the 750s it appears that parties in the clergy led both the Church and the Republic by means of loose coalitions that reached outside the Lateran into secular society. As long as the Byzantines represented a potential threat and the Lombards a very real one, the clergy's leadership was unchallenged. It is worth recalling the times when the pope deployed Roman troops: in Spoleto in 739; in the face of Aistulf's siege in 756; on behalf of Desiderius's quest for the throne in 756–57. After the major external threats to the Republic had been vanquished, the clergy tried to perpetuate its leadership, but the nobility, by means of its gradual penetration of the clergy, finally assumed control. Had the process of noble penetration been allowed to run its course, it is inevitable that the nobility would have come to direct the Church and the Republic at some time; probably in the first half of the ninth century. The nobility, however, cut short the natural process of social evolution within the Church and took over in 816. The pontificates of Paul I and Hadrian appear to have been transitional stages on the road to aristocratic dominance, and the tumultuous reign of Leo III was the last gasp of the old order.

Ironically, then, the clergy was always dominant in the Republic, but the ethnic backgrounds and bloodlines of that clergy changed dramatically in a century and a half. The old clerical order of the early eighth century gave way before a noble and Roman clergy of the dawning ninth. The principal consequence of this change was that by the early ninth century the struggles present in Roman society had been imported directly into the Lateran. By the time of Paschal, battles in the Lateran appear to have been little more than extensions of battles going on in the larger society of the Republic.

The papal office may have become the focal point of the battles of Roman politicians, but the popes did not completely succumb to the forces that might have transformed them into nothing more than secular potentates. Paul and Hadrian worked to reform the Frankish Church. Hadrian corresponded with English kings and prelates, and debated high matters of dogma with the Greeks. Leo counseled Charlemagne on biblical exegesis, settled quarrels among monastic communities in Jerusalem, and debated with Frankish theologians about the procession of the Holy Spirit. Paschal I and Gregory IV assisted in sending missionaries to win Scandinavia for the Church. The lofty and universal traditions of the papal office served as one shield against the "Earthly City."

Long and varied careers in the Church also insulated the popes from the purely secular interests of the society that surrounded them. If it is true that the popes did not fully escape the ties of class and party, then it is also true that the Lateran erected around the popes walls and barriers against the enticements of political involvement.

Seven

The Governance of the Republic

CONTINUING OUR look inside the Republic, we must now ask how, rather than by whom, it was governed. Actually, the "how" and the "whom" cannot be sharply distinguished from one another. That is, in describing the institutions through which the popes actually governed the Republic, it will be impossible to avoid commenting upon the persons who held offices of one kind or another.

But did the popes govern? A venerable tradition, once again going back in its modern form to Sickel, holds that the Republic possessed only ecclesiastical institutions and not clearly differentiated secular ones. The argument maintains that ecclesiastical institutions are inherently incapable of governing a state and therefore no true state existed. Many historians prefer to speak of "patrimonial administration" rather than true government. This old and almost universally held assumption imposes a double burden on the following account. It must describe institutions while simultaneously attempting to demonstrate that they were fully suited to the tasks of government in all necessary and effective respects.

Sancta Romana Ecclesia and the Lateran Administration

The papacy was the pivot around which the life of the Republic turned. Heretofore we have examined the men who held the office, its place in the social structure of the Republic, and the procedures whereby the papacy was attained. Now we turn to the papacy as an institution in a larger sense, and to the government over which it presided. The papacy became a political, even a "politicized," office but it began as and remained an ecclesiastical institution. Our point of departure, therefore, must be with the local religious community whose head was the pope.

To understand the organization of the Roman Church, and eventually of the Republic, it is necessary to retreat into the fourth century to observe the origins of certain institutions that were still very much an integral part of the Roman scene four or five centuries later. There was a numerous and well-endowed Christian community in Rome before the conversion of Constantine, but its history is shrouded in obscurity. As Richard Krautheimer says, "properly speaking the history of Christian Rome starts on 28 October A.D. 312, when Constantine wrested the city from his co-emperor Maxentius."[1] Constantine's seizure of Rome, and his conversion to Christianity, made it possible for the Church to operate as a licit and public institution. Most of our evidence for the organization of the Roman Church dates therefore from the fourth or subsequent centuries.

The "Roman Church" can be thought of in two distinct ways, only one of which is relevant to the present discussion. We are not here concerned with the idea of the Roman Church as the Church Universal, nor are we going to study in all respects the entirety of the Christian community within the Roman church province. Rather, our focus will rest upon the pope, the Lateran administration, and the churches and basilicas which, taken together, formed the *sancta Romana ecclesia* in the narrow sense. At the end of the eighth century, for example, there were some 130 churches in Rome,[2] but only about three dozen of them constituted the "Roman Church" as we shall use that term.

The pope, as bishop of Rome and as archbishop of the Roman church province, a region extending out into the countryside some forty or more miles in all directions, stood at the head of an ecclesiastical corporation that formed the Roman Church.[3] Rome was unique among Christian communities, however, in that its pastoral and liturgical activities were never centered in a single cathedral church.[4] The religious life of the Roman Church revolved around the *tituli*, of which at least twenty were pre-Constantinian.[5] By the time of Pope Stephen III there were twenty-eight *tituli*, and that

---

[1] Krautheimer, *Rome*, p. 3.
[2] Vielliard, *Recherches*, pp. 109–10.
[3] Hinschius, *Kirchenrecht* 1:212–13.
[4] Stephan Kuttner, "Cardinalis: The History of a Canonical Concept," *Traditio* 3 (1945): 146.
[5] Kuttner, "Cardinalis," p. 147ff; Vielliard, *Recherches*, pp. 32–53.

number remained firm for centuries thereafter.[6] Originally the *tituli* were unimpressive and unobtrusive meeting places for individual communities of worshipers. They were not, from a geographical point of view, evenly distributed throughout the city. Instead, they were clustered in zones of heavy population density. Actually, they tended to be situated on the fringes of the populous quarters of the ancient city. Rome evidently had no distinctively Christian quarter. Rather, groups of Christians could be found scattered almost everywhere. After the time of Constantine the *tituli* became quasi parishes, and some of the titular churches became impressive structures.[7]

Each *titulus* had as a rule two or three priests, the most senior of whom was the *presbyter prior*. The senior titular priest of the city was the archpriest of the Roman Church who, as we have seen, was one of the triad of officials who governed the Church *sede vacante*. The titular clergy were not ordained for their particular *titulus*, but for the Roman Church. They made up the Roman *presbyterium* and were a key component of the episcopal clergy of the city.[8] Priests in nontitular churches were not part of the *presbyterium* and did not figure among the episcopal clergy.

Ordinarily, within any Christian community, sacramental unity was focused on the bishop and preserved through his control or delegation of pastoral and sacramental celebrations. This was also true of Rome, but the size of the city and the magnitude of its Christian population, already large before Constantine and immense thereafter, meant that in practice the priests of the *tituli* took on very early a significant share in the sacramental functions of the bishop, who in Rome was of course the pope. Titular priests could absolve penitents by the time of Innocent I in 416, and in the late seventh century, maybe earlier, they could baptize infants and catechumens at the vigils of Easter and Pentecost. These priests also celebrated the eucharistic liturgy in their *tituli*, and often in one or more of the cemeterial

---

[6]Kuttner, "Cardinalis," pp. 147, 149–50; Fürst, *Cardinalis*, pp. 60–62; Hans Walter Klewitz, "Die Entstehung des Kardinalskollegiums," *ZRG, kA* 25 (1936): 149ff. Andrieu, "L'origine du titre de cardinal dans l'église romaine," *Miscellanea Giovanni Mercati* (Rome, 1946), 5:131ff, 135, thought that there were no more than 22 *tituli* in the time of Hadrian I and Leo III because of two passages in the *LP* (1:504; 2:20). Fürst, following Klewitz and Kuttner, argues persuasively that there were 28. Enrico Josi, "Titoli della chiesa romana," *Enciclopedia cattolica* (Vatican City, 1954), 12:153–54 believes that a full 28 was not reached until the twelfth century. On title churches see also Herman Geertman, *More Veterum: Il Liber Pontificalis e gli edifici ecclesiastici di Roma nella tarda antichità e nell'alto medioevo* (Groningen, 1975), pp. 106–11, 143–80.

[7]Vielliard, *Recherches*, pp. 53–55; Kuttner, "Cardinalis," p. 147.

[8]Kuttner, "Cardinalis," pp. 147–48; Fürst, *Cardinalis*, pp. 21–23.

churches located outside the city. Celebrations in the latter churches, however, seem to have diminished in importance during the Gothic and Lombard wars when regular services in these suburban churches became impossible.[9]

Inside Rome the titular priests gradually began to play an important role in celebrating masses in the city's great basilicas. Constantine established basilicas at St. Peter's tomb and at the Lateran, and his mother, Helena, created another at the former Sessorian palace. In due course several other basilicas were erected in various parts of the city. Rome's basilicas were in part the result of pious and generous benefactions, but they were also designed to create more capacious and commodious sites for the ever more numerous Christian assemblages of the city.[10] By the early eighth century five of these basilicas had come to be regarded as "patriarchal": St. Peter's, St. Paul's, St. Lawrence's, St. Mary Major, and the basilica of the Saviour at the Lateran.[11] Pope Simplicius (468–83) established the practice of appointing the titular priests to keep weekly liturgies at the basilicas.[12] In the fifth century, and for quite a while thereafter, the title priests celebrated at St. Peter's, St. Paul's, and St. Lawrence's, and perhaps also at the Lateran.[13] By the early eighth century St. Mary Major had been added to the list of basilicas served by the title priests. At that time there were twenty-five title priests, with five of them appointed to say daily masses, except on Fridays and Saturdays, at each of the five major, or patriarchal, basilicas.[14] During the eighth century, in a process brought to completion by Stephen III, the organization of the basilican services was restructured. Eventually, the priests of twenty-eight *tituli* were appointed to serve four of the basilicas on a daily basis and seven of Rome's suburbicarian bishops (Ostia, Albano, Palestrina, Porta, Silva Candida, Gabii, and Velletri) were appointed to serve in the Lateran basilica, which was increasingly regarded as the pope's own church.[15]

The twenty-eight *presbyteres priores* from each of the titular churches and the seven suburbicarian bishops posted to the Lateran basilica were in the eighth century called the cardinals of the Roman Church. The significance of the terms *presbyteri* or *episcopi cardinales* has been much debated.

---

[9]Kuttner, "Cardinalis," pp. 147–48; Fürst, *Cardinalis*, pp. 23–28.

[10]Vieilliard, *Recherches*, pp. 59–66, 68–71.

[11]Klewitz, "Entstehung," p. 149ff; Kuttner, "Cardinalis," pp. 147–48; Fürst, *Cardinalis*, pp. 27–29.

[12]*LP* 1:249.

[13]Klewitz, "Entstehung," p. 149ff.

[14]Fürst, *Cardinalis*, pp. 29–30. Mass was not celebrated Friday or Saturday.

[15]*LP* 1:423, 446, 478. Fürst, *Cardinalis*, pp. 29–30, 60–62; Kuttner, "Cardinalis," pp. 148–49.

According to one view they were called cardinals because, despite having their own churches, they were "incardinated" to serve in other churches.[16] A more recent and compelling view, however, holds that the cardinal clergy was a privileged group within the clergy of the Roman Church which alone belonged directly to the Roman *presbyterium*. In the eighth century the foundations were laid for the development of the cardinalate as a discrete institution encompassing bishops, priests, and deacons. The origins of the cardinalate, however, reside in the order of priests, in the *seniores* of the *tituli*.[17]

Within Rome and its immediate environs there were numerous monastic communities. Most of these were of Latin observance, but a few important houses were Greek. The vast majority of these monasteries had no formal connection with the Roman Church, but a few, called "basilical monasteries," were designated for special liturgical services in the city's patriarchal basilicas. Basically, some of the monks from each of the three or four communities appointed to each basilica had to see to the regular observance of the liturgy of the hours in the basilicas. In this way some at least of the many monks in Rome were integrated into the organizational structure of the local church.[18]

Naturally the pope could, and frequently did, move throughout the patriarchal basilicas and *tituli* to celebrate particular liturgies, called stational liturgies. There is in *Ordo Romanus I* a remarkably detailed description of one such stational liturgy.[19] The pope and his cardinal clergy thus provided for the pastoral, liturgical, and sacramental needs of the people of Rome and its immediate environs. It would be impossible to overemphasize the bonds of unity and cohesion produced in Rome by the unification and organization of the ecclesiastical life of the city. One has only to read in *Ordo I* the

---

[16]Traditions tending toward this position were put on a firm foundation by Kuttner, "Cardinalis," pp. 129–46. His views were called "the consensus position" by Karl F. Morrison, "Cardinal," *New Catholic Encyclopedia* (New York, 1967), 3:104–5.

[17]Fürst, *Cardinalis*, pp. 62–72. Fürst's interpretations are actually a refinement of a tradition that sees the cardinals as the most significant clergy of the Roman Church. For a resume of this view see Andrieu, "Cardinal," p. 130.

[18]Ferrari, *Early Roman Monasteries*, pp. 365–75. For an interesting study of the development of the basilical monasteries serving Santa Maria Maggiore see: Duchesne, "Les monastères desservants de Sainte-Marie-Majeure," *MAH* 27 (1907): 479–94. For some insights into papal concerns about the development of these monasteries see: *LP* 1:397 (St. Paul's: Gregory II), 419 (Lateran: Gregory III). See ibid, 1:418 for the posting by Gregory III of monks to a *titulus*, Santa Maria in Praesepe.

[19]*Ordines Romani*, ed. Andrieu, 2:67–108. For a discussion of the papal mass see Theodor Klauser, *A Short History of the Western Liturgy*, trans. John Halliburton, 2d ed. (Oxford, 1979), pp. 60–68.

account of the large and dazzling papal entourage passing from the Lateran to one of the *tituli* to form an impression of the impact such occasions must have had on the populace of the city. And, it should be noted, these spectacles were by no means rare. On the great feasts of the liturgical year, on the days of special sanctoral celebrations, and on numerous other occasions dictated by local custom, the people of Rome were reminded of the splendor, the power, and the majesty of their religious leaders. I am confident that centuries of religious leadership, symbolized by liturgical celebrations of all sorts, helped to pave the way for eventual political leadership.[20]

The Roman community differed from others not only in its extreme decentralization of religious functions, but also in its separation of pastoral from administrative duties. As the former depended directly on the pope, so too did the latter, but just as the pope could not personally provide for all of the liturgical and sacramental needs of his flock he also could not administer the ecclesiastical life of the city by himself.[21] In the third century Pope Fabian (236–50)[22] divided Rome into seven regions and provided for each a deacon and a subdeacon.[23] From Fabian's time or a little later each region also had a notary,[24] and by the fifth century each region also had a *defensor*.[25] By 680 or shortly after when *Ordo I* was compiled,[26] there were also regional acolytes who could step up in office to replace deacons who had died.[27] Under the Republic the regional administrative structure created in Christian antiquity still existed and, with a complement of Lateran officers, carried out a wide range of crucial tasks.

Rome's seven deacons were, in the beginning, essentially ministers for

---

[20]For an elegant and insightful discussion of the political significance of public ceremony in the late Roman world see: Sabine G. MacCormack, *Art and Ceremony in Late Antiquity* (Berkeley, 1981).

[21]Fürst, *Cardinalis*, pp. 14–15.

[22]Jaffé, *RP*, p. 15.

[23]*LP* 1:64. Duchesne, "Lés regions de Rome au moyen âge," *MAH* 10 (1890): 126–30. The ecclesiastical regions thus created owed nothing to the 14 civil districts into which the city had been divided by Augustus.

[24]*LP* 1:64; cf., however, 1:123 (Clement I), where the same thing is said. Harry Bresslau, *Handbuch der Urkundenlehre*, 4th ed. (Berlin, 1969), 1:191–92, says notaries surely existed by the time of Constantine and may be as early as Fabian. The statement about Clement is apocryphal.

[25]Balthasar Fischer, "Die Entwicklung des Instituts der Defensoren in der römischen Kirche," *Ephemerides Liturgicae* 48 (1939): 444–47; Guglielmo Felici and Giacomo Violardi, "Avvocato," *Enciclopedia cattolica* (Vatican City, 1949), 2:563–65.

[26]Andrieu, *Ordines Romani* 2:38–52, dates *Ordo I* to the very late seventh or early eighth century.

[27]*Ordo I*, cc. 2, 3, ed. Andrieu, *Ordines Romani* 2:67, 68.

charitable services. They looked out for the poor, for widows and orphans, for the infirm, and for pilgrims. They also had general custody of church property within their regions.[28] They were great, powerful, and influential officers of the Church, and they had their headquarters in the Lateran. The senior deacon was the archdeacon of the Roman Church and the pope's direct and chief representative in each region of the city.[29] The archdeacon was also, in all probability, the head of the administrative personnel as a whole,[30] and he was, as we have seen, one of the three officials who ruled the Church *sede vacante*. The regional deacons were independent of the priests of the *tituli*, but as both were *clerici episcopi* they were members of the Roman *presbyterium* which was headquartered in the Lateran. Thus was effected a junction between the pastoral and administrative staffs of the Roman Church. *Tituli* also had deacons, but they were clerics on their way to the priesthood and must be carefully distinguished from the regional deacons. The latter seldom went on to higher orders but often, as we shall see, assumed different offices within the Church. The seven regional deacons came to be called "cardinal deacons" by the late eighth century, and they were granted active rights in papal elections by the decree of 769 and, by that same decree, pronounced eligible for election as pope.[31]

Pope Fabian's biographer also says that each region had a notary whose duty it was "faithfully to collect the deeds of the martyrs."[32] It is possible that the notaries did function as quasi-official historians in very early times, but in later times they had more varied and important responsibilities. It may be that the Church began very early to appoint notaries by analogy to the public *tabelliones* at Rome. If so, they would have been charged to execute various kinds of documents necessary for efficient ecclesiastical record keeping.[33] Eventually, however, the notaries, whose total number cannot be estimated, began to write papal documents, oversee the papal archives, and

[28]Duchesne, "Notes sur le topographie de Rome au moyen âge II: Les titres presbytériaux et les diaconies," *MAH* 7 (1887): 217–18; Kuttner, "Cardinalis," p. 179; Llewellyn, *Rome in the Dark Ages*, p. 121.

[29]*Ordo I*, c. 4, ed. Andrieu, *Ordines Romani* 2:68 "archdiaconus, id est vicarius pontificis."

[30]Duchesne (*Temporal Sovereignty*, p. 62) believes the archdeacon was the head of the clergy as a whole but Fürst (*Cardinalis*, p. 41) doubts this. The evidence is scant but I incline toward Duchesne's view.

[31]I follow Fürst, *Cardinalis*, pp. 16–19, 20ff, 30, 40–46, 62. Kuttner, "Cardinalis," p. 178ff, has much of value to say on the deacons but, following Fürst, I disagree with him on the cardinalate of the deacons.

[32]*LP* 1:64.

[33]Guglielmo Felici, "Notaio," *Enciclopedia cattolica* (Vatican City, 1952), 8:1955–59; Reginald Lane Poole, *Lectures on the History of the Papal Chancery Down to the Time of Innocent III* (Cambridge, 1915), pp. 6–7, 12–19; Jones, *Later Roman Empire* 1:515–16.

work as the secretariat in papal synods. They were often among the pope's closest advisers and frequently served as his personal envoys. Their use as envoys, often on sensitive missions, probably resulted from their knowledge of state secrets gained through their secretarial work.[34] Documents refer to them as either *notarii* or *scriniarii*. Probably no sharp distinction existed between these two designations.[35] Notaries were always clerics, usually sub-deacons, and under the Republic were quite regularly noblemen.[36] By the time of Pope Gregory I (590–604) the notaries were organized into a *schola*, a corporation.[37] The seven regional notaries held pride of place, and the two senior regional notaries, called the *primicerius* and *secundicerius notariorum*, were high officers of the Roman Church. The *primicerius* not only headed the papal chancery and archive, but also was one of the triumvirate who ruled *sede vacante*.[38]

In the seventh century, and probably for a long time before then, the *primicerius* supervised not only the notaries but also the papal library and archives.[39] The *scrinium*, that is, the office where the notaries worked and perhaps the archive as well, was located in the Lateran palace near the main entrance and just off the reception hall.[40] The archives were in the Lateran by 649, although they had earlier been conserved at the basilica of St. Lawrence in Praesina, later called St. Lawrence in Damaso after Pope Damasus (366–84), who had installed the archive and perhaps the library there. Some documents were kept at St. Peter's, for example, the Frankish

---

[34]Hinschius, *Kirchenrecht* 1:375; Plöchl, *Kirchenrecht* 1:318; Bresslau, *Urkundenlehre* 1:194–97; Keith Hopkins, "Elite Mobility in the Roman Empire," in *Studies in Ancient Society*, ed. M. I. Finley (London, 1974), p. 114.

[35]Hinschius, *Kirchenrecht* 1:382, 433, assumed a distinction but Bresslau, *Urkundenlehre* 1:196, disproves it.

[36]Hinschius, *Kirchenrecht* 1:380. LD, nos. 69, 70, ed. Foerster, pp. 126–27, provides a few details.

[37]Gregory I, *Register*, 8.16, ed. Ewald and Hartmann, *MGH*, 2:18, proves that the *schola* existed by 598. Giuseppe Palazzini, "Primicerio e secundicerio," *Enciclopedia cattolica* (Vatican City, 1953), 10:20, cites epigraphic evidence for the *schola* as early as 565.

[38]Palazzini, "Primicerio e secundicerio," pp. 20–22; Bresslau, *Urkundenlehre* 1:194; Duchesne, *Temporal Sovereignty*, pp. 63–64. LD, nos. 59, 61–63, ed. Foerster, pp. 113–14, 117–21.

[39]On the development of the papal library see: Pierre Battifol, "Libraries byzantines à Rome," *MAH* 8 (1888): 297–308; H. I. Marrou, "Autour de la bibliothèque du Pape Agapit," *MAH* 48 (1931): 124–69. The records for the Roman synod of 649 say that the *primicerius* headed the library and archives: Mansi, *Concilia* 10:863. He also ruled the chancery, usually called the *scrinium*, although this term could be used synonymously with *archivium* as in LD, ed. Foerster (appendix), p. 429: "in archivio nostrae sanctae romanae ecclesiae scilicet in sacro lateranensi scrinio." See also: Bresslau, *Urkundenlehre* 1:196–97.

[40]Lauer, *Palais de Latran*, p. 60.

donations, but under the Republic the principal archive was in the Lateran.[41] The papal library was also housed in the Lateran by the eighth century, and probably earlier. Very little can be known about it. The oldest surviving catalogue of the papal library dates from the pontificate of Boniface VIII (1294–1303), and all efforts to reconstruct the early medieval holdings of the library have failed. More information is available about the archives. The registers of Pope Gregory I (590–604) provide some evidence for the kinds of documents which the Lateran administration kept, and at the same time give some indication of the daily work of the notaries: records of ordinations, papal privileges, donations to the Church, patrimonial records, synodal *acta*, correspondence.[42] Virtually all of this material has succumbed to the ravages of time. It is thought that papal registers began being compiled in the fourth century, but almost all of these letters and collateral documents have disappeared.[43] Over 850 letters of Gregory I survive, but even this large number represents only about 60 letters per year and must be a small fraction of the correspondence produced during this busy pontificate. It is widely thought that the so-called *Liber Diurnus* is a surviving copy of a formula book used in the papal chancery, but some believe it is an unofficial canonical collection.[44] Because of this division of opinion on the essence of the *Liber Diurnus*, the view that it represents a manual used for instructing young notaries and a ready-reference for veterans cannot be accepted without hesitation. Nevertheless, the *Liber Diurnus*, with its approximately 100 canonical formulae, most of which date from the period 680 to 790, stands today as a valuable witness to the many kinds of documents emitted by the papal chancery and conserved in the archives. The *schola notariorum* recruited and trained notaries, but nothing can be known for certain about their course of instruction.[45] It seems that in the seventh and eighth centuries a distinctive script began to be used in the papal chancery, but the oldest papal document that survives in a complete, original form is a letter from Paschal I

---

[41]Bresslau, *Urkundenlehre* 1:150–54; Poole, *Papal Chancery*, pp. 14–16.

[42]Gregory I, *Register*, 3.54, 4.17, 7.38, 9.135, 206, 220, 11.40, 12.6, 14.4, app. 3.2, ed. Ewald and Hartmann, *MGH* 1:212, 252, 487, 2:134, 194, 212, 314, 353, 434, 446.

[43]Poole, *Papal Chancery*, pp. 29–30. On the beginnings of papal registers and their significance see now Ullmann, *Gelasius I* (Stuttgart, 1982), p. 35ff. He makes the point that registering decretals carefully was one means employed by popes from Innocent I onward to establish their jurisdictional primacy.

[44]H. Foerster, "Liber Diurnus Pontificum Romanorum," *New Catholic Encyclopedia* (New York, 1967), 8:694; Giulio Batelli, "Liber Diurnus Romanorum Pontificum," *Enciclopedia cattolica* (Vatican City, 1954), 7:1262–67; Rudolf Buchner, *Die Rechtsquellen* (Weimar, 1953), pp. 55–57; Leo Santifaller, "Zur Liber Diurnus Forschung," *HZ* 161 (1940): 532–38.

[45]Poole, *Papal Chancery*, p. 17.

to Louis the Pious. Before this time there exist, in original form, only a few fragments from the time of Hadrian. This pope introduced some important reforms into the practices of the papal chancery, but little can be known about them because of the woeful state of the evidence.[46] In the end, a good deal can be known about the work of the notaries, but there is much about their training and work, as well as about formal chancery practices, that cannot be ascertained.

Whereas all of the writing and record-keeping offices of the Lateran tended to be centralized under the jurisdiction of the *primicerius* before the Republic, some interesting transformations began to appear in the eighth century. For example, the future Pope Gregory II was *sacellarius* (a financial officer: see below) and *bibliothecarius* (librarian) but not, as far as is known, *primicerius*.[47] Under Hadrian I we meet three men, Zacharias (773), Theophylact (781), and Anastasius (787), who appear to have had charge of the library alone.[48] By 829 this was a prestigious office and almost alone among high Lateran dignities was usually held by a suburbicarian bishop.[49] Probably the increase in record keeping occasioned by the creation of the Republic necessitated a separation of the library and archives with the latter remaining under the jurisdiction of the *primicerius*. During the republican years, however, the *primicerius* not only lost charge of the library, but he was also shorn of another of his responsibilities. In 861 there appears another officer, the *protoscriniarius* (or sometimes *primiscriniarius*). This official was not a member of the *schola* of the notaries, and on at least one occasion in the tenth century the office was held by a layman. Probably, the *protoscriniarius* replaced the *magister censuum*, who still existed in 758 and 821, at the head of the public *tabelliones*. Apparently the early Republic provided complete notarial services through its own staff, but later found it necessary to create a separate Lateran department to discharge public record keeping.[50] The *primicerius*, despite being shorn of some of his earlier responsibilities, remained one

---

[46]Poole, *Papal Chancery*, pp. 38–39. See also: Paul Rabikauskas, *Die römische Kuriale in der päptlichen Kanzlei* (Rome, 1958).

[47]*LP* 1:396.

[48]Jaffé, *RP*, nos. 2401, 2431, 2457. See also: Leo Santifaller, *Saggio di un elenco dei funzionari, impiegati e scrittori della cancellaria pontificia dall'inizio all'anno 1099* (Rome, 1940), 1:36ff. For *bibliothecarii* under the popes down to Gregory IV see ibid., 1:40, 42–43, 43–45, 45–46, 46f.

[49]Schramm, "Studien zu frühmittlelalterlichen Aufzeichnungen über Staat und Verfassung," *ZRG, gA* 49 (1929), 205; Bresslau, *Urkundenlehre* 1:211. Schramm, following earlier scholars, believes that the first permanent and exclusive *bibliothecarius* dates from 829 but, with Santifaller, I hold for Hadrian's pontificate.

[50]Bresslau, *Urkundenlehre* 1:205–8.

of the truly great officers of the Roman Church. Perhaps this was because, among all high Lateran offices, that of *primicerius* of the notaries was the oldest.[51] Over the years, whatever his particular duties may have been at a given time, the *primicerius* of the notaries was always, so to speak, the pope's prime minister.

In addition to the deacons and notaries, each region of the city also had a *defensor*. Clerical defensors, who first appeared in North Africa, emerged by analogy to the Roman *defensores civitatis* who are first detectable in the diocese of Oriens under the emperor Licinius and became generalized by the time of Valentinian I. The Roman defensors were not originally a constituent element of the imperial hierarchy of officialdom. They were specially instituted to protect the people, especially the poor, from malfeasance or misfeasance by Roman officials. In addition to serving as advocates for the poor, they had minor civil jurisdiction in cases involving less than 50 solidi. Justinian raised this amount to 300, but by then the bishops had achieved a decisive role in appointing the defensors. Eventually clerical defensors completely displaced the public ones. The clerical defensors continued to serve as advocates of the legal rights of the poor, of widows, and of orphans, as compared with the deacons who ministered to the material and spiritual needs of the unfortunate. They also served as advocates for the legal rights of the Church in particular regions.[52] In time the defensors acquired a wide range of duties of which it is possible to form some impression from the registers of Gregory I. They received and executed wills, dispensed alms, administered patrimonies, concluded contracts, judged legal cases, administered vacant bishoprics, supervised monastic discipline, and protected the lower clergy from arbitrary episcopal conduct.[53]

Probably because of their rising significance Gregory I organized the defensors into a *schola* in 598.[54] Henceforth the seven regional defensors formed the elite corps of a body of officials who were ubiquitous in the papal

---

[51]Halphen, *L'administration de Rome*, pp. 43–44, 89. The oldest known *primicerius* seems to be Laurentius between 420 and 430 but Santifaller (*Elenco dei funzionari*, 1:6) says 418.

[52]Armbrust, *Territoriale Politik*, pp. 18–26; Fischer, "Defensoren," pp. 444–54; F. Martroye, "Les 'defensores ecclesiae' au Ve et VIe siècle," *Revue historique du droit français et étranger*, 4th series, 2 (1923): 597–622; Annibale Bugnini, "Defensor Ecclesiae," *Enciclopedia cattolica* (Vatican City, 1950), 4:1301ff; Bresslau, *Urkundenlehre* 1:203ff; Hinschius, *Kirchenrecht* 1:377, 382; Jones, *Later Roman Empire* 1:144–45, 279–80, 286, 403, 479–80, 496–97, 500, 571, 521, 726–27, 758–59, 2:859, 897, 911.

[53]Gregory I, *Register*, 9.35, 9.37, 9.110, 9.123, 9.124, 9.128, 14.2, 14.4, ed. Ewald and Hartmann, *MGH* 2:65, 66–67, 117, 125, 128, 182, 420, 420–22, 423.

[54]Gregory I, *Register*, 8.16, ed. Ewald and Hartmann, *MGH* 2:18.

patrimonies, and later in the Republic generally. The senior regional defensor was called the *primicerius defensorum*, and he was another of the great officers of the Church with his headquarters in the Lateran.[55] Prior to Gregory's time defensors may regularly, or at any rate often, have been laymen, but after they were organized into a *schola* they were always clerics, though frequently only in minor orders and often married.[56]

The archpriest formed a bridge between the Lateran and the priests of Rome while the archdeacon, the *primicerius* and *secundicerius* of the notaries, and the *primicerius* of the defensors formed a similar bridge between the central government and the seven regions of the city. Although both the pastoral and the administrative staffs were headquartered in the Lateran, they were kept carefully distinct from one another. Altogether, these *ministri episcopi* helped the pope to bear his burdens and carry out his duites.

The republican Lateran had, again often as carry-overs from earlier times, other officers who contributed to the smooth and efficient functioning of the papal government. When the pope went in procession through the streets of Rome he was always accompanied by his highest-ranking associates, and from their places in the order of procession we can get a sense of their relative prominence. The officials already described rode immediately before the pope, and just behind him came the *vicedominus*, *vestararius*, *nomenc(u)lator*, and *sacellarius*.[57] These, plus a few other officials, made up the rest of the highest Lateran dignitaries.

The *vicedominus* was the majordomo of the Lateran palace.[58] The earliest known *vicedominus* was serving under Pope Vigilius in 554.[59] There is no evidence that the functions connected with this office changed in later days. At times this office was filled by a bishop,[60] which suggests that it was

---

[55]Bresslau, *Urkundenlehre* 1:203.

[56]Jones, *The Decline of the Ancient World* (New York, 1967), p. 266, says they were usually laymen but in *Later Roman Empire* 2:911, he argues that they were clergy in minor orders. They may have been laymen originally but when Gregory I organized them into a *schola* he gave them the right "sedendi in conventu clericorum." It is well known that Gregory disliked laymen serving in the Lateran. A century after Gregory the *primicerius defensorum*, often a deacon, had important liturgical functions in stational masses: *Ordo I*, cc. 69, 74, 81, 98, 113, ed. Andrieu, *Ordines Romani* 2:91, 92, 93, 99, 103–4.

[57]*Ordo I*, c. 10, ed. Andrieu, 2:70.

[58]Gregory I, *Register*, 1.11, ed. Ewald and Hartmann, *MGH* 1:12: "Anatholium ... vicedominum enim eum constituimus, cuius arbitrio episcopium commissimus disponendum." Also: 11.53, 2:328.

[59]Rohault de Fleury, *Latran*, p. 45.

[60]This was true under Zachary and Constantine II: *LP* 1:429, 470.

held in high regard and conferred considerable prestige upon its holder. Although the *vicedominus* does not seem to have had an area of administrative competence that extended outside the Lateran precincts, his control and supervision of the Lateran household staff must have made him an important and influential official.[61] He had under his charge functionaries called *basilicarii*, *cellerarii*, *cubicularii*, *custodes*, and *mansionarii*. With the exception of the *cubicularii*, we know next to nothing about these minor officials.[62]

The *cubicularii* were adolescents who served as the pope's personal attendants, and some of whom accompanied him on his travels. Usually they were youths from noble families who were getting an education within the Lateran.[63] Some were clerics in minor orders, and some remained laymen.[64] The papal *cubiculum* was a prime recruiting ground for the clergy of the Roman Church, and many papal *cubicularii* went on to higher orders and offices.[65] For example, Popes Gregory II, Stephen II, Paul I, Stephen III, Leo III(?), Stephen IV, Paschal I, and Valentinus were all *cubicularii*.[66] Nonnobles usually began their careers in the *schola cantorum*,[67] so under the Republic, it was the *cubiculum* that provided the avenue along which the Roman nobility penetrated and fused with the clerical elites of the papal government. It seems reasonable to propose that not least among the duties of the *vicedominus* was the recruitment, surveillance, and promotion of the careers of young aristocrats.

---

[61]Andrieu, *Ordines Romani* 2:42, 45; Hinschius, *Kirchenrecht* 1:383–84; Plöchl, *Kirchenrecht* 1:318–19; Duchesne, *Temporal Sovereignty*, p. 63. Without citing his evidence Llewellyn, *Rome in the Dark Ages*, p. 104, says that Gregory I reduced the significance of the archdeacon and replaced him with the *vicedominus*. Also without evidence Duchesne, *Temporal Sovereignty*, p. 36, says that in the late eighth century the *vicedominus* became the *superista*, that is a military officer of some sort.

[62]Hinschius, *Kirchenrecht* 1:377–79; Duchesne, *Temporal Sovereignty*, p. 63. *Mansionarii* received and transported liturgical books and sacred vessels on feast days: *Ordo I*, c. 22, ed. Andrieu, *Ordines Romani* 2:73. Duchesne, *LP* 1:364 n. 7, says *mansionarii* were customarily laymen whose functions were not unlike those of later sacristans.

[63]Hinschius, *Kirchenrecht* 1:378–80; Andrieu, *Ordines Romani*, 2:40.

[64]Gregory I disliked lay *cubicularii* and stipulated that only ordained ones could personally attend the pope: *Register*, 5.57, ed. Ewald and Hartmann, *MGH* 1:363. *Ordo I*, c. 23, ed. Andrieu, *Ordines Romani* 2:74, mentions *cubicularius laicus* and *cubicularius tonsoratus* so obviously laymen continued to serve in this department.

[65]Caspar, *Das Papsttum*, pp. 625–27; Duchesne, *Temporal Sovereignty*, 65.

[66]Hinschius, *Kirchenrecht* 1:380.

[67]*Ordo 36*, c. 1, ed. Andrieu, *Ordines Romani* 4:195: "Primum in qualicumque scola reperti fuerint pueri bene psallentes, tolluntur unde et nutriuntur in scola cantorum et postea fiunt cubicularii. Si autem nobilium filii fuerint, statim in cubiculo nutriuntur."

The *sacellarius* was one of the two chief financial officers of the Lateran administration. The other was the *arcarius*. The latter was the principal treasurer of the papal government and the former was the paymaster.[68] The *arcarius*, as the head of the papal *arca*, or treasury, was the older of the two offices. The earliest known *arcarius* was Anastasius in 559, whereas the first known *sacellarius* was the future Pope Gregory II.[69] The *sacellarius* also received petitions to the pope during processions.[70] Throughout the history of the Republic the *arcarius* retained his function as chief treasurer,[71] but it is interesting to note that in the ninth century bishops sometimes held the office and in the tenth century there were married *arcarii* who cannot have received orders beyond subdeacon.[72] Obviously no particular order of persons monopolized this office. The names of many *sacellarii* are known.[73] They were quite often notaries before taking on the second financial office, and they were regularly employed as envoys to the Frankish court.[74] The fact that the *sacellarii* were envoys implies that they ordinarily enjoyed the pope's full confidence, which is to be expected, one supposes, of the men whose primary duty it was to spend the Lateran's money.

Not much is known about the revenues that flowed into the papal treasury. More is known about how papal monies were spent, and we shall return to this subject several times below. Unquestionably the greatest source of income was the patrimonies, but foreign revenues such as "Peter's Pence," extraordinary pious donations, regular offerings, and fees also swelled the Lateran's coffers. Officials called *actionarii* were the primary revenue collectors under the *arcarius*.[75] Both revenues and expenditures were predictable enough by Zachary's time for a regular budget to be drawn up.[76] Regular budgeting under the Republic was a remarkable achievement, especially when it is remembered that elsewhere in the West medieval governments did not do this before the thirteenth century.

---

[68]Hinschius, *Kirchenrecht* 1:381–82; Duchesne, *Temporal Sovereignty*, p. 63; Bresslau, *Urkundenlehre* 1:201–3; William E. Lunt, *Papal Revenues in the Middle Ages*, 2 vols. (New York, 1934), 1:3–5, 29.

[69]Halphen, *L'administration de Rome*, pp. 115, 135.

[70]*Ordo I*, c. 13, ed. Andrieu, *Ordines Romani* 2:71.

[71]Schramm, "Studien," p. 212.

[72]Bresslau, *Urkundenlehre* 1:201–2.

[73]Halphen, *L'administration de Rome*, p. 135.

[74]*LP* 1:389, 469, 487, 491, 2:4; Jaffé, *RP*, nos. 2335, 2431.

[75]Lunt, *Papal Revenues* 1:29.

[76]*LP* 1:434, 439 n.53, provides the first hints of budgeting. Ferrari, *Early Roman Monasteries*, p. 390, assumes a budget by 684–85 but this is too early.

The *vestararius*, by about 640, had charge of the vestments and sacred vessels, as well as of the precious objects owned by the papacy. On special occasions he let these out to *mansionarii* with his seal.[77] He also had general supervision of the churches that belonged, *stricto sensu*, to the Roman Church.[78] In a sense, the *vestararius* was in charge of a large part of the capital wealth and his office was, therefore, a highly responsible one. We have already seen that the future Pope Leo III was once *vestararius*, but otherwise we know little about the persons who held this office. Although as we shall see the *vestararius* was occasionally employed as a judge after 772, no changes affected his basic duties under the Republic.

The last of the great Lateran officers under the Republic was the *nomenclator*. The office first appeared in the seventh century under Pope Agatho (678–81).[79] By the tenth century, often with the title *adminiculator*, the *nomenclator* had charge of charitable services,[80] but this cannot have been his original function. Duchesne believes he was the "grandmaster of ceremonies," and Bresslau considers it possible that he was the chief protocol officer.[81] Along with the *sacellarius* he also received petitions intended for the pope,[82] and again like the *sacellarius*, he was regularly used as an ambassador.[83] At some point in the history of the Republic the duties of the *nomenclator* were altered, but it is impossible to say when or why this happened. A reasonable hypothesis might be to suggest that as the Republic assumed greater responsibility for charitable services, these were gathered together under the charge of a person on the Lateran administrative staff with the result that the regionary deacons became more especially attached to the pastoral staff under whose aegis they had always stood.

Under the Republic, then, the administration of the papal government was in the hands of seven major officers: *primicerius* and *secundicerius* of the notaries, *primicerius* of the defensors, *sacellarius*, *arcarius*, *vestararius*, and *nomenclator*. In addition, the *vicedominus* was an important official

---

[77]The office is first mentioned about 640: *LP* 1:328. See: Hinschius, *Kirchenrecht* 1:384; Duchesne, *Temporal Sovereignty*, p. 63; Andrieu, *Ordines Romani* 2:43 and *Ordo I*, cc. 21, 22, 2:73.

[78]Geertman, *More Veterum*, p. 140.

[79]*LP* 1:350.

[80]Bresslau, *Urkundenlehre* 1:204–5; Schramm, "Studien," pp. 203, 209.

[81]*Temporal Sovereignty*, 63; *Urkundenlehre*, 1:205. See also: Llewellyn, *Rome in the Dark Ages*, p. 122.

[82]*Ordo I*, c. 13, ed. Andrieu, *Ordines Romani*, 2:71.

[83]*LP* 1:389, 473; *Annales qui dicuntur Einhardi*, annis 815, 821, 823, 826, 828, ed. Kurze.

and later so were the *bibliothecarius* and *protoscriniarius*. Looking at these officers a little differently, it will be seen that they can be divided into four major branches of activity: chancery, law, finance, household administration. Most of the officers antedate the Republic, but a few are contemporary with it, and many officers or branches experienced some reorganization or redefinition of their duties. It seems a fair assumption that under the Republic an increase in responsibility generally, and in specific responsibilities in particular, occasioned some altering and streamlining in the Lateran's administrative departments. The following table may help to recapitulate the basic facts concerning the principal Lateran branches and officers.

Branch Office(rs)	Date(s) of Origin	Date(s) of Alterations
CHANCERY	*saec.* IV?[a]	770s–780s
Notaries	ca. 250	565–98, *ante* 861
Archives	366–84	*ante* 649, *ante* 715, 780–829
Library	366–84?	*ante* 649, *ante* 715, 773–829
LEGAL	*saec.* V?	598, 772 *et post*[b]
Defensores	?	?
FINANCE	*ante* 559	*ante* 715, 740s[c]
Arcarius	*ante* 559	*ante* 715, 740s
Sacellarius	*ante* 715	?
HOUSEHOLD	?	598, 770s?[b], *ante saec.* X
Vicedominus	*ante* 554	?
Vestararius	*ante* 640	770s[b]
Nomenclator	678–81	*ante saec.* X

[a]On the assumption that the papal registers began being compiled then.
[b]See below, pp. 236–38, for possible changes in the judicature.
[c]If budgeting arose then and not earlier.

When the *Liber Pontificalis* makes one of its ubiquitous references to *proceres cleri*, *proceres ecclesiae*, or *optimates ecclesiae*, it is to these officers, and to the cardinal clergy, that the text calls our attention. They were the "nobles" of the Church, but their status derived in the first place from the offices they held and not from their social standing. To be sure, many of these nobles of the Church were genuine Roman aristocrats; from the pontificate of Zachary and perhaps already earlier most of them probably were. The Church thus provided ample scope for the talents and ambitions of the Roman upper class, and its members entered the clergy in significant numbers and attained great power and influence through its offices. Some of them rose to the summit, that is, to the papal office itself. The fusion of the social and clerical elites became quite complete by the early ninth century, but there is no evidence that an absolutely closed caste was created. Able persons from outside the Roman nobility could still aspire to and achieve prominence in the Republic.

The account just given of the pastoral and administrative branches of the Lateran will have made it clear why it is possible to characterize the republican popes as professionals. These were men who knew the system and how to make it work. Not everyone in this system could become pope, but a comparatively large number of men within it could hope to attain responsible offices. Indeed, all of the Lateran personnel were professionals and this made them, as a governing class, quite different from and far superior to the kinds of people who were available to execute the commands of, let us say, Charlemagne or Offa of Mercia. In short, in terms of institutional refinement or professional capabilities, the Republic of St. Peter was far ahead of its time in the medieval West.

Certainly many people in the Lateran administration received "on the job" training but only a few things can be known about their preparation in general. Highly specialized training was available in the various *scholae*. For example, notaries and defensors would have been introduced to the intricacies of their crafts by the accomplished staffs of their respective *scholae*. Training apart, it is rather difficult to form a picture of how Lateran careerists were educated. Boys, as already noted, entered the clergy through the *schola cantorum* if they were of humble state or through the *cubiculum* if they were noble. In practice, however, the distinction between these two institutions was not rigid. The *schola cantorum* was sometimes called the *orphanotrophium*, which suggests that it was a refuge for poor boys, but the later Pope Sergius II spent time there and he was noble. Moreover, it was possible to move from the *schola cantorum* to the *cubiculum*, as Pope Leo III, who was not noble, did. Direct entry into the *cubiculum* was probably a privilege of the nobility, but that was not a hard and fast rule. Duchesne supposed that the *schola cantorum* was a sort of minor seminary but this, in Andrieu's view, distorts and exaggerates the role of this *schola*. It was "exactement une maîtrise." That is, as its name implies, it trained boys and young men to chant in papal liturgies.[84]

Actually, it appears that there was in the Lateran a school where boys were educated regardless of the branch of the administration in which they

---

[84]Duchesne, *LP*, 1:321–22 n.3, 364 n.7; Andrieu, "Les ordres mineurs dans l'ancien rit romain," *Revue des sciences réligieuses*, 5 (1925), 232–74; Henri Leclercq, "Schola," *Dictionnaire d'archéologie chrétienne et de liturgie* vol. 15 pt. 1, (Paris, 1950): 1008–13.

were destined to serve. Gregory II, for example, was educated "from earliest youth in the *patriarchium*," that is, in the Lateran.[85] Leo III was "brought up and educated from earliest youth in the vestiary of the *patriarchium*."[86] Sergius II in the ninth century was similarly educated.[87] Not all Lateran careerists were educated in the *patriarchium*, however. Hadrian was educated by his family, presumably by tutors, and so was the later Pope Nicholas I. Some men, in other words, were educated outside the Lateran, even in monasteries, and then entered the papal government as adults.[88]

Of what did a clerical education in Rome consist? It is difficult to say precisely. Leo III was educated "both in the psalter and in sacred scriptures."[89] Sergius II learned "*communes litteras*" and also chant.[90] Evidently, then, education consisted of a basic grounding in the liberal arts plus instruction in scriptural studies. Sergius obtained this "dual" education in the Lateran, but Hadrian obtained it through his family and so did Nicholas I. The Lateran thus did not have the only schools in Rome. Nor were the subjects taught there unavailable elsewhere. Nicholas's father was a regionary notary and a "*liberalium amator artium*" who desired a "liberal" education for his son.[91] Presumably he obtained it outside the Lateran. Guillou has evidence for the basic clerical education in Ravenna, and he assumes that conditions in Rome would not have been significantly different.[92] If he is correct, then the Roman curriculum would have included grammar, rhetoric, dialectic, morals, physics, arithmetic, geometry, music, astronomy, theology, history, chant, and computus. All of this is likely enough as a broad outline of an ideal program, but it is nevertheless impossible to formulate a precise image of exact curricula, teachers, teaching methods, and textbooks. One can only say that in the Roman Church clergy received liberal and clerical educations that conformed to and perhaps somewhat exceeded contemporary standards.

---

[85] *LP* 1:396.

[86] *LP* 2:1.

[87] *LP* 2:86.

[88] Andrieu, "Ordres mineurs," pp. 256–68; Ferrari, *Early Roman Monasteries*, pp. 400–441.

[89] *LP* 2:1.

[90] *LP* 2:86.

[91] *LP* 1:498, 2:151.

[92] "L'école dans l'Italie byzantine," *SSCI* 19 (1972): 291–311, esp. 295–302. See also: Pierre Riché, *Education and Culture in the Barbarian West*, trans. John J. Contreni (Columbia, S.C., 1976), pp. 417–19. George Heinrich Hörle's old book has not lost all of its value: *Frühmittelalterliche Mönchs- und Klerikerbildung in Italien* (Freiburg, 1914).

The Lateran complex was the nerve center of republican Rome.[93] In the early eighth century it had fallen into disrepair, and this state of affairs caused John VII to contemplate moving the papal government to the old imperial precincts on the Palatine. Zachary, however, began refurbishing the Lateran, and later improvements were made by Hadrian, Leo III, and Gregory IV. The emergence in Sergius I's time of the term *patriarchium*, and then in the ninth century of *palatium*, conveys an impression of the extent to which the Lateran was understood to be a governing center. Unfortunately continuous remodeling and rebuilding have made it almost impossible to reconstruct the Lateran as it existed under the Republic. Primarily it consisted of the Lateran palace, donated to Pope Sylvester by Constantine, and the Constantinian basilica, which was regularly called St. Savior until the seventh century and St. John thereafter. There were other buildings as well, for instance, the house in which Gregory I installed the *schola cantorum* and a tower erected by Zachary, but little is or can be known about them. This lack of information about the early medieval Lateran is most disappointing because it would be interesting to know, in a physical, spatial sense, where the various branches of government were situated, how much space they occupied, and how they interacted with one another. All that can be said with confidence is that the Lateran complex provided quarters for schools and for a large and very refined pastoral and administrative bureaucracy.

Secular Administration

It might be argued at this point that the foregoing account proves only that that Lateran was eminently capable of governing a large and diverse Christian community. Certainly, the Lateran government was created, reformed, and refined to do just that. But, the governance of a Christian community may be understood in several ways. Did the Lateran provide what might be called secular services, or only ecclesiastical ones? Is it possible, in the eighth and ninth centuries, to draw sharp distinctions between the two? Perhaps these questions can be answered by examining some of the "secular" services provided by the papal government, and then by looking at the impact of the Republic on what remained of the secular institutions of Rome.

---

[93]The following account synthesizes the pertinent remarks of Rohault de Fleury, Lauer, and Krautheimer.

The papal sources for the fifth and later centuries are full of accounts of popes maintaining roads and bridges, restoring public buildings, or repairing aqueducts. These activities had all earlier been done at the expense of the Roman public treasury. Likewise, it had been to the Roman authorities that had fallen responsibility for the food supply. Gradually the Roman, actually the Byzantine, government showed itself either unwilling or unable to perform these tasks and the Church stepped into the void. Charitable benefactions had also been a prime expense willingly borne by imperial Rome, although over time the Church had come to play a significant complementary role in ministering to the unfortunate. The food supply and charity, therefore, provide two instructive examples of how the papal government stepped into realms formerly the preserve of the Roman state.

Pope Gelasius, his biographer says, "freed the city of Rome from the danger of famine."[94] Boniface II (530–32) did the same,[95] and Benedict persuaded Justin II to send grain from Egypt because of famine.[96] In the seventh century the papal biographers note Arab attacks in North Africa and Sicily whence Rome had always secured much of its food.[97] Popes John V and Conon secured fiscal exemptions for papal patrimonies in southern Italy and Sicily,[98] doubtless to enhance the agricultural productivity of these regions which sent a good deal of grain to Rome. From very early times, then, the papacy took pains to assure the food supply of Rome. By the eighth century much of Rome's grain was coming to the city from the patrimonies of the Church. Small wonder, then, that the popes were anguished by the impact upon their patrimonies of Lombard incursions and Byzantine fiscality. The pope had become Rome's grocer, and his supplies were being interrupted.

The number of hungry indigents in Rome appears to have been increasing in the late seventh and early eighth centuries, and the Byzantine government was powerless to do anything about the situation. It is therefore striking to observe that as the number and suffering of the indigents increased, as food supplies became threatened, and as relations with Byzantium began to be strained, the papal government created a new institution, the *diaconia*, to deal with these problems. This development cannot be mere coincidence and

---

[94]*LP* 1:255.

[95]Vielliard, *Recherches*, p. 117 (citing inscriptions).

[96]*LP* 1:308.

[97]*LP* 1:338, 346, 366. One is tempted to say something about the "Pirenne Thesis" in this connection!

[98]*LP* 1:366, 369.

is, in fact, a prime example of the early papal Republic taking cognizance of the full range of its responsibilities as it assumed the mantle of rulership formerly worn by the Greeks.

The Roman *diaconiae* had nothing in common with the regional deacons of Rome or the regions where the deacons officiated.[99] *Diaconiae* originated in fourth-century Egyptian monasteries as charitable institutions. Their name derives from the Greek verb διακονεῖν meaning "to serve" and in time διακονία came to have the specific meaning of service rendered to the poor, especially by monastic communities. In the sixth century the term διακονία (or now *diaconia*) passed to Italy, and in the time of Gregory I there were *diaconiae* at Naples, Pesaro, and Ravenna, but not yet at Rome.[100] The first Roman *diaconiae* appear in 684–85, and by then the word *diaconia* had changed from its original meaning of service to a name for a specific kind of charitable institution. From Benedict II to Leo III the *Liber Pontificalis* makes constant mention of *diaconiae*.[101] These references, along with an inscription,[102] and four formulae in the *Liber Diurnus*[103] make it possible to describe what the *diaconiae* were, how they worked, and what services they provided.

The *diaconiae* were essentially distribution centers for grain and other foodstuffs.[104] By the time of Leo III they numbered at least eighteen. Most

---

[99]Duchesne, "Titres presbytériaux et diaconies," pp. 236–37.

[100]Henri-Irenée Marrou, "L'origine orientale des diaconies romaines," *MAH* 57 (1940): 100–101, 110–15, 120–31, 132ff, 137; Bertolini, "Per la storia delle diaconie romane nell'alto medioevo sino alla fine del secolo VIII," in his *Scritti scelti* 1:319–30. A remark by John the Deacon in the ninth century (*Vita Greg.*, 2.24, *PL* 75:96, 98, 100) that there were *diaconiae* in Rome under Gregory I is patently anachronistic.

[101]*LP* 1:364, 367, 369, 410, 420, 434, 441, 501, 504, 505–6, 507, 509–10, 512, 2:9, 11, 12, 14, 16, 19, 21, 22, 26, 30, 33.

[102]From St. Maria in Cosmedin, 760s: transcribed in Bertolini, "Per la storia delle diaconie," pp. 458–59.

[103]*LD*, nos. 71, 88, 95, 98, ed. Foerster, pp. 127–28, 168–69, 173–75, 178–79.

[104]In addition to my own reading of the evidence, the following account depends mostly upon Bertolini, "Per la storia delle diaconie," pp. 311–458 passim. Marrou, "Diaconies," pp. 96–137, offers some valuable details but is strongest on the eastern origins and not on the Roman history of the *diaconiae*. Quite valuable, but flatly wrong on the role of laymen, is: J. Lestocquoy, "Administration de Rome et diaconies du VIIᵉ au IXᵉ siècle," *Rivista di archeologia cristiana* 7 (1930): 261–98. Worthwhile too, but necessarily brief, is: A. P. Frutaz, "Diaconia," *Enciclopedia cattolica* (Vatican City, 1953), 4:1521–35. Also brief but useful is: Ferrari, *Early Roman Monasteries*, pp. 355–61. Finally, a few good comments are offered by Geertman, *More Veterum*, pp. 111–14, 130–31, and numerous relevant statements can be found strewn throughout the notes to Duchesne's *LP*. Last but not least Krautheimer, *Rome*, pp. 74–77, is wise and helpful but places the origins of *diaconiae* in the mid-sixth century and Partner (reviewing

were located in the heavily populated central regions of but a few were in the suburbs, for example, at St. Peter's. The earliest ones were established in former Roman public buildings including *stationes annonae*. Others were placed in monasteries, and some were entirely new foundations. Influential laymen may have founded some of the first *diaconiae*, but the majority were created by the Church. At the head of each *diaconia* stood either a *pater* or a *dispensator*. The former were always clerics, the latter usually laymen. Regardless of their lay or clerical status, the heads of the *diaconiae* were appointed by the pope. Each *diaconia*, regardless of the means or place of its foundation, was staffed by monks, called *diaconitae* (διακονιταί), which explains the early references in the *Liber Pontificalis* to *monasteria diaconiae*. The *diaconiae* were not, however, monasteries. Eventually each of them had a small church or chapel and a priest who provided liturgical services. By the time of Hadrian I the poor of a particular district assembled at a *diaconia* on Friday, and then were led in procession, singing psalms, to the nearest baths. After bathing they received their food distributions.[105] The source of the food may be sought in the papal patrimonies generally, but from the pontificate of Gregory II it appears that specific estates were singled out as endowments for individual *diaconiae*.[106] In the early ninth century the *diaconiae* seem to have served as centers of food distribution not only "for the sustenance of the poor"[107] but for rich and poor alike, indeed for all of Rome.[108]

Ministering to the hunger of Rome's needy, or perhaps eventually to Rome's citizenry as a whole, was one kind of charity, or public service, and there were others. Pope Stephen II founded or restored several *xenodochia*, and Leo III endowed them even more richly.[109] Leo also founded a hospital for the poor, and for pilgrims.[110] Hadrian spent 100 pounds of gold refurbishing Rome's walls and towers,[111] and both he and Leo III, and later

---

Krautheimer: *Catholic Historical Review* 68 [1982]: 86) accepts this early date saying it will "command respect." I do not think so because all Krautheimer has demonstrated is that the buildings in which the *diaconiae* were instituted go back to the period just after the Gothic wars. This does not prove that the *diaconiae* themselves go back that far. Like other students of the subject I am struck by the fact that no Roman document mentions them before 684–85.

[105]*LP* 1:505–6.

[106]Kehr, *IP*, vol. 1, nos. 1, 2, p. 97; *LP* 1:441, 509–10.

[107]*LP* 1:420.

[108]*LP* 2:69. Vielliard, *Recherches*, p. 120.

[109]*LP* 1:440–41, 2:12, 25.

[110]*LP* 2:28.

[111]*LP* 1:501.

Paschal I, actively built or restored churches, monasteries, and other build-ings.[112] All of this construction must have provided employment for the large numbers of poor in Rome. This is not to imply that Hadrian and the others were engaged in a "New Deal" of public works projects, but someone had to do the work and it is reasonable to assume that the workers were paid. Much of the work of construction required only unskilled labor and Rome's poor would have been a natural workforce.[113]

Thus a sophisticated ecclesiastical apparatus governed the Church of Rome and provided certain kinds of services that had formerly been the responsibility of the Roman state. Earlier it was suggested that the organi-zation of pastoral arrangements in Rome may have helped to pave the way for political rule. Now it can confidently be proposed that the assumption of public charity and food distributions also assisted in cementing the leader-ship role of the Church in Rome. Rich and poor, cleric and layman, all had to eat, and the Lateran administration supplied the food. Many people, perhaps a large majority of the citizens, would have had recourse to one kind of charitable institution or another at some time. The continuous sig-nificance of the Lateran administration for the daily lives and well-being of huge numbers of people must have been immense.

In order to gain a complete picture of the government of the Republic, it is necessary to explore the fate of the secular institutional structure of Byzan-tine Rome as it was transformed into the Republic of St. Peter. More specif-ically, we must ask what remained of that structure, who staffed it, and who controlled it.

The chief civil and military officer in Byzantine Rome was the duke of Rome. He was subordinate to, and appointed by, the exarch of Ravenna.[114] It will be recalled that when Zachary left Rome to negotiate with Liutprand he left the city in care of the duke.[115] By 743, then, if not before, the office had become a papal appointment.[116] Dukes of Rome are still attested until 778–81, after which time the office disappears. The last dukes show very well the dependence of the office on the pope: Gratiosus was a relative of the *secundicerius* Sergius; John was a brother of Pope Stephen III; Theodore

---

[112]One may simply glance through *LP* 1:499–514, 2:1–4, 7–34, 52–63. The great study of all of this building activity is now Geertman, *More Veterum*.

[113]As much is stated by *LP* 1:513, where we are told that Hadrian gathered his work force from all about, paid them, and fed them.

[114]Hartmann, *Verwaltung*, p. 26ff.

[115]*LP* 1:429: "relicta Romana urbe iamdicto Stephano patricii et duci ad gubernandum."

[116]Halphen, *L'administration de Rome*, p. 1.

was a nephew of Hadrian.[117] Perhaps the final settlements between Charlemagne and Hadrian, and the finally won security of Italy, rendered the office obsolete. It may also be that the pope took over personal direction of the Roman militia through the *superista*, whom Duchesne considered to be the military governor of the Lateran.[118] Some support for this opinion may derive from the fact that in 823 Paschal sent, among his delegates to Louis the Pious, "Leo *magister militum*." One gathers that this officer enjoyed the pope's confidence. Later, under Leo IV, the *Liber Pontificalis* mentions a Gratianus who was "eminentissimum magistro [sic] militum et Romani palatii superistam ac consiliarium."[119] It is not beyond the realm of possibility that the pope, after his most serious foes had been beaten, did away with an office whose holder might have been a serious rival while at the same time instituting new and different military officers of his own choosing.

The Byzantine military organization of the city remained somewhat intact under the Republic. Rome was divided into twelve or fourteen regions,[120] or *scholae*, over each of which stood a *patronus*.[121] Each *schola* had a *signa*, a processional cross, and a *banda*, or *bandora*, a distinctive banner.[122] Charlemagne was met in 774 by "all the officials with their banners" thirty miles from Rome, and closer to the city, the Franks encountered "the venerable crosses."[123] Evidently, then, the imperial divisions of the city still had some civil and military significance and existed independently of the religious divisions of the city. What the civil roles of the divisions of Rome may have been cannot be said, but in a military sense they may have continued to represent contingents of the urban militia. Within the militia we hear of *duces, cartularii, comites, tribunes, patroni scholarum, primicerii domestici,* and *optiones*, but the precise significance and duties of these officers cannot

---

[117]Classen, "Karl der Große, das Papsttum und Byzanz," p. 545 n.22. Duchesne, *Temporal Sovereignty*, p. 62, thinks there were no "chief dukes" after Stephen II but this is not correct.

[118]*LP* 1:515 n.9, and following Duchesne, Llewellyn, *Rome in the Dark Ages*, p. 122.

[119]*LP* 2:134.

[120]Ancient Rome had been divided into 14 civil and 7 ecclesiastical regions. Halphen, *L'administration de Rome*, pp. 7–14, believes this situation persisted until the eleventh century when a single division into 12 regions was created. Duchesne, *Temporal Sovereignty*, p. 60, thinks the 12 regions had emerged by the seventh century. These are the two basic positions in a long and complex scholarly debate which, for lack of evidence, cannot really be terminated with a definitive answer.

[121]*LP* 1:497: "universas scolas militiae una cum patronis." The patrons, among other things, acclaimed a newly elected pope: *Ordo* 36, c. 54, ed. Andrieu, *Ordines Romani* 4:204.

[122]Duchesne, "Regions de Rome," pp. 130–31.

[123]*LP* 1:496–97.

be determined because documents are lacking.[124] Until the 770s it seems clear that the popes controlled the army of the Roman region and the urban militia. Down to the 720s the army protected the popes on several occasions. Thereafter it regularly did the pope's bidding. In 739 the pope put troops into Spoleto. In 756 the pope organized the defenses of the city, and in 757 troops were placed at the disposal of Desiderius. In 768 army contingents were sent into the countryside to put down the last remnants of Toto's rebellion. Finally, in 778 Hadrian sent the army out to recover Terracina. Between 778 and the commencement of the Muslim raids in the middle of the ninth century no more is heard of the Roman army or militia as discrete, identifiable entities. We shall see shortly that the apparent disappearance of the regular army and militia may be connected with the emergence of a distinct, papally controlled militia. The key fact is that, throughout the eighth century, the military forces of the Roman region were under papal control.

There is absolutely no evidence for the existence of a secular financial administration under the Republic. Available documents, for that matter, say very little about the inner workings of the papal treasury, but it appears to have been the only one in operation. There were still public notaries, but by the time the office of *protoscriniarius* was created and brought into the Lateran in the ninth century these officials too had become part of the papal administration. Of other kinds of officials, except for judges and diplomats, the sources are silent. The papal government sufficed.

The Roman judicature has attracted little attention in recent years, but when it was last discussed it evoked a lively debate. Because of a lack of judicial records certain things about the external structure and internal functioning of the courts will never be known. It is possible to paint a picture of the judicature but one must use broad strokes and muted colors.

The highest judicial officer in Rome was the urban prefect, but his role is difficult to follow because he disappears from the sources in the late sixth century and then reappears unexpectedly at the beginning of Hadrian's pontificate.[125] When he does reappear in the sources, the urban prefect was probably only the chief judicial officer for criminal cases. He was certainly a papal appointee.[126] Justinian had given bishops jurisdiction over the clergy

---

[124]Duchesne, *Temporal Sovereignty*, p. 61.

[125]On the Urban Prefect: Diehl, *Etudes*, pp. 127–29; Hartmann, *Verwaltung*, pp. 44–45. On the last mentions of the prefect in the sixth century: Diehl, p. 127; on his reappearance in the sources (*LP* 1:490) Halphen, *L'administration de Rome*, pp. 16–18.

[126]Theodor Hirschfeld, "Das Gerichtswesen der Stadt Rom vom 8 bis 12 Jahrhundert wesentlich nach stadtrömischen Urkunden," *Archiv für Urkundenforschung* 4 (1912): 444; Halphen, *L'administration de Rome*, pp. 16–19, 22ff; Brezzi, *Roma e l'empero*, p. 8. Halphen

as well as over cases between clerics and laymen.[127] During the eighth century virtually all civil jurisdiction seems to have passed into the courts of the Church,[128] but on the principle that clerics could not pass judgment in capital cases, criminal jurisdiction had to have remained extrinsic to the Church courts.[129] Thus one can say that, in general terms, the pope stood over the whole judicature and also that, under him, there were civil and criminal judges and other court officers. By the middle of the ninth century, and probably long before, there was a courtroom in the Lateran, but there is no evidence for the locations of other courts in Rome.[130]

Who were these judges? It is difficult to give a precise answer. Eighth-century sources make frequent use of the terms *iudices de clero* and *iudices de militia*,[131] but in papal Rome, as in Byzantine Italy generally, the word *iudex* simply means "official" and will not bear, in most cases, the more technical translation "judge."[132] In the eighth century, *iudices de clero* referred to the seven highest officials of the Lateran administration. They were the "officials" par excellence of the Republic after the pope himself.[133] In the late ninth century documents began to speak synonymously of *iudices de clero*, *iudices palatini*, and *iudices ordinarii*.[134] Again there are seven of these "palatine" or "ordinary" "judges," but they are not exactly the same as the seven Lateran *iudices*, or officials, of the eighth century. The *vestararius* has disappeared and the *protoscriniarius* has replaced him.[135] It is not at all clear that one can draw a straight line from the Lateran "officials" to the palatine "judges," however tempting it is to do so.[136] Hadrian once used his *vesta-*

---

assumed that the prefect continued to exist but Brown ("Social Structure," pp. 16–17) argues persuasively that Hadrian resurrected the office.

[127]Gregory I, *Register*, 13.50, ed. Ewald and Hartmann, *MGH* 2:414, 417.

[128]Hinschius, *Kirchenrecht* 1:382–83; Schramm, "Studien," p. 198ff; Toubert, *Latium* 2:1212–13.

[129]A *notitia* on Roman officials edited by Schramm ("Studien," p. 221) says: "Hi (scil. clerici) pro criminalibus non iudicant nec in quemquam mortiferam dictant sententiam."

[130]*LP* 2:139 n.66; Jaffé, *RP*, no. 2633.

[131]E.g., *LP* 1:470, 486, 490, 498.

[132]For examples of "iudex" meaning "official" in the times of Gregory I see his *Register*, 3.1, 3.2, 6.25, 10.15, 13.50, ed. Ewald and Hartmann, *MGH* 1:159, 160, 404, 2:249–50, 414. On the persistence of this general use of the term see: Diehl, *Etudes*, p. 135; Halphen, *L'administration de Rome*, p. 37; Brown, "Social Structure," pp. 18–22.

[133]Toubert, *Latium* 2:1201 n.3.

[134]Duchesne, *Temporal Sovereignty*, p. 64; Schramm, "Studien," p. 198ff, 206–7; Halphen, *L'administration de Rome*, p. 37ff.

[135]See the list of these judges edited by Schramm, "Studien," pp. 203–4. This list dates from the time of Anastasius Bibliothecarius, 860s or 870s according to Schramm, pp. 205–7.

[136]Plöchl, *Kirchenrecht* 1:307; Halphen, *L'administration de Rome*, p. 37–38; Schramm, "Studien," p. 198ff; Toubert, *Latium* 2:1200–1, 1212–13.

rarius as a judge,[137] and Leo III so used his *nomenclator, bibliothecarius,*
and *vestararius,*[138] so it may be that the Lateran officials were from time to
time designated ad hoc to sit in judgment of certain kinds of cases. But the
bibliothecarius was not one of the *iudices de clero* so it cannot have been
true that only the major officials could be used as judges. In the early
Republic there were probably no regular civil assizes, and then later as the
amount of judicial business increased, some routinization was called for.[139]
We simply cannot follow this process. There are two questions to which we
would like to have answers: Did the *iudices de clero* who were once "officials" become at a later time exclusively judges? Did the "palatine" or "ordinary" judges of later times possess jurisdiction especially within the administrative spheres of the former "officials" (e.g., did the *sacellarius* become a
judge for financial cases only)? Probably we will never be able to answer
these questions. To say that the pope controlled the civil judiciary of the
Republic is quite safe. To say more would be to engage in sheer speculation.

Criminal jurisdiction remained in the hands of the urban prefect, and
individual dukes and consuls presided over the tribunals and supplied police
functions to the city.[140] Their jurisdiction had originally extended to Rome
and its environs to a radius of one hundred miles,[141] but after the settlements
of the 780s would have extended only to the borders of the reconstituted
Duchy of Rome. We know that the pope appointed both the urban prefect
and the dukes,[142] and we also know that consul was a purely honorific title
probably reserved for persons who served in the courts.[143] We can therefore
say that a criminal judicature existed alongside the civil one, and that whereas
the civil was run from the Lateran, the criminal was directed by papally
appointed officials who were laymen and outside the Lateran administration
stricto sensu.

Not much, obviously, can be known about the fate of Byzantine Rome's
secular institutions, but in every instance where a determination of their fate
can be made it seems that either these institutions were allowed to lapse or
else they were absorbed into and controlled by the Lateran administration.

---

[137]*RF*, vol. 2, no. 90, p. 84; Jaffé, *RP*, no. 2395.

[138]*RF*, vol. 2, no. 199, pp. 162–63; Jaffé, *RP*, no. 2525.

[139]Toubert, *Latium* 2:1196.

[140]Halphen, *L'administration de Rome,* pp. 35–37; Brezzi, *Roma e l'empero,* p. 8; Toubert,
Latium 2:1213.

[141]See above n. 122; also Brezzi, *Roma e l'empero,* p. 8.

[142]Halphen, *L'administration de Rome,* pp. 35–36.

[143]Diehl, *Etudes,* p. 314; Halphen, *L'administration de Rome,* pp. 29–31; Toubert, *Latium*
2:1195–96.

This process of disappearance or transformation has left some tantalizing hints in the historical record, but in most instances these hints defy efforts at interpretation. The alterations sustained by Rome's judicature is one such instance, within which there are further interesting possibilities. For example, it is possible that the proliferation of dukes, who ought to have been military officers but who seem to have become officers of the courts, may be connected with the gradual eclipse of the Byzantine military structures and the assumption of control of the courts by the papal administration. That is, there ought to have been only one main duke around Rome, but by Hadrian's time there were many. It is clear that the old military organization was breaking up, and it is also clear that the urban prefect, as the head of the criminal judiciary, would have required assistants and assistance in carrying out his duties. Maybe the many dukes reflect a transformation of military officers into policemen and executive officers of the courts. This is, of course, only a hypothesis.

It is not clear that Byzantine Rome, as an outpost of the eastern empire, possessed a diplomatic service or a foreign ministry comparable to the rather elaborate structures that attended to foreign affairs at Constantinople. It follows, therefore, that no structures survived that could have been taken over by the papacy. The papal *apocrisiarii* resident at the capital from the fifth century to the 730s were not ambassadors,[144] and the Lateran administration had no other agents or departments specifically deputed to diplomacy. Under the Republic the popes regularly engaged in negotiations of all kinds with neighboring peoples, but the Lateran does not seem to have developed either a professional foreign service or a discrete department devoted exclusively to foreign policy.

A modern state would be unthinkable without ambassadors, but medieval governments began to create foreign services only in the late twelfth century. Even the papal legates of the types widely employed during and after the eleventh century were, as Donald Queller puts it, essentially messengers. That is, they were not plenipotentiaries "with authority to bind their principals." The legal effect of dispatching *legati* or *missi* was, under the Republic, roughly equivalent to sending a letter.[145]

---

[144]Garrett Mattingly, "The First Resident Embassies," *Speculum* 12 (1937): 425. But J. A. Abbo, "Papal Legates," *New Catholic Encyclopedia* (New York, 1967), 8:607, views *apocrisiarii* as "what may be considered the first manifestations of the papal right of external legation." This is doubtful.

[145]Queller, *The Office of Ambassador in the Middle Ages* (Princeton, 1967), pp. ix, 2–4, 6–9.

Sometimes the popes negotiated personally, and sometimes by means of intermediaries. Instances of the former would include Zachary's meetings with Liutprand, Stephen II's encounters with Aistulf and Pepin, and Hadrian's, Leo III's, and Stephen IV's dealings with Charlemagne and Louis the Pious. Intermediaries were so commonly used that it is pointless to begin citing examples. Moreover, when intermediaries were used there does not seem to have been a preference for any particular persons. Lateran bureaucrats were sent to Liutprand and Beneventan abbots to Aistulf. Lay and clerical dignitaries bearing numerous different titles were regularly deputed to the Carolingian court. The wide range of individuals employed on diplomatic missions by the popes tends to prove that no single Lateran office monopolized or had special responsibility for foreign affairs.

Whether special procedures were followed in negotiations is something we simply cannot know. It will be recalled that when Gregory III wrote to Charles Martel his letters, and Charles's, were carried by representatives who also transmitted oral messages. When Stephen II and Pepin corresponded between 753 and 756 messengers bearing oral instructions were again used. Hadrian was several times visited by Frankish agents whose specific words and actions are nowhere preserved in the surviving correspondence. If we had envoy's reports, council minutes, or even more correspondence, it might be possible to work out a hazy picture of papal diplomacy. But no evidence of these kinds survives. As a result, formal procedures, matters of protocol, and the details of actual negotiations are almost always lost to us.

The popes seem to have carried on diplomacy as well and as widely as any of their contemporaries except, perhaps, for the emperors. In short, what needed to be done was done even if no formal institutions were conserved or created to accomplish diplomatic representation. In part, the lack of regular diplomatic institutions under the Republic may derive from the ambiguity inherent in the pope's position as a the head of a state and of the universal Church.[146] That is, papal Rome was constantly kept abreast of problems on all fronts that touched upon the Church's interests. One thinks of the problem of iconoclasm, or of the adoptionist heresy that arose in Spain. Hadrian and Leo III erected and then suppressed an archbishopric at Lichfield in England and negotiated with a series of English kings about it. Greek and Latin monks in Jerusalem appealed to Leo III for arbitration of a

---

[146]S. Bakrouchine and E. Kosminski, "La diplomatie au moyen âge," in Vladimir Petrovich Potiemkine ed., *Histoire de la diplomatie*, vol. 1, trans. Xenia Pamphilova and Michel Eristov (Paris, 1948), pp. 94–97; Ganshof, *The Middle Ages: A History of International Relations*, trans. Rémy Inglis Hall (New York, 1971), pp. 36–55 passim.

dispute over the creed. The surviving records pertaining to these issues contain little more than a handful of details on the routine church business at hand. But, because we know that oral messages were transmitted in some instances, it is reasonable to assume that the popes regularly used the appearance of ecclesiastical envoys as a means of learning news about foreign lands and peoples. The Republic's popes, in other words, probably knew more about the totality of developments in their world than any one else, and if one function of diplomacy is the gathering of information, then the papacy had, as an ecclesiastical institution, a marvelous network of informants. In equal measure the Republic's lack of a sophisticated, institutionalized foreign ministry may be attributed to the military alliance concluded with the Franks in 754. From that time forward the security of the Republic was assured by the Carolingians, and this precluded the need for diplomatic agents assigned the task of procuring and preserving relationships essential to the survival of the Republic itself.

In the final analysis, the absence of formal diplomatic institutions in the Republic is less important than an awareness of the undeniable fact that the popes were able to carry on all necessary kinds of dealings with people from England to the Holy Land. In all that concerns institutions papal Rome was certainly less sophisticated than ancient Rome or Byzantium, and less routinized than medieval governments would later become. For their time and their needs, however, the popes had adequate diplomatic tools at their disposal. And the uses to which those tools were put prove quite compellingly that the Republic was regarded as fully capable of entering into extraterritorial relationships that were legal and binding.

Administration Outside Rome

Papal dominion truly extended to every feature of the religious, political, administrative, and judicial life of Rome and its environs. The Republic, however, consisted of more than just Rome and its *territorium*. The Duchy of Rome had been, since the 720s, the sturdy and solid core of the Republic, and so a determination of its governmental structures constitutes the most important part of the task of proving that the Republic really was a state with a government in the eighth and ninth centuries. Other regions claimed by, or donated to, the Republic have to be studied mainly to round out the picture. The task of describing papal rule outside Rome is difficult for at least three reasons. Some areas, like Venice and Istria or Benevento and

Spoleto, were long claimed but never effectively held or ruled. They must be left out of the discussion because any insights gleaned from them would of necessity be ephemeral. Indeed, analysis can only meaningfully be devoted to the territorial situation as it stood after 788. Then there is the problem of Ravenna. Some of the best documents come from the Ravennate, but from at least the 780s, this region possessed a split jurisdiction among its arch-bishops, the Franks, and the popes. Surely, therefore, one must avoid drawing overly bold generalizations from Ravenna. Finally, if the documentation for Rome itself is often frustratingly sparse, the evidence for the non-Roman sectors of the Republic is all but nonexistent for most times.

As archbishop of the Roman Church province, the pope had suffragan clergy throughout Latium and Campania, Tuscany, Umbria, Valeria, Pi-cenum, Samnium, Calabria, Lucania, Brutii, and Corsica.[147] Not all of these areas were included in the Republic, and to the south of Campania the Byzantine emperor Leo III had cut off the pope's control, in theory at least, after 732–33. Nevertheless, wherever the pope's provincial and republican boundaries were coterminous it was possible for the pontiffs to exercise appreciable control over the appointment of bishops, who may certainly be thought of as key local dignitaries. Throughout the period covered by this book the popes made large numbers of episcopal ordinations. The end of virtually every *vita* in the *Liber Pontificalis* records the number of bishops, priests, and deacons ordained by each pope.[148] The popes from John V to Gregory IV for whom figures exist ordained 1,082 bishops; each of them ordained an average of 72.1. How much control the pope exerted on a regular basis over these bishops is difficult to gauge. They had to swear a *promissio fidei*[149] and execute a *cautio*, which more or less spelled out their duties, responsibilities, and obligations.[150] Concessions of the pallium were strictly regulated,[151] and bishops were summoned to Rome annually on the anniversary of the pope's assumption of office.[152] Roman synods also served to collect episcopal clergy in Rome under the pope's watchful eye from time to time.[153] Within the individual dioceses of the pope's province the estab-

---

[147]Hinschius, *Kirchenrecht* 1:212–13 and 213 n.2.

[148]*LP* 1:367, 369, 376, 383, 386, 391–93, 410, 421, 435, 456, 480, 514, 2:34, 50, 63, 83. Figures are lacking for Paul I, Paschal I, Eugenius II, and Valentinus.

[149]*LD*, nos. 73, 75, ed. Foerster, pp. 128–32, 136–37.

[150]*LD*, no. 74, ed. Foerster, pp. 132–36.

[151]*LD*, nos. 45, 46, ed. Foerster, p. 101–8.

[152]*LD*, no. 42, ed. Foerster, p. 100.

[153]Jaffé, *RP*, p. 250 (Gregory II:721), 257 (Gregory III:731), 259 (Gregory III:737–39), 265 (Zachary:745), 271 (Stephen II:753, authenticity questionable), 276 (Stephen II: ca. 757),

lishment of monasteries, foundation of oratories and baptisteries, dedications of altars, and installation of relics were governed by privileges routinely issued by the papal chancery.[154] It is reasonable to assume that the pope's control of the clergy outside Rome was less strict and continuous than it was inside the city, but it would be a mistake to regard it as negligible. In a larger sense it is quite true that ecclesiastical and political control are different, but the one can considerably smooth the way for the other. Moreover, because rural clergy were enmeshed in the life of their local communities, papal control throughout Rome's province may be seen as a countering force to the power and influence of the rural nobility.

In addition to controlling the hierarchy, the pope influenced much of the countryside through his vast patrimonies. The *Register* of Gregory I, which has been minutely scrutinized by historians, yields a treasure of information about the patrimonies in the late sixth century, but conditions in the eighth and ninth centuries are more difficult to grasp. Certainly innmuerable documents concerning the papal patrimonies were kept in the Lateran archives, but except for some fragments of what may have been a register compiled under Gregory II,[155] none of these texts survives. Throughout the history of the Republic the papacy never ceased looking out for patrimonies in its possession and reclaiming ones that had been lost.[156] In the end, however, no estimate can be made of the total extent of the patrimonies,[157] the annual revenues derived from them,[158] or the precise locations of the great majority

---

279 (Paul I:761), 285 (Stephen III:769), 292 (Hadrian I:774), 310 (Leo III:800), 313 (Leo III:810), 321 (Eugenius II:826).

[154]For some examples: *LD*, nos. 10, 16, 17, 25, 29, 30, 64, 65, ed. Foerster, pp. 83–84, 86–87, 90, 92, 92–93, 121–22, 122–23. Here again we have some evidence for the work of the notaries and archivists.

[155]Jaffé, *RP*, nos. 2189ff.

[156]One thinks of the claims for restitutions pressed before Luitprand, or claims against Desiderius or complaints against the Beneventans. Dozens of examples could be cited.

[157]The locations of the great concentrations are known: Spearing, *Patrimonies*, pp. 5–14. They were (leaving out those not in Italy) located in Sicily, Bruttium, Lucania, Calabria, Apulia, Samnium, Campania, Naples, Sabina, Latium, Tuscany, Picenum, Ravenna, Istria, Liguria, Cottian Alps. All the patrimonies of southern Italy and Sicily were seized by Emperor Leo III. It seems doubtful that those in the western Alps and Istria were retained. Most of the others, at least to the extent that they fell within the borders of the Republic, probably persisted in at least an attenuated state.

[158]Ravenna was second to Rome in wealth, probably a distant second (Hartmann, *Verwaltung*, pp. 86–89), and by chance Agnellus has left an account of the revenues of the archbishops in the sixth century which has some value for purposes of comparison: 3,000 solidi, 880 fowls, 266 chickens, 8,800 eggs, 3,760 lbs of pork, 3,450 lbs. of honey, plus geese and milk: *Lib. pont. rav.*, c. 60, MGH, SSrL, pp. 319–20.

of individual estates.[159] That the Roman Church was the largest landholder in Italy, and that its holdings in every district of the Republic far exceeded the possessions of local laymen, is beyond dispute. That the possession of land in the early Middle Ages translated directly into power and influence is also beyond dispute. Unfortunately, these perfectly accurate qualitative judgments cannot be exchanged for equally accurate quantitative ones.

If the extent and locations of the papal patrimonies cannot be fixed, their organization can be. At least, there is no reason to believe that conditions evident in Gregory's *Register* had altered under the Republic, with one exception to which we shall return below.[160] *Patrimonium*[161] was a general name for a complex of localized estates called *massae*. The *massae* may have been discrete, individual donations to the church. *Fundi* were individual farms, a number of which made up each *massa*. Probably the *fundus*, like the *mansus* in Francia, represented the holding of one family. Texts also mention *casales*, which were not, as is sometimes maintained, a further subdivision of a patrimony, but the villages inhabited by farmers of *fundi*.

At the head of each major patrimony stood a *rector*. Before Gregory I, laymen and bishops, indeed all manner of persons, functioned as *rectores*, but after Gregory's time virtually all *rectores* were clerics. It was not uncommon for Roman deacons or subdeacons to be appointed, but very often *rectores* were either defensors or notaries. When *rectores* were chosen among the defensors or notaries, who belonged to *scholae* centered in Rome and headed by regionaries, the Lateran bureaucracy itself was extended into the countryside. Whether *rectores* came from the Roman clergy or were chosen locally—and the two possibilities are not mutually exclusive—they were appointed in Rome. The newly created *rector* was given a *breve* detailing his patrimony and a *capitulare* spelling out his exact instructions. The *rector* had to deposit an oath, a *cautio*, in the papal archives, and before he entered

---

[159]Castagnetti, *Organizzazione rurale*, pp. 169–204, points out that, later, around Ravenna and Ferrara one finds terminology almost identical to that used earlier in the patrimonies, which suggests the possibility of using later evidence to work backward, to proceed by analogy, and to illuminate earlier conditions. Alas, he makes a convincing case that such a procedure would be dangerous in the extreme, though not necessarily impossible.

[160]Jones, "L'Italia agraria," pp. 57–58.

[161]The following acount constitutes a synthesis of: Grisar, "Verwaltung"; Schwarzlose, "Patrimonien"; Spearing, *Patrimonies*; Hartmann, *Verwaltung*, pp. 49–51, 85–89; Bréhier and Aigrain, *Histoire de l'église*, pp. 543–53; Partner, *Lands of St. Peter*, pp. 1–10; and, now by far the best and fullest account, Recchia, *Gregorio Magno e la società agricola*, pp. 16–24 and passim. These studies are based upon the *Register* of Gregory I, the *LP*, and the *LD*, plus a few other scattered documents.

upon his duties a papal encyclical was sent to the inhabitants of the patrimony informing them that a new *rector* had been appointed and providing special details and instructions as necessary. As direct papal agents the *rectores* functioned as papal legates in the patrimonies. They had both ecclesiastical and administrative supervision, and their authority extended even to bishops and monasteries. *Rectores* had various subordinate officials, chief among whom were *defensores, notarii,* and *actionarii.* The defensors administered poor relief and guarded the peasants from oppression by local clergy and even by the *rectores.* Notaries were clerks. They kept records and drew up documents. *Actionarii* were inferior clerks, bailiffs, executive officers, and revenue collectors. Frequently they were laymen.

The peasants on the patrimonies paid fees, *pensiones,* in both money and in kind, though payments in kind seem to have predominated. Doubtless these payments in kind made possible the papacy's provision for Rome's food supply, and it is reasonable to suppose that the greater the pope's role in feeding Rome's populace, the stricter his management of the patrimonies. The *pensiones* were usually fixed by custom for very long terms, and they seem to have been modest. Possibly this owed something to the Church's sense of its charitable obligations, but it may also have been a result of the fact that the peasants were liable to the *tributum,* the Byzantine land tax, and the *coemptio,* the requisition for cause of goods in kind. If, as appears likely, papal exactions were not burdensome it is easy to see why Gregory II resisted so resolutely the tax increases of the 720s. Those increases would have jeopardized church revenues by placing a crushing burden on the patrimonial peasants, and by diverting to Constantinople funds or goods needed in Italy.

This rather elaborate bureaucratic system was not invented by Gregory I, and it long survived him. Alongside it, however, there gradually emerged a parallel structure. The Church had long been in the habit of leasing out its lands. Canon and civil law forbade the alienation of church property, but nothing really stood in the way of leasing it. It has been plausibly proposed that after the Gothic wars Italy was underpopulated and that the Church began, from the middle of the sixth century, to lease out considerable tracts of land because it had insufficient dependents to exploit them fully. After the time of Gregory I the commonest form of lease was the emphyteusis, which was originally a grant in perpetuity but became eventually a three-lifetime lease. The name derives from ἐμφυτεύειν meaning "to plant." The possessor of an emphyteusis was expected to enhance his holding, presumably by bringing it under regular and productive cultivation. All over Italy, soldiers of the *exercitus Italicus* sought to assure their fortunes by becoming lessees of church lands, and some individuals acquired enough leases to become real landed magnates. Often these holders of emphyteusis contracts appointed *conductores*, who managed their estates and collected revenues from them in money and in kind. From these revenues the papal treasury was paid the annual fee prescribed by the original lease. Naturally the emphyteuta kept a margin over their annual rents as profit, but the peasants probably did not fare badly because their dues were also fixed for long terms, and after the 720s, they were relieved of the *tributum* and the *coemptio*. In any case, there appear to have been defensors located even on the lands let out by the Church to look out for the interests of the Church and the peasants.

Such, then, was the patrimonial system within the Republic. The number of people who were, as a result of this system, directly dependent upon the Church, coupled with the pope's control of the hierarchy throughout the Republic, provides a crucial, albeit qualitative, index of the papacy's influence. Given that the pope was by a wide margin the greatest landholder within the Republic, it is only just to suggest that the great majority of the rural population were directly dependent upon the Church. This was true both of the peasants working on their *fundi*, and of the aristocrats drawing profit from their emphyteutic estates.

Hartmann has aptly noted that the Roman Church cannot be viewed as a "*Privatwirtschaft*," and that it would be a mistake to call it a "*geschlossene Hauswirtschaft*."[162] Indeed, by the eighth century it was the only functioning bureaucratic organism in central Italy. But, as Hartmann also observed, the pontificate of Zachary provides the first evidence that the papacy was beginning to find the existing order of things unsatisfactory.[163] Probably so much land had been leased, and so many leases had become tantamount to alienations, that the rural aristocracy was becoming simultaneously a rival to the Church in the countryside, a threat to the Church's livelihood, and a potential political opponent of major proportions.

Zachary's answer was the creation of a new type of rural institution, the *domusculta*.[164] Zachary established four or five of them and later Hadrian added four more.[165] During Hadrian's pontificate two individuals also be-

---

[162]Hartmann, "Grundherrschaft und Bureaukratie im Kirchenstaat vom 8. bis zum 10. Jahrhundert," *Vierteljahrschrift für Sozial- und Wirtschaftsgeschichte* 7 (1907): 147. This valuable study seems to have been sadly neglected.

[163]Hartmann, "Grundherrschaft und Bureaukratie," pp. 149, 151ff. David Miller graciously allowed me to consult an unpublished 48 page typescript entitled "The Establishment and Early Development of the Papal States: A Study in Feudal Politics" which treats some of these problems very imaginatively.

[164]*LP* 1:434–35; Kehr, *IP*, vol. 2, nos. 14, 15, p. 5, no. 5, p. 9, no. 14, p. 12, no. 1, p. 35.

[165]*LP* 1:501–2.

queathed lands for *domuscultae*. One was Leoninus "consul et dux . . . postmodum monachus" and the other was Mastalus, the *primicerius*.[166] Leo III also created *domuscultae*. They were attacked at the end of his pontificate. We do not know how many Leo created. The tiny amount of surviving evidence concerning the *domuscultae* has been carefully sifted, and it is now reasonably clear what they were and why they were created, but some controversial points have yet to be resolved.

The *domuscultae* were large rural estates and all of them were established very near Rome. Bertolini believes that they were new foundations that were erected on land that had been underpopulated and uncultivated.[167] Jones, on the contrary, thinks they represented a reorganization of the Church's rural landholdings.[168] The evidence will support both views but tends to lend more weight to Jones's opinion. At *Tres Tabernae* Zachary seems to have brought abandoned land under cultivation; hence Bertolini's interpretation. On another occasion, however, Zachary accepted a bequest of land, bought up surrounding parcels, and reorganized the whole mass into the *domusculta* of St. Cecilia.[169] This development, coupled with several *domuscultae* created by Hadrian on lands bequeathed to the Church or else on his own family land, supports Jones's view.[170]

The *domuscultae* were distinctive in several respects. First, Church authorities repeatedly emphasized that they could never be alienated, not even by lease.[171] Second, they marked efforts by popes, at least in some instances, to bring new land under cultivation and to use on that land peasants who were working directly for the Church. Third, the *domuscultae* had the result of taking certain lands out of emphyteutic circulation. The Church was moving from a bureaucratic system to *"Grundherrschaft,"* or landed lordship, on at least some of its property. The rural nobility, long accustomed to

---

[166]*LP* 1:505, 509.

[167]Bertolini, *Roma*, pp. 506–12; idem, "La ricomparsa della sede episcopale di 'Tres Tabernae' nella seconda metà del secolo VIII e l'istituzione delle 'domuscultae,'" *Archivio della società romana di storia patria* 75 (1952): 103–9; Wickham, "Etruria," p. 379, agrees.

[168]"L'Italia agraria," pp. 237–41.

[169]*LP* 1:434.

[170]Duchesne, *Temporal Sovereignty*, p. 67; idem, *LP* 1:439 nn.52–54, 518 nn.51, 52, 55, 56; Hartmann, "Grundherrschaft und Bureaukratie," pp. 151–52; Pepe, *Moyen âge barbare en Italie*, pp. 169, 187; Partner, "Notes on the Lands of the Roman Church in the Early Middle Ages," *Papers of the British School at Rome* 34 (1966): 68–79; Richards, *Popes and the Papacy*, p. 231.

[171]*LP* 1:435: "Statuit nulli quoque modo successorum eius pontificum vel alie cuilibet persone licere ipsas domus cultas ab usu ecclesiae quoquo modo alienare." Hadrian later demanded (ibid., p. 502) that his *domuscultae* had to remain in Church hands under pain of anathema.

holding vast tracts of Church land, cannot have liked this diminution of the
pool of available land in central Italy.[172] Fourth, the inhabitants of the *domuscultae* could be armed, whereas the ordinary clerical bureaucrats could
not be. This last feature of the *domuscultae* requires special emphasis.

While there is no reason to suppose that a desire to procure greater
economic efficiency did not play some role in the creation of the *domuscultae*, their military significance was very important as well and until recently
has been generally overlooked. Because the institution appeared under Zachary, when the Roman region was being threatened by the Lombards, it
may be that these estates of "soldier-farmers" were designed to play a role
in local defense. It is clear that, in the ninth century, they were expected to
play exactly this role.[173] In the long run, however, they proved ineffectual
against the Muslims and passed out of existence.[174] During their heyday,
however, the *domuscultae* not only played a role in local defense, but they
also got involved in Roman politics.

The *superista* was the chief military officer in the Lateran and the head
of a body of men called the *familia sancti Petri*. The latter were the soldiers
settled on the *domuscultae*.[175] Under Leo III the nobility ravaged the *domuscultae*, and under Paschal I the murderers of Theodore, Leo, and the others
were members of the *familia sancti Petri*.[176] From these few details it seems
possible to conclude that the papacy, as the Republic was coming into existence, began forming its own militia alongside the Roman duchy's regular
military structures. Friction between these two military bodies did not occur
while the Lombard threat was still very real, but may have broken into the
open at the time of Toto's rebellion in 767. Possibly by then the clergy
intended to use its own militia as a counterweight against the coercive force
of the military aristocracy in the countryside. Possibly too it was troops from
the *domuscultae* who kept Christophorus in power, and who carried out his
reprisals in the countryside after Desiderius withdrew from Rome in 768.
Hadrian founded several *domuscultae*. One of them was created at *Capracorum* near the lands of Toto of Nepi, whereas the others were scattered.
Perhaps this pope was seeking to assure the papacy of some forces against

[172]This is the thesis of Hartmann's article "Grundherrschàft und Bureaukratie."

[173]*LP* 2:100, 126, 137 nn.7, 47. Brown, "Social Structure," pp. 133–34; David Whitehouse, "Sedi medievali nella campagna romana: La 'domusculta' e il villaggio fortificato,"
Quaderni Storici 24 (1973): 861–76.

[174]Whitehouse, "Sedi medievali," p. 865.

[175]Brezzi, *Roma e l'empero*, pp. 25–26; Brown, "Social Structure," p. 134. That *familia*
means dependent populations on a *fundus* has also been pointed out by Bosl, *Gesellschaftsgeschichte*, p. 33.

[176]*Annales regni Francorum, annis* 815, 823, ed. Kurze, pp. 143, 162.

the possibility of another Toto. In 799 one of Leo III's attackers was Maurice of Nepi, and in 815 the rural nobility hatched another plot against Leo, and after it failed, they ravaged his *domuscultae*. Down to 816, then, the *domuscultae* may explain in part how the clergy was able to maintain itself against the nobility. Subsequently, with the noble takeover in 816, or at any rate by Paschal's time, the *familia sancti Petri* became a weapon in Roman factional strife.

Perhaps it is significant that the Duke of Rome disappears from the sources at just about the time that the *superista* appears. Perhaps as well it is not insignificant that from the time of Hadrian only a ceremonial role can be detected for the Roman militia. Likewise, it is curious that beginning with Hadrian's pontificate one discovers a proliferation of dukes with judicial responsibilities accompanying a progressive disappearance from the sources of clear traces of the role and activities of the traditional military structures. All of these coincidences require some explanation. A reasonable hypothesis would be that the popes of the Republic, by adjusting and reorganizing some of their rural holdings, attempted to create a military force independent of the Roman remnant of the *exercitus Italicus*.

If the older military structures are difficult to trace, the continued existence of dukes is not. Some of them certainly took on judicial duties, though it would be rushing far ahead of the scanty evidence to say that all of them did. Whether they remained military officers or became judicial ones, or perhaps both at the same time, they were papally appointed officials. Hadrian commended two dukes to Charlemagne.[177] Leo III speaks in a letter of a duke he instituted,[178] and in 815 he sent a duke as an envoy to Louis the Pious.[179] Paschal I twice sent military officers as envoys to Louis.[180] It seems quite clear that the republican popes appointed the dukes in the Duchy of Rome.[181] In so doing they maintained some control over the local aristocracy. The attack on Leo III, however, proves that the rural nobility could as easily turn against the pope as be employed by him. In the years after 774, and especially after the territorial settlements of the 780s, Rome was for a time

---

[177]CC, no. 90, p. 627.

[178]Jaffé, *RP*, no. 2516.

[179]Astronomer, *Vita Hludowici*, c. 25, *MGH, SS* 2:619.

[180]Astronomer, *Vita Hludowici*, cc. 34, 37, *MGH, SS* 2:626, 628. These accounts are a bit curious. On the first occasion the *superista*, or the military governor of the Lateran, was sent. On the second occasion "Leo magister militum" was dispatched. These were similar, perhaps identical, offices.

[181]This issue has not been studied recently (Toubert did not look in detail at this early period), but there seem to be no reasons to challenge the conclusions of Armbrust, *Territoriale Politik*, pp. 98–104, and Falco, "Amministrazione," pp. 681, 683.

without serious military opponents. This leads to the suspicion that the ducal title may have become largely honorific: a means of acknowledging and rewarding significant members of the local nobility.

Beyond the Duchy of Rome the situation is more complicated because in Emilia, the Ravenna region, and the Pentapolis new structures were created to introduce papal rule, but they appear to have been ephemeral and their workings cannot be observed closely. In Ravenna, Stephen II dispatched a bishop and a duke, named Philip and Eustacius, respectively, to represent the pope and to take up rule in his name. These officials received their instructions in Rome and appointed subordinate officials in Ravenna who had to go to Rome to be invested with their offices. All of our knowledge about Stephen's actions comes from a letter of Hadrian to Charlemagne written late in 774. This letter, as well as another from 775, make it clear that Hadrian considered papal control of Ravenna and the Pentapolis to be the usual and natural order of things.[182] The reality was different.

Officials for Ravenna were to be appointed in, instructed by, and supervised from Rome.[183] Officials in Emilia and the Pentapolis could be locals, but they also had to go to Rome to be invested with their offices and to receive their specific mandates.[184] The cities of Emilia and the Pentapolis were supposed to swear allegiance to the to the pope before papal envoys.[185] This was the ideal.

In fact, Archbishop Leo of Ravenna was impeding papal dominion at every turn. He was ordaining affairs in Ravenna himself,[186] and he had expelled papal officials from Bologna and Imola.[187] He seized the cities of the Pentapolis, refused to admit papal officers into them, and would not give loyalist Pentapolitans leave to go to Rome to obtain their offices and commissions.[188] Leo's conduct in Ravenna itself was certainly an outgrowth of the antecedent hostility between Rome and Ravenna. Hadrian disliked and considered illegal Leo's conduct in Ravenna, but the pope was especially outraged by the archbishop's actions in the Pentapolis, because if Hadrian's

---

[182]CC, nos. 49, 54, pp. 568–69, 577. Only Bertolini has studied in detail the introduction of papal rule into Ravenna, but his work is incomplete in several respects: "Gli inizi del governo temporale," pp. 31–32; idem, "Le prime manifestazione," pp. 602–3, 606.

[183]CC, no. 49, pp. 568–69.

[184]CC, no. 54, p. 577. I am not sure whether to take the papal "actores" mentioned in CC, no. 49, as locals responsible to the pope or as Romans introduced by the pope. In general, however, conditions were as they are described above.

[185]CC, no. 55, p. 579.

[186]CC, no. 49, p. 568.

[187]CC, no. 54, p. 577.

[188]CC, nos. 54, 55, pp. 577, 579.

words can be trusted, these cities desired to be loyal and obedient to Rome and Leo would not allow them to be.[189] Hadrian directed his complaints to Charlemagne because Leo himself had visited Francia and had also sent personal representatives there.[190] The Ravennese archbishop defiantly told the pope that Charlemagne had not given Ravenna, Imola, and Bologna to the pope but instead to him.[191]

After a flurry of correspondence and exchanges of envoys in 774 and 775, the whole Ravennese situation disappears from the sources for a few years. When it reappears in the 780s we find in place the division of authority which, in chapter 5 above, was called a "double dyarchy." I suggested at that time that some sort of a compromise settlement was arranged in 781 which guaranteed some rights to the pope, and which also respected the historic particularism of Ravenna. Only a few documents illuminate the dyarchy in operation. They make Charlemagne look a bit like a referee and prove that papal dominion outside the Duchy of Rome was attenuated but not abrogated.

On one occasion Charlemagne wanted to take some marble from Ravenna and he asked Hadrian for permission to secure it.[192] We have no evidence that he appealed in this matter to Ravenna's archbishop. On another occasion Charlemagne wished to get Venetian merchants excluded from Ravenna and he asked Hadrian to expel them.[193] Hadrian appointed a count in Gabello,[194] and later Leo III was instituting dukes in the neighborhood of Ravenna and charging them with the task of collecting certain unspecified revenues and sending the proceeds to Rome.[195] Hadrian continued to expect officials from Ravenna and the Pentapolis to answer to him for their conduct, but he had to appeal to Charlemagne to get guilty parties sent to Rome.[196] Several popes confirmed privileges for the Church of Ravenna, or for churches in the area of Ravenna,[197] but Charlemagne displayed

---

[189]CC, no. 49, p. 568; no. 54, p. 577: "Nam Pentapolenses omnes, oboedientes existentes in nostro apostolico servitio, ad nos proni sicut tempore praedecessore nostri, domni Stephani papae"; no. 55, p. 597: "nam illos omnes parati erant ad nos coniungere." See also: *LP* 1:496 for confirmation of the desire of the Pentapolitans to join Rome.

[190]CC, no. 53, p. 575.

[191]CC, no. 49, p. 568. This charge went back and forth several times.

[192]CC, no. 81, p. 614.

[193]CC, no. 86, pp. 622–23.

[194]CC, no. 55, p. 579.

[195]Leo III, *Epistolae X*, no. 2, *MGH, EKA* 3:89.

[196]CC, nos. 75, 86, 88, 94, pp. 606–7, 623, 624–25, 635.

[197]Kehr, *IP*, vol. 5, no. 1, p. 132, no. 77, p. 35, no. 92, p. 37, no. 5, p. 103, no. 93, p. 38, no. 94, p. 38, no. 95, p. 38.

great reserve in this region. He issued a diploma for the merchants of Comacchio, and ruled in a dispute between the bishop of Bologna and the abbot of Nonantula.[198] This last case is difficult to interpret in the present connection, however, because Nonantula was inside the *regnum*. Hadrian told Charlemagne not to interfere in episcopal elections in Ravenna and reminded the king that he had no right to do so.[199] In about 808 Leo III complained bitterly to Charlemagne about the conduct of imperial *missi* around Ravenna, but he did not assert that the emperor had no right to send *missi* there in the first place.[200]

No matter how this list of cases is read, it is difficult to draw firm conclusions. The pope both possessed and exercised power and authority in Ravenna and the Pentapolis. His power was apparently concurrent with both the archbishop and the king (or emperor after 800), and his power was effectively limited to the extent that he could get Charlemagne to do his bidding. It would be imprudent to try to make out a strong case for papal rule in northeastern Italy, but it would be completely incorrect to assert that the pope had no rights or powers there. It is interesting to note that after all the bitterness and acrimony of the years 774 and 775, all future references to Ravenna in Roman sources are quite routine and businesslike. It is a real shame that no trace survives of the Franco-Ravennese-papal settlement of 781, but it is apparent that that settlement was satisfactory to all sides.[201] Ravenna was not handed over integrally and absolutely to the papacy, but neither were the pope's legitimate claims ignored nor his modest rights trampled upon.

It is not surprising that things worked out the way they did in the Ravennese sector of the Republic. Ravenna and Rome had been allies only in the face of common threats. Otherwise, the history of these two cities, since the last days of the Roman Empire, under the Gothic monarchy, and during the period of exarchal rule, had been one marked by jealousy and hostility. Likewise, the archbishops of Ravenna were in Italy, and perhaps in all the West, second in rank and wealth only to those of Rome. Under these circumstances it is perfectly natural that after the Goths, Byzantines, and

---

[198]*MGH, DK*, vol. 1, nos. 132, 197, pp. 182–83, 265–66.

[199]*CC*, no. 85, pp. 621–22.

[200]Leo III, *Epistolae X*, nos. 2, 9, 10, *MGH, EKA*, 3:89, 101, 102. It seems clear to me that all three of these letters treat the same case.

[201]Hadrian admitted as much when between 787 and 791 he asked Charlemagne to expel an invader named Garamannus from Ravenna "ut et nostra territoria per vestram regalem tuitionem intacta permaneant": *CC*, no. 86, p. 623. The use of "tuitio" meaning "protection" is important.

Lombards disappeared as enemies, Ravenna should have returned to the path of independence. In the 750s, however, a third party had entered the scene: the Franks. In 755, 756, and 774 Frankish kings had promised Ravenna to the Republic. In 774, if not perhaps earlier, Charlemagne learned that domination by Rome did not gladden the hearts of the Ravennese, but he had his promises to keep. He kept them by admitting that the pope had claims in Ravenna, and by coming to the support of those claims. At the same time, because the pope obviously had inadequate coercive powers to make good his claims by himself, Charlemagne effected a compromise with the archbishop of Ravenna that was acceptable both in Rome and in Ravenna. He then made himself the guarantor of that compromise. In all his dealings with Italy Charlemagne was a great peacemaker. This is nowhere clearer than in Ravenna.

The Papal Government

The fact that the pope's primary responsibility, as a priest, was to convey souls from this world to the next did not prevent him from becoming a formidable and effective temporal ruler. His religious control in and around Rome, and across much of central Italy, caused large numbers of people to look directly to him as their pastor and spiritual leader. As he moved about in solemn processions, the pope was the most majestic and awe-inspiring personage that any Italian alive in the eighth or ninth centuries would have seen or could have imagined. Even Charlemagne, with his rough Franks, must have appeared a poor and distant second. Purely religious leadership, there can be no doubt, helped to prepare the way for other kinds.

As a dimension of his responsibility for Christian charity, and in succession to the Roman and Byzantine public authorities, the pope fed, housed, and healed many of the people within his area of direct influence. On vast estates scattered over the length and breadth of Italy, countless peasants worked on papal lands to earn their slender livings. Their labors were overseen by salaried papal officers. Papal building projects provided employment for some at least of the idle mob that had been a constant feature of the Roman scene since the days of the Gracchi. Within Rome and without papal defensors protected the poor from the rich and the powerless from the mighty. All of these people looked to the pope, as their pastor, for ultimate salvation from the sins of this world, but they looked to that very same pope for immediate alleviation of some of this world's burdens.

As the eighth century wore on, the Lateran housed the only real government in Rome and, not surprisingly, the flower of Rome's aristocracy entered
its offices and hoped for its summit, the pontifical throne. Short of the see of
Peter, however, there were other positions that conferred upon their holders
power and prestige, the two things that all noble Romans sought above
everything else. Administration of the papal treasury, or custody of the papal
palace were important and responsible offices worthy of these historic, but
not genetic, sons of those senators who had once ruled the world. As the
Lateran offices provided outlets for talent and ambition, they also conferred
less tangible but no less real rewards. The high officers were all clerics who,
in an unending cycle of liturgical celebrations, stood before the people of
Rome and, by their elegant clerical garb, by the mystical solemnity of their
liturgical offices, and by their proximity to the successor of St. Peter, silently
proclaimed their eminence. *Auctoritas*, to a Roman, always meant power in
a very practical way but also and just as importantly respect and recognition.
Papal Rome provided opportunities for both influence and recognition that
had been all but absent in Byzantine Rome.

The Lateran ordained everything within the Republic. Budgets were drawn
up, revenues collected, disbursements made. Courts of law sat and rendered
verdicts. Public works and charities were supplied for all who needed them.
A host of officials great and small were recruited, trained, appointed, transferred, and promoted. Virtually every public service that ancient Rome had
provided for its citizens, papal Rome provided as well. There was of course
one great exception. Papal Rome could not send out legions marching under
their eagles to the ends of the earth, or even, as things stood, to the borders
of the Republic. Thus Lombards early and Muslims late would prove redoubtable foes, and Pope Leo could be attacked in Rome, and Archbishop
Leo could be recalcitrant in Ravenna. But, just as ancient Rome finally
turned to the north for hearty Germanic soldiers, so papal Rome looked to
Francia, to the Carolingians, for military aid.

In all respects save the military it simply cannot be argued that the
Republic of St. Peter had no true government because it was a state run by
a church with essentially ecclesiastical institutions. Indeed, the Roman Church
was a large and sophisticated enterprise with a huge staff, vast estates, and
wide-ranging responsibilities long before it assumed the mantle of temporal
rule. When, during the eighth century, the Church took the lead in emanci-
pating Italy from Byzantium, it easily and smoothly adapted its own institutions to the needs of government on a grander scale. Witness the growing
sophistication and division of labor in the papal archives, reforms in the
collection and distribution of revenues, and the creation of *diaconiae* to

administer "poor relief." Likewise, it is worth reemphasizing the way the Church preserved certain necessary secular institutions such as the urban prefecture for criminal law and the public notaries for record keeping. Finally, it is worth repeating that, early in its history, the Church reached out more openly to embrace the Roman nobility while at the same time it sought to insure that nobles, once they had become clerics, would adhere faithfully to the aspirations, traditions, and policies of the ecclesiastical leaders of the Republic.

Eight

Amicitia, Pax et Caritas: The Franco-Papal Alliance

THE REPUBLIC'S relationship with the Franks constitutes the last significant element in its history. This relationship, which has already come to our
attention many times, has two dimensions which must now be confronted
directly: the precise nature of the bonds forged between the Carolingian
rulers and the popes; and the degree and kind of Frankish interference in
and influence upon the Republic of St. Peter. The present chapter will take
up the first of these problems, and chapter 9 will take up the second.

Neither Pepin nor Charlemagne created the Republic of St. Peter, but
they did inaugurate a close and complex association between the papacy
and the Frankish monarchy. Even if Lindner's remark, mentioned above in
the introduction, to the effect that the Franco-papal relationship is among
the most critical issues in medieval history, no longer rings true today, there
is no denying that an astonishingly lively debate on the subject has been
going on for a century. In 1938 Percy Ernst Schramm characterized well the
current state of the question when he wrote, "To pass in review in full
compass the state of research would be a hopeless task for there are num-
berless opinions, some of which diverge radically from one another, and
some of which merely accent one another."[1] Today it may be that the waters
are a little less muddy than they were when Schramm wrote these words,
but no clear consensus has emerged on the Franco-papal relationship, or on
its implications for the Republic.

It would be just as hopeless in 1984 as it was in 1938 to characterize all
of the major contributions to the ongoing debate. Certain trends in interpretation have been remarkably persistent for a century, however, and very
recently some wholly new departures have been taken. A discussion of some
of the major trends will help to define the precise dimensions of the problems

---

[1]Schramm, "Das Versprechen Pippins und Karls des Großen für die römische Kirche (754
und 774)," in his *Kaiser, Könige und Päpste*, 1:149.

at hand, while simultaneously acknowledging the work of some very great historians and laying the foundations for a new understanding of the Franco-papal bond.

A Historiographical Orientation

Modern thought on the Franco-papal alliance reaches back over dozens of studies to a two-part article written by Wilhelm Sickel, although a few relatively minor points seem to have survived from earlier studies by Karl Lamprecht and Wilhelm Martens.[2] Not many of Sickel's specific arguments have stood up to the test of time, but his work did establish conclusively in the minds of most scholars the idea that in 754 a formal treaty was concluded between Pepin, as the Frankish head of state, and Stephen II, as the head of the Church and, simultaneously, a quasi head of state.[3] The institution of this treaty has been regarded since Sickel's time as a product of the specific political environment of the 750s.

Perhaps it was only natural that German historians writing during or just after the chancellorship of Otto von Bismarck would have taken a decidedly political view of the treaty, or alliance, of 754. To most of the scholars who examined the issue, only brutally straightforward power relationships and political realities governed the bargains that were struck. Moreover, there is implicit in much of the early literature an assumption that the diplomatic démarche of 754 had a winner and a loser. One party, usually

---

[2] W. Sickel, "Die Verträge der Päpste mit den Karolingern und das neue Kaisertum," *Deutsche Zeitschrift für Geschichtswissenschaft* 11 (1894): 301–51, 12 (1894–95): 1–43; Lamprecht, *Die römische Frage* (Leipzig, 1889); Martens, *Die römische Frage*; idem, *Neue Erörterung über die römische Frage unter Pippin und Karl dem Großen* (Stuttgart, 1882).

[3] It is curious that virtually all of the great work has been done by German historians, right down to the present. Louis Duchesne made many worthwhile observations in the copious notes to his edition of the *LP* and said a little more on some subjects in his *Temporal Sovereignty*. Léon Levillain ("L'avènement de la dynastie carolingienne") addressed the alliance only indirectly, concentrating instead on chronological problems and textual analysis. Likewise, Louis Saltet and Elie Griffe devoted their attention to a generally pointless and destructive textual criticism. Lot, Halphen, and Ganshof tended, for the most part, to follow Levillain on some issues and the Germans on others. Among Italian scholars only Bertolini has had much to say, and he seems to draw heavily upon the results of German scholarship. Ullmann, an Austrian whose career was spent in England, has made some worthwhile points, but most English and American historians have been content to repeat, often via the French, what the Germans have said.

Pepin, is thought to have imposed his will on the other. Too often, then, nineteenth-century diplomatic values and attitudes have been read into eighth-century events. Only very recently has it become possible to attack this nineteenth-century conceptualization at its very foundations, even though in the second decade of this century some writers began to evince qualms about a line of interpretation that depended exclusively on power politics.

The first comprehensive effort to explain the events of 754 on a different basis was published by Johannes Haller in 1912.[4] In his view there were two separate acts of commendation at Ponthion: Stephen commended himself to Pepin, while Pepin commended himself to St. Peter. In each instance a vassalic relationship in Frankish law served as a model for the reciprocal arrangements of the contracting parties. Haller, in short, moved the discussion from the realm of Realpolitik to that of feudal law. This represented a commendable effort to find an appropriate eighth-century idiom to characterize the Franco-papal bond, but in later years Haller's specific theses were undermined, largely because no genuine evidence for commendation can be adduced.[5] Even in very recent studies, however, there is still apparent a tendency to enter the lists against Haller, perhaps because of the high visibility earned for his views as a result of their having been incorporated into his widely read history of the papacy.

Beyond question, the single most influential study yet written has been that of Erich Caspar published in 1914.[6] Caspar drew to some extent on the work of Martens and Sickel, but his interpretation is essentially original and has had at least some impact on almost everyone who has written on the subject since the First World War.[7] He maintains that at Ponthion Pepin alone swore to defend the Roman Church, and that later in 754 Pepin and Stephen entered into a reciprocal bond of love and friendship.[8] There were,

---

[4]Haller, "Die Karolinger und das Papsttum," pp. 38–76; idem, *Das Papsttum* 1:420–21.

[5]The first blow was dealt by Caspar; see below. The second came from Eduard Eichmann, "Die römische Eide der deutschen Könige," *ZRG, kA* 37 (1916): 145–49. The whole commendation theory was challenged in 1918 by Albert Brackmann, "Pippin und die römische Kirche," now in his *Gesammelte Aufsätze* (reprint, Darmstadt, 1967), p. 400, and then destroyed by Karl Heldmann, "Kommendation und Königsschutz im Vertrag von Ponthion," *MIÖG* 38 (1920): 541–70. The coup de grâce to what remained of Haller's theories was dealt by Schramm, "Versprechen." To my knowledge only Mohr, *Studien*, p. 38ff, still holds to Haller's interpretation.

[6]Caspar, *Pippin und die römische Kirche.*

[7]Eichmann, "Die römische Eide," pp. 144ff, 150ff; Brackmann, "Pippin," p. 498ff; Rassow, "Pippin," p. 494ff; Ullmann, *Papal Government*, p. 55ff; Fritze, *Papst und Frankenkönig*, pp. 92ff, 95ff.

[8]Martens, *Die römische Frage*, p. 26, had also noticed this "*Liebesbund*" but supposed it to be purely ethical and of no political import.

thus, two separate arrangements entered into in 754. Both were rooted in early medieval Germanic law. Caspar thus follows Haller's lead in trying to find eighth-century, rather than nineteenth-century, terms to describe the alliance of 754. Likewise, Caspar accentuates Haller's detection of genuinely mutual, reciprocal relationships in the alliance.

Schramm, in what has become a profoundly influential study, entertains Caspar's ideas at great length, but eventually rejects them in favor of a theory that reaches back over Albert Hauck to Wilhelm Gundlach.[9] He argues that at Ponthion Pepin swore to defend the Roman Church, and that the sources do not permit any firm determinations to be made about a second set of legally binding arrangements concluded in 754. Thus, half of Caspar's thesis is upheld by Schramm and, albeit with some reservations, half is rejected. Since the appearance of Schramm's article scholars have been about equally divided in arguing for one or two diplomatic arrangements in 754.

In the last ten years the nature of the debate has shifted somewhat. Wolfgang Fritze has investigated the bond of love and friendship in an effort to prove that it was, to use his term, a *Schwurfreundschaft*.[10] This "oath friendship," characterized in the sources as a bond of *amicitia, pax et caritas*, bound the popes and the Franks tightly, honorably, and reciprocally from 754 to 817. Although, as Fritze is aware, *amicitia* had been a formal, regular feature of Roman public life, he argues that the *Schwurfreundschaft* was a confection of the Merovingian period, and that its first truly significant application was at Ponthion in 754.[11] Fritze's arguments raise some serious questions. Was there actually such a thing as a *Schwurfreundschaft*? If it existed, was it used in 754, and does it adequately explain the Franco-papal bond?[12] One may have doubts about these issues, but Fritze's reading of the evidence is absolutely persuasive on one count, at least. The *Liebesbund*, already noted by Martens, was somehow a significant feature of the alliance of 754. Caspar nods at the *Liebesbund* but does not emphasize it sufficiently, and Schramm is certainly wrong to dismiss it so thoroughly. In other words, Fritze makes two positive contributions. First, he demonstrates that

---

[9]"Das Versprechen," pp. 150ff, 170–75; Hauck, *Kirchengeschichte Deutschlands* 2:20ff; Gundlach, *Kirchenstaat*, p. 36ff. He also thought (75–78) that Stephen commended himself in some vague, general way.

[10]Fritze, *Papst und Frankenkönig*, passim.

[11]Fritze, "Die fränkische Schwurfreundschaft der Merowingerzeit," *ZRG, gA* 71 (1954): 74–125.

[12]Fritze showed his work to Schramm in typescript and the latter wrote a detailed critique: "Das Versprechen," pp. 176–79; see also Morrison's review of Fritze, *Speculum* 50 (1975): 722–23: The book "has the character of a preliminary sketch, rather than that of a comprehensive analysis."

the bond of *amicitia, pax et caritas* was a central feature of the Franco-papal alliance. This remains true whether or not one accepts his judgments about what this *amicitia* bond actually was (i.e., a *Schwurfreundschaft*). Second, Fritze forces the debate onto a broader chronological plane. No longer will it be possible to look for interpretations drawn exclusively from, or only relevant to, the period from 754 to 774. With a wider chronological focus it has become possible, in fact necessary, to relate the Franco-papal alliance to a range of problems both greater than and different from the immediate difficulties of Pepin and Stephen II in the early 750s.

Shortly after the appearance of Fritze's book, Anna Drabek published an examination of papal-German treaties from the eighth to the eleventh century.[13] She, like Fritze, lays great emphasis on what she calls an *amicitia-Bündnis* but, unlike Fritze, she dismisses Caspar's bipartite explanation of the events of 754. Pepin's oath to defend the Roman Church was part, and at that only one part, of the *amicitia-Bündnis*. There were not two separate engagements in 754, or at any later time. The Franco-papal treaty did, according to Drabek, have two dimensions, but not in the way assumed by Caspar and his followers, including Fritze. First, there was a "friendship-alliance," and second there was a *pactum*. The latter was a written document containing the mutual and specific agreements reciprocally concluded. Over time the *amicitia-Bündnis* did not change, but the *pactum* could, and did. This gave to the Franco-papal alliance the essential flexibility that all successful diplomatic arrangements require.

The duality introduced by Haller and Caspar has finally been removed. There was only one comprehensive agreement entered into by Pepin and Stephen in 754, and between their respective successors in later years. To a limited extent, then, Sickel's view that there was only one, complex political alliance has been vindicated. Still, Drabek's work is flawed in a way because, like Sickel's, it provides an almost purely political interpretation of the essential features of the alliance. She writes about *Verträge* (treaties) and about "*zwischenstaatliche Beziehungen*" (interstate relations). Her orientation is almost exclusively political and institutional. Moreover, it is not at all clear that every renewal of the Franco-papal alliance produced a *pactum* in Drabek's sense of the term. Certainly there were *pacta* in 754, 755, 756, 774, 781, 787, 816, and 817. But there is no conclusive evidence for *pacta* in 757, 767, 768, 772, or 795, and the *pacta* of 755, 756, 781, and 787 were not directly connected with a renewal of the alliance. As we shall see, the alliance was frequently confirmed in writing by means of envoys. Still, it is a

---

[13]*Die Verträge der fränkischen und deutschen Herrscher mit dem Papsttum von 754 bis 1020,* (Vienna, 1976), p. 15–47.

bit risky to assume that "*pactum*" adequately characterizes each confirmation document. There is no reason to suppose, for example, that in 757 there was a *pactum* similar to the Quierzy document or to the Pavian treaty instruments. In short, Drabek's conceptualization of the alliance is valuable in broad outlines but a little weak in details.

Very recently some of the shortcomings of Drabek's work have been in part remedied by Arnold Angenendt.[14] He correctly sees the profoundly religious aspects of the Franco-papal alliance. In fairness, Angenendt was not the first to detect the religious features of the alliance, but his predecessors, especially Eduard Eichmann, have not always received the attention their work deserves.

Actually, Angenendt's study takes as its point of departure the *Liebesbund* of Martens and Caspar while pointing out, correctly, that these scholars, in their determined quest for political explanations, failed to see the religious significance of the documents upon which they were basing purely secular interpretations. Angenendt also comments on the work of Eichmann, who long ago commented on the adoption of the Franks by St. Peter, or by his vicar, the pope.[15] This was obviously a deeply religious type of spiritual kinship, and in various forms it existed throughout much of the Middle Ages. In short, the natural but erroneous tendency to view Franco-papal relations from an essentially, sometimes wholly, political point of view obscures the hints and clues, long lurking in the literature, that mark the path to a correct understanding of the engagements of 754 and their aftermath. Although there are certain shortcomings in the work of both Angenendt and Drabek, their important studies constitute a firm foundation upon which it has been possible to erect a new and less deliberately exclusive interpretation of Franco-papal relations. This interpretation must seek to grapple with the alliance as a unity, rather than as two or more independent parts, and it must accord a prominent place to religious elements alongside purely political ones. Likewise, this interpretation will have to account for repeated confirmations of the alliance until at least the 820s. This means that the obviously political features of the alliance must be explained in such a way as to accommodate a constantly fluctuating set of circumstances during three-quarters of a century.

---

[14]Angenendt, "Das geistliche Bündnis der Päpste mit den Karolingern (754–796)," *HJB* 100 (1980): 1–94.

[15]Eichmann, "Die Adoption des deutschen Könige durch den Papst" *ZRG, gA*, 37 (1916): 291–312; Zwölfer, *Sankt Peter*, pp. 136–43, also noticed this and Morrison, in his review (see n.12 above), criticized Fritze for omitting it.

The *Amicitia* Alliance

My aim in what follows is to prove that the Franco-papal alliance was one multifaceted set of agreements that was mutual, reciprocal, and equally binding upon both parties. In the process of demonstrating this I will discuss the exact obligations and duties incurred by both the popes and the Franks. Furthermore, I will demonstrate that the agreements reached in 754 persisted through at least 824 when Eugenius II ascended the papal throne and Louis the Pious was reigning in Francia.

Most efforts to comprehend what happened in 754 have been frustrated by the fact that, apart from a few lines in some Frankish sources, virtually all of the evidence emanates from Rome and, quite understandably, portrays things from the point of view of the papacy. This problem, coupled with the bewildering array of terms and phrases deployed by the sources to describe or refer to the events of 754, has produced most of the controversy discussed above. To gain a proper understanding of the Franco-papal alliance, it is necessary to avoid damaging and prejudicial preconceptions about what happened, or about what ought to have happened, and to sort out the evidence so that only those documents that are genuinely relevant are brought to bear on the issue.

The *Liber Pontificalis* reports that Pepin and Stephen met at Ponthion, that they concluded "treaties of peace," and that Pepin swore an oath to secure the rights of St. Peter.[16] It is upon this critical passage that Haller, Caspar, and all the others have built their theory that there were two separate arrangements in 754. In reality, there was only one alliance, or one *"pacis foedera,"* but the evidence that proves this must be sought in later years, because taken by itself, the evidence from the year 754 will not permit, let alone support, any valid conclusions applicable to later years, or even applicable to the circumstances surrounding Stephen's visit to Francia.

Paul I and Stephen III sought to confirm the alliance, and so did the usurper Constantine. There will be occasion to return to these confirmations below, but more important at present is the confirmation between Hadrian and Charlemagne in 774. On the day before Easter the pope and the king entered St. Peter's and "bound themselves mutually by oath."[17] Nothing in

---

[16]*LP* 1:447–48: "beatissimus papa praelatum christianissimum regem lacramabiliter deprecatus est ut per pacis foedera causam beati Petri et reipublicae Romanorum disponeret. Qui de praesenti iureiurando eundem beatissimum papam satisfecit." The principal Frankish accounts use different words but say much the same thing: *Annales regni Francorum, anno* 753, ed. Kurze, p. 10; *Annales mettenses priores, anno* 753, ed. Simson, pp. 44–45.

[17]*LP* 1:497: "seseque mutuo per sacramentum munientes."

the evidence suggests that anything unique or original was done in 774, so here the *Liber Pontificalis*, an official papal record, provides the first certain testimony that mutual oaths were sworn. We have already seen that in 774 Charlemagne willingly confirmed his father's territorial promises, and therefore it may be that he also swore an oath exactly like Pepin's.

There is evidence to which, again, we shall return that Charlemagne and Leo III confirmed the alliance in 796, but the next piece of really pertinent corroboration comes from the *Pactum Ludovicianum*. In chapter 5 we saw that the surviving version of this document dates from the early days of the pontificate of Paschal I, but that the extant copy is only a repetition of the pact concluded between Louis and Stephen IV in 816. Thus, one document provides evidence for two confirmations. Here is what the *Ludovicianum* says: "When he [i.e., the pope] has been consecrated, legates shall be sent to us or to our successors, kings of the Franks, who between us and them will ally in a bond of love and devotion and peace just as it was customary to do in the time of our grandfather [i.e., Pepin] and of our father, the lord emperor, Charles."[18] We see here quite clearly the mutuality of the alliance, but we also find in this document, for the first time, some clear testimony about the form of the bond. The words *amicitia, pax et caritas* are crucial. Louis's pact also proves that the alliance had been in force for three generations. With just these few facts in mind we can now return to 754 and begin reconstructing the Franco-papal alliance.

Historians who believe that there were two arrangements in 754, an *amicitia-Bündnis* and an oath by Pepin to defend the Church, have devoted most of their energy to an attempt to reconstruct only one of these elements, namely, Pepin's defense oath.[19] Many believe that the *amicitia* alliance was

---

[18] *MGH, Cap.*, vol. 1, no. 172, pp. 354–55. That this passage relates to the year 754 is the cornerstone of Fritze's argument: *Papst und Frankenkönig*, p. 15ff; see also Hahn, "Ludovicianum," pp. 112–15, who accepts the connection with 754 but basically rejects Fritze's interpretation.

[19] In 878 at the Synod of Troyes Pope John VIII (Mansi, *Concilia* 17:347) caused to be read the oaths sworn by Pepin and Charlemagne in order to establish Charles the Bald's obligation to defend the Church. Caspar, *Pippin*, pp. 18–19, assumed that this was exactly Pepin's "*Schutzeid*" of Ponthion and said that CC, no. 7, p. 491 ("vos beato Petro polliciti estis eius iustitiam exigere et defensionem sanctae Dei ecclesiae procurare") contains the closest surviving witness to the actual words of the oath. Schramm, "Versprechen," p. 153ff, believes that an oath found in a tenth-century coronation *Ordo* is actually Pepin's oath, but Drabek, *Verträge*, pp. 91–92, argues persuasively that Schramm's oath cannot be dated securely before the time of Pope John VIII (872–82). Eichmann, "Die römische Eide," p. 150ff, also believed the oath from the *Ordo* was Pepin's oath and he traced the history of this oath all the way to the twelfth century. I believe that Caspar was closer to the truth, even though I do not believe that there were two distinct oaths in 754.

formless, and that it cannot be reconstructed, while Fritze characterizes it as a *Schwurfreundschaft*, and Drabek essentially agrees with him. Decades of controversy can be overcome if an attempt is made to demonstrate that there was only one mutual *amicitia* alliance, of which Pepin's oath to defend the Republic was only a single constituent element. Hadrian swore an oath, as did Stephen IV and Paschal I, so it is quite reasonable to suggest that Stephen II did too. Fortunately, it is possible to resurrect his oath, at least in part, and also to recover Pepin's oath.

Eichmann correctly notes that a letter of Stephen III preserves, roughly at least, the language of the *amicitia* oath of 754: "For you promised to blessed Peter and to his vicar and to his successors that you would be a friend to his friends and an enemy to his enemies; indeed, we are known to remain steadfastly faithful in that same promise."[20] Several years earlier Paul I had used much the same language,[21] and in 783 Hadrian did again.[22] The Franks and the popes, thus, had sworn to be friends to one another's friends and enemies to one another's enemies. This language is not a literary or rhetorical flourish. *Amicitia*, expressed in the formula "*amicus amicis* . . . ," was a technical term in diplomatic terminology, and its use signifies a bond of formal alliance. These words were the result of a "deliberate choice."[23] With this "*amicus amicis*" formula we are very close to the "*amicitia, pax et caritas*" of the *Ludovicianum*, and to the "*pacis foedera*" of the *Liber Pontificalis*.

The *Codex Carolinus* and other papal letters contain numerous additional examples of this complex of ideas. The following list, which is not exhaustive, exemplifies well some of the many combinations of terms that were employed and, we may presume, perfectly understood in Franco-papal correspondence.

---

[20]Eichmann, "Die römische Eide," pp. 154–56. See also: Liutpold Wallach, "Amicus amicis, inimicus inimicis," *ZKG* 52 (1933): 614–15. Even Haller ("Karolinger," p. 70) and Caspar (*Pippin*, p. 32ff) thought that this was the oath of the *amicitia* alliance. For the letter: CC, no. 45, p. 562: "vos beato Petro et vicario eius vel eius successoribus spopondisse, se amicis nostris amicos esse et se inimicis inimicos; sicut et nos in eadem sponsione firmiter dinoscimur permanere."

[21]CC, no. 29, p. 534: "Quapropter—testatur veritas, quia—ubi vestros amicos agnoverimus, tamquam amicos et fideles sanctae Dei ecclesiae oblectare et amplectare cupimus, et, ubi vestros inimicos invenerimus, veraciter tamquam inimicos sanctae Dei ecclesiae et nostros proprios ita eos respuimus atque persequimur, quia vestri amici sanctae Dei ecclesiae et nostri existunt et hi, qui inimicitias contra vos machinantur, profecto inimici sanctae Dei ecclesiae et nostri esse conprobantur."

[22]CC, no. 75, p. 606: "qui prumpti fideles eiusdem Dei apostoli sunt, et vestri felicissimi regni fideles sunt, pariter et, qui eius inimici esse videntur, vestri procul dubio inimici sunt."

[23]Bertolini, *Roma e i longobardi*, p. 20.

1. in ea fide et dilectione et caritatis concordia atque pacis foedera, quae prelatus beatissime memoriae dominus et germanus meus, sacratissimus pontifex, vobiscum confirmavit, permanentes[24]

2. in vinculo spiritalis foederis pariter sumus adnexi[25]

3. in ea ipsa caritate et dilectione atque promissione vos firmiter esse permansurum[26]

4. et nos firmiter in vestra caritate et dilectione cunctus diebus vitae nostrae erimus permansuri, et nullus nos poterit per quamlibet temporum interruptionem a vestro amore et caritate atque dilectione separare[27]

5. firmi atque immobiles in vestra caritate ac dilectione . . . permanentes[28]

6. in ea caritate atque amicitia permanere[29]

7. in nostra fixi caritatis connectione[30]

8. firmi in vestrae caritatis dilectione permanemus[31]

9. persistentes etiam una nobiscum et in osculo caritatis[32]

10. in ea promissione amoris, [quam cum] vestro pio genitore, sanctae recordationis domino Pippino[33]

11. firmi et stabiles in vestra permanemus caritate[34]

12. una dilectio, una caritas . . . inter nos[35]

13. in vestro amore et dilectionis caritate[36]

14. magna inter nos atque insolubilis caritatis concordia . . . quae mutuo inter nos asserentes confirmavimus[37]

15. in vinculo caritatis atque dilectione[38]

16. in ea fide et dilectione simulque et promissione te confidimus permanere, in qua et nos firmi et stabiles, quod faciae ad faciaem polliciti sumus[39]

17. fidem atque dilectionem[40]

----

[24]CC, no. 12, p. 508.
[25]CC, no. 14, p. 511.
[26]CC, no. 21, p. 523.
[27]CC, no. 21, p. 523.
[28]CC, no. 22, p. 526.
[29]CC, no. 24, p. 528.
[30]CC, no. 34, p. 541.
[31]CC, no. 34, p. 541.
[32]CC, no. 37, p. 547.
[33]CC, no. 44, p. 559.
[34]CC, no. 51, p. 571.
[35]CC, no. 53, p. 575.
[36]CC, no. 55, p. 579.
[37]CC, no. 56, p. 581.
[38]CC, no. 59, p. 585.
[39]CC, no. 62, p. 590.
[40]CC, no. 73, p. 604.

18. fidem . . . ex intimo corde dilectionis amore[41]
19. amore nostraque paterna dilectione[42]
20. amor, caritas, dilectio, fides[43]
21. in ea caritate ac dilectione, qua cum nostris predecessoribus, domno Stephano ac Paulo, permansistis, nobiscum permanere iubeatis et in eadem amicitiae connexione cum mea fragilitate persistere[44]
22. de nostra fidelitate, quam erga vestram regalem potentiam gerimus[45]
23. amore et dilectione fideliter[46]
24. ut pax et concordia inter nos firma et stabilis Deo mediante constituatur[47]
25. Pro tanto amore tantaque dilectione atque fide, quam erga vestram serenitatem gerimus[48]
26. cum multo amore multaque fide erga vos[49]

With the evidence thus displayed, certain aspects of the Franco-papal alliance become abundantly clear. First, the alliance was genuinely mutual, not one sided (nos. 1, 2, 4, 7, 9, 10, 12, 14, 15, 16, 21, 24). Second, it was formal and binding, not some sort of purely ethical *Liebesbund*. Only twice does *foedera* appear, but its analogues *vinculum*, *connexio*, and *concordia* are ubiquitous (nos. 2, 7, 14, 15, 21, 24). *Amicitia* appears in almost every example, but it too has analogues in *caritas* and *dilectio* which are just as frequent. This constant repetition of *amicitia*, or its synonyms, stands at the heart of the alliance and effects an unbreakable connection with the *amicus amicis* formula. *Amicitia* had deep roots in both Roman and Germanic law, and it involved positive, objective obligations on the part of the contracting parties. They met as equals, pledged support for one another, and rejected coming to the assistance of one another's enemies.[50] The word *pax* must be understood in a similar way. The Carolingians and the popes had never been engaged in overt hostilities, so there was no need for them to conclude a peace treaty to put an end to difficulties. In fact, in the Carolingian period,

---

[41]*CC*, no. 83, p. 618.
[42]*CC*, no. 87, p. 623.
[43]*CC*, no. 94, p. 635.
[44]*CC*, no. 99, p. 652.
[45]*CC*, no. 99, p. 652.
[46]Hadrian I, *ep.* no. 2, *Epistolae Selectae Pontificum Romanorum*, MGH, EKA 3:6.
[47]Leo III, *ep.* no. 1, MGH, EKA 3:88.
[48]Leo III, *ep.* no. 2, MGH, EKA 3:91.
[49]Leo III, *ep.* no. 10, MGH, EKA 3:103.
[50]Drabek, *Verträge*, pp. 17–18; Fritze, "Schwurfreundschaft," pp. 77–87, 87ff, 121ff; idem, *Papst und Frankenkönig*, p. 20 and passim; Angenendt, "Das geistliche Bündnis," pp. 37–38.

at least to advanced thinkers, *pax* did not imply, negatively, a cessation of hostilities or the absence of war. Rather, its connotation was positive. It meant roughly the same thing as the *amicus amicis* formula, that is, good relations grounded in a convergence of interests and in a shared appreciation of Christian love.[51] The word *fides* (and its relative *fidelitas* could be tracked also) appears nine times in the examples quoted above (nos. 1, 16, 17, 18, 20, 22, 23, 25, 26). Its use in these contexts does not imply subjection, vassalage, or any kind of subordination of one party to the other. Instead, it means loyalty, or fidelity (*Treue*), and is exactly complementary to *amicitia* and *pax*, and to the *amicus amicis* formula. It meant that the Franks and the popes would be loyal to one another in all situations, and against all their mutual or individual enemies.[52] Finally, *caritas* was in two respects the cement that held the "friendship" and "loyalty" elements of the alliance together. First, it connoted a bond of Christian love wherein two people met as equals and pledged themselves to one another. Second, because Christian charity could mean either a giving of oneself or a giving of one's material possessions or personal services, *caritas* provided a formula under which the popes and the Franks could do concrete things for one another.

The Franco-papal alliance was therefore a mutual, binding agreement sealed by reciprocal oaths. For the sake of convenience it may be called a "friendship alliance," but it is crucial to see that it had public, legal force. It was not merely an ethical *Liebesbund* as Martens suggests.[53] The alliance was also deeply religious. Of course, it cannot be denied that the *amicus-amicis* formula was secular and political, and that it had antecedents in both Roman and Germanic law and custom. This formula provided a flexible arrangement to permit the Franks or the popes to come to one another's aid. In the 750s, any invocation of this formula was likely to bring the Franks

---

[51] See Roger Bonnaud-Delamare, *L'idée de paix à l'époque carolingienne* (Paris, 1939). Among other things, he notes that this positive conception of peace has patristic roots.

[52] Drabek, *Verträge*, p. 19ff, with further literature. Caspar, *Pippin*, p. 8, had already noted that the bond did not imply subordination. See also: Gundlach, *Kirchenstaat*, pp. 75–78.

[53] Martens, *Die römische Frage*, p. 26. Sickel, "Verträge," pp. 336–38, already saw the mutual, binding nature of the alliance and (p. 338) its possible connection with the "*amicus-amicis*" formula, but he did not develop this idea. When Haller and Caspar came to this question they blazed different trails. Fritze was correct to stress, against his predecessors, that the "*Liebesbund*" was formal and legal, and that its terms could be worked out. His insistence on calling the alliance a Frankish "*Schwurfreundschaft*," however, forced his work into too narrow a mold. Schramm, "Versprechen," pp. 176–79, correctly saw that the concept of "*Schwurfreundschaft*" did not fit all of the evidence, but he incorrectly insisted that the "friendship-alliance" was an informal by-product of Pepin's oath to defend the Church. Drabek, *Verträge*, pp. 15–47, does better when she asserts the public, binding nature of the "*amicitia-Bündnis*" while avoiding the "*Schwurfreundschaft*" model.

into Italy to combat St. Peter's enemies, but other and different possibilities also were taken into account—as we shall see in a moment—by these terms. *Pax* and *caritas*, however, describe personal and religious bonds which transcended purely political realities. They signify the creation between Stephen and Pepin of a bond whose ultimate sanction rested upon divine guarantees, and not upon the frail and fickle motivations of human conduct. It would be no exaggeration to say that the whole alliance was constructed in such as way that any breach of its provisions would have been not only an international provocation but also a sin. The importance of this spiritual sanction becomes quite clear when it is remembered that one of the two contracting parties was St. Peter—on whose behalf the pope acted—and that this saint was the "keeper of the keys." Papal correspondence rarely neglected to emphasize this attribute of St. Peter to the Carolingians.

But there were also several other very old traditions that met at Ponthion, and that contributed to what later papal correspondence regularly called the "spiritual bond" between the popes and the Franks. There was, first, a tradition at least as old as Ambrose that princes were the sons of the Church,[54] and papal letters often reminded the Carolingians of their obligations to their "Holy Mother," the Church.[55] In the second place, when Gregory III wrote to Charles Martel in 739 he called him a "beloved son of St. Peter."[56] The popes continually reminded the Carolingians of their duties to St. Peter, who stands in an eponymous sense for the Church itself.[57] Third, fictive kinships of various kinds played a prominent role in the diplomatic life of the early Middle Ages. It will be recalled that Charles Martel had established such a bond between his son Pepin and the Lombard king, Liutprand. Many other instances of this sort are known, and they illustrate one means whereby early medieval rulers cemented alliances.[58] Finally, in papal letters, beginning shortly after Stephen's sojourn in Francia, the popes regularly referred to the Carolingians as "spiritual co-fathers."[59] All of these interrelated phenomena have been the subject of the recent and penetrating analysis by Angenendt alluded to above.[60]

---

[54]Eichmann, "Die Adoption," pp. 291–92.

[55]This recurs constantly. CC, no. 89, p. 626 is a very good example.

[56]CC, no. 1, p. 476.

[57]This is so frequent that it suffices to call attention to CC, nos. 1, 2, 5, 6, 7, 8, 10, 14, 17, 19, 21, 22, 24, 25, 26, 29, 32, 33, 34, 35, 36, 37, 43, 44, 45, 51, 52, 53, 54, 55, 58, 60, 64, 68, 69, 94, 98, 99. These are not the only examples; just typical ones.

[58]Angenendt, "Das geistliche Bündnis," pp. 1–9. He draws heavily upon the work of Franz Dölger, "Die Familie der Könige," *HJB* 60 (1940): 397–420.

[59]CC, nos. 6, 7, 8, 11, pp. 489, 494–97 passim, 504–6 passim.

[60]Angenendt, "Das geistliche Bündnis," pp. 1–43.

In Angenendt's reconstruction, the Franco-papal alliance rested upon a quasi-sacramental bond of "compaternity." When Stephen II anointed Pepin's sons as kings of the Franks, he and Pepin became, in a spiritual sense, "co-fathers" (*compatres*, hence "compaternity") of Charlemagne and Carlomann. The role of Stephen and Pepin vis-à-vis the newly anointed kings was analogous to the role played by godparents in baptism or by sponsors in confirmation. Between the *baptizandus* or *confirmandus* and his godparent or sponsor there was created a deep and lasting spiritual kinship. In fact, this kinship, fictive though it was, was so strong that it served as an impediment to matrimony. In 754 Stephen and Pepin drew royal anointing into the realm of sacramental relationships. St. Peter and his vicar became "father" to Pepin's sons and at the same time *"spiritalis compater"* with Pepin himself. Later papal correspondence referred constantly to this spiritual kinship between St. Peter, the popes, and the Carolingians.[61]

The Carolingians were no less conscious than the popes of the spiritual kinship that had been created. In a dedicatory poem accompanying the "Godescalc Evangeliary," sent by Charlemagne to Hadrian, the king called the pope his *"compater."*[62] Also, Charlemagne called Leo III his spiritual father in 796.[63] Both Pepin and Charlemagne expressed in their official titles their gratitude to God, which meant to St. Peter and the pope, for their office.[64] In 781 Charlemagne had two of his sons anointed kings by Hadrian,

---

[61]*CC*, no. 6, p. 489: "per beatum Petrum principem apostolorum, qui vos in reges unxit"; *CC*, no. 10, pp. 501ff is a letter written by the pope as though he were St. Peter; *CC*, nos. 17, 19, pp. 515, 519–20: Pepin made promises to St. Peter to win salvation.

[62]Angenendt, "Das geistliche Bündnis," pp. 77–78 and n.350.

[63]*Apud Alcuini Epistolae*, no. 93, *MGH, EKA* 2:136–38.

[64]*DK*, vol. 1, no. 24, p. 33 (July 768): "Pippinus gratia Dei rex Francorum vir inluster"; no. 55, p. 81 (January 769): "Carolus gratia Dei rex Francorum vir inluster." See also no. 16, p. 22 (August, 762): "Et quia nobis providentia in solium regni unxisse manifestum est" or "Et quia reges ex Deo regnant nobisque gentes et regna pro sua misericordia ad gubernandum commisit." Scholars have always and properly emphasized the religious foundations and dimensions of Carolingian rule. See, recently, Hauck, "Die Ausbreitung des Glaubens," passim, and older studies by Werner Ohnsorge, "Orthodoxus Imperator: Vom religiösen Motiv für das Kaisertum Karls des Großen," in his *Abendland und Byzanz* (Darmstadt, 1956), pp. 64–78, and Mohr, *Die karolingische Reichsidee* (Munster, 1962), pp. 6–38. These studies take widely diverging perspectives but make valuable complementary points. This is not the place to attempt a summary of the literature on Carolingian political theory and theology. Even though she fails to cite many important studies Marta Cristiani surveys the major trends in interpretation quite clearly in *Dall'unanimitas all'universitas da Alcuino a Giovanni Eriugena: Lineamenti ideologici e terminologia politica della cultura del secolo IX* (Rome, 1978), pp. 7–79. I take strong exception to her effort to explain the Christianization of political thought as a consequence of usurpation.

and Louis was baptized by the pope, which created a new and special bond
of kinship, or compaternity, among Hadrian, Charlemagne, and Louis.[65]

Therefore, the mutual obligations of pope and king incurred under the
"friendship alliance" were in reality guaranteed by both the profound spiritual kinship created in 754 between Pepin and Stephen and the bonds of
Christian peace and love attendant upon the *amicitia-Bündnis*. Pepin did
swear to protect St. Peter and to secure his rights, but this was not an
independent, unilateral act on his part. He willingly assumed a duty to come
to the aid of his special patron and protector, his spiritual cofather, which
meant that, as St. Peter's friend, he had to oppose steadfastly the pope's
enemies. The friendship alliance, a multifaceted agreement to be sure, was
as spiritual as it was political because it was grounded in fundamentally
religious concepts. The truth of this contention can be seen most clearly in
an analysis of the obligations incurred by both the papacy and the Carolingians under the terms of their alliance.

The Terms of the Alliance

Probably the clearest statement of the terms of the Franco-papal alliance is
to be found in one of the most famous letters of the Middle Ages, namely,

---

[65]Angenendt, "Das geistliche Bündnis," p. 72ff (with sources). I admire Angenendt's study
and assign it a prominent place in the literature on Franco-papal relations, but I disagree with
some of the fundamental premises upon which it rests. He believes, for example, that Pepin's
relationship with Stephen and Paul "was wholly characterized by the alliance of compaternity"
(p. 63). This is inaccurate in two respects. First, the alliance was not merely one of *compater-
nitas*. Rather, compaternity was one element of the alliance. Second, the compaternal bond was
generally connected with the adoption of the Carolingians by the popes (cf. CC, no. 10, p. 501:
"apostolus Dei Petrus, qui vos adoptivos habeo filios, ad defendendam, de manibus adversa-
riorum hanc Romanam civitatem et populum mihi a Deo commissum") and specifically connected with sacramental compaternity only in 781. True, Pepin sent Paul I his daughter Gisela's
baptismal robe (pp. 57–59) and Stephen III sought to effect a direct compaternal bond with
the sons of Carlomann (pp. 64–65). Stephen II did not, however, baptize Pepin's sons and there
is no good evidence that he confirmed them, as some scholars have supposed: Oelsner, *Jahrbücher*, p. 160 n.8; Caspar, *Pippin*, p. 39; Brackmann, "Pippin," p. 402. Paul participated in
no sacramental union and neither did Constantine who still called the Carolingians his "*spiri-
tales filios.*" Perhaps Constantine was merely adhering to chancery practices but, even so, those
practices are nonetheless revealing. Neither Leo III nor any of his successors baptized or confirmed a Carolingian prince. Thus, Angenendt correctly perceived the bond of compaternity
(against Drabek, for example, who focused exclusively on the "*amicitia-Bündnis*") but he goes
too far beyond Eichmann who, without the richness of detail and insight that are the hallmarks

the one sent by Charlemagne through Abbot Angilbert of St. Riquier to Leo III in 796. The most critical passage of this letter reads as follows:

For just as I entered upon a pact of holy fatherhood with our most blessed father your predecessor, so with your blessedness I desire to establish an inviolable treaty of the same trust and affection, to the end that by the divine favor of your apostolic holiness invoked in prayer the apostolic blessing may follow me wherever I go, and that the Holy See of the Church of Rome may with God's grace be defended always by our devotion. It is for us, in accordance with the help of divine goodness, outwardly to defend by force of arms the Holy Church of Christ in all places from the incursions of pagans and the ravages of infidels, and inwardly to fortify her with our confession of the Catholic faith. It is for you, most holy father, raising your hands to God with Moses, to aid our armies, and to that end with you as intercessors and with God as guide and giver our Christian people may in all places have the victory over the enemies of its holy name, and the name of our Lord Jesus Christ may be renowned throughout all the world.[66]

It was Charlemagne's responsibility to defend Rome and the Catholic faith, and Leo's duty to support the king's efforts by his prayers. They were to stand in devotion and faith to one another in a bond of loving fatherhood and sonship. Here, in a letter from the Frankish court, and not from the Lateran, we have all the terms and concepts with which we have been dealing. We also see that each party had specific obligations.

Between 754 and 774 the popes constantly reminded the Carolingians of their obligations to defend the Republic.[67] After 774 Hadrian incessantly recalled to Charlemagne that he was the Republic's "liberator," "defender," "security," and "strong right arm."[68] Obviously, until Aistulf and Desiderius had been defeated, the Lombards represented the chief threat, and it was

---

of Angenendt's study, kept his vision fixed on the papal adoption of the Carolingians. In a sense, Angenendt's earlier article ("Taufe und Politik") had things in proper perspective and in his later study he seems to have gotten carried away with what is both a valuable idea and a crucial insight. My differences with Angenendt, then, turn on matters of perspective.

[66]*Apud Alcuini Epistolae,* no. 93, *MGH, EKA* 2:136–38. I cite the translation of H. R. Loyn and J. Percival, *The Reign of Charlemagne* (London, 1975), pp. 118–19.

[67]In the appropriate letters the Carolingians are reminded of their duty to defend Rome, the Roman Church, the Republic, St. Peter, St. Peter's "peculiar people," and the pope. They are called upon to secure Peter's rights (*"iustitiae"*): CC, nos. 5, 6, 7, 8, 9, 10, 11, 12, 13, 14, 16, 17, 18, 20, 21, 22, 24, 25, 27, 29, 32, 33, 34, 35, 36, 37, 38, 39, 42, 45, 47. Bertolini, "Problema del'origini," pp. 529–32, demonstrates the extent to which all of these expressions are synonymous.

[68]CC, nos. 51, 52, 54, 56, 57, 59, 84, 86, 89. 92.

defense against them, the pope's enemies, that the Franks, the pope's friends, had to provide. Later, Byzantines and Beneventans posed threats, both real and imagined, and the Carolingians were expected to protect the Republic from them also. In 806 Charlemagne, sensing the approach of death, divided his vast realm among his sons and enjoined them to protect the Church of Rome.[69] Leo III regarded Charlemagne, above all, as his defender.[70] Louis the Pious publicly stipulated his duty to defend in the *Ludovicianum*, and Paschal I later reminded him of his obligation.[71] The first key obligation incurred by the Carolingians was to defend the Republic.

Charlemagne's letter to Leo also says that he had to defend the faith. This the Carolingians did with a single-minded resolve. In 767 the Franks anathematized the Greeks for their stand on the *"filioque"* issue, and right through the entire period covered by this book, the Carolingians rejected and combatted Byzantine iconoclasm although, it is true, they sometimes did so more vigorously than the even popes themselves might have liked. Charlemagne and his court theologians rooted out and destroyed the Adoptionist heresy that arose in Spain and passed into Francia through the Spanish March. Pagan Saxons were beaten and forced to convert, and the Khan of the Avars received baptism at Charlemagne's capital, Aachen. The Republic itself, and the faith professed and propagated by it, were always and everywhere defended, just as Charlemagne promised they would be.

Turning to the pope's obligations, we find a slightly more complicated situation than Charlemagne's letter to Leo seems to depict. The popes did indeed support the Carolingians with their prayers. From Pepin's time through Charlemagne's, the *Codex Carolinus* provides constant evidence for this intercessory support.[72] Hadrian even inserted intercessions for Charlemagne into the regular Saturday prayers in the Roman liturgy,[73] just as Pepin had already been included in the liturgies of the hours said by monks in the Roman basilicas.[74] Leo III prayed for Charlemagne,[75] and Louis the Pious expected Stephen IV, and doubtless Stephen's successors, to pray for him.[76]

---

[69]*MGH, Cap.*, vol. 1, no. 45, c. 15, p. 129.

[70]Leo III, *epp.* nos. 1, 2, 6, 9, *MGH, EKA* 3:88, 89, 96–97, 100.

[71]*MGH, Cap.*, vol. 1, no. 172, p. 354; Paschal I, *Epp. Sel. Pont. Rom.*, no. 10, *MGH, EKA* 3:68.

[72]*CC*, nos. 50, 51, 52, 53, 60, 61, 62, 67, 72, 73, 74, 76, 79, 82, 83, 85, 87, 89, 92, 93, 94. Angenendt, "Das geistliche Bündnis," pp. 74–75.

[73]*Ordo* 22, c. 13, *Ordines Romani*, ed. Andrieu, 3:260–61.

[74]*CC*, nos. 11, 50, pp. 504, 570. Angenendt, "Das geistliche Bündnis," 45–46.

[75]Leo III, *ep.* no. 2, *MGH, EKA* 3:89.

[76]Ermoldus Nigellus, *Carmen in honorem Hludowici*, ed. Edmond Faral (Paris, 1932), vs. 1028–31, 1055.

Our age may be even more cynical than that of the nineteenth-century Realpolitiker who denied, or who failed to notice, the practical significance of the spiritual bond between the Carolingians and the papacy. Eighth- and ninth-century people thought differently. Prayer for them was a potent weapon against the evils of this world and a significant shield against its dangers. It was also an adequate reward in diplomatic bargaining. Papal prayers and the special intercession of St. Peter were desirable to the Carolingians as effective means of smoothing their paths to heaven, but they were no less avidly sought as immediately and immensely practical adjuncts to the force of Frankish arms.

Coupled with the heavenly fruits of the Franco-papal bond, however, were many earthly and practical ones. Stephen confirmed Pepin's crown, anointed his sons as kings, and forbade the Franks ever to choose a king from another family. The importance of these actions should not be under-estimated in view of the tenuous position in which Pepin found himself in 754. During his sojourn in Francia, Stephen conferred a pallium on Chrode-gang of Metz, an old and trusted associate of Pepin.[77] The significance of this act by Stephen lies in the fact that Chrodegang could, thanks to his pallium, consecrate bishops. After the retirement of Carlomann in 747, Pepin had not enjoyed uniformly good relations with the more progressive and influential elements in the Frankish Church. Stephen, through Chrode-gang, placed Pepin in a position to effect a real and thorough control of the Church in Francia; and there is evidence that Chrodegang did consecrate many bishops.[78] When Tassilo of Bavaria proved disloyal to Charlemagne, Hadrian used his good offices to support the Franks against the Bavarians, even though Rome and Bavaria had generally had good relations for three-quarters of a century.[79] This last case is interesting because Tassilo, as *inimi-cus* of Charlemagne, was perforce *inimicus* of Hadrian who was Charle-magne's *amicus*. The popes thus prayed for the Carolingians, but they also rendered other kinds of support of a more obviously practical nature.

The Duration of the Alliance

Evidence was adduced earlier to show that the alliance was initiated in 754 and confirmed in 774, 816, and 817. It remains to demonstrate that it was

---

[77]*LP* 1:456.

[78]Paul the Deacon, *Gesta ep. Mettensium, MGH, SS* 2:268. On Chrodegang's pallium see: Angenendt, "Das geistliche Bündnis," pp. 43–45.

[79]Reindel, "Zeitalter der Agilolfinger," 130–33.

also confirmed in 757, 767, 768, 795–96, and 824. Evidence is lacking for the years between 814, when Charlemagne died and Louis succeeded him, and 816, when Leo III died. That is, it cannot be determined if Louis and Leo III renewed the alliance, however likely this may be on general considerations.

Paul I wrote to Pepin shortly after his succession in 757 and said that he wished to confirm "the treaty and concord of peace and love and devotion and faith" previously concluded between Pepin and Stephen. He added that this was the desire of himself and of "all his people."[80] Later Paul wrote to say that he was glad that he and Pepin had been confirmed "*in vinculo spiritalis foederis.*"[81] Paul and Pepin had not met, so it is evident that the alliance could be, indeed was, confirmed in writing by means of envoys.

The usurper Constantine wrote to Pepin in 767 in an attempt to renew the alliance,[82] but there is no evidence that his effort proved successful. Perhaps it was not, because Frankish bishops, certainly with Pepin's blessing, participated in the synod that eventually condemned him. Stephen III in 768 attempted to renew the alliance, but his efforts were complicated by the death of Pepin and the initiation of hostilities between the late king's sons.[83] His letters are, however, full of the language of the alliance, and it is a fair assumption that it was at some point confirmed. I suspect that this confirmation may have occurred when Bertrada visited Rome, but I would not rule out other possible times and places. In neither 767 nor 768 was there a meeting between pope and king, so again, it is apparent that confirmations were sought in writing and through envoys.

In 796 Charlemagne and Leo confirmed the alliance, as is obvious from the letter of Charlemagne to Leo quoted above. The confirmation is also attested to in a letter sent by Charlemagne to Angilbert charging him to go to Rome.[84] Charlemagne and Leo did eventually meet, but only some three years after they had renewed the alliance. Once more, then, we see that the confirmation could be effected through emissaries.

The *Ludovicianum*, as we have already seen, required a confirmation of the alliance after each change on the Frankish throne or the chair of Peter, and specified that this confirmation should be accomplished by envoys. In 824 the *Constitutio Romana*—a crucial document to which we shall advert

[80]CC, no. 12, p. 508.
[81]CC, no. 14, p. 511.
[82]CC, no. 98, p. 651.
[83]CC, nos. 44, 45, pp. 558–63.
[84]*Apud Alcuini Epistolae,* no. 92, *MGH, EKA* 2:135–36.

repeatedly in the next chapter—reiterated the requirements contained in the *Ludovicianum*.[85]

These confirmations shed further light on the nature of the alliance itself. In every case, the new confirmation was related directly to the original pact of 754 and its successors. Thus, while the alliance was always understood to be durable, it had no set term. It was not, most assuredly, an ad hoc arrangement pertinent only to conditions in Rome and Francia in the middle 750s. The alliance had a personal dimension, in that it had to be confirmed each time that one of the contracting parties died. But, it did not have to be confirmed in a face to face meeting, although Pepin, Charlemagne, and Louis each confirmed it at least once in such a setting: Pepin and Stephen in 754, Charlemagne and Hadrian in 774, and Louis and Stephen IV in 816. Finally, both papal and Carolingian letters make it very clear that their respective peoples were bound by the alliance just as tightly as the concluding parties themselves.[86] The pope spoke each time for the people of the Republic, and the king for the Franks.

The Place of the Alliance in the History of the Republic

It is time now to harvest the fruit of all of those pioneer students of Franco-papal relations, most of whom apprehended a part of the truth but none of whom has seen it whole. In 754 a single alliance was concluded that was possibly foreseen to be perpetual. It may be called a "friendship alliance," but it must not be dismissed as merely ethical, because it possessed binding legal significance sealed by mutual oaths. The alliance was based on a spiritual bond of compaternity between St. Peter and the Carolingian monarchy, and also on a bond of Christian peace and love, but it carried potent practical force along with its religious elements. Pepin did swear to protect the Republic, or St. Peter's rights, or the saint's "peculiar people," but he did so as a part of the larger obligations which he incurred under the terms of the alliance. St. Peter, or his vicar, became Pepin's "friend" and the king was duty bound to fight all of St. Peter's enemies. These might be Lombards, or heretics, or pagans, but whoever they might be, and wherever they might emerge, Pepin had to defend St. Peter from them. The pope, acting for God

---

[85]*MGH, Cap.*, vol. 1, no. 161, p. 324.

[86]*CC*, nos. 8, 9, 13, 99, pp. 494, 498, 510, 652; *LP* 1:497–98. Only Drabek, *Verträge*, pp. 28–31, 43, has emphasized this crucial fact.

and St. Peter, had to support the Carolingian monarchy against all its foes, too, but papal prayers were supposed to keep the Carolingians favorably placed before the throne of God in good times as well as bad. The Republic's alliance with the Carolingians saved the infant state from a hideous threat and allowed it to survive and prosper, but it would be grossly erroneous and anachronistic to explain the basic features of the alliance in exclusively political terms. Charlemagne, the greatest of the Franks, did not lay a political memorandum before Leo. He asked his "father" to pray for him.

Sickel and his heirs were right to speak of a formal treaty between the Carolingians and the popes, but they have gone wrong in explaining this alliance with pointed reference to political realities in the 750s. Actually the alliance was from the beginning constructed so flexibly that it could, and in fact did, conform to many new and different situations that could not have been foreseen precisely when Stephen went to Francia. Caspar and his heirs were right to notice the *amicitia*-bond, but wrong to suppose that is was formless, extralegal, and secondary to the problems posed by Aistulf's attacks upon Rome. Schramm and his supporters were correct to emphasize Pepin's obligation to protect the Roman Church, but wrong to see this as a unilateral undertaking on Pepin's part unconnected to solemn obligations incurred by the popes. Virtually all scholars before Fritze and Drabek were shortsighted in studying only the years from 754 to 774 because the Franco-papal alliance remained in force at least until the 820s. It was proper for Fritze to emphasize the binding, legal nature of the "friendship alliance," but because he looked, as did Drabek, for only the Germanic antecedents of the alliance he failed to recognize its Christian elements. Angenendt, by following and amplifying upon the work of Eichmann, quite properly emphasized the spiritual side of the alliance, but he assigned too much significance to the bond of compaternity and too little to the other religious sides of the pact.

This alliance did not create the Republic of St. Peter, any more than did Pepin's campaigns against the Lombards. Rather, through its central *amicus amicis* formula, it secured for St. Peter's vicar and "peculiar people" durable and effective protection. Furthermore, nothing in this alliance assigned to the Carolingians any rights, duties, or responsibilities *inside* the Republic of St. Peter unless, as after the attack on Pope Leo III, the pope might call them in as protectors. In the next chapter we shall have to ask whether the Carolingians actually did have any rights, or exercise any authority, inside the Republic, and if so by what warrant these things were done.

Nine

The Republic and the Franks

THE VEXED and venerable question of the extent, origins, and bases of any rights, powers, duties, and responsibilities possessed by the Franks within the Republic must now be confronted. It has always been assumed that the Carolingians did possess a fairly broad range of rights alongside those held by the popes. The ease with which this assumption arose, and the equal ease with which it has been transmitted, have sometimes caused historians to neglect to ask a number of tough questions about Frankish rights in Rome. How and when did the Carolingians obtain whatever rights they are thought to have possessed? Under what legal or institutional entitlements were such rights exercised? Were papal and Carolingian rule in the Republic concurrent? Is it likely that the popes, having struggled so mightily to liberate themselves from the Greeks and defend themselves from the Lombards, would have turned straight around and handed themselves over to another power? Were there any real or potential benefits for the Carolingians in ruling the Republic?

Any discussion of the role of the Franks within the Republic is fraught with difficulties. First, given theses that have long since been inscribed in hard stone, it may seem as though there is something bold, reckless even, in broaching the issue at all. Second, the sources are cryptic, enigmatic, scanty, and in truth, susceptible of multiple interpretations. Third, the imperial coronation of Charlemagne in 800 ought to have produced a new constitutional and legal relationship between Francia and the Republic, and most scholars have assumed that it did. But, the impact of that coronation on Franco-papal relations is anything but clear. Fourth, it is often quite easy to say what the Franks did not do in and around Rome, but usually it is difficult to discern pattern and meaning behind what they actually did. This means that much of the scholarship is richer in assumptions and speculations than it is in concrete, sustained demonstrations. The following account, the reader deserves to be told, shares something of the speculative traditions transmitted by earlier historians, but it proceeds from different assumptions. It starts out by supposing that the popes never dreamed of sharing their rule with Pepin's family, and that the Carolingians had no reason to think of the Republic as though it were just another province of their far-flung kingdom (or empire after 800).

The Franks in the Republic Before 800

There is today a consensus that any rights or powers possessed by the Carolingians were attendant, before 800, upon the office of *Patricius Romanorum* and, after 800, upon the imperial office. To the imperial office we shall turn in due course. For the moment we must confine ourselves to the patriciate, and to the period between 754, when Stephen II made Pepin and his progeny *patricii Romanorum*, and 800, when Leo III made Charlemagne emperor. Although the conventional wisdom holds that Pepin and Charlemagne, as *patricii Romanorum*, became in some fashion lords of the Republic, there is little agreement on how this happened, or on what, exactly, was implied by the *patricius* title.[1] The meaning of this title itself, therefore, is the

---

[1]Some of those who maintain that Pepin, Charlemagne, or both were lords of Rome are: Halphen, *L'administration de Rome*, pp. 1–2; Arthur Kleinclausz, *L'empire carolingien. Sa vie et ses transformations* (Paris, 1902), p. 155; Schnürer, *Kirchenstaat*, pp. 94–95; Caspar, "Das Papsttum unter fränkischer Herrschaft," p. 63; Brezzi, *Roma e l'empero*, pp. 15–16; Classen, "Karl der Große, das Papsttum und Byzanz," p. 554; Ewig, *Handbook of Church History*, pp. 22, 59; Fleckenstein, *Early Medieval Germany*, p. 77. Some argue that the Carolingians were rulers of the Republic without drawing an explicit connection to the patriciate: Gundlach, *Kirchenstaat*, pp. 115, 121; Hartmann, *Geschichte Italiens*, 2.2:296; Haller, "Karolinger und das Papsttum," p. 40 (although in *Das Papsttum* 2:24 he draws the connection more tightly); Delaruelle, "Charlemagne et l'église," p. 177; Folz, *Coronation of Charlemagne*, p. 35; Tabacco, *Storia d'Italia*, p. 78; Jan Dhondt, *Le haut moyen âge (VIIIᵉ–XIᵉ siècles)*, trans. from German and revised by Michel Rouche (Paris, 1968), p. 5.

Partner, *Lands of St. Peter*, p. 37, expresses a middle view well when he says "within the judicial and administrative system of the Frankish dominions the Papal State was a privileged area, but it was within the system nonetheless." It is interesting that great legal historians like Heinrich Brunner (*Deutsche Rechtsgeschichte* 2:113 n.1) and Georg Waitz (*Verfassungsgeschichte Deutschlands* 3:85) were unwilling to say that any specific rights attached to the patriciate. Likewise, the pioneer student of the Franco-papal alliance, Wilhelm Sickel, said that nothing concrete resulted from the *patricius* title: "Verträge," pp. 340, 342–43, 346; idem, "Kirchenstaat und Karolinger," p. 405. This was also the position of the great student of Charlemagne's coronation: Karl Heldmann, *Das Kaisertum Karls des Großen* (Weimar, 1928),

necessary point of departure for an analysis, not only of the significance of the patriciate, but also, and more generally, of Carolingian rule, or the absence of such rule, inside the Republic down to 800.

It was F. L. Ganshof who first conclusively proved that the title was of Byzantine origin, and that it was largely honorific. That is, high Byzantine dignitaries were often called patricians, but their actual powers always derived from the possession of some other office. For example, the exarchs of Ravenna were usually patricians, and often the dukes of Rome were as well. Only the emperor could officially confer the patriciate, and he did this by means of documents that were quite different from the ones used to assign persons to other regular public offices (ἀξίαι διὰ βραβειῶν for the patriciate instead of ἀξίαι διὰ λογόυ, which were used for regular offices). At Byzantium, the title rarely had an ethnic component, such as the *Romanorum* in the Carolingian *patricius* title. The title bestowed upon Pepin and Charlemagne was, therefore, a papal creation rooted in Byzantine traditions.[2] Thus it is clear that at St. Denis in 754 Stephen II made Pepin and his sons Patricians of the Romans on his own initiative, without in any way having been mandated to do so by the emperor at Constantinople.[3] In no sense were the Carolingians meant to be successors to the exarchs, or to any other Byzantine officials. Essentially, the title was meant to express the Carolingian protectorate over the Republic[4] or, as one historian has put it, to provide public recognition that Pepin had become the Republic's *"generalissimo."*[5]

---

p. 345. Elie Griffe said the same thing: "Couronnement imperial," pp. 195, 197. Long before any of these historians Bernhard Niehues had already expressed this view: *Geschichte des Verhaltnißes zwischen Kaisertum und Papsttum im Mittlealter*, 2d ed. (Munster, 1877), 1:526.

[2]Ganshof, "Notes sur les origines byzantines du titre 'Patricius Romanorum,' " *Annuaire de l'institut de philologie et d'histoire orientales et slaves* (*Mélanges Henri Gregoire*) 10 (1950): 261–82. The fullest study of all the problems surrounding the *patricius* title is Josef Deér, "Zum Patricius-Romanorum-Titel Karls des Großen," in *Zum Kaisertum Karls des Großen*, ed. Gunther Wolf (Darmstadt, 1972), pp. 240–308. Valuable too is Herwig Wolfram, "Ac Patricius Romanorum," in his *Intitulatio* 1:225–36.

[3]The view that Stephen acted for Constantine V goes back most directly to Diehl, *Etudes*, p. 416ff. In recent times its chief advocate has been Deér, "Zur Praxis der Verleihung des auswärtigen Patriziats durch den byzantinischen Kaiser," *AHP* 8 (1970): 7–25. There is today broad agreement that Stephen acted on his own, although Guillou ("L'Italia bizantina," p. 231) still maintains that Stephen acted as a Byzantine agent.

[4]This is the position of Ewig (*Handbook of Church History*, p. 22) and Fleckenstein (*Early Medieval Germany*, p. 77) and I concur, although I cannot follow them in arguing that legal rights were attached to the patriciate. I agree with E. A. Thompson, *Romans and Barbarians* (Madison, Wis., 1982), p. 66, who says "the title of patrician [was] by itself a mere mark of status. It carried no powers in itself, either civil or military."

[5]Miller, "Roman Revolution," p. 127.

What the popes desired from their "patrician-friend-ally" was protection, and this is what they received. From 754 on papal letters to Pepin and to Charlemagne always addressed the Carolingians as patricians,[6] but it would be dangerous to deduce from this undeniable fact any broad set of rights or duties connected with the title because, except for defense, there is not one single document that establishes any sort of connection between the *patricius* title and anything that Pepin or Charlemagne ever did in Italy. Pepin never actually used the *patricius* title, as far as we know, and Charlemagne did so only sporadically between July 774 and June 776 when he commenced continuous use of it.[7] In short, if Pepin or Charlemagne had any rights or powers in the Republic, there is no way to demonstrate that these are attributable to the *patricius* title. Scholars, and there are many of them, who argue that specific rights attached to the patriciate are in reality guilty of engaging in speculation about the source of those rights.

But there is a larger issue involved here and it is this: Did Pepin or Charlemagne actually possess or exercise any sort of jurisdiction within the Republic, regardless of the source or foundation of that jurisdiction? The answer has usually been "yes." Long ago Albert Hauck listed several specific instances of Carolingian rule in the Republic, and it is easy to see that his list derives, at least in part, from the work of several of his predecessors.[8] It is also easy to follow this list, with or without acknowledgment, right down to 1965 when Peter Classen simply cited Hauck as though the matter were definitively resolved.[9] On closer inspection it will be seen that this scholarly tradition is wrong, almost completely, on every point. Therefore, the standard interpretation that, to use Tabacco's words, "Carolingian supremacy was everywhere recognized" in the Republic stands in need of revision. Perhaps the most convenient way to study the issue of Carolingian rights in the Republic is to take up Hauck's classic litany of "proofs" because they seem to provide the familiar terms around which the discussion has turned for half a century or more.

---

[6]E.g. CC, no. 6, p. 488. Angenendt, "Das geistliche Bündnis," p. 40, thinks that only Pepin's sons were called patricians but I do not read the addresses of the letters that way, nor has anyone else. Hadrian twice used the peculiar form "*patriciatus*" (CC, nos. 85, 94, pp. 622, 635) but in neither instance does the context permit firm conclusions to be drawn.

[7]Not one of Pepin's diplomas has the title. The first one of Charlemagne to bear it is DK, vol. 1, no. 81, p. 116. Down to no. 111, p. 156, we have 31 diplomas between the first to bear the title and the beginning of the series in which it always appears. Of these, 18 do not have the *patricius* title. For a while, evidently, Charlemagne did not know what to make of it.

[8]A. Hauck, *Kirchengeschichte Deutschlands* 2:87–93.

[9]Classen, "Karl der Große, das Papsttum und Byzanz," p. 574.

The first case involves Ravenna, specifically that Charlemagne is alleged to have been a supporter of Leo. We have already seen in chapters 5 and 7 that Ravenna was a special instance of shared rule in the Republic. Hauck's conclusion that Charlemagne's conduct there proves that "he considered himself highest lord of the papal lands" is therefore exaggerated. Charlemagne and Hadrian, on the basis of the compromise settlement of 781, agreed amicably to share jurisdiction in Ravenna. Additionally, Charlemagne may indeed have been kindly disposed toward Leo, but it is too much to say that he was a supporter of the archbishop. Finally, facts that pertain to Ravenna prove nothing at all about the Duchy of Rome which was, from beginning to end, the heart of the Republic.

Another case involves Città di Castello, which was seized by Duke Raginald of Chiusi in about 776. It is perfectly true that Hadrian complained to Charlemagne about the seizure of Città di Castello, and that he reported to the king a rumor that the city had been taken with the king's approval.[10] But, Hadrian said that he did not believe the rumor, and the existence of such rumors between 774 and 780–81 suggests that I was correct earlier in characterizing this period as one of profound uncertainty. In any event, in 781 Città di Castello was given to Hadrian definitively as a part of that year's comprehensive territorial settlements. Thus, any argument based on the disposition of Città di Castello before 781—here we are talking about 776—proves nothing about Charlemagne's "rule" in the Republic.

Hadrian's complaints about the Beneventan settlement are also taken as proof that Charlemagne acted decisively within the Republic as a result of his *patricius* title. In fact, the letters Hauck cites from the *Codex Carolinus* antedate the settlement of 787, and after that date, Benevento was no longer an issue in Franco-papal relations except for Hadrian's displeasure when Charlemagne named Grimoald duke. Hadrian's complaints on this score, however, prove nothing about Charlemagne's rights. Certainly, the Quierzy-Rome document laid claim to Benevento, but the duchy was never handed over to Rome. Instead, in 787 the Duchy of Rome was expanded to the south to compensate Hadrian for abandoning all claims in the lands of his southern neighbors. Thereafter, the Lombard duchy became a Frankish dependency and Charlemagne, as *rex Langobardorum*, had every right to treat it as he wished. Beneventan evidence tells us nothing about Carolingian rule inside papal Italy.

It is also argued that Charlemagne derived from his patriciate the right to hear appeals from papal justice. Now, the letter cited as evidence by

---

[10]CC, no. 58, p. 583.

Hauck does say that appellants were going from Ravenna and the Pentapolis to Charlemagne.[11] But Hadrian's words make it perfectly clear, on close reading, that the pope considered this to be irregular and unlawful. Hadrian said that just as he would never receive fugitives from Charlemagne's justice, so too the king should not entertain fugitives from the Republic. In this same letter, Hadrian raised a loud lament about simony in Tuscany and in Ravenna, and he complained about Tuscan bishops moving from see to see. He said that Charlemagne's own envoys were aware of these problems. The pope also spoke angrily about persons from Ravenna who refused to submit to papal jurisdiction. It is thus difficult to figure out what kinds of fugitives, or appellants, were going to Charlemagne, and for what reason. The fact that they were from Ravenna, however, ought to put us on our guard against drawing general conclusions about Carolingian rights in the Republic. In addition, the pope's letter says very explicitly that he did not consider Charlemagne to have any right to hear appeals from papal justice. What Charlemagne himself thought we do not know precisely. Still, it is difficult to read this letter as evidence that Charlemagne claimed the specific and defined right to inspect the fruits of papal justice inside the Republic generally.

The next two cases cited by Hauck are singularly meaningless. Charlemagne had heard a report that Christian slaves were being sold to Muslims in Rome and he wrote to Hadrian to express his grave concern. Hadrian wrote back to say that, in fact, Lombards were selling slaves to Greeks and that, as much as he detested this vile commerce, he could do nothing about it.[12] Hauck says that Hadrian "as was his custom" blamed someone else for his own failings and "never contested the formal right of the emperor to object." It is hard to say why Hauck would not believe Hadrian's plain testimony, but it is clear that no significance ought to be attached to his unexplained phrase "the emperor's formal right to object" (indeed, Charlemagne was not yet emperor). Moreover, without Charlemagne's letter to Hadrian it is gratuitous to try to make anything out of this affair. The king also wrote to the pope to get him to remove some Venetian merchants from Ravenna. Hadrian complied and so notified Charlemagne in a letter Hauck characterizes with the words, "Would a vassal have written differently?"[13] This particular affair actually works against Hauck's thesis in two ways. First, the Venetians and the Carolingians were regularly in open hostility during this period, and Venice displayed no noticeable partiality toward

---

[11]CC, no. 94, pp. 632–36.
[12]CC, no. 58, pp. 584–85.
[13]CC, no. 86, pp. 622–23.

Rome either. Thus, the expulsion of Venetian merchants from Ravenna and the Pentapolis is a perfect example of the Franco-papal alliance in operation. The Venetians were *inimici* of both the Franks and the popes who were, of course, *amici*. Second, we have repeatedly seen that Ravenna was a region of concurrent rule, and in the handling of the case of the Venetian merchants, we have an example of harmonious cooperation. Indeed, had Charlemagne fancied himself sole or highest lord of the Republic, would he not have sent his own agents into the Ravennate to expel the Venetians?

Hauck goes on to say that Charlemagne was the highest authority in the Church within Francia and that he extended his ecclesiastical control to include the Republic. His evidence is a letter in which Hadrian responded to the king's complaints about simony in Tuscany and Ravenna. In fact, Hadrian's letter demonstrates that he himself was deeply disturbed about this problem.[14] This letter in no way proves that the Roman Church passed under Charlemagne's control. Indeed, we have no evidence that it ever did.[15] Moreover, the letter Hauck cites refers to Tuscany, which was not a part of the Republic, and to Ravenna, a region that rarely yields evidence relevant to other sectors of the Republic.

Two other regularly cited cases are completely irrelevant. First, there was a mischievous monk, John, whom Charlemagne turned over to Hadrian with a plea on his behalf.[16] Nothing certain can be known about this John. He may or may not have come from the Republic, although it is possible that he was from the region of Ravenna.[17] Nevertheless, Hadrian wrote to Charlemagne to say that John was really a rather despicable fellow. Probably these words from the pope were in response to Charlemagne's plea on behalf of John. In the end, however, John's case proves only that Charlemagne left to the pope the disciplining of clerics. In other words, things appear to have been exactly as they ought to have been. Second, there is a bishop named Peter whom Charlemagne sent to Rome for consecration.[18] Hauck himself points out, following Gundlach, the editor of the *Codex Carolinus*, that this person was probably Peter of Verdun.[19] Peter may actually have been an

---

[14]CC, no. 94, p. 634.

[15]This is proved by Kempf, "Chiesa territoriale e chiesa romana nel secolo VIII," pp. 293–317, esp. 311–12.

[16]CC, no. 88, pp. 624–25.

[17]In CC, no. 86, pp. 622–23, Hadrian complained about depredations around Ravenna by a Duke Garamannus and in no. 88 Hadrian says he was informed about John by Garamannus who was then *missus* of Charlemagne.

[18]CC, no. 70, p. 600.

[19]CC, p. 600 n.2 with sources.

Italian, but his consecration by Hadrian as bishop of Verdun says absolutely nothing about Charlemagne and the Republic; as with the monk John, it suggests only that the king left routine ecclesiastical business to the pope.

In sovereign fashion Hauck concludes that, whether or not Charlemagne did these things as *patricius*, the king "acted quite clearly as overlord [*Oberherr*] of Rome. In his mind he possessed those rights which belonged to him in the Frankish kingdom. . . . Since the fall of the Lombard kingdom the pope was totally powerless against the Frankish king."[20]

Hauck's repeatedly cited litany of *exempla* simply does not prove that Charlemagne ever was, or ever claimed to be, "overlord" of Rome. Virtually all of Hauck's cases come from Ravenna, which was a zone of concurrent jurisdiction. Even where Ravenna is concerned, however, Hauck's "evidence" does not depict Charlemagne acting as sole ruler. The whole issue of who held jurisdiction within the Republic would be better understood if we had not only Hadrian's letters, but Charlemagne's as well. Still, my reading of Hadrian's correspondence does not lead me to characterize him as "powerless."

Classen cites Hauck on another point which actually reaches back over Gundlach to the great legal historians Brunner and Waitz.[21] Simply stated, this argument maintains that both Pepin and Charlemagne required the inhabitants of the Republic to swear a subject's oath to the Frankish king. If this argument is valid, then it means that, either as patricians or in some other capacity, the Carolingians truly were overlords of the Republic. If the pope's "peculiar people" swore allegiance to another prince, then the pope cannot be said to have been lord over them except in a very limited way.

This whole issue is, at first sight, highly complex for several reasons. In the first place, it is axiomatic today, although it was not in the days of Brunner and Waitz, that in Frankish law there was a sharp distinction between a subject's oath and a vassal's oath.[22] Throughout the period covered

[20]A. Hauck, *Kirchengeschichte Deutschlands* 2:92.

[21]Waitz, *Verfassungsgeschichte Deutschlands* 3:292–93; Brunner, *Deutsche Rechtsgeschichte* 2:59; Gundlach, *Kirchenstaat*, pp. 81–82; A. Hauck, *Kirchengeschichte Deutschlands* 2:93; Classen, "Karl der Große, das Papsttum und Byzanz," p. 560.

[22]Auguste Dumas denied the distinction but his conclusions have found no support: "Le serment de fidélité à l'époque franque," *Revue belge de philologie et d'histoire* 14 (1935): 405–26 and "Le serment de fidélité et la conception du pouvoir du Iᵉʳ au IXᵉ siècle," *Revue historique du droit français et étranger* 10 (1931), 30–51, 289–321. For authoritative views on the distinction between the oaths see: Ferdinand Lot, "Le serment de fidélité à l'époque franque," *Revue belge* 12 (1933): 569–82; Charles E. Odegaard, "Carolingian Oaths of Fidelity," *Speculum* 16 (1941): 284–96; idem, "The Concept of Royal Power in Carolingian Oaths of Fidelity," *Speculum* 20 (1945): 279–89; idem, *Vassi and Fideles in the Carolingian Empire* (Cambridge, Mass.,

by this book there is no evidence at all that anyone in the Republic ever swore a vassal's oath to the Frankish king.[23] This fact is of some general significance to the present discussion, but is not directly connected to the question of the presence or absence of a subject's oath. The Merovingians had betimes exacted a general oath of fidelity in the Frankish kingdom, but this practice had fallen into desuetude during the seventh century.[24] Charlemagne revived it in 789 and 802.[25] Basically, the subject's oath was a generalized oath of fidelity which bore essentially negative connotations. That is, it required anyone who swore it to refrain from conduct manifestly disloyal or deleterious to the king. It did not, as a rule, require the performance of specific services, or the fulfillment of concrete terms and obligations.[26] For our purposes, the question is, do we have evidence for such an oath in the Republic?

Historians have long pointed to certain Carolingian letters and diplomas wherein people from the Republic are referred to as "*fideles.*"[27] Because the form of the subject's oath used in Francia began "*fidelis sum . . .*" numerous authorities have jumped to the conclusion that the Frankish subject's oath was sworn in the Republic. This conclusion is not justified, however. Charlemagne demanded a general oath of fidelity for the first time in 789. All of the documents cited to establish the subject status of the inhabitants of the Republic antedate that year. Before 789 Charlemagne never referred to people in Francia in vague, general terms as *fideles*, so why would he have done so in the Republic? Why would Pepin have done so given that he never even exacted a general oath of fidelity in Francia? The answer appears to be that no subject's oath was sworn inside the Republic by any of its inhabitants.

1945); Marcel David, *La souveraineté et les limites juridiques du pouvoir monarchique du IXe au XVe siècle* (Paris, 1954).

[23]Karl Jordan tried to prove that Frankish feudal practices did enter the Republic, probably through Farfa: "Das Eindringen des Lehnwesens in das Rechtsleben der römischen Kurie," *Archiv für Urkundenforschung* 12 (1932): 13–110, esp. 24ff. Toubert, *Latium* 2:1093–95, proves that this was not the case. Likewise, Mengozzi, *Città*, pp. 211–17, cannot find feudal oaths or benefices in the Republic. On feudalism in Carolingian Italy generally see: Leicht, "Il feudo in Italia nell'età carolingia," *SSCI* 1 (1954): 71–107. He finds no evidence for vassals in the Republic.

[24]Odegaard, "Carolingian Oaths of Fidelity," p. 284.

[25]Ganshof, "Charlemagne's Programme of Imperial Government," and "Charlemagne's Use of the Oath," both in his *The Carolingians and the Frankish Monarchy*, pp. 58ff, 111–24.

[26]Ganshof, "Charlemagne's Use of the Oath," pp. 112–13.

[27]The texts most commonly cited are: *CC*, nos. 11, 13, 17, 55, 83, and *DK*, vol. 1, no. 132, pp. 182–83. Actually, this list could be expanded considerably but to no useful purpose.

The fidelity mentioned, or alluded to, in the documents usually called to witness refers only to the fidelity incumbent upon all parties according to the terms of the Franco-papal alliance. The pope and his "peculiar people" were all Charlemagne's *amici* and had to be loyal to him by refraining from supporting his enemies. But, these *amici* also had positive obligations under the alliance which subjects usually did not have. Likewise, Charlemagne and all the Franks were the pope's *amici,* and they had to help him against his enemies and to propagate the *fides catholica.* No bond of subjection was thereby created, and none is really implied by the language of the documents. Earlier generations of historians, trained under the influence of the legal and political norms of the nineteenth century, saw fidelity in the sources and immediately inferred subjection. Actually, there was fidelity, but no subjection of any kind. Thus, one can say that Peter's "peculiar people" were Charlemagne's *fideles,* but one must be very careful not to place this fidelity into the wrong context.

No one, finally, has ever been able to discover evidence for the actual swearing of the subject's oath within the Republic, and it is surprising that constitutional historians have not seen that their interpretations have placed them in a dilemma. In Francia, special *missi* were sent through predetermined *missatica,* regions incorporating as a rule several counties, to take up the oaths of 789 and 802.[28] No such *missi* are ever heard of in the Republic, and this area was never divided into *missatica.* Thus, had the will to exact this oath existed, and it did not, the machinery for exacting it was never in place.[29]

---

[28]Ganshof, "Charlemagne's Use of the Oath," pp. 113–14.

[29]Here a troublesome text must be confronted: *Annales qui dicuntur Einhardi, anno 796,* ed. Kurze, pp. 99: "Adriano defuncto Leo pontificatum suscepit et mox per legatos suos . . . regi misit rogavitque, ut aliquem de suis optimatibus Romam mitteret, qui populum Romanum ad suam fidem atque subiectionem per sacramenta firmaret. Missus est ad hoc Angilbert. . . ." This passage has been adduced as evidence for the subject status of the inhabitants of the Republic but the judgment is hasty. Only this one source uses this language. To be sure the "revised" *Royal Annals* were written by a person associated with the Carolingian court, but this does not guarantee that they are free of errors, anachronisms, or incomprehensible statements. See: Wilhelm Wattenbach, Wilhelm Levison, and Heinz Löwe, *Deutschlands Geschichtsquellen im Mittelalter* (Weimar, 1953), 2:247ff, 254–56, and Hartmut Hoffmann, *Untersuchungen zur karolingischen Annalistik* (Bonn, 1958), p. 17ff. Charlemagne's letter to Angilbert, and his letter to Leo, both of which were discussed above, never mention this oath, and no other source does either. This leads me to conclude that in 796 the Franco-papal alliance, with its general oath of fidelity, was confirmed and that the Frankish annalist erred by drawing a parallel between the subject's oaths of 789 and 802 and the alliance confirmation of 796. In 816, Stephen IV received the oath of the Romans before he set out to visit Francia (Thegan,

The various "proofs" for Charlemagne's overlordship turn out to be no proofs at all. The evidence that has been adduced is either irrelevant, or else it will not bear the interpretations that have been placed on upon it. Likewise, speculations about the significance of the patriciate are not very helpful in view of the fact that neither Pepin nor Charlemagne, nor any of their court theoreticians, nor any of the popes who were contemporary with them, ever bothered to write a "job description" for the office. The existing literature, in short, does not contain a single absolutely convincing case of Carolingian rule in the Republic outside the immediate area of Ravenna. And, as we have come to know, all evidence from Ravenna is riddled with ambiguities.

On more general considerations, it is not at all surprising that things should have turned out this way. For example, Charlemagne never minted money in Rome,[30] and before 800 he never participated in any kind of judicial proceedings there.[31] No evidence exists that he collected any taxes in the Republic, and he never summoned the inhabitants of the Republic to serve in his armies.[32] Neither Charlemagne nor Pepin ever interfered in a papal election, and they never asserted a right to do so.[33] With the possible exception of some involvement in archepiscopal elections at Ravenna, there is no evidence that Pepin or Charlemagne ever appointed an official of any kind anywhere in the Republic, or that they ever dismissed an official.

In the realm of symbolic deeds and gestures, much the same picture emerges. When Charlemagne visited St. Peter's in 774, it is interesting and

---

Vita Hludowici, c. 16, *MGH, SS* 2:594), and we have already seen that Louis and Stephen confirmed the alliance in conventional terms. Additionally, we have seen that on most occasions the alliance was confirmed by envoys (i.e., "aliquem de suis optimatibus"). In 796, of course, Angilbert was sent to Rome for just this purpose. Therefore, I conclude that the reviser of the *Royal Annals* made a small but significant error in his report for 796.

[30] Philip Grierson, "The Coronation of Charlemagne and the Coinage of Pope Leo III," *Revue belge* 30 (1952): 825ff, 829–30; Karl F. Morrison, *Carolingian Coinage* (New York, 1967), pp. 107–11, confirms Grierson's judgment that all of Charlemagne's Italian coins were minted in the *regnum.*

[31] Classen, "Karl der Große, das Papsttum und Byzanz," p. 574. But courts were held, and verdicts rendered in his name, in the *regnum.* See: Cesare Manaresi, *I placiti del 'regnum Italiae'* (*FSI*, vol. 92 [Rome, 1955]), nos. 1–11, pp. 1–30 (for Pisa, 1; for Trita, 1; for Lucca, 3; for Spoleto, 6).

[32] Philippe Contamine, *La guerre au moyen âge* (Paris, 1980), p. 103, notes, however, that Lombards from the *regnum* were called to serve.

[33] Bayet, "Les élections pontificales," p. 69–72; Ernst Mayer, *Italienische Verfassungsgeschichte,* 2 vols. (Leipzig, 1909), 2:64 and n.67; Ullmann, "The Origins of the *Ottonianum,*" *Cambridge Historical Journal* 11 (1953): 117.

important to note that he requested permission from Hadrian to enter the city of Rome.[34] Permission was granted, and Charlemagne celebrated Easter at the Lateran. His two substantive meetings with Hadrian, however, both took place outside Rome, at St. Peter's. In this same connection, it is worth noting that no Carolingian ever made use of the imperial palace in Rome on the Palatine. Constans II, the last Byzantine emperor to visit the city, resided there in 663, and the exarch usually stayed there when he was in Rome. The Carolingians avoided the place. In fact, they built their own residence out in the suburbs at St. Peter's, near the modern Vatican. It is not absolutely clear that Charlemagne himself created the Carolingian residence at St. Peter's, although most of the evidence leads to such a conclusion.[35] In any event, a remark by Peter Llewellyn is particularly appropriate. He says that that Carolingians were accredited, not to the pope, but to St. Peter.[36] It is difficult to escape the conclusion that the popes deliberately sought to avoid creating the impression that the Carolingians had any regalian rights in Rome. Finally, the pomp and ceremony amidst which Charlemagne and his entourage were received in 774 is curious. Hadrian sent the high officials of Rome out thirty miles, which was unprecedented. He also sent the *scholae* and their patrons to meet Charlemagne one mile out "as was the custom for receiving an exarch or patrician." Hadrian himself waited at the steps of St. Peter's, just outside the city.[37] All of this is odd because imperial protocol required the pope to go out six miles to receive an emperor and, evidently, one mile to meet an exarch or similar official.[38] Hadrian orchestrated a peculiar reception party that did not treat Charlemagne in any established, traditional way.

Arguments *ex silentio* are dangerous, of course, but it cannot be without significance that before 800 no Frank appears to have exercised any Byzantine or Frankish regalian rights inside the Republic of St. Peter. It is recognized today that Charlemagne kept the Lombard kingdom and the Republic administratively separate,[39] and that Carolingian institutions penetrated slowly into the *regnum*: the Lombard nobility was not immediately replaced; the

---

[34]*LP* 1:497.

[35]Brühl, "Die Kaiserpfalz bei St. Peter und die Pfalz Ottos III. auf dem Palatin," *QFIAB*, 34 (1954):1–30; idem, "Neues zur Kaiserrpfalz bei St. Peter," ibid. 38 (1958): 266–68; Ewig, *Handbook of Church History*, pp. 57–58.

[36]Llewellyn, *Rome in the Dark Ages*, p. 193.

[37]*LP* 1:496–97.

[38]Duchesne, *LP* 1:343, 378 n.15.

[39]This is implied by *MGH, Cap.*, vol. 1, no. 45, p. 126. See: Eiten, *Das Unterkönigtum*, pp. 19–20; Leicht, "Il feudale," p. 72; Fasoli, *Carlomagno*, pp. 106–7.

Frankish comital system was introduced slowly and unevenly; Frankish control of Italian bishoprics was never complete; the feudal system entered Italy slowly and struck shallow roots.[40] If Carolingian rule penetrated slowly, unevenly, and imperfectly into the *regnum*, where Charlemagne was unquestionably overlord, and if not one single source unambiguously documents Carolingian rule within the Republic, and if Hadrian—who as pope would have understood implicitly the power and meaning of symbolic, ritualistic gestures—studiously avoided allowing Charlemagne to appear as a ruler, how can Hauck and his many followers say that "one must consider Rome as totally ruled by Charles. . . . The development which we have observed is the transformation of the patriciate into rulership (*Herrschaft*)"?

Looking at the other side of the issue may be instructive. That is, did the popes express themselves on the matter of who ruled the Republic? Given the two sets of developments followed in the earlier chapters of this study— the effort to secure the Republic's existence and frontiers and the elaboration of its institutional structures—it is tempting to answer this question affirmatively and be done with the issue. There is, however, some positive evidence to which one can point. The forms of address used by the papal chancery in the letters of the *Codex Carolinus* always refer to the people of the Republic as "our people," that is, as the pope's people.[41] Beginning in 781, at the latest, Hadrian began issuing documents in his own name, and neither he nor any of his predecessors ever issued them in the name of, or with the regnal years of, Pepin or Charlemagne.[42] Hadrian issued coins

---

[40]This results from the major, substantial studies of early Carolingian Italy. See: Manacorda, *Studi sul'inizii*, passim; Fasoli, *Carlomagno*, pp. 103–19; Bullough, "Counties of the *Regnum Italiae*," pp. 148–68; Hlawitschka, *Franken, Alemannen, Bayern und Burgunder im Oberitalien*, passim; Fischer, *Königtum, Adel und Kirche*, passim; Toubert, "L'Italie rurale aux VIIIe– IXe siècles: Essai de typologie domaniale," *SSCI* 20 (1973): 95–132. See also chapter 5 n.38.

[41]Good examples: CC, nos. 13, 24, 37, 45, 52, pp. 509–10, 529, 547, 563, 574.

[42]Fichtenau, " 'Politische' Datierung des frühen Mittlealters," in Wolfram's *Intitulatio* 2:489– 93. The author assumes that Hadrian's use of his own name in documents may antedate 781. It is from that year, after a gap of nine years, that an original document survives: Jaffé, *RP*, no. 2435. Thus, one cannot safely say what form was used from 772 to 781. Leo III introduced a curious change in 798 by issuing documents with his own name followed by "atque domni Caroli excellentissimi regis Francorum et Langobardorum et patricii Romanorum, a quo cepit Italiam anno XXV": Fichtenau, p. 493; Jaffé, *RP*, no. 2498. I shall come back to this document but for the moment it suffices to say that it does not indicate an admission of Frankish overlordship because: (1) Leo's name appears first; (2) It dates from 774 but Charlemagne became patrician in 754, co-king in 768, and sole king in 771. Only Carolingian documents for Italy are dated from 774 when Pavia fell. In short, there is nothing "official" about this odd way of dating a document.

bearing his own name and image.[43] The *ius monetae* is an important bit of regalia. In 1951 Schramm looked at papal coins, documents, and other related items and concluded that Hadrian began early in his pontificate to transfer imperial prerogatives and the trappings of imperial rule from the Greeks to Charlemagne. By 795, in Schramm's opinion, Charlemagne was already "quasi-emperor."[44] Now, it goes without saying that a "quasi-emperor" is no emperor at all, but Schramm's argument has been countered from another direction by Deér who reviewed the same evidence and argued persuasively that Hadrian actually translated the regalia of imperial rule onto himself, not onto Charlemagne.[45]

The total corpus of evidence is not large, but it all leads to the same conclusion. The pope considered himself to be, and acted as though he was, the lord of his Republic. Neither Pepin nor Charlemagne claimed, was assigned, or exercised any of the obvious and ordinary rights of rulership in the Republic. To the limited extent that those rights can be observed in operation, it was the pope alone who pulled the levers.

Readers will have noticed that the foregoing account was cast almost entirely in negative terms. That is, old interpretations were denied and then testimony was heard on what the Carolingians *did not do*. Perhaps it will be objected that proving that the Carolingians did not do this or that does not establish that they were not all the while doing something else. One can only respond to the objection by saying that it is striking not to find in dozens of

---

[43]Hadrian issued two types of silver deniers. One bears a likeness of the pope and is clearly modeled on the coins of Byzantine emperors such as Leo III, Artavasdus, Constantine V, and Leo IV. The other coins, later but indeterminate in date, have Hadrian's name on the obverse and *Sanctus Petrus* on the reverse. For reproductions of type 1 see: Camillo Serafini, *Le monete e le bolle plumbee pontificie del medagliere vaticano* (reprint Bologna, 1965), vol. 1, pp. 4–5, nos. 3, 4, Tavola 1, nos. 3–5; *Corpus Nummorum Italicorum*, 15, pp. 62–4, nos. 1–14 and Tavola 4, no.1, 2. For type 2: Serafini, 1, Tavola 1, no. 5; *CNI*, 15, p. 64, nos. 15–17 and Tavola 4, no. 3,

There exist some copper "objects" struck under Gregory III and Zachary which may or may not be coins: Serafini, 1, p. 3, Tavola 1, nos. 1, 2; *CNI*, 15, Tavola III, nos. 29, 30. They have the pope's name on the obverse and *Sanctus Petrus* on the reverse. Serafini called them coins but one may doubt this. Even if these "objects" are only, perhaps, pilgrim's tokens, it is still interesting to see popes issuing such items bearing their own names so early in the eighth century.

These coins, like Hadrian's documents, are a significant indicator of the lack of Carolingian rule in the Republic. In 788 Charlemagne demanded that the Beneventans put his name on their coins and charters: Erchempert, *Hist. Lang.*, c. 4, *MGH, SSrL*, p. 236. Obviously no such command was ever issued for Rome.

[44]Schramm, "Die Anerkennung Karls des Großen als Kaiser," pp. 215–63.

[45]Deér, "Die Vorrechte des Kaisers in Rom," pp. 30–115.

letters, many diplomas, Italian capitularies, papal and royal *vitae*, chronicles, annals, and histories a single instance of unambiguously demonstrable Carolingian rule inside the Republic. Moreover, it is equally striking that one can compile a quite full and nuanced dossier on Carolingian governance in the Italian *regnum* after 774 without being able to discern anything about such governance in the Republic. Others have cited evidence that is not evidence at all, or else they have speculated that from the absence of evidence one is permitted to deduce the presence of rule. I speculate that from the absence of evidence one must deduce an absence of rule.

The Imperial Coronation of Charlemagne

So things stood down to 800, when Charlemagne was crowned emperor. This is not the place to attempt an exhaustive treatise on Charlemagne's imperial coronation, but some investigation of that famous act must be undertaken because there is a school of thought which maintains that, as emperor, Charlemagne was definitely lord of the Republic, and that his lordship derived from his constitutional position as emperor. To some extent, proponents of this view are just as guilty of speculation as are those who imagine all sorts of nonexistent rights to have inhered in the patriciate. In other words, it is not correct to argue without further ado that, as emperors, the Carolingians could automatically do everything that Roman or Byzantine emperors had done. It is wrong, certainly, to write and to interpret on the basis of a static, timeless conception of the imperial office. The imperial dignity assumed by the Carolingians was not exactly like any one that had preceded it and differed from all of those which followed. This deceptively simple fact must never be lost sight of; nor dare we forget that, over time, the Carolingian imperial ideal grew, evolved, changed. In truth, however, matters did become a bit more complicated after 800 than they had been before Charlemagne's last and most historic visit to Rome.

Thanks to nearly a century of sophisticated and penetrating historical research, there is broad consensus today that long before Charlemagne was crowned at St. Peter's on Christmas day in 800, the idea that he ought to be an emperor had been gaining currency. The coronation was, therefore, a culmination of several distinct but related historical developments. Some theologians saw in Charlemagne the fulfillment of an Augustinian program of world order, the Christian emperor for the Christian empire, both created to mirror the divine ruler and his universal realm. Others, perhaps reflecting on the numerous classical manuscripts available in Carolingian libraries, believed Charlemagne to be in some respects the natural heir of the ancient Roman emperors. There were also those who felt that the great Frank's remarkable conquests and achievements were inadequately encompassed within a mere royal title. There may have been a party at Rome that desired to have an emperor again, and of course there was the pope, Leo, who was Charlemagne's protegé and a political pariah at Rome. He crowned Charlemagne, perhaps thereby to render more secure and effective the Carolingian protectorate over the Republic generally, and over himself specifically. These are only some of the major highways along which thought has traveled, but they serve well to illustrate the complexity of the subject.[46] The development of an imperial ideology before 800 is not always easy to trace, and after 800 there is no denying Peter Munz's remark that the "coronation of Charlemagne meant different things to different people."[47]

The background to, and immediate aftermath of, the coronation may be set forth briefly. Leo III was attacked in Rome in April 799, and after a very brief incarceration, he fled to Francia where he was honorably received by Charlemagne at Paderborn. Charlemagne sent investigators to Rome, but they were unable to turn up any certain information concerning Leo's travails. Later in 799, Leo himself was accompanied back to Rome by a Frankish escort, and in August 800 Charlemagne decided to go to Rome. Ganshof has argued that Alcuin persuaded Charlemagne that his presence in Rome was necessary to salvage the tarnished reputation of the pope.[48] Alcuin had, however, already written to his friend, Arn of Salzburg, one of the men who had accompanied Leo back to Rome, to say that no one should presume to sit in judgment of the pope.[49] Charlemagne's closest advisers, then, did not

---

[46]Heldmann, *Das Kaisertum Karls des Großen*, while arguing that the coronation was largely the product of local Roman conditions, fairly and almost exhaustively discusses the literature down to its date of publication. More recently two anthologies have incorporated the major findings and diverging points of view: Richard E. Sullivan, *The Coronation of Charlemagne: What Did It Signify?* (Boston, 1959) and Wolf, *Zum Kaisertum Karls des Großen*. In addition to these anthologies, important perspectives are developed by: Werner Ohnsorge, *Das Zweikaiserproblem im früheren Mittelalter* (Hildesheim, 1947); Heinrich Fichtenau, *The Carolingian Empire*, trans. Peter Munz (New York, 1964), esp. chaps. 2 and 3; idem, "Karl der Große und das Kaisertum," *MIÖG* 61 (1953): 257–334; Peter Munz, *The Origin of the Carolingian Empire* (Leicester, 1960); Folz, *The Imperial Coronation of Charlemagne*; Schramm, "Karl der Große als Kaiser im Lichte der Staatssymbolik (800–814)," in his *Kaiser, Könige und Päpste* 1:264–302. Wolf's anthology has a splendid bibliography.

[47]Munz, *Origin of the Carolingian Empire*, p. viii.

[48]Ganshof, "Alcuin's Revision of the Bible," in his *Carolingians and the Frankish Monarchy*, p. 34.

[49]*Ep.* no. 179, *MGH, EKA* 2:297.

foresee for him any judicial role in Rome. Nor did they assume that he had any judicial authority there. On 1 December 800 Charlemagne held an inquest in Rome, but no one would come forward to accuse Leo of anything.[50] Three weeks later Leo publicly swore that he was innocent of any wrongdoing.[51] No Byzantine emperor had ever recognized the principle *"papa a nemine iudicetur,"* but Charlemagne did in 800.[52] Two days later Leo crowned Charlemagne emperor and the Romans acclaimed him. Shortly after Christmas the new emperor condemned to death the persons guilty of the attack on Leo, but the pope persuaded him to commute the sentence to exile.[53]

Behind this deceptively simple story there stand a number of elements that are both revealing and disturbing. We may at least express some curiosity at the fact that Charlemagne waited a year and a half before going to Rome. Perhaps he was unsure about how to proceed. As Leo's ally he had a duty to protect him from any misfortune, and it was certainly as an ally that the pope had appealed to the king in the first place.[54] An abrupt intervention was not possible, however, because Charlemagne had no clear right to hold a trial in the city or to pass judgment on Romans. In addition, with various charges against Leo being bruited about,[55] there was the possibility that the pope was actually guilty of some offense. The spectacle of putting the pope on trial appealed to no one in Francia, and this meant that Charlemagne had to find some other means of assisting Leo. Arn and his associates had held an inquest, but they were unable to learn anything concrete. When Charlemagne arrived in Rome he too held an inquest, but in the form of a Roman *synod*, not of a secular tribunal, over which he presided.[56] Unfortunately, no one would admit culpability. Had someone done so he would doubtless have been declared *inimicus* and sentenced, to either death or

---

[50] *Annales regni Francorum anno* 800, ed. Kurze, p. 112.

[51] *LP* 2:7 preserves a fragment of the oath Leo swore. This was demonstrated by Wallach, "The Genuine and the Forged Oath of Pope Leo III," in his *Diplomatic Studies in Greek and Latin Documents from the Carolingian Age* (Ithaca, 1977), pp. 299–327, esp. 301–3.

[52] Zimmermann, *Papstabsetzung*, pp. 25–36; Kempf, "Chiesa territoriale," p. 313.

[53] *Annales regni Francorum, anno* 810, ed. Kurze, p. 112.

[54] Sickel, "Verträge," pp. 333–34, appears to be the only scholar who has emphasized this point.

[55] Alcuin, *ep.* no. 184, *MGH, EKA* 2:309. This is the famous letter in which Alcuin says he had destroyed a report about Leo sent to him by Arn. Other information, or charges, probably circulated as a result of Arn's visit to Rome in 799.

[56] Wallach argues persuasively that this synod was judicial in nature: "The Roman Synod of December 800 and the Alleged Trial of Leo III," in his *Diplomatic Studies*, pp. 328–52. It was an inquest, however, and not a trial and it is necessary to emphasize that it was a *synod* and not a secular tribunal.

banishment, on the spot. Three weeks later Leo publicly swore to his own innocence. This had the result of putting the onus on his opponents. Still, there remained the question of what was to be done with those opponents. What would happen to Leo if Charlemagne left Rome? The events of 1 and 23 December shed light retrospectively on Charlemagne's position in Rome before the coronation. Neither the pope nor the Romans were his subjects. He could not sit in judgment of them. In short, down to 23 December the scanty and frequently enigmatic sources provide evidence of profound uncertainty on all sides.

On 25 December Charlemagne was crowned emperor and a few days later, "by the law of the Romans," Leo's attackers were sentenced to death for the *crimen laesae maiestatis*.[57] The old theory that Charlemagne was made emperor to procure a judge competent to pass a sentence in Roman law thus has some validity.[58] Likewise, Heldmann was at least partly correct in saying that the coronation was fundamentally the result of local events in Rome.[59] Only after Christmas did Charlemagne do what he apparently could not have done before he was made emperor, and only the attack on Leo had brought him to Rome in the first place.

At this point the perennially difficult questions raised by Einhard's account of Charlemagne's coronation must be confronted. He said, in perhaps the best-known passage of the *Vita Karoli*, that if Charlemagne had known what was going to happen on Christmas day he would not have gone to church at all despite the solemnity of the occasion.[60] It seems necessary to dismiss as unworthy of belief the idea that Charlemagne was totally surprised by what happened at St. Peter's. The king had been mulling over this whole situation for some eighteen months, and he had been in Rome for

---

[57]*Annales regni Francorum, anno* 801, ed. Kurze, p. 114: "Post paucos autem dies iussit eos, qui pontificem anno superiore deposuerunt, exhiberi; et habita de eis quaestione *secundum legem Romanam* ut maiestatis rei capitis dampnati sunt." *Laesa maiestatis* here does not necessarily imply treason in a Roman sense. Tassilo of Bavaria had been judged guilty of *lèse-majesté* in 788. Increasingly, Frankish law saw infidelity as a *laesa maiestatis*: Maxime Lemosse, "La lèse-majesté dans la monarchie franque," *Revue du moyen âge latine* 1 (1945): 5–24. It is not absolutely clear, however, that the guilty were condemned for infidelity to Charlemagne. It may have been that Leo was seen as the aggrieved party. We shall return to this issue below where fuller evidence can be brought to bear on the matter.

[58]Caspar, "Das Papsttum unter fränkischer Herrschaft," pp. 135–36. Classen, "Karl der Große, das Papsttum und Byzanz," pp. 570–71, 592–93, sees the issues in more or less the same terms.

[59]But he went too far in virtually denying that any other forces were at work. See the selection from his work in Sullivan, *Coronation of Charlemagne*, pp. 59–69.

[60]C. 28, ed. Halphen, p. 80.

more than four weeks. These weeks, it must be assumed, were filled with intense negotiations and discussions on a broad range of subjects. In addition, key persons around Charlemagne, and perhaps people in Rome also, had been contemplating the possibility of making the Frankish king an emperor for many years. Leaving the question of surprise aside, then, Einhard's remark must be examined on other grounds. He was, after all, one of Charlemagne's intimates and had to have had something in mind with his puzzling statement about the king's reaction to his imperial coronation. Because Einhard composed his *vita* in the 820s, long after the events it describes had taken place, it may be useful to expand our field of vision to include more than the exact moment of the coronation. It may be possible, in other words, to develop retrospectively an understanding of what Charlemagne and Einhard found troubling about, to use Viscount Bryce's words, the "central event of the Middle Ages."

The quasi-official *Royal Annals* contain an intriguing report about Charlemagne's activities immediately after the coronation. They say, "Having ordained the affairs, both public, private and ecclesiastical, of the Romans and of the apostolic city and of the whole of Italy—indeed throughout the winter the emperor did nothing else—he again sent an expedition under his son Pepin against the Beneventans and he himself, after Easter [25 April 801] set out from Rome for Spoleto."[61] If only more details survived about all of this activity by Charlemagne! The Beneventan campaign had nothing to do with the Republic. It represented an effort to break the incessant strivings for autonomy by Duke Grimoald. Probably the condemnation of Leo's attackers ought to be reckoned among the emperor's activities. Only one other detail can be filled in. On 4 March 801 Charlemagne pronounced judgment, at Rome, in a very old dispute between Siena and Arezzo.[62] Because, however, both of these cities were in the *regnum* and not in the Republic, Charlemagne's settlement of their controversy tells us nothing about his lawful position in the Republic, or about his conception of the imperial office.[63] It would be different if, for example, the struggle had been between the bishops of, let us say, Alba and Porto. The royal annalist thus portrays a winter bristling with activity, but he and other writers supply virtually no evidence about what was actually going on.

---

[61] *Annales regni Francorum, anno* 801, ed. Kurze, p. 114.

[62] *DK*, 1, no. 196, p. 264. The course of this dispute between Siena and Arezzo from Gregory II to Leo III may be followed in Kehr, *IP* 3:2, 127, 129, 147, 148, 368.

[63] Classen, "Karl der Große, das Papsttum und Byzanz," p. 593, wrongly cites this case as evidence of Charlemagne's imperial rights in Rome.

Charlemagne's diploma for Arezzo is interesting. It bears only his royal titles and contains no mention of the imperial office. Medieval chancery practices are always a valuable indicator of prevailing political and institutional notions. Therefore, it is striking to discover that in early March 801 Charlemagne had not yet officially styled himself emperor. Then, on 29 May 801 the emperor issued, at Bologna, a diploma for Nonantula which bears the official title Charlemagne used for the remainder of his life.[64] This long and cumbersome title reads as follows: "Karolus serenissimus augustus a Deo coronatus magnus pacificus imperator Romanum gubernans imperium, qui et per misericordiam dei rex Francorum atque Langobardorum." Prodigies of ingenuity have been devoted to the task of deciphering the meaning of this curious set of formulations. Apparently, it was meant to express at least four things: (1) Charlemagne did eventually come to view himself as a legitimate emperor, and he took the office seriously; (2) The imperial office was of divine, and not papal, origin—*a Deo coronatus* is the analogue of the *rex Dei gratia* in his former royal title; (3) The secure basis and genuine foundation of Charlemagne's rule was to be found in the two royal titles; and (4) The odd phrase *Romanum gubernans imperium*, which was not a recent invention but a formula taken over from Roman documents probably found at Ravenna, was designed to include the Romans in the empire without acknowledging that the empire itself was Roman, that it had been created by the Romans, or that it was centered on them.[65] To put all of this into slightly different terms, one might say that Charlemagne's empire, and his imperial office, were Christian and Frankish. Charlemagne did not see himself as a Roman emperor, and he in no way imagined himself to be a successor to or a replacement for the Byzantine emperors. Indeed, he spent

---

[64]*DK*, 1, no. 197, p. 265.

[65]There is a vast literature on Charlemagne's imperial ideas. I have been most influenced by: Classen, "Romanum Gubernans Imperium"; Beumann, "Nomen Imperatoris. Studien zur Kaiseridee Karls des Großen"; Arno Borst, "Kaisertum und Namentheorie in Jahre 800"; Beumann, "Das Paderborner Epos und die Kaiseridee Karls des Grossen" all in Wolf's *Zum Kaisertum Karls des Großen*; Schramm, "Karl der Große im Lichte der Staatssymbolik," (as in n.46); Stengel, "Kaisertitel und Souveranitätsidee," *DA* 3 (1939): 1–56; Ohnsorge, *Das Zweikaiserproblem*; Levillain, "Le couronnement imperial de Charlemagne," *Revue histoire de l'église de France* 18 (1932): 1–19; Folz, *The Coronation of Charlemagne*; idem, *The Idea of Empire in Western Europe*, trans. S. A. Ogilvie (New York, 1969), pp. 24–26; Tabacco, "L'ambiguità delle istituzioni nell'Europa costruita dai Franchi," in *Formé di potere e struttura sociale in Italia nel medioevo*, ed. Gabriella Rossetti (Bologna, 1977), pp. 73–81. Naturally, these studies do not all agree. They are, however, complementary and I have learned from each of them.

the next twelve years trying to win from Constantinople recognition of his equality with the eastern emperors.[66]

In 806 Charlemagne divided his realm and provided for the succession among his three legitimate sons.[67] The document issued at that time makes no mention of the imperial office but does tend to view the whole complex of Frankish territories in a unitary way. For example, the emperor's sons were enjoined to support one another in a spirit of fraternal concord, and jointly to defend the church against all its enemies. That Charlemagne did not in 806 confer the imperial title upon one of his sons does not prove that the old emperor considered the imperial office to be a purely personal dignity that would die with him. There is no reason to suppose that he did not plan, at some later date, to name one of this three sons as his imperial successor.[68]

In 813, Louis the Pious actually was made emperor by his father. By this time Louis's brothers, Charles and Pepin, had already died, and lengthy negotitations with Byzantium had culminated in a grudging recognition by the East of the new empire in the West. At Aachen, in the palace chapel, before the assembled Franks, Louis was made emperor on his father's command. Louis lifted from the altar a crown that had been placed there and put it on his own head. The Franks then acclaimed him, in much the same way that the Romans had acclaimed his father some years before. Here, in 813, we can see what Charlemagne had disliked about his own coronation, and why Einhard made his curious remark about his subject's displeasure. It was God and the Franks, as in 813, not the pope and the Romans, as in 800, who alone could create a Carolingian emperor.[69] It cannot be without meaning that Charlemagne did not bequeath his imperial title until after the Byzantine emperor had recognized its legitimacy. Charlemagne's years of

---

[66]Ohnsorge, *Zweikaiserproblem*, pp. 9–10, 24ff, and Schramm, "Karl der Große im Lichte der Staatssymbolik," pp. 290–96, are good on Franco-Byzantine relations.

[67]*MGH, Cap.*, 1, no. 45, pp. 126–30.

[68]The most sensitive analysis of the *Divisio regnorum* is Schlesinger, "Kaisertum und Reichsteilung. Zur Divisio regnorum von 806," in *Zum Kaisertum Karls des Großen*, ed. Wolf, pp. 116–73. See also: Schramm, "Karl der Große im Lichte der Staatssymbolik," pp. 296–300.

[69]*Annales regni Francorum, anno* 813, ed. Kurze, p. 138; Einhard, *Vita Karoli*, c. 30, ed. Halphen, 84. Thegan, *Vita Hludowici*, c. 6, *MGH, SS* 2:591 says Louis crowned himself which Simson (*Jahrbücher* 1:5) accepts but Waitz (*Verfassungsgeschichte Deutschlands* 3:222 n.3) and Ewig (*Handbook of Church History*, p. 101) disagree, believing that Charlemagne crowned Louis. On the coronation and its significance see: Eichmann, *Die Kaiserkrönung im Abendland*, 2 vols. (Wurzburg, 1942), 1:22, 35–36; Beumann, "Romkaiser und fränkischer Reichsvolk," in *Festschrift für E. E. Stengel* (Munster, 1952), pp. 157–80; Heldmann, *Das Kaisertum*, pp. 258–89; Ganshof, *Frankish Institutions*, p. 17 and n.96.

negotiations with the Byzantines suggest that he did not believe that the legitimacy of his imperial office depended upon the pope and the Romans; at least not upon them exclusively.

Given the religious and Frankish foundations upon which Carolingian emperorship rested, it would be hasty to assume that, after 800, Charlemagne immediately succeeded to the ancient rights and prerogatives of the Roman emperors.[70] The evidence for Charlemagne's imperial attitude toward Rome yields a picture that differs in few details from the one drawn earlier of his royal attitude. He condemned Leo's attackers, but he never rendered another verdict of any sort, as far as we know, in Rome. He sent *missi* into the Ravenna region, and evoked a loud retort for having done so, but sent no regular *missi* anywhere else in the Republic. No troops were levied, and no taxes collected. No Carolingian coins were minted in Rome. No Carolingian officials were placed in positions of authority or responsibility in the Republic. No papal officials were subjected to any sort of oversight. The fact that Charlemagne had been made emperor in Rome, and that the Romans had acclaimed him, certainly implies that, at least in an abstract constitutional sense, the emperor had rights in Rome which he had never possessed as *patricius*. When, however, Charlemagne's conduct vis-à-vis Rome between 800 and 814 is examined closely, it is absolutely impossible to ascertain what he imagined those rights to be. He never defined them, and there is little to be gained by engaging in idle speculation about them. When the old emperor died in 814 he left a very unclear situation for his son Louis.[71]

As seen from the point of view of the papacy, the relationship of the Republic with the Frankish empire is only a little clearer. Leo dated his documents by Charlemagne's regnal years, but he put his own name first.[72] This order would never have been tolerated by a Roman or a Byzantine emperor, and it does not conform to the formulations used in private charters in Francia where the name of the king, or emperor, always came first, and the name of a bishop or abbot or secular magnate came second. Leo's coins before 800 bore only his own name,[73] but after the coronation they had

---

[70]But this is the traditional view: Ficker, *Forschungen* 2:344; Sickel, "Verträge," pp. 26–27, 29; Caspar, "Das Papsttum unter fränkischer Herrschaft," p. 146.

[71]Ganshof has argued that many problems were left unsettled at Charlemagne's death. It should be no cause for surprise that relations with the Republic were among them. See: "The Last Period of Charlemagne's Reign: A Study in Decomposition," and "Charlemagne's Failure," in his *Carolingians and the Frankish Monarchy*, pp. 240–55, 256–60.

[72]Fichtenau, "Politische Datierung," pp. 493–94, 497. Jaffé, *RP*, nos. 2498, 2503.

[73]Only one coin survives from the years 795–800. See: Grierson, "Coronation of Charlemagne and Coinage of Leo III," pp. 826–28.

Charlemagne's name on the reverse and "*Sanctus Petrus*" and the papal monogram on the obverse.[74] This, again, was unprecedented in past imperial experience. Fichtenau believes that Leo was seeking to portray himself as "lord" of the Republic and Charlemagne as his "overlord."[75] This is possible. In his letters, however, Leo employed only the customary language of defense and protection.[76] And, like his predecessor Hadrian, he complained about Carolingian *missi* in Ravenna.[77] The most that can prudently be said is that Leo looked at his Republic as an autonomous region within the Frankish empire, and as somewhat more effectively protected by an emperor-friend than it had been by a king-friend. Nothing that Charlemagne said or did would have contradicted his understanding of the situation.

In 802 Charlemagne issued a capitulary that Ganshof, in a famous article, called "Charlemagne's Programme of Imperial Government." It does not mention the Republic or the pope. In the last few years of his life Charlemagne tidied up several discordant or deficient features of numerous contemporary law codes. The Republic's laws were unaffected. After 810 the old emperor embarked upon a massive program of ecclesiastical reform throughout his empire. As far as we know not one of the measures enacted between 810 and 813 touched the Republic.[78]

The very fact that Charlemagne's imperial ideal underwent a good deal of transformation between 800 and 813, and that it may never have assumed clear and precise proportions, ought to put us on our guard against supposing that the great Frank ever formulated an exact comprehension of his imperial relationship with the Republic. Likewise, why should we assume that, after 800, Charlemagne would have decided that his position in Rome had altered dramatically? Certainly his conduct vis-à-vis Rome after he departed in early 801 does not suggest that any new or different conceptions of the Republic were formulated in his mind.

The Republic and Louis the Pious: The *Ludovicianum*

In practice, then, very little had changed in the Republic of St. Peter between 800 and 814. Thus, Charlemagne's assumption of an imperial office, and

---

[74] Serafini, *Monete* 1:5, Tavola 1, nos. 7, 8; *CNI* 15:65, nos. 1–4.

[75] Fichtenau, "Politische Datierung," p. 497.

[76] Leo III, *epp.* nos. 1, 2, 6, 9, *Leo III Epp. X, MGH, EKA* 3:88, 89, 96–97, 100–101.

[77] Leo III, *epp.* nos. 2, 9, 10. *Leo III Epp. X, MGH, EKA* 3:89, 101, 102.

[78] *MGH, Cap.*, vol. 1, no. 33, pp. 91–99. Ganshof, "Charlemagne's Programme of Imperial Government," in his *Carolingians and the Frankish Monarchy*, pp. 55–85.

Louis's succession to that office, do not seem to make it possible to argue that, in theory, the whole situation had been radically transformed. By the time that both Charlemagne and Leo had died, Franco-papal relations were crying out for definition and clarification. Clarity first began to emerge when Stephen IV traveled to Francia in 816 to meet Louis. The result of their meeting was the issuance of the *Pactum Ludovicianum* which not only defined in detail the territorial holdings of the Republic and renewed the traditional "friendship alliance" but also spelled out explicitly the legal and political relationships between the papacy and the Frankish emperor. The fact that the *Ludovicianum* contains a confirmation of the old alliance of 754 with its mutual protection and defense obligations proves that the Republic continued to exist as an autonomous region. Louis would hardly have concluded a treaty—a treaty, it must be remembered, that Louis said replicated the pacts of his father and grandfather—with a people or a person who were his subjects. But, the definitions of both papal and imperial rights contained in the document also suggest that the Republic was no longer as fully independent as it had formerly been. The remarkable aspect of the *Ludovicianum*, however, is not that it represents an effort to define the place of the Republic in the new *Imperium*, but that in almost all critical respects it reflects a deliberate attempt to embalm traditions that reached back to 754.

The legal and political prescriptions contained in the *Ludovicianum* governing Carolingian and papal rights appear at first glance to be so favorable to the papacy that is has been customary to suspect that the document contains masssive forgery or interpolations, or to look at it as evidence of the pious incompetence of Louis *the Pious* who caved in under a papal assault on his imperial prerogatives. There is no need to repeat here what was said in chapter 5 about the authenticity of the *Ludovicianum*. There exist no substantial grounds for impeaching the document's testimony. As to Louis, work done on him in the last generation has gone a long way toward reversing the traditionally negative judgments about him.[79] He was, it is now

---

[79]The reorientation of thinking on Louis the Pious began with two articles: Ganshof, "Louis the Pious Reconsidered " (1957) in his *Carolingians and the Frankish Monarchy*, pp. 261–72, and Schieffer, "Die Krise des karolingischen Imperiums," in *Aus Mittelalter und Neuzeit: Festschrift für Gerhard Kallen*, ed. J. Engel and H. M. Klinkenberg (Bonn, 1957), pp. 1–15. I have surveyed the intervening literature and added perspectives of my own in: "The Monastic Ideal as a Model for Empire: The Case of Louis the Pious," *Revue bénédictine* 86 (1976): 235–50, and "Louis the Pious and His Piety Re-reconsidered," *Revue belge* 58 (1980): 297–316. Old ideas die hard, however. See the recent book by Gustav Faber, *Das erste Reich der Deutschen* (Munich, 1980), pp. 255–68, reflecting positions a hundred years old.

seen, a more active and effective ruler than had been admitted by his detractors. As we shall see, Louis and Stephen IV merely codified the status quo. If the *Ludovicianum* is favorable to the papacy, this is due only to the caution and reserve always shown by the Carolingians in their dealings with Rome. Actually, it ought to be argued that Louis took a decidedly positive step in clarifying and codifying a relationship that had for some sixteen years been left vague and ill-defined.

Louis had a more refined and sophisticated religious sense than his father, and his understanding of his own imperial responsibilities was more profound than Charlemagne's.[80] He styled himself merely *"Imperator Augustus,"*[81] and he called his office a *"munus divinum."*[82] Louis tended to regard the people of his empire not as an agglomeration of ethnic communities, but as the *populus Christianus*, whose souls had been committed to him for safe-keeping.[83] Political theologies that had long been latent, but perhaps only partially formed, in Charlemagne's time came to full fruition in the minds of Louis and his advisers.[84] The much more elaborate ideology evident in Francia after 814 may have been a potent impetus to a clarification of Franco-papal relations. The issuance of the *Ludovicianum* can also be located within a broad pattern of activity during the early years of Louis's reign. The years from 814 to about 819 were filled with political, institutional, and religious reforms of many kinds. The spirit that informed and inspired all of this reform was one of definition; quite often of definition,

---

[80]See my two articles cited in n. 79 and Josef Semmler, "Reichsidee und kirchliche Gesetzgebung," *ZKG* 71 (1960): 37–65.

[81]On Louis's title and its religious significance see: Sigurd Graf von Pfeil, "Der Augustus-Titel der Karolinger," *Die Welt als Geschichte* 20 (1960): 194–210.

[82]Schramm, "Die Siegel, Bullen und Kronen der Karolinger," in his *Kaiser, Könige und Päpste* 2:63–67.

[83]I discuss this in "Monastic Ideal." The classic study remains Henri Xavier Arquillière, *L'augustinisme politique*, 2d ed. (Paris, 1955). Valuable too is Lotte Knabe, *Die gelasianische Zweigewaltenlehre bis zum Ende des Investiturstreits*, (Berlin, 1936).

[84]On ideologies current at Louis's court see: Borst, "Kaisertum und Namentheorie," pp. 50–51; Ullmann, *The Carolingian Renaissance and the Idea of Kingship* (London, 1969), chap. 3; Mohr, *Die karolingische Reichsidee*, chap. 3; idem, "Reichspolitik und Kaiserkrönung in den Jahren 813 und 816," *Die Welt als Geschichte* 20 (1960): 168–86; idem, "Die kirchliche Einheitspartei und die Durchführung der Reichsordnung von 817," *ZKG* 72 (1961): 1–45; Folz, *The Idea of Empire*, pp. 26–29. The work of Ullmann and Mohr is stimulating but must be read very carefully to screen out excessive judgments. Among somewhat older studies these seem to me to have retained much of their value: Carl Erdmann, *Forschungen zur politischen Ideenwelt des früheren Mittelalters aus dem Nachlass des Verfassers* (Berlin, 1951); Roland Faulhaber, *Die Reichseinheitsgedanke in der Literatur der Karolingerzeit bis zum Vertrag von Verdun* (Berlin, 1934).

clarification, or completion of work left unfinished by Charlemagne.[85] One of the key actions taken by Louis involved the calling in of all ecclesiastical privileges in order to examine, confirm, and reissue them.[86] It is therefore not at all cause for wonder that upon the first change in the see of Peter, that is, at the first opportunity to renew the Franco-papal alliance, Louis undertook a fresh examination of the place of the Republic within the Carolingian Empire.

It is not at all clear, however, that Louis unilaterally sought a reckoning of accounts. No evidence exists for an imperial initiative along these lines during the two years when Louis's and Leo's reigns intersected (814–16), and the sources say quite explicitly that, immediately after his election, Stephen IV decided to set out for Francia to meet and negotiate with the emperor. Perhaps there were people in Rome who themselves wondered about the place of the Republic in the Carolingian empire. Such people had been given no clear signals during the fourteen years of Charlemagne's imperial tenure, and none in the first two years of Louis's. Moreover, Stephen was himself elected by, and representative of, the very people who had long and violently opposed Leo III, whose bold step had created the Carolingian imperial office in the first place. It is a fair assumption that Stephen and the Roman nobles saw in this new imperial regime the possibility of a recreation of the Byzantine tyranny of hateful memory. Stephen, in short, may have been encouraged by sixteen years of Carolingian reserve vis-à-vis Rome to travel to Francia in an effort to insure the Republic's independence.

While he was in Francia Stephen IV crowned Louis at Reims in a ceremony rich with religious and symbolic significance, but lacking totally in constitutive force.[87] The official *Liber Pontificalis* does report on Stephen's journey but omits all mention of the coronation. Louis desired this coronation as an enhancement of the Christian characteristics of the office conferred upon him by his father. The papal coronation of 816 did not, however, make him emperor; nor was this coronation the reason for Stephen's long journey. Actually, the recoronation of Louis in 816 is roughly analogous to Pepin's in 754. In each instance the pope, as vicar of Peter and high priest of the Church, added something to an office—once royal, now imperial— that already existed. These coronations were among the things that the popes had been doing for some time for their "friends."

---

[85]See my "Louis the Pious and His Piety," pp. 298–307; Ganshof, "Louis the Pious Reconsidered," p. 262ff.

[86]Thegan, *Vita Hludowici*, c. 10, *MGH, SS* 2:593.

[87]Eichmann, *Kaiserkrönung* 1:18–21; Brühl, "Fränkischer Krönungsbrauch und das Problem der 'Festkrönung,' " *HZ* 194 (1962): 283–311.

Other comments in the sources accurately reflect the true importance and purpose of Stephen's having taken the unusual step of leaving Rome. By drawing upon several surviving accounts we can see that the pope's journey actually was undertaken for the following reasons: to discuss the *"res,"* the property, of the Republic; to treat "other important matters of concern (*"aliisque utilitatibus"*) to the holy Church of God"; to negotiate concerning a number of hostages and fugitives then in Francia "on account of the crimes which they had perpetrated on the Lord Pope, Leo"; and, finally, to define the rights of the pope in Rome, and his political situation there.[88] It seems, then, that after sixteen years of impenetrable obscurity the hour had arrived for the pope to seek a clear statement from the emperor of his place within the Carolingian Empire.

In early October 816, Louis and Stephen carried on negotiations for several days, and the result was the issuance of the *Ludovicianum*. Because the pact deals with each of Stephen's stated reasons for going to Francia, and because the pope went home "having obtained everything which he desired,"[89] it seems reasonable to suggest that its issuance was the consequence of mutually agreeable deliberations.[90] Because parts of the pact echo the language of papal documents, while other sections are remarkably similar to the wording of Carolingian diplomas and capitularies, it is almost a certainty that both Louis and Stephen—or officials acting on their behalf—made important contributions to the shaping of the text.[91] If, then, the impetus to a clarification of Franco-papal relations came from Stephen, Louis showed himself perfectly willing to participate actively in the process. And Louis's participation fits neatly into the pattern of regularizing and routinizing activities that were the hallmarks of the early years of this emperor's reign.

The document itself declares that it was a *"Pactum confirmationis"* and a *"confirmationis decretum."* We have already seen that it contains a renewal of the Franco-papal alliance with its obligation on the part of the Franks to defend the Republic. Here, then, is one thing that was confirmed. The pact also contains a precise and detailed listing of the territories of the Republic. Probably this section of the *Ludovicianum* was a confirmation of a series of

---

[88]LP 2:49; *Annales regni Francorum*, anno 816, ed. Kurze, p. 144; Astronomer, *Vita Hludowici*, c. 27, MGH, SS 2:621; Ermoldus Nigellus, *In honorem Hludowici*, ed. Faral, vs. 936–40, 1034–39, 1040–47.

[89]Astronomer, *Vita Hludowici*, c. 27, MGH, SS 2:621.

[90]Thomas, "Pactum Ludovicianum," ZRG, *kA* 21 (1921): 145; Hahn, "Ludovicianum," pp. 24–25.

[91]Sickel, *Das Privilegium*, pp. 84–87, 120; Hahn, "Ludovicianum," pp. 40–41.

documents beginning with Fulrad's from 756, and proceeding through the Quierzy-Rome documents as emended in 781 and 787. There is no evidence that Charlemagne ever issued a single, comprehensive territorial inventory, although it is not impossible that he did so. Hadrian, it may be recalled, had continually spoken of "*multis documentis.*" More likely, Louis and Stephen pulled numerous instruments out of their respective archives, rationalized them, and put them together into one well-ordered text. In any event, the pact was a confirmation of republican land titles. It is interesting to note once again in this connection that all later papal territorial claims rest upon the *Ludovicianum*, and not upon earlier Carolingian donations.

Having held only these few aspects of the *Ludovicianum* up to scrutiny, we must pause to reflect upon two oddities. If, after 800, the Republic had passed integrally into the Carolingian Empire, why did Louis and Stephen confirm the old Franco-papal alliance? Would not such a confirmation have been appropriate only if Francia and the Republic had remained distinct entities as they had been between 754 and 800? Moreover, why did the pope and the emperor spell out in almost loving detail the territories of the Republic? If the Republic had become a mere annex of the empire in 800 would not an enumeration of its territories have been quite superfluous? When Louis provided for succession to his own throne in 817, he did not mention the Republic, but he did mention Italy in a context that makes it clear that he did not consider the former to be a part of the latter.[92] The dispository language of the *Ludovicianum* is revealing as well. Louis conceded the lands of the Republic into the pope's "*potestate et ditione,*" that he might "hold and dispose" of them as he saw fit. Then, after the long enumeration of lands, Louis repeated that the pope was to have these lands in his "*iure, principatu et ditione.*"[93] Obviously, if the Republic was indeed a part of the empire, it enjoyed an astonishingly privileged status.

The impression that the Republic was a privileged region is confirmed by the paragraphs in the *Ludovicianum* that correspond to the "*aliisque utili-*

---

[92]*MGH, Cap.*, vol. 1, no. 136, c. 17, p. 273.

[93]*MGH, Cap.*, vol. 1, no. 172, pp. 353, 354. This problem is discussed by Thomas, "Pactum Ludovicianum," p. 135ff. It would be hazardous to base any kind of a theory on these words because all of them lack technical precision. Some examples: *ditio* appears in grants of land from Louis's time which bear no similarity to grants to the Republic (*MGH, Formulae*, ed. Karl Zeumer, no. 27, p. 305) in annals referring to Barcelona (*Annales qui dicuntur Einhardi, anno* 797, ed. Kurze, p. 101) and appears repeatedly in the *CC* in all sorts of connections and contexts (nos. 11, 42, 53, 62, 64, 76, 83, 90, 94); *principatus* is used in *CC* (no. 96) to refer to papal authority in dogma, appears in the *Constitutum Constantini* as a term for papal control of bishops (c. 10, ed. Fuhrmann, p. 81) and signified once for the Metz annalist the office of mayor of the palace (*Annales mettenses priores*, ed. Simson, p. 1).

tatibus sanctae Dei ecclesiae" discussed by Louis and Stephen. Louis renounced in perpetuity any right or power of intervening in the Republic unless expressly requested to do so by the pope.[94] Some have thought that this passage must be a forgery,[95] while others hold it up as evidence for Louis's pious foolishness.[96] Both of these interpretations are wrong. Louis and Stephen merely confirmed and put into writing the status quo. No Frank had ever intervened in Rome before 800. Charlemagne did so once, but only on the urgent request of Leo III. When, in 815, Leo had new difficulties, Louis sent a mission to make inquiries and to help the pope if necessary, but it returned home satisfied with Leo's handling of the matter.[97] In short, Louis simply *confirmed* that in the future the Carolingians would not intervene in Rome without having been requested to do so, just as they had not, absent a request, done so in the past. There is no reason to see papal forgery or imperial weakness in this passage, unless one proceeds from incorrect assumptions about what had been customary before 816, and unwarranted speculations about how emperors ought to conduct their affairs.

The same paragraph in the *Ludovicianum* contains a clause about fugitives, another of the subjects that Louis and Stephen treated at Reims. Louis stipulated that if anyone should flee to him in an attempt to escape the pope's authority, Louis would return him. The emperor reserved the right to intercede for fugitives if they had committed trivial offenses, but major malefactors were to be returned promptly. Louis agreed, or perhaps he got the pope to agree, that only persons fleeing from violence or oppression would find refuge in Francia.[98]

---

[94] *MGH, Cap.*, vol. 1, no. 172, p. 354.

[95] Hauck, *Kirchengeschichte Deutschlands* 2:493 n.2; Brunner, *Deutsche Rechtsgeschichte* 2:127 n.57.

[96] A. Hauck, *Kirchengeschichte Deutschlands* 2:493ff (he tries to have it both ways!); von Schubert, *Kirche im Frühmittelalter*, pp. 396–97; Halphen, *Carolingian Empire*, pp. 163–64.

[97] Leo, it will be recalled, was himself attacked and then had his *domuscultae* plundered, Louis sent investigators who reported back to him, and Leo sent a delegation of his own. It is interesting and important to note that Leo condemned his opponents by Roman law of a *laesa maiestatis* and Louis, the situation having calmed, saw no reason to intervene personally. Llewellyn, *Rome in the Dark Ages*, p. 251, says "Leo appears to have insisted on the full sovereign rights of the papacy in Roman law." This is a bit strong, and too juristic, a line of reasoning. It is, however, a fair assessment of how Louis probably viewed his own position. Let us recall that in 800 Leo's first group of opponents may have been condemned for infidelity to the pope, and that *lèse-majesté* and infidelity were increasingly being equated in the Carolingian period. For sources see: *Annales regni Francorum, anno* 815, ed. Kurze, pp. 142–43; Astronomer, *Vita Hludowici*, c. 25, *MGH, SS* 2:619.

[98] *MGH, Cap.*, vol. 1, no. 172, p. 354: "Et si quilibet homo de supradictis civitatibus ad vestram ecclesiam pertinentibus ad nos venerit, subtrahere se volens de vestra ditione et potes-

In 790 or 791 Hadrian had written to Charlemagne to say that just as he would never receive a fugitive from Frankish justice, so Charlemagne should not harbor persons trying to escape papal jurisdiction.[99] This suggests that no firm rule was then in force governing fugitives, and that Hadrian did not believe that his subjects had some sort of a right of appeal to the Carolingian court. Louis thus merely confirmed that, except under limited and special circumstances, he also had no right or duty to receive fugitives from the Republic. Certainly the plight of appellants and of fugitives would have been much the same in practice; so if the Republic was securely a part of the empire, does it not seem strange that its inhabitants did not, like all other residents of the empire, possess, at least in theory, the elementary right of appeal to the emperor? Does it not appear that, again, the Republic enjoyed a peculiarly privileged status not accorded to any other region? Indeed, the fugitive clause seems more like an extradition treaty between two independent states than a political settlement between master and subject, or between two concurrent rulers within the same state.

A few tantalizing hints in the sources may make it possible to apprehend, at least to some extent, the true nature of the Republic's status. A guaranty of protection, coupled with a prohibition of access to public officials and a requirement to hand over fugitives, sounds very much like a regular institution in Frankish law: the immunity. The language of the *Ludovicianum* approximates in some ways the language of Louis's immunity formula,[100] and during the early years of his reign, Louis issued numerous immunity diplomas which—this was a novelty—also bore royal protection, to churches throughout his empire.[101] Ewig calls this a "comprehensive system" during Louis's reign,[102] and it seems that a special version of the system was applied to the Republic. More research will have to be done to complement the seminal study of Semmler, but I wonder if Louis's "comprehensive"

---

tate, vel aliam quamlibet iniquiam machinationem metuens aut culpam commissam fugiens, nullo modum eum aliter recipiemus nisi ad iustam pro eo faciendo intercessionem, ita dumtaxat si culpa quam commisit venialis fuerit inventa; sin aliter comprehensum vestre potestati eum remittamus: exceptis his qui violentiam vel oppressionem potentiorum passi ideo ad nos venerint, ut per nostram intercessionem iustitiam accipere mereantur; quorum altera conditio est a superioribus est valde disiuncta."

[99]CC, no. 94, p. 635.

[100]Hahn, "Ludovicianum," pp. 92ff, 128–29.

[101]Semmler, "Traditio und Königsschutz: Studien zur Geschichte der königlichen Monasteria," ZRG, kA 45 (1959): 1–33.

[102]Ewig, *Handbook of Church History*, p. 106; Semmler, "Kirchliche Gesetzgebung und Reichsidee," p. 42.

immunity-protection "system" was not itself patterned upon the Franco-papal alliance. Some historians have in the past noticed that there are similarities between the immunity and the customary treatment of the Republic by the Carolingians, but they have failed to draw out the full implications of their observation.[103]

It would probably be a mistake to push the analogy too far because the Roman Church and its Republic were demonstrably different in countless ways from the churches and monasteries of Francia. Still, the coincidences between the immunity-protection system so widely deployed by Louis and the terms of the *Ludovicianum* are too close to be dismissed. It was, I believe, by a system analogous to the granting of an immunity that the legal relations between the Carolingians and the papacy were defined. Today it is widely recognized that the grant of an immunity was not inevitably damaging to the rights of the monarchy for, in fact, the immunity created a strong legal bond between grantor and recipient.[104] From the "immunity analogy" theory just expressed, it is possible to say, finally, that the Republic definitely was thought by the Carolingians to be a part of their empire. From the beginning, however, they had possessed exiguous rights there, and the *Ludovicianum* merely confirmed that tradition.

The pope had reason to be satisfied with the *Ludovicianum* because he had given up little. Stephen and his successors continued to acknowledge a vague imperial overlordship by putting the emperor's name on documents and coins.[105] In day-to-day affairs, however, the pope continued to be master

---

[103]Brunner, *Deutsche Rechtsgeschichte* 2:120: "constitutionally the papal region may be described as a dominion equipped with comprehensive seigneurial and immunity rights lying inside the Frankish empire." See also: Gundlach, *Kirchenstaat*, pp. 79–80; von Schubert, *Kirche im Frühmittelalter*, p. 350; Thomas, "Pactum Ludovicianum," p. 133; Hartmann, *Geschichte Italiens* 3.1:99.

[104]For the older view that immunities were damaging to royal authority one can consult: Maurice Kroell, *L'immunité franque* (Paris, 1910). Walter Goffart, *The LeMans Forgeries* (Cambridge, Mass., 1966), chap. 1, takes a dim view of immunities as does Helmut Quaritsch, *Staat und Souveranität* (Frankfurt, 1970), 1:190ff, but they treat periods when the royal power in general was declining and thus the power of immunists was rising. This was not how the system was supposed to work, and it did work well under vigilant kings. See: Brunner, *Deutsche Rechtsgeschichte* 2:382–415; Ganshof, "L'immunité dans la monarchie franque," *Recueil de la société Jean Bodin* 1, 2d ed. (Brussels, 1958): 171–216; idem, *Frankish Institutions*, pp. 45–50. For some especially penetrating insights on the intended functioning of the immunity see Theodor Mayer, *Fürsten und Staat* (Weimar, 1950), p. 31, and Lot, "Le concept d'empire à l'époque carolingienne," in *Recueil des travaux historiques de Ferdinand Lot* (Paris, 1968), 1:351.

[105]For documents see: Jaffé, *RP*, no. 2549 (Paschal I); for coins, the series inaugurated by

of his own house. Relations between Rome and Aachen changed somewhat after 800, but they did not return to conditions like those that had obtained when central Italy had been Byzantine. The territorial integrity of the Republic was assured, and its defense was guaranteed. In short, the popes after 800 gave up very little to preserve what they had been seeking for a century, freedom and autonomy, while the Franks claimed little in the way of regalian rights, because for more than a half-century they had possessed none. It may be worth recalling, one last time, that the *Ludovicianum* was a confirmation.

The Republic and Louis the Pious: The *Constitutio Romana*

The next milestone in Franco-papal relations was reached with the issuance of the *Constitutio Romana* in 824. Traditionally this document has been interpreted as having inaugurated a radical departure from the regime instituted by the *Ludovicianum*.[106] This interpretation is flawed on at least two counts. First, it proceeds from the assumption that the *Ludovicianum* represented a gross abandonment of imperial rights that were then recovered in 824. This view totally misunderstands the place of the *Ludovicianum* within the long history of Franco-papal relations. Second, it incorrectly assumes that the *Ludovicianum* and the *Constitutio Romana* were radically different. In fact, the pact of 824 can be explained as a logical and coherent extension of the pact of 816–17.

It is important, but also very difficult, to ascertain why, after only eight years, it was felt necessary to emend the *Ludovicianum*. Moreover, it is curious to note that the *Constitutio Romana* appears to have been the result of unilateral action[107] by Louis's son Lothair, acting on his father's behalf,[108]

Leo III lasted for a century: Serafini, *Monete* 1:6–7 and Tavola 1, nos. 9–19 or *CNI* 15:66–69. It may be worth noting, also, that like his father Louis did not mint coins in Rome: Morrison, *Carolingian Coinage*, pp. 145–47.

[106]This interpretation is pervasive. For examples: A. Hauck, *Kirchengeschichte Deutschlands* 2:496–98; von Schubert, *Kirche im Frühmittelalter*, p. 398; Amann, *L'époque carolingienne*, p. 209; Seppelt, *Geschichte der Päpste* 2:208–10; Lorenz Weinrich, *Wala: Graf, Mönch und Rebell* (Lübeck, 1963); Halphen, *Carolingian Empire*, pp. 178–80; Ewig, *Handbook of Church History*, p. 112; Partner, *Lands of St. Peter*, p. 49.

[107]*MGH Cap.*, vol. 1, no. 161, p. 323: "Constitutum habemus. . . ."

[108]Those who see the act as a departure from the *Ludovicianum* assume that Lothair or his associate Wala were responsible for it. First, one must ask how they forced this act upon an unwilling Louis. Second, what are we to make of the statement in the quasi-official *Royal*

when the *Ludovicianum* had so obviously been the product of mutual discussions in 816. The text of the *Constitutio* itself, plus some related documents, provide insights into what came to be seen as shortcomings in the *Ludovicianum*, but absolute certainty about conditions in Rome between 816 and 824 is beyond reach, and it is in Rome, rather than in Francia, that one must seek the reasons for the issuance of the *Constitutio*.

The evidence may be scanty and enigmatic, but it points in a straight line to turbulence and unsavory behavior. Sometime between 28 June and 27 July 823 Louis received news[109] that Theodore and Leo, respectively the *primicerius* and *nomenclator* of the Republic, had been blinded and beheaded in Rome.[110] Apparently at least two other persons suffered a like fate.[111] According to some accounts, these men had been murdered for showing loyalty to Lothair, and there are intimations in these accounts that Pope Paschal was implicated.[112] Louis immediately decided to send *missi* to Rome to investigate, but before they had even departed a delegation from Paschal arrived in Francia. Louis dismissed Paschal's representatives quickly and sent his own envoys to Rome anyway.[113] When they arrived there they were unable to pursue an investigation because Paschal and a number of Roman clerics had purged themselves by oath of any wrongdoing.[114] Paschal did send a second delegation to Louis, but it merely asserted that the pope had had nothing to do with the deaths of Theodore and the others and that, because the perpetrators belonged to the *familia sancti Petri*, the pope had no intention of handing them over. Finally, the envoys, speaking of course for the pope, said that the two men had gotten what they had deserved because they had committed the *crimen laesae maiestatis* and had accord-

---

Annals that Louis sent Lothair to Italy "ut vice sua functus ea quae rerum necessitas flagitare videbatur" (*anno* 824, ed. Kurze, p. 164)? Lothair issued the edict in Rome but it was Louis's idea.

[109]*BM*, no. 778a.

[110]*Annales regni Francorum*, anno 823, ed. Kurze, p. 161.

[111]Considerations were made on behalf of a Floronis and a Sergius in the *Constitutio*: *MGH, Cap.*, vol. 1, no. 161, p. 323.

[112]*Annales regni Francorum*, anno 823, ed. Kurze, p. 161; Astronomer, *Vita Hludowici*, c. 37, *MGH, SS* 2:627–28.

[113]*Annales regni Francorum*, anno 823, ed. Kurze, pp. 161–62; Astronomer, *Vita Hludowici*, c. 37, *MGH, SS* 2:627–28.

[114]Howard Adelson and Robert Baker, "The Oath of Purgation of Pope Leo III in 800," *Traditio* 8 (1952): 35–80, believe that the procedure used in 823 was technically a "*purgatio canonica*" but Wallach, "Genuine and Forged Oath," p. 313ff, demonstrates that this procedure did not develop until the eleventh century. Paschal did, however, mimic the action of Leo III in 800.

ingly been condemned lawfully.[115] Louis sent this second delegation back to Rome and for several months nothing more was done.

In many ways these events are reminiscent of those of 799–800 and 815–16. Each time the pope was in trouble, charges of *lèse-majesté* were spoken, and Carolingian intervention was short-circuited by either a papal oath or preemptive papal action. Louis did send envoys to Rome without, as far as we know, having been asked to do so. No litigation of any kind ensued, however. The traditional Carolingian reluctance to interfere in the domestic life of Rome had apparently been affirmed. It is also striking that in 800, 815, and 824 Frankish sources mention the *crimen laesae maiestatis* in connection with the pope's travails. "Majesty breaking," in Roman law, was a crime only against the emperor. It amounted to treason. It was in a fundamental way a breach of sovereignty. In none of these cases had the emperor been attacked, although, of course, his protegé was; and when Leo was attacked in 799 there was no emperor. Still, if Romans could commit an offense tantamount to treason by attacking the pope, does this not speak eloquently for the independence of the pope's position within the empire?

When Paschal's second set of legates returned to Rome they found the pope ill; in fact he was on the point of death. A few days later he died, and there ensued a double election. The *Liber Pontificalis*, displaying characteristic discretion, does not mention electoral strife, or the fact that the Romans refused to allow Paschal to be buried at St. Peter's. Frankish sources add these details, while also reporting that Wala, a relative of Louis and long one of the Franks' "Italian experts," worked hard to get Eugenius II elected in order to effect, through him, necessary reforms.[116]

Reforms came quickly enough through the *Constitutio Romana*, although the *Liber Pontificalis* does say of Eugenius that he labored humanely in his own right on behalf of the poor and oppressed.[117] In other words, neither Frankish nor papal sources depict Eugenius as a Carolingian stooge. The *Constitutio* itself, whose provisions will be analyzed below, speaks of unjust seizures of land, depredations by papal officials, and ecclesiastical properties seized "as if with papal license."[118] Paschasius Radbertus, Wala's

---

[115]*Annales regni Francorum, anno* 823, ed. Kurze, p. 162; Astronomer, *Vita Hludowici*, c. 37, *MGH, SS* 2:628; Thegan, *Vita Hludowici*, c. 30, *MGH, SS* 2:597.

[116]*BM*, no. 785b; Jaffé, *RP*, p. 320. *Annales regni Francorum, anno* 824, ed. Kurze, p. 164; Thegan, *Vita Hludowici*, c. 30, *MGH, SS* 2:597; Paschasius Radbertus, *Vita Walae* 1.28, *PL* 120:1604; *LP* 2:69. See also: Weinrich, *Wala*, pp. 51–52; Amann, *L'époque carolingienne*, p. 208; Haller, *Das Papsttum* 2:27.

[117]*LP* 2:69.

[118]*MGH, Cap.*, vol. 1, no. 161, cc. 2, 6, p. 323.

biographer, hints at the existence of certain long-standing grievances without, unfortunately, specifying what they were.[119] A passage in the *Ottonianum*, the pact of Otto I granted in 962, mentions "inexcusable acts" committed before the issuance of the *Constitutio*.[120] This is all the evidence we have, plus of course the violence of the year 823, to try to fit together a picture of Roman conditions in the mid-820s, and to measure the Frankish response to those conditions.

A fully coherent and nuanced picture of those conditions simply cannot be drawn, but certain lines and features can be discerned. A late ninth-century treatise says that at the time of the deaths of Theodore and Leo all the "greater men of the city had become adherents of the emperor."[121] This cannot be literally true. Theodore and Leo were high officers of the Lateran and it is possible that they were imperial partisans. Paschal himself, however, must have retained the loyalty of other key people. Members of his two legations to Francia included Bishop John of Silva-Candida, the Archdeacon Benedict, the *bibliothecarius* Sergius, a subdeacon Quirinus, and the *magister militum* Leo. Moreover, a Frankish report, which may or may not be strictly accurate but which is certainly revealing, says that thirty-four bishops and five priests and deacons exculpated themselves by oath of any guilt in the deaths of Theodore and his associates.[122] These people must have been supporters of Paschal, and their numbers suggest that his power base was fairly broad. From these few details it seems safe to draw the inference that many papal officers supported the pope but that some did not, and that those who opposed Paschal had perhaps turned to Lothair, and maybe even to Louis, to seek redress of some sort. Lothair and several of his closest advisers had been in Italy frequently between 822 and 824, and in 823 this eldest son of Louis the Pious was crowned emperor by Paschal in a ceremony similar in significance to his father's coronation at Reims in 816. People in Rome who had grievances against the pope would have had ample opportunity to turn to the young emperor, and the *Ludovicianum* had provided that persons fearing violence or oppression could appeal outside the Republic. The sources that speak of long-standing grievances, depredations, prop-

---

[119]*Vita Walae*, 1.28, *PL* 120:1604.

[120]*MGH, DO*, vol. 1, no. 235, p. 326.

[121]*Libellus de imperia potestate in urbe Rome*, ed. Zuchetti (*FSI*, vol. 55 [Rome, 1920]), pp. 197–98. The editor comments that whereas the *Libellus* makes this remark right after narrating Leo's problems in 815 other statements in the text make it clear that the author was talking about 823–24. The *Libellus* is quite frequently wrong about such details. See also: Gregorovius, *Geschichte der Stadt Rom* 3:45.

[122]Thegan, *Vita Hludowici*, c. 30, *MGH, SS* 2:597.

erty disputes, and "inexcusable acts" surely evoke an image of violence and oppression, and that image is brought into sharper focus by the deaths of Theodore, Leo, and the others in 823.

It seems that the Lateran hierarchy was riven by factional strife. Ever since the pontificate of Zachary, but especially during and after the time of Hadrian, the Roman nobility had been merging with the ecclesiastical elite of the Republic. In the 760s there may still have been fairly clear lines drawn between the lay and clerical orders, but after that time the Lateran itself had become the cockpit for intramural and internecine struggles among noble factions constituted out of the same basic social groups. Evidently these disputes turned, at least in part, on issues of land rights and judicial manipulation, but in the absence of records there is no point in speculating about details. It also seems that the dispute of 823, whatever its precise instigation might have been, had spilled over into the countryside. The murderers of Theodore and company were members of the *familia sancti Petri*, that is, of the farmer-soldiers on the rural *domuscultae*. In addition, thirty-four bishops pled innocent of any wrongdoing. Rome had seven suburbicarian bishops, so if the pertinent Frankish report is literally accurate, twenty-seven rural bishops were involved somehow. Perhaps factions in Rome were unhappy about certain developments outside the city. Or, it may be that contending parties in the city were linked with opposed parties in the vicinity of Rome. The popes had a stranglehold on the institutional life of the Republic, and so during the 820s, the faction out of power turned to the emperor. This caused the faction in power to react brutally, but it should be remembered that their actions were by no means unprecedented. Let us recall the violence that marked the years from 767 to 772, and the attacks on Leo III in 799 and again in 815. As earlier disturbances had had a tendency to recur, so too the killings of 823 did not put a term to the problems of the 820s. There was a contested papal election in 824. Only the dim outlines of the real problems of these years can be perceived by historians because papal biographers usually supplied few details, and Frankish writers were generally in the dark because Carolingian inquests, of which there were many, repeatedly crashed against walls of silence. Factional squabbles, probably having something to do with land battles and court cases, seem to have been behind all of these difficulties. More cannot be said with confidence.

Since 754 the Carolingians had assumed a responsibility to protect St. Peter's "peculiar people." When it had been the Lombards trying to visit evil upon the Republic, the issues were clear for the Franks. When, after 799, St. Peter's people began doing violence to one another, it must have become extremely difficult in Francia to decide how and whom to protect. The

Constitutio Romana provided, for the Carolingian era and for a long time thereafter, the definitive answer.

Happily there is no need to enter into any detailed textual or diplomatic discussions of the *Constitutio*. Although fragments of it are transmitted in canonical collections, it also has an independent manuscript tradition, and there have never been any serious questions about its authenticity.[123] In some ways the *Constitutio* is a conservative document which honors the historically privileged position of the Republic. In other ways, however, the pact of 824 extended certain features of the *Ludovicianum* so as to create an imperial presence in Rome, and to tie the Republic more tightly to the empire than it had ever been tied before. It did not, however, resurrect a Byzantine type of control over Rome.[124] It was a Carolingian document, true to traditions seventy years old at its issuance. Also, if the Romans had behaved in a reasonably civilized way, the *Constitutio* would never have been issued at all. This must not be forgotten.

The first feature of the *Constitutio* which is simultaneously conservative and innovative has to do with papal elections. As in the *Ludovicianum*, the franchise was still extended to all Romans, but this time an imperial sanction was brought to bear upon anyone who might presume to interfere unlawfully in the electoral process. Troublemakers would henceforth be exiled by the emperor. Elections were to be carried out "justly and canonically."[125] All of this was profoundly conservative and exemplifies the traditional Carolingian reluctance to intrude into the elections of popes. Innovative, however, was a requirement that the newly elected pope had to confirm by oath the old Franco-papal alliance before he could be consecrated.[126] The intent here was evidently to remind the newly elected pope that he had reciprocal obligations vis-à-vis the Carolingians. There is no evidence that the Franks claimed a right to pass judgment upon the fitness of the newly elected pope. Byzantine emperors could have, in theory at least, rejected a newly elected candidate by witholding confirmation. Louis did not claim this right.

A second aspect of the *Constitutio* which looked both to the past and to the future is its treatment of the Romans. The clauses in the *Constitutio*

---

[123]See Boretius's introductory comments: *MGH, Cap.*, vol. 1, pp. 322–23.

[124]Schieffer thought so: "Krise des karolingischen Imperiums," p. 7.

[125]*MGH, Cap.*, vol. 1, no. 161, c. 3, p. 323.

[126]Sickel, "Verträge," pp. 40–41, and Bertolini, "Osservazione sulla 'Constitutio Romana' e sul 'Sacramentum Cleri e Populi Romani' dell'824," in *Studi medievali in onore di Antonio de Stefano* (Palermo, 1956), p. 53ff, correctly see that Eugenius was only required to confirm the alliance. On the oaths in the *Constitutio* see below.

dealing with the Romans have evoked some controversy, and, for the most part, the *guerre des savants* has been waged because of a misunderstanding of the issues involved.

The *Constitutio* concludes with an oath that all Romans were to be required to swear to the emperor. In order to understand this oath, its importance for the status of the Romans, and the historical controversies associated with it, a full citation of the text will be helpful.

Promitto ego ille per Deum omnipotentem et per ista sacra quattuor euangelia et per hanc crucem domini nostri Iesu Christi et per corpus beatissimi Petri principis apostolorum, quod ab hac die in futurum fidelis ero dominis nostris imperatoribus Hludowico et Hlothario diebus vitae meae, iuxta vires et intellectum meum, sine fraude atque malo ingenio, salva fide quam repromisi domino apostolico; et quod non consentiam ut aliter in hac sede Romana fiat electio pontificis nisi canonice et iuste, secundum vires et intellectum meum; et ille qui electus fuerit me consentiente consecratus pontifex non fiat, priusquam tale sacramentum faciat in praesentia missi domini imperatoris et populi, cum iuramento, quale dominus Eugenius papa sponte pro conservatione omnium factum habet per scriptum.[127]

There are quite clearly three distinct elements in this oath, and a proper understanding of them requires that we work backward, taking the third element first. We must begin, though, with a few preliminary considerations. The manuscripts of the *Constitutio* do not contain any part of this oath text. It is the Roman continuation of Paul the Deacon's *History of the Lombards* which transmits the document, although placing it in 825.[128] The papal oath has been interpreted as a revolution in Franco-papal relations,[129] and as a later imperial forgery.[130] Some scholars doubt that the oath was

---

[127]*MGH, Cap.*, vol. 1, no. 161, p. 324. A translation may be helpful: "I promise by almighty God, and by these four holy Gospels, and by this cross of our Lord Jesus Christ, and by the body of blessed Peter, the prince of the apostles, that from this day forward I shall be faithful to our lord emperors, Louis and Lothair, all the days of my life to the best of my ability and understanding, without fraud or evil intention, save for that loyalty which I have promised again to my apostolic lord; and that I shall not consent that in this Roman see there shall be a papal election conducted otherwise than canonically and justly, [I promise these things] to the best of my ability and understanding; and that he who shall have been elected shall not with my consent be consecrated pope before he shall have sworn an oath in the presence of the *missi* of the lord emperor just like the oath sworn by the lord pope Eugenius in writing, of his own free will and for the benefit of all."

[128]*Pauli continuatio Romana, MGH, SSrL*, p. 203.

[129]Halphen, *Carolingian Empire*, p. 180.

[130]Ullmann, "Origins of the Ottonianum," p. 117ff; idem, *A Short History of the Papacy in the Middle Ages*, corrected ed. (London, 1974), p. 92.

ever sworn at all,[131] while others believe that it formed part of a second, otherwise unattested, pact between Louis and Eugenius from 825.[132] Obviously, these problems need to be cleared up.

Ullmann challenged the authenticity of the oath, primarily because he believes that the *Constitutio* was designed to provide more effective imperial protection for the Republic and that making the pope an imperial subject was no good way to secure protection. Thus, he reasons, the oath was a later imperial forgery, and this explains how a mention of it found its way into the privilege of Otto I for the Roman Church. As we shall see, Ullmann is virtually the only historian who has properly understood the spirit of the *Constitutio*, but he misunderstood the nature of Eugenius's oath and blazed a trail that leads nowhere in attacking its authenticity.

The *Ottonianum* does contain reference to a papal oath, but required one to be sworn as it had been "by our venerable and spiritual father Leo."[133] Because virtually the whole of the *Constitutio Romana* was incorporated into the *Ottonianum*,[134] scholars have, not unnaturally, looked at this "Leo" and said that there cannot have been an oath by Eugenius in 824. This assumption was buttressed by the idea that the Leo in question had to be Leo VIII (963–65) because the language of the *Ottonianum* seems to speak of a living man. Then Paul Kehr demonstrated that the relevant passage of the *Ottonianum* was taken over verbatim from a nonextant imperial privilege from about 850,[135] and Karl Hampe proved that the Leo in question was actually Leo IV (847–55).[136] Thus, sources will sustain an argument that Leo IV swore an oath, and this ought to have removed the necessity of appealing to a tenth-century concoction. Further research turned up the fact that, for a time, Sergius II (844–47) adamantly refused to swear an oath,[137] which certainly points to the fact that the obligation was then in force. Finally, there is good evidence that Gregory IV (827–44) swore an oath.[138]

---

[131]Simson, *Jahrbücher* 1:230 n.4; *BM*, no. 1021. Von Schubert, *Kirche im Frühmittelalter*, p. 397.

[132]Brunner, *Deutsche Rechtsgeschichte* 2:127–28; Stengel, "Kaiserprivilegs," pp. 224–25.

[133]*MGH, DO* 1:326.

[134]The relationship between the *Ottonianum* and its predecessors has been comprehensively discussed by Zimmermann, "Das Privilegium Ottonianum und seine Problemsgeschichte," *MIÖG, Erganzungsband* 20 (1962): 147–90.

[135]In Kehr's review of Lindner, pp. 135–37.

[136]Hampe, "Die Berufung Ottos des Großen nach Rom durch Papst Johann XII," *Historische Aufsätze Karl Zeumer dargebracht* (Weimar, 1910), pp. 159ff, 163ff.

[137]*LP* 2:90. *BM*, no. 1115a. Halphen, *Carolingian Empire*, pp. 229–31; Ernst Dümmler, *Geschichte des ostfränkischen Reiches*, 2d ed., 3 vols. (1887; reprint, Hildesheim, 1960), 1:249–51.

[138]*Annales regni Francorum*, anno 827, ed. Kurze, pp. 173–74; Astronomer, *Vita Hludo-*

Nothing certain is known about Valentinus, the pope between Eugenius and Gregory, but all of the available evidence urges us to conclude that the oath was indeed required beginning with Eugenius.[139] There also appear to be no good reasons to assume that the oath was part of a second pact from 825.[140] In short, then, Eugenius did swear an oath, and the *Constitutio* required that all future popes would have to swear it before their consecrations.

So, Eugenius swore an oath. In other words, the third element of the "oath package" of the *Constitutio* is authentic and datable. Now we must try to see what kind of an oath it was. Some scholars have argued that the *Constitutio* marked a revolution in Franco-papal relations because the pope was required after 824 to swear a Frankish subject's oath. The assumption here is that the first part of the "oath package" attached to the *Constitutio* was actually a Frankish subject's oath. Again, it is necessary to turn first to the third portion of the oath package, a portion that has habitually been misread. The key words required the Romans to guarantee that they would not allow a pope to be consecrated until he had sworn an oath like the one Eugenius *had sworn*. The past tense was used in order to speak about what Eugenius had already done, not to describe what he was going to do upon or after the issuance of the *Constitutio*. The *Constitutio* was issued in mid-November 824[141] and speaks, therefore, about something that the pope had already accomplished. He was elected and consecrated in early June,[142] and we have already seen that the Frankish agent Wala was in Rome at that time. Thus, the only possible conclusion that can be drawn is that, shortly after his election, Eugenius confirmed in writing, probably in Wala's presence, the old Franco-papal alliance. That he did this in writing agrees perfectly with most previous confirmations of the alliance when there had been no face-to-face papal-Carolingian encounters (e.g., 757, 767, 768, 796, 817). In addition, the text itself speaks of an oath Eugenius made *"per scriptum,"* that is, in writing. The *Ludovicianum* had affirmed the obligation of confirming the alliance, and the *Constitutio* retained that affirmation while additionally demanding that it be accomplished before an imperial *missus* and before

---

wici, c. 41, *MGH, SS* 2:631; Benedict, *Chronicon,* ed. Zuchetti, p. 144. In my view Gregory later admitted to swearing an oath in a letter of his preserved with the correspondence of Agobard: *ep.* no. 16, *MGH, EKA* 3:230.

[139]On other grounds Bertolini, "Osservazione," pp. 50–52, disproves Ullmann's theory of forgery.

[140]Zimmermann, *Papstabsetzung,* p. 39 n.68; Ewig, *Handbook of Church History,* p. 112.

[141]Ewig, *Handbook of Church History,* p. 112, says, without sources, 11 November. *BM,* no. 793b, states only that Lothair was in Rome on 11 and 13 November.

[142]Jaffé, *RP,* p. 320.

consecration. It simply is not possible to read into this text a proof that Eugenius swore a subject's oath. Ullmann has astutely observed that turning the pope into a subject really would have been revolutionary, and that it would have evoked a loud howl of protest from Rome.[143] Eugenius did not complain precisely because no fundamental novelty had been thrust upon him. Quite simply, Eugenius's successors were to ally with the Franks before, and not after, they were consecrated. This relatively minor innovation changed nothing in the basic Franco-papal bond.

The second clause of the oath was also mildly innovative, but no radical departure from prevailing custom. All it did was to insure that the Romans would pledge themselves to fair and canonical papal elections. The *Ludovicianum* had insisted on the same electoral procedures without requiring the Romans to take an oath binding them to abide by them. Now an oath was required, probably as an effective means of rendering justiciable anyone who might presume to break it. Louis thus defined the terms of his defense a little more precisely and required the Romans to act a bit more responsibly. In 824, then, a rather general provision of the *Ludovicianum* was tightened up a bit. That is all.

Now we can return to the first portion of the oath package. There can be no doubt that the clause beginning "*Ego ille promitto . . .*" is a Frankish subject's oath. One has only to compare it to the preserved text of this oath as it was sworn in 802.[144] Even though it should now be clear that this is not the oath that the pope swore in 824, we must still ask whether, by requiring the Romans to swear a Frankish subject's oath, Louis did not take a revolutionary step designed to make the inhabitants of the Republic his subjects in a direct and explicit way. Was this oath a blatant manifesto of imperial sovereignty?

There is no denying that the requirement laid upon the Romans to swear this oath was a novelty. Leo III had tried to get Charlemagne to send "one of his magnates" to Rome to take up some sort of an oath in 796, and Stephen IV received some kind of oath before he went to Francia in 816. Nothing came of either of these schemes, however, and we cannot be certain

---

[143]Ullmann, "Origins of the Ottonianum," p. 120.

[144]*MGH, Cap.*, vol. 1, no. 34, p. 101: "Sacramentale qualiter repromitto ego, quod ab isto die inantea fidelis sum domno Karolo piissimo imperatori, filio Pippini regis et Berthanae reginae, puramente absque fraude et malo ingenio de mea parte ad suam partem et ad honorem regni sui, sicut per drichtum debet esse homo domino suo. Si me adiuvet Deus et ista sanctorum patrocinia quae in hoc loco sunt, quia diebus vitae meae per meam voluntatem, in quantum mihi Deus intellectum dederit, sic attendam et consentiam."

what the popes had in mind. There is, moreover, absolutely no evidence before 824 that the subject's oaths of 789 and 802 were ever sworn in Rome or its environs.[145] I suspect that Leo and Stephen were only referring in an oblique way to the fidelity owed by the Romans to the Franks as a component of the alliance. Therefore, we do have an innovation in 824, but what is to be made of it? Much less than some scholars have made.[146]

To my knowledge, no one has ever commented on the fact that the *Constitutio* oath contains a safeguard clause. The oath required persons to swear fidelity to the emperor "save for the fidelity *salva fide* which they had sworn to the pope." There are two clear precedents for this safeguard clause in earlier Carolingian documents. In Charlemagne's *Divisio Imperii* of 806, regulations regarding succession were set forth in detail, but the emperor reserved all imperial rights and prerogatives until his own death.[147] Likewise, in Louis's succession instrument, the *Ordinatio Imperii* of 817, there is a "*salva*" clause that expressly reserved the emperor's rights until his death.[148] These safeguard clauses should be taken seriously because they mean that no imperial rights were to be shared while the reigning emperors yet lived.[149] The presence of a *salva* clause in the *Constitutio* is thus striking because it can only mean that inhabitants of the Republic owed fidelity to the pope in the first place, and to the emperor in the second place. The *Constitutio* did not assert imperial sovereignty in unambiguous terms as, presumably, a revolutionary act would have done. At the same time, a similar regime of vaguely concurrent powers had long been in operation in Ravenna, so there was at least a rough precedent behind what the *Constitutio* did for the Republic as a whole.

Ever since 754 the Franks and the inhabitants of the Republic had had reciprocal obligations to one another because they were *amici*. For the Franks this meant, in practice, assuring the defense of the Republic from external threats, but it could also mean protecting St. Peter's "peculiar people" from themselves. Defeating the Lombards was a relatively clear-cut issue, but defending Leo against his attackers, or determining who, exactly, required

---

[145]That the oath of 802 was not sworn in Rome was demonstrated long ago by A. Laptre, *L'Europe et le Saint-siège à l'époque carolingienne* (Paris, 1895), pp. 212–13 and 213 n.2.

[146]Duchesne, *Temporal Sovereignty*, p. 130ff; Amann, *L'époque carolingienne*, p. 209; Brezzi, *Roma e l'empero*, pp. 46–48; Halphen, *Carolingian Empire*, p. 180; Bertolini, "Osservazione," p. 76; Schieffer, "Krise," p. 7; Ewig, *Handbook of Church History*, p. 112; Pacaut, *La papauté*, p. 79.

[147]*MGH, Cap.*, vol. 1, no. 45, c. 20, p. 130.

[148]*MGH, Cap.*, vol. 1, no. 136, p. 271.

[149]Brunner, *Oppositionelle Gruppen*, p. 98.

defense in the latter days of Paschal's pontificate, was quite another matter. Charlemagne, on one occasion, passed judgment in Rome when he condemned Leo's opponents. Whether, as is usually assumed, he actually rendered a verdict in Roman law, or whether he acted as Leo's *amicus* after the pope had publicly sworn to his own innocence, is difficult to say. It is clear, though, that neither Charlemagne himself, nor his successor, treated the case of 800 as a precedent for subsequent imperial intervention. In 816 and 817 the peoples of Francia and of the Republic confirmed their traditional bonds of "friendship, peace and love," but no further legal bonds were created. Gradually, after 799, the Republic became a coarsely tumultuous place. St. Peter's people began displaying an alarming tendency to mistreat one another often and viciously. Frankish inquiries repeatedly ran up against an unwillingness to respond to queries. By 824 it had become clear in Francia that more effective protection was needed, and that a new mechanism had to be found to provide it. Thus, the Romans were required to swear a subject's oath.

To confirm this line of interpretation, it is only necessary to go back to the year 786 when a shadowy Thuringian named Hardrad had rebelled against Charlemagne. The rebellion was rather easily suppressed, but its ringleaders, who came from powerful old families which had long been almost completely independent of the Franks, claimed that they had not been rebels at all because they had never sworn fidelity to Charlemagne.[150] Three years later Charlemagne required, for the first time, all inhabitants of his vast realm to swear fidelity to him. This action, which was repeated in 802 after the imperial coronation, made it possible for Charlemagne to demand loyalty, and to punish persons who were manifestly disloyal.

The oaths of 789 and 802 are traditionally called subject's oaths, and this appellation is acceptable as long as excessive burdens are not placed upon it. The nineteenth- and twentieth-century legal historians who have written on this oath sometimes fail to realize that modern conceptions of what a subject is frequently bear little resemblance to the realities of the eighth and ninth centuries. It is, for example, legitimate to draw, for the Carolingian period, a distinction between a subject's oath and a vassal's oath, but it must be realized that, whereas the latter carried concrete obligations, the former was primarily negative. It enjoined fidelity in a limited way, and prevented certain overtly unlawful, that is, disloyal, acts. It did not demand obedience in any clear, defined way. Germanic law, for that matter,

---

[150] Abel and Simson, *Jahrbücher* 1:520ff.

did not possess an abstract, objective requirement of obedience.[151] Charlemagne may have created an *Untertanenverband* (a union of subjects),[152] but this meant only a very free association of people pledged not to harm him or one another. Overt acts of disloyalty were punishable, but no positive standard of conduct was required. Charlemagne did not have subjects the way Louis XIV did; nor did he have fellow citizens the way a modern state does.[153]

In 824 Louis required the inhabitants of the Republic to swear a subject's oath, which it would be better to call a loyalty oath, in order that, if they committed overtly criminal acts of disloyalty, they could be punished. In 799–800, 815–16, and 823–24 the Franks had been virtually powerless to come to the aid of St. Peter's people because the alliance oath was too weak and inchoate a mechanism to render such domestic assistance possible. Carolingian traditions had always provided the emperors with only exiguous rights in Rome. Thus, the oath which the Romans had to swear beginning in 824 made them subjects, and therefore justiciable, in the same way that Hardrad and his kind had been brought before the bar of Frankish justice in 789. The *Constitutio* oath was neither more nor less than an efficacious protection device for the pope and for St. Peter's people.

Other provisions of the *Constituio* make it perfectly clear that, as only Ullmann has really seen, the purpose of the document was to provide more comprehensive protection for everyone in the Republic while preserving the pope's position as direct overlord.[154] Likewise, the Republic's remarkably privileged position within the Carolingian Empire was retained.

The *Constitutio* "decreed" that all dukes and officials were to be obedient to the pope. In fact, this requirement was stated twice.[155] Never are the Republic's officials called imperial officers, and nowhere did Louis assert a right to install or dismiss them. The emperor did say that once a year all officials who had judicial authority were to appear before him "so that he might know their names and their number and admonish them individually concerning the ministry assigned to them."[156] If anything, Louis's decree strengthened and guaranteed the pope's leadership within the Republic to a degree unheard of before. It is, in addition, hardly necessary to read between

---

[151]Fritz Kern, *Kingship and Law*, pp. xxiii–xxv, 97–117.

[152]Brunner, *Oppositionelle Gruppen*, pp. 40–53.

[153]Quaritsch, *Staat und Souveranität*, pp. 202–20.

[154]Ullmann, "Origins of the Ottonianum," pp. 117–20.

[155]*MGH, Cap.*, vol. 1, no. 161, cc. 1, 9, pp. 323, 324.

[156]*MGH, Cap.*, vol. 1, no. 161, c. 8, p. 324.

the lines of the *Constitutio* to see that its terms spelled out a more direct and specific kind of protection for the preeminent position of the pope in Rome.

As to St. Peter's people generally, several clauses are relevant. They were forbidden to make depredations against the pope, or against one another. Louis placed a permanent *missus* in Rome and required the pope to do the same. All persons who had complaints about the officials of the Republic were to appeal *to the pope* who would then select one of the two *missi* to adjudicate the case.[157] Louis commanded that all persons who had suffered unjustice should be compensated. These measures imply that Louis did not regard the officers of the Lateran administration as entirely blameless in recent years, and he served notice that his brand of protection did not include a toleration of official misconduct. Too much should not be made of the imperial *missus*, however, because he looks more like a referee, or an ombudsman, than a high official appointed to challenge the pope's authority. Finally, Louis required all inhabitants of the Republic to declare the law by which they wished to live, and then he commanded that everyone should have access to courts that were competent to handle their cases.[158] What Louis did here was extend the Germanic concept of personality of the law to the Republic, a region that had always lived by Roman law.[159] This step was doubtless appreciated by the many Franks, Saxons, and Lombards, not to mention countless other non-Romans, who lived within the Republic. It was a significant protective device for non-Roman republicans.

Despite a number of trifling innovations, the *Constitutio Romana* was a profoundly conservative document. It was at once fully consonant with the spirit of the *Ludovicianum*, and with the traditions of Franco-papal relations. It did not make the pope a Frankish subject, and it created only slightly stronger, and at that mediatized, bonds between the Franks and the inhabitants of the Republic. No permanent *missus* had been instituted before, and on no previous occasion had a Carolingian insisted so explicitly on ensuring justice in Rome. In 754 Stephen II had sought protection for himself and for St. Peter's peculiar people. In 824 Louis the Pious attempted to define in a new way how he might best provide that protection. Had not the Romans themselves served such frequent notice that they needed to be protected from

---

[157]*MGH, Cap.*, vol. 1, no. 161, c. 4, p. 323.

[158]*MGH, Cap.*, vol. 1, no. 161, c. 5, p. 323.

[159]Hirschfeld, "Gerichtswesen," pp. 435–36; Mayer, *Italienische Verfassungsgeschichte* 2:74. Partner, *Lands of St. Peter*, p. 49, believes that the intent was to permit Romans to escape the harshness of papal courts. This, although not impossible, is a bold reading of the text. There is no point in debating the far-fetched idea of Solmi, *Il senato*, pp. 14, 62–66, that Louis's intention was to take criminal jurisdiction away from the pope and assign it to the senate.

one another, there is no reason to believe that the *Constitutio Romana*, or anything like it, would ever have been issued.

Friendship, Protection, Administration

This history of Franco-papal relations between 754 and 824 has been a long and confusing one, but it can be reduced to a few common elements. In 754 Pepin and Stephen II inaugurated a Franco-papal alliance between themselves as individuals and between their respective peoples. The alliance was grounded in a complex bond that was an amalgam of Germanic, Roman, and eccelesiastical elements. It created a fictive, spiritual kinship between the reigning Carolingian and St. Peter's vicar, but the alliance also made them *amici* in a way that brought binding, reciprocal obligations. To put it as simply as possible, each contracting partner had to protect the other. For the Franks this meant defending St. Peter's people from the Lombards, protecting St. Peter's vicar from a Roman mob, and buttressing St. Peter's faith against attacks by pagans, iconoclasts, or adoptionists. The popes had, of course, to provide that special kind of protection that resulted from a constant flow of prayers on behalf of the Franks and all their works, but from time to time more tangible kinds of "protection" were supplied. For example, the Carolingian dynasty was assured against rival claimants in 754, Tassilo of Bavaria was chastized in 787, and divine intercession was invoked for the success of Carolingian military campaigns.

This fundamental alliance was never changed during our period. It was renewed every time a pope or a Carolingian "migrated from this world." The popes always and only demanded defense, and the Carolingians sought faithfully to supply it. The kind, but not the quality, of that defense did change over the years, however. Originally, the Romans required defense from foreign foes, but in the end they had to be defended from one another. Still, it was defense that Stephen II had sought in 754 and defense that Eugenius obtained in 824.

Charlemagne's coronation in 800 changed the Franco-papal relationship in subtle, but not fundamental, ways. Before 800 neither Charlemagne nor Pepin possessed any rights in the Republic, and they never acted as though they had any. The ingenious but speculative lucubrations of four generations of scholars have failed to turn up a single scrap of persuasive evidence that the Carolingians, as *patricii Romanorum*, were overlords of the Republic. Those same scholars who always assumed that Carolingian patricians ruled

Rome jumped quite naturally to the conclusion that Carolingian emperors ruled it even more decisively. Actually, Charlemagne and Louis strove mightily to avoid ruling the Republic. Their actions, and some actions by the popes, lead to the conclusion that the Carolingians did come to think of the Republic as a part of the empire. Had scholars not drunk so deeply at the well of Romano-Byzantine theory, however, they would have realized that after 800 the Republic possessed an independence so massive and pervasive that it can only be characterized as autonomy bordering on full independence. If sufficient attention had been paid to Charlemagne's reluctance to interfere in Rome, then there would not exist almost everywhere in the literature the mistaken notion that the *Ludovicianum*, now that we do at least know that it was not a clever papal forgery, did not represent a gross abdication of imperial rights by the pious and foolish Louis. If the *Ludovicianum* had been seen as a conservative, traditional expression of longstanding policies, then it would not have been possible to regard the *Constititio Romana* as a radical rejection of the pact of 816 when, in fact, it was merely a coherent extension of the *Ludovicianum*.

Symbol and Reality in the Lateran Mosaics

While Pope Leo III was carrying out some of his work of remodeling the Lateran palace, he redecorated the *triclinium*, the great meeting and banqueting hall. Two of the mosaics that he had installed are very revealing of how the popes viewed the Franco-papal alliance. Neither of these mosaics is extant today, but reasonably reliable drawings of both have survived. Each one contained a group of three figures. In the first, a seated Christ was flanked by St. Peter and Constantine, both of whom were kneeling. Peter was receiving the keys to the kingdom of heaven, and Constantine a banner. In the second mosaic the central figure is St. Peter. To his right, kneeling, was Pope Leo receiving a pallium. To Peter's left, also kneeling, was Charlemagne receiving, like Constantine, a banner.[160]

The banners in each mosaic represent secular, but especially military, rule. Christ and Peter are of the order of Melchisedek; they are priests; they cannot fight with this world's weapons. But they can define which fights are

---

[160]Gerhard Ladner, *Die Papstbildniße des Altertums und des Mittelalters* (Vatican City, 1941), 1:114–15, figs. 94, 95, 100, 101. For penetrating comments on these mosaics see: Schramm, *Die zeitgenössischen Bildnisse Karls des Großen* (Leipzig, 1928), p. 4–16.

God's, and they can command others to fight God's enemies. Also they can rule. Constantine, so the myth went, had vacated the West so as to leave Peter's vicars to rule there. Peter also allows or denies entry to heaven—a very particular and ultimate kind of authority. Leo's pallium pointed to his priestly rule. A pallium was a yoke, in a way, that symbolized the priest's bondage to his flocks. But, a priest was also the earthly counterpart of the ultimate priest, Christ. And Christ was "King of Kings" and "Lord of Lords." In some ways the Christ-Peter figures appear equal to the Constantine-Charlemagne ones, but in crucial respects the former were greater. So it was in the Republic of St. Peter.

Conclusion

"MODERN SOCIOLOGISTS and theorists of public law," says Sidney J. Ehler, "are unanimous in requiring for the state of today three characteristic signs: a territory, a population and an established governmental power."[1] Defining a state is risky business, and all definitions are subject to endless qualification. Still, Ehler's may serve as a useful point of departure for some concluding reflections on the Republic of St. Peter.

There can be no serious question that the Republic had a territory. Beginning in the 720s, as a result of problems that went back in a direct way to the 680s, the popes, along with prominent central Italians, sought to liberate from the Byzantine Empire and to defend against the Lombards all of the lands that had comprised the Exarchate of Ravenna. The regions to which the popes pressed their most urgent and consistent claims were more restricted, however. These included the Duchies of Rome and Perugia, Ravenna, and the Pentapolis. For a long time possession of Istria and Venice was asserted by the popes, but these former exarchal territories never really entered into the Republic. Venetian particularism assured the eventual independence of the "Jewel of the Adriatic," and Istria was too far from Rome to be effectively governed by the popes, and too strategically significant to the Franks to be handed over. In failing to acquire these lands the popes lost only a plethora of insoluble problems. From time to time the papacy claimed the old Lombard Duchies of Spoleto and Benevento. These lands, too, were to remain outside the Republic, but papal designs on them were bound to

---

[1] Ehler, "On Applying the Modern Term 'State' to the Middle Ages," *Medieval Studies Persented to Aubrey Gwynn S.J.*, ed. J. A. Watt et al. (Dublin, 1961), p. 496. For some lucid comments on the difficulty of defining the state see: Quaritsch, *Staat und Souverantiät*, pp. 11–19.

have been ephemeral because they were always rooted in very special circumstances. During the 730s and 740s the popes used the duchies as a part of a complicated and generally successful diplomacy designed to bring pressure to bear upon the Lombard kings at Pavia. Between 754 and 774 the papacy kept alive a tenuous claim to the duchies as a result of the contingent treaty of Quierzy. Because the contingencies upon which that treaty rested were never fulfilled, the duchies did not definitively enter into the Republic, although Hadrian did actually hold Spoleto for a short time between 774 and 776. Once the Republic secured protection from the Frankish monarchy its reasons for laying claim to the duchies disappeared. Ravenna was always problematical. Basically, the Ravennese sought independence in their own right, and therefore they studiously tried to avoid papal domination. On numerous occasions, however, the inhabitants of the Ravennate cooperated with the popes when it was in their interest to do so. What finally emerged in this area was an odd sort of condominium shared by the popes, the archbishops, and the Franks. After Hadrian and Charlemagne worked out a comprehensive territorial settlement in the 780s, the Republic possessed almost exactly the essential core of lands that the popes had been claiming for a half century.

The consistency of the papacy's claims was no less impressive than the determination with which they were advanced. Through a series of treaties with the Franks a remarkably precise inventory of the Republic's lands was developed. But that inventory was not novel when it was first committed to writing. The documents of the 750s reflected accurately aspirations that reached back decades. In 816 Louis the Pious confirmed the territorial status quo as of 788, and in 962 Otto I confirmed in all essential respects the situation as it had stood in 817. Early in the thirteenth century Innocent III set out to recover lands that the papacy had lost during the previous two centuries, and the initial basis for his planned recuperations was the *Ludovicianum*, which had itself defined the territorial contours of the Republic as they had evolved between the 720s and 788. In the nineteenth century the papacy was finally and forcibly ejected from most of those same territories.

Obviously, then, it was during the eighth century that the popes began to assert very specific claims to a body of carefully defined lands. Were those claims recognized by others? The Byzantines, of course, regarded the popes as usurpers. They must be looked at as hostile witnesses, but even their complaints down to the 750s evince an implicit recognition of de facto reality, namely, papal possession of a sizeable piece of central Italy. The Lombards dealt formally and officially with the popes on numerous occasions. Liutprand negotiated often with Gregory II, Gregory III, and Zachary.

Aistulf made treaties with Stephen II. Desiderius signed accords with Paul I and Stephen III. The Lombards certainly considered the popes to be fully competent partners in the process of defining borders in Italy. The very existence of Lombard-papal negotiations and treaties demonstrates an explicit recognition by the Lombards of the right of the Republic to exist within secure frontiers, even though heated arguments arose over exactly where those borders ought to be. The Franks, it goes without saying, always recognized the right of the Republic to exist. Indeed, they saved the Republic from annihilation and then helped to define its borders.

Likewise it cannot be doubted that the Republic had a population. This was true in the most basic sense: people lived in the Republic. More specifically and significantly, however, the popes claimed those people as their own. Always papal documents spoke of the inhabitants of the Republic as St. Peter's "peculiar people." Others, for example the Franks, might be St. Peter's friends or protectors, but they were never his "peculiar people." When the Lombards seized a town, the popes referred to its people as "lost sheep." On at least one occasion the Ravennese called the pope their "shepherd" and expressed sincere gratitude that he had left his "flocks" to come to the aid of other "flocks" who had been "lost." Hadrian complained when Leo of Ravenna prevented the agents of the Republic from exercising due authority over the people of Ravenna and the Pentapolis. In the 780s Hadrian expressed anger that cities in the Liri valley had been handed to him but that their inhabitants had refused to submit themselves to papal rule. Both the *Ludovicianum* and the *Constitutio Romana* recognized that the people of the Republic owed principal allegiance to the pope.

Sometimes papal documents expressed the relationship between the papacy and the people of the Republic in legal, jurisdictional terms. On other occasions papal language was pastoral. Nevertheless, in all instances the papacy regarded the inhabitants of the Republic as a single *populus*. It would be anachronistic to call St. Peter's "peculiar people" citizens of the Republic, but they were most assuredly its subjects. They looked for spiritual guidance and direction, of course, to the church over which the pope presided. In many ways the pope's spiritual leadership of his flocks preceded and smoothed the way for his direct rule over them. They eventually brought suits in his courts, labored on his lands, received food from his granaries, and answered to his officials. From the lowliest peasant to the mightiest aristocrat the economic, social, and political life of the Republic revolved around the papacy and the Lateran administration.

Gradually the ecclesiastical and the social elites of central Italy became virtually indistinguishable from one another. New elites actually formed, leadership in and around Rome changed hands, and classic Roman oligar-chies took shape. As this happened the papal government, and the people governed by it, became by dint of a common historical process and tradition inextricably intertwined.

Finally, the Republic possessed "an established governmental power." The papacy itself was an elective monarchy in both its spiritual and govern-mental manifestations. Individual popes were prepared long and carefully for their office, and they worked through and with officials similarly trained and educated. The papal government provided pastoral and sacramental services, as always, but with an ever quickening pace in the eighth century also supplied purely secular services as well. Central Italy's food supply was assured by the papal government, and as time passed, more and more char-itable benefactions were guaranteed by the Lateran. The papal court carried on a lively diplomacy. Courts of law were organized, and called into session, and they rendered verdicts. Revenues of all sorts were collected, budgeted, expended. Records and documents of many kinds were written and filed in archives by a trained staff. In eighth- and ninth-century Europe only the imperial government at Constantinople was more sophisticated in design than that of the Republic, and the institutions of the Basileus may not have been as continuously effective.

During the last years of the seventh century and the early ones of the eighth, the popes arrived at, or perhaps were driven to, the conclusion that central Italy had to separate itself from Byzantium. Murderously meddle-some officials, confiscatory fiscal measures, and odious religious policies all made important contributions to the emergence of the Republic, but condi-tions in Italy played a crucial role too. The pope did not drive Italy out of the Byzantine orbit, he led it out. Italians increasingly saw their fortunes and their futures to be located in an Italy independent of the dubious advantages of imperial control. Italian voices did not rise in a chorus of objections to the papal drive for independence. Rather, the Italians defended the popes, and thereby endorsed the goals and aspirations of those who were most immediately responsible for the creation of the Republic. Indeed, as the Republic was coming into existence prominent Italians ceased granting ac-tive or passive support from the outside, and they began entering the Lateran. There they fused with the clerical elites and began playing a role in formu-lating fundamental policies. By the pontificate of Hadrian the lands, the peoples, and the institutions of the Republic had been fashioned into a recognizable and potentially durable political entity.

Why, then, would Pierre Toubert say as recently as 1973, "It is commonly admitted that one cannot correctly speak of a 'Papal State' in the proper sense of the term before the thirteenth century"?[2] The answer lies more in historians that it does in history. Or, to put this a bit differently, Toubert, and all those whose views he represents, have fallen victim to certain prevalent notions about what actually constitutes a state. In this connection it is very important to notice Toubert's qualifying clause: "in the proper sense of the term." What, we may ask, is the proper way to think about a state?

For the liberal, nationalist historians of the nineteenth century, whose writings have directly or indirectly influenced almost all subsequent investigations, the whole historical process has been a long, steady march toward the modern, sovereign, omnicompetent nation-state. During the high and late Middle Ages, the period from the twelfth to the fifteenth centuries, it is argued, the germ of the modern notion of sovereignty first appeared.[3] During and after the Napoleonic wars the idea of sovereignty came to be associated with particular ethnic communities, geographical entities, and institutional structures. The nineteenth century, therefore, witnessed a culmination of conceptual, human, geographical, and governmental phenomena that reach back in some instances into the Middle Ages.

But never into the early Middle Ages: Joseph Strayer, for example, emphasizes the role of European institutional developments between 1100 and 1600 in the creation of the modern state.[4] An international colloquium held in 1965 focused on ethnic, geographical, and institutional developments after the breakup of the Carolingian Empire.[5] Fredric Cheyette believes the ideas unleashed by the Investiture Controversy were crucial in producing the ideology of the modern state.[6] Walter Ullmann and Michael Wilks place their stress on the canonists and political thinkers of the late Middle Ages,[7] while Gaines Post, concentrating his studies on the same kinds of writers, sees the origins of the state in the twelfth century.[8] Regardless of the specific issues under investigation, historians have worked from a certain model of

---

[2]Toubert, *Latium* 2:935.

[3]Ullmann, "The Development of the Medieval Idea of Sovereignty," *English Historical Review* 64 (1949): 1–33, remains a good discussion. For a more massive treatment see: Michael Wilks, *The Problem of Sovereignty in the Later Middle Ages* (Cambridge, 1963).

[4]Strayer, *On the Medieval Origins of the Modern State* (Princeton, 1970), p. 6ff.

[5]Tadeusz Manteuffel and Alexander Gieszytor, eds., *L'Europe aux IX*ᵉ*–XI*ᵉ *siècles: Aux origines des états nationaux* (Warsaw, 1968). In this collection, and disappointingly traditional in all key respects, one will find: Dupré-Theseider, "Sur les origines de l'état de l'église," pp. 93–103.

[6]Cheyette, "The Invention of the State," in *The Walter Prescott Webb Memorial Lectures*, vol. 12, ed. Bede K. Lackner and Kenneth Roy Philp (Austin, Texas, 1978), pp. 143–78.

[7]See n.3 above.

[8]Post, *Studies in Medieval legal Thought* (Princeton, 1964).

the state that was fashioned in the last century, and they have, in one way or another, found the remote antecedents for that model in Europe after about 1100.

To the extent that these scholars have focused on ethnic and geographical factors, there is no reason why their researches should not have taken them back into the early Middle Ages. The Republic of St. Peter, for example, had defined and internationally recognized frontiers in central Italy and a relatively homogeneous population. The frontiers of the Republic effectively excluded the more Germanic elements of the population of northern Italy as well as the more extensively Hellenized populace of the south. In addition, the Republic also had an effective government, or, in Post's words, a "constitutional order, without which the state is nothing."[9] But, it is thought, the Republic lacked at least one critical component of the modern state. It was not fully sovereign, because it owed allegiance to a higher authority; first to the Byzantines and then to the Franks.

There are several ways of assessing this supposed lack of sovereignty. One might first consider the wise observation of Cheyette who writes, "As we watch the nation-state gradually fade from its glory as the ultimate goal of all historical experience, we begin to understand that such concepts as 'public,' 'private,' 'central power,' and 'particularism' are themselves the value laden products of historical development and not atemporal categories of human thought."[10] In other words, our models, and the most fundamental bases upon which they have always rested, may be inadequate to the tasks we have assigned to them. Perhaps history has not been heading toward the nation-state and, if not, then it may be that we ought not to evaluate earlier political forms according to their degree of conformity to the nation-state model.[11]

Another approach would be to ask whether there existed in the early Middle Ages any complex of ideas that bears similarity to the doctrine of sovereignty insofar as that doctrine has become a part of the conceptual apparatus of the modern state. "There is no doubt," writes Stengel, "that in the imperial titles of the early Middle Ages there dawned already the same

---

[9]Post, *Studies in Medieval Legal Thought*, pp. 7–8.

[10]Cheyette, "The Invention of the State," p. 146.

[11]Otto Brunner, *Land und Herrschaft*, 5th ed. (Vienna, 1965), pp. 111ff, esp. 113–14, talks of the danger of applying modern theories of the state to the Middle Ages, but also speaks of the "fruitful" efforts of many scholars to seek the germ of the modern state in the later Middle Ages. Post, *Studies in Medieval Legal Thought*, pp. 10, 242ff, 247ff, also evinced qualms about the applicability of modern notions to the medieval period but then went ahead and applied them.

fundamental conceptions that were articulated later in the sovereignty formulae of the thirteenth and fourteenth centuries."[12] The key point here is "fundamental conceptions." Basic ideas are critical, not their pedigrees, or the particular institutional forms in which they are embodied. Early medieval kings and emperors did not answer to higher authorities, and they sought to command universal allegiance from those under their rule.[13] In the context of interstate relations, the various royal and imperial titles of the early Middle Ages were designed to express the independence and equality of each realm. Perhaps the Carolingian imperial title actually provoked others into the use of imperial titles of their own, as in Spain or England. That is, Anglo-Saxon or Spanish kings may have styled themselves emperors not to evoke universalist reveries of ancient Rome but, much more practically, to assert their independence from and parity with the Carolingians.[14] In what concerns intrastate relations we have already seen that Charlemagne revived the Frankish subject's oath in 789 and 802 in order to establish a minimal degree of allegiance owed to him by all the residents of the *imperium Francorum*.[15] To the extent that sovereignty implies complete independence from external control and a refusal to tolerate competing jurisdictions internally, the kingdoms of the early Middle Ages certainly possessed an adequate version of, perhaps an acceptable substitute for, the later full-blown doctrine of sovereignty.

In this connection it should be noted that the early Middle Ages knew the simultaneous existence of a bewildering array of institutional, geographical, and ethnic forms.[16] Within the limits of the present study, to go no

---

[12]Stengel, "Kaisertitel und Suveranitätsidee," *DA* 3 (1939): 44.

[13]David, *La souveraineté*, pp. 21–30; Quaritsch, *Staat und Souveranität*, pp. 26–32, 202–20.

[14]Stengel, "Kaisertitel und Suveranitätsidee," pp. 3–11, 24–31; Löwe, "Von den Grenzen des Kaisergedankens in der Karolingerzeit," *DA* 14 (1958): 345–74.

[15]Quaritsch, *Staat und Souveranität*, pp. 202–20; Lemosse, "Lèse-majesté," pp. 13–14, 19ff.

[16]Karl Ferdinand Werner, "Les principautés périphériques dans le monde franc du VIIIᵉ siècle," *SSCI* 20 (1973): 483–514; Herwig Wolfram, "The Shaping of the Early Medieval Kingdom," *Viator* 1 (1970): 1–20; idem, "The Shaping of the Early Medieval Principality as a Type of Non-royal Rulership," ibid. 2 (1971): 33–51; Gerhard Köbler, "Land und Landrecht im Frühmittelalter," *ZRG, gA* 68 (1969): 1–40; K. Hauck, "Von einer spätantiken Randkultur zum karolingischen Europa," pp. 3–93. My thinking has also been influenced by the following studies: Ganshof, "A propos de ducs et duchés au haut moyen âge," *Journal des Savants* (Jan.–Mar. 1972), pp. 13–24; idem, "Stämme als 'Träger' des Reiches?" *ZRG, gA* 89 (1972): 147–60; Walther Kienast, *Studien über die französischen Volksstämme des Frühmittelalters* (Stuttgart, 1968); idem, *Der Herzogstitel in Frankreich und Deutschland* (Munich, 1968); Karl Bosl,

further afield, we have talked of the Byzantine Empire, the Frankish monarchy and empire under two, or really three, different regimes, the Lombard monarchy in two very different manifestations before and after 774, independent and then subjugated ducal Bavaria, the virtually autonomous Lombard Duchies of Spoleto and Benevento, the almost independent Duchy of Benevento after about 812, Venice whose status almost defies precise description, and finally, the Republic itself. Amidst this array, and in a world where ideas analogous to the later and more familiar doctrines of sovereignty surely existed, we ought to be on our guard against connecting too tightly specific concepts of sovereignty with particular kinds of states or governments.[17]

Even if it were admitted that the early Middle Ages knew a vague doctrine of sovereignty, and that many different kinds of early medieval states were each in their own way sovereign, it would probably still be argued that the Republic was not sovereign, and that it was therefore lacking one critical criterion for statehood. The region answered to external authorities.

From the 730s to 800 the Republic was fully independent, even though it depended on the Franks for military security. That the Republic had recourse to a foreign power for military assistance in no way diminishes the extent of its independence. Throughout the Middle Ages and the Renaissance the papacy never ceased calling upon French, German, and Spanish princes, or even Italian *condottieri*, to fight its battles. In the nineteenth century Pius IX was still appealing across the Alps for aid against his own subjects and against the likes of Cavour, Garibaldi, and Mazzini who were seeking to incorporate the Papal States, whose sovereignty in this latter period has never been doubted, into a unified Italy. One suspects that Stephen II or Leo III would have understood Pius's predicament quite well. In short, before 800 the Republic appears to have met every possible criterion for statehood.

After 800 the Republic was an autonomous region within the Carolingian Empire. This has always made it easy to argue that no sovereign Republic could have then existed. There are, however, at least two problems with this point of view. First, the Carolingians struggled mightily to avoid ruling the Republic. The popes had always demanded from them protection and defense. This demand was never altered, although the nature of the protec-

---

"Herrscher und Beherrschte im deutschen Reich des 10.–12. Jahrhunderts," *Sitzungsberichte der bayerische Akademie der Wissenschaften, phil.-hist. Klasse*, no. 2 (Munich, 1963); Dhondt, *Etudes sur la naissance des principautés territoriales en France* (Bruges, 1948); Schlesinger, *Die Entstehung der Landesherrschaft* (Dresden, 1941).

[17]David, *La souveraineté*, p. 81; Stengel, "Kaisertitel und Suveranitätsidee," pp. 38–40, 47.

tion accorded to Rome and its environs certainly sustained a few transformations. In the 750s and 770s the Lombards were beaten back. In 800 the pope's personal enemies were brought to the bar of justice. In 824 a tumultuous Roman scene was pacified. Through all of this, however, the basic Franco-papal relationship, grounded as it was in a complex political and religious alliance, never changed dramatically. Second, it may be that Ehler is correct to say that the degree of interference by one state in the affairs of another ought to be the litmus test for independence and sovereignty, rather than an arbitrarily absolute standard of noninterference.[18] How much did the Carolingians interfere in the Republic? They did not interfere at all before 800. After Charlemagne's coronation and down to 824 they introduced no officials into Rome, played no role in papal elections, and did not, as far as we know, treat the Republic in any other respect like a constituent part of the empire. They continued to ally with the popes and continued to guarantee to the popes the undisturbed possession of a carefully defined block of lands. No such considerations were made on behalf of, let us say, the Saxons or the Bavarians. In 824 slightly more aggressive measures were taken, but only after the Romans had been commanded to observe primary allegiance to the pope, and only to supply more effective protection. In a word, the degree of Carolingian intereference in the Republic was slight, and throughout it was consistent with the Carolingian goal of protecting St. Peter's vicar and his "peculiar people."

In the end, one has three possible approaches for deciding if the Republic was a state. One can embrace a minimalist definition such as Ehler's. On this score, the Republic was unquestionably a state, although it might be objected that Ehler's definition is so chronologically and conceptually imprecise that it would permit the attribution of statehood to entities ranging from prehistoric villages, to the "turf" of an urban street gang, to the United States of America. Alternatively, one can suggest that modern models are relevant only to the modern world and assert that they simply cannot be applied retrospectively to the past. This approach has much to recommend it, but it runs the risk of making it impossible to speak of historical continuity, and it also begs a whole series of questions about how, precisely, medieval political forms ought to be labeled and described. In short, one can perhaps say that the Republic of St. Peter was a "state" and then say that it simply was not a modern state. This is true, but not very helpful. Finally, it might be argued that the best approach is the one that recognizes simultaneously the distinctiveness of the modern state and the historical emergence of the antecedents

---

[18]Ehler, "Applying the Modern Term 'State,' " p. 496.

of that state in the Middle Ages. Then, one can take this line of interpretation a step further and maintain that, to date, there has been a tendency to draw the line a bit short of the real mark in terms of when those antecedents actually began appearing. That is, one might productively look to the early Middle Ages rather than to the eleventh and twelfth centuries. On this reckoning, it is possible to call the Republic a state because it is comparatively easy to identify in the Republic a wide variety of characteristics that are partial or quite complete adumbrations of the essential criteria for statehood in the modern world.

Aristotle, one is reminded, said that man is a creature who by nature associates with his fellows. Following up on this assumption the philosopher and his students then proceeded to analyze nearly two hundred Greek *poleis*, all of which shared certain common features, but no one of which was exactly identical to any other. The Middle Ages, of course, saw the creation of a diverse array of political forms, and it has been one of the difficult—and to some exasperating—lessons of the recent past that if human beings are wont to associate in states of their own devising, then the particular forms in which they have chosen to embody their associations display little predictability. In a way, therefore, the perspective that ought to be applied to the history of St. Peter's Republic should not be a rigid and constricting one. Rather, it should be flexible and diverse enough to accommodate, and to hope to explain, the ever shifting course of historical reality.

Historians love paradigms, hate peduncles. Their aversion to the latter may help to explain the reasons why the Republic of St. Peter has been given short shrift. It did not, in its original form, last long beyond the 820s. This has perhaps made it appear as a less than legitimate historical mutation destined to have no traceable record. Appearances are deceiving, however, because in new forms, or at any rate in different ones, the Republic has not yet suffered extinction.

Late in the 820s tensions in the Carolingian family led to a generation of civil war in Francia. Under these straitened circumstances, the Franco-papal alliance, and Carolingian relations with the Republic generally, ceased to figure prominently in the thinking of Pepin's descendants. Once the Frankish civil wars were put to a term, the several subsequent Carolingian kingdoms were plagued by continuing internal dissension, economic dislocation, and marauding bands of Vikings, Muslims, and Magyars. As the Carolingian world cracked apart, St. Peter's "strong right arm" was too busy and distracted to continue bringing protection to the saint's "peculiar people."

When a new imperial order was resurrected in the tenth century by the

Saxon dynasty of German kings, the cautious and reserved Carolingian attitude toward Rome and the pope was jettisoned. The Saxon emperors, and this was true as well of their Salian and Hohenstaufen successors, retained the Christian content of the Carolingian tradition, but laid greater stress on the Roman elements of imperial rule. The Germans intervened and interfered in papal Italy in ways that the Carolingians never did. As a result, the popes suffered the blows of foreign domination until, feeling themselves able to endure no more, they cast the Occident into the impossibly complicated paroxysm that was the Investiture Controversy. Narrowly, but at great cost, did the popes escape becoming glorified German chaplains.

As the world around the Republic became more complex and turbulent after the 820s, so too conditions inside the region did not stand in static repose. Muslim raiders exposed the military weakness of the Republic and, for a time, threatened to capture a large part of it. No Frankish arms did, or could, rush to Italy to protect St. Peter from these new oppressors. As in the north, so too in Italy, defense against these new invaders was much more effectively secured at the local level. In no time at all fortified communities dotted the countryside, and their inhabitants eventually discovered that they could flaunt their growing independence from Rome. The Muslim attacks exacerbated this process, but in reality, it reached far back into the Italian past. The "localization" of society already apparent in late Byzantine Italy had been halted for a time by the centralizing tendencies of the Republic only to awaken with rejuvenated vigor in the ninth century.

Around the fringes of the Republic, partly because of the absence of the steadying hand of the Carolingians and partly because of historical forces that no one could have thwarted forever, the years after the 820s had as their hallmarks difficulty, disorder, disruption. Benevento encroached from the south as did the *regnum* from the north. Ravenna broke away almost completely, as did parts of the Pentapolis. Effective papal rule was soon confined to little more than the immediate environs of Rome, and even there, as noted, there was no lack of challenges. Not for nothing has the "political archaeology" of Italy been the despair of all students of her history.

Inside the Republic, again absent the possibility of effective Carolingian protection—which it might be more accurate to call pacification—the Roman nobility gave free rein to its historic penchant for confrontation and violence. The tenth-century papacy was secularized as at perhaps no other moment in history, and twelfth-century Rome witnessed the erection of a purely secular administration openly opposed to the pope.

Early in the thirteenth century Innocent III set out to procure domestic tranquility, freedom from foreign threats, institutional stability, and secure frontiers. In the fourteenth century, after the popes had removed to Avignon, Cardinal Albornoz tried to achieve these same things. So did the Renaissance popes. So did Pius IX. What they tried to do, however, had in most respects already been done by Gregory II and the popes who, in the century after Gregory, wore the crown and bore the staff that symbolized their rule over the peculiar people who lived in the Republic of St. Peter.

Bibliography

Abbo, J. A. "Papal Legates." In *New Catholic Encyclopedia* 8: 607–9. New York, 1967.

Abel, Sigurd, and Simson, Bernhard. *Jahrbücher des fränkischen Reiches unter Karl dem Großen.* 2 vols. 2d ed. Leipzig, 1883–88.

Adelson, Howard, and Baker, Robert. "The Oath of Purgation of Pope Leo III in 800." *Traditio* 8 (1952): 35–80.

Affeldt, Werner. "Das Problem der Mitwirkung des Adels an politischen Entscheidungsprozessen im Frankenreich vornehmlich des 8. Jahrhunderts." In *Aus Theorie und Praxis der Geschichtswissenschaft: Festschrift für Hans Herzfeld zum 80. Geburtstag,* edited by Dietrich Kurze, pp. 404–23. Berlin, 1972.

————. "Untersuchungen zur Königserhebung Pippins." *FMSt* 14 (1980): 95–187.

Amann, Emile. *L'époque carolingienne: Histoire de l'église depuis les origines jusqu'à nos jours.* Edited by Augustin Fliche and Victor Martin. Vol. 6. Paris, 1947.

————. "Léon III." *Dictionnaire de théologie catholique,* vol. 9, pt. 1, pp. 304–12. Paris, 1926.

Anastos, Milton V. "The Transfer of Illyricum, Calabria and Sicily to the Jurisdiction of the Patriarchate of Constantinople in 732–33." *Studi bizantini e neoellenici* 9 (1957): 14–31.

————. "Leo III's Edict Against the Images in the Year 726–27 and Italo-Byzantine Relations Between 726 and 730." *Byzantinische Forschungen* 3 (1968): 5–41.

Andreolli, Maria Pia. "Una pagina di storia langobarda: 'Re Ratchis.'" *Nuova rivista storica* 50 (1966): 281–327.

Andrieu, Michel. *Les Ordines Romani du haut moyen âge.* 5 vols. Reprint. Louvain, 1961–65.

————. "Les ordres mineurs dans l'ancien rit romain." *Revue des sciences religieuses* 5 (1929): 232–74.

————. "L'origine du titre de cardinal dans l'église romaine." In *Miscellanea Giovanni Mercati*, 5:113–44. *Studi e Testi*, vol. 125. Vatican City, 1946 113–44.

Angenendt, Arnold. "Taufe und Politik im frühen Mittelalter." *FMSt* 7 (1973): 143–68.

————. "Das geistliche Bündnis der Päpste mit den Karolingern (754–796)." *HJB* 100 (1980): 1–94.

Anton, Hans Hubert. *Fürstenspiegel und Herrscherethos in der Karolingerzeit.* Bonner historische Forschungen, vol. 32. Bonn, 1968.

Armbrust, Louis Heinrich. *Die territoriale Politik der Päpste von 500 bis 800 mit besonderer Berücktsichtigung der römischen Beamtenverhältnisse.* Göttingen, 1885.

Arquillière, Henri-Xavier. *L'augustinisme politique: Essai sur la formation des théories politiques du Moyen-Age.* 2d ed. Paris, 1955.

Ary, Mikel V. "The Politics of the Frankish-Lombard Marriage Alliance." *AHP* 19 (1981): 7–26.

Bakhrouchine, S., and E. Kosminski. "La diplomatie du moyen âge." In *Histoire de la diplomatie*, edited by Vladimir Petrovich Potiemkine, and translated by Xenia Pamphilova and Michel Eristov, vol. 1. Paris, 1946.

Battelli, Giulio. "Liber Diurnus Romanorum Pontificum." In *Enciclopedia cattolica* 7: 1262–67 Vatican City, 1951.

Baumont, Maurice. "Le pontificat de Paul Ier (757–767)." *MAH* 47 (1930): 7–24.

Bayet, C. "L'élection de Léon III, la révolte des romains en 799 et ses consequences." *Annuaire de la Faculté des lettres de Lyon*, vol. 1 (1883).

————. "Les élections pontificales sous les carolingiens au VIIIe et au IXe siècle (757–885)" *Revue historique* 24 (1884): 49–91.

Beck, Hans-Georg. "Die Herkunft des Papstes Leo III." *FMSt* 3 (1969): 131–37.

Belting, Hans. "Studien zum Beneventanischen Hof im 8. Jahrhundert." *Dumbarton Oaks Papers* 16 (1962): 141–93.

Berschin, Walter. *Griechisch-lateinisches Mittelalter: Von Hieronymus zu Nikolaus von Kues.* Bern, 1980.

Bertolini, Ottorino. *Roma di fronte a Bisanzio e ai longobardi.* Bologna, 1941.

————. *Roma e i longobardi.* Rome, 1972.

————. "La caduta del primicerio Cristoforo (771) nelle versioni dei contemporanei e le correnti antilongobarde e filolongobarde in Roma alla fine del pontificato di Stefano III (771–772)." In his *Scritti scelti di storia medioevale*, edited by Ottavio Banti, 1:19–61. 2 vols. Livorno, 1968.

————. "Longobardi e Bizantini nell'Italia meridionale: La politica dei principi longobardi fra Occidente ed Oriente dai prodromi della 'renovatio' dell'Imperio in Occidente con Carlomagno alla sua crisi con Carlo III 'Il Grosso' (774–888)." In his *Scritti scelti* 1:171–92.

————. "Per la storia delle diaconie romane nell'alto medioevo sino alla fine del secolo VIII." In *Scritti scelti* 1:309–460.

————. "Le prime manifestazione concrete del potere temporale dei papi nell'esarcato di Ravenna (756–757)." In *Scritti scelti* 2:593–612.

————. "Il problema delle origini del potere temporale dei papi nei suoi presuppositi teoretici iniziali: Il concetto di 'restitutio' nelle prime cessione territoriali alla Chiesa di Roma (756–757)." In *Scritti scelti* 2:485–547.

————. "Sergio, arcivescovo di Ravenna." In *Scritti scelti* 2:549–91.

————. "Il primo 'periurium' di Astolfo verso la chiesa di Roma (752-753)." In *Miscellanea Giovanni Mercati* 5:160–205. Studi e Testi, vol. 125. Vatican City, 1946.

————. "La ricomparsa della sede episcopale di 'Tres Tabernae' nella seconda metà del secolo VIII e l'istituzione delle 'domuscultae.'" *Archivio delle società romana di storia patria* 75 (1952): 103–9.

————. "I papi e le relazioni politiche di Roma con i ducati longobardi di Spoleto e di Benevento. III. Il secolo VIII: da Giovanni VI (701–705) a Gregorio II (715–731)." *Rivista di storia della chiesa in Italia* 9 (1955): 1–57.

————. "I rapporti di Zaccaria con Costantino V e con Artavasdo nel racconto del biografo del papa e nella probabile realta' storica." *Archivio della società romana di storia patria* 78 (1955): 1–21.

————. "Osservazione sulla 'Constitutio Romana' e sul 'Sacramentum Cleri et Populi Romani' dell'824." In *Studi medievali in onore di Antonino de Stefano*, pp. 43–78. Palermo, 1956.

————. "Riflessi politici delle controversie religiose con Bisanzio nelle vicende del sec. VII in Italia." *SSCI* 5 (1958): 733–89.

————. "I vescovi del 'regnum Langobardorum' al tempo dei Carolingi." In *Italia Sacra, 5: Vescovi e diocesi in Italia nel medioevo (sec. IX–XIII)*. pp. 1–26. Padua, 1964.

————. "Carlomagno e Benevento." In *Karl der Große: Lebenswerk und Nachleben*, edited by Wolfgang Braunfels, 1:609–71. 5 vols. Düsseldorf, 1965.

————. "Gli inizi del governo temporale dei papi sull'esarcato di Ravenna." *Archivio della società romana di storia patria* 89 (1966): 25–35.

————. "Le origini del potere temporale e del dominio temporale dei papi." *SSCI* 20 (1973): 231–55.

Beumann, Helmut. "Romkaiser und fränkisches Reichsvolk." In *Festschrift für Edmund E. Stengel, zum 70. Geburtstag am 24. Dezember 1949 dargebracht von*

Freunden, Fachgenossen und Schülern, edited by Erika Kunz, pp. 157–80. Münster, 1952.

————. "Zur Entwicklung transpersonaler Staatsvorstellungen." In *Das Königtum: Seine geistigen und rechtlichen Grundlagen,* edited by Theodor Mayer, pp. 185–224. *Vorträge und Forschungen,* vol. 3. Sigmaringen, 1956.

————. "Nomen Imperatoris. Studien zur Kaiseridee Karls des Großen." *HZ* 185 (1958): 515–49. See also under Gunther Wolf, pp. 174–215.

Bischoff, Bernhard. "Das griechische Element in der abendländischen Bildung des Mittelalters." *BZ* 44 (1951): 27–55.

Bonnaud-Delamare, Roger. *L'idée de paix à l'époque carolingienne.* Paris, 1939.

Borst, Arno. "Kaisertum und Namentheorie in Jahre 800." *Festschrift Percy Ernst Schramm,* edited by Peter Classen and Peter Scheibert, 1:36–51. 2 vols. Wiesbaden, 1964. See also under Gunther Wolf, pp. 216–39.

Bosl, Karl. *Gesellschaftsgeschichte Italiens im Mittelalter.* Monographien zur Geschichte des Mittelalters, vol. 26. Stuttgart, 1982.

————. "Herrscher und Beherrschte im deutschen Reich des 10.–12. Jahrhunderts." *Sitzungsberichte der bayerische Akademie der Wissenschaften, phil.-hist. Klasse,* no. 2. Munich, 1963.

Boumann, C. A. *Sacring and Crowning: The Development of the Latin Ritual for the Anointing of Kings and the Coronation of an Emperor Before the Eleventh Century.* Groningen, 1957.

Brackmann, Albert. "Pippin und die römische Kirche." In his *Gesammelte Aufsätze,* pp. 397–421. Reprint. Darmstadt, 1967.

Breckenridge, J. D. "Evidence for the Nature of Relations Between Pope John VII and the Byzantine Emperor Justinian II." *BZ* 65 (1972): 364–74.

Bréhier, Louis, and René Aigrain. *Grégoire le Grand, les états barbares et la conquête arabe (590–757).* Vol. 5 of *Histoire de l'église depuis les origines jusqu'à nos jours,* edited by Augustin Fliche and Victor Martin. Paris, 1947.

Bresslau, Harry. *Handbuch der Urkundenlehre für Deutschland und Italien.* Vol. 1. 4th ed. Berlin, 1969.

Breysig, Theodor. *Jahrbücher des fränkischen Reiches, 714–741.* Leipzig, 1869.

Brezzi, Paolo. *Roma e l'empero medioevale (774–1252).* Bologna, 1947.

Brown, T. S. "Social Structure and the Hierarchy of Officialdom in Byzantine Italy, 554–800 A.D." Ph.D. diss., Nottingham University, 1975.

————. "Settlement and Military Policy in Byzantine Italy." In *Papers in Italian Archaeology* 1: The Lancaster Seminar. BAR Supplementary Series, edited by H. McK. Blake, T. W. Potter, and D. B. Whitehouse, 4:323–38. Oxford, 1978.

————. "The Church of Ravenna and the Imperial Administration in the Seventh Century." *English Historical Review* 94 (1979): 1–28.

Brühl, Carlrichard. *Studien zu den langobardischen Königsurkunden.* Tübingen, 1970.

_____. "Die Kaiserpfalz bei St. Peter und die Pfalz Ottos III. auf dem Palatin." *QFIAB* 34 (1954): 1–30.

_____. "Neues zur Kaiserpfalz bei St. Peter." *QFIAB* 38 (1958): 266–68.

_____. "Fränkischer Krönungsbrauch und das Problem der 'Festkrönungen.'" *HZ* 194 (1962): 265–326.

_____. "Chronologie und Urkunden der Herzöge von Spoleto." *QFIAB* 51 (1971): 1–92.

Brunner, Heinrich. *Deutsche Rechtsgeschichte.* 2 vols. Vol. 1. 2d ed. Leipzig, 1906. Vol. 2. 2d ed. Edited by Claudius Freiherr von Schwerin. Leipzig, 1928.

Brunner, Karl. *Oppositionelle Gruppen im Karolingerreich.* Veröffentlichungen des Instituts für Österreichische Geschichtsforschung, vol. 25. Vienna, 1979.

Buchner, Maximilian. *Die Clausula de unctione Pippini eine Fälschung aus dem Jahre 880: Eine quellenkritische Studie, zugleich ein Beitrag zur Geschichte der Karolingerzeit.* Paderborn, 1926.

_____. "Rom oder Reims, die Heimat des Constitutum Constantini?" *HJB* 53 (1933): 137–68.

Buchner, Rudolf. *Die Rechtsquellen.* Weimar, 1953.

Bugnini, Annibale. "Defensor Ecclesiae." In *Enciclopedia cattolica* 4:1301–2. Vatican City, 1950.

Bullough, Donald. "The Counties of the *Regnum Italiae* in the Carolingian Period (774–888): A Topographical Study I." *Papers of the British School at Rome* 23 (1955): 148–68.

_____. "Leo, *qui apud Hlotharium magni loci habebatur,* et le gouvernement du Regnum Italiae à l'époque carolingienne." *Le moyen âge* 67 (1961): 221–45.

_____. "'Baiuli' in the Carolingian 'regnum Langobardorum' and the Career of Abbot Waldo." *English Historical Review* 77 (1962): 625–37.

_____. "Germanic Italy: The Ostrogothic and Lombard Kingdoms." In *The Dawn of European Civilization,* edited by David Talbot Rice, pp. 157–74. New York, 1965.

_____. "The Writing Office of the Dukes of Spoleto in the Eighth Century." In *The Study of Medieval Records: Essays in Honor of Kathleen Major,* pp. 1–21. Oxford, 1971.

Bund, Konrad. *Thronsturz und Herrscherabsetzung im Frühmittelalter.* Bonner historische Forschungen, vol. 44. Bonn, 1979.

Büttner, Heinrich. "Bonifatius und die Karolinger." *Hessisches Jahrbuch für Landesgeschichte* 4 (1954): 21–36.

_____. "Aus den Anfängen des abendländischen Staatsgedankens." In *Das Königtum,* edited by Theodor Mayer, pp. 155–67. Constance, 1956.

Caspar, Erich. *Pippin und die römische Kirche: Kritische Untersuchungen zum fränkisch-päpstlichen Bunde im VIII. Jahrhundert.* Berlin, 1914.

————. *Das Papsttum unter byzantinischer Herrschaft.* Vol. 2 of *Geschichte des Papsttums von dem Anfängen bis zur Höhe der Weltherrschaft.* Tubingen, 1933.

————. *Das Papsttum unter fränkischer Herrschaft.* Darmstadt, 1956.

————. "Papst Gregor II und der Bilderstreit." *ZKG* 52 (1933): 29–89.

Castagnetti, Andrea. *L'organizzazione del territorio rurale nel medioevo: Circonscrizione ecclesiastiche e civile nella "Langobardia" e nella "Romania."* Turin, 1979.

Cessi, Roberto. *Storia della Repubblica di Venezia.* Vol. 1. Milan, 1968.

————. "La crisi dell'esarcato ravennate agli inizi dell'iconoclastia." *Atti del reale istituto veneto di scienze, lettere ed arti* 93 (1933–34): 1671–85.

Chapin, J. "Liber Pontificalis." In *New Catholic Encyclopedia* 8:695–96. New York, 1967.

Charanis, Peter. "On the Question of the Hellenization of Sicily and Southern Italy During the Middle Ages." *American Historical Review* 52 (1946): 74–86.

Cheyette, Fredric L. "The Invention of the State." In *Essays on Medieval Civilization.* The Walter Prescott Webb Memorial Lectures, edited by Bede K. Lackner and Kenneth Roy Philp, 12:143–78. Austin, Texas, 1977.

Christophilopulu, Aikatherine. "SILENTION." *BZ* 44 (1951): 79–85.

Classen, Peter. "Romanum gubernans imperium: Zur Vorgeschichte der Kaisertitulatur Karls des Großen." *DA* 9 (1951): 103–21. See also under Gunther Wolf, pp. 4–29.

————. "Karl der Große, das Papsttum und Byzanz." In *Karl der Große*, edited by Wolfgang Braunfels, 1:537–608. 4 vols. Dusseldorf, 1965.

Congar, Yves. *L'ecclésiologie du haut moyen âge de Saint Grégoire le Grand à la désunion entre Byzance et Rome.* Paris, 1968.

Cristiani, Marta. *Dall'unanimitas all'universitas da Alcuino a Giovanni Eriugena. Lineamenti ideologici e terminologia politica della cultura del secolo IX.* Istituto storico italiano per il medioevo, Studi storici, fasc. 100–102. Rome, 1978.

Daly, William M. "St. Peter: An Architect of the Carolingian Empire." *Studies in Medieval Culture* 4, no. 1 (1973): 55–69.

Dannenbauer, Heinz. "Zum Kaisertum Karls des Großen und seiner Nachfolger." *ZKG* 49 (1930): 301–6.

David, Marcel. *La souveraineté et les limites juridiques du pouvoir monarchique du IXe au XVe siècle.* Paris, 1954.

Deér, Josef. "Die Vorrechte des Kaisers in Rom, 772–800." *Schweizer Beiträge zur allgemeinen Geschichte* 15 (1957): 5–63. See also under Gunther Wolf, pp. 30–115.

————— . "Zum Patricius-Romanorum-Titel Karls des Großen." *AHP* 3 (1965): 31–86. See also under Gunther Wolf, pp. 240–308.

————— . "Zur Praxis der Verleihung des auswärtigen Patriziats durch den byzantinischen Kaiser." *AHP* 8 (1970): 7–25.

Delaruelle, Etienne. "Charlemagne, Carloman, Didier et la politique du mariage franco-lombard (770–771)." *Revue historique* 170 (1932): 213–24.

————— . "Charlemagne et l'église." *Revue d'histoire de l'église de France* 39 (1953): 165–99.

Delaruelle, Etienne, and Jean-Remy Palanque. "La Gaule chrétienne à l'époque franque." *Revue d'histoire de l'église de France* 38 (1952): 52–72.

Delogu, Paolo. "Il regno longobardo." In *Longobardi e Bizantini*, vol. 1 of *Storia d'Italia*, edited by Giuseppe Galasso, pp. 1–216. Turin, 1980.

Devreesse, Robert. *Le fonds grec de la Bibliothèque Vaticane des origines à Paul V.* Studi e Testi, 244. Vatican City, 1965.

Dhondt, Jan. *Etudes sur la naissance des principautés territoriales en France.* Bruges, 1948.

————— . *Le haut moyen âge (VIIIe–XIe siècles).* Translated from the German and revised by Michel Rouche. Paris, 1968.

Diehl, Charles. *Etudes sur l'administration byzantine dans l'Exarchat de Ravenne (568–751).* Bibliothèque des écoles franaises d'Athènes et de Rome, vol. 53. Paris, 1888. Reprint. New York, n.d.

Dölger, Franz. "Die Familie der Könige im Mittelalter." *HJB* 60 (1940): 397–420.

Downs, Norton. "The Role of the Papacy in the Coronation of Charlemagne." *Studies in Medieval Culture* 3 (1970): 7–22.

Drabek, Anna M. *Die Verträge der fränkischen und deutschen Herrscher mit dem Papsttum von 754 bis 1020.* Veröffentlichungen des Instituts für Österreichische Geschichtsforschung, vol. 22. Vienna, 1976.

Duchesne, Louis. *The Beginnings of the Temporal Sovereignty of the Popes*, A.D. *754–1073.* Translated by Arnold Harris Mathew. London, 1908.

————— . "Notes sur la topographie de Rome au moyen âge II: Les titres presbytériaux et les diaconies." *MAH* 7 (1887): 217–43.

————— . "Les régions de Rome au moyen âge." *MAH* 10 (1890): 126–49.

————— . "Le *Liber Diurnus* et les élections pontificales au VIIe siècle." *BEC* 52 (1891): 5–30.

————— . "Le sedi episcopali nell'antico ducato di Roma." *ASR* 15 (1892): 478–503.

————— . "Les monastères desservants de Sainte-Marie-Majeure." *MAH* 27 (1907): 479–94.

Dumas, Auguste. "Le serment de fidélité et la conception du pouvoir du Ier au IXe siècle." *Revue historique de droit français et étranger* 10 (1931): 30–51, 289–321.

————. "Le serment de fidélité à l'époque franque." *Revue belge de philologie et d'histoire* 14 (1935): 405–26.

Dupré-Theseider, Eugenio. "Sur les origines de l'état de l'église." In *L'Europe aux IXe–XIe siècles: Aux origines des états nationaux*, edited by Tadeusz Manteuffel and Aleksander Gieysztor, pp. 93–103. Warsaw, 1968.

Ehler, Sidney Z. "On Applying the Modern Term 'State' to the Middle Ages." In *Medieval Studies Presented to Aubrey Gwynn S.J.*, edited by J. A Watt et al., pp. 492–501. Dublin, 1961.

Eichmann, Eduard. *Die Kaiserkrönung im Abendland*. 2 vols. Wurzburg, 1942.

————. "Die Adoption des deutschen Könige durch den Papst." *ZRG, gA* 37 (1916): 291–312.

————. "Die römischen Eide der deutschen Könige." *ZRG, kA* 37 (1916): 140–205.

Eiten, Gustav. *Das Unterkönigtum im Reiche der Merowinger und Karolinger*. Heidelberger Abhandlungen zur mittleren und neueren Geschichte, vol. 18. Heidelberg, 1907.

Erdmann, Carl. *Forschungen zur politischen Ideenwelt des Frühmittelalters; aus dem Nachlass des Verfassers*. Edited by Friedrich Baethgen. Berlin, 1951.

————. *The Origin of the Idea of Crusade*. Translated by Marshall W. Baldwin and Walter Goffart. Princeton, 1977.

Ewig, Eugen. "Das Bild Constantins des Großen in den ersten Jahrhunderten des abendländischen Mittelalters." *HJB* 75 (1956): 1–46.

————. "Zum christlichen Königsgedanken im Frühmittelalter." In *Das Königtum*, edited by Theodor Mayer, pp. 7–73. Constance, 1956.

————. "The Papacy's Alienation from Byzantium and Rapprochement with the Franks." In *The Church in the Age of Feudalism*, translated by Anselm Biggs, pp. 3–25. Vol. 3 of *Handbook of Church History*, edited by Hubert Jedin and John Dolan. New York, 1969.

————. "Die Petrus und Apostelkult im spätrömischen und fränkischen Gallien." In his *Spätantikes und fränkisches Gallien*, edited by Hartmut Atsma, 2:318–54. Munich, 1979.

Faber, Gustav. *Das erste Reich der Deutschen*. Munich, 1980.

Fabre, Paul. "Le patrimoine de l'église romaine dans les Alpes cottiennes." *MAH* 4 (1884): 283–420.

Falco, Giorgio. "L'amministrazione papale nella campagna e nella marittima dalla caduta della dominazione bisantina al sorgere dei comuni." *ASR* 38 (1915): 677–707.

Fanning, Steven C. "Lombard Arianism Reconsidered." *Speculum* 56 (1981): 241–58.

Fasoli, Gina. *Carlomagno e l'Italia.* Vol. 1. Bologna, 1968.

Faulhaber, Roland. *Die Reichseinheitsgedanke in der Literatur der Karolingerzeit bis zum Vertrag von Verdun.* Historische Studien, vol. 204. Berlin, 1934.

Felici, Guglielmo. "Notaio." *Enciclopedia cattolica* 8: 1955–59. Vatican City, 1952.

Felici, Guglielmo, and Giacomo Violardo. "Avvocato." *Enciclopedia cattolica* 2: 563–65. Vatican City, 1949.

Ferrari, Guy. *Early Roman Monasteries: Notes for the History of the Monasteries and Convents at Rome from the V through the X Century.* Studi di antichità cristiana, vol. 23. Vatican City, 1957.

Fichtenau, Heinrich. *Das karolingische Imperium: Soziale und Geistige Problematik eines Großreiches.* Zürich, 1949.

——————. *The Carolingian Empire.* Translated by Peter Munz. New York, 1964.

——————. "Karl der Große und das Kaisertum." *MIÖG* 61 (1953): 257–334.

——————. " 'Politische' Datierungen des frühen Mittelalters." In *Intitulatio*, edited by Herwig Wolfram, 2:453–548. 2 vols. Vienna, 1973.

Ficker, Julius. *Forschungen zur Reichs- und Rechtsgeschichte Italiens.* 4 vols. Innsbruck, 1868–74.

Fischer, Balthasar. "Die Entwicklung des Instituts der Defensoren in der römischen Kirche." *Ephemerides Liturgicae* 48 (1939): 443–54.

Fischer, Joachim. *Königtum, Adel und Kirche im Königreich Italien 774–875.* Bonn, 1965.

Fleckenstein, Josef. *Die Hofkapelle der deutschen Könige. I Teil: Grundlegung. Die karolingische Hofkapelle.* Schriften der MGH, vol. 16, pt. 1. Stuttgart, 1959.

——————. *Early Medieval Germany.* Translated by Bernard S. Smith. Amsterdam, 1978.

Foerster, H. "Liber Diurnus Pontificum Romanorum." In *New Catholic Encyclopedia* 8: 694. New York, 1967.

Folz, Robert. *The Concept of Empire in Western Europe from the Fifth to the Fourteenth Century.* Translated by S. A. Ogilvie. New York, 1969.

——————. *The Imperial Coronation of Charlemagne.* Translated by J. E. Anderson. London, 1974.

——————. "Charlemagne and His Empire." In *Essays on the Reconstruction of Medieval History*, edited by Vaclav Mudroch and G. S. Couse, pp. 86–112. Montreal, 1974.

Folz, Robert et al. *De l'antiquité au monde médiévale.* Paris, 1972.

Fournier, Paul, and LeBras, Gabriel. *Histoire des collections canoniques en occident.* 2 vols. Paris, 1932.

Fritze, Wolfgang H. *Papst und Frankenkönig. Studien zu den päpstlich-fränkischen Rechtsbeziehungen von 754 bis 824.* Vol. 10 of *Vorträge und Forschungen.* Sigmaringen, 1973.

————. "Die fränkische Schwurfreundschaft der Merowingerzeit." *ZRG, gA* 71 (1954): 74–125.

Fröhlich, Hermann. *Studien zur langobardischen Thronfolge von den Anfängen bis zur Eroberung des italienischen Reiches durch Karl den Großen.* 2 vols. Tübingen, 1980.

Frutaz, A. Pietro. "Diaconia." In *Enciclopedia cattolica,* 4:1521–35 Vatican City, 1950.

Fuhrmann, Horst. "Konstantinische Schenkung und Silvesterlegende in neuer Sicht." *DA* 15 (1959): 523–40.

————. "Konstantinische Schenkung und abendländisches Kaisertum." *DA* 22 (1966): 63–178.

————. "Das frühmittelalterliche Papsttum und die Konstantinische Schenkung: Meditationen über ein unausgeführtes Thema." *SSCI* 20 (1973): 257–92.

————. "Zu kirchenrechtlichen Vorlagen einiger Papstbriefe aus der Zeit Karls des Großen." *DA* 35 (1979): 357–67.

Fürst, Carl Gerold. *Cardinalis: Prolegomena zu einer Rechtsgeschichte des römischen Kardinalskollegiums.* Munich, 1967.

Ganshof, Franois Louis. *Frankish Institutions Under Charlemagne.* Translated by Bryce and Mary Lyon. New York, 1970.

————. *The Middle Ages: A History of International Relations.* Translated by Rémy Inglis Hall. New York, 1971.

————. "Observations sur le Synode de Francfort de 794." In *Miscellanea Historica in honorem Alberti de Meyer,* pp. 306–18. Louvain, 1946.

————. "Notes sur les origines byzantines du titre 'Patricius Romanorum.'" *Annuaire de l'institut de philologie et d'histoire orientales et slaves* 10 (1950): 261–82.

————. "L'immunité dans la monarchie franque." *Recueil de la société Jean Bodin,* 1:171–216 2d ed. Brussels, 1958.

————. "A propos des ducs et duchés au haut moyen âge." *Journal des savants,* Jan.-Mar. 1972, pp. 13–24.

————. "Stämme als 'Träger' des Reiches?" *ZRG, gA* 89 (1972): 147–60.

————. "Alcuin's Revision of the Bible." In his *The Carolingians and the Frankish Monarchy: Studies in Carolingian History,* translated by Janet Sondheimer, pp. 28–40. Ithaca, 1971.

————— . "Charlemagne's Programme of Imperial Government." In *Carolingians and the Frankish Monarchy*, pp. 55–85.

————— . "The Church and the Royal Power in the Frankish Monarchy Under Pippin III and Charlemagne." In *Carolingians and the Frankish Monarchy*, pp. 205–39.

————— . "The Frankish Monarchy and Its External Relations from Pippin III to Louis the Pious." In *Carolingians and the Frankish Monarchy*, pp. 162–204.

————— . "The Imperial Coronation of Charlemagne: Theories and Facts." In *Carolingians and the Frankish Monarchy*, pp. 41–54.

————— . "Louis the Pious Reconsidered." In *Carolingians and the Frankish Monarchy*, pp. 261–72.

————— . "Some Observations on the 'Ordinatio Imperii' of 817." In *Carolingians and the Frankish Monarchy*, pp. 273–88.

Garms-Cornides, Elisabeth. "Die langobardischen Fürstentitel (774–1077)." *Intitulatio*, edited by Herwig Wolfram, 2:341–452. 2 vols. Vienna, 1973.

Gasparri, Stefano. *I duchi longobardi*. Istituto storico italiano per il medio evo, vol. 109. Rome, 1978.

Gasquet, A. *L'empire byzantin et la monarchie franque*. Paris, 1888.

————— . "Le royaume lombard, ses relations avec l'empire grec et avec les francs." *Revue historique* 33 (1887): 58–92.

Gay, Jules. *L'Italie méridionale et l'empire byzantin depuis l'avènement de Basile Ier jusqu'à la prise de Bari par les Normandes (867–1071)*. Bibliothèque des écoles françaises d'Athènes et de Rome, vol. 90. Paris, 1904.

————— . "L'état pontifical, les Byzantins et les Lombards sur le littoral campanien (d'Hadrien Ier à Jean VIII)." *MAH* 21 (1901): 487–508.

————— . "Quelques remarques sur les papes grecs et syriens avant la querelle des iconoclastes (678–715)." In *Mélanges offerts à M. Gustave Schlumberger* 1:40–54. Paris, 1924.

Geertman, Herman. *More Veterum. Il Liber Pontificalis e gli edifici ecclesiastici di Roma nella tarda antichità e nell'alto medioevo*. Archaeologica Traiectina, vol. 10. Groningen, 1975.

Gericke, Wolfgang. "Wann entstand die Konstantinische Schenkung?" *ZRG, kA* 43 (1957): 1–88.

————— . "Das Constitutum Constantini und die Silvester-Legende." *ZRG, kA* 44 (1958): 343–50.

————— . "Das Glaubensbekenntnis der 'Konstantinischen Schenkung.' " *ZRG, kA* 47 (1961): 1–76.

————— . "Konstantinische Schenkung und Silvesterlegende in neuer Sicht." *ZRG, kA* 47 (1961): 293–304.

Goffart, Walter. *The LeMans Forgeries: A Chapter from the History of Church Property in the Ninth Century.* Cambridge, Mass., 1966.

Görres, Franz. "Justinian II und das römische Papsttum." *BZ* 17 (1908): 432–54.

Goubert Paul. *Rome, Byzance et Carthage.* Vol. 2 of *Byzance avant l'Islam.* Part 2 of *Byzance et l'Occident.* Paris, 1965.

Gouillard, Jean. "Aux origines de l'iconoclasme: Le témoignage de Grégoire II?" *Travaux et memoires: Centre de recherche d'histoire et civilisation byzantines* 3 (1968): 243–307.

Graf von Pfeil, Sigurd. "Der Augustus-Titel der Karolinger." *Die Welt als Geschichte* 19 (1959): 194–210.

Gregorovius, Ferdinand. *Geschichte der Stadt Rom im Mittelalter.* Vols. 2 and 3. 7th ed. Stuttgart, 1922.

Grierson, Philip. "Election and Inheritance in Early Germanic Kingship." *Cambridge Historical Journal* 7 (1941): 1–22.

————. "The Coronation of Charlemagne and the Coinage of Pope Leo III." *Revue belge* 30 (1952): 825–33.

Griffe, Elie. "Aux origines de l'état pontifical: Apropos de la Donation de Constantin et de la Donation de Quierzy (753–755)." *Bulletin de litterature ecclésiastique* 53 (1952): 216–31.

————. "Aux origines de l'état pontifical: Charlemagne et Hadrian Iᵉʳ (772–795)." *Bulletin de litterature ecclésiastique* 55 (1954): 65–89.

————. "Aux origines de l'état pontifical: Le couronnement impérial de l'an 800 et la Donatio Constantini." *Bulletin de litterature ecclésiastique* 59 (1958): 193–211.

Grisar, Hartmann. "Ein Rundgang durch die Patrimonien des heiligen Stuhles um das Jahr 600." *Zeitschrift für katholische Theologie* 1 (1877): 321–60.

————. "Verwaltung und Haushalt der päpstlichen Patrimonien um das Jahr 600." *Zeitschrift für katholische Theologie* 1 (1877): 526–63.

Grotz, Hans. "Beobachtungen zu den zwei Briefen Papst Gregors II. an Kaiser Leo III." *AHP* 18 (1980): 9–40.

Grumel, Venance. "L'annexion de l'Illyricum oriental, de la Sicile et de la Calabre au patriarchat de Constantinople: Le temoignage de Théophane le chronographe." *Recherches de science religieuse* 40 (1952): 191–200.

Guillou, André. *Régionalisme et indépendence dans l'empire byzantin au VIIᵉ siècle: L'example de l'Exarchat et de la Pentapole d'Italie.* Istituto storico italiano per il medioevo, Studi storici, fasc. 75–76. Rome, 1969.

————. "Demography and Culture in the Exarchate of Ravenna." *Studi Medievali,* 3d series, 10 (1969): 201–19.

————. "L'école dans l'Italie byzantine," *SSCI* 19 (1972): 291–311.

————— . "L'Italia bizantina dall'invasione longobarda alla caduta di Ravenna." In *Longobardi e Bizantini*, vol. 1 of *Storia d'Italia*, edited by Giuseppe Galasso, pp. 217–338. Turin, 1980.

Gundlach, Wilhelm. *Die Entstehung des Kirchenstaates und der curiale Begriff Res publica Romanorum: Ein Beitrag zum fränkischen Kirchen- und Staatsrecht*. Breslau, 1899.

Hahn, Adelheid. "Das Hludowicianum." *Archiv für Diplomatik* 21 (1975): 15–135.

Hahn, Heinrich. *Jahrbücher des fränkischen Reiches, 741–752*. Berlin, 1863.

Hallenbeck, Jan T. *Pavia and Rome: The Lombard Monarchy and the Papacy in the Eighth Century*. Transactions of the American Philosophical Society, vol. 72, no. 4. Philadelphia, 1982.

————— . "The Election of Pope Hadrian I." *Church History* 37 (1968): 261–70.

————— . "The Lombard Party in Eighth-Century Rome: A Case of Mistaken Identity." *Studi medievali*, 3d series, 15 (1974): 951–66.

————— . "Paul Afiarta and the Papacy: An Analysis of Politics in Eighth-Century Rome." *AHP* 12 (1974): 22–54.

————— . "Pope Stephen III: Why Was He Elected?" *AHP* 12 (1974): 287–99.

————— . "Rome Under Attack: An Estimation of King Aistulf's Motives for the Lombard Siege of 756." *Mediaeval Studies* 40 (1978): 190–222.

————— . "Instances of Peace in Eighth-Century Lombard-Papal Relations." *AHP* 18 (1980): 41–56.

————— . "The Roman-Byzantine Reconciliation of 728: Genesis and Significance." *BZ* 74 (1981): 29–41.

Haller, Johannes. *Das Papsttum: Idee und Wirklichkeit*. Vols. 1 and 2. Basel, 1951.

————— . "Die Karolinger und das Papsttum." *HZ* 108 (1912): 38–76.

Halphen, Louis. *Etudes sur l'administration de Rome au moyen âge (751–1252)*. *BEHE*, vol. 166. Paris, 1907.

————— . *Charlemagne et l'empire carolingien*. 2d ed. Paris, 1968.

————— . *Charlemagne and the Carolingian Empire*. Translated by Giselle de Nie. Amsterdam, 1977.

————— . "Les origines du pouvoir temporel de la papauté." In his *A travers l'histoire du moyen âge*, pp. 39–50. Paris, 1950.

————— . "La papauté et le complot lombard de 771." *A travers l'histoire du moyen âge*, pp. 51–57.

Hampe, Karl. "Die Berufung Ottos des Großen nach Rom durch Papst Johann XII." In *Historische Aufsätze Karl Zeumer zum sechzigsten Geburtstag als Festgabe dargebracht von Freunden und Schülern*, pp. 153–67. Weimar, 1910.

Hannig, Jürgen. *Consensus Fidelium: Frühfeudale Interpretationen des Verhältnisses von Königtum und Adel am Beispiel des Frankenreiches.* Monographien zur Geschichte des Mittelalters, vol. 27. Stuttgart, 1982.

Hartmann, Ludo Moritz. *Untersuchungen zur Geschichte der byzantinischen Verwaltung in Italien, 540–750.* Leipzig, 1889.

————. *Geschichte Italiens im Mittelalter.* 3 vols. in 5. Gotha, 1897–1911.

————. "Grundherrschaft und Bureaukratie im Kirchenstaate vom 8. bis zum 10. Jahrhundert." *Vierteljahrschrift für Sozial- und Wirtschaftsgeschichte* 7 (1909): 142–58.

Haselbach, Irene. *Aufstieg und Herrschaft der Karolinger in der Darstellung der sogenannten Annales Mettenses Priores.* Historische Studien, vol. 412. Lubeck, 1970.

Hauck, Albert. *Kirchengeschichte Deutschlands.* 5th ed. Vols. 1 and 2. Leipzig, 1935.

Hauck, Karl. "Von einer spätantiken Randkultur zum karolingischen Europa." *FMSt* 1 (1967): 3–93.

————. "Die Ausbreitung des Glaubens in Sachsen und die Verteidigung der römischen Kirche als konkurrierende Herrscheraufgaben Karls des Großen." *FMSt* 4 (1970): 138–72.

Hazlitt, W. Carew. *The Venetian Republic: Its Rise, Its Growth and Its Fall,* A.D. *409–1797.* Vol. 1. London, 1915.

Head, Constance. *Justinian II of Byzantium.* Madison, Wis., 1972.

Heldmann, Karl. *Das Kaisertum Karls des Großen: Theorien und Wirklichkeit.* Weimar, 1928.

————. "Kommendation und Königsschutz im Vertrage von Ponthion (754)." *MIÖG* 38 (1920): 541–70.

Hinschius, Paul. *System des katholischen Kirchenrechts.* Vol. 1. Reprint, Graz, 1959.

Hirsch, Ferdinand. "Papst Hadrian I. und das Fürstenthum Benevent." *Forschungen zur deutschen Geschichte* 13 (1873): 33–68.

Hirschfeld, Theodor. "Das Gerichtswesen der Stadt Rom vom 8 bis 12 Jahrhundert wesentlich nach stadtrömischen Urkunden." *Archiv für Urkundenforschung* 4 (1912): 419–562.

Hlawitschka, Eduard. *Franken, Alemannen, Bayern und Burgunder in Oberitalien 774–962: Zum Verständnis der fränkischen Königsherrschaft in Italien.* Forschungen zur oberrheinischen Landesgeschichte, vol. 8. Freiburg, 1960.

————. "Karl Martell, das römische Konsulat und der Römische Senat: Zur Interpretation von Fredegarii Continuatio cap. 22." In *Die Stadt in der europäischen Geschichte: Festschrift Edith Ennen,* edited by Werner Besch, pp. 74–90. Bonn, 1972.

Hodgkin, Thomas. *Italy and Her Invaders.* Vols. 5, 6, and 7. Oxford, 1895-99.

Hoffmann, Hartmut. *Untersuchungen zur karolingischen Annalistik*. Bonner historische Forschungen, vol. 10. Bonn, 1958.

―――――. "Französische Fürstenweihen des Hochmittelalters." *DA* 18 (1962): 92–119.

Höfler, Otto. "Der Sakralcharakter des germanischen Königtums." *Das Königtum*, edited by Theodor Mayer, pp. 75–104. Constance, 1956.

Holtzmann, Robert. *Die Italienpolitik der Merowinger und des Königs Pippin*. Darmstadt, 1962.

Hopkins, Keith. "Elite Mobility in the Roman Empire." In *Studies in Ancient Society*, edited by M. I. Finley, pp. 103–20. London, 1974.

Hörle, Georg Heinrich. *Frühmittelalterliche Mönchs- und Klerikerbildung in Italien*. Freiburger theologische Studien, vol. 13. Freiburg, 1914.

Hubert, Henri. "Etude sur la formation des états de l'église." *Revue historique* 69 (1899): 1–40, 241–72.

Huyghebaert, Nicolas. "La donation de Constantin ramenée à ses véritables dimensions." *Revue d'histoire ecclésiastique* 71 (1976): 45–69.

Irigoin, Jean. "La culture grecque dans l'occident latin du VIIᵉ au XIᵉ siècle." *SSCI* 22 (1975): 425–46.

Jarnut, Jörg. "Quierzy und Rom: Bemerkungen zu den 'Promissiones Donationis' Pippins und Karls." *HZ* 220 (1975): 265–97.

Jedin, Hubert, and John Dolan, eds. *The Church in the Age of Feudalism*, translated by Anselm Biggs. Vol. 3 of *Handbook of Church History*. New York, 1969.

Jones, Arnold Hugh Martin. *The Later Roman Empire, 284–602: A Social and Administrative Survey*. 2 vols. Norman, Okla., 1964.

―――――. *The Decline of the Ancient World*. New York, 1966.

―――――. "Church Finances in the Fifth and Sixth Centuries." *The Journal of Theological Studies* 11 (1960): 84–94.

Jones, Philip J. "L'Italia agraria nell'alto medioevo: Problemi di cronologia e di continuità." *SSCI* 13 (1966): 57–92.

Jordan, Karl. "Das Eindringen des Lehnwesens in das Rechtsleben der römischen Kurie." *Archiv für Urkundenforschung* 12 (1932): 13–110.

Josi, Enrico. "Liber Pontificalis." *Enciclopedia cattolica* 7:1278–82. Vatican City, 1949.

―――――. "Titoli della chiesa romana." *Enciclopedia cattolica* 12:152–58. Vatican City, 1954.

Kaminsky, Hans H. "Zum Sinngehalt des Princeps-Titels Arichis' II. von Benevent." *FMSt* 8 (1974): 81–92.

Kampers, Franz. "Roma aeterna und Sancta Dei Ecclesia rei publicae romanorum." *HJB* 44 (1924): 240–49.

————. "Rex et Sacerdos." *HJB* 45 (1925): 495–515.

Kehr, Paul. "Die sogenannte karolingische Schenkung von 754." *HZ* 70 (1893): 385–441.

————. Review of Lindner, *Die sogenannten Schenkungen* (see below). *Göttingische gelehrte Anzeigen* 158 (1896): 128–39.

Keller, Hagen. "Zur Struktur der Königsherrschaft im karolingischen und nachkarolingischen Italien." *QFIAB* 47 (1967): 123–223.

Kempf, Friedrich. "Il papato dal secolo VIII alla metà del secolo XI." In *Problemi di storia della chiesa nell'alto medioevo*, pp. 59–71. Milan, 1973.

————. "Chiese territoriali e chiesa romana nel secolo VIII." *SSCI* 20 (1973): 293–317.

Kern, Fritz. *Kingship and Law in the Middle Ages*. Translated by S. B. Chrimes. New York, 1970.

Kienast, Walther. *Der Herzogstitel in Frankreich und Deutschland*. Munich, 1968.

————. *Studien über die franzözischen Volksstämme des Frühmittelalters*. Stuttgart, 1968.

Klauser, Theodor. *A Short History of the Western Liturgy*. Translated by John Halliburton. 2d ed. Oxford, 1979.

Kleinclausz, Arthur. *L'empire carolingien: Sa vie et ses transformations*. Paris, 1902.

Klewitz, Hans Walter. "Die Entstehung des Kardinalkollegiums." *ZRG, kA* 25 (1936): 115–221.

————. "Die Festkrönungen der deutschen Könige." *ZRG, kA* 28 (1939): 48–96.

————. "Germanisches Erbe im fränkischen und deutschen Königtum." *Die Welt als Geschichte* 7 (1941): 201–16.

Knabe, Lotte. *Die gelasianische Zweigewaltentheorie bis zum Ende des Investiturstreits*. Historische Studien, vol. 292. Berlin, 1936.

Köbler, Gerhard. "Land und Landrecht im Frühmittelalter." *ZRG, gA* 68 (1969): 1–40.

Krause, Victor. "Geschichte des Institutes der missi dominici." *MIÖG* 11 (1890): 193–300.

Krautheimer, Richard. *Corpus basilicarum christianarum Romae*. Vol. 5. Vatican City, 1977.

————. *Rome: Profile of a City, 312–1308*. Princeton, 1980.

Kretschmayr, Heinrich. *Geschichte von Venedig*. Vol. 1. Gotha, 1905.

Kroeber, A. "Partage du royaume des Francs entre Charlemagne et Carloman Ier. *BEC* 20 (1856): 341–50.

Kroell, Maurice. *L'immunité franque*. Paris, 1910.

Krüger, Karl Heinrich. "Königskonversionen im 8. Jahrhundert." *FMSt* 7 (1973): 169–222.

Kuttner, Stephan. "Cardinalis: The History of a Canonical Concept." *Traditio* 3 (1945): 129–214.

Ladner, Gerhard. *Die Papstbildniße des Altertums und des Mittelalters*. Vol. 1. Monumenti di antichità cristiana, vol. 4. Vatican City, 1941.

Laehr, Gerhard. *Die konstantinische Schenkung in der abendländischen Literatur des Mittelalters bis zur Mitte des 14. Jahrhunderts*. Historische Studien, vol. 166. Berlin, 1926.

Lamprecht, Karl. *Die römische Frage*. Leipzig, 1889.

Lapotre, A. *L'Europe et le Saint-siège à l'époque carolingienne*. Paris, 1895.

Lauer, Philippe. *Le palais de Latran: Etude historique et archéologique*. Paris, 1911.

Laufs, Manfred. *Politik und Recht bei Innozenz III*. Kölner historische Abhandlungen, vol. 26. Cologne, 1980.

Lawrence, A. W. "Early Medieval Fortifications near Rome." *Papers of the British School at Rome* 32 (1964): 89–122.

Leclercq, Henri. "Liber Pontificalis." *Dictionnaire d'archéologie chrétienne et de liturgie*, vol. 9, pt. 1, pp. 354–460. Paris, 1920.

―――― . "Schola." *Dictionnaire d'archéologie chrétienne et de liturgie*, vol. 15, pt. 1, pp. 1008–13. Paris, 1950.

Leicht, Pier Silverio. "Il termine 'communitas' in una lettera di Gregorio II." *Bulletin Du Cange: Archivum Latinitas Medii Aevi* 1 (1924): 171–75.

―――― . "Il feudo in Italia nell'età carolingia." *SSCI* 1 (1954): 71–107.

Lemerle, Paul. "Les répercussions de la crise de l'empire d'orient au VIIe siècle sur les pays d'occident." *SSCI* 5 (1958): 713–31.

Lemosse, Maxime. "La lèse-majesté dans la monarchie franque." *Revue du moyen âge latine* 1 (1945): 5–24.

Lesne, Emile. *La hiérarchie épiscopale, 742–882*. Mémoires et travaux des Facultés catholiques de Lille, vol. 1. Lille, 1905.

Lestocquoy, J. "Notes sur l'église de St. Saba." *Rivista di archeologia cristiana* 6 (1929): 313–57.

―――― . "Administration de Rome et diaconies du VIIe au IXe siècle." *Rivista di archeologia cristiana* 7 (1930): 261–98.

Levillain, Léon. "De l'authenticité de la *Clausula de unctione Pippini*." *BEC* 88 (1927): 20–42.

————— . "Le couronnement imperial de Charlemagne." *Revue d'histoire de l'église de France* 18 (1932): 1–19.

————— . "L'avènement de la dynastie carolingienne et les origines de l'état pontifical (749–757)." *BEC* 94 (1933): 225–95.

Levison, Wilhelm. "Pippin und die römische Kirche." *Historische Vierteljahrschrift* 20 (1920–21): 330–37.

————— . "Konstantinische Schenkung und Silvester-Legende." In *Miscellanea Francesco Ehrle* 2:159–247. Studi e Testi, vol. 38. Rome, 1924.

Lindner, Theodor. *Die sogenannten Schenkungen Pippins, Karls des Großen und Ottos I. an die Päpste.* Stuttgart, 1896.

Lintzel, Martin. "Karl der Große und Karlmann." *HZ* 140 (1929): 1–22.

————— . "Der Codex Carolinus und die Motive von Pippins Italienpolitik." *HZ* 161 (1939): 33–41.

Llewellyn, Peter. *Rome in the Dark Ages.* London, 1971.

Loenertz, Raymond. J. "*Constitutum Constantini*: Destination, destinataires, auteur, date." *Aevum* 48 (1974): 199–245.

Lot, Ferdinand. "Le concept d'empire à l'époque carolingienne." In *Recueil des travaux historiques de Ferdinand Lot* 1:338–52. 3 vols. Paris, 1968–73.

————— . "Le serment de fidélité à l'époque franque." *Revue belge* 12 (1933): 569–82.

Löwe, Heinz. "Zur Vita Hadriani." *DA* 12 (1956): 493–98.

————— . "Von den Grenzen des Kaisergedankens in der Karolingerzeit." *DA* 14 (1958): 345–74.

————— . "Bonifatius und die bayerisch-fränkische Spannung: Ein Beitrag zur Geschichte der Beziehungen zwischen dem Papsttum und den Karolingern." In *Zur Geschichte der Bayern*, edited by Karl Bosl, pp. 264–328. *Wege der Forschung*, vol. 60. Darmstadt, 1965.

Lunt, William E. *Papal Revenues in the Middle Ages.* 2 vols. New York, 1934.

Luther, Paul. *Rom und Ravenna bis zum 9. Jahrhundert: Ein Beitrag zur Papstgeschichte.* Berlin, 1889.

MacCormack, Sabine G. *Art and Ceremony in Late Antiquity.* Berkeley, 1981.

McKitterick, Rosamond. "Charles the Bald and His Library." *English Historical Review* 95 (1980): 28–47.

Manacorda, Francesco. *Ricerche sugli inizii della dominazione dei Carolingi in Italia.* Istituto storico italiano per il medio evo, Studi Storici, fasc. 71–72. Rome, 1968.

Mandic, Dominic. "Dalmatia in the Exarchate of Ravenna from the Middle of the VI Until the Middle of the VIII Century." *Byzantion* 34 (1964): 347–74.

Mann, Horace Kinder. *The Lives of the Popes in the Middle Ages.* Vol. 1, pts. 1 and 2, and vol. 2. London, 1925.

Marcou, Giorgio S. "Zaccaria (679–752): L'ultimo papa greco nella storia di Roma altomedioevale. Note storico-giuridiche." *Apollinaris* 50 (1977): 274–89.

Marrou, Henri-Irenée. "Autour de la bibliothèque du Pape Agapit," *MAH* 48 (1931): 124–69.

————. "L'origine orientale des diaconies romaines." *MAH* 57 (1940): 95–142.

Martens, Wilhelm. *Die römische Frage unter Pippin und Karl dem Großen.* Stuttgart, 1881.

————. *Neue Erörterung über die römische Frage unter Pippin und Karl dem Großen.* Stuttgart, 1882.

Martroye, F. "Les 'defensores ecclesiae' au Ve et VIe siècle." *Revue historique de droit français et étranger,* 4th series, 2 (1923): 597–622.

Mattingly, Garrett. "The First Resident Embassies." *Speculum* 12 (1937): 423–39.

Mayer, Ernst. *Italienische Verfassungsgeschichte von der Gothenzeit bis zur Zunftherrschaft.* 2 vols. Leipzig, 1909.

Mayer, Theodor. *Fürsten und Staat: Studien zur Verfassungsgeschichte des deutschen Mittelalters.* Weimar, 1950.

————. "Staatsauffassung in der Karolingerzeit." In *Das Königtum,* pp. 169–83.

————, ed. *Das Königtum: Seine geistigen und rechtlichen Grundlagen. Vorträge und Forschungen,* vol. 3. Sigmaringen, 1956.

Mengozzi, Guido. *La città italiana nell'alto medioevo.* Reprint. Florence, 1973.

Michel, Anton. "Die griechische Klostersiedlungen zu Rom bis zur Mitte des 11. Jahrhunderts." *Ostkirchliche Studien* 1 (1952): 32–45.

Mikoletzky, Hanns Leo. "Karl Martell und Grifo." In *Festschrift E. E. Stengel,* pp. 130–56. Munster, 1952.

Miller, David Harry. "Papal-Lombard Relations During the Pontificate of Pope Paul I: The Attainment of an Equilibrium of Power in Italy, 756–767." *Catholic Historical Review* 55 (1969): 358–76.

————. "The Motivation of Pepin's Italian Policy, 754–768." *Studies in Medieval Culture* 4, no. 1 (1973): 44–54.

————. "The Roman Revolution of the Eighth Century: A Study of the Ideological Background of the Papal Separation from Byzantium and Alliance with the Franks." *Mediaeval Studies* 36 (1974): 79–133.

————. "Byzantine-Papal Relations During the Pontificate of Paul I: Confirmation and Completion of the Roman Revolution of the Eighth Century." *BZ* 68 (1975): 47–62.

Mohr, Walter. *Studien zur Charakteristik des karolingischen Königtums im 8. Jahrhundert.* Saarlouis, 1955.

————. *Die karolingische Reichsidee.* Münster, 1962.

—————. "Karl der Große, Leo III und der römische Aufstand von 799." *Archivum Latinitas Medii Aevi* 20 (1960): 39–98.

—————. "Reichspolitik und Kaiserkrönung in den Jahren 813 und 816." *Die Welt als Geschichte* 20 (1960): 168–86.

—————. "Die kirchliche Einheitspartei und die Durchführung der Reichsordnung von 817." *ZKG* 72 (1961): 1–45.

Morrison, Karl F. *The Two Kingdoms: Ecclesiology in Carolingian Political Thought.* Princeton, 1964.

—————. *Carolingian Coinage.* Numismatic Notes and Monographs, vol. 158. New York, 1967.

—————. "Cardinal, I (History of)." *New Catholic Encyclopedia* 3:104–5. New York, 1967.

Mühlbacher, Englebert. *Deutsche Geschichte unter den Karolingern.* Stuttgart, 1896.

Munz, Peter. *The Origin of the Carolingian Empire.* Leicester, 1960.

Niehues, Bernhard. *Geschichte des Verhältnißes zwischen Kaisertum und Papsttum im Mittelalter.* 2 vols. 2d ed. Münster, 1877.

Noble, Thomas F. X. "The Monastic Ideal as a Model for Empire: The Case of Louis the Pious." *Revue bénédictine* 86 (1976): 235–50.

—————. "Louis the Pious and His Piety Re-reconsidered." *Revue belge* 58 (1980): 297–316.

Nordhagen, Per Jonas. *The Frescoes of John VII (A.D. 705–707) in S. Maria Antiqua in Rome.* Institutum Romanum Norvegiae, Acta ad archaeologiam et artium historiam pertinentia, vol. 3. Rome, 1968.

Norwich, John Julius. *Venice: The Rise to Empire.* London, 1977.

Odegaard, Charles E. *Vassi and Fideles in the Carolingian Empire.* Cambridge, Mass., 1945.

—————. "Carolingian Oaths of Fidelity." *Speculum* 16 (1941): 284–96.

—————. "The Concept of Royal Power in Carolingian Oaths of Fidelity." *Speculum* 20 (1945): 279–89.

Oelsner, Ludwig. *Jahrbücher des fränkischen Reiches unter König Pippin.* Leipzig, 1871.

Ohnsorge, Werner. *Das Zweikaiserproblem im früheren Mittelalter.* Hildesheim, 1947.

—————. "Das konstantinische Schenkung, Leo III und die Anfänge der kurialen römischen Kaiseridee." In his *Abendland und Byzanz: Gesammelte Aufsätze zur Geschichte der byzantinisch-abendländischen Beziehungen und des Kaisertums,* pp. 79–110. Darmstadt, 1958.

—————. "Das Mitkaisertum in der abendländischen Geschichte des früheren Mittelalters." In *Abendland und Byzanz,* pp. 261–87.

_____ . "Orthodoxus Imperator: Vom religiösen Motiv für das Kaisertum Karls des Großen." In *Abendland und Byzanz*, pp. 64–78.

_____ . "Renovatio regni Francorum." In *Abendland und Byzanz*, pp. 111–30.

_____ . "Das Constitutum Constantini und seine Entstehung." In his *Konstantinopel und der Okzident*. pp. 92–162. Darmstadt, 1966.

Ortalli, Gherardo. "Venezia dalle origini a Pietro II Orseolo." In *Longobardi e Bizantini*, vol. 1 of *Storia d'Italia*, edited by Giuseppe Galasso, pp. 339–438. Turin, 1980.

Ostrogorsky, George. *A History of the Byzantine State*. Rev. ed. Translated by Joan Hussey. New Brunswick, N.J., 1969.

Pabst, H. "Geschichte des langobardischen Herzogthums." *Forschungen zur deutschen Geschichte* 2 (1862): 405–518.

Palazzini, Giuseppe. "Primicerio e secundicerio." *Enciclopedia cattolica* 10:20–22. Vatican City, 1953.

Partner, Peter. *The Lands of St. Peter: The Papal State in the Middle Ages and in the Early Renaissance*. Berkeley, 1972.

_____ . "Notes on the Lands of the Roman Church in the Early Middle Ages." *Papers of the British School at Rome* 34 (1966): 68–78.

_____ . Review of Krautheimer, *Rome* (see above). *Catholic Historical Review* 68 (1982): 85–87.

Pasztor, Lajos. "L'histoire de la curie romaine, problème d'histoire de l'Eglise." *Revue d'histoire ecclésiastique* 64 (1969): 353–66.

Patlagean, Evelyne. "Les armes et la cité à Rome du VIIᵉ au IXᵉ siècle, et le modèle européen des trois fonctions sociales." *MAH* 86 (1974): 25–62.

Pepe, Gabriele. *Le moyen âge barbare en Italie*. Translated by Jean Gonnet. Paris, 1956.

Perels, Ernst. *Papst Nikolaus I und Anastasius Bibliothecarius: Ein Beitrag zur Geschichte des Papsttums im neunten Jahrhundert*. Berlin, 1920.

_____ . "Pippins Erhebung zum König." *ZKG* 53 (1934): 400–416.

Pertusi, Agostino. "Ordinamenti militari, guerre in occidente e teorie di guerra dei Bizantini (secc. VI–X)." *SSCI* 15 (1968): 631–700.

Plöchl, Willibald M. *Geschichte des Kirchenrechts*. Vol. 1. 2d ed. Munich, 1960.

Poole, Reginald Lane. *Lectures on the History of the Papal Chancery down to the Time of Innocent III*. Cambridge, 1915.

Post, Gaines. *Studies in Medieval Legal Thought*. Princeton, 1964.

Poupardin, René. "Etudes sur l'histoire des principautés lombardes de l'Italie méridionale et leurs rapports avec l'Empire franc." *Le moyen âge*, 2d series, 10 (1906): 1–26, 245–74; 11 (1907): 1–25.

Prinz, Friedrich. *Klerus und Krieg im früheren Mittelalter: Untersuchungen zur Rolle der Kirche beim Aufbau der Königsherrschaft.* Monographien zur Geschichte des Mittelalters, vol. 2. Stuttgart, 1971.

Quaritsch, Helmut. *Staat und Souveränität.* Vol. 1. Frankfurt, 1970.

Queller, Donald. *The Office of Ambassador in the Middle Ages.* Princeton, 1967.

Rabikauskas, Paul. *Die römische Kuriale in der päpstlichen Kanzlei.* Miscellanea Historiae Pontificiae, vol. 20. Rome, 1958.

Rasi, Piero. *Exercitus Italicus e milizie cittadine nell'alto medioevo.* Padua, 1937.

Rassow, Peter. "Pippin und Stephan II." *ZKG* 36 (1916): 494–502.

Recchia, Vincenzo. *Gregorio Magno e la società agricola.* Verba Seniorum, n.s., vol. 8. Rome, 1978.

Reindel, Kurt. "Grundlegung: Das Zeitalter der Agilolfinger (bis 788)." In *Handbuch der bayerischen Geschichte,* edited by Max Spindler, 1:71–179. Munich, 1971.

Richards, Jeffrey. *The Popes and the Papacy in the Early Middle Ages, 476–752.* London, 1979.

————. *Consul of God: The Life and Times of Gregory the Great.* London, 1980.

Riché, Pierre. *Education and Culture in the Barbarian West.* Translated by John J. Contreni. Columbia, S.C., 1976.

————. *Daily Life in the World of Charlemagne.* Translated by Jo Ann McNamara. Philadelphia, 1978.

Riesenberger, Dieter. "Zur Geschichte des Hausmeiers Karlmann." *Westfälische Zeitschrift* 120 (1970): 271–85.

Rodenberg, Carl. *Pippin, Karlmann und Papst Stephan II.* Historische Studien, vol. 152. Berlin, 1923.

Rohault de Fleury, Georges. *La Latran au moyen âge.* Paris, 1877.

Sackur, Ernst. "Die Promissio Pippins vom Jahre 754 und ihre Erneuerung durch Karls des Großen." *MIÖG* 16 (1895): 385–424.

Saltet, Louis. "La lecture d'un texte et la critique contemporaine. La prétendue promesse de Quierzy dans le 'Liber Pontificalis.'" *Bulletin de litterature ecclésiastique* 41 (1940): 176–206; 42 (1941): 61–85.

Santifaller, Leo. *Saggio di un elenco dei funzionari impiegati e scrittori della cancellaria pontificia dall'inizio all'anno 1099.* Bolletino dell'Istituto Storico Italiano per il medio evo, no. 56. 2 vols. Rome, 1940.

————. "Zur Liber Diurnus-Forschung," *HZ* 161 (1940): 532–38.

Schäfer, August. *Die Bedeutung der Päpste Gregor II. (715–731) und Gregor III. (731–741) für die Gründung des Kirchenstaates.* Montjoie, 1913.

Schaube, Adolf. "Zur Verständigung über das Schenkungsversprechen von Kiersy und Rom." *HZ* 72 (1894): 193–212.

Scheffer-Boichorst, Paul. "Neuere Forschungen über die konstantinische Schenkung." *MIÖG* 10 (1889): 302–25.

————. "Pipins und Karls des Großen Schenkungsversprechen. Ein Beitrag zur Kritik der Vita Hadriani." *MIÖG*, 5 (1884): 193–212.

Schieffer, Theodor. *Winfrid-Bonifatius und die christliche Grundlegung Europas.* Reprint with corrections. Darmstadt, 1980.

————. "Die Krise des karolingischen Imperiums." In *Aus Mittelalter und Neuzeit: Festschrift für Gerhard Kallen zum 70 Geburtstag dargebracht von Kollegen, Freunden und Schülern*, edited by J. Engel and H. M. Klinkenberg, pp. 1–15. Bonn, 1957.

Schlesinger, Walter. *Die Entstehung der Landesherrschaft. Untersuchungen vorweigend nach mitteldeutscher Quellen.* Sächsische Forschungen zur Geschichte, vol. 1. Dresden, 1941.

————. "Karlingische Königswahlen." In his *Beiträge zur deutschen Verfassungsgeschichte des Mittelalters* 1:88–138. 2 vols. Göttingen, 1963.

————. "Kaisertum und Reichsteilung: Zur Divisio regnorum von 806." In his *Beiträge zur deutschen Verfassungsgeschichte*, 1:193–232. See also under Gunther Wolf, pp. 116–73.

Schmid, Karl. "Zur Ablösung der Langobardenherrschaft durch den Franken." *QFIAB* 52 (1972): 1–36.

Schmidt, Hermann Josef. "Die Kirche von Ravenna im Frühmittelalter (540–967)." *HJB* 34 (1913): 729–80.

Schmiedt, Giulio. "Le fortificazioni altomedievali in Italia viste dall'aereo." *SSCI* 15 (1968): 859–927, plates 1–40.

Schneider, Fedor. *Die Reichsverwaltung in der Toscana von der Gründung des Langobardenreiches bis zum Ausgang der Staufer (568–1268).* Vol. 1. Bibliothek des deutschen historischen Instituts in Rom, vol. 11. Rome, 1914.

Schneider, Reinhard. *Königswahl und Königserhebung im Frühmittelalter: Untersuchungen zur Herrschaftsnachfolge bei den Langobarden und Maerwingern.* Monographien zur Geschichte des Mittelalters, vol. 3. Stuttgart, 1972.

Schnürer, Gustav. *Die Entstehung des Kirchenstaates.* Cologne, 1894.

Schramm, Percy Ernst. *Die zeitgenössischen Bildnisse Karls des Großen.* Beiträge zur Kulturgeschichte des Mittelalters und der Renaissance, vol. 29. Leipzig, 1928.

————. "Studien zu frühmittelalterlichen Aufzeichnungen über Staat und Verfassung." *ZRG, gA* 49 (1929): 167–232.

————. "Die Anerkennung Karls des Großen als Kaiser (bis 800)." In his *Kaiser, Könige und Päpste: Gesammelte Aufsätze zur Geschichte des Mittelalters* 1:215–63. 4 vols. in 5. Stuttgart, 1968–71.

————. "Karl der Große als Kaiser im Lichte der Staatssymbolik (800–814)." In *Kaiser, Könige und Päpste* 1:264–302.

————. "Die Siegel, Bullen und Kronen der Karolinger." In *Kaiser, Könige und Päpste* 2:15–74.

————. "Das Versprechen Pippins und Karls des Großen für die römische Kirche (754 und 774)." In *Kaiser, Könige und Päpste* 1:149–92.

Schreiber, G. "Levantinische Wanderungen zum Westen." *BZ* 44 (1951): 517–23.

Schwarzlose, Karl. *Die Patrimonien der römischen Kirche bis zur Gründung des Kirchenstaates*. Berlin, 1887.

————. "Die Verwaltung und die finanzielle Bedeutung der Patrimonien der römischen Kirche bis zur Gründung des Kirchenstaates." *ZKG* 11 (1890): 62–100.

Sefton, David S. "Pope Hadrian I and the Fall of the Kingdom of the Lombards." *Catholic Historical Review* 65 (1979): 206–20.

Semmler, Josef. "Traditio und Königsschutz: Studien zur Geschichte der königlichen monasteria." *ZRG, kA* 45 (1959): 1–33.

————. "Reichsidee und kirchliche Gesetzgebung." *ZKG* 71 (1960): 37–65.

————. "A propos des abbayes royales." *Bulletin de la société nationale des antiquaires de France* (1968), pp. 160–61.

Serafini, Camillo. *Le monete e le bolle plumbee pontificie del medagliere vaticano*. Vol. 1. Reprint. Bologna, 1965.

Sickel, Theodor. *Acta Karolinorum Digesta et Ennarata*. 2 vols. Vienna, 1867.

————. *Das Privilegium Otto I. für die römische Kirche vom Jahre 962*. Innsbruck, 1883.

Sickel, Wilhelm. "Die Verträge der Päpste mit den Karolingern und das neue Kaiserthum." *Deutsche Zeitschrift für Geschichtswissenschaft* 11 (1894): 301–51; 12 (1894–95): 1–43.

————. "Kirchenstaat und Karolinger." *HZ* 84 (1900): 385–409.

————. "Alberich II. und der Kirchenstaat." *MIÖG* 23 (1902): 50–126.

Siegmund, P. Albert. *Die Überlieferung der griechischen christlichen Literatur in der lateinischen Kirche bis zum zwölften Jahrhundert*. Abhandlungen der bayerischen Benediktiner-Akademie, vol. 5. Munich, 1949.

Simson, Bernhard. *Jahrbücher des fränkischen Reiches unter Ludwig dem Frommen*. 2 vols. Leipzig, 1874–76.

Sirch, Bernhard. *Der Ursprung der bischöflichen Mitra und päpstlichen Tiara*. Kirchenrechtlichen Quellen und Studien, vol. 8. St. Ottilien, 1975.

Solmi, Arrigo. *Il senato romano nell'alto medioevo (757–1143)*. Rome, 1944.

Spearing, Edward. *The Patrimony of the Roman Church in the Time of Gregory the Great*. Cambridge, 1918.

Speck, Paul. *Artabasdos, der rechtgläubige Vorkämpfer der göttlichen Lehren: Untersuchungen zur Revolte des Artabasdos und ihrer Darstellung in der byzantinischen Historiographie*. Poikila Byzantina, vol. 2. Bonn, 1981.

Stein, Ernst. "Beiträge zur Geschichte von Ravenna in spätrömischer und byzantinischer Zeit." *Klio* 16 (1919): 40–71.

Steinacker, Harold. "Die römische Kirche und die griechischen Sprachkenntniße des Frühmittelalters." *MIÖG* 62 (1954): 28–66.

Stengel, Edmund E. "Kaisertitel und Suveränitätsidee." *DA* 3 (1939): 1–56.

————. "Die Entwicklung des Kaiserprivilegs für die römische Kirche, 817–962." In his *Abhandlungen und Untersuchungen zur mittelalterlichen Geschichte*, pp. 218–48. Cologne, 1960.

————. "Immunität." In *Abhandlungen und Untersuchungen*, pp. 30–34.

Strayer, Joseph R. *On the Medieval Origins of the Modern State*. Princeton, 1970.

Sullivan, Richard E. *The Coronation of Charlemagne: What Did It Signify?* Boston, 1959.

————. "Pope St. Leo III." *New Catholic Encyclopedia* 8:640. New York, 1967.

Tabacco, Giovanni. "La storia politica e sociale." In *Storia d'Italia*, edited by Giulio Einaudi, vol. 2, pt. 1, pp. 3–274. Turin, 1974.

————. "L'ambiguità delle istituzioni nell'Europa costruita dai Franchi." In *Forme di potere e struttura sociale in Italia nel medioevo*, edited by Gabriella Rossetti, pp. 73–81. Bologna, 1977.

Tangl, Georgine. "Die Passvorschrift des Königs Ratchis und ihre Beziehung zu den Verhältnis zwischen Franken und Langobarden vom 6.-8. Jahrhundert." *QFIAB* 38 (1958): 1–66.

————. "Die Sendung des ehemaligen Hausmeiers Karlmann in das Frankenreich im Jahre 754 und der Konflikt der Brüder." *QFIAB* 40 (1960): 1–42.

Tellenbach, Gerd. "Der großfränkische Adel und die Regierung Italiens in der Blützeit des Karolingerreichs." In *Studien und Vorarbeiten zur Geschichte des großfränkischen und frühdeutschen Adels*, edited by Gerd Tellenbach, pp. 40–70. Forschungen zur oberrheinischen Landesgeschichte, vol. 4. Freiburg, 1957.

Thomas, Hildegard. "Die rechtlichen Festsetzungen des Pactum Ludovicianum von 817: Ein Beitrag zur Echtheitsfrage." *ZRG, kA* 11 (1921): 124–74.

Thompson, E. A. *Romans and Barbarians*. Madison, Wis., 1982.

Toubert, Pierre. *Les structures du Latium médiéval: Le Latium méridional et la Sabine du IXe siècle à la fin du XIIe siècle.* 2 vols. Bibliothèque des écoles françaises d'Athènes et de Rome, vol. 221. Rome, 1973.

————. "L'Italie rurale aux VIIIe–IXe siècles: Essai de typologie domaniale." *SSCI* 20 (1973): 95–132.

Ullmann, Walter. *The Growth of Papal Government in the Middle Ages: A Study in the Relation of Clerical to Lay Power.* 3d ed. London, 1970.

————. *A Short History of the Papacy in the Middle Ages.* Corrected edition. London, 1974.

————. *Gelasius I. Das Papsttum an der Wende der Spätantike zum Mittelalter.* Päpste und Papsttum, vol. 18. Stuttgart, 1981.

————. "The Development of the Medieval Idea of Sovereignty." *English Historical Review* 64 (1949): 1–33.

————. "Leo III." *Lexikon für Theologie und Kirche* 7:947–48. Freiburg, 1963.

————. "The Origins of the *Ottonianum.*" *Cambridge Historical Journal* 11 (1953): 114–28.

VanDijk, S. J. P. "The Urban and Papal Rites in Seventh- and Eighth-Century Rome." *Sacris Erudiri* 12 (1961): 411–87.

Vehse, Otto. "Die päpstliche Herrschaft in der Sabina bis zur Mitte des 12. Jahrhunderts." *QFIAB* 21 (1929–30): 120–75.

————. "Benevent als Territorium des Kirchenstaates bis zum Beginn der avignonesischen Epoche." *QFIAB* 22 (1930–31): 87–160.

Vielliard, René. *Recherches sur les origines de la Rome chrétienne.* Rome, 1959.

Waitz, Georg. *Deutsche Verfassungsgeschichte.* Vols. 3, 4. 2d ed. Berlin, 1883.

Waley, Daniel. *The Papal State in the Thirteenth Century.* London, 1961.

Wallach, Liutpold. "Amicus amicis, inimicus inimicis." *ZKG* 52 (1933): 614–15.

————. "The Genuine and the Forged Oath of Pope Leo III." In his *Diplomatic Studies in Latin and Greek Documents from the Carolingian Age,* pp. 299–327. Ithaca, 1977.

————. "The Roman Synod of December 800 and the Alleged Trial of Leo III." *Diplomatic Studies in Latin and Greek Documents,* pp. 328–52.

Wattenbach, Wilhelm; Wilhelm Levison; and Heinz Löwe. *Deutschlands Geschichtsquellen im Mittelalter.* vol. 2. Weimar, 1953.

Weinrich, Lorenz. *Wala: Graf, Mönch und Rebell. Die Biographie eines Karolingers.* Historische Studien, vol. 386. Lubeck, 1963.

Werner, Karl Ferdinand. "Les principautés périphériques dans le monde franc du VIIIᵉ siècle." *SSCI* 20 (1973): 2:483–514.

————. "Important Noble Families in the Kingdom of Charlemagne: A Prosopographical Study of the Relationship between King and Nobility in the Early Middle Ages." In *The Medieval Nobility: Studies on the Ruling Classes of France and Germany from the Sixth to the Twelfth Century,* edited and translated by Timothy Reuter, pp. 137–202. Amsterdam, 1978.

White, Lynn T. "The Byzantinization of Sicily." *American Historical Review* 42 (1936): 1–21.

Whitehouse, David. "Sedi medievali nella campagna romana: la 'domusculta' e il villaggio fortificato." *Quaderni Storici* 24 (1973): 861–76.

Wickberg, Paul Gordon. "The Eighth-Century Archbishops of Ravenna: An Ineffectual Alternative to Papalism." *Studies in Medieval Culture* 12 (1978): 25–33.

Wickham, Chris. *Early Medieval Italy: Central Power and Local Society 400–1000.* London, 1981.

—————. "Historical Aspects of Medieval South Etruria." In *Papers in Italian Archaeology,* vol. 1 The Lancaster Seminar. BAR Supplementary Series, edited by H. McK. Blake, T. W. Potter, and D. B. Whitehouse, 4:373–90. Oxford, 1978.

Wilks, Michael. *The Problem of Sovereignty in the Later Middle Ages.* Cambridge, 1963.

Wolf, Gunther, ed. *Zum Kaisertum Karls des Großen.* Wege der Forschung, vol. 38. Darmstadt, 1972.

Wolfram, Herwig. *Intitulatio.* Vol. 1, *Lateinische Königs- und Fürstentitel bis zum Ende des 8. Jahrhunderts.* Vol. 2, *Lateinische Herrscher- und Fürstentitel im neunten und zehnten Jahrhundert. MIÖG, Erganzungsband,* vols. 21 and 24. Vienna, 1967, 1973.

—————. "The Shaping of the Early Medieval Kingdom." *Viator* 1 (1970): 1–20.

—————. "The Shaping of the Early Medieval Principality as a Type of Non-royal Rulership." *Viator* 2 (1971): 33–51.

Zielinski, Herbert. *Studien zu den spoletinischen 'Privaturkunden' des 8. Jahrhunderts und ihrer Überlieferung im Regestum Farfense.* Tübingen, 1972.

Zimmermann, Harald. *Papstabsetzungen des Mittelalters.* Graz, 1968.

—————. "Das Privilegium Ottonianum von 962 und seine Problemsgeschichte." *MIÖG, Erganzungsband* 20 (1962): 147–90.

Zwölfer, Theodor. *Sankt Peter, Apostelfürst und Himmelspförtner: Seine Verehrung bei den Angelsachsen und Franken.* Stuttgart, 1929.

Index

Throughout the index, *Sanctae Romanae Ecclesiae* is abbreviated *SRE.*

The Middle Ages
Edward Peters, General Editor

The Middle Ages